Fritz Steegmüller / Ottersheim
A Home Town History

About the Translation

This translation is offered as an expression of gratitude to Fritz Steegmüller. His detailed historical account of Ottersheim has given me a unique perspective on the life and times of my ancestors. Even more, this book provided insight into German history and culture; and in doing so gave me an appreciation for the village of Ottersheim and her people.

In his preface, Steegmüller expressed a hope that one day his book might "reach the hands of the descendants of the Ottersheim emigrants so that they may know the home of their ancestors." May this translation be a step towards achieving that goal.

The translation diverges little from the German book published in 1968. It attempts to maintain the same formatting, writing style, and voice of the author. Not translated are German place names, proper names, personal names, street names, landmarks, monetary values, and terms of measure. We also keep the German sharp Ess (ß), the umlauted vowels, and the author's original quoting and parentheses. Additions not in the original book include many footnotes and a biography of the author, which can be found in the back matter. Three persons helped make this translation possible.

Edith Lueke provided the translation. She was unrelenting in her pursuit of a consistent and accurate translation in spite of a fair amount of old and regional German dialect, poetry, and colloquialisms. The German reviewers often commented on the quality of her work.

Bernhard Steegmüller, who as son of the author, helped acquire and grant the necessary approvals, provided supplementary information, answered all of our linguistic, cultural, and historical questions, and completed several reviews. His dedicated support and encouragement would make his father very proud.

Waltraud Krieger, a descendant of Ottersheim ancestors herself, helped establish the initial contact with the Steegmüller family. She also gave of her time to review the translation and provided impromptu historical perspectives. Her knowledge of the original book and the local area provide further confidence in the translation presented.

"Vielen Dank - Edith, Bernhard und Waltraud!" A simple "thank you" does not seem an adequate expression of my gratitude. May you take pride in knowing you helped make the hope of Fritz become reality. It was my privilege to know you and to have worked with you these past several months. "Gott segne Euch."

Stephen Hank
Descendant of Ottersheim Shepherds
Markus Hanck and his son Stephan

Fritz Steegmüller

OTTERSHEIM

in District Germersheim

A home town book celebrating 1200-years of the village in year 1968

The original German language version of this book was published in 1968
Publishing House: Druckerei Dr. A. Kraemer KG.; 674 Landau (Pfalz), Schulhof 5
Publisher: Ottersheim Community Government

The original book is archived at the Palatinate State Library
Speyer, Rhineland-Palatinate, Germany
Shelf mark: 4.9853
Media number: 011861553107

The original book can be found on the internet in PDF format at the
Rheinland-Palatinate Digitisation Portal
http://www.dilibri.de; keyword: Ottersheim.

Permission to translate and publish this book was provided by the
Children of Fritz Steegmüller
(Bernhard, Hermann and Monika)
and the
Ottersheim Community Government

Permission to use the Ottersheim Coat of Arms was provided by the
Ottersheim Community Government

Translated by Edith L. Lueke / USA
Composition by Stephen P. Hank / USA

Translation and historical assistance provided by
Waltraud Krieger / Gleisweiler
Caecilia Kröper / Ottersheim
Bernhard Steegmüller / Speyer
Paul Steegmüller / Ottersheim

Translation reviewed by
Waltraud Krieger / Gleisweiler
Bernhard Steegmüller / Speyer

Table of Contents

Message from the Mayor of Ottersheim

For the 1200-year anniversary of our village, Municipal Director Mr. Steegmüller, a son of our community, presents us this book, "Ottersheim through changing times." With no gaps, in detail, and in simple terms, the fate of our local village and its inhabitants is documented from its first recorded mention in 768. Through years of painstaking work, Director Steegmüller has gathered the material for this book. Now that it is finished, I would like to recommend it to all, inside and outside the local community of Ottersheim.

Since the production of a book with such a small number of copies can only be done at a high cost, no one will experience material gain from it. I would therefore like to thank the council warmly for providing the money that was necessary to produce this work at all. My thanks also go to the District of Germersheim, especially to Councilman Mr. Weiß, for the approval of an additional stipend.

So now, in the year 1968, we would like to celebrate the 1200th birthday of our home village with joy and festivity. In joy and sorrow, war and peace, sickness, misery and death, in sad and happy days, it has survived the centuries. May all people of Ottersheim, "inside and outside," be filled with joy, pride, and love for their home village. May all continue to help it flourish and prosper. Now we want to ask the Lord, "O good Father above, protect the home place. And bless it with peace, grant all that is good to our home, now and forever."

We would like to accept this book now from the author with heartfelt thanks, as a treasure for future generations and ourselves.

Wünschel, Mayor

Ottersheim, in November 1967

Epigraph

Blessed is he who holds dear the memory of his fathers,
Who happily entertains the listener with their deeds,
Their greatness; and quietly rejoicing
When they have been told, feeling
Himself one with them!

Johann Wolfgang von Goethe
in the play
Iphigenia in Tauris

Author's Preface

When this history appears in print, it will have been 1200 years since Ottersheim was first mentioned in a historical document. This proves that this place belongs to the oldest settlements of the Palatinate. May this be a welcome occasion for residents and friends alike, to concern themselves with the emergence and development of the village and to remember the many fateful happenings. Ottersheim was at no time the center of great historic events. Nor was it so remote that the waves of history would not have reached it. The events, happy and tragic, that passed by our fatherland left their mark on our ancestors. Bearing witness to this are the many letters, notes, documents, essays, and reports from times gone by. It was a tedious and time-consuming task to track down all these sources and evaluate them. In fact, this task was almost insurmountable. Therefore, it is my sincere desire to thank all those who have helped me. Thanks are due to the State Archives in Speyer and local government of Ottersheim who have made many files and documents readily available to me. I must also thank the Catholic parish rectory in Ottersheim and the Protestant parish rectory in Offenbach for allowing me access to the parish books. Also, my uncle, Spiritual Adviser Otto Steegmüller who painstakingly researched and documented many details of Ottersheim history should not be forgotten. Also deserving thanks is Jean Benz, former Raiffeisen accountant, who from his youth has kept a diary of village events, and has collected and organized many newspaper clippings from past decades that he willingly provided to me. I must also thank my sister Elisabeth who clarified many an open question by interviewing older village citizens. I would also like to include in my thanks Deputy Headmaster Philipp Stürmer of Gleisweiler, all the many volunteers who contributed advice and assistance to the success of the work, and those whom I cannot all mention by name. Special thanks to the community of Ottersheim and the district of Germersheim who made this printing possible.

May this book find acceptance in the village community and be welcome reading for young and old! Last but not least, the history is intended to assist the local schools in teaching home lore and history. It would be gratifying if the book would also come into the hands of those whose origins are in Ottersheim, but who no longer live here because they or their ancestors emigrated and live in other places. They should know that their home of old has not forgotten them. May the book be a greeting to them and an invitation to renew their bonds with their relatives in the homeland or to strengthen existing connections.

Speyer, in December 1967
Fritz Steegmüller

Location and Character of the Village of Ottersheim

In his description of the Electoral Palatinate on the Rhine in 1785, Widder states that Ottersheim in the District of Germersheim is "a considerable village," although at that time it only consisted of 597 souls with 135 families. At the same time, Knittelsheim had 443 inhabitants, Bellheim had 1,215, and Offenbach had 1,128. Today, we must classify Ottersheim with its 1,272 souls as one of the smaller villages of the Palatinate. From a district perspective, there are 161 people per square kilometer.

Ottersheim[1] is located about 2 kilometers south of the Queich[2] River on Highway 509 that runs from Bellheim to Landau. The village is located almost equidistant from the Rhine River to the east and the Haardt Mountain Range to the west. The distance to Germersheim is 12.5 kilometers and to Landau is 9.2 kilometers. Good connections exist only to the east and west, while villages to the south and north are at best reachable through roundabout means. This was beneficial in the past in that Ottersheim was only affected by troops moving in east-west directions, while those moving north to south and vice versa used roadways either along the Rhine or on the edge of the Haardt. The neighboring villages of Knittelsheim and Offenbach are a distance of 1.8 kilometers and 3.0 kilometers from Ottersheim respectively. It is 4.1 kilometers to Bellheim.

Like all early Frankish settlements, Ottersheim was created near a stream. Because the Queich valley was partially swampy wetland in the old days, the Ottersheim settlers chose to settle on the *Brühlgraben [swampy meadow trench]*.[3] The brook did not have much water. However, it was suitable for agriculture and animal husbandry because both sides contained fertile loess and clay soils.

The center of the village lies 125 meters above sea level. To the south, the Kahlenberg rises 145 meters and slopes gently towards the Queich. At the lowest point, it is 120 meters above the sea. The village plat resembles a rectangle that is slightly more than 4 kilometers long and not quite 2 kilometers wide. The northern part of the village plat is covered with meadows and forests while the central and southern parts contain farmland and vineyards. Not only grain, potatoes, and root vegetables thrive there but also tobacco, onions, and vegetables of any kind. Apart from a few artisans and merchants, all the inhabitants were formerly engaged in agriculture. Today, 60% of the villagers are still engaged in agriculture. This is also reflected in the construction of the houses. In addition to the house, almost every property has a barn, a shed, and a hay or granary structure that can be reached across a long yard, and these are constructed in Frankish fashion like the home.

In the center of the village is the Catholic Church with its massive tower rising proudly above the houses. The church stands on an artificial hill that served as a cemetery until

---

[1] See "Present Day Ottersheim Region" on page C of the back matter.

[2] The Queich is a 52 kilometers long tributary of the Rhine River with head waters in the Palatinate Forest. It flows through Offenbach an der Queich, then north of Ottersheim, and joins the Rhine at Germersheim.

[3] Brackets identify information not found in the original book, mostly translations of imbedded German text.

1824. Based at the churchyard wall is the community hall. Built in 1555, it is the oldest building of the village. In the immediate vicinity of the church are the old schoolhouse, the rectory, and the Nurses' Station. Only in recent years, a kindergarten and the new school building were constructed a little further north on the Schulstraße[4] [School street].

The population of Ottersheim is hardworking and ambitious. It is quite open to new ideas in spite of its ties with tradition. Ottersheim residents are jokingly called the `Bears´ in the surrounding area. That this says something about the villagers' character cannot be totally dismissed out of hand. In any case, the people are good-natured and harmless as long as they are not consciously provoked. A sense of community is still very much alive among the villagers. One not only willingly helps a neighbor, but the people also gladly volunteer for community tasks. Almost all adults address each other with the familiar form *Du [You]*. As for older men and women, the older form *Ihr [Thou]* is still commonly used.

Throughout its long history, Ottersheim was always managed under the District of Germersheim. During the Electoral Palatinate time, it belonged to the *District Office of the Fautei [Bailiwick] of Germersheim,* in the French time to the *Canton of Germersheim,* in Bavaria's time to the *Country Commission or District Commission of Germersheim,* and since the last War, to the *Administrative District of Germersheim.* Even though the official name is *Ottersheim bei Landau,* this means only that Landau is the nearest city from which also the mail is delivered to Ottersheim. The post buses between Ottersheim and Landau are very frequent, while the connections to Germersheim are pretty bad. Persons who have no vehicle must use the train. However, the train stations are in Bellheim, Offenbach, or Hochstadt.

The unfavorable traffic situation has undoubtedly contributed to the fact that Ottersheim has grown little over the past 100 years. So far, there is no factory in the village that could give the people work and wages. Therefore, it is not surprising that in the past not just a few sons and daughters moved away and sought their living in the city or in industrial locations. Today, having a car allows them to maintain their residence in the village if they have found a job elsewhere.

Besides Ottersheim in the district of Germersheim, there is another town of the same name in Germany. This is the Catholic parish of *Ottersheim bei Kirchheimbolanden,* which counts 293 inhabitants and is one of the smallest villages of the Palatinate. Also mentioned in the Lorsch Charter,[5] this place belongs to the Diocese of Worms and will soon celebrate its 1200th anniversary.

---

[4] *Straße* is a street, road, or highway. Synonyms are a *weg* which is defined as a way, road, path, route or passage; a *gasse* can be a street or alley (Cassell's German Dictionary, 1958, Funk & Wagnall's). The designation of straße, gasse, or weg is typically determined by the type and amount of traffic.

[5] The *Lorsch Charter,* also called the *Lorsch Codex,* is a historical, 460-page book created in the late 12th century that lists gifts given to the Lorsch Monastery

A View of the Community of Ottersheim

(According to official surveys of 6 June 1961)

1. District area: 790 hectares (Ha.)   [1952 acres]
   This includes 119 hectares on forest land
2. Mean annual temperature: 9-10⁰ Celsius [48⁰-50⁰ Fahrenheit]
3. Annual rainfall: 600 millimeters   [23.6 inches]
4. Main wind direction: Southwest to West
5. Population: 1,233 people: This includes 45 or 3.6% displaced persons and refugees.

Male	588	47.7%
Female	645	52.3%
Catholic	1,059	85.9%
Protestant	174	14.1%

6. Age distribution of the Population:

			Palatinate	
Under 6 years:	167	13.6%	Palatinate	10.3%
From 6-15 years:	174	14.1%		13.4%
From 15-21 years:	78	6.3%		7.8%
From 21-45 years:	374	30.3%		32.9%
From 45-65 years:	302	24.5%		25.7%
Over 65 years:	138	11.2%		9.9%

7. Occupation structure:

Agriculture:	425	61.0%	Palatinate:	15.8%
Manufacturing:	161	23.1%		50.2%
Trade and Transport	59	8.5%		14.7%
Services	52	7.4%		19.3%
Total:	697	100%		100%
Female	332	47.6%		37.0%
Employment rate		56.5%		47.4%

8. Social Structure:

Self-employed:	227	32.6%	Palatinate:	13.5%
Helping family members	243	34.8%		11.4%
Officials and employees:	41	5.9%		23.1%
Laborers:	168	24.1%		47.0%
Apprentices:	18	2.6%		5.0%
Total labor force:	697	100%		100%

9. Commuters and their main places of work

Outbound Commuters:	189	27%	of labor force
Inbound Commuters:	12		
Working in Ottersheim:	520		
Working in Landau:	109	57.7%	
in Germersheim:	22	11.6%	
in Bellheim:	16	8.5%	
in Ludwigshafen:	12	6.3%	
in other communities:	30	15.9%	

10. Size of agricultural enterprises:

Under 2 hectares:	106	operations
From 2-5 hectares:	98	operations
From 5-10 hectares	42	operations
From 10-20 hectares:	—	
Total:	246	operations

The target size of a family farm operation in Ottersheim is 12 hectares of land.

11. Land usage:

(Some of this land lies in the area belonging to the Knittelsheim and Offenbach districts.)

		Other acreage:	
Arable land:	546 Ha.	Forest:	119.5 Ha.
Meadows/pasture:	169 Ha.	Wasteland:	1.5 Ha.
Grape vines:	16 Ha.	Roads/Paths:	16.0 Ha.
Gardens:	8 Ha.	Water bodies:	6.5 Ha.
Total:	739 Ha.	Buildings/Farms:	12.5 Ha.

12. Livestock:

Horses:	55	
Cattle:	748	which includes 385 cows
Pigs:	345	

13. Non-agricultural work places:

Crafts:	26	workplaces with 54 employees
Other establishments:	27	workplaces with 54 employees
Total:	53	workplaces with 108 employees including 33 women

Among the other companies are 16 commercial firms with 28 employees.

14. Tax revenue

Total: 71,124 deutschemarks (DM.) including 26,953 DM. from business taxes

Per capita in Ottersheim:	58 DM.
Per inhabitant in the district of Germersheim:	90 DM.
Per capita in the Palatinate:	161 DM.

15. Residential buildings/housing conditions:

Number of dwellings:	274
Number of apartments:	366
Number of households:	378

16. Age of residential buildings:

Built before 1919:	179	65.3%
Built from 1919-1948:	41	15.0%
Built from 1949-1961:	54	19.7%
Total:	274	100%

17. Local facilities:

Ottersheim has a Catholic Church, a Protestant Church, a community hall, a new and an old school building, a gymnasium, a kindergarten, a Nurses' Station, a new and an old cemetery, a Raiffeisen Bank, a branch of the County and City Savings Bank, a sports field, a fire hall, and a parish library.

18. Responsible Offices:

Labor Office:	Neustadt an der Weinstraße
Labor Office Extension:	Germersheim
District Court:	Germersheim
Tax office:	Germersheim
Forest District:	Germersheim in Bellheim
Police station:	Bellheim
Health Department:	Germersheim
Cultural Affairs:	Neustadt an der Weinstraße
District Court:	Landau in the Palatinate
District Office:	Germersheim
Post Office:	Landau in the Palatinate
Tax and Collection authority:	Bellheim
Roads Authority:	Speyer
Surveyor's Office:	Speyer

19. Health Care:

Ottersheim has a Nurses' Station but no doctor. Anyone who is sick can contact the doctors in Bellheim, Offenbach, or Landau. The nearest pharmacies are in Offenbach and Bellheim. The nearest hospitals are located in Landau and Germersheim. A midwife lives in Ottersheim.

20. Schools:

The upper grades of elementary school attend the school in Bellheim. The responsible professional school is in Germersheim. Those wanting to attend a secondary school usually go to Landau in the Palatinate.

Ottersheim through Changing Times

The 1200 Years of History of the Village of Ottersheim and Human History

Measured on a single human life, the village of Ottersheim is very old. If one measures three generations per century, then 36 generations have lived and worked in this spot on earth since the first time the name Ottersheim was recorded. But more likely, the Frankish settlement of Ottersheim is at least 1,500 years old, so that a total of 45 generations have lived in the village since its inception in the early Middle Ages to the present day. Not every village and much less every city is able to look back on such a long history. However, this timeframe is quite modest when measured by the total history of humankind. According to prehistoric research, the first evidence of human existence was about 600,000[6] years ago. Materials used in tools of old can be divided into those from the stone, bronze, and iron ages.

A) The *Stone Age* (about 600000 to 2000 B.C.)

   The *Early Stone Age* dates from 600000 to 10000 B.C. The people of that time were initially collectors and hunter-gatherers. A higher level of hunting developed later. About 20000 B.C., people began to cultivate plants. In the *Middle Stone Age,* from 10000 to 5000 B.C., people were primarily shepherds. Not until the *Late Stone Age,* from 5000 to 2000 B.C., did the history of farming begin. People used plows, and grew grain and fruit. Also, people raised cattle.

B) The *Bronze Age* (from 2000 to 800 B.C.)

   People mined copper and tin from which they made bronze for jewelry and tools. As with the Stone Age, the Early, Middle, and Late Bronze Ages distinguish the Bronze Age.
   The *Early Bronze Age* lasted from 2000 to 1600 B.C.
   The *Middle Bronze Age* ranged from 1600 to 1100 B.C.
   The *Late Bronze Age* from 1100 to 800 B.C.

C) The *Iron Age* (from 800 B.C. to the Birth of Christ)

   Bronze is replaced by iron. Based on the most important archaeological sites, we distinguish the *Hallstatt Culture or Early Iron Age* from 800 to 450 B.C., and the *La Tène Culture or Late Iron Age* from 450 B.C. up to the Birth of Christ.

Among the high civilizations of antiquity, only the Romans left their mark on the left bank of the Rhine. In 58 B.C., Julius Caesar began the subjugation of the area. The area remained occupied by Roman soldiers until the year 406 A.D. With the fall of the Western

---

[6] This was the extent of the knowledge available when this book was written some 45 years ago.

Roman Empire in 476 A.D., a new time began for the Germanic tribes on the right and left banks of the Rhine - the *Middle Ages.*

The *Middle Ages* cover approximately the period from 500 to 1500 A.D. The Middle Ages can be broken down as follows:

1. The *Early Middle Ages* from the 5th to the 10th century

   This is the time of the Merovingian and Carolingian Dynasties. The Merovingian Dynasty began in 481 A.D. with King Chlodwig and ended in 751 A.D. with King Childerich III. The reign of the Carolingian Dynasty lasted from 751 to 911 A.D. Progenitor of the dynasty was Pepin the Short, King of France, and the most important member was Charlemagne (768-814).

2. The *High Middle Ages* from the 10th to the 13th century

   In this golden age of the Holy Roman Empire, the German rulers were the Saxon, the Salian, and the Hohenstaufen emperors. The Saxon emperors ruled from 919 to 1002 A.D., the Salian from 1024 to 1125 A.D., and the Staufer from 1138 to 1254 A.D. The most important rulers were Otto the Great (936-973), Konrad II (1024-1039) who built the Cathedral of Speyer, and Friedrich Barbarossa (1152-1190).

3. The *Late Middle Ages* from 13th to the 15th century

   This period of history begins with the election of Rudolf von Habsburg (1273-1291) as King of Germany. In addition to the Habsburgs, other kings ruled from their respective kingdoms.

The *Modern Era* began in 1500 A.D. with the discovery of America (1492) and the religious schism in Germany (1517).

The events of the 20th century are often grouped together under the term *Modern History or Contemporary History.*

If we now place the emergence of the Ottersheim village into this comprehensive chronology, the first mention of this place would be in the Early Middle Ages. The name of the village Ottersheim was first mentioned in 768 A.D. in documents called the Lorsch Charter.[5] This places the founding of the village in the Merovingian period.

Prehistoric and Early Historical Discoveries In and Around Ottersheim

When the area of Ottersheim was first settled cannot be determined with certainty. It would have been very early however. This is suggested by the skeleton of an elephant that was found in January 1950 on the estate of the Dumser brothers at 52 Lange Straße. At that time, a well was being dug about 11 meters away from the street in the yard between the two houses. When they had dug almost 6 meters deep, the skeleton of a large animal was discovered whose name and age were obtained from the Historical Museum. According to the expert, it was a so-called *straight-tusked elephant (elaphas antiquus),* which lived about 100,000 years ago during the next-to-last interglacial period. Two pieces of ribs and a vertebra piece were salvaged. The bones lay in the gray sand under a layer of blue to blue-purple sediment. The relative placement of the remains to each other allows one to assume that the complete skeleton of this animal can be found in this location. Given that this is true, then the first complete skeleton of a Pleistocene elephant could be uncovered in our area. Unfortunately, the dig could not take place due to financial and technical issues.

The strata at the site was:

0.0 - 0.3 meters:	topsoil, humus layer
0.3 - 1.5 meters:	fine, red sand mixed with gravel and boulders
1.5 - 3.0 meters:	coarse red sand mixed with gravel and boulders
3.0 - 4.5 meters:	yellowish clay sediment
4.5 - 5.9 meters:	blackish-blue to violet clay sediment
5.9 - 6.1 meters:	gray sand (location of the straight-tusked elephant)

When the straight-tusked elephants lived in the forests of the river valleys of our homeland about 100,000 years ago, there were already people living here at the time. They had a stocky build and lived in caves and grottoes. People at that time knew how to keep a fire burning and make simple tools from stone and bones. They subsisted on fruits and meat. They preferred the two-horned rhinos, elk cows, and the straight-tusked elephants, which they killed with spears after the animals had fallen into pits they had dug. The territory of the Palatinate today was a favorite hunting ground for the people of the Early Stone Age due to its favorable climatic conditions.

Stronger evidence of human life in Ottersheim and the surrounding area has been found from the New Stone Age. A stone ax was discovered in the Ottersheim district in 1918 that is now preserved at the Historical Museum of the Palatinate in Speyer. It was found by former workers of the Schott Company of Knittelsheim and it dates from the period 5000-2000 B.C. Similar discoveries of tools from the Stone Age had been made in the neighboring community of Knittelsheim. A stone ax was found on the Gollenberg, another on the church square in Knittelsheim, and a third in the woods. In Offenbach, a burial mound from the Stone Age has even been found in the forested area north of the Queich. The fact that prehistoric finds in Ottersheim have been sparse so far is perhaps connected to the population of the village paying too little attention to the remnants of the past and not looking at removed stones when working their fields.

Surprisingly, no objects from the Bronze Age that covers the period from 2000 to 800 B.C. have been found in Ottersheim. In the Knittelsheim district however, twelve clay pots dating to the Early Bronze Age were recovered from a cremation site in the middle sand layer and placed in the Historical Museum of the Palatinate. From the Iron Age, which extends from 800 A.D. until about the Birth of Christ, only finds from Knittelsheim and Offenbach have been reported so far. In the Hohweg of Knittelsheim, a vessel from the Hallstatt period (800-450 B.C.) and a bowl from the La Tène period (450 B.C. to the Birth of Christ) have been discovered. Remains of vessels from the La Tène period were also found in the pastures of Knittelsheim. A burial site from the Hallstatt period has been found in the Offenbach forest. These finds along with the other finds show that our country was inhabited by people during the last millennium before the Birth of Christ.

From the conquest of Gaul in the years 58-52 B.C. by Julius Caesar to the year 406 A.D., the left bank of the Rhine was part of the Roman Empire. The Romans built forts and roads. While numerous finds from Roman times were made in the Knittelsheim district on the Gollenberg, in the Hohweg, or in the forest, no artifacts from Roman times could be identified in Ottersheim for a long time. It was not until 1945 during the excavation of ditches to pave the Landauer Straße that fragments of Roman brick, also parts of a vessel with a fine pattern *(Terra Sigillata)*,[7] and a black perforated sphere the size of an apple were found. The objects were in the field of farmer Emil Kern, halfway to the border to Offenbach about 1.8 meters deep in the sand. Unfortunately, the items were lost in the chaos of war at that time. It is likely there is additional proof of Roman times existing within the Ottersheim district. These items will only be discovered when houses are built and similar opportunities arise to uncover the remains of ancient graves, buildings, vessels, and the like, and reports of such discoveries are brought to the attention of the *State Office for Pre- and Early History of the Palatinate* in Speyer. If this was done consistently then such finds can be dated and documented, like the stone coffin that was reportedly uncovered at 6 Ludwigstraße when a shed was being built decades ago. Also, the centuries-old Ried Well at 45 Ludwigstraße would have been found more quickly had the observations immediately been passed on to an interested agency.

---

[7] *Terra Sigillata* is Latin for "sealed earth" and refers to a high satin gloss coating on clay used instead of a glaze in the making of pottery.

How Ottersheim Originated

In the middle of the 5th century, the Mongolian Huns stormed into Europe from the Far East around the year 375 A.D. and established themselves in the Hungarian Plain. Under their king, *Attila the Father,* the Huns dominated the tribes and peoples from the Baltic Sea to the Lower Danube and from the Rhine deep into the Ukraine. Fear and terror held the vast empire together. The *Song of the Nibelungs* tells of their victory over the Burgundians. Attila, also known as *Etzel,* called together all his subject populations in the summer of 451. He wanted the Western Roman Empire brought under his control, particularly Gaul.

Huge armies on horseback soon steamrolled out over the Rhine near the mouth of the Neckar scorching and burning. Between the Marne and the Seine and on the Catalaunian Fields there was a fierce battle between the Roman legions with their auxiliary Germanic peoples on the one hand and the Huns with their subject populations on the other. As the story goes, the battle was so bloody even the dead continued to fight in the air. Attila was undefeated when night put an end to the struggle. He retired to his battlements and constructed a pyre from wooden saddles. If the enemy stormed the camp then the Huns would not fall alive into their hands.[8] But the attack did not happen and Etzel could leave unhindered. When he died suddenly two years later, the vast empire fell apart under the rule of his sons.

Because of the Hun invasion and the bloody battles, the territory of the Palatinate of today was almost completely depopulated. The depopulated land was a popular settlement area for both the Alemanni in the south and the Franks in the north. Their advance from opposite directions made a collision inevitable. Bloody conflicts ensued. A decisive battle took place at Zülpich around the year 500. In the bitter struggle, the Frankish King Chlodwig (481-511) remembered his vow should he win, to accept Christianity and to convert to the God of his Catholic wife, Chlotilde. Indeed, the fortunes of war inclined to his side. Soon after, King Chlodwig was baptized with 3,000 Frankish nobles by Bishop Remigius of Reims.

The defeated Alemanni were forced back to the south. Frankish King Chlodwig moved selected military families into the area of present-day Vorderpfalz [the eastern part of the Palatinate]. These so-called *settlements* took place along the old Roman roads between the Rhine and the Haardt where the water supply could be assured by local streams. The warrior *Udomar* and his family were assigned to the parcel south of the middle Queich where some dwellings were probably already in existence, the Ottersheim district of today. The family of *Knutil* received the parcel to the east, while the warrior *Ballo* was rewarded with the adjacent area - now Bellheim. It should have been expected that the Frankish tribes of these three places would settle on the Queich. However, that was not possible at that time because the site to the right and left of this stream was marshy and very wet, until a thousand years later when it was drained through artificial trenches. The village of

---

[8] Attila had made up his mind to throw himself on the pyre rather than give the enemy the satisfaction of wounding or killing him.

22

Udomar was called by the inhabitants of surrounding villages *Udomarsheim*. That name became *Ottersheim*[9] over the course of time. Some old documents that provide evidence to the development of the name are:

Name	Document
Udomarsheim:	Deed of gift dated 12 August 768 at the Monastery of Lorsch.
Udemarsheim:	Deed of gift dated 30 August 775 at the Monastery of Lorsch.
Hudamareshaim:	Deed book at the Monastery of Fulda from the time of Charlemagne, written 780-802.
Otteresheim/ Hoteresheim:	Commodity Classification at the Monastery of Weißenburg from Charters of the 9th and 10th centuries by Abbot Edelin written in the 13th century.
Othersheim:	In 1231, the Cleric Hugo transfers an estate in Othersheim to the Monastery of Hördt.
Ottersheim:	In 1318, the widow Katharina Rorhus gives her properties in Ottersheim and Knuttelsheim to the Monastery of Hördt.

First Historical Evidence of the Place Name Ottersheim

The name Ottersheim is first mentioned in a deed of the Monastery of Lorsch dated 12 August 768. At that time, a nobleman named Erkenbert gifted his estate in Ottersheim, including cultivated and uncultivated land, to the Benedictine Abbey of Lorsch, which was founded in 763 under Pepin the Short, the father of Charlemagne. The deed of gift, written in Latin, reads as follows:

In Christi nomine sub die II id. aug., anno XVI Pippini regis, ego Erkenbertus pro remidio anime mee dono ad. S. Nazariem e. c., mansum 1 in pago spirensi in Udomarsheimer marca, cum terra culta et inculta que ad ipsum mansum pertinent ...

The translation of the deed of gift is as follows:

I Erkenbert give in the name of Christ, on 12 August in the 16th year of the reign of Pepin, for the salvation of my soul, to Saint Nazarius and companions, an estate in the Speyer valley, in the Udomarsheimer district with the developed and undeveloped land that belongs to it ...

The 16th year in the reign of Pepin the Short was the year 768. Charlemagne took over the government of the Frankish empire in the same year

---

[9] Martin Dolch and Albrecht Greule in the book, "Historisches Siedlungsnamenbuch der Pfalz" [Historical Settlement Name Book of the Palatinate], 1991, dispute the previous historical opinion that the name Ottersheim was derived from the names Udomarsheim, Udemarsheim, and Hudamareshaim.

riḡ. anno· xvii· karoli regis· Don ꝉ erkenbꝛ.

IVDO GISREH EIMER mrca·

H xp̄i nomine· Subdie·ii Id· Aug· anno·xvi·
Pippini regis· Ego Erkenbert· p̄ remedio ani
me̅ mee· dono ad· s· h· mr̄em· qui req̄·incor
pore inmonaſt̄· lauriſḡ· ubi uene̅r· bunde
land?· alꝫ· p̄ eſſe uidet̄· manſum ·i· inpago Spi
renſi· in Vdomarſheimer· marc̄· cum terra
culta oꝛ inculta que adipſum manſu̅ p̄ti
net· ſtipuꝉ ſubnixa· dctum inmonaſt̄· lau
riſḡ· die ꜫ ꞇ· q· s· Donmo ꞇ R C H e ꜫ

Be R ꞇ ꜫ· iii ſup̄dict̄ iii A R c ꜫ·
H xp̄i nomine Anno· xv Pippini reḡ· Ego Er
kenbertuſ dono ad· s· h· mr̄em qui requieſ
cit incorpe inmonaſt̄· lauriſḡ· ubi uenerab·
bundeland?·alꝫ· p̄ eſſe uidet̄· quidq̄d habere
uideor: meadem marca ſup̄adicta p̄ ecualit̄
adpoſſidendum· ſtipuꝉ· ſubnixa·dctum inmo
naſtio lauriſḡ· ꞇ· q· s· Donmo A c h ꜫ
oꝛ dꜧ· ꜧ G undeflebis coniugis eius·
Hxp̄i nomine Subdie·iii· kꝉ· Sept̄ Anno
vii karoli regis· Ego lechiolꞇ· oꝛ coniux mea·
Gundefled· donamus· ad· s· h· mr̄em qui re
quieſcit incorpe inmonaſt̄· lauriſḡ· ubi ue
ne̅r· bundeland?·alꝫ· p̄ eſſe uidet̄· unu̅ man
ſum īpago Spurenſi· in Vdemarſheimer· mar
ca· cum campiſ prauſ· ſiluiſ aquiſ· ſtipulat̄
ſubnixa· Actu̅ inmonaſt̄· laur꜠· ꞇ· q· s·

The Deed of Gift from the Lorsch Monastery
(where Udemarsheim is mentioned)

Another deed of gift dates from the 15th year of the reign of Pepin the Short. It was written in the period from November 766 to November 767. Although it is about a year older than the previous certificate, it is listed second in the Lorsch Charter. The transcript reads:

In Christi nomine anno XV Pippini regis, ego Erkenbertus dono ad S. Nazariem. Gundelandus ... quidquid habere uideor, in eadem marca supra dicta perpetualiter ad possidendum, stipulatione ...

The translation of this deed of gift is:

In the name of Christ, in the 15th year of the reign of Pepin, I Erkenbert give to honor the Saints Nazarius ... Gundelandus ... whatever I have in the same district, in perpetuity for ownership by contract ...

Ottersheim is mentioned a third time in the Lorsch Charter in a deed dated 30 August 775. The text of this document is:

In Christi nomine sub die III kl. sept. anno VII Karoli regis, ego Acchiolt et coniux mea Gundefled donamus ad S. Nazariem ... Gundelandus ... unum mansum in pago spirensi in Udemarsheimer marca, cum campis, pratis, Siluis, aquis, stipulation ...

The translation of this deed of gift is:

In Christ's name, on 30 August 775, in the 7th year of the reign of Charlemagne, we, Acchiolt and my wife Gundefled, in honor of Saint Nazarius ... Gundelandus ... an estate in the Speyer region, Udomarsheimer district, with fields, meadows, forests and waters by contract ...

Ottersheim in the Deed Book of the Monastery of Fulda

According to the deed book of the Monastery of Fulda, during the reign of Charlemagne a certain Acbuto deeded to the Fulda Monastery: a church, a manor house, twenty hufe[10] [parcels] of land at Höfen (Kandel), a church in Geinsheim, enough vineyards for twenty fuder[11] of wine at Weyher, and 63 or more indentured people at the places of Leimersheim, Rülzheim, Hördt, Hudamareshaim (Ottersheim), Walsheim, Gommersheim, Mußbach, Mulinhuson (Mühlhausen at Landau), Mörzheim, Offenbach, Mörlheim, Godramstein, and Nußdorf.

The donation falls within the period of 780-802. It is listed under number 403 in the deed book.

---

[10] A *hufe* (also *hube*) was considered to be the amount of land necessary to support and maintain a farmer and his family. It could vary in size from 7.5 to 30 hectares depending on the region and soil quality.

[11] A *fuder* was either a cartload, or an oak barrel having a volume of approximately 1000 liters.

Ottersheim in the List of Goods of the Monastery of Weißenburg in Alsace

Ottersheim is mentioned several times in the *Traditiones Possessionesque Wizenburgensis (Johann Kaspar Zeuss, 1842)*. The texts are written in Latin. Translating the meaning, we read in the *Liber Donationum [Book of Donations]*:

> In the 8th year of the reign of Charlemagne (i.e., the year 808 A.D.), a nobleman named Erbio bequeathed to the Abbot of Weißenburg his possessions in Alsace. For this, he and his children have a right to use possessions of the Monastery of Weißenburg in the Speyer region, including in Ottersheim, Knittelsheim, and Hochstadt. The properties had been in the possession of the Noble Irminolfus in Ottersheim. It was a feudal manor with associated buildings. Belonging to the feudal properties were four servant parcels with buildings upon two of them.

In *Liber Possessionum [Book of Possessions]* of the Abbot Edelin in the 13th century, we read in entry IX:

> From Ottersheim: Belonging to the manor in Hoteresheim are arable land, meadows, and vineyards. From the meadows, 106 loads of hay, and from the vineyards, 4 fuder of wine are to be delivered. Also, belonging to the manor are 13 full parcels and 5 half parcels. Three days of each week, work is to be done for the manor. In autumn, three morgen[12] of land are to be plowed, and likewise in the spring. Each occupant of a full parcel must provide 13 piglets, and the occupant of a half-parcel provides 6 Denar, 5 hens, and 15 eggs. All must provide the use of a team three times each year. The women must make a half bolt from their own linen. For military service, the property occupant must provide an ox, a half wagon, and a man.

The following list of possessions can be found in entry LXXI of the Monastery of Weißenburg directory:

> From Ottersheim: In Ottersheim, the monastery owns a manor house, a church with tithes[13] that includes a feudal manor. The manor includes nine land parcels, vineyards yielding 3 loads of wine, meadows that yield 60 carts of hay, a mill from which 14 measures of grain must be delivered, a woodlot where 30 pigs are kept. Also belonging to the manor are 14 parcels with buildings, from each of which a piglet or a gold coin is to be delivered, along with 5 hens and 15 eggs. The wives of the parcel dwellers must deliver linen cloth of 10 elles[14] length and 4 elles width. In the event of war, an ox, half a cart, and a man are to be provided. Three days of each week, work is to be done for the manor. Three times a year a

---

[12] A *morgen* was a common unit of land measure having an inconsistent area depending on the region and quality of the soil. A morgen could range from 1/4 to-1 hectare.

[13] *Tithes* were required contributions to religious organizations or taxes to governments typically paid using agricultural products.

[14] An *elle* was a dry unit of length equaling the distance from the elbow to the tip of the middle finger.

team is to be provided and 2 morgen of land are to be plowed. Moreover, grain and hay are to be harvested to prepare beer and bread. From the 8 parcels that are partly built upon, a third of the grain is to be handed over.

Ottersheim was mentioned a fourth time in the list of goods from the Monastery of Weißenburg under entry CCCXI. Translating the meaning, it states:

When the minor-aged Emperor Otto III (983-1002) took over the government after the death of Otto II (973-983), the Monastery of Weißenburg suffered a severe affliction. Duke Otto of Worms, the grandson of Otto the Great, used the situation to attack the monastery and disperse among his own subjects the feudal properties of the monks and the parcels used for their maintenance. Among the numerous benefices that were affected was the monastery in Ottersheim. That happened in the year of our Lord 991, under Otto III.

How Ottersheim Probably Looked Around the Year 800

No one can say with certainty how Ottersheim looked during the time of Charlemagne (768-814). Nevertheless, if one attempts here to create a picture of the village and its inhabitants around the year 800, then this venture relies on the fact that the list of goods of the Monastery of Weißenburg includes some information about Ottersheim that can be evaluated for such a description. However, it must be stated explicitly that by no means is a claim being made to draw a historically accurate picture of Ottersheim around the year 800. A factor of uncertainty exists even in the selected time frame, because it cannot be determined exactly to which century the Weißenburg list refers. With certainty, we know that the Abbey at Weißenburg in the time of Charlemagne had land in Ottersheim that was lost to Duke Otto of Worms in 991. Like Fulda and Lorsch, Weißenburg at that time was a small principality that was one of the most important abbeys of the kingdom. Weißenburg owned 10,000 morgen of farmland in at least 28 places in and around the area. The vineyards yielded 300 wagonloads and the meadows 2,000 wagonloads. In these 28 villages, 765 homesteads were required to pay tributes.

Ottersheim also was one of the villages that belonged to the Abbey of Weißenburg. The place at the least had a church at that time to which a property was connected. This property included, depending on the quality of the soil, about 20 to 30 morgen of fields and meadows so that one peasant farmer could live from it. The main purpose of the church property was to secure the maintenance of the clergy. Since the church was equipped with tithe law, it must be assumed that even then there was a parish in Ottersheim. The clerics probably worked the Abbey of Weißenburg for which it received a third of the tithes. The second third was used for the upkeep of the church, while the last third of the tithe was for the poor. In all probability, the small wooden church stood on the square now occupied by the Catholic Church. The feudal land possessions of the Monastery of Weißenburg, consisting of a house, stables, barns, and sheds, were probably located in an area south of the church. Belonging to the manor were nine parcels of about 200 morgen of fields and meadows that were largely in the immediate vicinity of the feudal manor. The property was managed by a peasant or steward who was placed there by the Monastery of Weißenburg. The meadows that belonged to the manor seem to have been very extensive, because 60 loads of hay were delivered off them. However, considering the bad roads of the time, a load would have been much smaller than today. A large part of the meadows lay on both sides of the *Quotgraben [Big trench]* on the *Oberbrühl [Upper swampy meadows]*. However, it is likely that the *Vorderwiesen [Front meadows]* were present even then.

The Weißenburg goods directory also mentions a mill in Ottersheim that had to deliver 14 measures of grain. This small mill, which is never mentioned in later documents, probably stood at the present *Mühlwiesen [Mill meadows]* and got its water from a trench that was dug from the Queich. No mill could be built on the Queich itself in the Ottersheim district, because the land on both sides of the creek was quite swampy. That a water trench ran through the front meadows is attested in later documents. The mill itself, which was surely small and insignificant due to the weak water power source, seems to have been abandoned during the Middle Ages. At any rate, the peasants of Ottersheim were obliged during the Palatinate times to have their grain milled at the Germersheim mill. Also belonging to the Weißenburg feudal manor in Ottersheim were vineyards of which three loads or about three fuder of wine were to be delivered. The vines most likely stood near the church and in the *Gröhlig [Ravine]*, the farmland west of the south village exit. It is likely the arable land was mostly located south of the village. To the north of the Brühlgraben, land was hardly cultivated past the road to Offenbach. The area north of the village up to the Queich was almost entirely covered with woods and bushes, and primarily served as grazing land with the exception of the Vorderwiesen. Unlike today, the Kahlenberg and Gollenberg were still covered with trees. This forest, which stretched from west to east, was gradually cleared and cultivated during the course of the 9th century. As far as the wooded area north of the village that belonged to the Monastery of Weißenburg, it was used for raising pigs. Thirty pigs could be kept there.

In Ottersheim, 14 full hufe owed tributes to the Abbey of Weißenburg. That is to say, that the occupants of 14 properties, of 20 to 30 morgen each, had to provide labor and goods to the Monastery of Weißenburg. These obligations are described in detail in the goods directory. Therefore, the peasant had to work three days a week at the manor without pay. This forced labor was carried out in the fields, the meadows, or at the manor itself. The men not only helped in the planting and harvesting, but also in clearing roads, improving land, preparing and mending fences, and working on buildings at the manor. The women had to lend a hand in the hay and grain harvest, milk, and make bread, malt, and mead. In addition, each year they had to deliver a bolt of linen ten elles long and six elles wide. Each parcel occupant had to provide a team three times each year. These were typically used to collect any surpluses of hay, grain, wine, and so on, and to take these to the Monastery of Weißenburg or to a specific collection location. In addition, each had to plow two morgen of the landlord's fields using his own team. A piglet or lamb, or in its stead a gold coin had to be provided to the manor from each parcel. In addition, 5 hens and 15 eggs were to be provided at Easter. In the event of war, all parcel occupants were obliged to provide half an ox cart and a man. For the eight parcels that were only partly built upon, one third of the grain was to be provided to the manor. Even running errands was among the obligations of the dependent peasants towards the monastery. There was at that time no mail or public transport, so that the connection between the monastery and the manor was maintained through messengers.

Also, sentinel duties on the pastures and in the manor yard was among the duties of the parcel occupants. A final duty of the parcel occupants was to fatten the pigs during the winter. During the summer and fall, the pigs were driven into the manor forest where they fed on acorns and other fruits of the forest. However, in winter the 30 pigs were distributed to the various parcels and fattened there. Since the forested areas of the village were rather small, the Monastery of Weißenburg seems to have made an exception in Ottersheim with timber deliveries.

From this compilation of the various obligations and duties of the parcel occupants, one could get the impression that the peasants of that time were enslaved and exploited, which was not so in reality. Basically, their dependence consisted mainly in that in addition to their own fields, they also had to provide for the convent. This settled all their obligations to community, church, and state. Moreover, one must remember that the work of the peasant farmers in those days was much less and easier than today. Specialized crops were not yet known. The fields were mostly rye, spelt,[15] oats, barley, flax, and hemp that only had to be sown and harvested. The cattle grazed from spring to late autumn at the community pasture or common land and had to be fed hay only in winter. In the vineyards, one was satisfied with what grew on the vines. One knew nothing of pesticides, artificial fertilizers, potatoes, vegetables, and onions at that time. The work largely consisted of plowing, sowing, and harvesting. The food was accordingly simple and humble. The main diet consisted of porridge, bread, eggs, butter, and meat. Honey was used as a sweetener, and was consumed as honey wine when in fermented state. In addition, there existed by now gardens where cucumbers, melons, and pumpkins were planted as well as flowers and roses.

The peasants would build their wooden houses themselves and with vigorous assistance from their neighbors. Also, they built their own wooden plows and other equipment. The only artisans of the village were the blacksmiths. In Ottersheim, the blacksmith likely had his workshop to the south of the Weet on the grounds of the Weißenburg feudal manor as in the Late Middle Ages. The blacksmith was in some sense a municipal employee and was appointed by the community. The forge was provided for a small fee by the community.

---

[15] Spelt was a type of wheat and is considered of subspecies of present-day common wheat.

The affiliation to the Monastery of Weißenburg imposed various obligations on the peasants of Ottersheim. But they were released simultaneously from a burden that formerly lay heavily on their shoulders, the obligation for military service. That is to say, every free peasant who owned a large property had to go to war with the King at his own expense. In addition to horses and equipment, he had to pay for his own food. There was no lack of war during the Merovingian and Carolingian Dynasties. Many peasants were gone for years and work in the fields had to be done by women and children. Therefore, many peasants voluntarily entered into the protection of a landowner who could release them from the obligation to military service. This was likely the reason that the Ottersheim parcel inhabitants owed tributes to the Monastery of Weißenburg. Together, they were obliged to provide only one soldier along with one ox and a half cart. The ox served as food and the cart as transportation. Ottersheim likely traded with other locations from campaign to campaign in providing a cart since only half a cart was required.

The Weißenburg feudal manor, with its tributary land parcels, was lost in 991 to Duke Konrad of Worms. Under the Salian dynasty, the manor went to the Palatinate and was property of the Poppelmann Dynasty until the French Revolution. It would be nice to know whether other such landlords were present in Ottersheim around the year 800. Unfortunately, the historical sources tell us nothing in this regard. However, it is known that the Klingenmünster Abbey in Ottersheim owned 41.5 hectares of land and had a feudal manor that stood on the east side of the Deich[16] during the Middle Ages. This was probably owned by King Dagobert indicating the Klingenmünster Abbey in Ottersheim was also well off. In all likelihood, the conditions at the feudal manor of the Klingenmünster Abbey would not have been much different from those of the Weißenburg feudal manor. However, Klingenmünster was never owner of the Ottersheim parish because its significance was lower.

Ottersheim in the High Middle Ages

Little information about Ottersheim has been passed on from the 10th to 13th centuries. We are told that in the year 1106, Hermann von Spiegelberg gave his cultivated fields, vineyards, and pastures in Ottersheim to the Augustinian Monastery in Hördt. In 1231, the Cleric Hugo from Speyer also gave to the Hördt Monastery an estate in the Ottersheim district. And the Cistercian Abbey of Eußerthal received property in Ottersheim from the hands of Mechthild von Hovenstein in 1269.

---

[16] The author references the *Deich [Dike]* throughout the book. This was the Deich Gasse, an early road on the west side of the village that crossed the dike that created the Weet. It connected the Große Gasse in the north by the Catholic Church to the Landauer Straße in the south.

However, the most interesting data of note from that time is that a knighted family was located in Ottersheim or at least owned property there in the 13th century. We hear that in 1249, in the time of King Friedrich II (1215-1250), a Knight Hugo von Offenbach sold his property in Offenbach to the Abbot of Eußerthal and that Knight Konrad von Ottersheim was witness thereof. Knight Konrad von Ottersheim appears for the second time in 1283, being present for the proceedings at the great Knightly Court in Eußerthal regarding basic rights. In 1292, a Knight Hartlieb von Ottersheim is mentioned in an exchange of land between the community of Queichheim and the Eußerthal Monastery. In addition, a Knight Konrad von Ottersheim appears again in 1299. Finally, a Squire Resche from Ottersheim is mentioned in 1300. Unfortunately, we do not know whether any knights were resident or at least owned property in Ottersheim during the 11th and 12th centuries. It cannot be readily dismissed, especially since many neighboring towns housed knights within their walls at that time.

It is generally known that knights were bound to their lord for military service, and they went with the king or prince on horseback into battle. A knight was not allowed to "speak or act against the Holy Religion or against the German Reich, to insult a woman or virgin, breach good faith, or to flee from battle." All the knights together formed the military having divorced themselves from the working class. The king was responsible for the well-being of his warriors. He paid the knight not with money but with a large piece of land called a *fief.* While the property rights were retained by the feudal lord, the income of the estate belonged to the knight as a vassal. The knight had to provide his own horse, armor, and food, and be ready to serve his lord at anytime and anywhere. It is very likely that such a manor was present in Ottersheim. This was probably the former lands of the Monastery of Weißenburg that were lost in 991 to Otto of Worms, who was a grandson of Otto the Great. This estate was later transferred to the Salian Imperial family by inheritance. However, when the Salian dynasty went extinct with Heinrich V in 1125, the property fell to the Staufer who ruled from 1138. We may assume with great probability that when the royal family owned the Ottersheim property, such property would have been awarded to a deserving feudal knight as was common practice at the time. However, there remains the question whether the knight and any family lived in Ottersheim, or whether the knight owned other property where he may have had a permanent residence. It is also conceivable that in the course of an inheritance a side branch chose to live in Ottersheim. In any case, the mention of Knight Konrad von Ottersheim or Hartlieb von Ottersheim supports the idea that these knights lived around Ottersheim.

What is striking is the fact that knights from Ottersheim are not mentioned until the second half of the 13th century, while the golden age of chivalry falls in the 11th and 12th centuries. The role of Knights decreased steadily in importance with the death of Hohenstaufen King Konrad IV in 1254. Clearly, in the "ruler-less, terrible time" from 1256 to 1273, many families fell into such poverty that they turned to street robbery or mugging. It is very well possible during this time that later-born sons of knights had to make do with smaller parcels. If in fact a knighted family lived in Ottersheim, then certainly he did not live in a magnificent castle, as was such the case in other places. Perhaps the knight family inhabited the manor west of the Deich, while servants and maids would have cultivated the fields and meadows.

Around the year 1400, when Ottersheim was already part of the Palatinate, the Poppelmann family was in possession of the former monastery and later the knightly manor in Ottersheim. Through several generations, the Poppelmann dynasty was the caretaker of the castle in Germersheim, and they took orders from the local castellan.[17] They were required to do service as arms-bearers in the castle and to serve in any wars. They lived in Weingarten and also had a large property in Knittelsheim. After the Poppelmann family died out, the Palatinate awarded the Ottersheim property to individual tenants. It was not until the French Revolution at the beginning of 18th century that the 37.2 hectares of fields and meadows were finally divided and sold by the French to private individuals.

Later Medieval Documents about Ottersheim

(These documents are in the Bavarian State Archives in Munich. Excerpts of the content are provided in the following text.)

1231:   The Cleric Hugo passes an estate in *Ottersheim* to the Monastery of Hördt.

1249:   Knight Hugo von Offenbach sells his possessions in Offenbach to the Abbot of the Monastery of Eußerthal. Witness to the transaction is Knight Konrad von *Ottersheim.*

1269:   On 31 May 1269, Mechthild von Hovenstein transfers her possessions in Königsbach, Gimmeldingen, Winzingen, Haardt, and *Ottersheim* to the Eußerthal Monastery.

1279:   On 25 October 1279, Konrad Stolle sells certain possessions in the Village of *Ottersheim* to the Cathedral Chapter in Speyer.

1292:   On 12 October 1292, the community of Queichheim traded a meadow for two jauchert[18] with the Monastery of Eußerthal. Witness to this transaction is Knight Hartlieb von *Ottersheim.*

1299:   On 31 March 1299, Graf Friedrich von Leiningen, Imperial Governor in the Speyer region, awards a property called Melnfurt to the village and Monastery of Hördt in a dispute between the village and Monastery of Hördt on one hand, and the village of Dettenheim. Witness was Knight Konrad von *Ottersheim.*

---

[17] A *castellan* was the governor or captain of the castle.

[18] A *jauchert* was a parcel of land equivalent to a morgen.

1310: On 14 January 1310, Speyer citizen Ulrich von Rorhus gives the new Saint Georg Hospital in Speyer possessions and rights in *Ottersheim* as well as a forest near Lingenfeld.

1318: On 28 January 1318, Katharina, widow of Speyer citizen Ulrich von Rorhus, gives her possessions in *Ottersheim* and Knittelsheim to the Monastery of Hördt in exchange for an annuity.

1327: On 6 February 1327, Nikolaus of the Staffelhofe at Weißenburg relinquishes all claims of a property to the Hördt Monastery in *Ottersheim,* which at that time belonged to Ulrich von Rorhus.

1328: The Monastery of Hördt exchanged its properties in Mühlhausen (by Landau) for those of Merkel at Landau to *Ottersheim.*

1357: On 29 March 1357, Johann, Pastor of *Ottersheim,* Peter, Pastor of Knöringen, and Wolf, son of Peter of Walsheim sell to the Monastery of Eußerthal their own free properties in the villages of Knöringen, Essingen, Dammheim, Burrweiler, Landau, Nußdorf, and Walsheim for 714 pfund-hellers.[19]

How Ottersheim Came to the Electoral Palatinate

In an effort to affect the well-being of their souls, the descendants of the Noble Udomar bequeathed large parts of their possessions in Ottersheim to the flourishing monasteries in the near and further surroundings. Around the year 800, the Benedictine Abbey of Weißenburg already owned a sizable feudal manor in the western part of the village upon which also stood the church. Presumably, this was the property on the west side of the Deich that was later owned by the Poppelmann dynasty. Weißenburg was also owner of the Ottersheim parish at that time. The abbey most likely took over the parish and church as a gift of a nobleman; because, the church was not consecrated to Saint Peter, the patron saint of Weißenburg, but instead to Saint Martin. The manor at the Monastery of Weißenburg also included several full hufe and half hufe parcels for which the occupant owed tributes to the monastery. In the year 991, the entire property of the Abbey of Weißenburg in Ottersheim was lost through the robbery of numerous monastic properties by Otto of Worms, a grandson of Otto the Great. The property was later given to the disposal of the royal family by Otto of Worms. It is therefore no surprise that King Heinrich VII (1308-1313) gave the rights of patronage in Ottersheim to the Cistercian Monastery of Eußerthal in 1311.

---

[19] In 1356, a *pfund-heller* (later just pfund) was equal to 1 gulden or 120 pfennigs or 240 hellers.

The successor of Heinrich VII, King Ludwig the Bavarian (1314-1347), often faced financial troubles. He placed his cousin, Palatinate Count Rudolf II, in charge as governor of the Speyer region on 16 September 1338 in Frankfurt am Main, as recognition of his service to the kingdom. In the document, King Ludwig the Bavarian decreed that all lords, earls, freemen, serfs, towns, castles, monasteries, markets, villages, and other people who belong to the jurisdiction must serve and obey the Count Palatinate or his deputy. The ruling dynasty had thus come to the Speyer region in the Palatinate, and the start was made for incorporating the Speyer region with the adjacent Palatinate land to the north. Already by the year 1347, electoral governor Jakob von Flersheim appears as a bailiff. He was entrusted rights associated with the protection of the Elector in the Speyer region. Since that time, the former royal estate in Ottersheim was subject to the Electoral Palatinate.

Like the Weißenburg Monastery in the western part of the village in the Early Middle Ages, so also the Benedictine Monastery of Klingenmünster had a feudal manor east of the Deich. This manor and its properties came later as a fief to the Ochsenstein dynasty of the Castle of Meistersel at Ramberg. About Otto of Ochsenstein, we are told that he mortgaged half of the property in 1369 to Konrad Landschad von Steinach of Ottersheim. Excluded from the pledge were 30 eighths of grain rent[20] that was passed to the Lords of Meckenheim in feudal tenure, and 20 eighths of grain rent which was awarded to Bock von Erfenstein. The Klingen fief of the Ochsenstein dynasty in Ottersheim was probably transferred at that time by the treaty between the Abbot of Klingenmünster and Elector Philipp in 1484, but no later than 1489 with the extinction of the Ochsenstein dynasty. Since that time, the Palatinate was the sole ruler of the Ottersheim village. Frey's opinion in his description of the Rhine district, that Ottersheim was for a time in the possession of the Archbishop of Speyer, cannot be verified.

The village is also not mentioned in the exchange agreement of 1709 in which a series of Palatinate communities were named and where "the exasperating general rule" between the bishop and the elector was removed.

The Rulers of Ottersheim during the Electoral Palatinate

Rudolf II.	1329-1353	
Ruprecht I.	1353-1390	
Ruprecht II.	1390-1398	
Ruprecht III.	1398-1410	From 1400-1410, he was also German King Ruprecht I.

---

[20] *Grain rent* was payment in grain or other crops for the use (lease) of the land.

Ludwig III.	1410-1436	
Ludwig IV.	1436-1449	
Friedrich I.	1449-1476	He was also known as: The Victorious.
Philipp I.	1476-1508	He was also known as: The Sincere.
Ludwig V.	1508-1544	
Friedrich II.	1544-1556	
Ottheinrich	1556-1559	He led the Reformation in the Palatinate. With him, the Heidelberg line of the Wittelsbach family was extinguished.
Friedrich III.	1559-1576	He came from the Simmer's line.
Ludwig VI.	1576-1583	
Johann Casimir	1583-1592	He reigned as guardian for the minor Friedrich IV.
Friedrich IV.	1592-1610	
Friedrich V.	1610-1632	In 1619, he was elected King of Bohemia. As the Winter King, he lost the Battle of White Mountain near Prague. Thereby the 30-Years War was introduced to the Palatinate.
Karl Ludwig	1632-1680	His daughter, Liselotte, married the Duke Philipp von Orleans.
Karl	1680-1685	He died without children. With him, the Simmer's line was extinguished.
Philipp Wilhelm	1685-1690	He came from the Neuburg line and was Catholic like his successors.
Johann Wilhelm	1690-1716	
Karl Philipp	1716-1742	
Karl Theodor	1742-1799	He came from the Sulzbach line and lived in Mannheim. When the Bavarian main line of Wittelsbach was extinguished in 1777, Karl Theodor received the Land of Bavaria. He then moved to Munich.

Ottersheim in the Late Middle Ages

When Palatine Elector Ruprecht III, known as the Clement or the Benevolent, died in 1410, the Electoral Palatinate lands were distributed to his heirs. Germersheim, which also included Ottersheim at that time, went to Ludwig III the Bearded of the Heidelberg line.

Around the middle of the century, Friedrich I became Elector of Heidelberg. The Elector's reign from 1449 to 1476 was full of fights and feuds that he had to endure with his cousin, Duke Ludwig I of Zweibrücken. In 1459, he moved against the Veldenzers from Zweibrücken who had allied themselves with Count Emich of Leiningen and the Bishop of Mainz. Early in the fighting, half the village of Kandel was burned to the ground. In the week before Palm Sunday in 1460, the Faut [governor] of Germersheim advanced against Dörrenbach with 1,000 men, knights, and foot soldiers, and set the village in flames. The villages of Minfeld, Oberotterbach, and Rechtenbach suffered the same fate soon after. The feud ended when Friedrich the Victorious defeated these opponents in the battle of Pfeddersheim in 1461, and the Veldenzers and their allies surrendered.

Friedrich led successful battles against Württemberg, Baden, and the Bishop of Metz in 1462. He was involved in the Weißenburg feud from 1469 to 1471. In spite of a settlement of the war, it ended with the Veldenzers losing a number of towns in the Palatinate and Weißenburg, thereby recognizing Friedrich's rights in the Palatinate. When Elector Friedrich I the Victorious died in 1476, his holdings included a total of 18 jurisdictions resulting from numerous acquisitions. Of course, the many battles and feuds did not take place without leaving their mark on the inhabitants of the Palatinate. Ottersheim surely did not escape unscathed either.

The successor of Friedrich the Victorious was Elector Philipp the Sincere (1476-1508). Under him, the Bavarian-Palatinate War of Succession began in 1503. Duke Georg the Rich of Bavaria-Landshut had his son-in-law, Ruprecht, the son of Elector Philipp von der Pfalz, in mind as heir and successor in his country. Duke Georg's brother-in-law, Duke Albrecht von Bayern-München, disagreed. He was instead of the opinion that the inheritance should be his own. So it came to war. The opponents of the Elector assembled on the Rhine. The Elector fortified his towns and had the movable possessions of its inhabitants brought there for safety. To make it more difficult to burn the houses down, the thatched roofs were removed from the buildings.

The Palatinate was devastated when the war ended in 1505 and many valuable possessions were lost. Moreover, the debt burden of the State had grown considerably. When Elector Philipp the Sincere died in Germersheim three years later, his son, Ludwig V, took over the government in the Palatinate. Ludwig V is known in history as the Peaceable, because no feud took place during his long reign from 1508 to 1544. All the more depressing for him was the bad news of the peasants in Nußdorf going to war against monks and aristocrats in 1525, thereby threatening to plunge the country into misery through looting and arson.

The Peasants' Revolt in 1525

With the decline of chivalry in the Late Middle Ages, there grew self-confidence in the peasants who did not want to be permanently counted as people with fewer rights. Rural people claimed the same Christian dignity as noblemen and town residents. In particular, the peasants demanded the abolition of the small tithes, the abolition of serfdom, free access to hunting and fishing, abolition of forced labor and feudal dues, free choice of the clergy, and pure interpretation of the Holy Scriptures. Finally, there was a series of uncoordinated uprisings in the 15th century when the property owners tried to compensate for the declining value of money through increased mandatory services from the rural population. Following the example of Swabian peasants, an uprising took place by the peasants of Malsch near Heidelberg in the region under the Prince Bishop of Speyer during Holy Week of 1525. From there the flames burst through to the left bank of the Rhine. A bunch from Baden moved across the Rhine near Maximiliansau. They plundered first the Monastery of Hördt and then the Eußerthal Mönchshof [Monk's estate] in Mechtersheim. Then the rebels returned to the right side of the Rhine for safety.

Another group of disgruntled peasants invaded the Palatinate from the Alsace, and plundered the palaces at Lindelbrunn, Gräfenstein, and Landeck as well as Ramberg and various other castles. Often the castles were set ablaze when they withdrew. In the Palatinate itself, the peasant war began in Nußdorf. There the Church dedication festival was underway on the Sunday after Easter. About 200 young peasants from Nußdorf and the surrounding area gathered. While drinking their wine, they swore to march against monasteries and nobility and to free themselves from servitude and tithes. The crowd grew to 500 men in the Siebeldingen valley. The watchful bailiff in Germersheim hurried with a small force to meet them and was successful in getting the rebels to retreat back to their villages.

Hardly had the bailiff and his companions returned to Germersheim when the peasants banded together again. A crowd overwhelmed the Monastery of Klingenmünster and the house of the Knights of Saint John in Haimbach near Zeiskam. A second band turned towards the Rhine and took from the Monastery of Hördt and the Mönchshof in Mechtersheim that which the peasants from Malsch had left, especially wine, grain, and livestock. Under the leadership of the Nußdorf peasants, other bands from the Siebeldingen and Annweiler valleys sacked the Cistercian Abbey at Eußerthal, the Convent of Heilsbruck in Edenkoben, and the Bishops' palaces in Edesheim, Kirrweiler, Kropsburg, and Maxburg. They were aiming mainly at the rich wine cellars. The wine they did not drink was dumped into the cellars. The very large crowd of rebellious peasants rested at the Mönchshof in Mörlheim after most of the monasteries, castles, and palaces were burnt down.

Elector Ludwig V of Heidelberg, who had always tried to end the uprising of his Palatine peasants amicably, eventually decided to proceed with armed force. On 23 May 1525, his soldiers marched from Heidelberg on a punitive expedition. Among his 8,000 soldiers were about 1,200 cavalry. The Elector was sorry to have to spill the blood of his country's children, but he saw no other way to avert the chaos.

On 23 June 1525, a bloody confrontation took place near Worms between the army of the Elector and the Palatine peasants. At first, the rebellious peasants on the right side of the Rhine were beaten and severely punished. Some 8,000 rebels had taken up residence in the town of Pfeddersheim and intended to defy the Electoral power. An ill-advised foray out of the town cost about 4,000 peasant lives and the rest managed to escape back behind the walls of Pfeddersheim. On the following day, the white flag was hoisted as the Electoral soldiers readied to attack the town. During the unconditional surrender, some rebels tried to escape and cost another 800 peasant lives. The Elector released the remaining peasants after the execution of the ringleaders.

The rebellious peasants were lords of the Palatinate for nine weeks. During this short time, they destroyed 18 monasteries, 7 palaces and 10 manors of the church as well as 37 castles and palaces of worldly ownership. They almost exclusively destroyed non-religious goods. Only in Dirmstein were 16 opponents' lives lost during a raid. It is likely that some Ottersheim peasants were involved in the uprising. Unfortunately, we have no record that could give us verifiable information. It deserves to be noted that all the monasteries that were well off in Ottersheim were plundered and burned during the Peasants' War.

From the District Office in Germersheim

The District Office in Germersheim emerged little by little from the original small office through purchase and conquest. Most of the growth occurred in the 16th century as the Palatine Electors took over a number of convents and monasteries in the wake of the Reformation. In 1577, the District Office counted 4 cities and 54 villages, and it had more than 100 cities and villages by 1664. Before the 30 Years War, the District Office of Germersheim was considered one of the largest and richest offices of the Electoral Palatinate. At that time, it included the following areas:

1. The Fautei (Bailiwick) of Germersheim with the city of Germersheim and the villages of Bellheim, Knittelsheim, Ottersheim, Böbingen, Zeiskam, Sondernheim, and Hördt.
2. The Priory (tithe management) Offices of Hördt and the villages of Leimersheim, Kuhardt, and Pfotz.
3. The official Hagenbach Winery with the City of Hagenbach and four villages.
4. The Seltz Customs Office (in Alsace) with the City of Seltz and the village of Münchhausen.
5. The Office at Altenstadt near Weißenburg, with nine villages under the joint management of the Weißenburg Monastery and the Palatinate.
6. The Monastery (tithe management) of Klingenmünster with four villages.
7. The Office at Landeck with 14 villages under the joint administration of the Bishopric of Speyer and the Palatinate. The Landeck Office included the villages of Insheim, Offenbach, Oberhochstadt, and Schwegenheim, among others.

8. The Winery at Landeck with seven villages in the Wasgau, including Lug, Stein, Gossersweiler, and others.
9. The Office at Billigheim with the city of Billigheim and the villages Klingen, Erlenbach, Impflingen, Rohrbach, and Steinweiler.
10. The Eußerthal Abbey with the villages of Albersweiler, Gräfenhausen, and Nußdorf. Also belonging to the Eußerthal Abbey were cloisters in Mörlheim, Landau, Göcklingen, Bergzabern, Winzingen, Speyer, and Mechtersheim.
11. The Land offices of the Siebeldingen Valley with the villages of Siebeldingen, Godramstein, Birkweiler, and Gleisweiler.

Not all villages in the vicinity of Ottersheim belonged to the Palatinate. Herxheim and Rülzheim belonged to the Bishopric of Speyer, while Niederhochstadt, Oberlustadt, and Niederlustadt belonged to the Order of Saint John. Landau was a free Imperial City until after the 30 Year's War when it came under French dominion. The inhabitants of the District Office of Germersheim were either free Imperial people or they were serfs. Because these places had come to the Palatinate from the former Roman Empire, the Imperial freemen inhabited the four towns of Germersheim, Hagenbach, Seltz, and Billigheim, as well as the villages of Bellheim, Knittelsheim, Ottersheim, Böbingen, Zeiskam, Sondernheim, Hördt, Godramstein, Siebeldingen, and Rohrbach. Whoever wanted to move to these places had to have his marriage certificate and his letter of free birth or evidence of his redemption from bondage.

The residents of the other towns of the District Office of Germersheim who did not transfer from the Roman Empire to the Palatinate were considered serfs. While the freemen mainly paid land taxes as free citizens, the serfs owed the Electors an annual body tax and other tributes. In particular, contrary to the freemen the so-called *death-rule* required the following to be delivered to the Electors upon death of a serf:

Man: the best head of cattle
Woman: the best dress

However, usually a cash equivalent was paid in lieu of goods.

At the top of the District Office of Germersheim was the *Faut [Governor]* who was usually of noble birth. Toward the end of the 17th century, the term for the office changed from *Vogt [Bailiff]* to *Oberamtmann [Administrator]*. To accomplish his various administrative duties, he employed a *Landschreiber [Magistrate's clerk]*.

This clerk kept books on not only the revenue and expenditures of the District Office, but he also had a major word to say in legal, forestry, and police cases. From the beginning of the 18th century, the District Office clerk was the most important man in the office, and as a representative of the governor, he was responsible for literally everything. A staff of assistants consisting of various officers and employees were available to help. A person who oversaw the serfs, the orphans, the illegitimate children, the Jews, and the refugees was called any one of the following titles: *Hörigenvogt, Waisenvogt, Höerfaut, or Ausfaut*. He had to advise them and represent them in court. He also had to ensure that the serfs paid their dues on time. Another clerk, who reported directly to the District Clerk, kept the protocol during meetings, wrote up contracts, and kept the District books up-to-date, among other tasks. Other agents at the District offices were the collector's office, office runner, the official physician, the customs clerk, the cellar clerk, the fruit clerk, the forest manager, and forest clerks, one on foot and one on horseback. The administration of church property was carried out by administrators and collectors called *Schaffner.*

In all forests of the District Office, only the Palatine Elector was allowed to exercise the right to hunt. This was also the case when the forest was owned by the community as in Ottersheim. The hunting of deer and wild boars was reserved by the Elector for himself and his entourage, while the Faut was required to be content with taking hares. Several hundred red deer and wild boar were killed by the District Office of Germersheim every year. It is no coincidence that in 1550, Elector Friedrich II of Heidelberg (1544-1556) built a hunting lodge called *Friedrichsbühl* in the Bellheim forest on the Sollach. However, the proud Renaissance structure did not survive the 30 Years War. The last remains of the walls were demolished and sold around 1725. A single outbuilding is said to have survived the ravages of time. The timber-frame building was taken down and then reassembled at the Römerplatz in Knittelsheim.

The peasants of these villages were less pleased with the rich hunting grounds in the forest area north of Bellheim, Knittelsheim, and Ottersheim. Only through many fences could they protect their fields and meadows from damage caused by wildlife. The fishing rights on the Queich were also reserved for the Electors. No one was allowed to fish in the Queich without approval of the District Office of Germersheim. Even today, we feel the far-reaching requirement that the residents of Ottersheim, Knittelsheim, Bellheim, Hördt, Sondernheim, and Dettenheim only mill their grain at the so-called *Bannmühle [Spelt mill]* in Germersheim. The regulation to use only one mill within the District was mainly economic. This ensured that not only the incomes of the hereditary tenant of the mill but also the tributes to the District Office were guaranteed. It was not until around the year 1700, when the area south of the Queich was occupied by the French, that a second mill in Bellheim was approved.

Together with the Palatinate, the District Office of Germersheim was eliminated in the Napoleonic period at the beginning of the 19th century. The present-day Germersheim district covers only a small part of the territory of the former District Office.

Essentially, only the Fautei in Germersheim, the Priory Offices at Hördt, and the Official Winery at Hagenbach remain as part of the Germersheim County or region, while the other parts were assigned to the counties of Bergzabern and Landau, provided they had been not previously been ceded to France.

Elector Ottheinrich Introduces a New Religion to Ottersheim in 1556

Luther's doctrine quickly became known throughout the German land after his public appearance in 1517. The peasants in Ottersheim were also not averse to hearing the call for freedom by Christians. Abuses in ecclesiastical life had convinced them that a reform of the Church from top to bottom was necessary. Initially, no one thought of founding a new church however. Rather, it was intended that the original form of the Catholic Church be restored, that the Church should be reformed. That changed the moment Luther broke with the Catholic Church and refused to obey the Pope in Rome.

The nobility of the time soon recognized the big advantages offered them by turning to the teachings of the Reformation. They could not only increase their land holdings and income significantly through the taking over of church possessions, but they also had the opportunity to rule their lands autocratically in both secular and ecclesiastical matters. Neither bishop nor pope would have anything to say in their affairs.

Of the Palatine Electors, Friedrich II (1544-1556) was the first to turn seriously to Lutheranism. His successor, Ottheinrich (1556-1559), completed the work of his predecessor and issued a religion order for the entire Palatinate on 4 April 1556. All clergy were commanded to preach the faith in the spirit of Luther or resign from their office. Ottersheim received its first Lutheran pastor at that time, Valentin Kempfer from Ladenburg. He lived in Knittelsheim however. The Catholic priest, who had led a less than exemplary life, was removed. Ottersheim had become a Lutheran village overnight with the change of the pastor. The Cistercian Monastery at Eußerthal, who owned a feudal manor in Ottersheim, had provided the Catholic priest up to this point. Now the Palatine Elector appointed the clergy in Ottersheim.

Pastor Kempfer from Ladenburg was active in Ottersheim for 32 years (1556-1588). In his religious beliefs, he seems to have adapted smoothly to the flow of the times, or he would have probably been let go by 1563. By this time, so it was that Ottheinrich's successor, Friedrich III of Heidelberg (1559-1576), turned from Lutheranism to Calvinism [Reformed] and declared so openly. All clergy had to accept the so-called *Heidelberg Catechism* and explain it on Sundays to the faithful in the Church. The Saints' Days were abolished and the celebration of Mass disappeared. Altars, statues, and paintings were destroyed. The Lord's Supper was to be celebrated on a wooden table. Instead of wafers, bread was used. The marriage blessing was no longer allowed to take place. Clergymen who refused to accept the new church order were asked to leave the country. The religious beliefs of the people were not considered. The process followed the familiar principle of, *"Cuius regio, eius religio,"* that is, *"Whose realm, his religion."* The Elector did not reject the use of police coercion to give the people a life of Christian character. He ordered that anyone who health-wise was able to attend church on Sunday be required to do so. Cursing, excessive eating, and drinking were forbidden and punishable. Bounds were set on any waste, carelessness, and lack of discipline at weddings and other festivities. An electoral order of 15 July 1570 established presbyteries in all municipalities that consisted of the ministers and the community representatives. These "elders" were the moral monitors and had to impose penances on the stiff-necked. A protocol of 12 November 1598 reported that an Ottersheim peasant was sentenced to two gulden,[21] because he had cursed "blasphemously."

Elector Ludwig IV took over the government after the death of Friedrich III in 1576. Because he was a supporter of the Lutheran faith, his subjects had to accept that belief. The Lutheran Church was again introduced everywhere in the Palatinate. Images of Christ, organs, altars, baptismal fonts, Latin hymns, communion wafers, and chalices were returned. The pastors and teachers who did not adopt the Church Order of 20 August 1577 were relieved of their offices. About 600 families of Calvinist preachers and teachers became unemployed throughout the Palatinate.

When Elector Ludwig IV passed away in 1583, his whole work collapsed again. His successor, Johann Casimir (1583-1592), forced the inhabitants of the Palatinate for the fourth time in 27 years to change their religion and accept the Calvinistic faith. About 500 Lutheran preachers and teachers lost "bread and country." The Protestant clergymen who had been expelled as heretics eight years before returned to their offices.

With brief interruptions during the 30 Years War, Ottersheim remained a Reformed congregation from 1583 for nearly 100 years. A document from the year 1671 confirms this in which is stated that among the 40 households of Ottersheim none is Catholic.

The greatest zealot for the introduction of the Calvinistic faith was Elector Friedrich III (1556-1576) of Heidelberg. In addition to the violent conversion of his subjects, he closed a number of monasteries and took over their land. Of these, all religious institutions in Ottersheim that were well off were involved. Eußerthal was closed in 1561, the Monastery at Germersheim in 1563, the Monastery at Hördt in 1566, and the Priory at Klingenmünster in 1567. The peasants had hoped that the monastic property would fall to their ownership. They were to be disappointed in this regard because for them everything remained the same. Instead of the monasteries, there was now an officer of the Electors to collect their taxes in cash and equivalent goods. One must even fear that from now on, less forbearance would be practiced with them than with the spiritual masters. There is a reason for the medieval proverb: *"It is good to live under the crosier."* The confiscated monastery lands were administered by the secular office steward. Later, an office known as the *Spiritual Goods Administration* was created in Heidelberg for the whole Palatinate. In order to manage the clergy and teachers of both denominations, it was to administer the income from the secularized monastic property, by constructing churches and schools and through other charitable endeavors,

But what did the Bishop of Speyer have to say about the measures taken by the "Pope of Heidelberg," as Elector Friedrich III was sometimes called by his neighbors? When the new teachings were introduced into the Palatinate, Rudolf von Frankenstein was the Prince Bishop in Speyer. He died in 1560 of mental derangement, so one could hardly expect any effective actions. However, his successor, Marquard von Hattstein (1560-1581), did not

---

[21] The gulden was the currency used in the Palatinate during the Late Middle Ages. One gulden was equal to 60 kreutzers or 15 batzen or 240 pfennigs or 480 hellers.

42

want to do anything either, because he was more a secular prince than he was a spiritual director of the diocese. The construction of a new castle in Udenheim (Philippsburg) was more important to him than his spiritual duties. Hardly a word of protest was heard from him as the monasteries were dissolved, and the Catholic priests were replaced by the Electors. Bishop Marquard was satisfied that the Bishopric of Speyer and Catholic belief was mostly kept intact in his territory, and that he was able to save the properties of the Speyer Bishopric through the tortuous times. What happened beyond the borders of his land bothered him very little. So the people remained without responsible spiritual leadership during the fateful years of the religious schism in the Palatinate.

Electoral Law in Ottersheim in 1565[22]

Today, Tuesday, 16 August 1565

I, Peter Brechtell, Clerk of the District Office in Germersheim, arrived in Ottersheim and there called the Mayor and the Court before me as required, and in whose presence I am to describe the rules and laws of the Electoral Palatinate, including taxes, tributes, and so on for the places within the District of Germersheim. Whereupon, that they be duly reminded of their oath and vow to the Electoral Palatinate, that they document and report in the village of Ottersheim the persons of said Palatinate and individual taxes on goods or otherwise and provide them to me. Those who have done this with their answer and report are named as follows:

Veltin Draut, village mayor
Dieter Renger
Jacob Markh
Ulrichs Mathis
Wendel Grunwaldt
Hanß Trauth
Jost Lauß

First, those from Ottersheim have vowed and sworn by God the Almighty to recognize the Electoral Palatinate and none other as their sovereign land and hereditary lord.

---

[22] This is a transcript of the governing laws that were read to the Ottersheim villagers at a yearly meeting in the community hall. The transcript in the original book was written in old German, an excerpt of which is shown on the following page. An interim, modern German transcript provided by Bernhard Steegmüller was used for this translation.

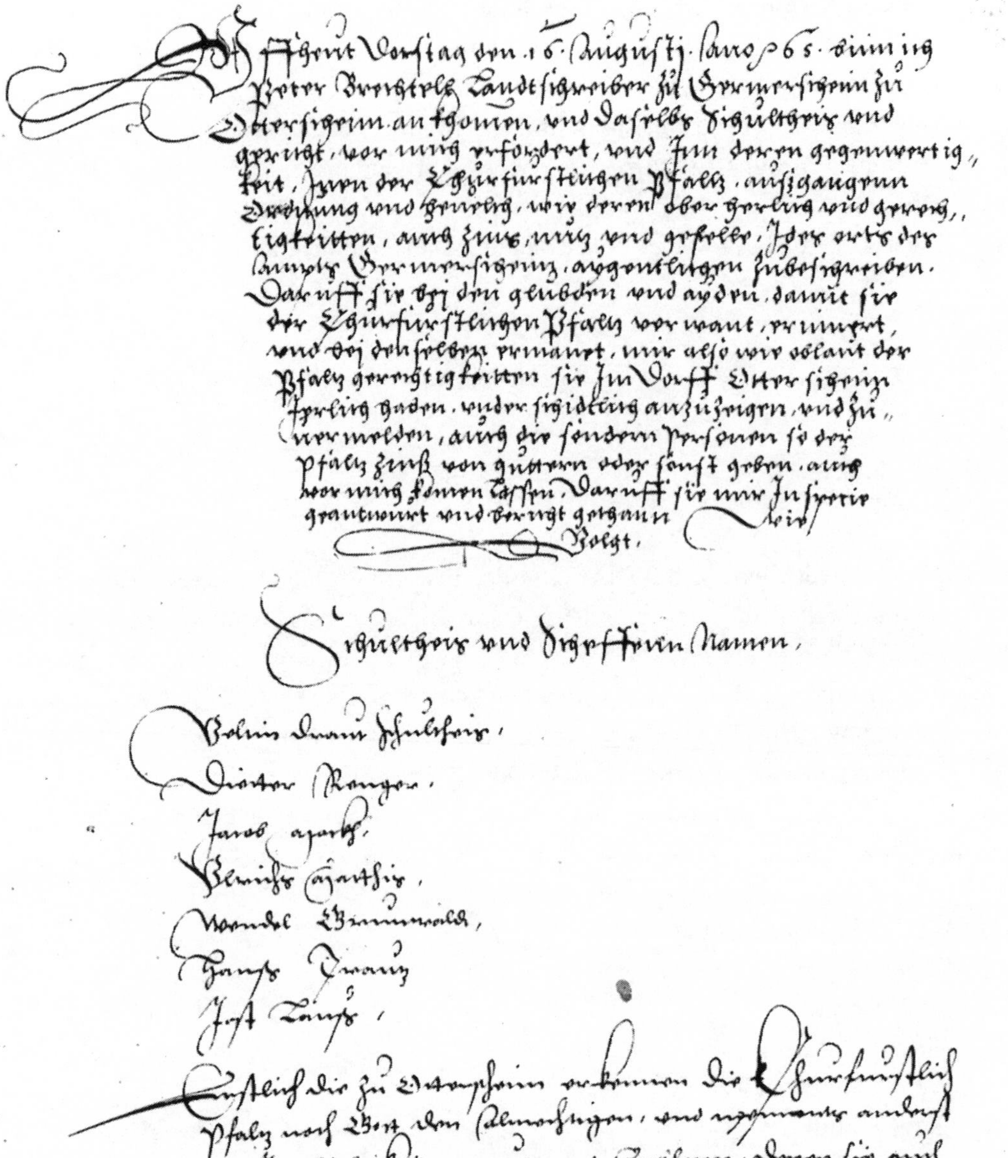

Electoral Law In Ottersheim in 1565 (Page 1)

High and Low Officials

The Electoral Palatinate has both high and low sovereignty, including over Ottersheim. The commands and prohibitions they are to obey are spelled out, and such wisdom or statutes that the Electoral Palatinate announces yearly being hereafter set forth and documented. The court is called the *Herrengericht [Lords court]*.

Common Rules

This list of rules is recorded in a yearly summary for the High Elector's and the community's glory by the court in Ottersheim.

For the first item so we show our gracious Lord Elector's sovereignty over the water and meadows of the community. For the use of which the poor shall give the gracious Lord their labor and tributes.

Also be it noted that we have a path up along the village between Jörg Seldnern[23] and Simon Nauertt. Whoever needs it may use it at the proper time.

Also after that we note a trench called the Quotgraben [Big trench] that runs through the entire community. This trench is to be cleaned. When this is required, the village master orders it. And if one refuses to do it, we will reprimand him vehemently.

Also after that we note a path down in the village between Ulrichs Mathissen and Dieter Renger. Whoever in the community needs it may use it

After that we note a well called the Ried Brunnen [Reed well], which the community is to keep up half.

Also we note an alley called the Riedtgaß [Reed alley]. Whoever in the community needs it may use it.

Also we note a path through the Oberalming [Upper commons] across the Priory of Hördt to the five morgen that abuts the Mittelgraben [Middle trench]. Whoever may need it may use it.

Also note a way through the Wehr gasse [Weir road] across the Priory of Hördt up to that of Niederhochstadt. If one wants to go this way, he has to see for himself how to continue on.

Also note that the Wasserbeiz path and the Henndweg belong to all, the poor as well as the rich.

Also whoever wants to collect rushes or wood chips [fire wood] must do so after Saint Michael's Day[24] until Saint Jörg's Day[25] but without harm to the community.

Also note that if the Lord God has allowed acorns to lie in the forest and these have not rotted, then these may be used by anyone to feed swine.

---

[23] Addresses were not used in these times. Instead, properties were identified using the names of the property resident, and if he was not well know, the name of the previous property resident.

[24] Saint Michael's Day is celebrated annually on 29 September by the Catholic and Lutheran Churches.

[25] Saint Jörg's (George's) Day is celebrated on 23 April, the traditionally accepted date of Saint Jörg's death.

Also note that after Saint Andreas Day,[26] if one has raised his swine at his place, then let him send them into the forest if it is not prevented by the community. He need not pay for this.

If an outsider has properties within our community and damages occur to these properties by his horses or other animals and if he has driven them out of our community, then we reprimand him before our master as malicious. In such case, the village master may order the damages to be replaced. Wherefore, the Village Master must stand judgment over this damage.

Also note that for dry goods measure and for wine measure, whoever needs them the village master is to calibrate and rectify them.

Note that whoever in the community has not sworn allegiance he must do so today.

Also note that if a citizen works too little we hold him accountable.

Also note that if a citizen was ordered before the court today, whether he answers or not, the proceedings shall continue.

Also note that if a citizen owns property in another district, he is required as of old to pay taxes in Ottersheim.

Also note that if a foreigner has property in our district, he must pay taxes here, except citizens of Bellheim and Knittelsheim.

Note a path down in the Ried between Ulrichs Mathis and Dieter Renger. This path was bought from the community by Ulrichs Mathis for 2 gulden as witnessed by Marten Marckhartt, poultry warden in Germersheim, and Mayor Niklas Kopf, as well as by the community. It was also agreed that if the community needs the path, the current owner must sell it back for 2 gulden. As far as it was improved, the community will pay the current owner a reasonable price.

Homicide, Theft

Whoever commits homicide, theft, or similar crimes in Ottersheim, judgment is not to be handled but the criminal is to be delivered to Germersheim. There the law will be applied and if applicable, punishment by the Electoral Palatinate High Officials.

In the case of other violence, fighting, bloodying, or punching, also insults, the Palatinate's law applies in the village of Ottersheim or its lands. If such lawlessness requires a court action, which takes place four times a year, such cases are handled by the officials in Germersheim. The Electoral Palatinate appoints and removes the Mayor and the court in Ottersheim.

Keeping Animals

Mayor and court give notice that in the Palatinate, neither the village nor the community of Ottersheim has kept or boarded animals for free, now or ever.

---

[26] Saint Andreas' Day is celebrated on 30 November.

Military

Who from Ottersheim is called in time of war or need must provide for himself according to his means; however, if he cannot the Palatinate will provide food and upkeep, but it can happen that the community may provide for these.

Serfdom-Compulsory Labor

Anyone from the Palatinate with handcart and wagon who takes a day trip to Heidelberg, Iggelheim, or the like is required to pay when asked. The Palatinate has always required of the Ottersheim citizens that when ordered to make trips to Heidelberg or other places, they must provide feed for their horses.

Appraisal and Taxes

As obedient subjects, the Ottersheim people recognize the authority of the Electoral Palatinate to appraise and their own duty to pay taxes according to their wealth.

Taxes

The Electoral Palatinate requires continuous payment from Ottersheim of 75 gulden. This is to be collected by the clerk in Germersheim in two parts, half at Easter and half at Saint Michael's Day. How the same is collected from each individual is described and recorded in the special tax book.

Further, they are to deliver to the Palatinate each year at Saint Michael's Day 12 schillings[27] and 9 pfennigs[28] as feudal tax, called the *Altbedt*. Further, the community of Ottersheim is to provide yearly to Germersheim, to the wine cellar of Germersheim, 9 malters[29] of grain that is called the feudal grain.

Death Tribute

The Palatinate requires no death tribute, that is, neither best animal nor best dress from the citizens of Ottersheim.

Immigration

Whichever foreigner moves to Ottersheim and becomes a citizen, whatever he gives to the community he must also give that amount to the Palatinate, which the clerk will collect and account for. But they are not to accept any citizen without first informing the officials at Germersheim.

---

[27] A schilling was a silver coin having a value of 17-1/2 pfennigs.

[28] A pfennig was a small silver coin. One pfennig was equal to 2 hellers; 4 pfennigs was equal to 1 kreutzer; 16 pfennigs was equal to 1 batzen; 240 pfennigs was equal to 1 gulden.

[29] A *malter* was a measure of volume. A light malter was equivalent to 142 liters while a heavy malter was equivalent to 127 liters.

Emigration

Whoever moves from the village of Ottersheim outside of the Palatinate to another authority, from that person will be deducted 5 pfennigs according to the Electoral Palatinate's order.

The view of the Electoral Palatinate regarding serfs, if they move to other masters or they or their children marry, the change in body tax has special rules, not only for the Ottersheim citizens but also for other subjects of the District of Germersheim.

Hens

In Ottersheim, the Palatinate will take neither hides nor hens as body [serf] tax from their subjects, not now and not in the future.

Payment of Taxes

The Palatinate requires payments from Ottersheim as in other villages under the District Office in Germersheim, also according to the special payment order set up and given by Elector Prince Friedrich.

Toll Road Payment

The Palatine Elector has no old or new customs rules in Ottersheim, either in coming or in use.

Fences, Hunting

The Prince Elector has the right to set fences in the Ottersheim fields and forests as he sees fit to facilitate his hunting rights.

Acorns, Beechnuts

Should acorns or beechnuts be found in the meadows of Ottersheim, these belong to the community to enjoy and need not give the Palatinate anything for them or owe anything.

Milling Tax

There is no mill or grinder in Ottersheim, so they must grind in Germersheim, as do other villages as has been ordered.

Brook (River) Rights

The Queich brook that flows from Landau through Ottersheim territory is reserved for the Prince Elector of the Palatinate. No one is allowed to fish in it without permission. And to prevent damage to such river as flows through the District of Germersheim, it should be cleaned of wood or hedges that may have grown in it by the villagers living near it. This includes the community of Ottersheim according to its proclamations.

Fair

In Ottersheim there is to be a fair on the Tuesday after Saint Martin's Day[30] by order of the Faut, which was established in Ottersheim about five years ago by the Schultheiß [mayor] and has been carried out since then. Regarding what money from the booths of the peddlers for horses sold, this should be collected by the clerk of Germersheim and kept by the Mayor. However, as ordered by the Director, the Mayor should keep and record 4 pfennigs from each horse, giving half to the Palatinate and the other half to the community.

Tithes

The large tithes in Ottersheim territory for the manor called the Poppelmann manor are owed entirely to the Electoral Palatinate according to the Mayor and the courts. The remaining territory is divided into thirteen parts. Specifically, one part from the Poppelmann property upfront, then six parts, half of the tithes. Further, the parish gets four parts, the Commander of the Order of Haimbach one part, the Provost of Hördt a half part, and also a half part for the nobleman in Zweibrücken, named Henrich Balwein, which earlier the von Fleckenstein is said to have had.

Small tithes

As the large tithes were distributed, so also are the small tithes to be distributed. In contrast, a pastor was paid according to his competence.

---

[30] Saint Martin's Day is a popular German holiday celebrated on the 11th day of the 11th month at exactly 11 minutes passed 11 o'clock in the morning.

Ottersheim around the Year 1600

1. The Village Layout

Based on the present-day location and expansion of the village, it seems rather odd that the street that is now the smallest was once the center of the village and the entrance to Ottersheim. Yet the documents leave no doubt the *Deich,* which is the stretch of road between the church and Quotgraben, is where the growth of the village began. On this road that leads from Germersheim to the Haardt, there was at this location still two old and important feudal properties in 1600, the feudal manor of the Klingenmünster Monastery on the east side and the Poppelmann property to the west. Where this road crosses the Quotgraben it was even piled up into a dike and secured with stones at that time.

The Deich was there not only to facilitate through traffic but also to dam the water of the Quotgraben, thereby providing water for cattle and creating a wetland environment, the so-called *Weet.* On the west side of the Deich around the year 1600 stood the church, the community (town) hall, and two former Poppelmann manor yards that were managed by the Audit Chamber of the Palatine Elector. The first house was inhabited by former mayor Hans Trauth, the second by community council member Martin Ludwig. The descriptions of the time leave no doubt that these were properties 8 and 10 on Germersheimer Straße. Even today, the property boundaries between the two houses run very irregularly. A barn and several sheds belonged to each of the two houses in the 16th century. To the north of the two manors was a "Wingart" [Vineyard] that apparently covered the land to the west of the church. The church was small and not in the best condition because only a few years later (1618) it was demolished and replaced by a massive stone building. In the church tower hung a bell that was operated on a regular basis by a bell ringer. The cemetery grounds were artificially heaped up but were not quite as large as today. In any case, the present stone boundary wall was not built until 1789.

To the south of the Poppelmann manor houses in 1600, there was an open space to which four house plots were attached. Originally belonging to the two feudal properties were the meadows of the upper Brühl where the horses, cows, cattle, and pigs of the Germersheim nobleman Poppelmann once grazed.

On the east side of the dike was the feudal manor of the Klingenmünster Monastery to which at that time belonged 150 morgen of arable land and 12 morgen of meadows. A document from 1571 reports three houses belong to this property as well as yards, stables, and barns. The manor served to collect the goods that had to be surrendered by the tenants of the fields and meadows. These goods were probably stored in the barn that existed on what is now property number 6.

The Klingenmünster Monastery was confiscated by the Palatine Elector in 1567. In the 16th century, the three houses of the Klingenmünster feudal manor in Ottersheim were awarded as hereditary property to the peasant farmers: Gangolf Dörrzapf, Adam Moock, and the heirs of Valentin Doll.

The drinking water for the residents of the Deich was provided by a well that was located near the church, the upkeep of which both the community and the Poppelmann manor were responsible. South of the Quotgraben or "big trench" at that time was a small blacksmith house that was leased for a gulden a year from the community to the village blacksmith.

The present-day Lange Straße [Long Street] was called at that time strangely enough *Die Hintergasse [The Back alley].* Though it was considerably longer even then than the Deich, in the minds of the people it took second place. Viewed from the Deich, the Große Gasse[31] [Large alley] lay behind. All indications are that the Dorfbach[32] [Village stream] was dug in the 15th or 16th century by human hands. In a contract dated 30 October 1599, the community committed itself to "hereby dig a village trench through the properties," to clean this trench regularly, and also to sweep the culverts. It is noteworthy that this village trench was not extended on the north side of the Lange Straße since it turned in that direction anyway at the rectory. This suggests more significant properties stood on the south side of the Hintergasse than on the north side. In fact, the Dorfbach touched not only the manor of the Klingenmünster Monastery at the beginning of the Hintergasse but also the Eußerthal manor in the middle of the street and the two houses of the Hördt manor at the east end of the village.

The Eußerthal courtyard stood on the property of what is today 65 and 66 Lange Straße belonging to the Emil Rund (his widow)[33] and Emil Gutting. The Eußerthal manor was only one house with various outbuildings in 1599. The property was presumably sold in 1595 by the Spiritual Goods Administration in Heidelberg to Ottersheim citizens Heinrich Dachenhäußer and Sebastian Degen for 250 gulden and other annual charges. The Eußerthal manor owned approximately 100 morgen of fields and meadows at that time.

The parsonage was also a Eußerthal possession. From 1311 until the introduction of the Reformation in Ottersheim during 1556, the Cistercian Monastery at Eußerthal had the obligation to provide the priest in Ottersheim. For this, the abbey received five-sixths of the large tithes as well as the small tithes, some of which had to be partially used for the construction and upkeep of the parsonage. When Friedrich III became Palatine Elector, he took over the Eußerthal Monastery in 1561, and the obligations of the Abbey went to him along with the possessions. Presumably, the Reformed teacher of Ottersheim lived in the rectory in 1599 and taught the children of the community while the minister was based in Knittelsheim. The rectory then was still a simple half-timbered building with barn, stables, and gardens.

At the end of the 16th century, the main manor of the Hördt Priory stood at the east end of the Hintergasse. Most likely, these were properties 15 and 16 on the Lange Straße that belong to Ludwig Sauther and Wilhelm Breßler. To the property of the main manor belonged three morgen of the Brühl meadows that stretched to the south past the Quotgraben.

---

[31] So as not to be confused, the *Hintergasse* over time became the Große Gasse, which in turn was renamed the Lange Straße of today.

[32] The Dorfbach was a second waterway in the village that aligned with the Hintergasse.

[33] It was common practice at the time to list only males as property owners. This reference and others of similar type that follow indicate an owner was deceased and his widow was occupying the premises.

The western boundary of the Hördt main manor was probably the present Riedgasse[34] [Reed alley]. To the east of the courtyard stood a barn "where the tithe was brought." Next to the main manor to the west lay the Hördt lower manor. Probably it is the present property of the Johann Brüderle heirs. Also included in the lower manor were three morgen of Brühl meadows that served as a cattle pasture. The boundary of the lower manor to the west formed the marsh area that apparently reached quite close to the Hintergasse then. Belonging to each of the two cloister manors was a house and a yard along with stables, barns, and sheds. The two properties owned approximately 790 morgen of land. A "path" led to the "Provost's Middle Brühl" which was separated by a gate. The fence that surrounded the Brühl meadows and the gate was intended to keep the grazing cattle together. For pedestrians there was a "Stiegel" [Stairway] next to the gate.

The drinking water for the inhabitants of the lower village was supplied by a well called the *Ried Brunnen [Reed well]*. It was on the property of what is 45 Ludwigstraße today. Half of the well's maintenance had to be provided by the community.

On the north side of the Hintergasse, a cottage for the two community shepherds stood between other houses. For a small fee, the shepherds, who usually did not own land, drove the cows, cattle, pigs, and geese to and from the large pastures that stretched to the left and right of the Gänsehaardt [Goose forest]. The *Viehtrift*, that is, the *cattle run*, was along the new road that stretched from above the parsonage to the forest.[35] On the west side, the Dorfbach prevented the animals from breaking out. On the east side, the fields were protected by a fence. Only at the present-day Falltorweg[36] [Drop gate road] would the herd have had the opportunity to get into the fields and cause damage. This was prevented by a gate that by virtue of its own weight closed automatically when it was opened by human hands. It was a portcullis, some of which can still be found today in fenced pastures in the Alps.

The new roads called Bauernweg [Peasant road] and the Riedgasse [Reed alley] were by now mentioned in documents from 1590. In the case of the Riedgasse, the document defines the road that leads from the east end of the Große Gasse in a southerly direction toward the highway just as it still is today. Among other things, this route served the brisk horse and cart traffic that traveled year in and year out between the Hördt Monastery and its manor yards within Ottersheim. Here rye, wheat, spelt, oats, and so on were brought to the Hördt, while the timber had to be delivered from the Hördt forest to Ottersheim.

Of the Kleine Gasse (Ludwigstraße), we read nothing in the documents of the 16th century. The homes of the about 300 inhabitants of the Ottersheim community seem to have lived mainly on the Deich and on the Hintergasse (Lange Straße). It is reported that there was a quarter vineyard in the Kröling (Gröhlig) that belonged to the church property.

---

[34] Later it was to be named the Ottostraße.

[35] The Viehtrift [Cattle run] over time became the Neuweg [New road] and later was named the Waldstraße [Forest Street].

[36] The Falltorweg was the east-west passage north of and parallel to the Große Gasse that connected with the Neuweg on the west end to the Bauernweg on the east end. It was renamed to *Schulstraße* in 1962.

2. The District Layout

Unfortunately, accurate records of the size and shape of the Ottersheim district from the period around 1600 are missing. But it must be assumed that the district boundaries differ little from those of today. The Insheimer Weg had a "stone foundation" even then. It led to the Kahlenberg where grapes had been planted by that time. Vineyards existed even in the low fields that abut the Herxheim district. Fields mentioned in the documents are the Schlegel, the Langgewanne, the Großstück, and the Gänsweidegärten.

From the Landauer Straße, the Mühlweg [Mill road] led to the Obersand [Upper sand]. The Neuweg and Bauernweg were connected by a path called the Falltorweg while the Schlittweg [Grassy road] led from the Bauernweg up to the Knittelsheim border. Meadows mentioned by name are the Mühlwiesen, Rechhagwiesen, Hörsten, Dämmel, Rödel, Wiesen am Wehr, Neuwiesen, Haimbacher Freiwiesen, and the Stöcken, among others. In addition, names appear that are now no longer used such as Bayerswiese, Münchswiese, Ölwiesen, and Biengarten.

The forest extended much closer to the village than it is today. The considerable demand for fuel wood and timber (for half-timbered houses) had noticeably thinned the stock of old large trees at that time, such that the forest close to the village consisted mostly of shrubs or bushes. Here the village cattle grazed from spring to late autumn. The actual meadows were largely surrounded by fences that protected them not only from grazing cows, cattle, and sheep but also from deer and roe deer.

The entrances to the meadows, pastures, and to the forest were often undeveloped paths. They are therefore referred to in documents as *Fahrten*. The terrain at the Queich was partly marshy especially below the dam. Here the water wound its way to the northeast through many turns, while the Buschgraben was still small and narrow at that time. The records from that time speak of an old quarry that is said to have lain on the north side of the Queich and that could be reached by crossing over the Queich. In addition, a Wehrgasse [Weir road] is mentioned that led over the Queich toward Niederhochstadt. The Wasserbeiß is also mentioned several times.

3. The residents

At the head of the village in 1600 was Mayor Hans Trauth. The six men on the tribunal were Jost Lausch, Jakob Renger, Jakob Metz, Simon Moock, Valentin Trauth, and Peter Trimpler. Village Master was Hans Kuntz, the "assistant" of Peter Trimpler. Like the mayor, the village master was responsible for order in the village. He had to determine when the Quotgraben had to be cleaned. He was responsible for the supervision over the Dorfbach. If the culverts were overgrown or blocked, then he had to have them "cleared and swept." In general, the village master at that time appears to have had the combined duties of a water overseer, a land warden, and a bailiff.

During the course of the 16th century, by order of the Governor in the District Office at Germersheim, a knacker named Franck was placed in Ottersheim. Faut Heinrich Riedessel chose Ottersheim as the place for the office of butcher and executioner because the village lay in the center of the District. The animal warden or butcher received 1 schilling for skinning a cow and 1 batzen[37] for skinning a horse. He had to return the hides to the peasants. Knacker Franck had also the task to carry out death orders that were spoken by the courts in the name of the sovereign. The office of executioner and skinner remained for more than 200 years in the Franck family in Ottersheim.

Most families in the village worked, in addition to their own fields, the rented properties from the manor for which they were paid in either money or goods. In the course of the Reformation, Elector of the Palatinate Friedrich III confiscated the properties of the monasteries and turned over the management to the Spiritual Goods Administration in Heidelberg. By order of this secular property administration, the subject offices for collection and storage of properties leased the fields and meadows to interested peasants.

Most contracts were made for a number of years. Toward the end of the 16th century, some properties, especially the buildings and their contents belonging to the monasteries, were often given as a hereditary lease to specific families. The new owners had to pay a severance sum in addition to small annual fees. Apparently, the State used this means to spare themselves the expense of upkeep and management of the houses, barns, and stalls. So it is understandable that in later records no mention is made of these monastery properties.

Absent any list of agricultural products from those years, documents describing interest obligations for leased land provide valuable insight. In many cases, the rent is paid in grain, wheat, spelt, oats, or barley. Also, lentils, peas, hemp, and hay are often mentioned. When the Ottersheim citizens Dachenhäußer and Degen acquired the Eußerthal manor for a purchase price of 700 gulden as a hereditary lease in 1596, they had in addition the duty to deliver a cartload of wine to the Pastor of Ottersheim each year. Wax and oil tithes were usually paid in cash in those days. By contrast, it was common to deliver live or slaughtered geese, roosters (capped), hens, sheep, and lambs for rented land. A document from that period reported that the community of Ottersheim was to deliver 360 Easter eggs and 6 geese annually to the District Office of Germersheim. The top bailiff received 200 eggs, the clerk received 100, and the forest supervisor received 60. Of the geese, the head bailiff was to receive four and the clerk two.

Presumably, Dyer's Madder was also cultivated in Ottersheim at that time. The plant was called *Röt (Rödt, Röthe)* because the root yields a red dye that was used to dye clothing material. The redness was prepared from the dried roots of the madder plant. A reminder of madder cultivation in Ottersheim today is only the field called "Bei der Rötdarr" at the south entrance of the village near the Insheimer Weg. Presumably, a large building stood there where the roots of the plant were dried. Raising madder likely enjoyed great popularity, not least because it brought much more money than raising grain.

Livestock played a large role in those days in addition to agriculture. Because the grazing land was common property, the number of animals individual families could have was established by statute. A cattle statute from that time divides the peasants into Wagenmänner [wagon owner], Kärcher [drayman], and Handfröner [hand laborer]. The

---

[37] A batzen was a small silver (later alloy) coin. One batzen was equal to 4 kreutzers or 16 pfennigs or 32 hellers; 15 batzen was equal to 1 gulden.

54

wagon owner was allowed 3-4 horses, 4 cows, 1 calf, and 13 sheep. The drayman as the owner of a 2-wheeled cart could have 2 horses, 3 cows, 1 calf, and 7 sheep. The hand laborer or anyone who had 1 horse was allowed to keep 2 cows, 1 calf, and 4 sheep. From this list, it is surprising that even the low-ranking peasant had a horse to call his own. It was his proud and his most valuable possession.

With administrative authorization, a horse market took place in Ottersheim each year since 1563 on the Tuesday after Saint Martin's Day. This market had been a "yearly event" by this time. Presumably, it was held in the open space next to the courtyard of the Poppelmann manor on the Deich. A four-pfennig tax had to be paid for each horse sold from which the Palatinate and the community each received two pfennigs.

The lower court overseeing the villagers was comprised of a set of judges that was chaired by the mayor. The rights and obligations of the citizens of Ottersheim were captured in a statute that has been preserved in several versions as a "Rulebook of the Ottersheim Community." The various provisions had to be read to the villagers on the *Great Day of Judgment.* Violations of the regulations were punished by the court people with penalties that were in part noted in the rulebook. Serious offenses and crimes were referred to the District Office of Germersheim. If a criminal was captured in Ottersheim, so the mayor had to put the person behind bars at the community hall and report to the District Office. Then the criminal was taken to the castle prison by the District Office of Germersheim where he was tried. Death sentences were carried out at the execution site in Germersheim by gallows and later also by the sword.

4. Ottersheim family names in the year 1600

A complete list of names of residents of Ottersheim in 1600 is not available. The following names are compiled from purchasing and leasing contracts that have survived from that period. Though the list may come pretty close to reality; nevertheless, it can make no claim to completeness.

1.	Antoni	(Anthoni)
2.	Apfel	
3.	Aude	
4.	Burggraf	(Called Borggraf der Bauer!)
5.	Dachhäußer	
6.	Deidesheimer	
7.	Degen	
8.	Doll	
9.	Dörr	(Dürr)
10.	Dörzapf	(Dörrzapf, Dürrzapf)
11.	Franck	
12.	Fuchs	
13.	Gensheimer	(Geinßheim, Geinßheimer)
14.	Grünewald	(Grünwaldt)
15.	Hannß	

16. Hatzenbühler   (Hatzenbüehel, Hatzenbüel, Hatzbül)
17. Klein
18. Kopf   (Kopff)
19. Kuhn   (Khun)
20. Kuntz   (Cuntz)
21. Kurt
22. Lausch
23. Ludwig
24. Martin
25. Merdian   (Märdian)
26. Metz   (Mez)
27. Meyer
28. Michel
29. Moock   (Mock)
30. Nauerth   (Nauerdt, Nauhardt
31. Österreich   (Osterrich)
32. Ringer   (Renger)
33. Rink   (Ringkh)
34. Röder
35. Rormayer
36. Sauer
37. Schaller
38. Schell
39. Söldner   (Soldner)
40. Spindler
41. Spitzfaden   (Spizfaden)
42. Steimer
43. Stein
44. Steinlein
45. Stiebig   (Stibich)
46. Trauth   (Trautt, Traut, Draut, Drautt)
47. Trimpler   (Drumpler)
48. Vetter
49. Voltz   (Volz)
50. Weinbühel   (Winbeyel, that is, Weinmesser)
51. Winkelblech
52. Wolf   (Wolff)

Ottersheim in the 30-years War, 1618-1648

The religious wars of the 16th century divided the German people into two hostile camps. In spite of the Emperor's attempts to unify the divide between Catholics and Protestants, the rift grew larger from year to year such that it appeared an armed conflict was inevitable. In 1608, the Calvinist Palatine Elector united several Protestant estates of the empire into a federation that was called the Union.[38] Standing against this association was the Catholic League of Bavaria.[39] Both leagues were obviously preparing for a war.

Only a spark was needed to ignite the flames of war. This spark was the Defenestration of Prague in 1618. A radical Protestant group was carrying out a free election for the King of Bohemia. In a confrontation with the Catholic group, the Protestant group moved to the castle and threw two Imperial governors out of the window. Thus began the fateful 30-Years War.

For Ottersheim, the first year of war in 1618 was marked by a very peaceful event. At that time, the construction of the present-day Catholic Church had begun. In line with the commitment of the population of Ottersheim, it was to be a Reformed Church. A cornerstone found in 1946 during renovation work in the tower had a lead tablet (28 centimeters by 14 centimeters) that contained some information worth noting. According to the stone, at that time Friedrich V was Palatine Elector, Johann Friedrich von Stockhe was the bailiff in Germersheim, Johann Konrad Glaser was pastor in Ottersheim, and Peter Trimpler was mayor of the village. Another tablet contained some significant maxims. Anyone who has ever built a house will be able to empathize when it states "Peter Trimpler, mayor here has much work with this building!" Another saying: "God defend against false teaching!" reminds that the Reformed faith was not unchallenged. The third thought: "God keep the community small!" would have been better not spoken. Most likely, no one at that time suspected that this wish would predict the fate of the village population. Like an evil curse, 30 long years of war did not allow the number of villagers to increase in any way; instead, their numbers decreased in such a frightening way as a result of hunger and misery that it took more than a hundred years before the initial population number would again be reached. It happened like this.

In 1619, Elector Friedrich V of the Palatinate, as head of the Protestant Union, was moved to accept the royal crown of Bohemia from the hands of the Bohemian Estates. He moved from Heidelberg to Prague with his entourage that same year. In foreboding of the coming disaster his mother exclaimed, "Oh, now the Palatinate is moving to Bohemia!" The armed conflict that had been confined to Bohemia affected all of Germany from here on. In 1620, the Catholic party under Maximilian of Bavaria won the Battle of White Mountain near Prague over the "Winter King" of the Palatinate.

---

[38] The author refers to the Protestant Union or Evangelical Union.

[39] The Catholic League of Bavaria was a loose confederation of Catholic German states formed in 1609.

Elector Friedrich V of Heidelberg had to flee. He lost his Elector status, which the Emperor transferred to Maximilian of Bavaria. Archduke Leopold, the brother of Emperor Ferdinand II, and Count Tilly [Johann Tserclaes] each conquered a number of Electoral Palatinate cities on the Rhine and in Alsace during 1622. In August 1622, the fortress of Germersheim was captured. Great havoc was wreaked in and around Germersheim through scorching, burning, and robbing during the siege by the Imperial Cavalry. A few feudal manors in Ottersheim were also vandalized at that time.

Archduke Leopold took possession of most of the District Office in Germersheim. On 23 November 1622, the villages Bellheim, Knittelsheim, Ottersheim, Böbingen, Zeiskam, Sondernheim, and Hördt had to pay homage to the Imperial Governor in the castle courtyard of Germersheim. In religious matters, the new government favored the Catholic faith but without exercising religious coercion. That changed in 1626. Worship by Reformed clergy was halted and their salaries were to be paid only to the end of the current quarter. Those of the Reformed ministry who did not want to change over to the Catholic religion had to leave the District Office of Germersheim.

The Reformed Pastor Johann Glaser of Sinsheim was also removed from office at that time. He still lived in Ottersheim but he was not allowed to exercise his office as pastor. Catholic priests from Lorraine, Holland, Bavaria, and from the adjacent cloisters assisted with the care of the previous Reformed parishes. As the chronicler reports, most subjects were "rather soft" and accepted the Catholic faith without resistance. The Catholic clergy again introduced the Holy Mass, had a burning light hung before the Blessed Sacrament, and set up holy water and baptismal fonts. The Ottersheim baptismal font dates from this period and now stands in the tower of the Catholic Church bearing the date 1629.

The endless accommodation of troops in the District of Germersheim led gradually to a complete impoverishment of the population. The levies of money, livestock, and food were so great that hunger and poverty moved into the villages. In particular, the Widdenhorst horsemen spread fear and terror in the villages of the district. Not infrequently, the residents were forced by the riders with beatings and debauchery to procure food.

There was so much uncertainty that hardly a peasant could dare to be seen with horses on the street or in a field. Therefore, it is not surprising that many residents of the District Office emigrated out of fear of wickedness, leaving house and yard behind for more peaceful countries. The first Spaniards arrived in Germersheim during the second decade of war. But they left the town and office to the Swedes by 1631, who in association with French Catholics, rushed to help the oppressed Protestants in Germany. The Swedes brought new suffering to the villages of the District Office of Germersheim. High taxes were laid and recklessly collected on all food and consumer goods. The District Office of Germersheim changed hands several times at that time; until from 1635 on, it was under Austrian rule for nine years with short interruptions

What went on in Ottersheim back then is evident in the statements of Reverend Hoerner from Siebeldingen in his book, "Der Geilweilerhof und das Kloster Eußerthal," in which he writes:

"The poor subjects of Bellheim, Zeiskam, Ottersheim, Knittelsheim, Böbingen, Hördt, and Sondernheim complain that the fields have been looted, the houses in the

village communities vandalized and destroyed, such that neither man nor animal could live in them, and all the fields lie barren and desolate, that now for a year and a half no plow has been there, and that to date most of the poor peasants do not live at home but instead linger in manor yards, forests, and cities, and out there even now a third have died or are depraved from hunger and worries."

This sad picture from 1635 is supplemented by additional records from the period that report some people ate wild herbs and unnatural foods in those years, even human corpses and dead animals. How much the population of the District Office of Germersheim had decreased and its former prosperity had vanished through the long years of war emerges from a compilation of country recorder Hiltebrandt from August of 1644. There we learn the following:

During the "good" period of peace, the District Office of Germersheim counted 3,559 people; in May 1644 only 601 souls (that is, 17% of the former population). Before the war, the inhabitants had 4,228 horses, 6,204 cows and cattle, 8,485 pigs, and 7,300 sheep. In 1644 there were only 375 horses (8.8%), 329 head of cattle (5.3%), 700 pigs (8.2%), and 0 sheep (0.0%). The fruit tithes had fallen to one seventh and the wine tithes to one twentieth. A morgen field or meadow that had cost 100 gulden before the war, cost four to six in 1644, the maximum being seven to eight gulden.

The French occupied the District Office of Germersheim in the last years of the war. The catastrophic conditions did not change. The 30-year struggle that began because of religious differences had long become a struggle for earthly goods. The states fought the war for power and possession of German land, the armies on both sides for prey and wild enjoyment, at most for military honor. The end was a general exhaustion that gradually brought the peace negotiations into motion. In 1644, negotiations were started in Münster and Osnabrück; a peace treaty was signed on 24 October 1648.

Of the fate of the Ottersheim village and its families in those terrible times of war, we understandably have no accurate records. Where hunger prevailed and the daily question was of existing or not; where epidemics and disease were prevalent and death took a huge toll; where the houses, stables, and barns had been plundered and the people abducted; where people temporarily lived in the forest or fled from their homeland; where no priest and no teacher ever stayed in the village and consoled the people; no one invested the time and effort to record the plight of a small village and its people for posterity. Nevertheless, we can draw from some general hints and valuable conclusions in lease agreements and petitions.

Around the year 1600, about 50 different family names were represented in Ottersheim. They had dwindled to slightly more than half that after the war. Names that disappeared by 1663 include Antoni, Apfel, Burggraf, Dachhäußer, Deidesheimer, Fuchs, Kurt, Lausch, Martin, Michel, Ringer, Rink, Sauer, Schaller, Schell, Spindler, Spitzfaden, Steimer, Steinlein, Vetter, Voltz, Weinbühel, and Wolf. Appearing after the 30-year war are some new names, such as Ferber, Hochdörfer, Kreiner, Schilling, Schwartz, and Schwaab. Managing to survive the chaos of war include the families of Degen, Doll, Dörzapf, Dörr, Gensheimer, Grünewald, Hatzenbühler, Klein, Kuhn, Ludwig, Metz, Mayer, Moock,

Nauerth, Österreich, Röder, Söllner, Stein, Stiebig, Trauth, Trimpler, and Winkelblech. Quite often the term, *widow or heirs,* stands behind the family name. This shows that the man of the house is no longer alive. A document dated 1663 speaks of "extinct and corrupt" tenants who have left nothing behind for their heirs. No doubt, family names vanish and new ones appear even in normal times. However, the scope of the documented changes suggests that the 30 Years War intervened mercilessly in the fate of the villagers.

It deserves to be noted that some of the fields, meadows, and gardens were still uncultivated 15 years after the war. In the documents, some of the land parcels are mentioned with the added comments:

"... is desolate and overgrown with weeds."
or
"... is bleak and is still covered with hedges."

It is reported that the quarter garden [the vineyards] in the Gröhlig lies there "deserted." This is understandable when we consider the many difficulties of a new beginning. The peasants could not expect help from outside. Not only was there a lack of seed and farming tools, work animals, and breeding stock, but also a lack of strong hands of men who could undertake cultivating the wasted lands. Some soldiers returned to their old home only after years while others remained missing altogether.

But what was the spiritual result of the war? In 1618, the armies were set in motion not in least part in order to re-institute the unity of Christendom. It was the unattainable goal of the two religious camps to subdue and try to force one's will on the other side. At the end of the 30-year struggle, both had to realize that unity in faith and doctrine through the power of the State could no longer be realized. So at the peace negotiations at Münster and Osnabrück, the Catholic, the Reformed, and the Lutheran faiths were recognized in principal as equal. As for the state of the religions and of church property, 1624 was designated as the "normal" year. From that point on, the Reformation rights of the authorities were repealed, and thus a change in the relationship between the faiths was stabilized. In our Palatinate, the counter-reformation that was carried out during the war was reversed. This meant for the District Office of Germersheim that the Reformed Church alone was granted the right of toleration.

On 10 July 1650, when France returned the District Office of Germersheim to Karl Ludwig, the son and successor of the unfortunate Winter King Friedrich V, the old state was restored everywhere. The Reformed preachers who were scattered during the war to other countries returned. On the other hand, the Catholic religious orders, which were established in Hördt, Eußerthal, and Klingenmünster, and had helped out at the former Reformed churches of the District Office of Germersheim during the war, were required to vacate the monasteries and abbeys again. The Reformed Pastor Salomon Walther, who was appointed to Offenbach in 1650 and worked there until 1659, was also responsible for the villages of Ottersheim and Mörlheim.

Ottersheim as a French Border Village, 1680-1702

Toward the end of the 17th century, Ottersheim was a French border town for over 20 years. Actually, the District Office of Germersheim belonged legally to the Palatinate at that time. However, the area south of the Queich was occupied by France in 1680 and administered under French law. It happened like this:

Louis XIV of France (1643-1715) had used the 30 Years War and subsequent decades of German weakness to extend his dominion along the Rhine. It served him in good stead that the Emperor in Vienna had been hard pressed by the Turks since 1678 and was involved in a fight to the death. Therefore, Leopold I had no time or strength to protect the borders of the empire in the west. To disguise his power politics, Louis XIV wanted to support his territorial acquisitions through judicial procedures. He therefore set up courts, the so-called *Chambers of Reunion,* which were to determine those areas that had once belonged to France as part of Alsace. One such Chamber of Reunion was established in Metz during 1679. It was to determine those areas that had belonged to the former French Bishoprics of Metz, Toul, and Verdun since 1552.

It was found that during King Dagobert's time (623), large parts of the District Office of Germersheim were owned by the Benedictine Monastery of Weißenburg. Therefore, a judgment of the Breisach Chamber of Reunion declared the river Queich to be a border to France in March 1680. That same year, French dragoons were ordered to march and quarter themselves in the villages south of the Queich. In all the reunified places, French crests were hung and the residents were ordered to swear an oath of allegiance to the French king.

When French City Mayor Pape d'Espel appeared on 4 May 1680 in Billigheim, he forbade the people to obey the commands of the Elector of Heidelberg under pain of body and life sentences. He quickly ordered the communities of Billigheim, Ottersheim, Knittelsheim, Bellheim, Sondernheim, Böbingen, and "Merlem" to remove the Palatinate "mandates and patents" that were posted in the villages. To make the change palatable to the people, they were told that the King of France could provide better protection than the Elector of the Palatinate, and that they therefore should have a strong rather than weak protector.

Complaints of the Palatine Elector in Paris remained unsuccessful. Louis XIV considered the District Office of Germersheim in particular to be part of Alsace and he had no intention to return it. His desire to maintain this area was supported in large part by the economic conditions in the Palatinate. Elector Karl (1680-1685) did not have the economical sense of his father, Karl Ludwig. He had debts and needed money. So in 1682, he transferred the District Office at Germersheim to France for payment of annual cash compensation. There it remained until the Ryswick Peace.

To safeguard the newly won land militarily, fortifications were built from Annweiler to Hördt. These so-called *Queich Lines (see page 326)* led along the northern edge of Ottersheim to Knittelsheim and Bellheim. Until 1704, the French kept the Queich line occupied. When the Queich lines had to be abandoned in the War of Spanish Succession in 1704, the town was instead fortified by both sides.

Toward the end of the 17th century, when the land south of the Queich was administered by France, profound changes took place with respect to the religion of the inhabitants. Like all rulers of that time, Louis XIV wanted to have unlimited power over the secular and ecclesiastical affairs of his subjects. He saw in the religious unity of his country an important prerequisite to political unity. Therefore, the newly won territory south of the Queich was to be brought into line with religious and cultural France as quickly as possible. To this end and according to the will of the French kings, the Calvinistic faith was to be eliminated and the District Office of Germersheim was to become Catholic again. To accomplish this, Louis XIV acted under the principle: *"un roi, une loi, une foi"* meaning, *"one king, one law, one faith."*

According to a decree of 26 August 1683, the Catholics were forbidden to accept any other religion under threat of heavy fines. Those who did it anyway had to reckon with permanent expulsion and confiscation of their possessions. The same punishment was to be expected by anyone who married someone from a different faith, or raised the children of an existing mixed marriage in any other than the Catholic religion. But whoever changed from a different religious denomination to Catholicism was tax-exempt from 1683 for three years. He was also exempted from the burden of quartering troops and did not need to help provide food for the troops.

Louis XIV acted with the utmost severity against relapsed converts in 1686. Apostatized Catholic men who had refused the sacraments on their sickbed were sentenced to a substantial fine, life-long galleys, and confiscation of their possessions after recovery. For fallen women, the imposed punishment consisted of payment of a fine, imprisonment, and confiscation of possessions. When relapsed converts died, their bodies were dragged through the streets and buried by the knacker in his yard where animal corpses were also brought.

A decree dated 5 June 1686 ordered the subjects to send their children to school in their own parishes. Children of recalcitrant parents were taken from their parents and educated at the parents' expense in Catholic schools or monasteries.

The consequences of these strict religious policies were inevitable. Many villages in the District Office of Germersheim, including Ottersheim, accepted the Catholic faith while others became mostly Catholic. According to a control visitation in 1701, 51 families in

62

Ottersheim had forsworn the Calvinistic faith. However, a small minority remained Reformed but did not show it outwardly. The Catholic parish that was disbanded in 1556 by order of Elector Otto Heinrich of Heidelberg was restored and the ministry was probably transferred to monasteries. The church sanctuary, which was probably still in the tower then, was turned over to the Catholics of Ottersheim for their use at the beginning of 1684. It was the same in Bellheim and Offenbach, while in Germersheim the whole church went to the Catholics. Petrus Otto was the designated Catholic priest for Ottersheim and Knittelsheim from 1695.

The Palatinate Simmern line ended in 1685 with the death of Elector Karl, who had promoted Calvinism in the Palatinate for over a hundred years and had helped that faith to victory. Louis XIV used the occasion to register his inheritance claims to the Palatinate. His own brother, the Duke of Orleans, was married to a sister of Prince Karl, the famous Liselotte von der Pfalz. Although Liselotte had dispensed with all rights of inheritance in her contract of marriage, Louis XIV demanded from the Palatinate the counties of Simmern and Sponheim and the rule of Kaiserslautern and Oppenheim. In 1688, the French invaded the Palatinate and occupied Kaiserslautern, Neustadt, Speyer, Heidelberg, and Frankenthal, among other places.

Most Palatinate cities went up in flames, and the fields and vineyards were devastated when they retreated in 1689. Only the cities and villages south of the Queich were spared, because these were to remain permanently under the dominion of the French King. The desire of Louis XIV was not fulfilled. In the Peace of Ryswick of 1697, the District Office of Germersheim was explicitly returned to the Palatinate. Nevertheless, France did not withdraw its troops until five years later.

The Ryswick Peace also stipulated that the re-Catholicized French regions should continue to remain Catholic. At that time, the church in Ottersheim was turned over completely to the Catholics. In view of the fact that almost all the villagers had accepted the Catholic faith, this right of possession has remained undisputed to this day. A change in the existing religious situation in the Palatinate was less expected, because the Palatinate had been ruled by Catholic Electors of the Palatinate-Neuburg line since 1685. After the Ryswick Peace, Elector Johann Wilhelm (1690-1716) openly began to favor the Catholic religion in his country. Some of the former Calvinists, who had become Catholic under pressure from Louis XIV, returned to their Reformed faith after 1697.

In the District Office of Germersheim, 150 families of this kind were counted at a visitation, 28 of them in Bellheim. Should they not change their religious commitment, these families were threatened with confiscation of all their possessions and expulsion from their homeland. In Ottersheim, there were also some persons who had accepted their Reformed faith again after 1697 and who were therefore called to bear responsibility. In 1700, they lodged a complaint in one of the Electoral offices because of their poor treatment, but they were not successful. In 1704, there were only five Reformed clergymen in the District Office of Germersheim where there had once been 21. In contrast, more than twenty Catholic priests were hired, according to the Reformed.

The death of Emperor Leopold I in 1705 forced the Catholic Palatine Elector Johann Wilhelm to change its church policy. King Friedrich I of Prussia, as a protector of the Protestants, demanded that the Reformed and Lutherans in the Palatinate be treated as the Catholics. So the Religions Declaration of 21 November 1705 came to be, thereby granting all faiths freedom of conscience. Each subject was to have the right to choose his religion freely. Of the seven churches in the countryside, five were to go to the Reformed and two to the Catholics. Similarly, the church property in the Palatinate was to be shared in the same proportions.

However, this regulation specifically excluded the District Office of Germersheim. Thus, the existing religious conditions remained by and large as before; 25 churches were assigned to the Catholics, 20 were to be used by Catholics and Protestants simultaneously. In twelve other places that were exchanged in 1709 to the Bishop of Speyer, the Catholics kept their churches. However, for the administration of church property the Elector installed a general lease owner who allegedly abused his office for personal profit.

In an ancillary judgment to the Religions Declaration of 1705, it was declared that the income from the rich abbeys and monasteries of Eußerthal, Hördt, Klingenmünster, Seltz, and Germersheim should fall to the Catholics. Of all other properties and possessions, one-third was assigned to the Reformed and Lutherans for the upkeep of their clergy. Even after the religious policy declaration of 1705, the religious situation in Ottersheim changed little. Responsible for the support of the Reformed was the Pastor of Bellheim to which also the communities of Knittelsheim, Hördt, Kuhardt, and Leimersheim belonged. As in Ottersheim, because the church and the schoolhouse both belonged to the Catholics, a Reformed teacher, who taught the Reformed children and performed the functions of a pastor if necessary, was most likely hired by the church council. He lived and worked at 22 Germersheimer Straße. He received his compensation from the Spiritual Goods Administration in Heidelberg. The Catholic priest of the Ottersheim parish lived opposite the church that was maintained by the Monastery at Eußerthal. The community was responsible for the Catholic schoolhouse. The cemetery near the church was used by Catholics and Protestants together.

Summary of Rights in the Village of Ottersheim - 1740

(A rough reproduction of a copy from the year 1740)

Praised be Jesus Christ!

A description of traditional laws of the community of Ottersheim, including what is to be reprimanded and to be punished; also descriptions of the paths and cattle runs in the meadows, gardens, trenches, roads, and bridges; plus everything else from ancient documents and descriptions of what usually was read aloud at full court each year.

As extracted by me the sworn city and district clerk, Johannes Rothuth, in the presence of the magistrate, the court, and the committee.

Ottersheim, 23 June 1740

First, what the Palatinate as well as any sovereign has in the way of rights and possessions, as they were renewed on 28 July 1599.

1. The Electoral Palatinate has all high and low sovereignty and rights; however, the community is exempt from care and feeding (shelter money, shelter penny), common law (duty of the best head of cattle on the death of the man and the best garment in the death of the woman), body tax (annual payment by the serfs of 1 shilling and 1 chicken), duty to provide a chicken at the beginning of lent, and the like, as is also the case in Bellheim, Knittelsheim, and Zeiskam.

2. The Electoral Palatinate has a rental property called the Poppelmann property from which the Palatinate alone may collect the tithes. As can be seen from the writing, the annual tax came to 7 gulden and 30 kreutzers.[40]

3. The Hördt Monastery has two good properties of the same type. The writing provides insight into the taxation.

4. The Klingenmünster Monastery also possesses a rental property as is described in the writing. It is a rental property used as personal property like the preceding. In addition, it must give the two horse caretakers twelve bundles of fruit. For this, the horse caretakers must help the tenants cut grain for six days and spelt for six days.

5. The Eußerthal Monastery has a rental property from which the grounds were sold long ago to Heinrich Dachenhäußer and Sebastian Degen for 250 gulden in addition to other charges.

6. The large and the small tithes have the following framework: The large and small tithes, except the fruit tithe from which the community is exempt under the old tradition, together are divided into twelve parts. Except the tithes from the Poppelmann manor which go entirely to the Palatinate. The Palatinate gets six of the twelve parts, the parish gets four parts, the Commander of the Order Haimbach gets one part, the presence or the Priory of Hördt gets a half part and the community gets a half part.

---

[40] A kreutzer was a small silver coin. One kreutzer was equal to 4 pfennigs or 8 hellers; 4 kreutzers were equal to 1 batzen; 60 kreutzers were equal to 1 gulden.

Note: These tithe collectors are required to build and maintain the church and to provide the bell ringer 13½ malters of grain as payment. Just as everyone receives, he must also give.

7. As salary, the Catholic schoolmaster here is appropriated the hay tax of 3-3/4 morgen of meadows in the Hundsloch and 4-1/2 morgen of meadows in the Neuwiesen near the stone weir.

8. The Eußerthal ministry has to build and maintain the parsonage here that up to now it has done.

Following are the traditional laws which otherwise were read on the day of hearing.

1. We acknowledge our most gracious sovereign's power over water and pasture, the poor as well as the rich. The poor are to provide work, value, and taxes.

2. Anyone who desires to be accepted in the community should first and foremost prove his independence, his departure from any office, he or she descends from honest parents, and is not bound to any servitude. He will immediately pay the imposed entry fee amounting to 60 gulden and then vow and swear. In the event of this not happening, he will be banned from water and pasture. And if one does not abide by this rule and makes use of water, pasture, and anything else in the community, he will be punished by the community.

3. If someone wants to move away from this community and make a home in a different place, so we will provide a written document stating that he does not owe the sovereign and is not connected to any other power.

4. If one is so small as to not appear at the judgment, we reprimand him as audacious and guilty before the court.

5. Note also that when one is ordered to court and charged, he may give an answer or not. The charge will still be pursued.

6. No one is to complain to an exile court or provide reply unless he has permission. Where one does not comply, we judge him to be audacious and guilty before the court.

7. Complaints about anything contained in the Electoral Palatinate police order and land rights of the most gracious sovereign are criminal.

8. Complaints about tree sticks or staffs and wood (brushwood, firewood that was cut with the sickle, or sickle knife); whomever this concerns, it should be given to him. But the great oak is to be given as of old, after one has paid for it.

9. We give warning, where one wrongfully cuts or steals timber or bush from another or from a community; he shall stand punishment in the community.

10. We also claim that whoever spreads straw or chaff in the woods or on community property before Saint Michael's Day, so he shall stand punishment in the community.

11. No one should dare to assemble (act of insolence) in the woods, or to chop down anything green, or oaken, or of beech with the exception of thorns. Whoever is caught shall stand punishment in the community.

12. He who wants to build and desires a half-timber foundation, the village master should perform an inspection to determine whether it is necessary. Then he should inspect and measure the construction and provide the desired timber.

13. No one from the marked land parcels who owns possessions in this district that were damaged by horses or other animals should drive them to another location. Instead, there are estimators here who are to estimate the damage. He who does it anyway, we reprimand him as insolent.

14. Complaints regarding dry goods measure and wine measure, the village master will calibrate and rectify the measures and provide these in exchange for a fee.

15. Complaints also when the village master orders something done on a path, bridge, or other in the community, each person is to obey or pay five gulden punishment.

16. The village mayor and master should keep order, and at all times ensure that the deer fences, field fences (that belong to a given person) and meadow fences as well as all trenches are closed or stopped, and punish the criminals as often as they are asked to perform these tasks each year. To support them, the village masters should have sheriffs and bailiffs who force compliance of the guilty, who collect the fines every four weeks, and deliver them to the village masters who are to record them in the village accounts.

Regarding the trenches

First, the Dorfgraben [Village trench] should be seven schuhs [227.5 centimeters] wide from the Schoßbrett (on the Queich) up to the Obersand.

Also, the rear meadow trenches and forest trenches should each be kept five schuhs [162.5 centimeters] wide.

Also, the same regarding the front meadow trenches and all water trenches as far as these are the main trenches.

Also, the *Trückelgräben* (dry trenches, drains) and the *Trückelrenden* (discharge chutes) are to be raised four schuhs [130 centimeters] and the others two schuhs [65 centimeters], as is the custom for main Trückelgräben.

The Quotgraben [Big trench] is sufficient for the district (as far as it flows through the district) because it is cleaned (swept) as often as the village master orders it done, on penalty of two gulden fine.

The Wassergraben [Water trench] on the Obersand from Offenbach territory up to the Großstück is to be kept at its width of four schuhs. Where one is found to be otherwise, he (the responsible party) is to be fined two gulden.

The above-mentioned trench flows over the Großstück from the Obersand up to the Neuweg. It is three quarters of a rute wide at the Obersand and one rute wide at the lower end. It belongs to the community.

All Pfluggraben [Plow trenches] should be two and a half schuhs wide, by penalty of a two gulden fine. Deer and field fence assemblies are each two gulden fine, that is, whoever does not keep the deer or field fences in order, and is called to account for this must pay two gulden as punishment.

Meadow fence assembly, it is one gulden each.

Meadow trench assembly, it is one gulden each.

For disobedience, it is five gulden.

As by ancient custom, if one desires a foundation block [for a half-timbered house] and it is given him but has not been built before Saint Michael's Day, he shall pay the community ten gulden and the wood is to be given to the community.

We declare that the well called the Ried Brunnen must be maintained half by the community. And if the community provides the rope and handle, the others must provide the container (bucket). Whoever may need it may use it.

Regarding an alley called the Riedgasse, whoever may need it may use it.

Note that a well up in the village near the church must be maintained half by the community. What needs to be done to this well, for this the community is to give 36 pfennigs and the Poppelmann manor 24 pfennigs. Whoever may need it may use it.

Declare also a path up in the village near the Schießberg (some of the lines, French fortress grounds). Whoever may need it may use it from the street up to the Schießberg.

Declare also a path through the Wehrgässel (on the Queich) lain with pebbles between Master Johann Conrad Glaser, Pastor Emeritus (1613-1626), from the forest across the Queichbach up to the (district limits) of Niederhochstadt. Should one want to go further, he has to see for himself how to proceed.

The Gässel was offered for sale by Hans Rudolf a few years ago for 20 gulden, but the community has reserved judgment. Now the Pastor has reported that it should get a gate and steps. However, when the community wishes such again for that money (20 gulden), so it should be given to them as the old document states.

This community, Zeiskam, and Niederhochstadt have a half morgen of meadow near the Oberschoßbrett and lease and maintain it together, sharing the interest annually in equal parts.

The following are the paths, roads and cattle tracks in the meadows

A path from the meadows into the forest.

A path across the Huggraben onto specific meadows.

A cattle run previously that of Theobald Pferd from the Wehr across the Huggraben and into the woods.

A path out to the Wehrgässel.

A path down across the Queichbach to the Priory of Hördt.

A path up onto the community meadows at the lower village.

A path in the lower village over the Queichbach to the old quarry.

A cattle run across the Queich onto the Haimbach free meadows.

A cattle run onto the Rödel meadows at the lower end previously that of Nicholas Trauth.

A path of Gall Stiebig from his Rödel meadows to the woods of Stoffel Trauth.

A path of Rudolf Kröper previously that of Christoph Busch, the community keeps a bridge in the woods from the Priory of Hördt.

A path on the Poppelmann five morgen into the woods.

A cattle run across the Queichbach from said Poppelmann property.

A path in the woods of former mayor Ulrich Grauels heirs to Niederhochstadt.

A path in the woods previously that of Peter Trimpler from the Provost's long morgen.

A path previously that of Burgers widow in the woods out to his own meadows.

A path out of Johannes Seither and the community keeps a bridge to the Rohrbusch. What lies below it should descend below.

A path of Valentin Rebstock from the Bayerswiesen to his own meadows.

A cattle run from the Bayerswiesen onto the Dämmelswiesen, the community keeps a bridge at the lower end over the Dolgraben.

A path of the Provost's three morgen, beginning with the outside edge onto the Dämmelswiesen, across the Wassergraben bridge, and towards the road by the Oberallmend. The community maintains the bridge. Salomon Moock and Georg Seither have this meadow.

A cattle run of the fenced meadow between Velten Herbergen and Georg Mayer. Each has half in the Oberallmend.

A path out of Peter Schopf von Sondernheim to the small Dämmel, to the Hörsten, going over to previously that of Hans Georg Schardt.

A cattle run down to the Scheerwiesen in the small Dämmel previously that of Wendel Wolf's child.

A path onto the Scheerwiesen to the Oberallmend of Johannes Glatz.

A path on the Abbot meadows to the Haardt to their own Abbot meadows previously that of Jakob Hatzenbühler.

A cattle run across the Wassergraben from previously that of Hans Trauth.

A path down to Wendel Julich from the Priory meadows, Georg Moock.

Also, a path on the Frühmeßwiese across the Wassergraben and the Flachsgraben.

A cattle run from the provost meadow across the Flachsgraben.

A path of the community from above the Neuweg.

A cattle run previously that of Village Mayor Peter Trimpler and Bartel Degen (his widow) from the Stöcken.

A path below it from the Niedervorderwiesen across the Münster manor.

A path on the Provost's Mühlwiesen to Johannes Seither in the Neuweg.

A path out of the Provost's Stöcken, called the nine morgen, into the woods.

A path into the woods previously that of Philipp Scherff from the Mühlwiesen.

A path of Ägidius Mau and Konrad Müller from their Mühlwiesen in the Niederallmend.

A path coming from the Niederallmend to the Vorderwiesen, provided by Bernhard Kopf.

A path previously that of Theobald Pferd from the seven morgen.

A cattle run previously that of Georg Herbig to the fermentation ponds at the lower end into the Gärtengasse.

A path toward Georg Moock to the meadows and provides stairs to Mathäs Glatzen heirs.

A path out to Paulus Burgermeister then to the fermentation ponds.

A path out to the Hundsloch, then to Lorenz Ludwig's heirs to access their meadows.

A cattle run out to the Münchswiese across the Flachsgraben previously that of Velten Berberich.

A path to the Rechhag previously that of Hans Georg Bechten's child.

A cattle run previously that of Gall Stiebig from the Neuweg

A cattle run previously that of Peter Schöpfen (his widow), Hans Georg Schard.

A cattle run in Flachengärten previously that of Hans Doll and Georg Grünwald.

The Farrenwiese [Bullock meadows]

There is a path from the Niedersand from the provost's three morgen whenever the Sand lies empty. But in the event it is not, they should use the Maryen path, the path up to Christian Walken (his widow), and the path to the Riedgasse.

A path previously that of Christian Walken (his widow) to the Niederbrühl.

A path from Konrad Dörzapf down from the Riedgasse to the provost's Niederbrühl.

A path to the provost's Mittelbrühl and the provost keeps a gate and stairs alongside.

A water way and two bridges, on the road below the Viehweiden [Cattle pastures] and Neuwiesen [New meadows] over the Quotgraben and Dorfgraben are kept up by the community and they fill any holes.

A path of Peter Trimpler to his Neuwies and the community maintains the bridge. Those on the Neuwiesen and Viehweiden have no further path down at that point to previously that of Peter Ludwig's meadow; others up there include bridges to previously that of Jakob Renger.

The path previously that of Jakob Renger heirs to previously that of Martin Job and the bridge is kept by the community.

Above the bulwark on the Viehweiden is a path provided by the community to the Obersand and a bridge over the Quotgraben. So when the Sand is empty, the Viehweide can be reached over the Sand.

A path to Martin Job's small farm Neuwies from the Viehweide by way of George Lauschers (his widow). Otherwise to Martin Job, the same as to Peter Trimpler.

A path from the Viehweide to the Eußerthal meadow.

Follow the paths in the Niederfeld which are used and should be used; criminals will be punished every time.

Note a road called the Grasweg [Grass road], which begins at the Hohl or street and goes up to the Herxheim district, it is laid with pebbles.

Note also a road from this road, within Schital's Baum, stretching over to Peter Dörr and the Priory manor of Peter Schaaf and goes out this road up to the Schliedweg.

Note after that a road down from Kappenmorgen up the field over to Velten Dörzapf and Georg Gensheimer provost's morgen up to this field and from there it continues.

Note also a road from the Grasweg to the Hintergrund that continues to the Schliedweg and to the fields in the Hintergrund.

The owners of the properties above the Insheimer Weg and the street (which are both laid with pebbles), as far as these lie out near there, they should use these paths to get to their fields; however, others should use the paths on the open fields.

Note the road called the Schliedweg from the Insheimer Straße stretching to the Hintergrund fields. Whoever may need it may use it.

In the Oberfeld [Upper Field]

First, we note two main roads toward Insheim up to the Offenbach district, that is to say the Altsheimer Weg and the Hauptstraße.

Also note a road from the Insheimer Straße past Provost Claudius Kreiner property out through the Langgewanne past Michel Hilsendegen and the Ludwig Busch Probst property next to the Niederfeld on the Berg.

Next then the open field stretching out to the Provost Bernhard Kopf property out above the Eußerthaler manor property to the open field.

Also a road out over the Provost property on the low side to Peter Dörzapf downward then up to the Mulde fields.

Also on the Schwalbenberg, a path to the Oberfeld has been reported.

Also a road along the Bill. From the Insheimer Weg over the Münster property stretching to the Provost property between Konrad Dörzapf and Lorenz Hatzenbühler and out to the Kahlenberg.

Also a road from the Insheimer Weg over the Provost's Zwanzigmorgen, out to the field stretching to the Münster property provided by Peter Schaaf.

Also a road out from the Insheimer Weg out the Hochangewanne stretching to the Offenbach district.

Also a road from the Insheimer Weg below the Zwanzigmorgen out to the Berg, over the Provost property between Georg Bahlinger and Bernhard Kopf stretching to the top of the Berg.

Obersand [Upper Sand]

Also a road from the Landauer Straße above to the Kaspar Benzen riding manor, down by Bastian Hatzenbühler user of the Brühl, arrives at the Stücken and the Brühl.

Also a road further up across the Poppelmann property, to the Poppelmann's Brühl.

Also a bridge over the Dorfgraben by the middle track to the Poppelmann manor, then out the trench, to the Rechhack [Rechhag] fields.

Mittelsand [Middle sand]

Also a road from the Neuweg over the Provost and next to the Münster property, then over the outgoing and incoming fields stretching to the Bauernweg.

Niedersand [Lower Sand]

Also a Schliedweg from the Bauernweg stretching to the Knittelsheim Scheid.

Following is the livestock policy, as it was renewed in year 1631

A coachman who has three or four horses should keep four self-raised cows, a calf, and thirteen sheep.

A carriage driver with two horses should keep three cows and a calf, and seven sheep.

A hand servant and anyone who has one horse should not hold more than two cows and four sheep. And no one should buy a calf in the pasture.

Moreover, whoever from outside the community drives one head too many (into the forest and onto the meadows), is to pay 10 schilling penalty the first time and again as much after that (double the amount).

Also, a coachman is to provide two sows as maintenance allowance whether he has them or not, and a carriage driver or a hand servant provides one sow.

Regarding the community meadow parcels, each citizen should pay 16 schillings each year from his parcel.

And when someone dies, his parcel should fall to whoever came first to the community.

Also, be it ordered that he who without permission and inspection separates something out and takes it away from the cattle pasture, he must pay a gulden as punishment.

Therefore, the mayor and village master should inspect (check) so that the common property is not spoiled and no harm happens to neighbors.

Ottersheim accessory facts

For the small tithes, on young breeding stock annually by Saint Georg's Day:

A suckling calf:	2 pfennigs
A young pig:	2 pfennigs
A suckling pig:	1 pfennig
A lamb:	3 pfennigs
A young goose:	4 pfennigs

The communities of Ottersheim and Knittelsheim are required to deliver each year: 600 Easter eggs as follows:

Ottersheim:	200 eggs to the bailiff
	100 eggs to the district clerk
	60 eggs to the forest warden
Knittelsheim:	100 eggs to the cellar master
	100 eggs to the poultry warden
	40 eggs to the forest warden

In addition, Ottersheim and Knittelsheim have to provide ten geese (without pay for them) as follows:

Ottersheim:	4 geese to the bailiff
	2 geese to the district clerk
Knittelsheim:	1 goose to the cellar master
	2 geese to the poultry warden
	1 goose to the forest warden

General debt

The debts mentioned in the old account were paid in full by the community in years 1733 and 1738 so that the community is currently completely debt free.

On Tithes

Four capons (fattened hens or roosters) are provided by the community each year from the community place on the Große Gasse. Top Mayor Wendelin Müller, assistant Stefan Gadinger.

(The community place was at 60 Lange Straße. It was still undeveloped in 1788.)

Also, the community of Ottersheim provides 14 malters of seed grain yearly to the cellar at Germersheim.

Ottersheim in 1788, On the Eve of the French Revolution

Thanks to three fortunate circumstances, we have today after nearly 200 years been able to create a fairly accurate picture of the plat and expansion of the village of Ottersheim, the number and names of residents as well as their occupations and possessions in 1788 on the eve of the French Revolution.

In 1787-1788, a census of all the faithful of the Diocese of Speyer was performed as instructed by the Bishop of Speyer, August von Limburg-Stirum (Bishop from 1770 to 1797). Pastor Georg Günther, who served from 1785 to 1801 in Ottersheim, created the required statistics very carefully. This is not surprising considering that previously he was a professor at Heidelberg before, and he returned there again as dean in 1801. According to Pastor Georg Günther, a total of 650 people lived in Ottersheim in 1788. Of these, 507 were Catholic and 143 were Reformed or Lutheran. The 507 Catholics were distributed in 105 households. The father and mother were living in 81 families and one parent was dead in 24 families. During the year, 24 children were born and baptized as Catholic. Four couples closed the marriage covenant. During the year, 12 Catholic citizens of Ottersheim died, including 9 adults and 3 children.

You could almost call it a coincidence that in the same year of 1788, the Palatinate Court Chamber in Heidelberg carried out an extensive survey of Ottersheim. On behalf of the Elector Karl Theodor of the Palatinate (1724-1799), Renovator Boltz was busy documenting all land, meadows, and households in Ottersheim. This book has been preserved. It is 40 centimeters high, 25 centimeters wide, 10 centimeters thick and comprises 1,110 pages. For measurements, the terms rute [3.75 meters], schuh [32.5 centimeters], and zoll [2.7 centimeters] are used. For land parcels, Boltz used a new measurement. Instead of the usual 100 ruten, a morgen of land was calculated using 160 ruten. One hectare thus became 2.5 of the new morgen measure where previously 4 morgen had formed a hectare.

It is amazing how much care and accuracy Renovator Boltz took in creating the record book with the help of Mayor Georg Kopf, Attorney (adjunct) Nikolaus Merdian, and court people: Johannes Seither, Konrad Kopf, and Jakob Kröper. At each land parcel and building lot, the length and width of the upper and lower end were measured and the surface area calculated. Property owners and all direct neighbors were named. At the end of the book, an alphabetical overview of all landowners is listed where each field, each meadow, and each house lot is mentioned. The third circumstance to which we owe thanks for our knowledge about Ottersheim toward the end of the 18th century were several statistical surveys in the years 1791 and 1792 that were ordered by the Electoral Palatinate. These special registries primarily provide information about the structure of the population, age distribution, and about the professions as well as the buildings and the livestock in the village.

1. The Village Layout

In 1788, Ottersheim was half as large as today, not only in the number of houses but also in the number of residents. As for the north side of the upper village, there were no houses along the Neuweg, and there was a single building on the Bauernweg where the Wiegehalle [Weighing hall] stands today. The area east of the road in the Gröhlig was also undeveloped. The Catholic Church that has belonged exclusively to Catholics since 1697 was somewhat smaller than today. It had only three pairs of windows instead of the current five. The altar was in the lower part of the tower. Like almost all the churches of the Middle Ages, it was pointed to the east so the gaze of the faithful during services faced the rising sun, the light from the east. The house of God could be entered from the south. A narrow staircase served as the entrance that led from the east side to the cemetery. The churchyard was also the cemetery. In this way, the dead should stay closely connected with the church and the parish. At every funeral, the coffin was first carried into the church and placed in front of the altar. After the funeral mass of the deceased, the departed was buried in the churchyard with the participation of the whole parish. The custom of erecting a *Tumba*[41] at the first mass of the dead was a common practice until recently.

It had become necessary to enlarge the church by 1788 due to the increase of population. The funds for this purpose had to be raised by the Electoral Court Chamber, by the Eußerthal Abbey, by the Monastery of Saint John in Haimbach, by the Provost of Hördt, and by the community of Ottersheim, according to their share of the tithe. Of the inhabitants of the Ottersheim community, only free handymen and horse or ox cart labor were expected. The church was to be extended to the west. In fact, already in 1789 steps were taken to begin the work. As the church, so also the cemetery was enlarged and surrounded with a new wall. The western part of the wall had to be built up.

The community hall, which in 1788 was at that time called the Rathaus, stood in front of the church as it does today. In its appearance, it would hardly have differed from its present form. The building was presumably built in 1555. The rectory, with its almost meter-thick walls, was the most beautiful stone house of the entire town in 1788. It was built in 1752 to replace an old and dilapidated house. The cost of the new building had to be borne by the Abbey of Eußerthal, because the Eußerthal Abbey was the former owner of the Ottersheim parish and received a third of the tithes. Wood and stones were brought in from the

---

[41] The *Tumba* was a makeshift coffin placed at the altar and draped with a cloth for the first of three traditional Masses of the Dead. It was intended to remind the churchgoers of the recently deceased.

Eußerthal area free of charge by the peasants of the village. The sand also had to be brought in by carts. It was a very extensive work that took a lot of time and led to a protracted dispute with the Ottersheim community regarding credit for the horse cart labor. A stone was placed over the entrance as a reminder of the building of the parsonage. This stone was decorated with the pelican representing the Eußerthal coat of arms, a partial inscription believed to represent 'Probstei Eußerthal', along with the Christian characters 'IHS'. Belonging to the parsonage were also a barn and an elongated side building with stables, a laundry, and a bakery. The barn was built between 1732 and 1733. During demolition in 1959, a 5-meter long beam was found with the following inscription:

CLOSTER EU 1733 SERSTHAL

Many outbuildings were necessary because the pastor back then worked his own parcel of approximately 20 morgen with the help of day laborers. Rectory and vicarage gardens were 0.2 hectare in size. An equally large plot lay east of the rectory in 1788 that was the property of then mayor Georg Kopf. This mayor was the richest peasant farmer in the village with nearly 40 morgen of his own property. In the year 1795, he was carried off in the plague shortly after he had replaced his house with a two-story building. His son, the 'famous' Kopp-Maire[42] sold this house to the community in 1827, which was then set up as a schoolhouse. The Catholic school stood on the property at 62 Lange Straße in 1788. The house is now occupied by Emil Brüderle. The knitting school was still held there during the 19th century. Teacher Georg Kern taught the Catholic children of the community in a single class of nearly one hundred students from 1778 to 1791.

On the north side of the Große Gasse, from the Neuweg to the Bauernweg, there were a total of 24 house lots in 1788, not counting the rectory. The lot listed in the record book as that of a certain Johann Philipp Störzer was just a garden behind the houses at 49, 51, and 54 Große Gasse. Property 54 where Alfred Scherff lives today was then owned by the community. In the lower village east of the Bauernweg, five houses (13, 14, 17, 18, and 21) stood on the north side of the Große Gasse and there were four properties (11, 12, 15/16, and 20) on the south side.

The south side of the Große Gasse counted a total of 25 house lots from the Riedgässel up to the Deich. As previously mentioned, among these was the Catholic school at property 62, what is now the residence of Emil Brüderle. The eastward bordering house on lot 60 of Eugen Leingang (his widow) was owned in 1788 by the Reformed community of Ottersheim. An old barn and a grass garden stood there. Note incidentally that houses 64 and 66 at the time had one owner. It was the pub or small restaurant "Zur Krone" that was inhabited by Andreas Müller, the son of former mayor Georg Müller, and his brother-in-law Markus Lorentz from Bellheim. The Große Gasse ended at the Deich with the half-timbered house of peasant Valentin Burgermeister. This is house 79 now occupied by the widow of Ludwig Föhlinger. The former "Zur Traube" Inn was probably built before the 30 Years War and to date has kept its original form as a half-timbered house. However, the yard and garden of the property were significantly larger in 1788 than now. At that time, the house lots at 77 Große Gasse and 4 Germersheimer Straße also belonged to this

---

[42] Maire is French for mayor, and Ottersheim was under French rule when the son became mayor.

property. The garden extended to the Quotgraben so that the whole manor yard was 0.2 hectare. The Ottostraße of today was called the *Riedgässel [Small Reed road]* in 1788. On its eastern side were only two small properties each having an area of 200 square meters. Today, these are house number 1 of Emma Sauther and house number 2 of Paul Romanowski. On the west side of the Riedgässel were five houses of which only four remain, specifically properties 3, 6, 8, and 10. In the lot of the fifth house is now the shed of Franz Benz. The area next to house number 10 of Oswald Moock was at that time owned by the executioner and skinner, Johannes Franck.

The Kleine Gasse already had essentially its present appearance in 1788. On the north side, there were 14 house lots at that time, and on the south side there were 13 house lots. Property 24 of Ferdinand Kröper was already there but the garden to the east was 25 ruten smaller than today. The rendering place of the butcher Johannes Franck was in the courtyard of lot 31, that of the widow of Peter Bischoff. The plan of 1788 recorded a second house on property 13 of Hermann Kröper that apparently stood in the backyard on the south side but has since been demolished. The site where the Protestant Church now stands belonged to property 3 of Ludwig Herrmann.

In the Gröhlig, a total of nine lots were counted up to the Quotgraben and all on the west side of the road. Four larger properties stood on the northern part of the Gröhlig and five smaller ones on the southern part. House 22 of Wilhelm Hoffmann that in 1963 gave way to a new building was at that time the Reformed schoolhouse. Reformed teacher Friedrich Ruppertus lived and taught there. From the Weet to the church on the west side of the road stood seven farmhouses and four stood on the east side. The land was undeveloped from house number 11 to the Quotgraben. In the upper village on the south side of the road were only five houses. The common road to the Ruschgarten, now the Tuchbleichpfad [cloth bleaching path] of today, formed the western village boundary. The north side of the road was undeveloped. A document from the 18th century reports that visible remains of the French fortifications could be seen there. A total of 1 morgen and 22 ruten of farmland on the north side of the road and on the Neuweg were "buried or unusable."

Ottersheim thus counted 120 house lots in 1788, including parish and community hall. From an exact statistic taken in 1791, we know that on these house lots there were 112 homes and 71 barns. The water supply was assured by the Quotgraben, the Dorfbach, and the Dorfgraben. The course of the Quotgraben has hardly changed since then. Where it touched the Deich, it was artificially dammed so that a large retention pond was created, the so-called *Weet.* The term *Weet* comes from the Old High German word *Wat* and it refers to the shallow standing water that is used as a village watering place. Even in the twenties of this century, it was common that the horses were ridden there in the evening for a refreshing swim. This was done with special fondness by the schoolboys who thus were able to test their riding skills. In recent decades, the Weet increasingly lost its usefulness until it was eliminated entirely.

The Dorfbach (Village creek) was an artificial diversion of the Queich excavated in the 16th century and it experienced hardly a change up to 1788. The Kleine Gasse was supplied with water from the Dorfgraben (Village trench). The Dorfgraben is an artificial trench diversion of the Quotgraben (Big trench). The Dorfbach and Dorfgraben were of great importance to our ancestors. Since there was no plumbing and only a village well, citizens not only washed clothes and shoes but also the face and hands at "the creek." In cases of fire, water was immediately available anywhere in the village and was carried in pails and buckets to the fire. In case of an emergency, water was also taken from the Weet. The danger of fire in earlier centuries was much greater than today because most houses were built of wood. If intervention was too slow, whole blocks could be destroyed by fire. The issue of a water supply for humans and livestock was an important reason that Ottersheim was built to the left and right of the Quotgraben.

The record book contains no information about the appearance of the houses in the 18th century. However, we may assume that with few exceptions there were mostly single-story half-timbered houses in Ottersheim. About 18 houses had two stories. Some of the buildings are preserved in their original condition today. The base was usually made of sandstone that had to be brought by carriage from the Haardt. The wood for the half-timbered houses came at least partly from the local forest. The community provided the base timber free of charge for a new building back then. Moreover, all the villagers actively helped with building a house. This beautiful custom in Ottersheim has been preserved into this century and served the village as a special honor.

2. The District

In 1788, the Ottersheim district included cropland, grassland, forest, and pastureland totaling about 790 hectares of land. Basically, that has not changed. The district boundaries, which were monitored annually by the land survey team, had remained the same except for the Amtmannswiesen. The breakdown into arable land, grassland, and forest does not correspond entirely to the present conditions. The total forest area in 1788 was approximately 123 hectares. It was comprised of the following:

Vorderwald [Front forest]:	24.40 hectares
Hinterwald [Back forest]:	80.14 hectares
Vorderer Niederwald [Front lower forest]:	18.45 hectares
Total:	122.99 hectares

The Vorderer Niederwald that stood next to the Wasserbeiz was deforested after 1788, as was a part of the Dämmel [Dark forest]. If in spite of this deforestation, the forested area is still 114 hectares in size. This can be explained by the fact that a part of the earlier meadows is now forest.

In 1788, the majority of the arable land was south of the village as it still is today. The Stockäcker, the Rechhag, and the Gänsweidegärten comprised the last open fields in the north. The fields were divided into six districts.

a) *Oberfeld [Upper field]:* The boundary was formed in the north by the Altsheimer Weg, in the east by the Herxheimer Weg, in the south by the Herxheim District, and in the west by the Offenbach District. The Oberfeld comprised a total of 44 open fields, among them the vineyards on the Kahlenberg, and on the Berg near the vineyard of Lorenz Ludwig.

b) *Niederfeld [Lower field]:* It stretched from the Herxheimer Weg up to the Knittelsheim District and from the gardens of the Kleine Gasse; that is, from the Brühlwiesen to the Schwalbenberg. In all, the Niederfeld contained 29 open fields.

c) *Gröhlig:* This is the name of the arable land west of the south exit of the village. The Gröhlig was bounded on the north by the Brühlwiesen at the Quotgraben and in the south by the Altsheimer Weg.

d) *Obersand [Upper sand]:* The southern border of the Obersand was formed by the Waalen and the upper Brühl, the eastern boundary by the Neuweg. The Obersand had 14 open fields.

e) *Mittelsand [Middle sand]:* The four open fields of the Mittelsand lay between the Neuweg and the Bauernweg.

f) *Niedersand [Lower sand]:* The Niedersand was the arable land to the east of the Bauernweg up to the Knittelsheim District. The meadows in the lower Brühl, also called the Faselbrühl, formed the south border. The Niedersand had 6 open fields.

In 1788, the Ottersheim had a total of 98 arable open fields comprising 505.45 hectares of fields. Meadows present at that time were:

9.75 hectares	in the upper Brühl and the Viehweide
1.75 hectares	in the middle Brühl
3.28 hectares	in the lower Brühl (Faselwiesen)
3.27 hectares	Rechhag
5.38 hectares	in Gärtelswiesen
2.33 hectares	on the Seemorgen
10.95 hectares	on the Niedervorderwiesen and in the Hundsloch
5.44 hectares	on the Mühlwiesen
6.08 hectares	on the Obervorderwiesen
6.00 hectares	in the Stöckwiesen and Scheerwiesen
9.52 hectares	on the Hörst meadows
2.76 hectares	in the Dämmelswiesen (Dümmelswiesen)
2.63 hectares	on the Börstwiesen (Berschwiesen)
6.85 hectares	in the Rohrbusch and in the Schwenkpfuhl
2.13 hectares	in Schuster's Eck
6.71 hectares	on the Hinterwiesen
1.80 hectares	in the Rödel
2.91 hectares	on the Neuwiesen
4.12 hectares	on the Seewiesen
1.53 hectares	on the Sechsmorgen on the other side of the Hubgraben

0.58 hectares	On the Freiwiesen, (The remaining 7.5 hectares belonged to the Monastery of Saint John in Haimbach. They were managed by a bailiff.)
11.23 hectares	over the Queichbach
107.00 hectares	of grasslands in total

The house lots, including their yards, comprised 14 hectares of land. Arable and grassland areas in 1788 therefore amounted to 612.45 hectares of land.

To the right and left of the present-day Gänsehaardt at that time were two large meadow areas belonging to the general public and were therefore called *Allmend or Ganerb.* The pasture was of grass that was riddled with hedges, small trees, and bushes. Here cows, cattle, pigs, sheep, and geese found nourishment from spring to late autumn. At the beginning of this century, the cow herder and swine herder still came through the village in the mornings with a signal horn and picked up the animals. They drove the animals back to the individual barnyards with stomachs full in the evening. There was a large pond where the geese could splash and swim during the day in the center of the Gänsehaardt.

The stock book of 1788 separated two large grazing areas east and west of the Gänsehaardt of today. The so-called *Oberweide* or upper pasture that also belonged to the Gänsehaardt stretched from the Neuweg to the Offenbach District and from the Vorderwald to the Stockäckern and to the Rechhag. The Oberweide consisted of 18.3 hectares or 73 morgen. The forest names *Oberalmen* and *Viehtrieb* still remind us today of the former meadowlands. Also, the name *Haardtstücke* points to the forestland of old.

The so-called *Niederweide [Lower pasture]* reached from the Gänseweidegärten (Goose grazing gardens) to the Niedervorderwiesen and from the Neuweg to the Vordere Niederwald, the present-day Wasserbeizäckern and Wasserbeizwiesen. The Niederweide was, with its 22.86 hectares or 91 morgen of land, about 4 hectares larger than the Oberweide. The meadows in the Niederalmen remind us still of the former Niederweide. At that time, a total of 41.16 hectares or 164 morgen of pasture was available to the Ottersheim peasants for grazing.

The network of roads has remained broadly unchanged to the present time. Not until the land consolidation were the pathways eliminated that probably were a thousand or more years old. Also, the path or road names in the 18th century were the same as today with very few exceptions. The Altsheimer Weg led to the defunct village of Altsheim that probably lay between Ottersheim and Offenbach. It was surely only a small Frankish settlement that disappeared around 1600. It cannot be ruled out that the open field called *Goldgrube [Goldmine]* at the District boundary of Offenbach is connected with the village of Altsheim. Perhaps gold coins buried by the residents of the village of Altsheim during times of war were found while plowing or digging in the Löchel [Small hole] as this field was called in 1788.

The Insheimer Weg does not lead directly to the village of Insheim; however, it is an imaginary extension point to this place. Already in the 16th century, this path was fortified with stones. The Rülzheimer Weg established the shortest route between the villages of

Ottersheim and Rülzheim, while the Herxheimer Weg provides access to the open fields toward Herxheim. The Mühlweg [Mill road] in the northwest of the district points in its imaginary extension to the Fuchsmühle [Fox mill] and the Neumühle [New mill] on the Queich. The Neuweg, upon which no house stood in 1788, served mainly as a cattle run. It is, as is the Bauernweg, already mentioned in the 16th century. The Falltorweg of today was called *Mittelsporweg* in 1788 while the name *Grübenweg* is not mentioned. Grübenweg reminds of the trenches that served the preparation of flax and hemp in the 19th century. The local people called these pits *Dulflöcher*.

As with the open fields, so also the roads have grown slowly over the centuries. Development centered on creating the shortest possible connection between the village and the fields. So is it only understandable that important field access roads were created in addition to the intersections in the main compass directions. That these pathways partially run crooked or angular is explained by the fact that they were not created on the drawing board but were gradually expanded with the clearing of new open fields in the course of centuries.

The Queich took its present course in the 18th century within the area of the local district. Although the community of Ottersheim possessed no land at the so-called *wooden Weir* near the Neumühle of Offenbach; nevertheless, it was required to maintain the mill together with the communities of Zeiskam and Niederhochstadt, because the Electoral Palatinate gave them the rights to obtain water from the Dorfbach for the mill. In 1723, when Master Carpenter Martin Burgard and Master Millers Jakob and Johannes Reyland wanted to erect two mills with the permission of the Palatinate Court Chamber, they had to conclude a contract with the communities of Ottersheim, Zeiskam, and Niederhochstadt, and explicitly recognize in that contract the water rights of these villages. Otherwise, the construction of the mills would not have been permitted.

In 1788, the Queich was separated at the so-called *stone Weir* into two equally strong arms, the so-called *old Queich* and the *Hubgraben*. A drawing in the National Archives in Speyer shows that the Hubgraben probably was broadened and strengthened by the hand of man in the 18th century, as it was originally a narrow trench. The open meadows beyond the Hubgraben belonged only in a very small part to the Ottersheim district in 1788. They were owned mainly by the Commandery[43] of Haimbach, whose house stood at the crossroads two kilometers north of Zeiskam. Since 1512, the Monastery of Saint John had been administered by a warden who also had to lease the 30 morgen of open meadows.

In the course of secularization, these meadows were purchased in 1809 by the Reformed adjunct Konrad Humbert of Ottersheim, the citizen Bernard Bernion of Germersheim and a certain Josef Spitz of Speyer for 10,200 francs.[44] They were mainly Ottersheim peasant farmers who had held these meadows as leased land or property. Therefore, they belong today to the Ottersheim district, although they are closer to Zeiskam than to Ottersheim. On the other hand, the history of these meadows makes understandable the controversy that ran for decades about the boundary of the district beyond the Hubgraben.

---

[43] A *Commandery* was a small unit of Knights who discharged all powers of the provincial administration.

[44] The franc was the unit of currency used by the French beginning in 1795.

3. Property ownership

The exact details of the record book provide valuable insight into the ownership of properties in Ottersheim at the end of the 18th century. Of 790.6 hectares of land, 306.6 hectares, or 40%, belonged to the rulers. These are primarily the estates properties confiscated by the Palatinate during the 16th century, the Priory of Hördt (192.9 hectares), the Klingenmünster Monastery (41.5 hectares), the Eußerthal Monastery (21 hectares), and around the Poppelmann manor (37.2 hectares). These lands were scattered in larger or smaller parcels throughout the district, although some areas are unmistakable. Thus, the Priory of Hördt had property, especially near the Altsheimer Weg, Hochangewanne, Zwanzigmorgen, Linsenäckern, Langgewanne, Schlittweg, Hintergrund, Muld, Berg, Brett, and Schlegel. The fields of the Klingenmünster Monastery were mainly near the Hochangewanne, Offenbach's Corner, Bild, Linsenäckern, Schlittweg, Langgewanne, Hintergrund, Berg, and Langenstein. The Poppelmann manor properties included, in addition to 36 morgen in the Großstück, 11 morgen in the Elfmorgen, 6 morgen in the Knopfgewanne, 15 morgen in the Hintergrund, and 4 morgen on the Kahlenberg. In addition to fields, also belonging to the manor properties were appropriate meadows. For example, the Priory of Hördt possessed 10 morgen in the Mühlwiesen and 9 morgen in the Stöckwiesen. An exchange of letters in 1543 reported that 9 morgen in the Stöckwiesen was exchanged for 9 morgen of meadows in the Biengarten. The Biengarten laid in the Wasserbeiz "inside the Loch."

Smaller plots of fields and meadows in 1788 belonged to the Commandery of Haimbach (2.6 hectares), the Cathedral Chapter of Speyer (2 hectares), the Collection Agency of Zeiskam (4.1 hectares), the hospital of Germersheim (3.3 hectares), the winery of Germersheim (1.5 hectares), and the church in Zeiskam (0.5 hectares).

The parish property was 8.15 hectares, and the community property was 19 hectares that consisted mainly of meadows. In addition to the forest and the two meadows, the Stockäcker also belonged to the community. The Allmendstücke comprised 173.85 hectares of land. In possession of individual peasants were a total of 283 hectares of fields and meadows. Twelve peasants had 5-10 hectares and eleven had 3-5 hectares of land. These 23 peasants cultivated a total of 122.9 hectares. The 142.6 hectares that remained was distributed among a total of 136 owners of Ottersheim. The residents of neighboring communities owned 17.5 hectares of fields and meadows. Also, it should be noted that the cemetery at that time was owned by the community. Overview:

Public property:	173.85	hectares	=	21%
Peasant properties:	283.00	hectares	=	36%
Community property:	19.00	hectares	=	2%
Parish property:	8.15	hectares	=	1%
Manor property:	306.60	hectares	=	40%
	790.60	hectares		100%

4. The population

The special directories from the years 1791 and 1792 give us valuable insight into the population of Ottersheim. At the head of the village at the time was Mayor Georg Kopf (1780-1795). He owned the most land (9.64 hectares) among all citizens of the village, which he managed with the help of a servant and a maid. At his side stood lawyer (adjunct) Nikolaus Merdian who lived at 3 Kleine Gasse. The lower court was exercised under the chairmanship of the mayor with three court people.

In charge of the Catholic parish in Ottersheim was Pastor Georg Günther (1785-1801), while the parishioners of the Reformed were under Pastor Stephan Karl Kasimir Riehm (1787-1792) of Offenbach. The Catholic teacher's name was Georg Kern (1778-1791); the teacher for the Reformed was Friedrich Ruppertus. Ottersheim counted 710 residents in 1791, including 126 men, 140 women, 221 boys, 203 girls, 7 servants, and 13 maids. The two schools were attended by 140 children. There were 11 boys in the craft apprenticeships. Living with their parents were 137 sons and 136 daughters. Both father and mother were alive in 121 of a total of 141 families. Fourteen people were known local indigents. In 1791, 35 children were born, 13 people had died, and 3 couples joined the covenant of marriage. There were a considerable number of tradesmen in addition to many country people.

The directories counted:

7	Linen weavers	4	Tailors
4	Shoemakers	3	Blacksmiths
3	Carpenters	3	Innkeepers
2	Masons	2	Butchers
2	Coopers	1	Joiner
1	Merchant	1	Bag or sack maker

Of the livestock kept in Ottersheim, there were 50 horses, 185 cows, 19 cattle and calves, 250 sheep, and 105 pigs. The sheep were cared for by shepherd, Stephan Hanck, the cows by cow herder, Bonifaz Kölsch. Most peasants lived with their modest self-possessions on rented land upon which they grew grain (rye), wheat, spelt, barley, oats, turnips, cabbage, flax, hemp, poppy (spells), canola, camelina (false flax), onions, peas, lentils, vetch, corn (maize), potatoes, sorghum, and tobacco. Wine grapes grew on the Kahlenberg and in several other fields in the southern part of the district. Wine cultivation was first documented in 1103 in Ottersheim but it is probably much older.

The former monastery lands were leased mostly for a set number of years in parcels called *Pflug*. Thus is reported that four pflüge of the Klingenmünster Monastery were auctioned for tenures of 15 years in 1780. The Hördt Priory manor was divided into 46 *pflüge*. Each pflug consisted of approximately 15 morgen of farmland and 1.5 to 2 morgen of meadow. As a rule, the leased land that lay in various field areas remained in the hands of the same family or their nearest relatives.

A lawsuit from that time deserves to be mentioned because it gives us an insight into concerns and needs of our ancestors that we no longer know about in our century. In 1791, the Ottersheim citizen Michael Müller of 19 Kleine Gasse bought an estate in Mechtersheim from the Eußerthal properties as a hereditary property. He wanted to move to Mechtersheim, and to the chagrin of the community, wanted to take with him his "substantial house together with stables and barn." Mayor Kopf, lawyer Merdian, and the court people turned to the Electoral Court Chamber of Karl Theodor in Mannheim with the request to forbid this house transport from Ottersheim to Mechtersheim. They had a valid reason to bring to bear. It was to be expected that at the place where the house would be demolished the successor would have to build a new house. For this house, it would be required that the community provide the wood and in Ottersheim wood was quite rare. But Müller did not want to budge. He insisted that a house belonged to movable property and the owner should therefore be allowed to take it when moving. He asserted that in Mechtersheim it was very difficult to procure timber and stone for a new building. Also, he should not be treated differently from other citizens of Ottersheim. Müller pointed out that about ten years previous a certain Jost Ludwig sold his house at 10 Riedgässel to Schwegenheim. Even Mayor Georg Kopf, who had built a new house about six years previous, was not been prevented from selling his old house out of the village. In addition Müller added, in previous years when his house was built the community provided only the base timber but not the timber for the entire house, which was at his disposal. He was willing to pay to the community treasury the usual price of 15 gulden for the base timber. The dispute dragged on for a long time until finally the Court in Mannheim ruled that Müller had to leave his house in Ottersheim. However, the treasury agreed to help him in the procurement of wood and stones for a new building. The value of the Ottersheim property was estimated at 800 to 900 gulden. It is likely that Müller sold his farm for that price and built a new house in Mechtersheim.

5. The Family Names

The record book of 1788 allows us to establish a fairly complete list of all surnames in Ottersheim and also to specify the number of the respective families and the single adults.

1.	Bär	1		35.	Jost	1
2.	Bahlinger	3		36.	Keller	1
3.	Baumann	1		37.	Kern	1
4.	Becker (Reformed.)	1		38.	Knöll	3
5.	Bischoff	1		39.	Kölsch	1
6.	Brand (Reformed)	1		40.	Kopf	2
7.	Burger (Reformed)	1		41.	Körper (Reformed)	2
8.	Burgermeister	1		42.	Kreiner	5
9.	Burry	2		43.	Kröper	12
10.	Busch	2		44.	Küburz	1
11.	Conrad (Reformed)	1		45.	Ludwig (Reformed)	3
12.	Dörr (Reformed)	1		46.	Mangold	1

13.	Dörzapf	11		47.	Merdian	5
14.	Doll (Reformed)	2		48.	Müller	5
15.	Eibler	1		49.	Moock	3
16.	Föhlinger	1		50.	Muth	1
17.	Franck	1		51.	Rösch	1
18.	Frey Reformed)	1		52.	Rohrmeier	1
19.	Gadinger	1		53.	Roth (Reformed)	3
20.	Gebhard	1		54.	Ruppertus (Reformed)	1
21.	Gensheimer (Reformed)	5		55.	Sauther (Reformed)	1
22.	Gib	1		56.	Schaf (Reformed)	1
23.	Glatz	2		57.	Scherff (Luthern)	1
24.	Günther (Reformed)	1		58.	Seither	4
25.	Gutting	1		59.	Stadel	2
26.	Hanck	1		60.	Störtzer	4
27.	Hatzenbühler	19		61.	Wagner	3
	(Reformed and Catholic)					
28.	Hilsendegen	3		62.	Walk	2
29.	Hindert	1		63.	Weiß (Reformed)	3
30.	Hofner	1		64.	Winkelblech	1
31.	Hörner (Reformed)	1		65.	Witz	1
32.	Humbert (Reformed)	1		66.	Zerrmann (Reformed)	1
33.	Jeckel	1		67.	Zimmer	1
34.	Job	9		68.	Zwißler	3
	(Reformed and Catholic)					

The following family names were the most common at the end of the 18th century:

Hatzenbühler:	19 times		Kreiner:	5 times
Kröper:	12 times		Merdian:	5 times
Dörzapf:	11 times		Müller:	5 times
Job:	9 times		Seither:	4 times
Gensheimer:	5 times		Störtzer:	4 times

These ten family names are still to be found in Ottersheim. Of the 68 above-mentioned names, about half died out over the course of not quite 200 years.

6. The Owners of the Houses or House Sites

Property Number	The owner of the house in 1788	The owner of the house in 1966
	Deich (gasse)	*Germersheimer Straße*
1	Community Hall	Community Hall
5	Andreas Walk	Robert Frey
6	Anton Knöll	Herrmann siblings
7	Anton Bischoff	Walter Fischer / Eugen Mohr

9	Johannes Knöll (Senior)	Karl Ettmüller (Branch Office of the County and City Savings Bank)
10	Konrad Föhlinger	Alois Walk
11	Valentin Zerrmann	Werner Hoffmann I.
12	Rudolf Hatzenbühler	Bernhard Kröper (his widow)
14	Theobald Hatzenbühler	Ludwig Ritter
15	Konrad Hatzenbühler (unmarried)	Ludwig Burgermeister
18	Georg Hatzenbühler (Junior)	Robert Kröper
19	Johannes Kröper (Senior)	Oskar Kuntz

Im Gröhlig

20	Dieter Wagner	Paul Dörzapf
21	Konrad Dörzapf	Albert Kröper
22	The Reformed Schoolhouse	Wilhelm Hoffmann II.
24	Johannes Bahlinger	Hugo Gutting (his widow)
25	Valentin Job	Fritz Gensheimer
26	Jakob Brand	August Walk (his widow)
27	Georg Hatzenbühler (the middle one)	Eduard Kröper
29	Jakob Muth	Eduard Jeckel I.
30	Jakob Ludwig	Severin Lerch

Große gasse — *Lange Straße*

11	Peter Moock	Richard Kreiner
12	Karl Weiß	Alois Reichling
13	Claudius Dörzapf	August Kuhn (his widow)
14	Jakob Conrad	August Zwißler
15/16	Georg Kreiner	Anna Sauter / Wilhelm Breßler
17	Andreas Rösch	Otto Bauchhenß
18	Konrad Kopf	Otto Merdian
20	Theo Hatzenbühler	Franz Schwaab
21	Valentin Dörzapf	Ludwig Gadinger I.
	Pankratius Hindert	Wilhelm Lutz (his widow)
22	Johannes Dörzapf	Franz Benz
23	Josef Keller	Eduard Dörzapf
24	Philipp Jakob Weiß	Alois Wingerter
25	Johannes Knöll (Junior)	Eugen Job I. (his widow)
26/27	Rudolf Merdian	Old Raiffeisen Warehouse / Emil Hünerfauth
28	Georg Gebhard	Theodor Weisbrod
29	Jakob Kröper	Josef Müller (his widow)
30	Johannes Franck (knacker)	Julius Job
32	Peter Körper	Franz Josef Kröper (his widow)
33	Georg Burri	Otto Glatz (his widow)
34	Salomon Job (his widow)	Otto Job I.

35	Georg Nikolaus Humbert	Alfons Zwißler
36	Andreas Gutting	Anton Zwißler
39	Johannes Zwißler	Eugen Jochim
40	Johannes Job (his widow)	Richard Hoffmann / Josef Dörzapf
41	Johannes Seither (Senior)	Stefan Hörner
42	Philipp Scherff	Alwin Seither
43	Georg Günther	Albert Hilsendegen (his widow) / Franziska Huwe
44	Johannes Busch (two-story house)	Erich Kern II.
45	Andreas Zimmer	Erwin Wünschel / Ludwig Detzel
46	Georg Hatzenbühler (Senior)	Julius Seither
47	Johannes Moock	Magdalena Weinmann (widow)
48	Claudius Dörzapf	Franz Föhlinger
49	Nikolaus Witz	Willi Röhrig
50	Georg Jakob Stadel	Edwin Hilsendegen
51	Andreas Job	Josef Weimann
53	Nikolaus Kröper (his widow)	Dumser siblings
54	Property of the community	Alfred Scherff
55	Georg Job (Junior)	Alois Kopf (his widow)
56	Konrad Kopf	Otto Job II.
57	Johannes Kreiner	Eduard Lavo (his widow) / Vinzenz Gläßgen
59	Johannes Böhm from Bellheim	Walter Kopf
60	Reformed Congregation Ottersheim (Empty house lot with yard)	uninhabited
61	Jakob Kröper	Alois Hilsendegen
62	Catholic Schoolhouse	Emil Brüderle
63	Johannes Anton Seither	Willi Hindert
64	Markus Lorentz (Merchant)	Emil Rund (his widow)
65	Johannes Hatzenbühler (Senior) Margarete Kröper	Eugen Gensheimer
66	Andreas Müller (two-story house) Restaurant "Zur Krone"	Emil Gutting
68	Georg Lorenz Gensheimer	Eduard Steegmüller (his widow)
69	Wilhelm Weiß	Friedrich Blattmann
70	Wendel Dörzapf	Ludwig Kreiner (his widow)
71	Georg Job (Senior)	Joh. Josef Job
73	Martin Dörzapf	Willi Faath (his widow)
74	Johannes Gadinger	Rudolf Metzger (his widow)
75	Katharina Körper	Severin Zwißler (his widow)
76	Johannes Seither (Junior)	Georg Kruppenbacher

78	Georg Kopf (Mayor) (two-story house)	Old Schoolhouse, built in 1902 now teachers' residences
79	Valentin Burgermeister (two-story house)	Ludwig Lorenz Föhlinger
—	Catholic rectory (two-story house, Rev. Günther	Catholic Rectory until 1959 (demolished)

Oberdorf

83	Nikolaus Witz (his widow)	Catholic Sisters' Home
85	Johannes Kröper (Junior)	Franz Müller (his widow)
87	Hans Georg Hatzenbühler (the middle one)	Otto Ettmüller (his widow)
89	Johannes Moock	August Faath
91	August Ruf	Wilhelm Dotterweich

Riedgässel   *Ottostraße*

1	Sebastian Hatzenbühler	uninhabited
2	Rudolf Glatz	Paul Romanowski
—	Jakob Dörzapf	Benz garden shed
3	Johannes Rohrmeier (Grass garden)	Alois Gadinger (his widow)
6	Jakob Mangold	Julius Hoffmann (his widow)
8	Ägidius Burri	Ferdinand Job / August Job
10	Johannes Jost Ludwig (Empty house lot with yard)	Oswald Moock / Jakob Moock
—	Johannes Franck (Empty house lot with garden)	Garden

Kleine Gasse   *Ludwigstraße*

2	Abraham Humbert	Arnold Zwißler
3	Nikolaus Merdian (Attorney)	Ludwig Herrmann
4	Johannes Jost Ludwig	Ferdinand Föhlinger
5	Georg Heinrich Hatzenbühler	Alois Benz
6	Georg Jakob Doll	Jakob Eichenlaub (his widow)
7	Dieter Wagner	Hubert Kramer
8	Heinrich Gensheimer	Ruprecht Hindert
9	Peter Zwißler	Kurt Kröper (Elisabeth Job)
10	Salomon Job (his widow)	Hugo Seither
11	Andreas Kreiner	Hugo Seither
12	Dieter Hilsendegen	Alois Merdian
13	Rudolf Moock	Hermann Kröper
—	Peter Hilsendegen	demolished
14	Josef Müller	Helmut Seither
15	Salomon Job (his widow)	Hugo Müller / Emma Müller / Ruprecht Job

16/17	Anton Bischoff	Franz Ludwig Dörzapf
18	Valentin Baer (his widow)	Eugen Dörzapf
19	Michael Müller	Karl Detzel (his widow)
20	Georg Gensheimer	Ludwig Disqué
21	Jakob Doll	Ludwig Braun / August Schaller
23	Franz Merdian	Emil Kern
24	Georg Zwißler	Ferdinand Kröper
—	Rudolf Merdian (Empty house lot with yard)	
25	Georg Jakob Job	Franz Moock II.
26	Johannes Nikolaus Sauther	Albert Dörzapf
28	Margarete Ludwig	Josef Michalczyk
31	Johannes Franck (butcher/skinner)	Peter Bischoff (his widow) / August Schreiber

	Bauernweg	*Maxstraße*
1	Jakob Hilsendegen	Weighing Hall

The Queich Lines at Ottersheim

The Sun King Louis XIV of France, who after the 30 Years War had brought the city of Landau under his control, wanted to move the French border to the Queich at the end of the 17th century. The legal basis for this measure was to be delivered by the Breisach Reunification Ruling of March 1680. On his orders, French soldiers occupied the southern Palatinate. Construction of fortifications along the Queich was started immediately in order to secure the country against attacks by German troops. These so-called *Queich Lines* reached from Annweiler to the Rhine. In Ottersheim, they went from Offenbach along the Brühl- or Bordgraben to the Tuchbleichpfad on the west side of the village. Then they led north around the town and reached the Bordgraben again at the Faselbrühl at the east end of the village. In the War of Spanish Succession (1701-1713), the French gave up the Queich Lines and set up new positions at the Lauter (left tributary of the Rhine). But in the Austrian War of Succession (1740-1748), they returned again to the Queich. Now the lines were not only repaired but also greatly expanded.

In the city archives at Landau, there are numerous maps showing the events at the fortification facilities from the year 1740. These show that among the villages south of the Queich, Ottersheim was especially well fortified. This was not only due to the special location of the village in the middle between the Rhine and the Haardt, but also due to the fact that the largest part of the Ottersheim village lay north of the Brühl- or Bordgraben, the last place where a German attack should break down according to the French plan. The fortifications on the western, northern, and eastern edge of Ottersheim consisted mainly of a high rampart and the Wassergraben [water trench or moat].[45] The moat was about ten meters wide at the top. Gun emplacements were built with access roads at points with a clear view and with a corresponding field of fire. One such "Schießberg" [Shooting hill] was the Tuchbleichpfad about midway between the county road and the Bordgraben. It was not easy to fill the moat with water because of the height difference of the ground that led around the north side of the village. For this purpose, a strong defense with a dam and a wooden closure was built east of the present day Friedhofstraße through the Brühl. Part of the water seems to have also come from the Dorfbach that crossed the fortifications at the Neuweg.

A particular problem was the exits of the streets and roads in the west, north, and east of the village. To allow traffic to flow, it was necessary to build bridges across the rampart trenches. Such bridges existed at the Offenbach Straße near the Tuchbleichpfad, in the Neuweg at the north end of the Pfarrgarten, in the Bauernweg just north of the present day Weighing hall, in the lower village near property 6 of Otto Morio, and in the present Riedstraße near the Faselbrühl. We can estimate from the extent of the fortifications that about 20 morgen of arable land were "buried" as the old documents report at that time. In addition, land for the Queich Lines was needed outside of the village. At the Offenbach border, entrenchments had been built that used three morgen of land. The meadows to the right and left of the Bordgraben were also to be used for defense in the event of an emergency. The plan was to block the flow of water and flood the Brühl with the help of dams. There were three such dams in the Ottersheim district. The first was near the Offenbach border, the second at the Friedhofweg [Cemetery road], and the third at the Faselbrühl. The latter was removed only recently in the wake of land consolidation, while the dam at the cemetery still exists.

Presumably, the lines that were started in 1740 were still not quite finished when these had to be vacated by French Marshal Noailles in 1743 on the approach of the Pragmatic Army. Two thousand peasants were ordered to raze to the ground the ramparts and trenches between Annweiler and Germersheim. Probably only the largest hindrances were removed, while the fortifications in the open fields remained intact for the most part. This assumption is even more likely since most of the fields that were "buried" did not belong to private owners but were manorial estates. As in the wake of the Revolution of 1789, the French returned to the Palatinate and they immediately repaired the Queich Lines again. About 1,300 peasants and 1,500 French soldiers were busy with the extension of the fortifications between Annweiler and Germersheim in 1794. Later, they were joined by 6,000 French recruits who were required to alternately drill and work on the entrenchments. "There were constantly Frenchmen in Ottersheim," noted Dieter Job in his house booklet. Two of them even married Ottersheim peasant daughters and remained to

---

[45] See the placement of the Queich Lines and moat in the illustration on page 326.

live in the village. A lot of wood was necessary for the extension of the lines. Unfortunately, for the population in Ottersheim numerous forest trees were felled. "That was the greatest damage we had," wrote Dieter Job in his notes.

These fortifications played no large military role in the war between France and Germany, much like the Western Wall[46] in our century. There have never been major battles in Ottersheim even though the lines have been repeatedly occupied by French soldiers. Dieter Job tells us the French "manned the lines" as they marched in from Landau in 1792. The soldiers arrived midday at 2 o'clock in the afternoon, but by evening the Austrians advanced and beat the French to flight. French troops returned and again "set up position in the lines" in 1795. The lines had become militarily irrelevant after the inclusion of the left bank of the Rhine to the French Republic. It remained so also during the Napoleonic wars where the battles were fought at other theaters of war.

There is some evidence for the extension of the French forts in the Ottersheim district in the land registry of 1802. Specifically, there is marked for each parcel how many morgen of land was "buried," that is, how many morgen of land were used for the lines.

At the Offenbach Scheid: "In der Schanz":	3.3	morgen
In the Oberbrühl:	1.8	"
On the Viehweide:	0.8	"
In the Ruschgarten:	2.0	"
In Gröhlig:	0.5	"
On the Großstück:	1.2	"
On the Münster Property:	1.8	"
In the Gartenstücken:	3.0	"
Above the Bauernweg:	2.8	"
Below the Bauernweg:	1.8	"
In the Ried:	0.6	"
Under the common road at the Faselbrühl:	2.8	"
Total:	22.4	morgen

The lines in Ottersheim were gradually leveled when the Palatinate went to Bavaria in 1816. The soil from the Schießberg in the Ruschgarten was used to fill the building lots to the north of the Weet on the Germersheimer Straße. The soil from the walls in the Ried was partially used to pave the Lange Straße. Houses, barns, or sheds were constructed at various points on the former fortification lands in the upper village, the Neuweg, the Bauernweg, and the lower village. There are frequent references to the former lines in the planning applications at the local government. The poor ground soil often caused cracks in the buildings that were built there, such as the barn of Philipp Müller. When a well was dug

---

[46] This refers to the West Wall, a 630 kilometers long defensive bulwark which Hitler had built between 1938 and 1940 along the western edge of the old German Empire stretching from the Netherlands to Switzerland.

90

or foundation excavated, one often hit black dirt at two or three meter depth that originates from the former water trench or moat. For example, Otto Morio experienced this as he was excavating a cellar. Hardly anything can be seen of the extensive French fortifications today. Only an expert can still find one or the other trace when carefully observing the soil types and composition. Also, the name *Linien or Lin-chen* is only known to a few villagers, even though it used to be the commonly used term for the former fortifications.

Ottersheim during the French Revolution

The storming of the Bastille, a State prison in Paris, on 14 July 1789 was the beginning of profound political and social upheaval that occurred in not only France but spread all over Europe. The French Revolution, with its demands for freedom, equality, and fraternity, abolished the privileges of the nobility and high clergy and laid the foundation for democracy. Unfortunately, the years of revolution were characterized by a sea of blood and tears. In addition to the French King, Ludwig XVI, thousands of nobles, innocent priests, and simple religious people were forced to climb to the gallows. Even its own children were not spared by the revolution.

When the Revolutionaries saw their work in danger from Austria and Prussia, they preempted the impending attack and declared war in 1792 on the "old powers." Impulsively, French General Custine occupied the left bank of the Rhine that same year, even though the Palatinate had declared its neutrality. Of those times, Dieter Job reported in his home booklet, "French soldiers occupied the Herxheim heights in 1792 at harvest time." They remained there about twelve days. Then the Austrians came across the Rhine and occupied positions at Schwegenheim. Suddenly, the French were gone but only for a short time. Then they moved from Landau to the Queich Lines at Offenbach, Ottersheim, Knittelsheim, and Bellheim. But even that was not of long duration. The French had to retreat when the German troops attacked during March of 1793, thereupon the Imperials took outpost positions at Herxheim and Offenbach. But already in May 1793, General Custine pushed the outposts back to Ottersheim and Knittelsheim. Part of the population fled in fear to Germersheim. The records and books of the Ottersheim community hall were taken to the magistrate's office at Germersheim in a box at that time. There, they were soon lost forever.

There were still bloody clashes between the Germans and the French in the summer of 1793. After a skirmish near Bellheim, the Imperial soldiers took up positions in Germersheim and on the north side of the Queich, while the French occupied the south side of the Queich. The French attacked the German troops in mid-July. The fight took place along the Queich from Germersheim to the Haardt. The French advanced and occupied the Bellheim forest after a heated battle near Bellheim. Then the Imperialists turned back the French counter-attack. The Germans finally managed to repel the French invaders back beyond Weißenburg. This victory was short-lived however. Already in December 1793, the Imperial Army had to move back over the Rhine leaving the whole Palatinate to the French. The French immediately established themselves in the villages of the District Office of Germersheim. What happened back then in Ottersheim is reported for us by Dieter Job in his home booklet.

"Our misery grew more than ever. We had to provide quarters for soldiers, and we had to provide them with provisions, hay, and oats. The population had to pay a lot for fire protection.[47] The paper money saw its beginning and all trading ended. So many zentners[48] of hay had to be delivered, so many malters of oats, so many malters of grain that it was impossible to raise it all. Then the French employed violence and took away our horses and cows. Not a tail remained. They came with carts and emptied the barns. When spring came and the fields were to be sown, there were no cattle. We had to work the fields by hand. The barley was chopped with a wide hoe. Then people gradually bought back cattle, but because the money had lost its value, the shortage kept increasing. The malter of grain rose to 36 gulden, the malter of spelt to 18 gulden. A horse that could only walk cost 100 gulden, and a small cow also cost up to 100 gulden."

According to the records by Gretchen Kopf, 157 Ottersheim citizens had to spend around 22,000 gulden in war taxes. The most highly taxed were:

Philipp Borger:	619 gulden	Jakob Job:	326 gulden
Johann Kopf:	462 gulden	Johann Seither:	319 gulden
Valentin Burgermeister:	456 gulden	Konrad Föhlinger:	271 gulden
Andreas Walk:	329 gulden	Nikolaus Sauther:	269 gulden

With the occupation of the Palatinate, the French attempted to spread their revolutionary concepts among the population. According to their philosophies, a cult of reason should replace Christianity. Therefore, church services were banned. The churches and monasteries were looted and the bells were carried off. Dieter Job noted in his house booklet, "Each village was allowed to keep only one bell, as a police bell." Ottersheim Pastor Georg Günther fled across the Rhine to Heidelberg in 1794. It was only in September 1796 that he was allowed to return. To make matters worse, at that time in Ottersheim a plague broke out that swept away no fewer than 90 people over the course of 17 months, including 53 adults and 5 couples. The victims could not be provided for nor could they receive a religious burial because the pastor was expelled. Mayor Georg Kopf was also among the

---

[47] It is believed Dieter is referring to extortion payments of money or valuables to the French troops who otherwise threatened to burn down the homes in the village.

[48] A *zentner* was the unit for mass for weighing crops. Also called hundred-weight it was equal to 100 pfunds or 50 kilograms. One pfund was equal to 1/2 a kilogram.

dead. The newborns were baptized at that time out of town, and the young couples were married in Bellheim or Germersheim.

Dieter Job recorded in his home booklet, "The French were continuously in Ottersheim during 1794." They were mainly engaged in rebuilding the Queich Lines. These fortifications stretched from the Offenbach Scheid [Offenbach border] across the Viehweide to the Ruschgarten. Then they followed the northern boundary of the village across the Neuweg and Bauernweg to the Ried in the lower village. At the Faselbrühl, they turned to the east. With the help of appropriate weirs, the defensive moat could be filled with water. The French moved out of Ottersheim for a short period after the lines were expanded. But on Saint Martin's Day 1795, they came back "like snowflakes" and positioned "themselves in the lines." In doing so, as Dieter Job notes, "30 to 40 men were accommodated in a single house." At that time, French soldier Franz Maillot from Besançon married the single woman Eva Maria Busch of Ottersheim. The marriage produced three children. Three years later, Maria Elisabeth Seither closed the bonds of marriage with a Sergeant of the 62nd Brigade, Johann Claudius Waçon of Poisson. The last bearer of the name Waçon (pronounced: Wasson) died in 1938 in Ottersheim.

After 1796, the French saw the Palatinate as a region of France. Prussia had given its approval to the assignment of the left bank of the Rhine in a confidential agreement in 1795, and Austria did the same thing two years later at the Peace of Campo Formio. In 1797, Citizen Rudler was appointed by the French Republic as governor, marshal, and administrator of the conquered Rhine country. As he saw it, his job above all was to implement the changes from the French Revolution into the Palatinate and other areas to the left of the Rhine.

In all places, the population had to swear the French oath of allegiance under a poplar tree, the freedom tree of the French Republic. To the delight of peasants, tithes and feudal rights were abolished. Those who occupied manorial estates with hereditary rights were allowed to keep them. Leaseholders were able to purchase their land. Hereditary holders were such families who constantly had in their possession the fields, meadows, and homes of manorial origin. At the first-time transfer, the hereditary owners paid a large sum. In addition, they paid some form of rent yearly, in kind or in money. As long as the hereditary owners had descendants, the land or the house remained in the family; otherwise, the estate fell back to the rulers. In addition to the hereditary properties, there were in Ottersheim many manorial properties that were leased for periods of 6 to 15 years. For example, the Priory manor of Hördt was divided into 46 so-called *Pflüge* that were leased out every nine years to the highest bidder. To be sure, it was customary that each pflug, which consisted of approximately 15 morgen of fields and meadows, mostly stayed in the same family. The possession of leased properties was considered by the French as so-called *National Property* that was forfeited to the State. The French Republic took for itself the right to claim these fields and meadows to sell at will, even though the rightful owner was mostly the church.

But what happened to the more than 300 hectares of land that had been former monastery or manor property that was confiscated and managed by the Electoral Palatinate? First, the French demanded a list of fields and meadows. Agent Konrad Hatzenbühler, a novice who took over in 1797, reported to Germersheim that in the community of Ottersheim some 265 Nürnberg morgen of land (about 106 hectares) existed that stemmed from the Spiritual Goods Administration in Heidelberg, and which had been given out "before the beginning of time" as hereditary parcels. In addition, there were 15 morgen of meadows (about 6 hectares) that stemmed from the house of Haimbach and were cultivated by Niederhochstadt citizens. Mayor Hatzenbühler probably gave this inaccurate information because he wanted to spare his fellow-citizens, and all other relevant documents had been lost in Germersheim a few years before. In a later review of the information by the French, it was discovered that not 106 but 250 hectares were in question that were also largely only time lease parcels. If the tenants were willing to buy these parcels, then the French government would agree to this. As far as this was not the case, the fields and meadows were sold at auction.

In the years 1807 to 1810, hundreds of morgen of land from the Ottersheim feudal manors were auctioned off. Buyers were mostly peasants in the village, some of whom had already been leasing the land. However, the shares of individual families were quite different. Some doubled or tripled their land ownership, such as then-Mayor Johann Kopf. Also, Daniel Schott of Knittelsheim acquired more lands, including nine morgen in the Reiterspieß. A portion of the property was bought by Landau citizens. The names of these successful bidders were Theodor Schmitt, Johann Jakob Schneider, H. Regenauer, Heinrich Otto Pauli, Friedrich Knoderer, and Jakob Klaus. Among other things, the large Poppelmann estate went to the above named Landau citizens.

The Amtmannswiesen, also called Schafswiesen or sheep pasture, was auctioned in 1809. This consisted of 30 morgen (7.5 hectares) and belonged to the Commandery of Saint John in Haimbach. The buyers were adjunct Konrad Humbert of Ottersheim, mill owner Johann Bernhard Bernion of Germersheim, and Josef Spitz of Speyer. The purchase price was 10,200 francs. This corresponded at that time to the value of about 3,400 zentners of hay or 5,100 zentners of straw.

The ability to acquire land for relatively little money was welcomed by the peasant population. They were less happy with other changes from the French Revolution. For example, French was imposed as the official language in 1797. The mayor had to create birth, marriage, and death records that were all written in French. So far, only the parishes had maintained such documents. The previous calendar was also abolished and replaced with a new system in 1798. In the opinion of the revolutionaries, the last vestiges of royal, aristocratic, and priestly rule should be eliminated through these changes. The first year of the Frankish era began on 22 September 1792. The *Republican Calendar* took effect in the Palatinate during March 1798 and lasted until December 1805. Each month had three equal parts of ten days each. The tenth day, the *Dékadi,* was a day of rest. Whoever celebrated Sunday instead of the Dékadi had to face severe punishment. No more bells could be rung for religious purposes, and any religious instruction was prohibited at school. It was not until Napoleon concluded a Concordat with the Pope in 1801 that religious conditions improved in the Frankish State. In the contract and approved by the pope was the secularization of church property, among other things. Since the tithe was abolished, the clergy lost almost all their income. The clergy was granted a small State salary by Napoleon as replacement. The church property in the Palatinate was also returned to the parish priests in 1803.

One was not pleased in the Palatinate about the general conscription that was introduced during the revolutionary period. In 1799, a legion was established in northern Franconia[49] in which many from the Palatinate had to serve. As far as the peasants were allowed to remain home during the constant campaigns of Napoleon, they were required to supply the armies with war charges of all kinds. So the community of Ottersheim had to raise 30,000 francs in 1808, whereby Peter Borger alone had to raise 745 francs. To be sure, the tithe was abolished, but the new property taxes, window taxes,[50] and the like often weighed more heavily on the shoulders of the peasants than did the lease tax that they had had to pay under the old system. They only had the satisfaction of knowing that there were no longer any privileged classes, and that each had to contribute to the common burden according to his property and income.

Important changes were also introduced in the community. Ottersheim and Knittelsheim were united under one mayor (maire in French) in 1800. Daniel Schott of Knittelsheim was ordered to the maire office, as it was called then, while Johann Kopf of Ottersheim was appointed adjunct. Kopf became head of the maire office for Ottersheim and Knittelsheim four years later. The unforgettable Kopf stood at the head of the village for ten years. With the downfall of Napoleon, he also had to make his office available. His father, Georg Kopf, had already been mayor of Ottersheim. He possessed a considerable fortune and a two-story house that he had built in 1785 next to the rectory. When Georg Kopf died from the plague in the year 1795, he left his son, Johann, 40 morgen of land. Kopf used the auction of the former monastery lands to increase its land holdings considerably. It was said of him that he could walk from the village exit to the Kahlenberg, halfway to Herxheim, and not have to leave his own property. In the Hintergrund, he possessed a whole open field alone that gave it the name *Kopp-Maire Field.*

Mayor Johann Kopf was married to Apollonia Helmer of Queichheim. The marriage produced ten children. There was neither order nor discipline in his house. Children and servants were allowed to follow their will and pleasure. When spring came, the food stocks were mostly used up so that a lot of money had to be spent to purchase hay and turnips.

---

[49] Franconia is the northern region of the state of Bavaria in southern Germany.

[50] This was a 17th and 18th century addition to property taxes based on the number of windows in a house.

Over time, field after field was auctioned until finally the richest farmer of the village became the poorest. He even sold his house to the community in 1827, which was used from then on as a schoolhouse. He moved to Mörlheim near Queichheim. At his age, the former mayor of Ottersheim fell into such distress that he went begging in his hometown. Death relieved him of his miserable existence at the age of 71 years. Mayor Kopp lives on in the memories of the people as an example of the saying, "Easy come, easy go." His youngest son, Johann Georg, applied in 1834 at age 20 for the job of school assistant at the elementary school in Ottersheim. The job was given to him, but he died just a year later.

The saying, "Easy come, easy go" was fulfilled even through the greatest man of the French Revolution, Napoleon Bonaparte. Born in Corsica, he received his education in French military schools. It was not until he was nine years old that he learned to speak French. During the revolutionary years, the "little corporal" rose quickly as an artillery officer. He took over the State power in 1799 as First Consul at age 30. The people cheered him when he crowned himself Emperor of France in Paris five years later. With this step, Napoleon had detached himself from the political ideology of the revolution without touching the liberal achievements. Rights and obligations of citizens were summarized in the Napoleonic Civil Code that put an end to the despotism of the first years after the Revolution. The Napoleon Civil Code was very much appreciated in the Palatinate. August Becker writes:

> "Although not every Palatine peasant carries the Napoleonic Code around in his pocket, everyone is at least familiar with the content and regulations, and respects it and judges it to be his most valuable asset. "

Napoleon freed the peasants on the Rhine from the feudal system, gave them personal freedom, and equality before the law. He gave them the land they cultivated, largely as their own property. Was it any wonder that the name of Napoleon sounded good to the village populations? The veneration that the Corsican enjoyed among the common people was particularly and clearly demonstrated when his marriage with the daughter of the Austrian Emperor, Marie Louise, brought forth a son. To commemorate this happy event, the so-called *Napoleon benches* were built. Even today on the road between Hochstadt and Dammheim, two such stone benches can be seen. The inscription reads:

> "A la naissance du Roi de Rome."

It says that the benches were set up to commemorate, "The birth of the King of Rome."

Napoleon's son was born on 20 March 1811 and he died at age 21 of consumption. Napoleon's star was already in decline when his son was born. Disaster overtook him in 1812 when his army of 600,000 men was wiped out almost entirely in Russia. Among the dead and frozen to death were also some Palatines who had gone to Moscow with Napoleon. The Battle of Leipzig sealed his fate. The remains of the French army retreated to the left bank of the Rhine and remained there until 1 January 1814. Then the Austrians and Prussians together with soldiers of the smaller German principalities marched across the Rhine and routed the French from the area. Landau was then besieged by the Russians until it surrendered on Easter of 1814. Gretchen Kopf reported that many Russians were quartered in Ottersheim. At their command, the girls of the village were to report to the old cemetery to "dance." Many hid out of fear. An old woman from Ottersheim was still able to sing Russian songs in 1898 that she had heard as a child.

The allied forces returned from France during June of 1814. But when Napoleon surprisingly returned from exile and many French soldiers rallied anew around him, the monarchs pulled their troops together and marched them against France. About 50,000 Austrian, Wuerttemberg, Bavarian, and Russian soldiers at that time made their camp at Knittelsheim for a few days. Dieter Job states in his home booklet, "During the advance of the allies, he had to put up and feed 21 men already in the first night." The following night, eight Russian Hussars, and several days later, twelve Westphalian soldiers were quartered with him, which cost him at least 50 gulden.

The allies pulled their troops back from France after Napoleon was overthrown on Saint Bartholomew's Day [24 August] in 1815, and Ludwig XVIII reigned as King of France. For four weeks soldiers marched in retreat through Ottersheim. These were largely Russians who had to be fed. Dieter Job had a loss of about 60 gulden. King Max of Bavaria took possession of the Palatinate on 1 May 1816. Job states in his house booklet, "Inflation came with the peace." The canton divisions of the French period were for the most part taken over by the Bavarian government. Ottersheim, Knittelsheim, and Bellheim, which had belonged to the canton of Germersheim, remained with Germersheim as the seat of the District Office. The mayor of Ottersheim was Bernhard Flory who was born in Großfischlingen. He had been living in the village for 20 years and married the widow, Maria Elisabeth Gutting née Gadinger of Ottersheim.

The years that followed the war turmoil of the Napoleon Era were hard ones. Because of bad weather in 1816, there was such a famine as had not been known since time immemorial. A malter of grain that had usually cost 3 to 4 gulden rose to a price of 40 gulden. A malter of spelt cost 22 gulden, a malter of barley 36 gulden, and a malter of oats 14 gulden. Prices declined slightly in 1817. But one still paid 18 gulden for a malter of grain, 9 gulden for a malter of spelt, 10 gulden for a malter of barley, and 6 gulden for a malter of oats. In 1818, the number of mice increased incredibly. Many millions were trapped or poisoned. They took out 20-30 of them from a single hole. It is any wonder that this year went down in history as the year of famine.

Goods that Georg Wagner Bought at Auction in 1807

1	morgen	in Offenbach's Corner:	165	francs
2	viertels[51]	in the Kurzen Gewanne:	35	"
1	morgen	in the Höhlchen:	130	"
2	morgen	in Schafdarm:	290	"
1	morgen	below the village:	515	"
1	morgen	of meadows in the lower Vorderwiesen:	255	"
1	morgen	on the Obersand:	70	"
1	morgen	on the Rülzheimer Weg:	85	"
1	morgen	Of meadows on the Hörst:	396	"
2	viertels	in the Altsheimer Weg:	225	"
4	viertels	in the Gartenweg:	535	"
		Together:	2,701	francs

Georg Wagner was the son of Dieter Wagner who lived on the Deich (now 20 Germersheimer Straße). Dieter Wagner, with his 6.3 hectares of land, was one of the wealthiest peasants in Ottersheim. Georg Wagner was born during 1760 and died in 1830. He was married to Maria Elizabeth Knöll and had nine children, of whom two died as infants. Georg Wagner's brother, Johann, emigrated in 1809 to the Franzfeld colony along the Black Sea where he became mayor. He later returned to his home and died here.

The Wedding Expenses of Georg Wagner on the Occasion of His Daughter's Marriage to David Job in 1813

For wedding dresses:	22	gulden	12	kreutzers
For bonnets:	6	"		
For 2 scarves and glove:	5	"	12	kreutzers
To carry out the ceremony:	10	"		
To identify the friendship:	6	"	30	kreutzers
For a ticking duvet:	15	"		
For a new Köln-style coverlet:	5	"	30	kreutzers
For 2 new Köln-style shoulder pads:	7	"		
For 2 new Köln-style duvets:	3	"	50	kreutzers
For a knitted chaff bag:	1	"	30	kreutzers
For 1 hemp and 2 knitted sheets:	3	"	30	kreutzers
For 1 hemp and 2 knitted tablecloths:	2	"	30	kreutzers
For 1 hemp and 2 knitted towels:	1	"		

---

[51] Viertel refers to one fourth of a morgen or a quarter morgen.

For a pregnant cow, estimated:	66	"		
2 suckling pigs:	6	"		
For an old crate:	1	"	40	kreutzers
For half a zentner of hemp:	7	"		
For a new bodice:	1	"		
For 1 pair of shoes:	2	"		
For 1 pair of socks:	1	"		
For 1 pair of wedding shoes:	2	"	45	kreutzers
2 malter sacks:	1	"	40	kreutzers
2 malters of spelt:	14	"		
1 new purchased bedstead:	5	"	30	kreutzers
An old partly damaged plow:	4	"		
1 pair of old cart wheels:	7	"		
1 yoke chain:	1	"	30	kreutzers
A scythe for the meadow:	1	"		
1 old sieve and 1 large wedge:	—	"	40	kreutzers
1 hay rope:	—	"	24	kreutzers
An old trough:	—	"	30	kreutzers
Total:	213 gulden		11	kreutzers

The Bavarian Kings as Rulers of Ottersheim

The ancestor of the Kings of Bavaria is Count Otto von Wittelsbach of the Palatinate to whom Friedrich Barbarossa awarded the Duchy of Bavaria in 1180. When the Bavarian main lines of the Wittelsbachs died out in 1777, the country fell to Palatine Elector Karl Theodor who came from a side branch of the Wittelsbach house. He was followed by:

Maximilian I.	from 1799 to 1825
Ludwig I.	from 1825 to 1848
Maximilian II.	from 1848 to 1864
Ludwig II.	from 1864 to 1886
Prince Regent Luitpold	from 1886 to 1912
Ludwig III.	from 1912 to 1918

Under Napoleon in 1806, Bavaria was raised to the rank of a kingdom. The Palatinate became part of Bavaria in 1816. It was first called the *Rhine Province* and then called the *Rhine District.* In 1838, the Rhine District was renamed the *Palatinate* under Ludwig I. On their journeys through the Palatinate, the Bavarian kings passed through Ottersheim several times.

The Horrors of 1822

In 1822, an insidious disease raged in Ottersheim. No fewer than 54 inhabitants had succumbed to typhoid fever over the course of twelve months. In the month of October alone, 21 people lay dead, the youngest at eleven and the oldest at 59 years of age. There was hardly a house where one was not sick. All joy and hope was gone from the village. There was not a single wedding during the year. The contagious disease became a catastrophe, because the village's Doctor Hoffmann treated the fever patients incorrectly. Only when the young physician, Dr. Geil from Harthausen, suggested fresh air and clean water for the people did the disease die out. How deeply the horror year of 1822 affected the residents is illustrated by a poem that remained alive among the people for a very long time. Composed at that time by the village poet, the poem reads:

Proud world, ephemeral being
To whom everything was entrusted
Tell me where were you
Ere the creator formed you?
Yes, the whole noble world
The Lord created from nothing.
And it will again be so,
Unless the Lord watches over it.
Young people have to die,
Their parents cry: Oh,
No one can save them,
Because Doctor Hoffmann said:
"Everything, everything is lost,
And the plague is really here! "

Then we seemed lost,
But God is still close by.
Medicine that he prescribed
And that only causes death,
He should have kept from us
Rather than let us die in fear.
But Dr. Geil, the "good"
Has replaced the "evil."
He brings back courage to all
And has redeemed many from death.
Thanks be to this noble gentleman,
Thanks be to this good man,
For people are happy to see him
Here in our fatherland.

Daily life again demanded its rights once the plague was gone. Widowers and widows soon married in order to provide for their children. The dictum: "Meine Kinder, deine Kinder, unsere Kinder" [My children, your children, our children] originated at that time and still survives in the vernacular to this day. Also, the years 1831 and 1837 display a high mortality from infectious diseases. A total of 62 deaths were recorded in 1831 while 20 people died at most in other years. In 1837, 40 Ottersheim citizens were swept away by death.

The Revolution years, 1848-1849

When the King of France was forced to abdicate during the February Revolution of 1848, the time had come for the bourgeois world in Germany to put their political ideas into practice. In particular, a united free Germany with a freely elected parliament was sought. In the year 1848, a sea of black-red-and-gold flags moved into Saint Paul's Church in Frankfurt am Main to conduct the "German National Constituent Assembly" meetings. Among the 800 assemblymen, there were no hourly wage earners and only one small peasant compared to 60 manor owners and many representatives of professional occupations. The parliament soon divided into the party of the moderates and the party of the radicals. The moderates would like to have seen an emperor at the head of the German Empire, while the radicals sought a republican state under removal of any princely ruler. All 14 members of the Palatinate belonged to the radical wing of the Frankfurt Parliament. In the discussions on the constitution, the Left most always remained in the minority.

The Frankfurt National Assembly accepted the Constitution in its entirety on 28 March 1849. Hereditary Emperor of the German Empire was to be Friedrich Wilhelm IV of Prussia. However, he stated that he could accept the Imperial Crown only if the German princes and the free states of Germany were in agreement. King Maximilian II of Bavaria was not prepared simply to approve the proposed regulation. Thus, the work of the Frankfurt Parliament was called into question by Bavaria. And now the radical wing of the National Assembly wanted to implement the Constitution by force.

The representatives from the Palatinate called on their compatriots, "with their wealth and blood to defend the Imperial Constitution and to withstand any attack from where ever it may come." A defense committee was formed in Kaiserslautern on 2 May 1849 under which a people's militia was placed. Herewith, the path of revolution was taken. Already on 17 May 1849, the revolutionaries instituted a "provisional government" in Kaiserslautern. When the royalist government of Speyer fled to the fortress of Germersheim, the "provisional government" was moved shortly thereafter to Speyer. Meanwhile, revolutionary citizens and disgruntled soldiers took up arms to overthrow the monarchy. The insurgents, as they were popularly known, wore blouse and a Hecker[52] hat with a feather. A group under Captain Brunner of Rheinzabern had set up their headquarters in Offenbach. The rebels, who included women, came to Ottersheim on horseback, equipped with rifles. Before the community hall, Captain Brunner with a drawn sword called for the citizens of the village to get their arms and to fight. But the residents of Ottersheim wanted nothing to do with the revolution, with few exceptions. Many hid in their homes. Some brave souls even publicly acknowledged their loyalty to the King, but

---

[52] So named after the revolutionary leader, Friedrich Hecker.

others set up barricades on the Deich Bridge. Only two soldiers from Ottersheim who served in the garrison of Landau joined the rebels. A certain Hilsendegen shot a bullet against the church tower. But soon, he lost his courage and fled from Germany to seek safety in America. A certain Kröper returned the same day to the garrison in Landau at the urging of his family.

The rule of the insurgents did not last long. Prussian troops were engaged to put down the revolt at the request of Bavaria, Baden, and Hesse. They entered Palatinate territory on 13 June 1849 under the leadership of Prince Friedrich Karl, while three days later a Bavarian division that was ordered to occupy the Palatinate crossed the Rhine at Oppenheim. A small battle took place at Bellheim between the insurgents and the troops advancing from the east. Some of the insurgents fell in battle, others fled, and the rest were imprisoned in the fortress of Germersheim. It is reported that in April 1850, 128 insurgents were imprisoned in Germersheim. The state of war was not repealed until 22 June 1850.

Although the population of Ottersheim wanted nothing to do with the revolution, they did not quite remain unscathed. When the insurgents were in the village, the peasants had to board them and contribute horses and equipment. Confiscations included wine, bread, hay and straw, a cavalry saddle, a coat, and a hunting rifle, among other things. For these the community paid to the victims a total of 121 gulden and 12 kreutzers.

The additional burden for the villagers did not stop with the departure of the insurgents, because the pro-government troops also had to be housed and fed. The people were therefore delighted when the war was over in 1850.

Ottersheim Emigrants

To Russia

Already in the late 17th century, many residents of the Palatinate left their homeland to establish new lives in America, Hungary, Yugoslavia, or Romania. In spite of the bans on emigration, the emigrant flow did not stop in the 18th century either. In the years of 1764 to 1767, some 30,000 peasant families followed the call of the Russian Empress Catherine and settled on the Volga. At the beginning of the 19th century, more Palatinate families left their ancestral homeland and moved to the Odessa area in Southern Russia. From this time, the names of those Ottersheim residents who made the arduous journey to the Empire of the Czar are known.

The emigrants had to make the journey on foot up to the Danube. Their few belongings were carried either on their backs or in carts that they pushed in front of them. Some traveled by boat to the Black Sea, while others chose to go by land for which they needed two summers and one winter. Those with strong resistance reached the long yearned for settlement area penniless, while the weak were often swept away by deadly diseases.

The area north of the Beresan River to the northeast of Odessa was settled in 1809. It was the richest of all the colonized districts, which had familiar village names like Landau, Speyer, Karlsruhe, Rohrbach, Worms, Rastatt, and München. There were also the villages of Kuhardt, Kandel, Mannheim, and Heidelberg along the Black Sea.

The emigrant Ottersheim families at the time settled largely in Franzfeld and took the fertile land under the plow. In the course of more than 100 years, the "Palatinate" by the Black Sea developed into a flourishing land. The German settlers were characterized by diligence, efficiency, and cleanliness. Their villages had broad streets and the houses resembled the farmyards in Germany. Churches and schools were also established and diligently attended. Since these were purely German settlements, the common language was German. There were some 400,000 inhabitants of German origin along the Black Sea in 1926 while along the Volga there lived about a half million Germans.

Of the Ottersheim emigrants, we know that a Peter Hilsendegen was mayor of Baden around 1900. A. Hilsendegen was a teacher in Kandel and another Hilsendegen was a teacher in München. A certain Johann Wagner of Ottersheim was mayor of Franzfeld. Also, the ancestors of Catholic priest Kreiner from Landau very likely descended from Ottersheim.

The October Bolshevik Revolution in 1917 did not spare the German settlements. The previously independent peasants were dispossessed and their land was consolidated into collective farms. It did not come to a radical displacement the ethnic German population until the Second World War. Those who were not called up for military service were carted off to Siberia and placed on collective farms or in industrial enterprises there. So it was not at all uncommon that prisoners of war beyond the Urals heard the purely Palatinate sounds from seemingly Russian voices or were awaken at night to the sounds of the song: "Horch, was kommt von draußen rein?" [Hark, what's coming in from outside?]

I also will never forget that in 1949, I was questioned by a "Russian" political officer (NKVD)[53] with the good German name of Wagner about some partisan activities and then was sent back home unexpectedly. It is not completely impossible that the ancestors of this political officer came from Ottersheim, since a certain Johann Wagner emigrated to southern Russia in 1809.

As a closed group, the Palatinate settlers have now disappeared in Russia. Although they speak only Russian in public, in many cases they have preserved their local Palatinate dialect however. Anyhow, whether their children and grandchildren will be able to preserve their German identity now and in the future is doubtful. In praise of the Germans from Russia, it must be said that they still stick together and stand together, even if their homes on the Volga and by the Black Sea have been taken from them.

List of Ottersheim emigrants to southern Russia

1809	Konrad Busch with family	to Franzfeld near Odessa
1809	Andreas Merdian with family	to Franzfeld near Odessa
1809	Nikolaus Franck, knacker, with family	to Franzfeld near Odessa
1809	Johann Wagner with family	to Franzfeld near Odessa
1809	Jakob Bischoff, shoemaker, with family	to Franzfeld near Odessa
1809	Johann Philipp Job with family	to southern Russia
1809	Johann Moock with family	to southern Russia
1809	Johann Dörzapf, mason, with family	to southern Russia
1809	Michael Rösch with family	to southern Russia
1810	Franz Koch with family	to Karlsruhe near Odessa
1810	Anna Maria Hatzenbühler with man	to Karlsruhe near Odessa
1810	Johann Hilsendegen, shoemaker	to southern Russia

North America

When the first emigrants from Ottersheim moved to North America can no longer be determined with certainty. At any rate, more than 9,000 people left their Palatinate home in 1709 and sailed from England to settle in the English colonies in North America. Part of the reason for leaving was economic need and also their yearning for freedom of religion, which especially drove the Palatinate folk to foreign lands. Of course, adventurers and soldiers of fortune were not lacking. When Palatine Elector Karl Theodor issued an ordinance in 1752 making emigration a criminal offense, not just a few fled their ancestral homeland of Ottersheim under the cover of darkness. Ottersheim emigrants from that time included Georg Kuhn (1747) and Konrad Doll (1753), among others.

---

[53] NKVD was the *Narodnyy Komissariat Vnutrennikh Del*, the People's Commissariat of Internal Affairs, the Soviet police and secret police.

More information about emigration to North America by citizens of Ottersheim is available from the 19th century. In the course of 100 years, more than 300 men, women, and children of the village left to establish a new existence beyond the great water. Most of them traveled by way of Paris to the sea port of Le Havre on the Seine estuary. About 600 kilometers had to be made on foot or by cart. Often-tortuous scenes took place at their departure, especially if parents with small children in their arms had to take leave of their grown sons and daughters. The thoughts and feelings of the emigrants have been recorded in a song that stems from those years and contains the following words:

Now the time and the hour have arrived
We travel to America.
The cart is ready and waiting,
With wife and children, we travel.
Your friends are all well known,
Give me your hand for the last time!
You friends, do not weep so much,
We will see each other nevermore!

Now we sail on the high sea,
There we'll see no more Germans,
We fear no waterfall
And recall that God is everywhere.
We now come to Baltimore,
As we extend the hand 'up
And shout: Victory!
Now we are in America!

We also know from the letters of Nikolaus Job, who lived in Lancaster in the State of Pennsylvania, emigrants from Ottersheim had already settled in North America in the middle of the 18th century. These letters lie in the Government Files at the State Archives in Speyer. Job was apparently poor and relied upon his inheritance in Germany. For that reason, he wrote several times to his relatives in Ottersheim and Niederhochstadt asking that his inheritance be sent. Since he himself had no money for travel, his friend Jacob Henning of Lancaster, who was travelling to Germany to visit, was to pick up the amount and bring it to America. To this end, Job gave Henning a letter for his cousin Johannes Ludwig in Ottersheim. He wrote:

God bless you dear cousins! We dearly hope that these few lines reach you in good health. As far as we are concerned, thankfully we are still all fresh and healthy. Further, we received your writing and learned from it that you planned to send me that which is mine from grandfather's bequeathed property, by way of a trusted man named Jakob Henning, who lives in Lancaster with wife and child. Trust this man as though I myself were there... Moreover, I hope you will send me that which is mine with this man (to America) for you know yourselves that my father, that is to say Georg Job, received little or nothing. So I leave it to your discretion and conscience. Do with me what you think is right because I ask for no more than what belongs to me. So you can leave it with this man because he is a local man by the name of Jakob Henning, resident of Lancaster, for I will most likely not get such an opportunity any time soon.

Further news regarding cousin Thomas Kern (from Freisbach) who lives a day's trip from us. But as we have heard they are still healthy. As far as we are concerned times are bad, for over a year nothing but war and rumors of wars. No one knows how this all will end. The wild people (Indians) have already killed many, and burned the houses and the barns with the crops. They handle people in a murderous way. They pull the skin off the heads of living people and bring them to the French. The French pay the Indians for the scalps. I know nothing further to write but that I, Nikolaus Job, owes my cousin, Appolonia Ludwig, a silver ring as a souvenir.

And remain your true friend

Nikolaus Job

Written on 8th December 1755

From other letters of Nikolaus Job, we know that Konrad Doll of Ottersheim moved to Pennsylvania. However, we may assume that these surely were not the only Ottersheim emigrants during the 18th century. We have a much better picture of the America travelers during the 19th century. A letter from Peter Kröper of 1861 states the ocean crossing at that time lasted 30 days. Later, travel from the Hamburg harbor went somewhat faster.

The Palatines in America settled mostly as farmers or craftsmen. The emigrant wave did not wear down throughout the entire 19th century. Now and then, one person or another returned after decades to visit or to remain in the old home, but others remain missing. It seems that no Ottersheim emigrants in America became rich.

Today, about a quarter of Americans are of German descent but few of them have retained their German language. However, there are still areas in North America where a true Palatine dialect is spoken. Many Ottersheim emigrants in America are known to us by name. This we owe to the father of former mayor Ludwig Job (1905-1920), a certain Johann Job, who wrote down a complete list of all emigrants from the year 1852. The register was later continued. The names of the emigrants in the first half of the 19th century were gathered by the Vocational Trade School Spiritual Adviser Steegmüller in painstaking detailed work. However, there is no guarantee that this list of names is complete.

Overview of the emigrants to North America

1832	Adam Metz with family	7
1832	Joh. Jakob Hoffmann, 19 years old	1
1832	Franz Dausch	1
1837	Sebastian Job, shoemaker, and family	4
1837	Christoph Gensheimer, 20 years old	1
1839	Andreas Kröper, mason, and family	3
1840	Ludwig Jost	1
1844	Johann Borger and his wife and children	10
1846	Johann Hilsendegen with his wife and child	3

1846	Georg Hoffmann, weaver, and family	4
1847	Franz Merdian with family	5
1847	Johann Müller and family	8
1848	Anton Gaab and family	5
1849	Andreas Franck and family	6
1849	Valentin Hatzenbühler, 14 years	1
1850	Johann Gerstner and family	7
1852	Heinrich Günther with wife and child	3
Jan. 1852	Johann Stadel and Sebastian Bischoff	2
20/03/1852	Konrad Kölsch, Eva Franck and Margarete Ludwig	3
25/04/1852	Heinrich Müller and family, Johann Merdian with family, and Johann Bumiller	15
11/10/1852	Joh. Georg Kröper, Katharina Hindert and Katharina Kröper	3
21/10/1852	Katharina Pfeifer from the rectory	1
11/11/1852	Valentin Job and wife	2
Nov. 1852	Adam Heckmann, Jakob Hatzenbühler and Johannes Kopf	3
22/12/1852	Rosa Kopf and her youngest daughter	2
12/03/1853	Georg Ehli and Ludwig Ehli	2
18/03/1853	Elisabeth Hanck and Anna Maria Müller	2
11/08/1853	Johann Hatzenbühler, Wilhelm Hoffmann, Johann Gutting and Johann Hindert	4
16/08/1853	Katharina Günther, Barbara Conrad and son Wilhelm who had already been in America for 21 years	3
18/09/1853	Elisabeth Dörzapf	1
23/09/1853	Georg Jakob Ludwig, wife and 5 children	7
22/11/1853	Joh. Georg Hindert, wife and 5 children, Konrad Hanck, Konrad Zwißler, Eva Merdian and Klara Merdian	11
12/12/1853	Anton Merdian, wife and daughter, with 2 children	5
22/12/1853	Johann Pfeifer and Elisabeth Zwißler	2
13/01/1854	Franz Adam Kröper, wife and 5 children, Jakob Hatzenbühler	8
22/01/1854	Theobald Ludwig, wife and 5 children	7
22/05/1854	Jakob Scheurer and Katharina Hatzenbühler	2
03/08/1854	August Kölsch and Anton Moock, soldier	2
12/10/1854	Peter Franck, 5 children and Barbara (sister-in-law)	7
12/01/1855	Konrad Dörzapf, Peter Dörzapf and Martin Winkelblech	3
Mar. 1856	Litzelberger, wife and 5 children	7
03/04/1856	Anton Hanck and Barbara Kröper	2
Nov. 1856	Andreas Seither	1

09/02/1857	Jakob Schuster, wife and four children from 1st marriage, and 4 children from a second marriage. Konrad Dörzapf, wife and stepbrother of the wife.	13
Apr. 1857	Jakob Hatzenbühler and Jakob Bischoff	2
27/10/1857	Joh. Georg Kröper, tailor, with wife and 3 children, Jakob Gaab	6
14/01/1858	Margareta Rösch	1
25/08/1858	Margareta Heider with 3 children and father Jakob Heider	5
03/05/1859	Michael Michleder and Katharina Müller with 2 children	4
15/11/1859	Georg Dörzapf, Johann Georg Dörzapf	2
July 1860	Paul Dörzapf	1
05/04/1861	Peter Kröper	1
04/10/1861	Widow Günther	1
27/02/1862	Franziska Stadel taken along by Jakob Bischoff	1
01/07/1862	Johann Kröper, shoemaker	1
27/06/1863	Eva Braun and Maria Damen	2
26/10/1863	Christina Decker	1
25/08/1864	Barbara Damen and Appolonia Damen	2
14/05/1865	Barbara Damen, widow, and 4 children, Anton Bischoff and Karl Dörzapf	6
06/06/1865	Konrad Zwißler, barber	1
11/10/1865	Eva Störtzer and Elis. Reg. Hatzenbühler	2
30/11/1865	Friedrich Ludwig with wife and two children	4
01/11/1865	Ludwig Damen	1
Feb. 1866	Georg Wingerter, tinsmith, Valentin Kröper and Eva Reichling	3
25/06/1866	Heinrich Hatzenbühler, blacksmith	1
01/07/1866	David Dörzapf and Katharina Reichling	2
21/10/1866	Anton Hertel with wife and child	3
25/02/1867	Anton Böhm	1
May 1867	Valentin Burgermeister, baker	1
12/07/1867	David Hatzenbühler (taken along by Franz Adam Kröper, who has been in America for 13 years)	1
24/07/1867	Josef Merdian	1
02/08/1867	Ludwig Knöll, Johann Kreiner and Elis. Moock	3
Dec. 1867	Regine Hatzenbühler, the large Regine	1
1869	Johann Busch	1
May 1870	Valentin Zwißler, locksmith	1
03/06/1870	Peter Müller, mason (well builder)	1
Apr. 1871	Franz Kröper and wife	2
Aug. 1871	Georg Gaab and Christine Gaab	2
16/02/1872	Julchen Burgermeister and Ludwig Burgermeister	2
16/03/1872	Adam Kröper	1

May 1872	Adam Günther	1
July 1872	Peter Job, teacher, and Michael Job, tinsmith	2
1872	Adam Jennewein, tailor	1
02/04/1873	Anton Müller, weaver	1
17/10/1874	The three youngest children of the baker, Valentin Burgermeister	3
08/06/1880	Fritz Hanck	1
20/07/1881	Wife of Peter Moock and Konrad Moock	2
21/08/1881	Konrad Merdian with his wife and six children	8
27/08/1882	Andreas Störtzer, called the White	1
05/09/1882	Anton Glatz with his wife and ten children, also Katharina Glatz and son	14
07/12/1882	Konrad Müller, shoemaker	1
07/04/1883	Johann Brüderle and Johann Föhlinger	2
30/08/1883	Regine Glatz and two children from the White Störtzer	3
13/01/1884	Nikolaus Reichling	1
28/08/1884	Johann Kopf, butcher	1
25/04/1885	Franz Leonhard Job	1
29/12/1887	Johann Gadinger, husband of Margaret Hanck	1
1888	Franz Kopf (taken along by Peter Kröper)	1
Oct. 1889	Elisabeth Kopf	1
Sep. 1892	Otto Kopf (was taken along by his brother Johann)	1
1882	Michael Hatzenbühler (son of Georg Hatzenbühler)	1
10/11/1893	Ludwig Kreiner	1
1900	Jakob Hatzenbühler (b.1873)	1
13/09/1902	Katharina Kopf (taken along by her uncle Johann Kopf, married a certain Henry Fink in America. Embarked in Hamburg 13 Sept. 1902. Arrived in New York 24 Sept. 1902	1
1903	Peter Moock, brother of Jakob Moock, 15 years old	1
1904	Maria Kuhn, born 1884, in Chicago, Illinois died 1948	1
09/09/1905	Anna Kopf and Lisa Kopf	2
1906	Franz Zwißler, hairdresser, son of "Zum Hirsch" innkeeper, born in 1874, uncle of Ernst Jochim	1
24/08/1909	Rosa Kopf (sister of Katharina Kopf)	1
1909	Julius Kuhn, mason, Chicago, Illinois, married in America, a Viennese	1
20/12/1925	Eva Föhlinger born Kopf, followed her daughters to America after 60 years and died there in 1939	1
1929	Ernst Jochim, son of "Zum Hirsch" innkeeper Georg Jochim, born 1903.	1
	Total:	321

To Africa

The French took over Algeria in the years 1830 to 1847 and turned the country on the north coast of Africa into a French colony. To build up unexploited areas there, European people were to settle them. Therefore, agents traveled through France, Germany, and Poland to recruit colonists for Algeria. The first settlers from Ottersheim who were willing to emigrate to Africa were Konrad Dörzapf (b. 1791) and his wife Katharina née Eibler of the same age. They traveled from Weißenburg in 1846 by fast carriage to Le Havre on the Seine estuary, where they embarked with other colonists and took transport to Algeria. According to her oldest daughter Elizabeth, the Dörzapf couple died later in Philippeville on the north coast of Africa. Like many others, they seem to have been victims of cholera, which raged at that time in Algeria and harvested richly especially among the colonists.

Two more Ottersheim residents tried their luck in Algeria in 1857. They were 28-year-old Theobald Seither and 27-year-old Andreas Dörzapf. Both left their home village on February 9th and probably joined the French Foreign Legion. Dörzapf died at age 75 in his home in Ottersheim while Seither remained missing.

In the middle of the 19th century, 15 people from Freckenfeld emigrated to Algeria. They were unable to handle the strain and left the barren land just a few years later. But today it is said that descendants of Palatinate settlers live in North Africa who have preserved some of their native Palatine language.

To Australia

The couple, Rudolf Müller and Martha Müller née Herrmann, emigrated to Australia In 1952 where the man found a job in an airplane factory. Müller was from Nuremberg and his wife from Ottersheim.

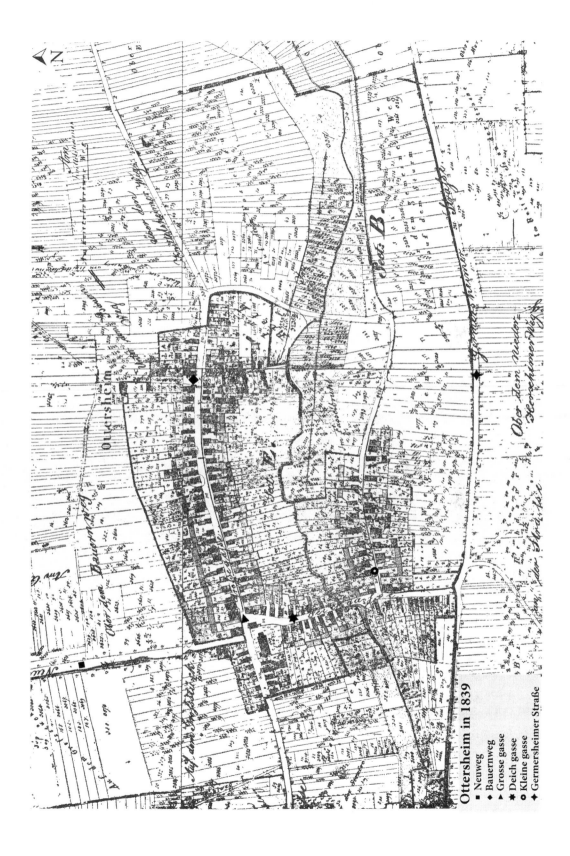

Ottersheim in 1839

- ■ Neuweg
- ◆ Bauernweg
- ▲ Grosse gasse
- ★ Deich gasse
- ○ Kleine gasse
- ◆ Germersheimer Straße

111

Ottersheim in the Year 1864

In the year 1864, 198 houses, most of them 1-1/2 story houses, stood in Ottersheim with 392 outbuildings. The houses were painted white and in good condition. The main village roads were already paved. The Dorfbach along the Große Gasse and Dorfgraben along the Kleine Gasse had been bordered with sandstone. The Dorfbach along the Neuweg was also bordered with sandstones in the years 1862 and 1863. The heavy blocks had to be brought from the quarries of Neustadt and Gimmeldingen. The construction work was conducted in two phases by foreign masons and cost the community approximately 1,500 gulden.

The road that leads from Germersheim to Landau experienced bustling traffic even then. The road was used not only by rural horse-drawn wagons and pedestrians but also by the parcel carrier and by a riding postman. This road, which had been built and maintained by the community, was taken over by the District in 1852. And in 1862, a new and sustainable bridge was built over the Deich near the Bordgraben.

Ottersheim was considered one of the richest villages in the District of Germersheim in the 19th century. On average, the total annual revenue amounted to about 7,000 gulden of which around 6,000 was spent. The community treasury was estimated at 167,000 gulden in 1864. The major revenue sources were the land and home property taxes. These brought in 2,500 gulden while the business taxes brought 180 gulden. Property leases from community-owned land brought in 2,200 gulden. Wood from the community forest accounted for 1,200 gulden, and the proceeds of the hunt amounted to 115 gulden.

In 1864, 73-year-old Valentin Seither stood at the head of the community as mayor. Seither had also occupied this office from 1835 to 1853. Adjunct Valentin Scherff had mainly policing duties. Town clerk was Adam Horn from Bellheim. Collector Franz Josef Klein was also located there. The office of community and police deputy was occupied by Peter Glatz, who also wore an appropriate uniform. Field warden was Konrad Störtzer, and forest ranger was Georg Haury. Ottersheim had two meadow watermen at that time. Linen weaver Johannes Bischoff supervised the canals, pastures, and Brühl meadows, while August Hindert was responsible for the front and back meadows. In the village at that time were also two night watchmen, specifically Johannes Kröper and Sebastian Dörzapf. Their police station was located in the community hall. An oil lamp burned there all night. The community had to provide 22 gulden and 30 kreutzers annually for the wicks and oil. On his nightly rounds through the village, the watchman carried a horn. He had to monitor streets and pay attention to fire hazards.

Ottersheim counted 262 families in 1864 with a total of 974 residents, 208 families with 781 souls were Catholic, and 54 families with 193 souls were Protestant. Of the 225 schoolchildren in the weekday and Sunday school, 180 were Catholic and 45 Protestant. In the weekday school, there were 128 Catholic and 33 Protestant children.

There were 176 of the 262 Ottersheim families working exclusively in agriculture, another 60 had businesses alongside the agriculture, and 26 families were day laborers. The day laborer had a fairly good income for the conditions at that time.

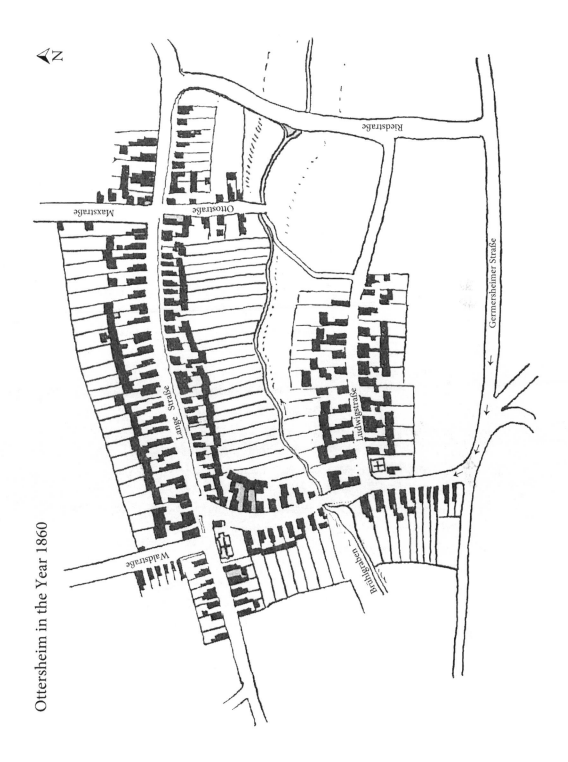

Ottersheim in the Year 1860

When they worked with privilege, that is, without food, men earned 40 kreutzers daily and women 28 kreutzers. The wage with food came to 18 and 16 kreutzers respectively. A pfund [about 1/2 kilogram] of pork cost was about 16 kreutzers at that time. The annual salary of a servant amounted to 80 gulden and a maid 50 gulden. The servants belonged to the family and ate at a common table.

Regarding the entire population, we are told that they lived in harmony with each other. They were religious and visited church services regularly. Not much time was devoted for pleasure and recreation. Taverns were visited only on Sunday and then only sparingly. The adult youth were also modest and diligent. Dance music was usually provided for the church fair. Catholic priest Matthäus Dotterweich and Protestant pastor Karl Anton Scherer from Offenbach had every reason to be satisfied with their community. There was a singing group with 50 members in the village. Only one farmer belonged to the agricultural society. But five other farmers joined the association in 1864. The clothing or costumes as these were worn at the beginning of the 19th century were mostly gone by 1864 and replaced by urban clothing.

Active teacher Anton Decker of Klingenmünster taught in Ottersheim for five years. At his side stood school assistant Peter Dausch from Eschbach. For the Protestant school, teacher Johann Ludwig Ecarius had been responsible for more than 30 years. The community was responsible for the salary of all teachers. Decker received 326 gulden annually, Ecarius received 330 gulden, Dausch received 250 gulden, and needlework teacher Barbara Damen was owed 30 gulden. The teachers also had to ensure that the school was provided with fuel for heating. For this purpose, the community provided 40 gulden per teacher. The mayor drew a salary of 95 gulden and the adjunct 25 gulden. The town clerk was paid 200 gulden a year. The night watchman had to settle for 30 gulden. The community administrators and police were entitled to 116 gulden. Forest and field wardens were each entitled to 130 gulden. Meadow irrigation officer Hindert received 50 gulden and meadow irrigation officer Bischoff 35 gulden. Franz Adam Winkelblech received 9 gulden compensation for winding the church clock. For the village paupers, of whom the number was very few, 120 gulden went to the community poor fund.

In 1864, the district land arrangement was as follows:

Arable land:	1,474.00	day's work[54]	491.33	hectares
Meadows:	381.20	day's work	127.66	hectares
Vineyards:	16.12	day's work	5.37	hectares
Non-arable land:	20.02	day's work	6.67	hectares
Road and pathways:	52.37	day's work	17.46	hectares
Buildings, courtyards and gardens:	46.12	day's work	15.37	hectares
Total:	1,989.83	day's work	663.86	hectares

---

[54] A *day's work* was an early measure of land area equaling the amount of land one man could plow in one morgen [morning] using oxen. In this table, a 1 hectare area was equivalent to a little over 3 day's work.

114

A day's work of arable land cost between 600 and 1,200 gulden in a good location and between 300 and 700 gulden in a bad location. For each day's work of arable land, 40 gulden was paid as rent, and 36 gulden was paid for each day's work of meadows.

The representative ownership is apparent from the following table:

6	families owned over	30	day's work of usable area,
40	families had	20-30	day's work,
80	families had	10-20	day's work, and
130	families had	5-10	day's work.

The fields were cultivated diligently and skillfully. Fertilizer consisted mainly of stall manure from leaves and straw. In addition, compost was made from manure, street waste [such as fallen leaves], and cut grass. Almost every farmer had a compost barrel. The farm implements corresponded to ancient custom. Farm machines were not available. Manure pits were still mostly located in the middle of the courtyard and were therefore subject to the effects of weather conditions. Sometimes people had to drive over the manure pits because of tight space conditions. In contrast, the community compost holes were better than other places. Irrigation of the meadows was carried out with great care. Only the Amtmannswiesen and the Freiwiesen showed defects because the miller wanted to restrict or even prevent irrigation to maximize the water power to the mill. The road and pathways were patched from time to time with sand and gravel, yet these still left much to be desired.

The following overview provides valuable information about the crop types, the yields, and the prices in 1864. At that time, the following were produced:

375 day's work	Spelt	at	16 zentners	for	3 gulden 40 kreutzers
220 day's work	Wheat	at	15 zentners	for	4 gulden 50 kreutzers
100 day's work	Grain	at	14 zentners	for	3 gulden 30 kreutzers
80 day's work	Barley	at	13 zentners	for	3 gulden 20 kreutzers
20 day's work	Oats	at	14 zentners	for	3 gulden 50 kreutzers
230 day's work	Potatoes	at	100 zentners	for	1 gulden 30 kreutzers
200 day's work	Clover	at	36 zentners	for	1 gulden 45 kreutzers
30 day's work	Canola	at	12 zentners	for	10 gulden 30 kreutzers
28 day's work	Tobacco	at	12 zentners	for	12 gulden
20 day's work	Hemp	at	6 zentners	for	20 gulden
1 day's work	Flax	at	5 zentners	for	24 gulden
10 day's work	Poppies	at	10 zentners	for	11 gulden
2 day's work	Camelina (false flax)	at	9 zentners	for	8 gulden 30 kreutzers
5 day's work	Cabbage	at	10,000 head	for	3 gulden per 100 head
2 day's work	Beans	at	18 zentners	for	4 gulden
1 day's work	Corn	at	12 zentners	for	3 gulden 40 kreutzers
381 day's work	Hay (Cuttings 1 & 2)	at	33 zentners	for	1 gulden 45 kreutzers
16 day's work	Vineyards	at	3000 liters		

Unlike other villages in 1864, restrictions existed in Ottersheim on field and meadow use. This was due to the inadequate roads that were not accessible at all times for wagons. The district was divided into two large parcels to avoid unnecessary damage to fields and meadows; one parcel was dedicated to summer crops and the other to winter crops. Some exceptions were allowed provided the access roads were available. In general, the following crop rotation was observed: clover, spelt, canola (sown in the stubble), grain, turnips (as subsequent crop), potatoes, and oats.

Raising livestock was always a high priority in Ottersheim. The village had an especially rich count of livestock in 1864 compared to other communities. Present were:

74	Horses and 8 foals (from the State stud of Zweibrücken)
19	Oxen and 3 draft animals
335	Cows, 150 cattle, and 15 Calves of the Glan-Donnersberg and Swiss race.
200	Pigs
35	Sheep
20	Goats
1000	Geese as well as ducks and chickens in large quantities.
45	Bee hives

The butter was bought from dealers who came to the village two to three times weekly. Market areas were mainly Karlsruhe and Edenkoben. The pigs were purchased from dealers as piglets from Westrich or from Prussia. After they were fattened up, they were partly consumed by the villagers themselves and partly sold. The sheep were kept for the wool. Poultry was kept in large quantities by all. The bee keeping was done old style using straw baskets.

Firewood was obtained from the community or State forests as well as from the wood stockpiles in Landau and Annweiler. Poorer people had to collect their wood from the community forest floor. In many cases, coal was also used as fuel. About 6,000 zentners [about 300,000 kilograms] of coal was picked up yearly and brought by wagon to Ottersheim from the rail station in Landau. Before the Landau-Neustadt train was put into service in 1855, many traveled by horse and wagon to the Saarland and brought coal from there. For this, they needed three days.

Ottersheim was hit by a strong heavy storm with hail on 13 August 1863. Many buildings sustained considerable damage that was not fixed in some cases until 1864. The community spent over 800 gulden for repairs to the tower, the roofs, and the glass windows of the Catholic and Protestant churches alone. Even the parish hall, the rectory, and the two schoolhouses had suffered damage and had to be repaired.

Ottersheim in the Franco-German War, 1870-1871

The Franco-German War of 1870-1871 affected Ottersheim only marginally and therefore left no traces. No sooner had France declared war on Prussia on 19 July 1870, than Bavaria sided with the Prussian King and his Prime Minister Bismarck and issued a mobilization order on the following day. Immediately, the fortresses of Germersheim and Landau, where some Ottersheim men also served, went into a state of war. The Third German Army, under the leadership of Prussian Crown Prince Friedrich, started their operations against France from Germersheim. They crossed the border into Alsace already on 4 August 1870. The main part of the French army was locked in the fortress of Sedan on 2 September and Emperor Napoleon III was captured. Soon, the fortresses of Strasbourg and Metz fell into German hands. The attack on Paris began on 5 January 1871, and the armistice was signed 23 days later. The Treaty of Frankfurt was signed on 10 May 1871. France had to give up Alsace, a large part of Lorraine, and also pay five billion gold francs as a war indemnity. During the Franco-German War, King Wilhelm of Prussia was crowned Emperor of Germany in the palace at Versailles on 18 January 1871.

Some soldiers from Ottersheim were also involved in the war between Germany and France. If they were in active service, then they had to pull out to the front with their garrisons. A few older soldiers were classified into the supply columns with vehicles. Veteran Valentin Stadel of Ottersheim (1847-1928) was wounded at Sedan. So after his return his fellow citizens called him only "Sedan." Several collections were organized during the war. The community donated 100 gulden for the wounded and sick soldiers on 15 November 1870. Some 2,000 French prisoners of war were interned in the fortress of Germersheim at that time. On 7 November 1870, 1,088 prisoners arrived from Metz, and another 1,029 men arrived on 17 December who had been captured near Orleans.

Even before peace was concluded, victory celebrations were held in March of 1871 in many towns and villages. Ottersheim was also involved. Here, the peace celebration took place on 5 March 1871. The community bought 18 elles each of black, red, and yellow flag fabric for the celebration, to add to the already existing blue and white flags. The two churches, the community hall, and the schoolhouse were decorated with these flags. Bells were rung and gun salutes were issued to begin the festivities. Pretzels were distributed among the village youth. A victory fire was kindled during the evening in an open space that was surrounded by the singing villagers. Seven men were hired to ring the church bells for which they received 8 gulden and wine. Costs incurred by the community for the victory celebration in March of 1871 amounted to 55 gulden and 12 kreutzers.

The victorious troops returned to their garrisons at Germersheim and Landau in June 1871. On their march through Ottersheim, they were received with flowers and wreaths

117

while the houses were decorated with flags. About that same time, the French prisoners of war were allowed to return to their homes. The Franco-German war was followed by a brief economic recovery, and in turn a stock market crash occurred already in 1873 in which thousands lost their assets and tens of thousands lost their jobs. Agriculture was also in big trouble, because cheap foreign grain flooded the German market. Only the protective tariff laws of 1879 brought a slow economic recovery that cannot compare to present-day conditions. How low the income was for working people at the time is evident from the following table. In 1888, the following annual wages were paid in agriculture and forestry:

Men and young men over 16 years:	420 marks
Women and young women over 16 years:	240 marks
Male youth under 16 years:	150 marks
Female youth under 16 years:	100 marks

Even if one considers that the employer provided lunch and dinner, and that consumer goods of daily life were a lot cheaper than today, still the earnings hardly met the needs of an individual let alone those of a family back then. Also, economic conditions improved only very slowly in the first decade of the 20th century. Nevertheless, through their great diligence, admirable thrift, and frugality, the citizens of Ottersheim ascended gradually to wealth and prosperity. With its gold and silver coins, this was the so-called *good old time* that the people often remembered with melancholy when placed against the times of the First World War.

Ottersheim in the First World War, 1914-1918

On 28 June 1914, Austrian Archduke Franz Ferdinand was murdered in Sarajevo. This bad news traveled with lightning speed to the most remote villages. In Ottersheim, the newspaper reports about the unfolding course of events were followed with trepidation. Very often, people stood together in groups and discussed the political situation, while the fieldwork remained almost entirely undone. War was in the air. Therefore, hardly anyone was surprised when general mobilization was ordered on 1 August 1914. With bells in their hands, the policemen marched through the streets of the village and announced "Mobilization has been ordered!" As a four-year-old, I stormed into my parent's home and joyfully repeated this call. But when I saw father and mother in the living room with eyes red from crying, I realized that this event must be something serious.

Already on 1 August 1914, many young men from Ottersheim entered the military. In the following days, the village was the scene of lively troop and equipment transports. Convoys of trucks and ambulances drove through Ottersheim, which was an extraordinary occurrence at the time. Because farm horses were mustered out in Bellheim, traffic on the roads was nonstop. In Landau, a large field bakery was built across from the prison, and barracks were built on the Ebenberg for prisoners. There were strict controls everywhere since one had to reckon with enemy spies. Whoever wanted to walk or drive to another place needed an identification record from the mayor's office. A guard stood day and night in front of the community hall.

When Germany declared war on France on 3 August 1914, an advance by the French from Alsace was expected. For that reason, a defensive position was built up in the shortest possible time in the foreyard of the Germersheim fortress. Trenches were dug, and barbed wire was laid on the Gollenberg and in the forest. A portion of the forest was cut down. Trucks from the fortress at Germersheim brought stone, wood, and barbed wire to the construction sites. A light railway led from Germersheim via Bellheim to the Gollenberg. The development of defense systems was conducted by non-combatant workers who were housed in Germersheim, Bellheim, Rülzheim, Knittelsheim, Ottersheim, and other locations. About 1,000 non-combatant workers were housed in Ottersheim. The men wore civilian clothes with red and yellow armbands. They were initially fed by their hosts at first. Later, the housewives had only to prepare the food, because they could pick up food for the workers at specific outlets. Such dispensaries were in the schoolhouse, and at the homes of Ludwig Seither I and Georg Burgermeister. The allocations of bread, meat, potatoes, coffee, and the like were so abundant that they could hardly be completely used up.

The non-combatants went to work at 5 o'clock in the morning and returned again at 5 o'clock in the evenings. The work was not interrupted on Sundays. In the evenings, the taverns were so full that tables and chairs had to be set up in the courtyards and in the streets. Two field services were held, one for Catholics at the old cemetery and another for Protestants on the festival grounds in the woods. King Ludwig of Bavaria came once by car through Ottersheim to inspect the fortifications during construction. When that occurred, we children ran through the streets shouting: "De König kummt, de Fahne raus!" [The King is coming, get out the flags!] When the danger of the French breaking through had passed, the work was stopped and the non-combatants were discharged and sent home. The workers were in Ottersheim about eight weeks. After they left, the defenses were guarded by the military.

Then young pioneers came to Ottersheim. A spotlight department joined them who carried four large and several smaller, portable spotlights with them. The group often conducted exercises at night along the road to Knittelsheim that the villagers observed closely. When the spotlight department moved off to the front, the locals adorned the soldiers' vehicles and horses. Then field artillery was quartered in Ottersheim. Under cover from bombers, its guns stood partly in the Bellheim forest and partly at the Knittelsheim mill. At the beginning of 1915, all soldiers from Ottersheim were at the front. By contrast, in Offenbach and Herxheim there were still parts of an infantry replacement battalion whose members built trenches and dugouts in the local woods, especially in the "Kühnen."

Meanwhile, life in the village became more difficult day by day. More and more able-bodied men and young men were drafted into the military, while women, children, and old people had to work in the fields and homes. On 12 July 1915, the first captive Russians came to Ottersheim and others were soon to follow. The Russians worked during the day for the peasants, who in turn cared for them. They slept in the Raiffeisen warehouse at night, guarded by two militiamen. They were Russian peasants and most were also trained in a craft. A prisoner named Alexander, who was very clever with tools, told the children that he was going to build a balloon and fly to Russia. Although his plan never materialized, he wrote letters for years to his former hosts when he returned to his homeland after the war.

For help in households, one could get refugees from Alsace who had been collected into camps at the beginning of the war. A number of Ottersheim families took advantage of the offer. So it happened that about 40 women, children, and elderly men arrived by wagon in Ottersheim on 19 September 1915. They came from near Colmar and Münster in Alsace. When the refugees arrived in Ottersheim, they were picked up at the community hall by their hosts. Most of them were large families who were distributed in the village. Only in exceptional cases was it possible that members of a refugee family could be accommodated in the same household. The names of the Alsatian families were: Breitenstein, Delagod, Füßner, Gutekunst, Haxer, Heinrich, Hellig, Herrmann, Sonntag, Wehrei, Wiehn, and Wittemann. The refugees could not return to Alsace until 15 February 1919. Some of them were still connected with their former hosts by letter for many years.

The longer the war lasted, the more difficult it was to supply the population in Germany with food and the economy with raw materials. The hunger blockade by the British meant that everything had to be rationed and distributed to the people through the use of ration cards. As in other rural villages, no farmer in Ottersheim was allowed to dispose of his products from field and stables freely. As soon as the grain harvest was completed, everything that exceeded their private consumption needs was brought to designated collection points for appropriate payment and delivery. The farmer, as the owner-producer, was allowed one pfund (about 1/2 kilogram) of bread per person each day. All cattle were carefully registered. Whoever wanted to butcher had to get a permission slip from the mayor's office. Farmers had to turn in most of their pigs and calves. And the farmers also could not freely dispose of milk and butter. It was therefore not surprising that the so-called *Local Government Association* was not very popular among the village population and that many tried to circumvent the drastic provisions, at least partially. Prohibited slaughtering was not a rare occurrence and not every pfund of butter arrived at the collection point in spite of high penalties. As justification of this behavior, one pointed to a sentence of the Bible that reads, "Thou shalt not muzzle the ox when he treadeth out the corn."

Finally, you could not demand that a farmer, who at that time had to work twelve or more hours daily, should have to suffer hunger. Even the police who were entrusted to ensure compliance with the provisions empathized and often closed their eyes to the occurrences. For example, the police knew that at night many a farmer drove to the mill to have grain or wheat ground. But it was only rarely that anyone was caught. Not all of the additional food that the farmers possessed was used in their own household. Very often strangers came to the farms in addition to friends and relatives. Sometimes even hordes came from Ludwigshafen. They never left the village with filled bags and sacks, because no farmer had large stores to draw from. The police had been ordered to intervene when the hamster lines of city dwellers became more frequent. Former police officials Burkhardt and Rölle could not bring themselves to take food from weeping women, children, and old people, such that another command had to be given their duties. These new officers also soon found reason to discontinue actions.

In addition to agricultural products, sugar, coffee, fat, soap, clothing, and shoes became scarcer from day to day. Resourceful people searched for and found many substitutes for these goods. In the farmhouses, people roasted barley and brewed black coffee from it. Syrup from sugar beets was used to replace sugar. The farmers again planted canola and poppies to grind the seeds for oil. The schoolchildren went into the forest to collect leaves that were used as a tobacco substitute. The so-called wartime brown-shirt soap had only its name in common with the peace [pre-war] soap. It felt like clay and hardly foamed. Clothing materials could be bought only rarely, and if you happened to find some in a store, then it was of poor quality. It was said then that nettles were processed into clothing material. Sacks were made of paper, and hardly any real leather could be found in shoes. If one wore wooden clogs in the winter during peacetime in Ottersheim, so now people often had to be content with galoshes in the summer. Rubber hoses and rubber for bicycles was not available anywhere for purchase. Some people helped themselves by using wooden tires mounted to rims on steel springs. In the city, bread flour was mixed with potato flour, and yes, some said that even sawdust was added to bread. In spite of all the hardships at home, they were not comparable to the suffering of the soldiers at the front.

The trench warfare demanded thousands of victims each day. Again and again, bad news arrived in the village about a husband, son, or fiancé who had been killed or wounded. The war materials became increasingly scarce as the war continued. In 1917, a collection of precious metals began across the country. Two bronze bells of the Catholic Church and a bronze bell from the Protestant Church were confiscated and melted down. Gold, copper, and nickel coins disappeared from circulation entirely. These were replaced by paper money. In order to mobilize the last reserves of gold and silver, a collection ran in each school under the slogan, "I gave gold for iron!" The schoolchildren bought nails with items of jewelry or precious coins to make an iron cross on a shield.[55] All this was of course insufficient to turn the tide of the war. Germany was surrounded and the collapse only a matter of time.

The enemy sent aircraft into border towns in order to weaken the morale of the German hinterland. So you could observe at 12 noon in Ottersheim on 24 December 1917, 14 aircraft flying to Ludwigshafen to drop their deadly bombs there, and see them returning shortly after 1 o'clock in the afternoon. One of the aircraft had to make an emergency landing at Herxheim. The occupants, two French officers, set their airplane on fire. Then they were met by a man at the vineyard cottage on the Kahlenberg and arrested. The enemy attacks on Ludwigshafen continued through the spring of 1918. On Pentecost Monday, 20 May 1918, Landau was struck by enemy aircraft at lunchtime. Several bombs were dropped and several people killed in this attack. Although the bombs rained down all over town, there was little damage to buildings other than smashed out windows.

On 8 August 1918, enemy tanks managed to advance far behind the German defenses. This "black day of the German army" shattered not only the fighting spirit of the soldiers, but also called those at home onto the scene who wanted peace at all costs. The war was coming to an end. A republic was proclaimed in München on 8 November 1918. Workers' and Soldiers' Councils took over in Berlin and Cologne on 9 November and forced the emperor to abdicate. On 10 November, a rally was held in Landau at which a Workers' and Soldiers' Council was formed. Finally, an armistice was declared on 11 November 1918. The German army had to be on the right bank of the Rhine within 14 days. In fact, the German General Staff was successful in withdrawing the troops in full order.

Day after day, trucks and hospital cars came through Ottersheim. They were on the way to Germersheim where they crossed the Rhine. On the night of 19 to 20 November, an Austrian provision convoy was quartered in Ottersheim. About a hundred vehicles were parked at the village exit road toward Knittelsheim. The horses remained in the open air, while the soldiers warmed themselves at a bonfire. During the following days, there was also no end to the billeting. All morning on 22 November 1918, Austrian troops passed through Ottersheim nonstop with field kitchens, field bakeries, guns, machine guns, and vehicles. In addition to horses and mules, they drove before them cows with abnormally

---

[55] To raise money for the war effort, the German public could sell their precious gems, gold and silver in the form of jewelry, or coins to buy ornamental nails. The nails were then pounded into wooden forms in the shape of the Iron Cross. When completed, the finished cross could then be used as a monument or memorial.

large horns and a herd of pigs. Württembergers and Bavarians came with artillery vehicles and ambulances the following day. With them were some Czechs and Slovaks who took the Choral Society's flag from the "Zum Gambrinus" Inn. The last quartering in Ottersheim was on 25 November; the withdrawal was over. On the same day, the Russian prisoners of war were brought to Germersheim.

For about a week it was quiet in Ottersheim. Then French soldiers entered the village for the first time on Monday, 2 December 1918. They belonged to the 147th Infantry Regiment that was stationed in the 12 barracks in Landau. Alternately, a portion of the regiment moved into position at Hördt, another remained in reserve at Ottersheim and Knittelsheim, and the remainder stayed in the Landau barracks at rest. These troops were replaced by the 51st Infantry regiment during January of 1919. From late January to March, a French convoy column lay at Ottersheim that had pontoons for use in building bridges. Their horses were housed in the barns of the farmers. On 13 May 1919, Marshal Foch and General Petain paid a visit to the city of Landau and its French occupation troops. Meanwhile, the Allies had drawn up a peace treaty that they presented to the German Commission for signature in June 1919. Because the French were not sure whether Germany would submit to the conditions, they had prepared to occupy the areas on the right side of the Rhine as a precaution. An ammunition convoy, with some 400 men and as many horses, came to Ottersheim on Sunday, 18 May 1919 to prepare for this. The quartering ended on 20 June 1919. The German Peace Commission put their signatures to the Treaty of Versailles eight days later.

Henceforth, French soldiers marched back to the garrison towns of Landau and Germersheim where they were stationed in the barracks as occupying forces until 1930. Their presence was felt in Ottersheim only when they held target practice on a certain days of the week from the Ebenberg in Landau to the Kahlenberg and the Gollenberg; and no one was allowed to enter the endangered areas.

Although the war ended in 1918, the German prisoners of war largely did not return to their homes until 1920. If they had been on the eastern front in Russia, they often had an incredibly long way to go until they could arrive on horseback or on foot in their homeland. Forty-four hopeful young men and fathers would of course never see their beloved native village again. They died for their country, and they were almost all buried in foreign soil.

Roll of Honor of the Dead of the First World War

At the front and at home, they died for Germany:

Eugen Bischoff	19/05/1898-17/06/1918	Merris
Friedrich Blattmann	04/08/1886-03/07/1916	Guillemont
Heinrich Dörzapf	28/12/1886-11/11/1914	Wytschaete
Otto Dörzapf	04/03/1894-18/10/1916	Rumania
Emil Föhlinger	17/11/1893-20/08/1914	Mörchingen
Adolf Frey	19/06/1895-22/07/1917	Kirschina (Russia)
Heinrich Frey	25/08/1889-26/04/1915	Czirak (Carpathia)
Wilhelm Frey	10/11/1898-30/12/1920	Germany (wounded)
Otto Gensheimer	15/08/1889-05/11/1914	France
Otto Gensheimer	09/06/1895-08/11/1916	Lille
Heinrich Glatz	13/05/1890-15/09/1917	Somme
Karl Glatz	1892-01/12/1917	Northern Italy
Hermann Greichgauer	29/11/1897-07/11/1917	Lavu
Otto Greichgauer	31/01/1886-19/12/1916	Freudenstadt (hospital)
Richard Greichgauer	30/03/1893-06/11/1917	Flanders
Siegmund Günther	05/06/1881-10/09/1916	Longueval (Somme)
Eduard Hilsendegen	01/09/1889-23/12/1915	Hulluch
Eugen Hilsendegen	20/05/1891-23/01/1917	Lille
Ludwig Hindert	14/06/1879-24/10/1917	Kortemarkt
Heinrich Hoffmann	17/10/1894-13/09/1916	Martinpuich
Heinrich Kaiser	26/12/1887-02/07/1915	Arras
August Kreiner	20/11/1892-15/03/1915	Saint Eloi
Peter Kröper	12/02/1871-29/03/1916	Bellheim (hospital)
Otto Leingang	05/10/1885-17/08/1918	Vaulx-Vraucourt
Adolf Merdian	30/09/1892-09/12/1914	Wytschaete
Alois Moock	17/09/1897-23/06/1917	England (captivity)
August Moock	25/10/1894-31/07/1916	Somme
Alois Seither	11/06/1888-22/10/1915	Serbia
Hubert Seither	25/05/1889-26/09/1914	Marie Court
Otto Stadel	19/01/1892-12/11/1914	Flanders
Martin Walk	03/11/1882-09/02/1918	Rum (war hospital)
Julius Winkelblech	24/05/1886-05/08/1916	Maurepas
Eugen Winkelblech	06/10/1889-20/08/1914	Saarburg
Eduard Zwißler	26/01/1885-13/09/1916	Somme
Richard Zwißler	25/02/1894-14/04/1917	Arras

Peter Bischoff	22/03/1893-08/06/1915	Russia
Alfred Glatz	1888-1914	Mörchingen
Albert Hilsendegen	03/03/1888-17/09/1916	France
Friedrich Kuhn	11/09/1897-15/07/1918	Allibandiers (Aube)
Josef Woock	31/08/1891-16/09/1916	Somme

The Turbulent Post War Years, 1918-1932

Hardly anything was felt in Ottersheim of the revolution that displaced King Ludwig III of Bavaria in Munich on 8 November 1918 and swept away Emperor Wilhelm II in Berlin on 9 November 1918, thereby replacing the monarchy with a republic. People took note of the events in the papers of course, but they went about their own business for the most part. The women and children were glad when many fathers and brothers in those days returned home and took up their work again. As in the preceding war years, only the bare essentials could be done and there truly was never a lack of work remaining. Since hunger was rampant in the cities, it was worthwhile to be a farmer. Not only could he eat his fill, but there also were always buyers for his products. Vegetable, onion, and tobacco cultivation flourished in Ottersheim at that time. With their large harvests, the small farmers of Ottersheim were usually at the top of the southern Palatinate communities. Annual yields of 15,000 zentners for onions, 8,000 zentners for carrots, 3,000 zentners for red cabbage, and 2,000 zentners for tobacco were not uncommon. Only in 1921 was there a bad harvest due to an ongoing drought. In spite of this, the wine yield was that much better.

Prices had begun to rise noticeably after the war but this started to cause concern by 1922. The large sums of annual reparations that Germany had to pay emptied the coffers of the country and forced the government to set the printing presses in action. New money was printed day and night and lost its value with the same speed. Inflation could no longer be stopped. If a gold mark was equal to 2,800 paper marks at the beginning of the struggle in the Ruhr[56] in 1923, so by November of the same year this gold mark cost one trillion. No longer could the government print enough to meet the demand for money. So states, cities, and even companies printed their own money. The wage and salary earners had to turn their money into goods immediately on payday, because a week later the money would be completely devalued. The farmers were somewhat better off as they could manage to get

---

[56] This refers to the invasion of the Ruhr Valley by France as a measure to pressure Germany into paying on defaulted war reparations.

clothing, shoes, and other items through bartering. The rapid development of prices is illustrated in the following overview:

It cost	Before 1914	1918	1922	Summer 1923	November 1923
1 pfund potatoes:	0.04 M	0.12 M	80 M	2,000 M	50 million M
1 egg:	0.08 M	0.25 M	180 M	5,000 M	80 million M
1 glass of beer:	0.13 M	0.17 M	60 M	3,000 M	150 million M
1 pfund of meat:	0.90 M	2.00 M	1,200 M	90,000 M	3,200 million M
1 pfund butter:	1.40 M	3 00 M	2,400 M	150,000 M	6,000 million M

M = marks

On 25 November 1923, a ticket for the mail coach from Landau to Ottersheim cost 360 billion marks. Typical for the situation at the time is the following episode. On 6 August 1923, an outsider set up a boat swing in Ottersheim. Five young boys jokingly expressed the wish to buy the swing. The owner closed the business a few minutes later; the swing, organ, and all the accessories went to the young people for 40 million marks.

The end of the year 1923 was also the end of inflation. The *rentenmark* was introduced by a law passed on 15 November 1923 at the recommendation of Currency Commissioner Schacht. That was replaced on 30 August 1924 by the *reichsmark*. From then on, 1 trillion marks was valued the same as one rentenmark or one reichsmark. In this way, the zeros could be deleted. However, the effects of the inflation were not removed by this measure. Many people who had saved all their lives for their old age no longer possessed anything. Hardest hit were those people who could no longer work because of age or disability. They had become beggars who from now on had to be cared for by the State and localities. Only those with their savings in properties had suffered no loss.

At the same time as the inflation, a separatist movement in the Rhineland and in the Palatinate was making its rounds. Supported by France, some separatists wanted to separate the left bank of the Rhine from Germany and make it independent. In the Palatinate in 1923, the separatists called for an "Autonomous Palatinate" government. The legitimate Palatinate government had to flee to Heidelberg along with numerous officials and employees. Those who refused to obey the new regime were expelled. At that time, 5,120 railroaders with over 12,000 family members departed the left bank of the Rhine and sought refuge on the right bank. Most of the villagers in Ottersheim wanted nothing to do with the separatist movement. Only a few members of the so-called *Free Peasantry* sympathized with the Separatists who were led by farmer Heintz from Orbis in the district of Kirchheimbolanden. But the Separatist movement quickly fell apart when President Heintz of the Autonomous Palatinate Government was shot by nationally minded men in the Wittelsbacher Hof in Speyer on 9 January 1924, whereby the freedom fighters Hellinger and Wiesmann were also killed. Already in February 1924, the legitimate government took office again in the Palatinate. Some of the expelled families could not return to their homes until the fall.

After inflation and the separatist scare, the German economy took a noticeable upswing with the help of foreign loans. Even the agricultural economy improved. The farmers could generally be satisfied with sales and prices. The prosperity at the time was also reflected in numerous festivities that were celebrated in the cities and in the country. But it was obvious after a few years that the economy was built on sand. In general, the German imports were more than exports. When the American Great Depression began in 1929, Germany was very quickly caught up into the downward spiral because of its close ties with foreign countries and its enormous debt. Exports decreased, short-term loans were called in, the public treasury was emptied, and the unemployment rate increased from day to day. There were more than three million unemployed in 1930 and their numbers rose in the following year to five million. The German foreign debt, which was subject to interest payments, grew to 20 billion marks in 1932.

Fortunately, there was not much of a trace of all this misery in Ottersheim. At the head of the community during this decade stood Mayor Franz Steegmüller who held the community finances in order with an iron fist. Ottersheim had no part of the $24 billion reichsmarks debt that was owed by the states, towns, and villages at the time. The community budget was balanced without missing out on needed acquisitions and updates. The village residents had also stretched as far as they could and consumed only what they had in fact raised or earned. There were hardly any indebted farms in Ottersheim. In fact, most residents had a small savings account at the Raiffeisen Bank as a fallback in old age. The only people in Ottersheim who were suffering during that time were some workers who had previously earned their money abroad and now had to collect unemployment. However, most of these people cultivated a few skills such that they did not have to rely entirely on the meager unemployment benefits.

Chancellor Brüning tried to become master of the economic crisis with rigorous austerity measures. The crisis increased in strength and size, because foreign countries did not act on his well-thought out proposals for reparation concessions. It was already too late when the necessary allowances were finally made in 1932 to his successor in the Chancellery office. In the Reichstag elections during 1932, the right and left wing radicals received enough votes together to form an absolute majority. Subsequently, 85-year-old President Hindenburg appointed Adolf Hitler as Chancellor on 30 January 1933. Although the NSDAP [Nazi party] at that time held only 34% of the parliament seats, the *brown*[57] rulers understood how to usurp absolute authority for themselves within a relatively short time. That they used any means they chose to get what they wanted is well known to anyone who experienced those times. And so the fate of Germany ran its course.

---

[57] This refers to the brown-colored shirts that served as the uniform of the Sturmabteilung (SA), the paramilitary wing of the Nazi Party; its members were known as "brownshirts."

Ottersheim in the National-Socialist Time

The political affiliations of the Ottersheim population were nowhere more evident than in the election results before Hitler took power in 1933. Here, each voter could select in a secret ballot the party to which he felt connected. An objective count of the votes was guaranteed by the fact that the representatives of the various parties sat in the election committee and mutually monitored the vote count. A fundamental change took place when the law regarding equality of the states and communities took effect. Now only those party members who were considered reliable by the Nazi party leadership were chosen for the election committees. The committee members had to remain silent about the processes used in the election. Only through man-to-man discussion could one find out about the falsifications that were commonplace at the Nazi elections. In some cases, there was not even an effort to count the yes and no votes at all; instead, results of 97%, 98%, or 99% were reported to the higher authorities as ordered by the district leadership. Some witnesses are still living who would swear to this claim at any time, at least for Ottersheim. This was also the reason why the ballots from the elections of 1933 had to be destroyed in contrast to the traditional practice.

In the period after the First World War until Hitler's takeover of power, many parties had sought the favor of the voter. Many of these parties were constantly below the 5% threshold and were therefore relegated to insignificance. In Ottersheim, the following parties were represented:

NSDAP:	National Socialist German Laborers' Party (Hitler's Nazi Party)
DNV:	German National People's Party (Hugenberg)
DV:	German People's Party
DDP:	German Democratic Party (later the German State Party)
DB:	German Peasants' Party
	Christian-National Peasants' and Country Folk Party
C. and BVP:	Centre and Bavarian People's Party (Catholic Party)
SPD:	Social Democratic Party of Germany
KPD:	Communist Party of Germany
Other:	For example, Christian Social People's Service (Protestant Party), Economy Party, and so on.

	07 Dec. 1924	20 May 1928	14 Sep. 1930	31 Jul. 1932	06 Nov. 1932	03 Mar. 1933
Voting:	597	636	697	685	692	685
Valid votes:	379	395	426	535	552	617
Turnout:	63.5%	62.1%	61.1%	78.1%	80.0%	90.0%
NSDAP:	1	7	29	123	107	177
	0.3%	1.8%	6.8%	23.0%	20.0%	28.7%
DNV:	18	2	1	3	—	—
DV:	54	26	17	—	8	—
DDP:	5	—	15	—	—	—
DB:	—	91	30	5	3	1
Centre and	280	235	313	378	399	411
BVP:	73.8%	60.0%	73.5%	70.6%	72.2%	66.6%
SPD:	18	31	16	20	20	21
KPD:	1	2	5	4	14	3
Other:	2	1	—	2	1	4

An analysis of election results in Ottersheim shows that the Centre and Bavarian People's Party possessed an absolute majority at all times. Even in the election in 1933 when Hitler was already in power, two thirds of all residents voted for the Catholic Centre and Bavarian People's Party. The Social Democratic Party was also successful in keeping their followers in line all in all. The successes of the Nazi Party at their highest point of 28.7% of the votes cast in 1933 were mainly at the expense of the liberal right-wing parties and of the pure professional parties such as Farmers' Party or Country People's Party. Without a doubt, the Nazi Party in 1933 was elected by people who up to this point had stayed away from the elections. Then there were the voices of the many hybrid grape growers to whom the Nazi propagandists had promised the fulfillment of their wish to keep the hybrid grape vines. From among the traditional voters of the Centre and the Bavarian People's Party, only a few swung to the Nazi Party. Perhaps they hoped that this party might eliminate unemployment or they might gain personally. They may also have belonged to the group of people who at that time were of the opinion that Hitler should be given a chance. He might "wear down his horns" within a short time and then disappear forever. In their shortsightedness, these people had not recognized that the democratic system of government would find its grave with Hitler.

This would soon be felt personally by the residents of Ottersheim. Until 1933, it was a matter of course that the village mayor was elected using a free and secret ballot by the village population. Under these democratic rules, a follower of Hitler would never have been elected to the top village office. This was only possible via the notorious law concerning equality of the states and municipalities that was issued in 1933 and was widely practiced. According to this law, all senior posts were to be occupied only by people who either were members of the party or at least were close to the party. The selection of the mayor was the job of the community council. Now in 1933, the old council was still in office in Ottersheim. It chose incumbent Mayor Emil Zwißler as head of the community by a 7-3 vote. However, the enforcement agency of the Nazi party denied its consent to this election because Zwißler was not a party member of the District Office. Therefore, the election had to be repeated on 11 May 1933. With eight votes, Alois Kopf I was elected as first mayor and teacher Ludwig Stibitz as deputy mayor. However, Kopf was unwilling to accept the office. So Konrad Hoffmann was simply appointed by the District Office as first mayor of Ottersheim on 30 May 1933.

Once the community leadership was replaced, the community council was to be purged of all "unreliable elements." In particular, all supporters of the Centre and the Bavarian People's Party were to disappear from the community parliament. To this end, a police action was started by order of the Nazi party. In June 1933, a police officer from Bellheim appeared with instructions to arrest and remove council members Josef Seither and Peter Müller. At the same time, a troop of SA[58] people came from Bellheim to justify the action to the public. These people acted as if they were the "angry" people from whose "rage" innocent and honest farmers supposedly needed "protection." Cell leader Stibitz, who did not trust the idea of the need for "protective custody," used the local bell to order that no one leave their home for the duration of the action. Then Seither and Müller were taken away and imprisoned with the help of "auxiliary police." For the majority of the population, the arrest of innocent citizens aroused disgust and resentment. But nobody dared to express his opinion publicly. They knew only too well from the news of the Strasbourg radio station what persecution to expect and by what means opponents of Hitler were silenced in concentration camps.

The June action that was directed by the Nazi party led to a completely new composition of the community council in Ottersheim. Of eight council members, seven were maneuvered out and replaced with Hitler supporters. However, the new mayor and councilors were just mindless tools in the hands of Hitler and his party. For example, the Ottersheim council aptly demonstrated this with the introduction of a citizen's tax.[59] The Nazi supporters who had decided to introduce this tax in 1933 had fought with all their might against the alleged citizen tax and rejected it just a short time before during the pre-election campaign. Now the tax was for anything, ordered and even wished for by the "beloved" leader.

---

[58] The SA or Sturmabteilung (storm troopers) or Brownshirts, the paramilitary wing of the Nazi Party.

[59] In 1930 the German President introduced a so-called citizen tax by emergency decree. The State was badly damaged economically and financially from the great depression and implemented a tax on every citizen over the age of 20 to gain desperately needed revenue.

Although we must reject Hitler's political system as undemocratic and inhuman, so also must an objective historical document not overlook the fact that National Socialism had some positive accomplishments to report. Thus, meeting the approval of the population as early as 1933, the residents of Ottersheim were not reluctant to see men of the volunteer work service begin to regulate the flow in the Quot- or Bordgraben, establish a large tobacco shed on the Falltorweg in August 1934, and a new milk collection building opposite the community hall. In addition, the elimination of unemployment that Hitler had set as a goal made slow but noticeable progress. There were 13 officially registered unemployed in Ottersheim when he came into power in 1933. Three years later that number had dropped to seven. First, relief work was used to employ these people. The Dämmel forest that had been already cut down in 1932 was leveled, plowed, and sown to oats by the unemployed in 1935. Also in that year, two settlement houses were built and sold to people of moderate means.

However, many a farmer who had voted for Hitler because of the Americanized grape vines waited in vain in the early years of Nazi rule for a satisfactory solution to the issue. Meanwhile, word had gotten around that Gau[60] Leader Bürckel had promised the winemakers at the Haardt before the power takeover that he would have all hybrid vines torn out, while in the same breath he promised the winemakers on the lower plain that they would be allowed to raise the American hybrid vines if they so desired. Now good advice was expensive. Konrad Hoffmann, the annoying reminder and vice president of the District Wine Growers Association for American hybrid vines, was removed from office in November 1934. Reluctantly, teacher Stibitz now became the community leader until tavern owner Edmund Bischoff was appointed and sworn in to the office in September 1935. Teacher Stibitz succeeded after repeated requests to be transferred to Oppau. So he was able to escape a political struggle that he considered to be hopeless. In one of his petitions to the government, it was confirmed by a leading party member that the political situation in Ottersheim was very unfavorable for National Socialism and that Ottersheim was still a stronghold of Catholicism.

In 1937, the time was right for Gau Leader Bürckel to resolve the question of cultivation of American vines once and for all. He ordered that all hybrid vines were to be removed within three years. Those who wanted could grow classic vines. Most farmers followed the Bürckel order with reluctance and at first destroyed a third of their hybrid vines themselves. Only two planters refused. Then the Office destroyed the vines of those who refused. Those who had refused also had to bear the costs while the obedient farmers were given a small compensation in money. Typical of the hypocrisy of the National Socialist press is the reporting of the hybrid action in Ottersheim. National Socialist press wrote on 16 November 1937, "Satisfaction was expressed at the order of the Gau Leader to remove

---

[60] The term *Gau* referred to the subdivisions of a country and was used in the 9th and 10th centuries in early Germany. It was revived in the 1920s to define the administrative regions of the Nazi Party.

the American vines. It gives the individual growers the opportunity to convert their plantings to noble vines within three years." But everyone knew that conversion from hybrid vines was always possible but had been rejected constantly and firmly. Note that the last American vines were uprooted in Ottersheim in June 1941.

The unsatisfactory manner in which the district leadership handled the question of American vine cultivation cost the Nazi party in Ottersheim some supporters in the rural population who had previously been loyal to the cause of Hitler. Thus, the handful of the "reliable" was so small that larger political actions were abandoned, and influence over the populace was eventually sought through the National Socialist associations and subdivisions. First and foremost, they made use of the agricultural association, because hardly any of the rural populace could escape the actions of the Reich's nutrition organization. This organization also received a capable leader in farmer Ludwig Gensheimer after the former leader of the rural peasantry was removed from office for disloyalty in 1937. In larger meetings, local rural leader Gensheimer explained the Nazi land policy to the people. If even the fewest of them could befriend the laws concerning the hereditary farms, then many would have approved of the market order of the Reich's nutrition organization.

The hearts and minds of village youth were mainly recruited through the *Hitlerjugend [Nazi youth]* organization. The *Bund Deutscher Mädel [League of German Girls]* and *Jungvolk [Young people]* were not very successful with their recruitment in Ottersheim. Few joined these organizations except the children of those families who felt connected to Hitler out of conviction. It was particularly difficult to find appropriate leaders for the youth groups, such that they had to be borrowed in part from neighboring villages. The National Socialist Women's group also remained a small group that barely kept itself above water. Moreover, there was also a lack of suitable homes for the organizations, so that meetings had to be held in the local party halls.

Even the school was to follow the will of the Nazi leaders and become a propaganda tool. The Catholic denominational school was not suitable for this. Here, there was no guarantee that Catholic-minded teachers would not secretly work against National Socialism. Therefore, the Catholic and Protestant elementary schools in Ottersheim were converted into a community school in 1937. Press reports showed that 97% of the population in the Palatinate chose this type of school. Town clerk Luitpold Stadel ventured to doubt this newspaper report. He was relieved of his duties for this! How this came about is characteristic of the tyranny of the Nazis. In the written vote on the introduction of the community school, most of the community officials from Ottersheim had refused their signature. Then on 22 March 1937, there appeared a representative of the Germersheim District Office at the mayor's office in Ottersheim to take the council members to account in the presence of the mayor. Among other things, he wanted to know the reasons why they had rejected the community school. After lengthy discussion, the representative of the

District Office asked Town Clerk Stadel if he wanted to add his name to the opinion of 97% of the Saar-Palatinate population. Stadel said, "I do not believe in the 97%." After additional forceful questioning as to what he meant by that Stadel continued, "I have been present at a lot of counts, and the result was often completely different than was reported." This statement was enough to remove the "black"[61] town clerk and father of six children from his office and livelihood on the spot. Such measures were of course little suited for awakening the sympathies of the law-based thinking of village residents for the National Socialist party. For Stadel, there was no way at that time to have an arbitrary decision of a lower authority reviewed in court.

Ottersheim in the Second World War

What was rumored in 1935 became apparent in 1938 - Hitler was preparing for war. The newspapers were not allowed to print a line about anything happening at that time in Ottersheim and in other places. Luckily, Jean Benz kept a diary in those years so that we can be quite accurately oriented about the details in Ottersheim.

In July 1938, officers of the Wehrmacht [Defense Force] appeared in Ottersheim and marked out specific land parcels. They were followed a few days later by labor service men from Schifferstadt and Speyer. They had orders to first remove the topsoil and then to dig basement foundations up to four meters deep. The excess soil was dumped in part on the Riedweg. Soon after, a convoy of trucks brought gravel, crushed stone, Rhine sand, and later also concrete iron and iron supports. To camouflage the sites, wire nets were stretched across them. Masons, carpenters, and laborers began with the construction of the bunker in late July. The concrete was prepared in large mixing machines and processed in day and night shifts without interruption. Strict controls ensured that no unauthorized persons approached the construction sites.

The bunker workers were housed partly in private homes and partly in barracks. Mail and private buses brought such bunker workers to Ottersheim daily from the barracks camp in Dammheim. Flak soldiers, and later infantry, were quartered in the village even before the fortifications were done. The soldiers left when the occupation of the Sudetenland[62] was over in October. Now work was begun to camouflage the bunkers to look like sheds, homes, and garden houses and to create tank traps. Dragon's teeth were constructed in the area outside the forest, and iron gates were built on the forest roads. The

---

[61] In German politics, the color red identified a socialist, green an environmentalist, yellow a liberal, and black a Christian conservative.

[62] This was the western regions of Czechoslovakia inhabited mostly by ethnic Germans.

dragon's teeth consisted of large concrete blocks that were rammed into the ground by machines. Once the bunkers were completed, they were guarded day and night. Because the forest and field paths were in bad shape due to the construction, they were later repaired by work service men from Schifferstadt and Speyer. Finally, the various bunkers were connected to each other by telephone cables so that the crews could easily communicate with each other in an emergency. The National Socialist propaganda described the construction of this "Western Wall" as a defensive measure to serve the peace exclusively. However, only a blind man would not perceive that the war had already begun.

A week before the official declaration of war, 50 men from Ottersheim were called to arms on Saturday of 26 August 1939 at 1 o'clock in the night. The induction notice was followed because there was no other choice. No hint of enthusiasm was felt anywhere. Soon, an anti-aircraft battery took up the position in Ottersheim. The guns were partially buried in the bunkers. The bunkers themselves were filled with ammunition that was brought in by trucks. Soldiers laid a network of telephone wires in forest and field.

On 3 September 1939, the population was ordered by local bell ringer to prepare an air raid shelter. Basement windows were to be covered using dung or sand bags. At night, light was to be turned on only in shaded rooms. Soon, the first refugees arrived from the Bergzabern[63] area. They had brought only the bare essentials in their carts. In the night, a hundred men in Ottersheim were summoned to collect the cattle in Herxheim from the vacated border villages and deliver them to Bellheim. The first enemy aircraft flew over the village on 6 September and dropped leaflets. Motorized artillery came to Ottersheim on 10 September. Also, three flak companies were quartered in the village.

During the French campaign in May and June of 1940, Ottersheim was spared from fighting. Beginning 20 August, French prisoners of war were brought as agricultural laborers to Ottersheim. They were housed in the hall rooms of the "Zum Gambrinus" Inn and guarded by two German soldiers. At the end of November, seven farmers from the village answered a call of the Gau leadership to settle in Lorraine. Another interested party had gone earlier to the occupied western territories. One must keep in mind that these settlers mostly did not know what role Gau leader Bürckel intended for them. In fact, they were to take over farms from which the owners had previously been expelled because they had stood by their traditional folk customs. In this process, the French simply had to leave their belongings behind.

Most Ottersheim settlers returned to their home village by Christmas of 1940, because they had lost interest in taking over foreign places in Lorraine. But the Gau leadership launched a new campaign in February 1941. The local peasant leader and two party comrades spoke personally with a large number of farmers to persuade them to settle in

---

[63] The municipality of Bergzabern lay on the French Germany border about 9 miles southwest of Landau.

Lorraine. Farmers were to decide whether they would accept the offer or not after a cooling off period of a week. The stubborn ones were threatened that they would be transported to Poland and settled in that province. The anger in the community was so great that the matter was soon called off. Probably the upcoming Russian campaign contributed to the deferral of the settlement of the issue for the time being. However, after winning the war the intention was to finish the work in this matter. Presumably, a dozen or two hereditary farmers would have been left in Ottersheim while the others would have been transferred to Poland, Russia, or France as so-called *soldier farmers*.

During the war, Ottersheim even had a train station. So it was that lanterns were set up on the Schwalbenberg and lit at night in the winter of 1940-1941. The lights were meant to mimic a train station so that enemy planes would dump their deadly load onto open fields. Responsible for the station lights was its own command of soldiers. However, apparently the enemy squadrons did not fall for this little trick and continued to drop their bombs in the larger cities and industrial settlements.

The focus of the war shifted to the eastern front with the beginning of the Russian campaign on 22 June 1941. In that year, it was not allowed to celebrate the Feast of the Ascension as a religious holiday any longer. After the rapid advance to the gates of Moscow in the winter of 1941, it turned out that for millions of fighters in Russia there were no warm winter clothes available. Hundreds of thousands suffered frostbitten hands and feet until Hitler finally decided that help was needed. In Ottersheim as in other places, the National Socialist Women's League conducted a successful action to collect woolen garments. Who would have wanted to refuse their own fathers, brothers, and sons some protection against the cruel Russian winter?

The Protestants had to give up the bronze bell from their church in March of 1942. The war industry was initially not interested in the steel bells of the Catholic Church. Toward the end of the year, the enemy air raids increased in strength. On 6 December 1942, a large number of explosive and fire bombs were dropped in the area in and around Ottersheim destroying 36 barns in Herxheim alone. For unknown reasons, the barns of Herrmann, Ettmüller, and Hoffmann on Germersheimer Straße went up in flames in April 1943. These were followed in May by the barns of Ripp and Dörzapf on the Ludwigstraße. In the years 1943 and 1944, often hundreds of bombers flew over Ottersheim towards the cities on the right bank of the Rhine to drop their deadly loads. During a major attack on Ludwigshafen and Mannheim on 26 August 1944, you could see the firelight from Ottersheim. The last emigrants returned from the Lorraine in those days. They carried all they had with them in back packs. "Wrong doing is not good," thought the others and were silent.

Now the war was approaching from the west; the invasion force was coming. On 11 September 1944, all male residents in Ottersheim aged 15 to 65 were called for labor service. They had to dig trenches every 50 meters on the roads to Offenbach and

Knittelsheim. Two days later, the people were sent to the border near Hagenbach in order to dig tank trenches 5 meters wide and 3.5 meters deep. Returning emigrants from the Palatinate border areas came to Ottersheim along with the supply transports of the fighting troops in December 1944. On the night of the 14 December, 200 Pioneer soldiers[64] moved into the bunkers and took up machine guns and bazookas positions on the streets and on the roads. Even the Home Guard was mobilized. It had been reported that the enemy had broken through at Weißenburg. The infantry and pioneers were transferred from Ottersheim to Germersheim on 16 December and were replaced by armored forces. Enemy artillery was already attacking Landau. All male and female residents of Ottersheim were put to building trenches in the area around the village on 19 December. All shelters were occupied by soldiers. A major transfer of wounded passed through the village in January 1945. Four-engine bombers laid bomb carpets. The explosions were so strong that the earth trembled. Low-flying aircraft attacked trucks inflicting deaths and injuries.

On 24 February, men of the Territorial Army occupied the halls of the school and the inns while Infantry Regiment 107 withdrew to Bellheim. The 16th of March brought a heavy attack on the city of Landau, whereby Pastor Knöll was killed. The French prisoners of war in Ottersheim were deported across the Rhine on 20 March. The attacks of the enemy artillery came dangerously close. No vehicle could venture into the streets or fields by day. In the evenings, enemy planes dropped firebombs on Ottersheim. In no time, the sheds at the Weet, the barn of Georg Jochim, the barn and the back building of Stefan Hörner, and the barn of Andreas Kuntz went up in flames. Fortunately, with united force the fires were brought under control. Large columns of French prisoners of war and scattered German troops came through Ottersheim on the 21st and 22nd of March 1945. They were followed by about twenty American prisoners of war who were to be brought across the Rhine at Germersheim. For Ottersheim, the war was coming to its end. The villagers were filled with fear and anxiety. What will the next day bring? Would the village be a battle area and be reduced to a heap of rubble, or would the fury of war once again graciously pass by? No one knew.

---

[64] The Pioneer soldiers typically took on the roles of construction and engineering in support of advancing or retreating infantry forces. Also, it was not uncommon for them to take up arms in defensive situations.

The End of the Second World War

(Excerpt from a letter written in those days by Hildegard Steegmüller to her sister Maria in India.)

Dear Maria!

The fear and excitement that the days from 21 to 24 March 1945 brought can hardly be expressed in words. As a precaution, we had built a small bunker for ourselves in our yard. Aunt Liß and the children stayed mostly in its proximity, but I felt safest in the house. In the basement, we had set up a makeshift sleeping area for the children. But because we were 25 people in the house, only the little ones were able to lie down there. The artillery fired continuously over our heads; fighter-bombers were our regular guests covering the whole area with bombs.

The German Army flooded back towards the Rhine. Since the bridges in Ludwigshafen and Speyer had been blown up, everyone squeezed to the Germersheim Bridge. American prisoners were led through the village. Dutch, Poles, Ukrainians, and other foreigners who for years had to work in Germany ran around abandoned. The ragged figures had orders to settle across the Rhine. Many preferred to hide and wait for the end of the war. Even German soldiers flooded individually or in large columns toward the east, exhausted, emaciated, with and without weapons: Victorious Retreat!

The 23rd of March was relatively quiet. At the Chapel stood four big guns that fired all day at the American front at Essingen and Hochstadt. Fränzel visited the German gun emplacement off and on and always brought the latest news. When the final rounds were fired, two guns were blown up; the soldiers took the other two during their retreat. Now we no longer see soldiers anywhere in the village. Only in the Gröhlig were the Waffen-SS settled in. We prayed that they might pull off soon so there would be no further military action. That resistance would only mean bad luck and death was clear to all rational thinking people. Finally, the Waffen-SS received the orders to move to the east after the enemy troops had already taken Herxheim and Hochstadt. At midnight, we heard tanks rolling in the area around Herxheim. Now for us there were no doubts, Ottersheim would be occupied on the following day.

At 6 o'clock in the morning, we went to Holy Mass. Afterward there was silence everywhere, as on Holy Saturday. More and more rumors raced through the village until Gutting came with the news; he had seen the leading American tanks at the Neumühle [New mill]. At 8 o'clock in the morning, a white flag flew from the Ottersheim church steeple. At this moment, four or five of the French prisoners of war appeared who had worked for years in the village and spent the last days hiding. It was a joyous welcome! Because the farmers always treated them humanely as prisoners of war, you could possibly hope for their help and intercession.

Meanwhile, the enemy tanks had reached the forest at the "Kühnen." They were accompanied by an observation plane, the so-called *lame duck*. The tanks first remained stationary in the uncertainty whether German troops were still in Ottersheim. Only when Hindert Bäcker and Robert Zimmer approached them on bicycle and explained the situation did they roll toward the village. Nobody had expected that the Americans would choose this path. In order to express their desire for peace, many village residents decked their houses in white, particularly in the Neuweg. All were glad that after the heady days, the occupation expired without a struggle. Once in the village, an American asked to speak to the mayor. He explained that all people were to go to their homes and close the windows. We sat in our living room and prayed the rosary and the Te Deum[65] in thanksgiving for the apparent protection of God in these perilous days and hours. No bomb had landed in the village; only three barns and two sheds had become victims of the flames.

Tanks rolled incessantly through the village followed by huge motorcades. Even after the noon meal, new surprises were waiting for us. About half of all houses had to be evacuated at short notice. Thirty Americans moved into our house. They cooked on large kerosene stoves in the back room for a whole company. The food was distributed in the courtyard. We were amazed at the quality and quantity of the meals. Some American soldiers secretly gave us some food. But no one dared get caught at this, as it was strictly forbidden to talk to us or to give us anything. On Sunday, we were able to go to church. It was Palm Sunday and Palm Procession as always. Then a military service was held but it was only sparingly visited. On Sunday, the Kleine Gasse had to be vacated entirely. In the evening, it was ordered that the population were not allowed to leave their homes for 48 hours. That was a shock because there was only one hour before this curfew would start. The necessary food had to be provided for as quickly as possible. We spent two full days in living rooms, chambers, barns, and stables. Then the curfew ended. On Thursday, the Americans left the village, and we moved back into our homes. They looked terrible. We cleaned out the stable and settled down there.

But quarters were again demanded by evening. This time French officers were to come. But there were only two officers' cooks who slept at night in the chamber. An order came to vacate the house within 30 minutes on Good Friday morning at 7:30. That was a shock! Beds and furniture had to stay. A soldier used a stopwatch to mark the time, and after half an hour, no one was allowed to enter the house. As we discovered later, our house had become the officer's kitchen and quarters. Approximately eight to ten men ate and lived there.

---

[65] The Te Deum is an early Christian song of praise.

What the people of the village had to deal with in the following days is indescribable. A veritable hunt for women and girls took place. The blacks,[66] of whom there were quite a few, acted like savages. We in our barn were lucky because where the officers lived no black robber dared to come inside. Our French chef was a kindhearted man. In Lorraine dialect, he told us "As long as I'm here, you do not need to fear the blacks." He also allowed us to get a bed and a sofa out of the house and set them up in the barn so that we did not have to sleep on straw. These conditions lasted until noon on Wednesday, then most of the French withdrew, and we were allowed back into our house.

In the coming days and weeks, we had no more billeting in the village. In contrast, in Knittelsheim a band of robbers was left behind who also molested our village with their daily or nightly visits. On 8 May, the day of the unconditional surrender, a new set of occupiers came to Ottersheim. Now the people were allowed to remain in their homes. Once again, we got the officers' mess. Usually five men ate in the living room while the food was prepared in our kitchen. That was tolerable. The troops were replaced at the beginning of July. Now we ourselves had to cook for three officers who treated us very humanely. No more billeting occurred in the village after they left.

---

[66] These were soldiers from the French African Colonies who had joined the French army.

Roll of Honor of the Dead of the Second World War

At the front and at home, they died for Germany:

Richard Bischoff	13/12/1913–30/12/1942	Stalingrad
Theo Böhm	27/10/1915-15/11/1942	Russia
Helmut Breßler	17/01/1926-04/04/1945	Germany (Ems River)
Ernst Brüderle	24/08/1920-16/12/1941	Russia
Otto Brüderle	28/11/1919-__/06/1944	France
Erwin Detzel	10/07/1918-01/07/1944	France
Ludwig Detzel	04/09/1914-26/12/1941	Russia
Erwin Disqué	15/09/1912-12/10/1943	Russia
Karl Disqué	09/01/1905-30/08/1944	Russia
Emil Dörzapf	12/10/1919-11/11/1942	Africa
Otto Dörzapf	08/09/1912-10/08/1941	Russia
Erwin Eichenlaub	22/01/1921-29/11/1942	Russia
Otto Ettmüller	22/03/1913-13/09/1944	Saint Wendel
Heinrich Faath	15/10/1901-07/10/1946	Russia
Otmar Föhlinger	16/01/1921-04/08/1942	Russia
Theo Föhlinger	11/11/1921-28/01/1942	Russia
Franz Frey	12/03/1909-15/12/1942	Russia
Richard Gaab	03/03/1909-12/08/1945	Russia
Werner Gaab	28/03/1927-01/02/1945	Ludwigshafen am Rhein
Alfred Gadinger	10/06/1919-08/03/1942	Russia
Hans Gadinger	23/11/1924-16/03/1945	Russia
Karl Glatz	23/07/1918-03/02/1942	Russia
Hugo Gutting	21/10/1912-07/05/1945	Mannheim
Franz Herrmann	04/01/1927-29/09/1944	Karlsruhe (flyer)
Otto Hilsendegen	19/03/1915-29/08/1942	Russia
Peter Hilsendegen	12/11/1913-26/12/1944	Niederlahnstein
Hugo Jeckel	13/12/1907-02/08/1944	France
Ludwig Jeckel	24/01/1922-29/11/1942	Russia
Alois Job	19/04/1922-11/11/1942	Stalingrad
Emil Job	02/01/1899-09/05/1945	Silesia
Leo Job	05/07/1925-29/12/1943	Russia
Willi Job	07/04/1920-04/09/1941	Russia
Oskar Knöll	29/06/1923-10/02/1945	Russia
Jakob Knöll, Pastor	10/02/1900-16/03/1945	Landau (Pfalz)
Alois Kopf	18/07/1899-02/04/1945	Ottersheim
Richard Kopf	18/01/1920-14/11/1941	Russia
Alois Kreiner	15/02/1909-07/08/1944	France
Emil Kreiner	21/04/1911-23/03/1945	Russia
Klemens Kröper	20/12/1913-20/11/1943	Russia
Otto Leingang	17/07/1911-05/10/1943	Russia

Ernst Moock	18/12/1920-04/03/1942	Russia
Ludwig Moock	17/02/1917-13/03/1942	Russia
Robert Moock	13/04/1915-26/07/1941	Russia
Hermann Morio	04/09/1914-26/11/1948	Russia (prison camp)
Ludwig Müller	07/12/1920-30/12/1941	Russia
Emil Ößwein	18/02/1917-10/04/1943	Kuban bridgehead
Emil Reichling	20/02/1920-23/09/1942	Stalingrad
Richard Reichling	28/04/1913-28/02/1942	Russia
Albert Ripp	23/05/1919-24/09/1944	Russia
Fritz Stadel	09/02/1925-14/01/1945	Russia
Ludwig Stadel	17/04/1921-27/12/1943	Russia
Ferdinand Walk	30/06/1911-05/09/1943	Russia
Ludwig Walk	18/07/1914-12/03/1943	Russia
Bruno Weisbrod	01/01/1924-16/01/1944	Russia
Hugo Wingerter	14/04/1921-27/12/1941	Russia
Ernst Winkelblech	21/05/1919-21/04/1945	Lithuania
Kurt Winkelblech	17/11/1921-17/03/1944	Russia (died Itzehoe)
Ludwig Wünschel	05/03/1915-30/04/1945	Breslau
Albert Zwißler	29/07/1905-15/10/1944	Ruhr
Alfred Zwißler	21/04/1926-01/01/1945	Belgium
Egon Zwißler	13/03/1921-23/03/1945	Baden (air raid)

The missing of the Second World War:

Hermann Faath	09/09/1919-__/__/1944	Russia
Otto Detzel	14/07/1912-24/02/1945	East Prussia
Siegmund Günther	24/04/1917-13/05/1944	Crimea
Heinrich Herrmann	13/09/1912-10/01/1943	Stalingrad
Helmut Jennewein	17/09/1924-__/__/1944	Russia
Erich Job	10/06/1923-29/06/1944	Russia
Ludwig Kramer	25/08/1913-31/12/1945	Goslar
Alois Kreiner	01/06/1919-07/08/1944	Ukraine
Josef Kreiner	13/05/1916-06/01/1945	Russia
Franz Anton Kröper	13/02/1915-18/08/1944	Russia
Ludwig Stadel	24/05/1916-__/08/1945	Russia
August Walk	26/01/1908-31/12/1945	Russia
Wilhelm Walk	07/02/1910-__/03/1945	Dresden
Josef Weisbrod	19/05/1922-16/06/1944	Russia
Oskar Winkelblech	25/07/1905-__/01/1945	Silesia
Alois Zwißler	18/11/1903-21/08/1944	Russia
Edgar Zwißler	08/01/1924-14/08/1944	Russia

The Post War Years, 1945-1949

The end of the war was the end of Nazi domination. Mayors, local farmer leaders, and various other persons were soon removed from their posts. Emil Zwißler was appointed first mayor and Josef Herrmann as deputy on 1 May 1945. Luitpold Stadel, who was dismissed because of his Catholic leanings in 1937, again received his old position as town clerk of Ottersheim. He was even promoted to administrative assistant a few months later. The Catholic Sisters were able to reopen their kindergarten already in April, and the elementary school began giving lessons again. The former Hitler supporters had to fill in and level off the trenches using spades and shovels. On 24 May 1945, the party members together with members of the Sturmabteilung [storm troopers], the Nazi women's organization, the Hitler Youth, and the men's organization were taken to Bellheim and interrogated in the brewery cellar. Already on the next day, most were allowed to go home again. The National Socialist mayor, the local peasant leader, the cell leader, and three other party members were taken to the Landau Fort barracks where they were employed in clean-up work. Not only they, but also all the villagers were to face hard times ahead.

The victorious troops used their absolute power to force the community to supply food and utensils. On 18 April 1945 for example, the mayor had to produce 300 eggs, 40 pfunds of butter, 40 pfunds of beans, 60 pfunds of sugar, and a calf at a moment's notice. Soon thereafter, the usable bicycles, motorcycles, cars, and rubber tires were confiscated. On 22 April, the soldiers came and took 50 blankets, and also from each household: eggs and butter as well as a cup or a mug. Almost every day French commandos came to the village and demanded chickens, geese, or ducks. At the victory celebration on 9 May 1945, all traffic on Germersheimer Straße was blocked from 5 o'clock in the morning on. At the high mast that was erected at the church, the tricolor was raised and everyone had to salute. The French decided that the residents on the Ludwigstraße had not properly cleaned their street for the celebration, so they were assessed a penalty of 200 reichsmarks. The French soldiers also considered themselves "masters" of field and woodland hunting. They shot at two cows once while stalking deer on the upper Mühlweg [Mill road]!

At the instruction of the French after the War, the Western Wall had to be destroyed. The bunkers north of the village were blown up by civilian commandos in September 1946. The recyclable material was saved by the villagers, while the concrete rubble was used to repair field roads. They began with the removal of the tank traps in June 1947. However, the villagers had already excavated numerous concrete blocks and brought them home. Some of the dragon's teeth with pyramid-shaped ends that once ran through the meadows and fields to the forest still remain as gate pillars today. The bunkers near the village were prepared for demolition in November 1947. All openings were cemented shut and the inside was filled with water. Walls made from bundles of sticks were built to protect the surrounding buildings. The houses and barns remained intact in spite of the strong explosions. Unfortunately, they failed at that time to remove the debris so that now the ruins provide a less than beautiful sight. The first postwar years were also marked with begging trips by the urban population to the countryside. All traffic was prohibited by the occupying forces without special permissions until June 1945. When this order was relaxed, day by day more and more people streamed into the villages in order to get themselves food. So for example, on 11 September 1945 at least 500 people from the cities in the Saarland came by way of Landau to Ottersheim to get potatoes, vegetables, and onions. Police had to be used to keep order. These "hamster" trains continued through 1946. A contemporary picture of those days is provided by Spiritual Adviser Steegmüller who wrote on 20 August 1946:

"The first train arrived at 8 o'clock in the morning in Offenbach and released its cargo from the Saarland, from Neustadt, and from Landau. Men, women, children, and old people enter the village by foot, bicycle, or handcart in groups of four, six, or ten people. Equipped with suitcases, bags, and backpacks, they throw themselves at gates and doors. Everyone wants to be the first. Many had been in Ottersheim often. They know their houses and their people and know where things can be had. Others feel their way more slowly and tend to have less luck. Though the field work needs attention, the yellow, narrow faces of the hungry with hands open for a piece of bread, a few potatoes, or some vegetables, yet awaken compassion. Some also follow the farmers on the field and draw from the source, with and without money. Once the bags and sacks are filled by midday, people wait for carts or cars to take them to the train or perhaps even to their homeland. Tips flow freely, but not all are in a hurry to get home so that not infrequently 30 to 40 people spend the night at the Sisters' Home. In addition to hungry city residents, there are also hoarders and smugglers who trade wine, household goods, and fabrics for wheat, flour, and ham. Finally, relatives and friends from the city come by bicycle in the evenings to pick up milk, flour, bread, or vegetables. In this way, between 300 and 400 people rely daily on the products of the Ottersheim farmers for their lives."

At that time, the overwhelming majority of the villagers shared their bread honestly with the hungry out of Christian responsibility. However, the large number of needy made it impossible to meet every need. As the saying goes, "one misfortune seldom comes alone." The winter of 1946-1947 brought four months of frigid weather. Even in the usually warm Rhine valley, the thermometer dropped to minus 15 degrees Celsius [5° Fahrenheit]. Sufficient heating fuel was lacking everywhere. There was no coal and the allocations of wood allowed for makeshift cooking of meals at best. It is no wonder that the forests were swept clean. Ex-President Hoover of the United States of America traveled to Germany and brought the attention of the world to the German famine. Everywhere there was a lack of clothing, underwear, shoes, sewing thread, and paper. That Americans helped us at that time should not be forgotten by future generations.

After the icy winter of 1946-1947, the longest and toughest in living memory, the summer started suddenly on 18 May 1947. The thermometer climbed to 38 degrees Celsius [100° Fahrenheit]. The cloudless sky provided no rain for months so that crop development stagnated after a good beginning. The hay harvest was still acceptable, but the second cutting was very poor. Until the beginning of cold weather in mid-October, the farmers drove their cattle in herds to the meadows. There were very few potatoes, and fodder beets remained small. The soil was dried out up to a depth of 1.8 meters, so it was difficult to plow and to sow the seed into the earth. Nevertheless, there were incessant columns of begging people from the cities hoping to get something to eat. In their distress, many were not deterred from sneaking back during the dark of night to steal the fruits of the fields.

To add to the full measure of misery, the French continued with their requisitions. Potatoes, onions, carrots, hay, and straw had to be delivered. The food was loaded in French cars and taken away. Even the tobacco went to the French processing plants in Strasbourg. Not only the townspeople but also the farmer looked with fear toward the coming winter for which they were barely ready. Finally, the year 1948 brought an end to the famine. The crops flourished with good weather, sunshine, and rain. The grain yielded a full harvest and the root crops were good.

The currency reform of 19 June 1948 contributed significantly to normalizing economic conditions. Previously, you could generally only get goods in exchange for other goods. Now, money was again the accredited medium of exchange. With that the vital nerve of the black market and profiteering were hit. People were relieved that stores offered their wares again at reasonable prices. Only now could one think of gradually getting rid of food ration cards.

The political situation also began gradually to return to a normal state. On 18 May 1947, the constitution of Rhineland-Palatinate went into effect and largely replaced the occupation regime. Two years later on 23 May 1949, the Basic Constitution of the Federal Republic of Germany was declared. The German people had thus recovered their State sovereignty. Meanwhile, the victorious powers had undergone a spiritual transformation. In view of the communist threat from the east, the German people were to be included as equal partners in the group of western-culture nations. Germany accepted the outstretched hand, thus creating the conditions for the unprecedented economic boom of the following years in which the village of Ottersheim had its share.

Germersheimer Straße with view of the Catholic Church

The old school house and the half-timbered house of
Ludwig Föhlinger (formerly the "Zur Traube" Inn)

The Ludwigstraße

The Kindergarten

The New Elementary School with School Gym

Gärrerbuben (Rattle boys)

The Weir at the Queich

Summer Day Parade

Floods of March 1965

In the Meadow

Tobacco Scale

Ottersheim in the Years 1950-1967

The rapid economic growth of the Federal Republic since the early fifties has had its effect on Ottersheim. It was expressed not only in unusually strong construction activity but also in a restructuring of agricultural practices, an increase in industrial undertakings, and an increase in the number of workers. Although the population of the village had grown only slightly, the number of significant properties increased. Seven new houses alone were built in 1952. Most new buildings were constructed on the Riedstraße and the extended Ludwigstraße. But the village grew also on the Waldstraße and the Friedhofstraße. Currently, Ottersheim has 288 homesteads, 55 more than in 1950. In spite of this positive development, there are still a number of people who wanted to build but who lacked the necessary building site. For this reason, the community wanted to extend the Schulstraße and the Waldstraße to create more building sites. Appropriate plans were drawn up and were implemented.

Among the new buildings from the past years, several craft or commercial enterprises deserve special mention. Motor Vehicle Master Otwin Zwißler built an agricultural machinery and auto repair shop in 1956 on the road to Knittelsheim, including a gas station. Ten years later, he built a large exhibition hall at his business that was used to house agricultural machines and tractors. With the steady progression of motorization, such an operation had good prospects for the future. Similar conditions existed for the spacious manufacturing hall of Hubert Gadinger that was completed and put into operation in 1967 on the Riedstraße. Gadinger received his certificate of Master Smith in 1953. Due to the switch to using tractors for agriculture, he saw few prospects for the future in his learned profession. He therefore sought a new field of work. In 1957, he introduced at his parents' property on the Ottostraße an automatic machine with which he manufactured the first hydraulic grease fitting for vehicles. He was already taking orders a year later from car companies for products of electronic parts. The operation took a sharp upturn in the early sixties when brass heel protectors were needed for millions of women's shoes. Soon there were eight fully automatic machines in action that could produce twenty tons of brass rods each month. On average, 120,000 parts were turned out daily. Even though only two people were needed to operate the machines, at least twenty persons were employed with sorting, counting, packing, and shipping. Today, the manufacturing of brass for women's heels has decreased but now accessories for bags and purse closures are made as well as valves and screw ends for hydraulic lines and the like. The tight spatial situation at his parents' property caused Gadinger to plan and build a new factory hall on the Riedstraße in 1967. The hall will accommodate the machines and make possible a more rational workflow.

A fresh-beverage plant also appeared in Ottersheim after the Second World War. It was founded in 1949 by Franz Steegmüller, transferred to Leo Lutz in 1955, then moved from the upper village to the Ottostraße in 1961 where the owner had built and furnished appropriate space. Deserving mention is also the carpenter store that Herbert Merdian built in the sixties at the east end of the Lange Straße. The home, which is reminiscent in appearance of a Black Forest house, was built mainly from wood and fitted with an unusually large roof. In addition to private buildings, several new public buildings have been erected in the past decade. The Raiffeisen Cooperative built a freezing facility in 1958 on the Germersheimer Straße at the former Weet. A new warehouse was built for the Raiffeisen Bank two years later, and an office building in 1963 that was occupied in 1964. The Catholic Church officially opened its new rectory in 1959 and a new kindergarten on the Schulstraße in 1962. The Protestant religious community was able to put their new meeting and youth facility on the south side of the church into service in 1965. The largest and most expensive construction project in the past though is the new school building and new gym. This building project was ready for use in 1965. Considering further that in the past decade the village received a water line, the village roads were repaired, and the field roads were renewed or even paved, objective observers would be convinced that these years belong to the most successful in the history of the village of Ottersheim. While all have helped, special praise is deserved for the men who held the positions of responsibility during this period, Mayor Paul Dörzapf and Pastor Josef Scherübl.

With the construction during the post war years, there was also a noticeable change in occupations in Ottersheim. For centuries, the place was a typical rural village, especially since the few artisans and merchants of earlier times maintained a few fields and some cattle. As a result of the land redistribution, there existed in Ottersheim hardly any large farms such as are common in Bavaria or in Northern Germany. In the Third Reich, there were only two hereditary farm owners among the 241 independent farmers. Today, not even one operation reaches the desired size of twelve hectares of land. Nevertheless, the small farmers generally did well. This is mainly due to special crops that have been successfully grown in Ottersheim for decades. However, this cannot conceal the fact that the profession of independent farmer was no longer desirable for many young people. So of eleven boys and girls who completed school in 1963, only one boy and one girl chose agriculture. The irregular working hours and the permanent attachment to house and stall at all times of the year keep many from the occupation of their fathers and mothers. This has meant that the number of laborers, employees, and officials has almost doubled from 1939 to 1961, while the number of independent farmers in Ottersheim has decreased accordingly. This trend will likely continue into the future. The result will be fewer but larger and more yield-capable farms that are worked largely by machine. But this shift needs time and will not proceed without conflict. In particular, many an old farmer will

146

look wistfully at his son, who is no longer willing to follow in the footsteps of his ancestors to become a farmer. The development itself is not stoppable; it can be delayed at best.

As the economy, so also the cultural life of Ottersheim had taken an encouraging upswing. The Cäcilien Club, male voice choir, band, and sports clubs had not only continued their activity, but they had sometimes been able to increase it significantly. Highlights were the various jubilees that these clubs were able to celebrate during this time. The Kolping Family joined the existing associations in 1952 and enriched the cultural life of the community through its amateur theater. Also, that the marching band of the Gymnastics Club had appeared for the first time in public in 1962 must be mentioned as a cultural factor. Something new for Ottersheim is represented by the Community Education Organization that Pastor Scherübl brought into being in association with the teachers. It gave the people an opportunity to expand their knowledge and to continue their education through lectures and other events. Church life in Ottersheim was enriched by new organs. In 1955, the Protestants dedicated their new organ, as did the Catholics in 1967. The Feast of Corpus Christi is still a public holiday that is celebrated with special solemnity by the Catholic religious community as in the past. The population not only decorates the houses and streets with love and devotion but also participates in the complete morning procession through the streets.

Finally, we should not fail to mention that the inhabitants of Ottersheim always had an open heart and an open mind to the plight of others during the years of economic upswing. Not the least proof for this was the results of the *Misereor* and *Adveniat*[67] collections, where Ottersheim stood percentage-wise at the head of Southern Palatinate communities. Also gratifying is the fact that in spite of all the care for the people, the animals were not forgotten. Bird lovers from Ottersheim have hung over a hundred boxes in the forest in the past years to give the feathered singers a nesting opportunity. In addition, feeding stations were set up to prevent bird deaths in winter. Here Jean Benz, Johann Gadinger, and Emil Kröper and his son have stood prominently in the service of a good deed. It would be desirable that the work of these and other people in Ottersheim be continued and expanded in the future by the youth of the village for the good of all.

---

[67] *Misereor* and *Adveniat* are German Catholic relief organizations which help the poor, sick, hungry, and disadvantaged in Africa, Asia and Latin America.

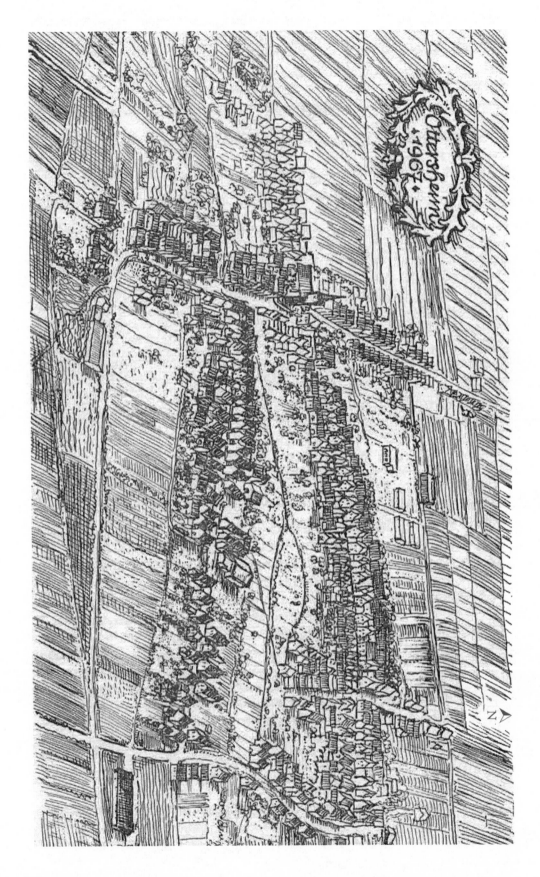

Ottersheim
1967

148

Displaced Persons and Refugees in Ottersheim

He who sows wind shall reap a storm. This adage applies not only in daily life but also in politics. The wind that Hitler sowed during the war with the expulsion of thousands upon thousands of Polish from the Warthegau produced a hurricane after the war that swept millions of Germans from their ancestral homes in Silesia, Pomerania, West Prussia, and East Prussia. Of the ten million Germans beyond the Oder and Neisse rivers, more than 9 million were deported and replaced by Polish settlers. In addition, many ethnic Germans from Czechoslovakia, Yugoslavia, Hungary, Romania, and Russia were forced to take to the roads heading west. More than 2 million Germans died during this flight, or they were deported to Siberia. Today, in the Federal Republic there are a total of 10.6 million displaced persons, while 4 million have found a new home in the Soviet-occupied zone. In addition, there are also 3.4 million refugees in the Federal Republic. By these are meant, especially those who left central Germany in the fifties under cover of darkness and fled to the west because they did not want to live under communist rule. So currently, about 14 million displaced persons and refugees live in the Federal Republic. This is around 18% of the total population.

It was a very difficult task to accommodate these people in the west and incorporate them into the economic process. As long as the French occupation zone existed, displaced persons came only sporadically to this area to settle. That changed after the founding of the Federal Republic in 1949. From then on, displaced families were systematically moved from the right bank to the left-bank areas by the District Offices and distributed to individual communities. In this manner, Ottersheim was assigned a total of 182 displaced persons in the course of ten years. Most of them were spared nothing in distress and want. The families Knebl, Weimann, Schwendemann, and Auer had to leave their home village of Karawukowo back in October 1944. They moved with bag and baggage from Yugoslavia, via Hungary and Austria to Germany, where they worked in Silesia, then Thüringia. Finally, they found shelter in the Bavarian Forest area. From there the way led via the transit camp of Osthofen to Ottersheim at the beginning of the fifties. Johann Sentz and Susanne Kremer also fled from their village of Lowas in Yugoslavia on October 1944. They were allowed to take from their possessions only what would fit on a farm wagon. They were underway four weeks before they found a place to stay in Hunding in November 1944, a small community in Austria in the district of Braunau. There they both worked in agriculture. They married in 1948. Of the four children who were born in Hunding, one son died in the first year of life. After 13 years of residence in the small town, they had to choose between German or Austrian citizenship. They chose German citizenship and then came to Schalding near Passau. From there they came to the transit camp of Osthofen in Rheinhessen two weeks later. Although the Sentz family registered in the district of Germersheim, they were initially assigned to Rockenhausen where they were placed for two months into temporary housing. Then they got a larger apartment in the small village of Würzweiler near Rockenhausen; however, they left the apartment already in January of 1958. So the displaced family came that same month to Ottersheim where three more children were born. Placed in emergency housing at first, they were able to move into their own home in 1965 on the Riedstraße.

It was not easy for the Mayor of Ottersheim to obtain decent housing for the 182 displaced and refugees who were assigned to the village over time. Empty houses or apartment buildings did not exist. Therefore, the locals had to squeeze closer and make room for the newcomers. Even more difficult was the task to find work and income for the displaced, because larger factories and companies were lacking. As far as the newcomers could not be placed in agriculture, they sought work outside of Ottersheim. Not surprisingly, they moved to their work location when the opportunity allowed. Due to this situation, 143 of the initial 182 displaced persons assigned to Ottersheim have left. Currently, 32 still live in the community. Of these, 20 come from Yugoslavia, 8 from the eastern territories of Germany, and 4 from Czechoslovakia. Seven displaced persons died, and they were buried in the cemetery. As far as the refugees who remained in Ottersheim, they have become so well integrated into the village community that they no longer are seen or treated as foreigners. Some of them have even built a house, and thus demonstrated their desire to remain permanently in Ottersheim. Only their somewhat unusual family name will remind later generations that they were among the displaced from the Second World War, who lost their ancestral homeland but found a new home in Ottersheim.

Residents displaced in Ottersheim according to the status in March 1967

First and last name	Number of people	Original Home	Month of Admission
Franz Knebl	2	Yugoslavia	November 1950
Jakob Knebl (his widow)	2	Yugoslavia	April 1952
Sebastian Knebl	1	Yugoslavia	November 1950
Josef Michalzyk	1	Upper Silesia	May 1950
Maria Morisak	1	Yugoslavia	October 1959
Willibald Richter	3	Czechoslovakia	June 1952
Paul Romanowski	1	East Prussia	May 1952
Charlotte Sablotny	2	West Prussia	October 1948
Johann Sentz	8	Yugoslavia	January 1958
Peter Schwendemann	2	Yugoslavia	September 1951
Franz Uterhardt	2	Pomerania	November 1950
Josef Weimann	4	Yugoslavia	October 1950
Werner Wenzel	1	Pomerania	1945
Maria Wrobel, married to Stadel	1	Upper Silesia	July 1961
Rudolf Zeisberger (his widow)	1	Czechoslovakia	November 1952

Deceased displaced according to the status in March 1967

	Number of people	Original Home	Year of death
Juliane Auer	1	Yugoslavia	1956
Josef Gaube	1	Romania	1959
Adamine Gaube	1	Romania	1963
Anna Langer	1	Czechoslovakia	1951
Heinrich Paszehr	1	Memelland	1957
Josef Schwendemann	1	Yugoslavia	1953
Elisabeth Schwendemann	1	Yugoslavia	1953

Displaced and refugees who temporarily lived in Ottersheim

	Number of people	Original Home	Range of years
Maria Amann	2	Yugoslavia	1955-1960
Gertrud Baum	2	Pomerania	1953-1954
Josef Blachut	3	Thüringia	1953-1960
Gerhard Bräuer	4	Saxony	1958-1959
Anna Cichy	4	Silesia	1953-1957
Martha Fidelak	5	Poland	1950-1960
Hans Gräf	6	Romania	1949-1952
Katharina Glas	1	Romania	1949-1952
Josef Hahn	4	Czechoslovakia	1955-1956
Erwin Hartkopf	3	Pomerania	1950-1956
Paul Hohn	4	West Prussia	1955
Gerhard Hoppenheit	4	Brandenburg	1953-1957
Johann Kaip	3	Yugoslavia	1953-1954
Willi Kenzler	6	East Prussia	1950-1951
Irmgard Kilka	1	Brandenburg	1953-1954
Franz Kramer	2	Thüringia	1958-1961
Friedrich Krull	5	Saxony	1953-1957
Erich Künstler	4	Yugoslavia	1953-1955
Gerhard Kuhn	4	East Prussia	1956-1957
Jakob Langeneck	5	Yugoslavia	1951-1959
Gerhard Loeck	3	Pomerania	1956
Karl Müller	5	Czechoslovakia	1950-1951
Kurt Opitz	2	Silesia	1957-1960
Hanna Oßke	4	Saxony	1956-1958
Johanna Pahlke	1	East Prussia	1948-1951
Roman Pasieka	9	Ukraine/Poland	1951-1956
Hermann Peukert	3	Lower Silesia	1950-1952

Alfred Poppitz	3	Saxony	1954-1956
Samuel Prechtel	5	Czechoslovakia	1953-1959
Friedrich Przygoda	4	East Prussia	1957-1958
Johann Sabo	4	Yugoslavia	1954-1955
Magdalena Sentz	1	Yugoslavia	1955-1960
Georg Schätzlein	4	Brandenburg	1953
Ida Schmidt	1	Silesia	1953-1963
Ernst Schmidt	1	Silesia	1953-1954
Richard Schmidt	1	Silesia	1952-1953
Franz Steidl	4	Czechoslovakia	1950-1951
Katharina Tengler	1	Hungary	1956-1959
Franz Watzl	2	Czechoslovakia	1950-1953
Jakob Zapilko	7	Czechoslovakia	1950-1953
Fritz Zapletal	2	Czechoslovakia	1950-1951
Wilhelm Ziegler	4	Silesia(Breslau)	1950-1953
	143		

The Ottersheim Coat of Arms

In 1954, the Ministry of the Interior of the Rhineland-Palatinate approved the use of a new coat of arms that was designed by the State Archives in Speyer. By design, the crest was somewhat amply filled due to the rich local history that was reflected in its symbols that date back to the early Middle Ages. Originally, the thought was to use the crests of the local Knights who are mentioned in documents dating back to the 13th century. However, the coat of arms of these families was not known.

Ottersheim Coat of Arms
(Full color version
shown on the front cover)

The Knights von Ochsenstein from the Castle Meistersel near Ramberg, who were the feudal lords in possession of the village and district property in the 14th and 15th centuries, were of particular importance for the development of the Ottersheim community. The Cistercian Abbey of Eußerthal, as the proprietor of the Ottersheim parish since 1311, played an important role in the history of the village. Finally, Ottersheim for centuries belonged to the Palatinate's Upper or District Office in Germersheim and formed the Fautei (Bailiwick) of Germersheim that included Knittelsheim, Bellheim, and other places.

This membership in the Electoral Palatinate is represented in the local coat of arms by the blue-white diamond fields that fill the upper-left part of the shield. To the right, we see two silver crossbars on a red background like those the Ochsensteiner had in their crest. The crossbow that is placed on the upper right field was the symbol of the Monastery of Eußerthal for a time. The lower half of the Ottersheim crest shows a black ring with a button-like peg on a gold background. In the middle of the ring hangs a red, six-pointed star. [See the full color version on the front cover.]

The lower part of the crest refers to the private seal of Mayor Wendelin Müller, who was at the head of the village from 1730 to 1746 and lived on the estate of the former monastery at 66 Große Gasse. His house was the "Zur Krone" Inn that was still in operation in the 19th century. The inn was marked with a sign that apparently was used as a model for the private seal. The inn sign contained a golden crown and a red star that sat upon a button. For his private seal, Wendelin Müller added to the inn sign the first letters of his name: WM. Because Wendelin Müller was later followed in office by his son Georg, the seal remained nearly unchanged. With Mayor Georg Kopf (1780-1795), who lived east of the rectory on the site of the old schoolhouse, there was no longer a reason to keep the crown in the seal. But he did not want to throw out lock, stock, and barrel what had already been in use for half a century. He used the existing forms and transformed them free-style.

At the beginning of the 19th century, the depiction of ring, peg, and star, which by then was perceived as representative of the village, was placed in a new shield and used as border markers district in 1827. In the year 1839, the supposedly ancient coat of arms was officially awarded to the community because of its considerable age; after all, it was the wish of the population that these coats of arms not disappear completely. The official seal of the community from the year 1925 had even reinterpreted the ring and peg into a snake that is biting itself in the tail. What remains are the ring with the peg and the star in the middle. Therefore, it was set in the bottom half of the new emblem after the worst distortions had been eliminated.

For those who know how to read it, the crest recalls not only the Palatinate, the Ochsensteiner, the Eußerthal manor, the long gone "Zur Krone" Inn, but also a flourishing time during the 18th century when the population and the number of houses in Ottersheim nearly doubled under Mayors Wendelin and Georg Müller.

Overview of the Number of Inhabitants

Year	Catholics	Protestants (Reformed)		Total	Comments
1557	—		—	~300	58 hearths
1671		Reformed	~180	~200	40 house foundations
		Lutheran	~20		
1707	188		~40	~228	—
1785	—		—	597	—
1788	507		143	650	—
1791	558		152	710	112 homes
1798	556		—	—	—
1802	512		132	664	—
1806	650		130	780	—
1823	—		—	927	—
1836	777		209	986	—
1855	—		—	933	—
1856	856		195	1,051	—
1864	791		183	974	—
1866	885		175	960	—
1871	—		—	975	—
1875	803		170	973	—
1880	965		149	1,114	—
1890	876		132	1,008	—
1895	836		178	1,004	—
1900	810		177	987	—
1905	871		158	1,029	—
1910	880		181	1,061	—
1917	—		—	1,010	—
1920	—		—	1,061	—
1925	923		146	1,069	214 residences
1928	934		152	1,086	—
1933	996		156	1,152	—
1935	923		156	1,069	—
1939	1,020		155	1,175	311 households
1946	—		—	1,211	—
1950	—		—	1,240	—
1952	—		—	1,282	—
1955	—		—	1,276	—
1961	1,093		169	1,262	378 households
1963	1,066		164	1,230	—
1966	1,111		161	1,272	—

(~ Denotes an approximation.)

Church, School and Kindergarten

The Catholic Church of Ottersheim

The Catholic Church of Ottersheim stands on an artificial elevation where the Landauer Straße makes a knee-shaped turn to the west in the middle of the village.[68] The church faces west contrary to tradition. The altar stands in a non-attached chancel from which a retracted flat apse extends on the west side. The older sacristy rises on the north side and the new sacristy on the south side. A 30-meter high tower completes the church on the east. The tower has five floors and a spire on top. Cornices are visible on the second and fifth floors. The lower tower room had a vaulted, gothic-ribbed ceiling with fluted ribs that connect directly to the walls. The north and south sides of the tower each have a large, pointed arch wall niche. Small windows are built into the third and fourth floors of the tower while the sound openings are paired and have slanted Gothic panels.

The classical entryway on the east side of the tower has straight sides. The walls are made of diamond mogul stone masonry (rustic work). Several tri-glyphs are visible under the cornices that complete the walls. The nave contains a flat ceiling that rests on a filleted flat slab. The neo-Gothic style of the Church is expressed especially by the pointed-arch windows. However, the south and north entryways are round-arched. A wooden gallery has been inserted in the rear of the church that also contains an organ in addition to pews for churchgoers. Three steel bells from the year 1924 hang in the tower. They are tuned to the notes D sharp, F sharp, and G sharp. The tower clock has four faces so that the time can be read from all sides. In the nave are 390 seats, 84 of them in the loft.

Until recently, it was believed that the Ottersheim Church was built in the years 1680-1689. This assumption is based on a report of Catholic priest Georg Uth from the year 1747. Uth writes in the report that the parish Church in Ottersheim was newly built in the style of the Reformed during the time of the Elector Karl Ludwig (who lived 1618-1680), and was made available to the Catholics around 1685, at the time of the reunion with the French crown. The writer, who came from Fulda, must have used older sources in his report, and he apparently interpreted these somewhat inaccurately. One only needs to remember the birth year of Elector Karl Ludwig for the information of Pastor Uth to be correct.

In fact, building of the Ottersheim parish Church was begun in 1618 and completed one year later. The last doubts about the founding date were removed by the discovery of the corner stone. The stone, found at the right corner of the entrance to the nave, was uncovered as a complete surprise during a church restoration project in 1946. It was 1 meter long, 95 centimeter wide and 60 centimeters high. The cornerstone contained a greenish glass ampoule with dried wine, a lead tablet 28 centimeters by 14 centimeters in size, and a smaller 13 centimeters by 3 centimeters tablet with these epigraphs:

---

[68] The Landauer Straße and the Deich are today the Germersheimer Straße.

God defend against false teaching.
God keep the community small.
Peter Trimpler, mayor here has much work with this building.

The whole thing was closed with a copper lid. The Certificate of Foundation on the larger tablet reads as follows:

"Under the government of his Excellency, Highborn Prince-Elector and Lord
Friedrich V of the Rhine: Under the officials of the Germersheim Office, the noble
Johann Friedrich von Stockhe, also Herr Eusebio Menio, district clerk here, on 28
May MDCXVIII (1618 A.D.) for the new church here the cornerstone was laid and
this document enclosed on 8 July in the cornerstone at the tower. At that time
Johan Conrad Glaser was pastor, Peter Trimpler mayor, Johann Schock of
Heidelberg master builder, Johann Bechtel von Frankweiler and Velten Ulrich von
Klingenmünster, stone masons."

On the back of the tablet is written:

A malter of grain is worth 3 Gülden
A fuder of wine XXVIII (28) Gülden.

With this, it becomes clear that the church was founded at the beginning of the 30-Years War in 1618. Whether the new church building was meant to give thanks to the Electoral House for the happy birth of an heir and crown prince cannot be proven but it is probable. Because at that time the whole village belonged to the Reformed faith, the church was certainly built as a Reformed house of prayer on the site of the old dilapidated church. One can construct the approximate original appearance of the church provided one ignores all that has proved to be built later.

It was actually a simple and unadorned church. The tower back then looked almost as it does today except for the entryway. However, the nave was much smaller and included only three pairs of windows. The church was then as now 11 meters wide and only 18 meters long but without the tower and chancel. At present, its length is 27 meters without the chancel shell. One could reach the interior of the house of prayer through the two side entrances to the south and north. The furnishings of the church would be very simple according to the Reformed view. A table and a lectern were most likely placed in the chancel while pews were installed in the nave. A loft was not present. In the tower hung two bells that were rung by the teacher of the village. Presumably, there was already a church clock present that regulated the daily tasks of the villagers.

It is probably not exaggerated that the Foundation Certificate made a brief reference to Mayor Trimpler having a lot of difficulty during the building. However, this comment would not have related to a concern with financing the construction as one nowadays might assume. As it was, collecting of the money was very exactly regulated at the time in that all recipients of tithes had to share the cost according to the percentages they collected. Of the running financial costs, the following had to muster:

Electoral Court Chamber:	6/12 [or 1/2]
Parish of Ottersheim via the Eußerthal Monastery:	4/12 [or 1/3]
House of Haimbach:	1/12
Priory of Hördt together with the community of Ottersheim:	1/12

But because the church properties were already confiscated in the 16th century by the State, the Spiritual Goods Administration in Heidelberg in fact had to finance nearly all of the new construction of the tower, the main nave, and the chancel for their sub-offices. The Administration even had to pay for the utensils of the house of prayer, because they had confiscated the income from the early Mass readings[69] in addition to the properties. The community was responsible for the churchyard wall, the bells, and the clock, while the village residents were required to provide labor and dray services as the Elector had explicitly pointed out to his subjects in 1614.

The procurement of construction materials, as was required of the citizens, should not be imagined as an easy task. That is to say, at that time the sandstone and construction wood had to be driven over 20 kilometers on two-wheeled carts to Ottersheim from the Haardt Mountains. Presumably, the Eußerthal Abbey, as owner of the parish, made their quarries and their forest available as they did later for the parish house building. Organization of work and the transportation was in the hands of Mayor Trimpler. Because all transportation and labor was carried out as feudal serf labor, it is not surprising that Mayor Trimpler had to invest a lot of effort with the distribution, control, and accounting of the work. Given the bad roadways, hundreds of cart trips were necessary in order to bring the quarry stone, the construction wood, and the sand to the site. Fortunately, the 30 Years War that broke out during 1618 in Bohemia spared the District Office of Germersheim until 1622, thus allowing the new construction to be completed. The date 1619, which points to completion of the construction in that year, was found in two places in the tower beams during the renovation.

Pastor Konrad Glaser could of course enjoy his new place of worship for only a short time. In the wake of the new religious policy of the victorious Austrians and Bavarians, he had to abdicate as Pastor of the Reformed Congregation of Ottersheim already by 1626. Although he lived in the village for another three years, he was not allowed to practice his office. In his place, a temporary Catholic clergyman took over the care of the community.

---

[69] The early mass readings were typically performed by a Catholic priest in the morning before work began. He received for this a stipend.

By State order, as did his Catholic brethren in other places in the District Office of Germersheim, he was to celebrate the Holy Mass on a regular basis, the Homily was to be used above all to explain the Sacrifice of the Mass, the Blessed Sacrament was to be installed, and an Eternal Light set up before it. He was also instructed to set up a holy water fountain and a baptismal font. It is therefore not surprising the baptismal font in the church today bears the date: `1629´.

When the 30 Years War ended in 1648, essentially the old religious practices were to be reinstated as a result of the Treaty of Münster and Osnabrück. The residents of Ottersheim, who had dwindled to a small number again, received a Reformed pastor in 1650 and henceforth practiced the beliefs of Calvin without exception. The church building itself seems to have survived the decades-long chaos of war without serious damage.

Fundamental changes in the ecclesiastical relations in Ottersheim did not occur until about the end of the 17th century. As we know, the Sun King Louis XIV occupied the area south of the Queich in 1680 and for all intents and purposes annexed it to France. At the instigation of the French Government during the first years of the occupation, a number of Ottersheim residents accepted the Catholic faith. For their sake, a Simultaneum was ordered by the State in the year 1684 establishing that Catholics and Reformed were to both make use of the church building, whereby the Catholics were given use of the chancel. In the following decade, nearly all residents of Ottersheim changed over to the Catholic faith. When Petrus Otto was named permanent Catholic pastor in 1695, 51 families had renounced the Calvinist faith and accepted the Catholic faith. So it was no surprise when the Catholics were awarded exclusive use of the church building by the Treaty of Ryswick in 1697. This ownership has remained undisputed since then.

No major construction or repairs to the Catholic Church in Ottersheim were performed during the second half of the 17th century. Presumably, there would have been no one who would have assumed the costs given the confused political situation at that time. The Electoral Palatinate, which by law would have been required to do so, had more or less given up the territory south of the Queich to France; and the French king needed his money for other purposes. So it is not surprising to us that a pastoral description from the year 1707 states, "The church is in total decline." It was 90 years old already and needed to be renovated from the ground up. The repairs needed at that time required 100 cubic meters of wood, 2 reams of slate stone, some 5,000 bricks, 4 malters of lime, 300 laths, and 5,000 nails. The carpenters received 50 gulden, 2 malters of grain, and 2 malters of spelt; the masons 24 gulden, 2 malters of grain, and 2 malters of spelt; the roofer got 90 gulden, 2 malters grain, and 2 malters spelt. A generation later under Pastor Uth, another renovation was conducted in 1740 for which 119 gulden were contributed from tithes.

Toward the end of the 18th century, the Catholic Church in Ottersheim essentially reached its present form. In 1707, the village counted 188 Catholics; however, by 1788 the number was already at 507. The House of God had to be extended to make room for the large number of churchgoers. The extension was begun in 1789 at the outbreak of the French Revolution. While maintaining the current design, the nave was extended to the west by two window pairs and finished off with a flat chancel shell. To this end, the cemetery was also enlarged to the west. The main entrance was moved into the tower at that time. In the eastern part of the nave, a wooden loft was moved in that was somewhat smaller than the current loft. The church expansion was also connected to the construction of a new sacristy on the north side of the nave.

The cost for the construction of tower, nave, and chancel at that time still had to be met by the tithe recipients. In 1788, the community had the clock installed by Elias Möllinger from Neustadt, and later they extended and renewed the churchyard wall. The staircase on the east side of the churchyard with the exposed gate pillars was also built at that time while the exit on the north side of the churchyard wall was built a hundred years later. Since the Church expansion in 1789, the Catholic Church in Ottersheim has experienced no more fundamental changes other than a new sacristy that was added in 1912 on the south side. During the 19th and 20th centuries, the upkeep and internal furnishing of the House of God remained an ongoing task of the Catholic community of which the following overview documents the most important measures.

1816:   Under Mayor Flory, the Catholic Church community receives a small bell (364 pfunds) from Frankenthal.

1821:   In Kaiserslautern, a second larger bell (614 pfunds) is procured. Apparently the old bells were carried off during the French Revolution and melted down

1842:   A new high altar with the likeness of Saint Martin is installed.

1853:   Two side altars are procured from voluntary donations.

1865:   New bells are purchased under Pastor Dotterweich. The three bronze bells are tuned to the notes G Flat, B Flat, and D Flat.

1868:   The church roof is replaced. The cost amounts to 3,000 gulden.

1874:   Since the "back-breaking" old benches are worthless, 44 oak pews are purchased by the Parish Community. Price: 992 gulden.

1877:   The church is painted, the high altar is restored, and side altars renewed. The church gets 14 Stations of the Cross. Plaster pillars are attached to the chancel shell. Over time, seven statues worth 2,000 marks are purchased from voluntary donations.

1880:   The church receives a new organ for 5,750 marks and a communion rail for 200 marks. Because the "inferior organ" is no good, it must be thoroughly overhauled already in 1881 by another organ builder. Cost: 250 marks.

1892:   Widow Knöll née Burck donates an oil lamp: the Eternal Light.

1896:   In the course of three years, Ottersheim citizens donate ten painted windows from Weißenrieder of Speyer. In total 2,870 marks are spent.

1901:   The tower is repaired and thereby the cross and rooster placed on it. Organ builder Poppe of Offenbach overhauls the organ.

1908:   From 1908 to 1912, the church is renovated from the ground up and painted by Fußhöller of Landau. Donations made by the community reached the considerable sum of 30,000 marks. The cost of the inside painting was 5,150 marks. Katharina Kopf donates a Lourdes Grotto in the tower.

1909: Widow Knöll née Burck donates a new high altar. Price: 3,800 marks. The two side altars are paid for by Valentin Seither VI. Price: 4,840 marks. The Mörlheim Parish gets the old altars.

1909: The loft is expanded. The organ has to be removed. It receives a new, pneumatic action organ by builder Poppe of Offenbach and it is mounted again in 1911.

1911: From 1911 to 1912, a new sacristy in Gothic Revival style is added to the south side of the church. Cost: about 5,000 marks.

1917: In order to obtain metal for war purposes, the large and small bronze bells as well as the large bell of the Protestant Church have to be surrendered. Only the middle bell is allowed to remain.

1924: From Bochum, three new steel bells are delivered. The bells were already paid in full for 66,560 marks in 1922. Because of the devaluation in 1923, the bells were bought for practically nothing. They are tuned to the tones D sharp, F sharp, G sharp. The bell set now consists of three steel and one bronze bell.

1925: The church receives electric light.

1931: Under Pastor Knöll, the church is plastered and the aisle is laid with limestone plates from Solnhofen.

1937: A nativity scene was set up.

1938: Organ builder Sattel of Speyer overhauls the organ from the ground up.

1946: The church receives a hot water heating system. Organ and bellows are moved. Artistic painter Heller from Mundenheim paints the church interior.

1947: The church gets new confessionals.

1954: The community has a new tower clock installed that is run by electricity. The old tower clock did its duty for better or worse for 165 years.

1955: The heirs of Philipp Benz donate a Madonna window in the church. Price: 1,000 deutschemarks

1957: Widow Berta Hilsendegen donates a new communion rail. Price: 935 deutschemarks. The chancery floor gets new tile. Price: 1,200 deutschemarks

1958: Lina Job donates a chalice. Price: 798 deutschemarks. The August Zwißler family donates a chasuble. Price: 820 deutschemarks

1959: Beams, slate, and belfry of the tower are completely replaced. The Diocesan Curia in Speyer gives 17,000 deutschemarks, the Rhineland-Palatinate government 13,000 deutschemarks.

1960: The former founders or their descendants have the church windows renewed. The church interior is painted. The pulpit is removed. A public address system is installed.

1961: The baptismal font is refurbished and placed in the tower. The church gets new pews, a lectern, and an electric heating system. The new high altar is dedicated by Bishop Doctor Isidor Markus Emanuel of Speyer.

1967: Consecration of the new organ that was built by Organ Master Paul Zimnol in Kaiserslautern. Diocesan Administrator Thiebes gives the keynote address. Cathedral organist Doerr demonstrates the successfully built instrument to the community. The new organ costs over 60,000 deutschemarks that was mainly raised through free-will donations from the community.

The Catholic Church in Ottersheim today was built in 1618 and had a predecessor that was built on the same spot. A remnant of the church seems to be the trough-shaped stone found in the rectory yard in 1966 that had been buried in the ground. It is probably the remains of a Romanesque baptismal font that was no longer needed and stood in the old church until the new Reformed Church was built in 1618. Presumably, it was used as a water reservoir in the rectory garden. In a competency book from the year 1605, it is stated that the old church was "pretty dilapidated." More than this about the old church has not been passed on. However, we can safely assume that this church stood on an artificial elevation with its spire towering over the half-timbered houses of the small village. There was most likely a predecessor to this church. The first church in Ottersheim was probably built well before the year 1000. As proof, one can refer to the records of Abbot Edelin of Weißenburg who names the church in Ottersheim as item 71 in his Possessions. The name of the church patron also suggests an old age. Saint Martin was the Merovingian national saint and was very popular among the Franks as church patron. Churches dedicated to Saint Martin are therefore usually very old churches, some of which were already built in the 6th, 7th, or 8th century. Stamer writes:

> "The fact that the church (of Ottersheim) does not have the Weißenburg patron indicates that this church came from foreign owners to the Saint Peter Monastery without changing its patron, which is usually an indication of venerable age."

Therefore, the possibility that the Ottersheim church already stood at the time of Charlemagne (768-814) should not be discarded.

The Franconian Knights who were located in Ottersheim could presumably have built the church. These Knights likely lived on the west side of the Deich where the Electoral Palatinate owned a feudal manor until the French Revolution in 1789, the so-called *Poppelmann Manor.* According to the custom of that time, the Knights would have built the church on their own property right next to the manor as a so-called *private church.* According to the will of the builder, the church was to be not only a House of God but also a defense site for protection against enemy attacks. Therefore, the church was built on an artificial hill that was surrounded by a wall. In case of enemy attacks, man and beast sought and found refuge in the cemetery. It is for good reason that in the Middle Ages the word *Freithof [Cemetery]* meant *protected* as much as *enclosed place.* The church with tower and nave was the last stronghold where residents could flee from the enemy. For this reason, it was equipped with thick and resilient walls. So in the Middle Ages the church was not only a place of worship but was also a stronghold for the protection of residents of the village.

Like other private churches, the Ottersheim church changed over in the course of time from private to monastic property. According to the writings of the Abbot Edelin, the Priory of Weißenburg owned a manor with house in Ottersheim, and in addition, a church with tithes to which belonged a Mansus (about 20 to 30 morgen of land). All these possessions of the monastery were already lost in 991 to Duke Otto of Worms, the grandson of Otto the Great. This property together with the church later went into the possession of the Palatine Counts. In the year 1311, Heinrich VII gave the patronage rights to the Eußerthal Monastery in Ottersheim. Bishop Emich of Speyer, with the consent of the Cathedral Chapter and the responsible Archdeacon, transferred the parish on 5 July 1314 to the Cistercians in Eußerthal, who from then on provided a secular priest to Ottersheim. For this, the Eußerthal Monastery received tithe rights in the parish. However, part of the proceeds had to be used for the construction and maintenance of the church. So we may assume that the predecessor of the Parish Church in Ottersheim of today was once built mainly at the expense of the Eußerthal Abbey. The church patron, Saint Martin, remained true to the House of God over the centuries. His name was not forgotten during the 130 years that the village belonged to the Reformed faith. Whether the present church was ever dedicated cannot be proven with certainty but it is not very likely that it was. A visitation protocol from 1701 notes the church had not yet been consecrated. The expansion of the church in 1789 would have provided an opportune occasion to make up for this omission. This was prevented by the turmoil of the French Revolution, during which not only the Pastor of Ottersheim but also the Bishop of Speyer were forced to flee. Since that time, nothing more was undertaken retroactively to consecrate the church.

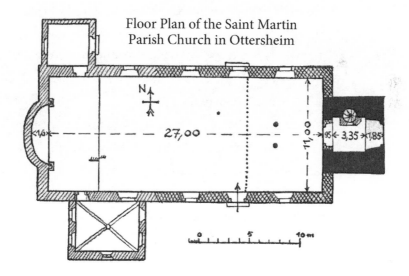

Floor Plan of the Saint Martin
Parish Church in Ottersheim

Saint Martin, Patron Saint of Ottersheim

During the reign of Emperor Constantine the Great (306-337), who in the year 313 officially recognized Christianity, Martin was born as the son of a high-ranking Roman soldier. Thanks to his ability, he rose in early years to the rank of officer's personal guardsman. He became acquainted with Christianity in Pavia where his father was from. He would have preferred to join the desert monks had he not been sent beforehand by the Emperor to Gaul, that is, present-day France. Martin was not only a conscientious soldier, but also a noble man who catered especially to the needs of the poor. Although he was not baptized, he observed always and everywhere the commandment to love your neighbor. As a 19-year-old officer on a wintry ride to Amiens in the year 335, he gave half of his cloak to a freezing beggar. According to tradition, in the night after he shared his cloak, Christ himself appeared to Martin wearing the other half and said to the angels who accompanied him:

"Martin, who is still a baptismal candidate, clothed me with this cloak."

Distinguished by God in this manner, the young officer decided to give up the military service and henceforth only serve God. He was baptized and two years later released as a soldier. Then he traveled to the Holy Bishop Hilarius in Poitiers (Tours) where he received the Minor Orders [was Ordained]. Later, he moved to Hungary, the home of his mother, and to Italy. He returned to Poitiers after five years. In the meantime the Holy Hilarius had died. Not far from the city, he founded the first cloister in the western world and led a hard life of penance there together with a few companions.

Martin was held in high esteem by the people. It was therefore not surprising that in the year 371 he was unanimously elected Bishop of Tours. Without changing his habits as monk, Martin submitted to the yoke imposed upon him. From then on, he moved back and forth across Gaul to spread the Christian faith and eradicate the rampant paganism. The trail of his life is marked by healing the sick and raising the dead. Also, his many enemies were not excluded from his love. Martin was held in especially high esteem by ordinary people, and he already enjoyed the reputation of sanctity at that time. When he died on 11 November 401, he was buried at Tours. As early as 472, his grave was overlooked by a basilica. This was the national shrine of the Franks.

Under the Merovingian royal family, who governed the Frankish Empire until 751, Saint Martin was honored as a national saint. In present-day France alone there are 3,360 churches dedicated to him. There existed as many Saint Martin churches in other countries. The Saint Martin churches in the Palatinate are, with very few exceptions, venerable houses of worship, even if the buildings themselves had to be renewed over time.

The Catholic Parish of Ottersheim

It is not known when the private church of the Knights of Ottersheim was converted to a parish church. But to all appearances, it must have existed before the year 1000. While a private church served more or less as a house of prayer, a parish church was equipped by the bishop after its consecration with the full rights of pastoral care. In the church, baptisms could take place, the Sacraments of Penance and Holy Communion provided, and Holy Mass could be read. In addition, the pastor had the right to bury the dead in the yard surrounding the church. All residents of the parish were required on Sundays and public holidays to visit their own parish church. At the service, those assembled were posed the question of whether someone from a foreign parish was present. He had to be removed and urged to return to his own parish. In the early Middle Ages, the pastor was responsible for the church building and the equipment. He was also responsible for the care of passing strangers.

The main source of income of a parish was the tithe. The large tithes were paid from grain, wheat, spelt, barley, and oats while all remaining agricultural products fell under the small tithes. The so-called *blood tithe* had to be paid from slaughtered animals. One third of the tithes went to the pastor, another third was to be used for the poor, and the final third was intended for the maintenance of the church building. In addition to the large and the small tithe, the parish benefice[70] was an important source of income for the pastor. In Ottersheim, this was about twenty morgen of fields and meadows that the pastor himself managed with the help of servants. The immovable assets of the parish, also called *Wittum,* were tithe-free. In addition, the pastor was allowed to use a part of the offering from Holy Mass for himself. Such offerings were ears of grain, grapes, oil, candles, incense, and the like.

The first definite documentation of the Ottersheim parish dates from the 14th century. In 1311, King Heinrich VII gave the patronage rights of Ottersheim to the Monastery of Eußerthal, and Bishop Emich of Speyer himself incorporated the church into the monastery in 1314. The latter was repeated again in 1327 when secular priest Konrad von Rodenberg was allocated as income: 30 malters of grain, the small tithe, half the vegetable tithe, double timber rights, and other similar items. The transfer of the rights of patronage to the Eußerthal Monastery was confirmed by Pope Boniface IX in 1403. It meant that from then on, the Abbey was owner of the Ottersheim parish with all rights and obligations. Eußerthal, which already had a sizable monastery in Ottersheim with about 100 morgen of land, commissioned a secular priest with the ministry in the Ottersheim parish. The Monastery of Eußerthal was required to build and maintain the house this priest lived in. The parsonage stood opposite the church on the property to the east of the Neuweg.

---

[70] A *benefice* was the products and revenue generated from the properties owned by the parish.

Because the Eußerthal Abbey was owner of the Ottersheim parish and not the secular priest, the tithes had to be delivered to the monastery. The extent to which donations from the villagers were handed directly to the currently assigned secular priest was left to the discretion of the abbey. Generally, it was customary that the priests received only a portion of what the Abbey of Eußerthal collected each year.

In the Middle Ages, the Ottersheim parish belonged to the Herxheim church district. In addition, the Ottersheim parish also had an Early Mass Reader. Testimony to this is contained in the parish registers of the Diocese of Speyer by Bishop Matthias Rammung (1464-1478). The Early Mass Reader's benefice was for priests whose holder was required to celebrate certain Masses early in the morning on weekdays before people went to work. The benefice for Early Mass Reading in Ottersheim consisted of approximately 12 morgen of fields and meadows. It was donated by residents of the village with the instruction that certain Masses were to be read for the peace of their souls. The Early Mass Reader benefice was not under the control of the parish priest. The village priest of the Middle Ages had usually enjoyed only a low level of education. They spent most of their time during the week in the field and in the rectory garden. During a visit by Elector Otto Heinrich in 1556, it was found that the Ottersheim priest was married. It therefore caused no stir when this pastor was removed from office and replaced by a Lutheran minister at the beginning of the Reformation.

There was no Catholic parish in Ottersheim from 1556 to 1684. The villagers confessed without exception to the Lutheran or Reformed faith during this time, as commanded by the Elector of Heidelberg. Only during the 30 Years War, when the Catholic Austrians and Bavarians occupied the District Office in Germersheim for several years, was the Catholic religion reintroduced. But during the second half of the war, Ottersheim had neither a Catholic nor a Protestant pastor. This only changed when the previous state was restored in 1650 according to the peace treaties of Münster and Osnabrück. Ottersheim again received a Reformed pastor, but he lived in Offenbach however. There were no Catholics among the 40 households in Ottersheim during 1671. Thirty-six families were Reformed and four were Lutheran.

The occupation of the southern Palatinate by soldiers of Louis XIV in 1680, and the assumption of management by the French government was of profound importance for the development of ecclesiastical affairs in the District Office of Germersheim. As is well known, the Sun King acted on the same principle as the Elector of Heidelberg before. The religion of the ruling house was also the dictated religion of the country's inhabitants. However, a government order was no longer enough in those days. The people had to be won over with temptation and force, and the commissioners of Louis XIV were not lacking in either. In the years 1683 and 1684, the Jesuits conducted missions in the villages of the occupied territories. The initial focus of the mission work was in Klingenmünster but moved in April 1684 to Bellheim, a village that not only "exceeded the other villages in importance, but also in its stubborn adherence to the Calvinistic doctrine." From this action, Catholicism was probably once again propagated to Ottersheim. Already in 1684, the chancery of the church was granted to the Catholics; after the Ryswick Peace of 1697, they were awarded the entire church for their sole use. In addition to the missionary work of the Jesuits, Louis XIV sought to push forward the re-Catholicization of the population through economic benefits. All who had become Catholic by 1 January 1683 would not have to pay taxes for three years. In addition, they were freed from any requirement to house soldiers or to pay for their upkeep. By a decree from 5 June 1686, all Reformed pastors were finally expelled from the country with the exception of Reformed Inspector Reinach of Impflingen. So it is not surprising that in the course of a few years all the villages south of the Queich were again Catholic. A visitation protocol from 1701 reported that 51 families of Ottersheim had renounced Calvinism and had returned to the Catholic Church. With somewhat more than 200 residents, this meant that the whole population became Catholic. This is also confirmed by a protocol from the year 1699 that states of Ottersheim, "All the subjects are Catholic." But it must not be denied that a fifth of the population was only Catholic in appearances while their heart continued to belong to the Reformed faith.

After the Peace of Ryswick in 1697, when the French returned the District of Germersheim to the Palatine Electors, the people hoped to be allowed to profess their Reformed beliefs openly again. However, they had to learn that Catholic Elector Johann Wilhelm (1690-1716) showed little sympathy for their cause. It was not until the Religion Declaration of 21 November 1705 that the residents received the right to decide freely among the Catholic, Reformed, or Lutheran faiths. As a result, about 40 residents of Ottersheim identified themselves with the Reformed Church while approximately 180 residents of the village remained Catholic.

After re-Catholicization of the villages south of the Queich in the years 1683-1684, it was difficult to provide Catholic clergy for the individual parishes. According to a visitation report from 1699, it must be concluded that the parishes of Ottersheim and Knittelsheim were served provisionally by the Jesuits and later by Reverend Franz Gundermann from Bellheim. Gundermann was a papal missionary and a native of Keffershausen in the Region of Eichsfeld. He was Pastor at Bellheim from 1685 to 1700 where he steadfastly persevered in spite of many persecutions. For Ottersheim and Knittelsheim, a dedicated priest named Petrus Otto from the Archdiocese of Trier was assigned in 1695, but he had not yet taken over the parish by 1699 for unknown reasons. Holder of the Ottersheim parish at that time was Pastor Reinhard Geist who was replaced around 1700 by Johann Jäger from the seminary in Würzburg. When Jäger died already in 1701, the parish was transferred to the existing Pastor of Mörzheim, Georg Weißhaupt, who remained in Ottersheim for 16 years.

As before the Reformation, the Ottersheim parish again belonged to the Church District of Herxheim. From a parish description of the year 1707, it can be seen that Pastor Weißhaupt drew the same income as his Reformed predecessor. The parish property consisted of 20 morgen of fields and meadows. From the large and small tithes, he could claim a fourth, plus a fuder of wine from the Monastery of Eußerthal. He received 21 gulden from the collections in Zeiskam and 12 gulden from the Eußerthal manor. As Pastor of Knittelsheim with 121 Catholics, he also drew the revenues collected from the parish property, which amounted to about 40 morgen of land.

A visitation report from the year 1718 is revealing in that the number of Catholic families in Ottersheim is indicated to be 41. The decrease is likely due to the fact that after the Religion Declaration of 1705, about 10 families from Ottersheim reassumed the Reformed faith while 7 or 8 from Knittelsheim did also. It is also noted in the report that the Knittelsheim families were dissatisfied because the Sunday services were held there only once every three weeks. These complaints are repeated again and again in later decades. These were only silenced when Knittelsheim again received its own pastor. We owe a thorough description of the Catholic parish from the year 1747 to Catholic priest Georg Uth who was transferred from Mörlheim to Ottersheim in 1734. This report was almost literally transcribed nearly 100 years later to the parish memorial book by Pastor Pfeiffer. In the description, among other things is reported a dispute that arose over the rectory and the schoolhouse. The community argued that the rectory on the Neuweg across from the church was the actual school building and that it should be used again for that purpose. The opinion was correct insofar as the rectory building was in fact used as a schoolhouse before and after the 30 Years War, because the Reformed pastors lived for the most part elsewhere. However, the population had overlooked that this building was always the Catholic rectory before 1556 and had been built and maintained by the Eußerthal Monastery.

Ottersheim received a chaplain for the first time in 1733; he was to care mainly for the Knittelsheim parish. The motivation came from the Knittelsheim Catholics who brought their request to the responsible Diocese through their Mayor Daniel Schott and lawyer (adjunct) Boos. For their justification, they pointed out that they did not have a preacher in Knittelsheim every Sunday, and Christian doctrine was taught only every three weeks. Moreover, the village had 40 Catholic families, a rectory with a beautiful pastoral garden, and pastoral property consisting of 36 morgen of fields and 5 morgen of meadows. The Knittelsheim Catholics would prefer to have their own pastor. To fulfill their wishes at least partially, Prince Bishop Damian in Bruchsal decreed that henceforth a chaplain was to be assigned to the Pastor of Ottersheim in order to better support the parish in Knittelsheim. Fifty years later, Elector Karl Theodor finally ordered the separation of the two parishes of Ottersheim and Knittelsheim on 18 March 1785. He transferred Georg Günther to Ottersheim, who was until now Professor at the Electoral Gymnasium (High school) in Mannheim, and he transferred Michael Schwoll to Knittelsheim, who was Mentor of Philosophy at the Electoral Seminary in Heidelberg.

Under Pastor Georg Günther and shortly before the outbreak of the French Revolution, the church was expanded to the west by two pairs of windows and by a sacristy at the northwest corner. The congregation had the churchyard wall updated and installed a clock in the tower. No sooner was the work completed in 1789 when the land left of the Rhine was flooded with revolutionary armies. Pastor Georg Günther had to flee in January 1794.

He stayed in Heidelberg until September 1796. Unfortunately, he left no information about what happened to the church during this time. However, we know the Board of the District of Weißenburg issued a decree to all the communities on 8 January 1794 ordering the systematic looting of the churches by their own commissioners. Everything had been confiscated from the churches within a very short time that was made of gold, silver, copper, tin, lead, or iron. The vestments also were not to be spared. About Ottersheim, it is known that the two bells were taken away by the revolutionaries. For the twenty months that Ottersheim was without a pastor, the dying often had no spiritual solace; and during that time, no fewer than 90 people were affected by plague, almost half having been swept away. Newborns were baptized by either a teacher or the midwife, and the church marriages were held partly in Bellheim and partly in Germersheim.

In the Peace of Lunéville in 1801, when the left bank of the Rhine went to France, it also had a profound impact on the church situation in these areas. Under the Concordat that Napoleon signed with the Holy See the same year, the majority of the present-day Palatinate was annexed to the Diocese of Mainz under the leadership of Bishop Josef Ludwig Colmar of Strasbourg. Because Ottersheim belonged to the Canton of Germersheim, like the other parishes of the Canton it was considered to be a so-called branch or auxiliary parish reporting more or less to the Canton priest in Germersheim. The pastor had no claim to a State salary. In the meantime, his income was limited to what the parish property yielded because the tithe system had been abolished. This new situation may have prompted the previous Pastor of Ottersheim, Georg Günther, to transfer to Heidelberg in 1802 as City Church Administrator where he had resided for some time already during the Revolution years. In the same year, the previous Pastor of the Knittelsheim parish, Michael Schwoll, received the parish in Ottersheim while former Pastor Josef Schöpf was assigned to the parish in Knittelsheim. At first, Pastor Schwoll had to live on the income that the parish properties yielded. Ottersheim had not yet been added to the list of those parishes that were entitled to a State salary of 500 francs until 1807. However, any proceeds of church property were subtracted from this salary. After the economic conditions had for the most part normalized under this rule, it seems odd that Pastor Schwoll gave up the parish of Ottersheim already in 1809 and went to Bechtheim in Hesse. This had a strange reason that at the same time sheds light on the characteristic religious attitude of the population and the government at the time. Specifically, in 1809 three women in Ottersheim and Bellheim simultaneously became ill. Quickly the rumor spread that the illness of these women was not of a natural kind, and the people demanded that the pastors of Ottersheim and Knittelsheim should exorcise the three patients. Without the examination and approval of their superiors in the government, both pastors followed the wishes of the people. This caused a large public outcry and a complaint at the prefecture. Upon hearing of this, the responsible French Minister of Culture ordered that the pastors of Ottersheim and Bellheim should be exiled. The punishment was mitigated and converted to transfers thanks only to the personal intervention of Emperor Napoleon. Pastor Wengler of Bellheim was sent to Ramberg and Schwoll of Ottersheim to Bechtheim in Hesse. The vacant pastorate in Ottersheim was then given to the previous Pastor of Harthausen, Franz Christoph Günther.

Pastor Günther was born in Bruchsal in 1770 and was the son of a court sculptor. He became Pastor at Harthausen in 1801 and pastor of Ottersheim in 1809. Already after 5 years he was called to Speyer as Canton pastor in 1814 where he first held the office of an Episcopal Pro-vicar, and from 1821 on he held a leading position in the newly established Diocese of Speyer. Before the election of Bishop Georg Matthäus of Chandelle, Vicar Günther was Administrator of the new diocese. He died in 1848 as Cathedral Capitular [Diocesan Administrator] in Speyer; he was buried in the new cemetery. Today his grave is located in the Cathedral Chapter Cemetery of Saint Bernard Church in Speyer. His whole life long, Günther did not forget his former parish. In his will, he donated to the poor of the town a capital of 1,000 gulden from which the interest was to benefit the village poor of Catholic faith. The charity foundation was intended primarily for the maintenance of the needy when ill, for the purchase of clothes for poor first communicants, and for extraordinary costs for births of children of poor parents. Not until the inflation of our century was the capital of Günther's charity foundation exhausted.

When Pastor Franz Christoph Günther went to Speyer in September 1814, the Ottersheim parish remained vacant until June 1817. The ministry was carried out temporarily by Dean Metz of Offenbach and by Chaplain Schaub of Bellheim until Pastor Märdian took over the Ottersheim parish in 1817. Meanwhile, the Palatinate had been awarded to the Kingdom of Bavaria. In 1818, the newly established Diocese of Speyer received its first bishop in Georg Matthäus of Chandelle; he did not take his office until 1822 however. Regulation of Church affairs in the Palatinate was now directed by the Concordat that the Bavarian government had signed with the Papal Court in 1817. Ottersheim, which had already belonged to the Church District of Germersheim under French rule, remained under the jurisdiction of Germersheim. Like the other parishes of smaller communities in the area on the left side of the Rhine, the Pastor of Ottersheim was also entitled to a State salary of 500 francs or 232 gulden, whereby the income from the parish property and other income from baptisms, weddings, and funerals were subtracted from that sum.

Of Reverend Märdian (1817-1839), we are told that he, as the pastor of Ottersheim in 1835, received free lodging and a State salary of 129 gulden and 56 kreutzers. The proceeds of the church property were estimated at 300 gulden and 51 kreutzers. Information on the income of his successor, Johannes Pfeiffer (1839-1859), is provided by the parish memorial book. As Pastor of Ottersheim, he moved into free housing in 1849 with 129 gulden and 56 kreutzers of State salary, whereby the living quarters were estimated at 37 gulden and 48 kreutzers. The proceeds from the parish property were figured at 242 gulden and 9 kreutzers, and he was owed 19 gulden and 34 kreutzers from the coffers of the church. In addition to this income was that from the Knittelsheim parish that was of a similar in amount. The net income totaled 792 gulden and 56 kreutzers. Father Pfeiffer performed an outstanding service in 1856 when he started a parish memorial book that included earlier events taken from historical records. He relied particularly on the "in-depth description of the Ottersheim parish" by Pastor Uth from the year 1747.

In addition to the ministry, especially dear to the hearts of the Ottersheim pastors was the decoration of the church in the second half of the 19th century and at the beginning of the 20th century. Among other things, new bells and a new organ were purchased, new altars and statues were erected, and the church interior was painted in those years. A memorable event of that time was the First Mass celebration of a new priest, Otto Steegmüller, on 21 August 1892. The church was filled to over capacity by visitors near and far, because he was the first priest in living memory that came from the Ottersheim parish.

At the turn of the century, the number of Ottersheim Catholics had grown to 810 souls. Because the Knittelsheim parish also had to be supported, Ottersheim received a chaplain in 1898 who was assigned mainly to Knittelsheim. Since 1910, the work had to be managed again by the current pastor alone. This was not always easy. From Pastor Michael Schmitt (1917-1929), we know that he was driven every Sunday and Holyday to Knittelsheim for services. Otherwise, he would have hardly been able to read Mass in the morning at both places and hold the usual extensive sermon.

Hardly had Pastor Schmitt taken over the parish in 1917 when the order came from the top War Ministry to deliver two of the three bronze bells. On 5 July 1917, the smallest was taken down from the church tower by Master Mason Valentin Winkelblech together with Peter Glatz, and the next day the largest bell. Also, the next day they brought with them to the collection point in Germersheim the larger bell of the Protestant Church. The grief of the community was so great that some people during the night of the 5th and 6th secretly dragged the smaller bell in the direction toward Offenbach and buried it in a field. There the bell was discovered by the policeman and returned. The Catholic religious community received 3,865 marks as compensation for the two bells.

After World War I, the church administration decided in 1921 to have three steel bells forged in Bochum. The contract with the Bochum Association of Mining and Steel Casting was signed in December with a negotiated price of 33,280 marks that was paid immediately. To accommodate for the progressive inflation, the same amount was paid again in 1922. The bells could not be delivered until 1924 because of the occupation of the

Ruhr by the French and the associated passive resistance that had paralyzed the railway traffic on the left of the Rhine. The bells arrived at the Bellheim station on 7 January 1924 where they were met with decorated floats, driven to Ottersheim, and accompanied by a solemn procession to the church. The bells were dedicated by Bishop Doctor Ludwig Sebastian with great participation of the entire population on the following Sunday. They were rung for the first time on Wednesday the 16th of January 1924. The old bronze bell that remained hanging in the tower was to be used in the future only at baptisms and funerals of children. Later, this so-called *children's baptismal bell* was given to the Catholic Cultural Center in Weingarten after completion of the new church building in 1950. There it faithfully performed its duty until 1954 when the Weingarten Catholic community was able to purchase a new set of bells. At the initiative of Alois Kröper, whose wife comes from Böbingen, the children's baptismal bell then went to Böbingen where it rings the small Catholic community to prayer and service to this day, and together with the bells of the Protestant Church accompanies the dead of both faiths on their way to the cemetery.

In 1929, Pastor Michael Schmitt took over the small parish at Schweighofen. To relieve his burden, Ottersheim received for the first time in 29-year-old Cathedral Chaplain Jakob Knöll, a young pastor who went to work with aptitude and enthusiasm. Of him, Spiritual Adviser Otto Steegmüller writes in the parish memorial book:

> *"With Pastor Knöll the old church has been replaced by the young one. Schedules and daily happenings were changed. Schott became the new Missal for old and young, the Salve Regina provided its wealth of songs and prayers. The old devotions were shaped into new ones in a colorful exchange. So all had to work and think together, there was no boredom and there was no time for babble. On Sunday afternoon, it was no longer Christian doctrine, traditional devotions, and rosary (with continuous repitition!), instead Christian peoples' doctrine with ten minutes devotion with a full Church."*

The renewal of life within the church found its complement in the renovation work at the church, organ, and cemetery. Unfortunately, the political situation after Hitler took power in 1933 was not likely to support and promote religious renewal. Quite the contrary! Hitler and his comrades wanted to systematically limit the Catholic lifestyle and let it gradually die off. Catholic youth were only allowed to be active within the church walls. Christian symbols, Christian prayers, and Christian faith were banned from public schools. In the community, the non-Catholics and non-baptized rather than practicing Catholics set the tone. Even the pastor's sermons were monitored. The skill with which Pastor Knöll confronted the enemies of faith was admirable. Without mentioning any names, he always knew how to express himself so that every listener knew what was meant. In this way, he provided the spies no basis for intervention. When Pastor Knöll went to Landau as city pastor in 1939, he left behind a community that was set fast in their faith and held a high level of skepticism against National Socialism. The ideology of the Third Reich was consciously rejected by most. This was demonstrated clearly in the behavior of the

Ottersheim Catholics towards the French prisoners of war. Also, after 1933 the Jewish merchants went freely in and out of the farmhouses until they were deported to Lorraine or to the occupied territories of western Poland at the order of Gau leader Bürckel. The French prisoners of war, who were employed as workers in agriculture, were secretly provided with food in spite of the stringent ban, or they were allowed to eat at the farmers' own table.

What Pastor Knöll had begun in the way of liturgical renewal, his successor Pastor Funk (1939-1950) actively continued. During the difficult years of the Second World War, where the fight at the front and at home exacted many victims, he was at the side of the stricken families with spiritual solace. When the guns finally fell silent in 1945, in spite of hardship and misery, a sigh of relief went through the Catholic population of the community. At last, one could again speak what one thought and felt and what one held to be true or false. Without hindrances, religious life was free to develop. The services that had always been well visited were overcrowded, and anything that had legs and could walk participated in the processions. Although there was no lack of other worries, is not the religious attitude of the villagers significant in that just a year after the war ended, the restoration of the church began? Even though prosperity was increasing over time, the initial enthusiasm declined slightly. Ottersheim is still one of the communities where church life plays a decisive role in the thoughts and actions of the population. Though the "bears" sometimes growl, they still have a good heart that is not closed to any need. Hardly anyone stands aside for charitable collections although few are particularly richly blessed with earthly goods. As Pastor Scherübl began with the construction of the new parsonage in 1959, the community collected not only a hefty sum in voluntary donations but also laid proficient hand to the excavation of the basement and the construction of the house. It was similar in the construction of the kindergarten in 1963. Ottersheim is still one of the Catholic communities where an essential part of public and private life centers on religion. Few people miss Sunday Mass without good cause and other church events generally have good attendance. That their active participation in church life is not based only on habit was shown during the years of the Third Reich when personal decisions had to be made. Then as now, the majority of the villagers acted purposely according to the Bible verse: *We must obey God rather than men.*

The Catholic Priests of Ottersheim

1311-1556: Secular priests who were sent from the Provost in Eußerthal to the Ottersheim parish.

1327: In a document, the Priest *Konrad of Rodenberg* is listed as Pastor of Ottersheim.

1357: On 29 March 1357, *Johann - Pastor of Ottersheim* sells freely owned property to the Monastery of Eußerthal.

1556-1684: The villagers are committed to the Lutheran or Reformed faith.

1695-1699: *Petrus Otto* is the designated Pastor of Ottersheim and Knittelsheim.

1699-1700: *Reinhard Geist*

1700-1701: *Johann Jäger from the Seminary of Würzburg:* Jäger belonged to an association of clergy who lived together in a community. He died in 1701.

1701-1717: *Georg Weißhaupt:* He was previously Pastor of Mörzheim.

1717-1728: *Jakob Macke from the Seminary in Mainz:* He was born in Duderstadt / Eichsfeld in 1679 and died in Ottersheim. His gravestone originally lay in front of the high altar. Now it is located at the south side of the tower where it was placed in 1909.

1728-1732: *Josef Marianus Cäsar:* He was later transferred as Pastor to Hambach.

1732-1734: *Johann Stefan Fahlbusch from the Seminary in Mainz:* He was born in 1682 in Wolbrandshausen / Eichsfeld. He came from Oberlustadt to Ottersheim where he died in 1743. Fahlbusch was buried in the church.

1734-1748: *Georg Uth from the Seminary of Fulda:* He was born in Lower Franconia in 1705 and died in 1748 in Ottersheim. From 1729 to 1734, he was pastor in Mörlheim. Under Pastor Uth, the Crucifixion scene was erected in the old cemetery

1748-1778: *Heinrich Altzen from the Seminary of Fulda:* He was born in Limburg an der Lahn in 1709 and died in 1782. He resigned in 1778 in favor of his nephew Hartmann.

1778-1785: *Heinrich Josef Hartmann:* The "trained in science, excellent but ailing" pastor died already at the age of 43 years and was buried at the foot of the high altar in Ottersheim. He was born in 1743 at Limburg an der Lahn.

1785-1802 *Georg Günther:* Prior to his appointment as pastor of Ottersheim, he was a professor at the Electoral High School (Gymnasium) in Mannheim. In 1802, he was transferred to Heidelberg as a city Dean. In the wake of the French Revolution, he had to flee and was located at Heidelberg from January 1794 to September 1796. He died in 1819.

1802-1809: *Michael Schwoll:* He was Mentor of Philosophy at the Electoral Seminary in Heidelberg until 1785. Then he applied for the newly established parish at Knittelsheim, which he received in 1785. He was transferred to Ottersheim in 1802. From there he went to Bechtheim in Hesse in 1809.

1809-1814: *Franz Christoph Günther from the Seminary in Bruchsal:* He was born in 1770 as son of a court sculptor in Bruchsal where he attended high school. In 1801, he became Pastor at Harthausen and came from there to Ottersheim in 1809. The zealous priest went as Pro-vicar and Canton Pastor to Speyer in 1814. As Apostolic Vicar, he was Administrator of the new Diocese of Speyer from 1821 until the election of Bishop Georg Matthäus von Chandelle. He died in 1848 as Cathedral Capitular [Diocesan Administrator]. He was buried in the new cemetery at Speyer. Günther wrote "Kurze Geschichte der Bischöfe zu Speyer" [A Short History of the Bishops of Speyer]. In his will, he remembered his former parishioners in Ottersheim with a charity foundation in the amount of 1,000 gulden.

1814-1817: The parish is vacant. Assistant Chaplain *Dean Metz* of Offenbach and Chaplain *Schaub* of Bellheim are assigned.

1817-1839: *Rudolf Märdian from the Seminary in Bruchsal:* He was born in Knittelsheim in 1762. He came to Ottersheim from Freinsheim where he died in 1839. He was buried in the new cemetery, which he had personally dedicated in 1823.

1839-1859: *Johannes Pfeiffer:* He was born in 1782 in Brockscheid near Trier and was ordained in 1811 at Metz. Pfeiffer came from Saint Ingbert to Ottersheim where he died in 1859. He began the parish memorial book in 1856.

1859-1863: *Johann Georg Ullrich:* He was born in 1806 in Dammheim / Lower Franconia and was ordained at Speyer in 1831. He died in 1863 from injuries received in an accident while riding in a chaise.

1863-1875: *Matthäus Dotterweich:* He was born in 1806 in Strullendorf near Bamberg and was ordained in 1835. He was pastor in Godramstein prior to his transfer to Ottersheim where he died in 1875.

1875-1889: *Wilhelm Schecher:* He was born in 1830 at Lohr in Lower Franconia and was ordained at Speyer in 1855. He died in 1900 as Pastor of Roschbach.

1889-1896: *Sebastian Ettmüller:* He was born in 1838 in Rödersheim and was ordained at Speyer in 1863. Ettmüller died at Ottersheim in 1896.

1897-1902: *Friedrich Höffler:* He was born in 1840 in Hochstein and was ordained as was Ettmüller at Speyer in 1863. Previously he was Pastor in Fehrbach and Kandel. He died in 1905 as Pastor of Flemlingen.

1903-1909:   *Johann Rudolf Schwarz:* He was born in 1860 in Niederwürzbach / Saarland and ordained in 1884 at Speyer. Schwarz died in 1909 and was buried in the new cemetery at Ottersheim

1910-1916:   *Heinrich Theobald Eckel:* He was born in 1863 in Edesheim and was ordained in 1888 at Speyer. Previously he was pastor in Nünschweiler and Oberhochstadt. He died in 1916; he was buried in Ottersheim.

1917-1929:   *Michael Schmitt:* He was born in 1865 and was ordained in 1890 at Speyer. Previously he was pastor in Wiesbach and Contwig. In 1929, he went to Schweighofen where he died in 1939.

1929-1939:   *Jakob Knöll:* He was born in 1900 in Neustadt an der Weinstraße and ordained in 1923 at Speyer where he was a Cathedral Chaplain. In 1939, he was transferred to Landau as pastor. There he became the victim of a bomb attack in 1945. His former parishioners from Ottersheim dug him from the rubble of the rectory and buried him in the old Ottersheim cemetery south of the church.

1939-1950:   *Karl Funk:* He was born in 1904 in Hochdorf and in 1929 was ordained at Speyer. Prior to his transfer to Ottersheim, he was pastor in Großkarlbach. In 1950, he went to Münchweiler on the Rodalb, and he took over the parish of Saint Joseph at Speyer in 1955.

1950-1959:   *Bernhard Kern:* He was born at Niederwasser in the Black Forest during 1901 and was ordained in 1927. In 1933, he became Pastor in Stetten and from there came to Ottersheim. After his departure in 1959, he took a job as a curate in Erfenbach near Kaiserslautern.

1959 —   *Josef Scherübl:* He is born in 1907 in Zweibrücken was ordained at Speyer in 1932. Before his transfer to Ottersheim, he was Pastor of Hermersberg for nine years. For the construction of the new rectory and kindergarten, he was the driving force.

Chaplains in Ottersheim

The two independent parishes in Ottersheim and Knittelsheim were served by a single pastor after re-Catholicization of the communities south of the Queich in the Palatinate. At the insistence of the Knittelsheim Catholics, the bishop decreed that Knittelsheim would get no pastor, but at least Ottersheim would get a chaplain who was mainly to serve Knittelsheim. These chaplains were:

       1733:   Johann Peter Karl Bettendorf
1733-1740:   Johann Nikolaus Becker: Born in Duderstadt / Eichsfeld.
       1740:   Johann Rhode: Born in Scheckendorf: Ordained at Fulda.
1741-1743:   Lorenz Faber from Sondermann, Würzburg diocese: Ordained at Fulda. He died from consumption in 1743; he was buried in the church.
1743-1744:   Kaspar Schmitt

1744:	Johann Adam Schüßler of Fulda
1744-1746:	Johann Mörchen from Hallenberg, Diocese of Cologne: Ordained at Fulda.
1746-1748:	Adam Folles: Born in Fulda
1749-1752:	Franz Eberhard Peez
1752-1753:	Anton Maierhöfer
1753-1754:	Martin Hausmann
1755-1756:	Johann Mollié
1756-1763:	Wilhelm Wittmer
1764-1769:	Johann Philipp Becker
1770-1774:	Johann Christoph Behren
1774-1775:	Klemens Bauer
1775-1780:	Wilhelm Diebold
1780-1785:	Nikolaus Walger

Knittelsheim received a pastor for the first time on 18 March 1785, Michael Schwoll from the Electoral Seminary in Heidelberg. From 1802 to 1809, his successor was Pastor Marcellinus Josef Schoepp. Then Knittelsheim was again cared for by the priest in Ottersheim. Only toward the end of the century was a chaplain again sent to Ottersheim.

1898-1899:	Josef Löffel
1899:	Heinrich Kästel
1907-1908:	Karl Klein
1908:	Otto Abel
1908-1909:	Johann August Hartard
1909:	Eduard Weigel

Thorough Description of the Ottersheim Parish in 1747

As taken from the present state and in part from existing documents from the then current Pastor,

Johann Georg Uth

Signed by the mayor and by a court person, in the year of 1747.

1. The religions

Ottersheim is a village of the Electoral Palatinate. It belongs to the Fautei (Bailiwick) of Germersheim and is located in the District Office of Germersheim.

In this village there are three religions that are recognized in the Roman (German) Empire: Catholics, Reformed, and Lutherans. Jews have not been tolerated in Ottersheim to date.

a) The Catholics are the most numerous. They own the parish and the Mother Church as their property. The Catholic priest has his residence here.

b) The Reformed come together in a former barn that they have prepared as a church. They are served by the Reformed Pastor from Bellheim.

c) The Lutherans do not have a meeting place of their own. They go on Sundays and on their prayer days to Offenbach, Bellheim, Zeiskam, and elsewhere. In death cases, they are served by the Lutheran Pastor of Germersheim. (By the way, in 1749 four Ottersheim residents were Lutheran.)

2. The parish church

The parish church was built as a Reformed Church completely new during the time of the Elector Karl Ludwig (born 1618) to his glorious memory. Around 1685, during the time of the War of the Reunions, it was made available by the French Crown to the Catholics. The Palatinate Church Division also gave it to the Catholics and it has remained theirs ever since. The church is consecrated to Bishop Saint Martin but the year of consecration is not known. It has three altars.

The community has to purchase and maintain the bells, the clock, and the churchyard wall.

The construction and maintenance of the choir, the nave, and the tower is the joint responsibility of the Electoral Court Chamber, the Provost of Eußerthal, the Monastery of Haimbach, the Priory of Hördt, and the community of Ottersheim according to their share of the tithes.

Vestments and other items for worship are the responsibility of Catholic Spiritual Goods Administration, because they confiscated all church property and the income from the Early Mass fund and have kept these to this day.

The cemetery is used by Catholics, Protestants, and Lutherans together.

The church bells consist of two bells, one of which, particularly the largest, belongs to the Catholics. The second bell is the property of the community and may also be rung by the Reformed and Lutherans. However, at funerals for the Reformed and Lutherans, the Catholic teacher was required to ring the bells. For a "large corpse," he is entitled to 30 kreutzers, at the funeral of a child 15 kreutzers.

3. Local church celebrations

Ottersheim has no special religious festivals except the church dedication festival that is celebrated annually on the Sunday after the feast of Saint Martin.

4. The processions

On Saint Mark's Day (25 April), there is a Procession that goes to the fruit fields. The parishioners from Offenbach, Knittelsheim, and Bellheim go in procession to Ottersheim on Monday in the Week of the Cross (the week before Ascension Day).

Tuesday during the Week-of-the-Cross, the Ottersheim parishioners go in Procession to Offenbach, and on Wednesday, they go to Bellheim.

On Ascension Day, the Ottersheim parishioners "Proceed" to Knittelsheim.

At Corpus Christi, the Blessed Sacrament is carried through the village.

At Four Altars, the four Gospels are sung. The Procession participants receive the Blessing during the celebration.

5. The parish, its income, and rights

The pastor is entitled to a third of the large and the small tithes in addition to the existing parish properties. Moreover, a third each of the blood and lamb tithes.

Since time immemorial, the pastor has received a tree for firewood from the forests of the two communities, Ottersheim and Knittelsheim. The two communities do not want to provide a tree any longer but will give the pastor double timber and fishing rights instead. Of the other common rights, the pastor is entitled to a "double portion."

6. Description of land assets comprising the parish properties:

1 morgen	in the Mittelsand
10-3/4 morgen	in the Oberfeld
8 morgen	in the Niederfeld
1/4 morgen	in the Viehweide meadows

7. The tithes

The large and the small tithes are each divided into 12 parts. From these is received:

The Palatinate Court Chamber:	6 parts
The Ottersheim parish via the Monastery of Eußerthal:	4 parts
The Monastery at Haimbach:	1 part
The Provost of Hördt and the community:	1 part

The large tithes include grain, wheat, spelt, barley, and oats. All other plants belong to the small tithes: wine, beets, cabbage, hay, flax, hemp, lambs, geese, piglets, poppy, canola, camelina (false flax), onion and onion seeds, peas, lentils, peas, corn, ground berry (potatoes), millet, tobacco, and so on. The tithe order is as follows:

For the large tithes, the tenth sheaf [bundle] is left lying on the field. However, if the piece of land is so small that it only yields 6, 7, or 8 sheaves, one sheaf must also remain

179

lying on the field. For the small tithes of hay, flax, hemp, poppy, camelina, millet, and tobacco, a tenth or the tenth "Bert"[71] (bundle) is separated out. So is also the process with peas, lentils, vetch, and corn (maize). Beets, potatoes, and onions are measured by the root. The wine tithe is paid by separating out each tenth basket. The blood tithe is paid with money. To be paid are 3 pfennigs for a dairy calf, 4 pfennigs for a pig, 2 pfennigs for a suckling pig, 2 pfennigs for a lamb, and 1 pfennig for a young goose.

The obligations of the tithe recipients

The respective Provost of Eußerthal has the obligation to build and maintain the rectory along with other relative equipment, including barn and stables. In accordance with this obligation, he built a new barn and associated stables in 1732.

8. The church patronage

The right of patronage belongs indisputably to the Elector of the Palatinate.

9. The present-day parish

The current Pastor is Johann Georg Uth, born at Fulda in 1705. There he was also accepted into the Papal Seminary in 1727. A year later, he became a chaplain in Eschbach. He took over the Mörlheim parish in 1729 and the parish of Ottersheim in 1734. He now stands in his 19th year of services to the Diocese of Speyer.

10. The parish property

Some in the local community believe and assert that the actual parish property was lost in bad times of the past. The place where the priest lives now was originally the community school property and this condition should rightfully again be established.

The current contentious parish property lies opposite the church and the cemetery. It borders on the common road in the front, the Eußerthal manor in the back, up to the Viehtrift or the Neuweg at the top, and Theobald Weber's place at the bottom.

The rectory, including barn, stables, and equipment, are to be built and maintained by the Provosts of Eußerthal. The rectory and the wooden fence around the rectory yard are in very bad condition. The parish barn and necessary stables were newly built in 1732 by Eußerthal.

The property also contains a garden of about one quarter morgen of land. The garden is surrounded partly by a living fence and partly by a plank fence, "but is very poorly maintained."

---

[71] A *Bert* was a bundle of approximately 200 fresh green tobacco leaves.

180

11. The school system

The right to hire a teacher has been carried out by the Palatinate government up to the present. So in 1727, they employed the current teacher, Augustin Schultz. Just as the community raised objections concerning the parish property, viewing it as their own property, so also they view the actual school property (that is, the schoolhouse) and the current schoolyard as property of the community. This property, which includes the dwelling place, is situated in the middle of the village on the Große Gasse. It borders the Quotgraben (Schlammgraben [Sludge trench]) on the outside, the Große Gasse on the inside, Wendel Müller (Mayor) on the upper side, and the community on the lower side. Said property, including the dwelling and garden, is built and maintained by the community and is temporarily assigned to the current teacher until the dispute over the parish and school property has been decided by the court.

The annual income of the teacher comprises:

1. From the Provost of Hördt: 6 malters of grain
2. From the Klingenmünster Monastery: 10 gulden
3. In addition, from an old authority registry book:
    As bell ringer from the tithes: 13 malters and 4 simmers grain
    To be paid as follows:
    > The chief official winery of Germersheim: 6 malters and 4 simmers
    > The parish; that is, the respective priest: 4 malters and 4 simmers
    > The House of Haimbach: 1 malter and 1 simmer
    > The community of Ottersheim: 4.5 simmers grain

    Note well, the Provost of Hördt as a tithe receiver should also contribute 4.5 simmers of grain. But that has not happened in the last 30 years.
4. From 9 morgen of meadows, the teacher is entitled to the hay tithe. The meadows lie equally distributed at the stone weir and in Hundsloch.
5. The teacher is also entitled to:
    a)   From each school child every 3 months: 15 kreutzers
         In winter from each child daily: 2 sticks of wood
         Note well, the school fees for poor children are paid from the charity fund.
    b)   From each wedding: 45 kreutzers
    c)   From a christening: 15 kreutzers
    d)   From the funeral of an adult: 45 kreutzers
    e)   From the funeral of a child: 15 kreutzers
         Note well, these amounts have been increased because at weddings and funerals the teacher must operate the bellows.
         Note: Because the Reformed do not have their own bells, the small community-owned bell is rung at their funerals. This is carried out by the Catholic teacher who alone is entitled to do so. The Reformed must pay him:
         At the funeral of an adult: 30 kreutzers
         At the funeral of a child: 15 kreutzers

In addition to these income sources, the teacher like any other citizen has the right to wood, to fish, and to other rights common to all.

"We, the undersigned Mayor and court have read, pondered, and verified word by word the present description of our church and parish together with all that it comprises, that all is grounded in truth, is drawn up honestly, and without malice according to its current condition so that with good knowledge and conscience as required of us with respect to truth, justice, and harm to none, we have all hereby personally signed and attached our Court Seal."

Ottersheim, 17 August 1747
Wendel Müller, Mayor
Johannes Seither of the court

Paper seal
(National Archives Speyer: Bishopric Speyer Fascicle 428)

The Catholic Rectory in Ottersheim

Like the Catholic Church itself, the rectory has not changed its location over the centuries. It was always on the property north of the church where the Neuweg enters into the Große Gasse. Probably the Eußerthal Abbey, the owner of the Ottersheim parish since 1311, was the first to build a rectory there. This was even more likely because the local fields belonged to the Eußerthal manor and these were classified as completely tithe-free. The rectory was first mentioned in the *Summary of Rights in the Village of Ottersheim from the year 1599.* Then, it included a house and a garden in addition to farm buildings. After the introduction of the Reformation, the property seems at times to have been used as a schoolhouse because the Reformed pastor lived in Knittelsheim.

The rectory was assigned to the Catholic priest after re-Catholicization of the village by Louis XIV toward the end of the 17th century. As owner of the parish, the Eußerthal Monastery built a barn in 1732. While the abbey had to pay for the building material and wages for craftsmen, the inhabitants of the village were required to bring stones and wood from the Haardt as feudal serfs (that is, without pay) and to help in the construction as day laborers. When the barn was demolished in 1960, they found a five-meter-long beam with the inscription:

CLOSTER EUSERTHAL 1733

Because the rectory was also in poor condition, as reported by Pastor Uth in 1747, construction of a new building was started in 1752. The financing was the duty of the Abbey of Eußerthal whose possessions were administered by an electoral caretaker.

182

The new rectory was probably the largest and most solid stone house in the whole village in its time. It was two stories and was covered by a hipped roof with four windows on one side and five on the other. There were three rooms and a kitchen on the ground floor, and upstairs there were six additional rooms, above which were two sizable storage spaces. A stone staircase led into the house from the east lying courtyard. Above the entrance was a stone with the pelican as the Eußerthal coat of arms, mounted above that is the sign of Christ, `IHS´, and to the left and right of the stone, the following letters:

BRO TH EIS STA

We can hardly be wrong if we denote these letters to be: "Provost Eußerthal." The Walls of the house were often almost a meter thick. Because the building had only a partial basement, moisture collected in the walls. The rectory was still surrounded by a wooden fence that was "in a most ruinous state" in 1747. Also, the garden fence, which was partly comprised of hedgerows and partly of wooden planks, was "very poorly kept." All these shortcomings were eliminated in 1785 when Pastor Georg Günther had a stone wall built around the property. The outbuildings that served commercial purposes were also built at that time. They included a woodshed, a wagon shed, pigsties, chicken coops, a laundry house, and a bakery.

The new rectory construction in 1752 required a lot of extra work on the part of the villagers. As the documents report for example, 80 klafter[72] of brick and 1,320 carts of sand had to be brought in. In addition, there were 32 loads of wood from the Eußerthal forest. It would have cost 250 gulden had the peasants been paid for their work on the construction project. All the work was done as serf duty to which the people were obligated based on the laws of that time. However, the villagers had expected that this work would be counted against the manorial service obligations that were required of them. This was not done sufficiently according to their judgment so they turned to the Electoral Court Chamber in Mannheim to lodge an official complaint. The trial at the Upper Appellate Court in Mannheim lasted until 1766 before the citizens of Ottersheim were granted their rights.

Just as the construction of the Ottersheim rectory was the obligation of the Eußerthal Abbey, so also was the maintenance. However, this changed in the time of Napoleon when the tithe was abolished and the property of the monasteries was sold. Many of the Spiritual Goods Administration obligations were turned over to the communities. Therefore, the Ottersheim community has been responsible for the maintenance of the rectory and the associated out buildings since the beginning of the 19th century. Because the Pastor of Ottersheim also managed the parish of Knittelsheim since 1808, the maintenance obligation for the Ottersheim rectory was extended by an Administrative Court verdict in the 1880s to include the Knittelsheim parish. The rectory in Ottersheim fulfilled its purpose by providing a total of 19 pastors with an apartment for over 200 years. Meanwhile, it

---

[72] A cubic klafter pile of wood was 1 meter high, 2 meters wide and 2 meters deep.

became old and in need of repairs. The strong walls most likely would have survived for many decades, but the woodwork was rotten and had to be completely replaced. Moisture had also penetrated deep into the walls, because the foundation was not insulated. Added to this was the inconvenience from the traffic that grew from year to year. Faced with the question of construction or renovation, it was finally decided by the Diocese in Speyer for a new building in the former rectory yard. Work began in 1959 under Father Josef Scherübl. Voluntary donations from the faithful brought the parish a total of 40,000 deutschemarks while the Diocese made the same amount available for the structure frame. During the construction, many Ottersheim Catholics provided volunteer help with the project. They dug the basement, brought in construction materials, and provided general labor without payment. So in 1959, the house could be occupied after only seven months of construction time. According to the technical accomplishments of our time, the new rectory was outfitted with an oil furnace and a garage. Its quiet location is an advantage that is especially appreciated by the spiritual worker.

The Kindergarten

Most likely, an Association of Saint Elisabeth group was already founded under Pastor Schwarz at the beginning of the 20th century but nothing was seen or heard of it for ten years. Not until after the death of Pastor Eckel in 1916 was it given a new lease on life. The association had set itself the goal to build a kindergarten and to establish an outpatient medical care center. Both facilities were to be run by nuns. In December of 1916, many people joined the club and paid dues regularly. But because of inflation, the entire assets of the association were lost and all activities of the organization had ceased by 1922. A renewed start took place on 8 January 1928 under Pastor Michael Schmitt. Of the 240 families in the village, 221 Catholic and Protestant families joined the club. It was possible to establish and operate a Nurses' Station with vigor using the financial contributions of its members.

Already by 12 February 1928, the Institute of the Poor School Sisters at Speyer provided a nurse and an administrative sister. The two sisters were housed, free of charge, on the top floor of Josef Seither's home on the Ludwigstraße. The furnishings for the apartment were donated by Ottersheim Catholics. Already during the first year of operation, Nurse Lamberta developed a beneficial set of activities. In addition to many people with light illness, they had no fewer than 138 people admitted who had been sick for more than three weeks.

Because available space was limited, it was not possible initially to think about the establishment of a kindergarten and a needlework school. This became feasible in July 1931 when the Association of Saint Elisabeth purchased the estate of Philipp Benz for 18,000 reichsmarks. Located to the west of the Catholic Church, a Nurses' Station was set up there.

The barn and stables were demolished, and a kindergarten and a needlework room were built in their place. Sister Sapientia Härder was able to begin needlework classes on 16 November 1931, while the kindergarten was opened to the delight of the villagers on 4 July 1932.

When the Nazis came to power in 1933, an attempt was made to paralyze the activities of the Catholic Church outside the church walls. Even the Catholic kindergarten was to be dissolved and replaced by a Nazi unit. However, in the early years no one dared to force the Catholic nuns from the kindergarten. To this end, the Nazi leadership took advantage of the turbulent times during World War II, when the men were at the front and the women were more than busy with work and other worries. On 16 March 1941, a quarter of a year before the start of the Russian campaign, a National-Socialist kindergarten that was run by brown sisters was launched in the orphaned rooms of the Protestant school. The Catholic kindergarten had to be abandoned. The infant care home of the Association of Saint Elisabeth had to be closed; it had been in existence for a year at the time. A Nazi infant care home was opened later by the Nazi People's Welfare organization as a replacement.

The Nazi kindergarten and infant home existed for four years and then disappeared without a trace. However, already by April 1945 the Catholic sisters had resumed their activities and reopened the new kindergarten of the Association of Saint Elisabeth. The acceptance by the villagers was so great that it was soon necessary to think about an expansion. Many plans were devised and discarded until it was finally decided by Pastor Scherübl to build a new kindergarten using the church property on the Falltorweg. A similar decision was made on 24 September 1961 at the general assembly of the Association of Saint Elisabeth.

Minister Scherübl went to work with great care and energy. Because a new rectory had been built shortly before, procuring the necessary funds would be difficult, given the cost estimate for the new building by Architect Knoll of Herxheim came to over 200,000 deutschemarks. The lion's share of this total could be obtained from government and ecclesiastical authorities. The county government in Neustadt gave 70,000 deutschemarks; the Diocese of Speyer gave 60,000 deutschemarks; the District of Germersheim gave 25,000 deutschemarks. The Ottersheim community contributed 17,500 deutschemarks that left a remainder of some 60,000 deutschemarks to be raised by the religious community or Association of Saint Elisabeth. One third of this amount was attributable to contributions made by the club members.

Certified Architect Knoll from Herxheim created a design and took over construction management. Many volunteer villagers helped dig the basement in January of 1962. The Ludwig Ripp Company of Ottersheim had completed the framing by the end of June. The internal work was also completed toward the end of the year so the inauguration could take place on 16 December 1962. As Charity Director of the Diocese of Speyer, Diocesan Administrator Eisner gave the keynote speech. District Administrator Weiß congratulated the community on the success of their work and praised the selfless efforts of the villagers in the construction of the kindergarten. There was great joy among the population, especially among the Catholic and Protestant children of the community for whom the house was built.

The Protestant Church of Ottersheim

The Protestant Church of Ottersheim stands at the southern corner where the Ludwigstraße connects to the Germersheimer Straße. It is 14.5 meters long and 10 meters wide. The church, whose front is directed to the south, has arched windows and a flat ceiling. On the northern gable end is a pilaster entryway with an arched door opening. Above the cornice in the arch is the following inscription:

"The citizens of the Reformed Congregation of Ottersheim built this church from the ground up in 1813."

The number '1816' is mounted in iron figures on the north gable and presumably denotes the completion year of the structural work. On both sides of the entry way are arched windows with a small circular window above. Rising above the gable was an octagonal roof turret with slate trim and cupola. The building exterior is plastered.

A room was added to the south side of the church in 1965 to serve as space for not only storage of liturgical items and clothing but also as a meeting place for church groups. In addition, the room is used by the pastor as a lounge before and after the service. The construction costs were estimated at 20,000 deutschemarks. Half of this sum was saved through voluntary work performed by members of the Protestant Church community.

The Protestant Church has two bronze bells that were cast at the Bachert Foundry in Karlsruhe. The bells were acquired in 1960 because the two existing bells did not harmonize when sounded together. An iron bell tower was erected for the new bells while the electric ringing station had been installed already in 1959. Since 1955, the Protestant religious community has also owned a new organ that was built by the Oberlinger firm in Windesheim near Bad Kreuznach. The cost of 6,703 deutschemarks was covered by voluntary donations from the parishioners. The new organ replaced its predecessor that had embellished the worship services of the Protestant community for over a hundred years. Inside the church, there is a simple altar behind which stands a pulpit that is accessed by a staircase.

It was a long and arduous journey before the Reformed Church in Ottersheim was completed. As previously stated, toward the end of the 17th century at the behest of Louis XIV of France, all residents of Ottersheim accepted the Catholic faith though a part of the population did so only externally. The church, school, and rectory were transferred into the hands of the Catholics at that time. After the Religious Declaration of the year 1705, when about ten Ottersheim families returned to the Reformed faith, they had no place to hold their worship services. So they bought the property at 22 Germersheimer Straße where Wilhelm Hoffmann lives today using private funds. They set up a school in the house and used the barn as a church. The makeshift church was in poor condition in spite of the repairs that were made to the barn. Even then, deliberations took place to replace it with a new building. However, it took over a hundred years for this dream to come true. The delay was due primarily to the fact that the small Reformed community did not have enough funds at their disposal to finance a new building through their own means. So the project was postponed again and again until finally toward the end of the century the dilapidated state of the temporary church forced a decision. Under Pastor Riehm of Offenbach (1787-1792), the Reformed families of Ottersheim pledged a sum of monetary contributions for the new church according to their respective financial circumstances. So in 1791 donations were as follows:

	Gulden		Gulden	Kreutzers
Philipp Peter Borger	15	Johannes Hatzenbühler	12	
Georg Jakob Conrad	12	Nikolaus Humbert	8	15
Georg Jakob Deschler	9	Valentin Job	15	
Jakob Doll	15	Georg Jakob Job	10	
Rudolf Doll	10	Johann Jost Job	12	
Johannes Frey	15	Georg Heinrich Körper	18	
Johannes Gensheimer	15	Georg Körper	5	30
Heinrich Gensheimer	14	Jakob Ludwig	8	
Lorenz Gensheimer	12	Johann Jost Ludwig	8	
Georg Lorenz Gensheimer	15	Margareta Ludwig	3	
Georg Gensheimer (his widow)	3	Nikolaus Joh. Sauther	9	
Anna Kath. and Maria Gensheimer	6	Wilhelm Weiß	15	
Valentin Günther	11	Philipp Weiß	6	
Georg Günther	10	Philipp Jakob Weiß	12	
Georg Hatzenbühler	9			
		Total:	312	45

Only a single Reformed citizen of Ottersheim, Jakob Brand, was not willing to contribute his part for the new church. All others had committed in writing to contribute the same amount in 1792 and 1793 as in 1791. Because 450 gulden was available from previous collections, there existed a foundation for hope that a new building could soon be realized.

A corresponding planning application, with building plan and cost estimate, was submitted on 6 February 1791 to the chief official of Germersheim, whereby the Reformed community of Ottersheim also asked for an appropriate grant. Because no reply had arrived by the end of 1792, a second application was sent via the official messenger from Klingenmünster. Presumably, the first petition never reached the proper authorities because by now the left bank of the Rhine was occupied by French revolutionary armies who had the motto "Fight against all Christianity" on their flags. No one could expect from them that they would allow building a new church let alone provide financial subsidies. So for the moment nothing changed. Not until the status of churches gradually normalized under Napoleon could the project again be pursued.

The Reformed congregation of Ottersheim bought a building site at the west end of Ludwigstraße in 1808 from the widow of Johannes Zwißler for 300 francs. A total of 2,000 francs had been collected through voluntary donations by 1812 while pledges for another 1,000 francs were already present. A sum of 300 francs was expected from the sale of the barn that served as a temporary church so that a total of 3,500 francs was available from the start. Overall, the cost would be 5,000 francs for the construction of the building, which was planned to be 21 meters long and 11 meters wide. Worth special mention is the fact that 19 towns from the surrounding area declared themselves willing to donate one or two tree trunks for the new building. These towns were Insheim, Kuhardt, Hördt, Leimersheim, Sondernheim, Neupotz, Zeiskam, Lingenfeld, Schwegenheim, Weingarten, Oberlustadt, Geinsheim, Waldsee, Haßloch, Iggelheim, Böhl, Schifferstadt, Otterstadt, and Neuhofen.

So on 24 January 1812, Mayor Kopf was able to venture and seek permission from the authorities for construction of a Reformed Church in Ottersheim.

Construction work started in 1813. Because no written records about the construction process were preserved, we must be satisfied with the few clues represented by the church itself or by descriptions found in the parish of Offenbach. From the community council protocols, we know the political community of Ottersheim donated 670 francs for the purchase of the windows in 1816. The time between the beginning of construction and the dedication of the church was remarkably long. In addition to the turbulence from political events, the lack of money is likely the most important reason for the slow pace of construction between 1813 and 1820. Oral tradition has reported that even the Netherlands was approached with requests for donations. Even before the new church could be put into service, the ramshackle makeshift church at the schoolhouse across the street was auctioned for demolition. So it happened that the Reformed community of Ottersheim was without a meeting room of its own from 1817 to 1820. For this reason, Catholic priest Rudolph Märdian allowed the Protestants the temporary use of the Catholic Church for religious activities such as baptisms, confirmations, sermons, and the like. The Reformed Church was finally consecrated on 20 August 1820. In addition to Ludwig Heintz, the responsible pastor from Offenbach, Pastor Wagner from Niederhochstadt appeared, who as former pastor, had provided an exceptional contribution to the planning of the new building. The festival sermon was given in the afternoon by Vicar Zinn. The joy of all parties was great because they had succeeded after over a hundred years in establishing a worthy house of worship for the Protestants of the Ottersheim community.

The interior furnishings of the church were reduced to a minimum then. A simple altar with an altar cloth stood at the front. Behind it was the raised pulpit that could be entered through a stairway as it still is today. At the back of the church was a small gallery with a humble organ that probably originated from the makeshift church. The organ had to be repaired often until it was replaced by a brand new one in 1852. The new organ was provided by organ builder Schlimbach from Speyer for 800 gulden. Half of the sum was assumed by the civil community of Ottersheim, while another 400 gulden were raised from voluntary donations from the Protestant parishioners.

On 14 April 1856, lightning struck through the roof of the church into the new organ. The damage was so great that 200 gulden had to be spent on repairs. The Protestant

Church most likely had a set of bells from the beginning. A description of the parish from 1866 mentions two bronze bells that were housed in the turret. The larger bell had to be sacrificed in 1917 to the First World War. It was melted and used as war material like the two bells of the Catholic Church. After the war ended, the Protestant religious community bought two new bronze bells from the Hamm Bell Foundry in Frankenthal in 1921 that were used until 1942. The larger bell had to be sacrificed as a consequence of total war. Another bell was purchased in 1949. An electrical bell ringing facility was added ten years later. But these bells were replaced by a new bell set in 1960 because the tones of the two bells were not harmonized.

For the maintenance of the Protestant house of worship, the civil community of Ottersheim has repeatedly contributed actively during the past 150 years, as has also been the case for the Catholic Church. In 1835 and 1837, 150 gulden were spent on repairs to the Protestant Church. When a hailstorm severely damaged the roofs of both churches in 1864, the community donated 440 gulden for the repair of the two roofs. The Protestant religious community was given 267 marks for repair and new exterior paint for the church in 1897, and another 100 marks for renovation work in 1910. Lightning rods were installed on both buildings at the expense of the community in 1908 while electric lights were not installed until 1925.

In 1921, the Ottersheim civil community bought the land south of the church in exchange for a field in the Hochgewanne. This was then provided to the Protestant teacher for cultivating as payment for the required organ services. The site was then sold by the community as building land. By the way, there stood directly adjacent to the south wall of the church a small, nondescript house in which Richard Jeckel lived until 1936. Due to its ugly appearance, the house was demolished at that time and the land was used as a garden. A newly built lounge and group room is located there now.

In commemoration of the beginning of the Reformation 450 years ago, the Protestant cultural community renovated their church from the ground up in 1967. Roof and turrets were repaired and the outside walls re-plastered. The cost for the renovation inside and outside amounted to more than 100,000 deutschemarks, which was collected in part from donations.

The Protestant (Reformed) Parish of Ottersheim

The turbulent times, after Luther posted his Theses on 31 October 1517 until the Peace of Augsburg in 1555, had little noticeable impact on the rural population of Ottersheim, if one disregards the Peasant Riots of 1525. That changed in 1556 when Lutheran-minded Elector Ottheinrich of Heidelberg took over as ruler of the Palatinate. Since every prince in Augsburg was granted the right to act on the principle *Cuius regio, Eius religio* to determine the faith of his subjects, Ottheinrich made immediate use of this right and introduced the Lutheran faith in the Palatinate.

In Ottersheim, the former Catholic priest was removed from office for his nonreligious way of life, and because he enjoyed no great reputation anyway, he was replaced by Lutheran-minded Valentin Kempfer from Ladenburg. This new pastor lived in Knittelsheim however. The Lutheran faith changed very little in the liturgy or in the traditional church life. The Mass was celebrated as usual except that the canon and the Transubstantiation[73] were omitted. That the Latin language was almost completely displaced in favor of the German language certainly found more support than rejection among the village population. Baptism, Eucharist, and Confession continued to be provided to the faithful. Since the altar, vestments, chalices, hosts, baptismal font, organ, and images of Christ were kept, the transition from Catholic to Lutheran faith was easy for most people, especially because the population could neither read nor write and probably took little notice of the theological changes.

That was certainly different from when the successor of Elector Ottheinrich, Friedrich III of Heidelberg, introduced the Reformed faith in place of the Lutheran faith in 1563. Nuntius Morone writes to Karl Borromäus in 1563 of the changes at that time in the Palatinate:

> "A new, very Calvinistic catechism (the so-called "Heidelberg catechism") must be accepted and explained each Sunday. There may be no more Holy Days other than Sundays. Altars, statues, and pictures are to be destroyed. The Lord's Supper must be celebrated on a wooden table using bread, not hosts. The consecration of marriages is to be abolished."

It is not known how popular these changes were in Ottersheim. However, because Pastor Kempfer was retained in the parish and not expelled from the country, as were other Lutheran clergyman of the Palatinate region, leads one to conclude that these rather drastic orders were accepted and were followed by him and by the community. Resisters were allowed to emigrate into other territories. But, they had to leave their belongings behind. Ottersheim once again became a Lutheran parish for seven years under Elector Ludwig IV

---

[73] Transubstantiation is the Catholic doctrine which believes the bread and wine used in the Sacrament of Holy Communion is changed into the Body and Blood of Jesus.

in 1576. Then, the Reformed faith was again declared to be the State religion and so it remained during the 30 Years War with few years of disruption until 1684.

When Pastor Glaser of Sinsheim took over the Ottersheim parish in 1613, there was hardly anyone in the village who had not been raised and educated in the Reformed faith from childhood. Only the dilapidated church remained of the Catholic past, which was to be replaced in the near future by a church in the Reformed style. A simple unadorned church, a castle of God that could protect the villagers in times of war was planned. The Elector selected Johann Schock from Heidelberg for master builder. The costs were almost entirely borne by the State. The villagers had to bring the stones and timber as well as help the artisans. Construction commenced in 1618, and a year later, the structural work was done. No one imagined how much misery and suffering the next 30 years would bring to the village and its residents.

The year 1626 was of particular importance to the Calvinist community of Ottersheim. The victorious Austrians and Bavarians had set themselves the goal to convert the Reformed parishes to Catholic parishes. Therefore, they prohibited Reformed pastor Glaser from performing any official act in Ottersheim. Instead, Catholic priests from out of town were to lead the way back to the Catholic faith. Mass was again read on Sundays, and a stone baptismal font was installed in 1629. The sacraments were also performed again according to the Catholic rites. However, an orderly church life was unthinkable in the chaos of war. Ottersheim had neither a Catholic nor a Reformed local pastor until the year 1650. This did not change until the departure of the French two years after the end of the 30 Years War. In accordance with the provisions of the peace agreement of Münster and Osnabrück, the District Office of Germersheim had to reverse the Counter Reformation and reintroduce the Reformed faith. Because the number of residents in villages and towns throughout the long war had dwindled greatly by 1650, the villages of Ottersheim, Offenbach, and Mörlheim were combined under the care of Pastor Salomon Walther who lived in Offenbach. Although the three communities had a common pastor, Ottersheim placed great weight to be regarded as an independent parish. A count of the 40 households in Ottersheim in 1671 listed 36 families as Reformed and 4 as Lutheran. Catholics were not present. The Pastor in Offenbach received the small tithes for his work in Ottersheim, while the large tithes were collected by the Office in Germersheim. The parish property in Ottersheim was listed as vacant in 1674.

The year 1684 brought significant changes to the Reformed parish in Ottersheim. A short time before, Louis XIV of France had used the weakness of the German Reich to have his soldiers occupy the areas south of the Queich. Like all the absolutist rulers of the time, he demanded of his subjects that they accept the religious faith of their ruler. The king willed that the villages south of the Queich were to become Catholic. This of course could not be accomplished by a simple command. It was also simply not enough to replace the pastor as was done the previous hundred years. Rather, those carrying out the orders of Louis XIV had to adopt a large quantity of targeted measures to suppress the Reformed faith in favor of the Catholic faith. Since Ottersheim did not have a resident priest, it seems that resistance was less initially than in other Reformed communities of the southern Palatinate.

The Counter-Reformation was carried out by the Jesuits, who were first stationed in Klingenmünster and then in Bellheim from 1684. Representatives of the king supported the activities of the members of the Order through civil measures. For example, anyone who became Catholic by 1 January 1683 was not required to pay taxes for three years. In addition, they were freed from the requirement to provide board and provisions for French troops. It is therefore not surprising that a report from 1699 states that all residents of Ottersheim were Catholic. Additionally, in the year 1701 a report states that:

"Recently 51 families renounced Calvinism and returned to the Catholic Church."

It is therefore not surprising that in 1697, the Peace of Ryswick granted sole use of the church in Ottersheim to the Catholics. As justification for this measure, the Chamoy Lists[74] documented "a conversion of the inhabitants," that is, the change of faith of the people of Ottersheim. At any rate, since 1686 there was no longer a Reformed Pastor in Offenbach, because he had been expelled like almost all other pastors in the villages in lands south of the Queich. Thus, the Reformed parish in Ottersheim was dissolved, although not legally but by default.

Although it has not been documented, later developments provide proof that the change of religion under Louis XIV was not accepted by all residents in Ottersheim out of inner conviction. Some complied with the order, but others remained true to the Reformed faith in their hearts. However, they dared not openly return to the old faith, because the French king had threatened hard punishments in case this happened. If relapsed converts, the so-called *heretics,* should die, their corpse would be dragged through the streets and thrown into the bone yard while their assets would fall to the State. Apostatized men who refused the sacraments on their sickbed and then recovered would be sentenced with substantial fines, lifelong galleys, and confiscation of their possessions. Fallen women would be sent to prison.

When the Ryswick Peace reversed France's territorial claims in 1697 and the Palatinate was again awarded the area south of the Queich, the followers of the Reformed faith saw that the time had come when they could again openly profess their religious beliefs. The Reformed-minded residents of Bellheim, Knittelsheim, and Ottersheim were encouraged

---

[74] This is a reference to a list created by French Ambassador to Germany, Louis Rousseau de Chamoy, at the request of the Sun King Louis XIV that identified those places in the German territory previously held by France that should be allowed to remain Catholic.

by Reformed Pastor Müller of Zeiskam, although this was forbidden by the government. Pastor Müller therefore had to defend himself before the District Office in Germersheim on 4 October 1698. He was accused of "offering the sacrament to new converts who now became apostate" without Electoral permission. In 1700, the Reformed from Ottersheim were ordered to Germersheim where they were sometimes mildly, sometimes with harsh words, told that they should again become Catholic. However, all those subpoenaed with the exception of two people declared that they would remain with their Reformed religion. In the same year, they were subjected to billeting of soldiers and horsemen who behaved very badly. Among other things, the soldiers emptied the beds of feathers and poured the wine on the ground. When the people complained in Germersheim, they were told that they had to become Catholic, this was an order from the Elector. The costs associated with the quartering in Ottersheim and Knittelsheim amounted to about 200 gulden that had to be raised by the Reformed.

The suppression of the Reformed faith did not end until the Religions Declaration of 21 November 1705, whereby all subjects of the Palatinate were granted the right to decide for themselves whether to belong to the Catholic, the Reformed, or the Lutheran faith. At that time, about ten Ottersheim families chose to profess publicly the faith of their parents and formed the Reformed parish of Ottersheim. From 1706, they were cared for by the Reformed Pastor in Bellheim to which also belonged the subordinate parishes of Knittelsheim, Hördt, Kuhardt, and Leimersheim. At that time, in Ottersheim there lived alongside 188 Catholics about 40 Reformed, and a few Lutherans for whom the Lutheran Pastor of Germersheim was responsible. In the period 1706-1763, a Reformed church book was kept in Ottersheim that was still kept at the Mayor's Office during the 19th century. Unfortunately, it is nowhere to be found today. The small Reformed parish in Ottersheim had to begin completely from scratch in 1706. They had no school to educate their children in the Reformed faith, and no church where they could gather together to conduct services. Because a few wealthy farmers belonged to the Reformed community, they bought property on the Germersheimer Straße with private money. That was house number 22 that is now occupied by Wilhelm Hoffmann. The barn was set up as a temporary church and the home as a school. The salary of the teacher was paid by the Spiritual Goods Administration in Heidelberg. The number of Reformed grew from about 40 to 152 souls from 1707 to 1791 while the Catholics grew from 188 to 558 souls. Since the situation in Bellheim and Knittelsheim was similar, the Reformed Church established new parish lines in 1763. The Reformed parish in Ottersheim became a branch of the Reformed parish in Offenbach to which Mörlheim also belonged. The first pastor to serve the daughter parish in Ottersheim from the base in Offenbach was Elias Philbert of Hospital from Weingarten near Durlach.

The members of the Reformed congregation of Ottersheim desired above all that a new church be built to replace the dilapidated barn. However, they realized that the plan failed repeatedly because sufficient funds could not be made available by the community members. Under Pastor Riehm (1787-1792), a collection had begun and a plan for the new building had already been drafted. But when the French revolutionary armies overran the Palatinate in 1792, the project had to be postponed until calmer times should arrive. Construction work could not begin until 1813 and that dragged on for several years. The church inauguration ceremony was held on 20 August 1820. Now the Protestant community, which numbered about 150 souls, finally had a worthy place for holding their religious services.

For the Reformed and Lutheran Christians from our home the year 1818 is of particular importance. In the 16th and 17th centuries, while the followers of Calvin and the followers of Luther in the Palatinate stood in an often-hostile relationship to each other, they now joined together in the *United Protestant-Evangelical Church.* Since only a few Lutherans lived in Ottersheim, events remained by and large the same as before. The union was agreed to by all community members. From now on, the parish of Offenbach and its daughter community of Ottersheim were no longer called *Reformed* but instead *Protestant.* As before, the pastor came from Offenbach to Ottersheim on Sunday and held the church service. It was common that an Ottersheim coach went to Offenbach to fetch the pastor. Later, there arose a dispute between the pastor and his community over this matter that could only be resolved when modern transportation methods made the use of a coach unnecessary.

Two decades after the inauguration of the Protestant Church, the Protestant community erected a new school building next to the Catholic schoolhouse on the Lange Straße. The construction cost was paid mainly by the civil community while a portion of the funds came from the proceeds from the sale of the old schoolhouse. A schoolroom and a service apartment for the teacher were housed in the one-story building. It was in use from 1832-1902, until it was replaced by a common school for Catholics and Protestants. It was often difficult to get a suitable teacher for the small, one-class school. When teacher Ecarius died in 1877, no one could be found for three years who was willing to take the orphaned position. During this time, the Protestant children attended the Catholic school. The organ service in the Protestant church was also provided by the Catholic teachers.

If the Protestant church community in Ottersheim did not grow in the past hundred years, this can be blamed on the small number of children and also on the emigration to North America. The highest population level of Protestants was reached in 1836 where 209 of the 986 village residents were Protestant. The number dropped to 175 in 1866 where it has basically remained. Striking is the fact that only a few family names from previous centuries have remained to this day. Gone are the Protestant names of Borger, Conrad,

194

Doll, Deschler, Humbert, Körper, and Ludwig. For this, new names have emerged through marriage such as Bauchhenß, Blattmann, Brüderle, Disqué, Hühnerfauth, Kern, Lösch, Scherff, and Scheurer.

Those familiar with historical development will not be surprised that in the 18th and also partly in the 19th century, tensions existed between the Catholic and the Protestant populations in Ottersheim. But a very good relationship had developed in the last hundred years. In spite of the imbalance in population, the Catholics always took care to ensure that the position of an adjunct or second mayor was granted to a Protestant. When updates to the churches were necessary, both churches were taken into account by the civil community, although there is no legal obligation to do so.

It deserves to be noted that the Protestants of Ottersheim always stood firmly together when maintenance or interior updates of the church demanded offerings. Since the Second World War up to the year 1965, a new organ, two bronze bells, and an electrical ringing system were purchased and paid for largely by voluntary donations. A meeting and youth room was added to the south side of the church in the year 1965 for which the costs were estimated at 20,000 deutschemarks. Half of the sum was saved through voluntary assistance in the construction work. From this came a thorough renovation of the entire church in 1967 for over 100,000 deutschemarks.

The Protestant (Reformed) Pastors of Ottersheim

Valentin Kempfer from Ladenburg, living in Knittelsheim		1556-1588
Leonhard Weidner of Schabatz (Thuringia)		1588-1603
Johannes Regius (Reckius)		1603-1613
Johannes Konrad Glaser of Sinsheim. He was removed from his office with the introduction of the Catholic faith in 1626. He lived in Ottersheim until 1628.		1613-1626
Unassigned:		1626-1650
Salomon Walther, Pastor of Offenbach, Ottersheim, and Mörlheim, living in Offenbach		1650-1659
Johannes Kluck	(assigned)	1669
Melchior Philgesius	(assigned)	1680
Heinrich Wetzel. He was expelled from the country under Louis XIV.	(assigned)	1685
Without a pastor:		1685-1706

From 1703 to 1763, the Reformed Pastor of Bellheim served the Ottersheim parish. He also served Knittelsheim, Hördt, Kuhardt, and Leimersheim.

The Reformed pastors of Bellheim were:

Johann Bernhard Serini	1706-1725
Johann Christian Simon from Kreuznach	1725-1728
Johann Jakob Müller	1728-1730
Johann Georg Keßler	1730-1734
Abraham Wittner from Niederhochstadt	1734-1743
Philipp Nikolaus Kling	1743-1750
Johann Nikolaus Schwarz	1750-1759
Johann Valentin Hoffmeister	1759-1762
Karl Ludwig Kleinmann	1762-1763 (1774)

Since 27 February 1763, Ottersheim had no longer been an independent parish. Ottersheim became a branch parish of Offenbach in 1763, and since then was served by the pastor of Offenbach. The names of the Offenbach pastors are:

Philbert Elias of Hospital from Weingarten by Durlach	1763-1776
Johannes Hoppe	1776-1785
Abraham Horn	1785-1787
Stephan Karl Casimir Riehm of Kreuznach	1787-1792
Johann David Geul	1792-1797
Johann Jakob Gulden	1797-1805
Johann Jakob Wagner	1805-1813
Ludwig Philipp Wilhelm Heintz	1814-1820
Dietmar Wilhelm Brämer	1821-1824
Philipp Jakob Höpffner	1825-1833
Johann Jakob Bruckner	1834-1858
Johann Daniel Stepp	1858-1863
Karl Anton Scherer	1863-1868
Jakob Münch	1868-1884
Leonhard Welker	1885-1889
Jakob Herancourt	1889-1907
Karl Wilhelm Reichhold of Feilbingert	1907-1931
Temporary pastor	1931-1936
Ottheinrich Reichhold, Son of Karl Wilhelm Reichhold	1936-1952
Wolfgang Jung	1952—

The School Buildings in Ottersheim

In the last decades of the 16th century, when the elementary school was established in Ottersheim in the wake of the Reformation, the former rectory opposite the church was used as a schoolhouse at first. Such a solution was possible without difficulty because the Reformed pastor of Ottersheim lived in Knittelsheim. The house stood at the corner of the Lange Straße and the Neuweg, and even then was not in top condition. It was demolished in 1752 and replaced by a new stone building that also served as the Catholic rectory until 1959.

After re-Catholicization of the village toward the end of the 17th century, the existing school building was again used as a rectory. So the community was forced to look for new housing for the schoolchildren. To this end, they bought the property at 62 Lange Straße from an Ottersheim citizen and outfitted a school for the village children there. The teachers most likely also lived in this house. Because the space no longer sufficed for the many children at the beginning of the 19th century however, the community purchased the two-story property of the impoverished former mayor, Johann Kopf, and moved the school there in 1827. The house stood on the Lange Straße to the east of the rectory and had space for two classrooms, a teacher apartment, and a room for the teacher's aide. The barns and stables were available to the teachers for their gardens. This building served as the Catholic school until 1902.

A private school was available for the Reformed children of Ottersheim. The house stood at 22 Germersheimer Straße. It was purchased by the Reformed community with private funds at the beginning of the 18th century. Reformed teacher Friedrich Ruppertus of Ottersheim lived there also. The barn on the property served as a makeshift church for a long time. At the time of the retirement transfer of teacher Ruppertus in 1831, who had worked in Ottersheim for 51 years, the Reformed school building was in such poor shape that the community was forced to look for a new building for the Protestant school. To this end, the old schoolhouse in the Gröhlig was sold, and a small stone building was built to the east next to the Catholic schoolhouse on the Lange Straße. It had a classroom and an apartment for the teacher that teacher Ecarius occupied in 1832. So from then on, the two schoolhouses stood next to each other. The schoolyard was shared by all children.

These conditions remained essentially the same for the seven decades that followed. Toward the end of the century, it was determined that the two schoolhouses were not just old and in need of repair but had also become too small for the many schoolchildren. Therefore, the Electoral District Office in Germersheim, as overseer, pressed for an improvement to the school conditions in Ottersheim. The community was initially undecided whether to renovate the two buildings or to demolish them and erect a new building. One thing was clear to everyone; any construction project would cost money! In 1896, there was already a basis of 6,093 marks available. The community council wanted to begin construction once this sum reached 20,000 marks. However, the Regional Office pushed for an earlier date given the poor condition of the schools. District Master Builder Ginand was commissioned to develop a plan for a new building. This plan was submitted in 1901 to the community council together with the cost estimate. The new school building was to cost 31,100 marks. A full year passed before they reached agreement on all the details. In addition to three classrooms, two teacher apartments were planned. In order to finance this, a sum of 25,000 marks had to be borrowed and repaid over the course of 20 years.

The construction work was awarded in January 1902, whereby a number of Ottersheim craftsmen were considered. So the masonry work went to the brothers Winkelblech, the structural carpentry work went to the brothers Glatz, the cabinetry work went to Hanck and Kröper, the plumbing work went to Walk and Zwißler, and the metal work went to Johann Kröper in conjunction with Seuffert of Bellheim. The stone masonry work was given to Jakob Hoffmann from Knittelsheim and the roofing work to August Hornbach from Landau. Because the district architect had to make additional changes requested by the community council, the new construction could not be started until 1902, and not before the buildings of the old school had been demolished. The stones taken from the Protestant schoolhouse were used to construct the house at 52 Lange Straße currently belonging to the Dumser siblings. With pride, Mayor Lorenz Föhlinger and his council were able to inaugurate the new school building in 1903. The building contained three classrooms, two spacious teacher apartments, and a smaller two-room assistant's apartment. However, the money was insufficient for new school furniture. So they continued to use the old oaken benches that sat up to eight children. New benches were purchased for the lower classes in 1906. Also not updated at that time were the toilets although they represented no ornament to the house. It was not until 1930 that these were demolished and replaced with new ones.

As long as Ottersheim had one Protestant and two Catholic school classes, the schoolhouse built on the Lange Straße in 1902-1903 was sufficient. But in the thirties when a third Catholic school classroom became necessary, the space issue was the cause of many headaches within the community school board, until finally the Association of Saint Elisabeth offered space in their extended house west of the church in 1933, a hall about 60 square meters in size. For this, the community was to pay 300 marks rent yearly.

After the collapse in 1945, all school halls were occupied by troops such that instruction even had to be conducted in a barn for a short period. By May 1947, three rooms in the school building could again be used. So when the fourth schoolroom was outfitted in June 1949, one class had to move to a needlework room at the Sisters' Home until finally the former assistant's and later caretaker's apartment on the ground floor of the school building was outfitted for teaching in June 1950. However, this fourth room was significantly smaller than a conventional schoolroom so the children of an average class could not be accommodated. Therefore, the teacher of this class had to teach all grades in one room. Another major shortcoming was that neither a room for the teacher, nor a special room for needlework, home economics, nature studies, carpentry, or physical education was available. So the film presentations, needlework, and religion lessons had to be held temporarily in the basement. Therefore, the demands from teachers, schoolchildren, and parents for new classrooms became louder and louder.

Considering the difficult financial situation of the community, initial thoughts were of an extension to the existing school building. However, when county and State government declared their willingness to grant substantial subsidies, it was decided unanimously for a new school building on the Falltorweg. A corresponding decision was concluded by the Council on 13 September 1961. Planning and supervision were awarded to the architect, Goldaté of Jockgrim. On 5 October 1963, the ceremonial laying of the cornerstone took place in which the school youth, the village Council members, numerous villagers, and District Administrator Weiß participated. Mayor Paul Dörzapf read the certificate of founding, and then placed it with several important documents into a time capsule that was built into the foundation. The topping out ceremony was in the summer of 1964. Due to rain, frost, and other difficulties, the construction work had been somewhat delayed so that the deadlines were not strictly met. On Saturday, 23 October 1965, the new elementary school was inaugurated in the presence of numerous local residents and many guests. Government Director Fritz Steegmüller gave the keynote speech on behalf of Minister of Culture Dr. Orth. Mayor Wünschel thanked all participants and expressed the pleasure brought by the successfully completed work.

The new school building included a two-story main building and a single-story pavilion, both connected by a covered concourse. These buildings are adjoined to the west to the sanitary facilities and in the southwest to the gym with its associated rooms. The school had five classrooms, a multipurpose room, a training kitchen, carpentry space, a teacher's room, teaching materials room, and a janitorial room. All rooms were equipped with new furniture and heated by a central hot water heating system with an automatic oil furnace. The gym was 300 square meters in size. It was the pride of the community who had waited more than a half century for a sports hall. School building and gymnasium cost about 1.1 million marks. For the financial expenses, the State of Rhineland-Palatinate gave a grant of 600,000 deutschemarks, and the District of Germersheim contributed 150,000 deutschemarks. Approximately 45 companies were involved in the construction. The mason work was done by the construction companies, Ludwig Ripp of Ottersheim and Hubert Vogel of Bellheim.

The Elementary School of Ottersheim

Until the mid-16th century, there was no school in Ottersheim for the 58 households that totaled approximately 300 residents. This is quoted from a competency book of the District Office of Germersheim from the year 1557 that states,

"There is no school yet in Ottersheim."

The neighboring villages of Knittelsheim and Offenbach also had no school like most of the villages in the District. Only Bellheim, Germersheim, Hagenbach, Kandel, Billigheim, Steinweiler, and Rohrbach were notable exceptions. The acting pastor was responsible for the instruction of the children in Ottersheim. He generally contented himself with teaching the children and adults in faith and morals, because as a secular priest he typically had only a modest education himself. It was certainly not an everyday occurrence when a gifted boy would be sent to the convent school in Hördt to prepare for a religious vocation or an administrative position. It was not until the century of Reformation that the traditional circumstances were shaken, thereby ushering in new developments. The founding of the elementary school in Ottersheim took place during that time.

In 1582, 50 pastors and 60 teachers were counted in the District Office of Germersheim, and they reported to the three superintendents in Germersheim, Hagenbach, and Billigheim. This fact suggests that there was at least a school in each parish in the District Office of Germersheim. An important impetus for the promotion of education appeared to be grounded in the Church Council Order from the year 1564 that demanded the establishment of good schools to educate "competent and learned ministers of religion" and to preserve the Christian religion. It was most likely during that time when the Ottersheim elementary school was established. The fact is corroborated by an entry in the competency book from the year 1605 where it says of Ottersheim:

"Three morgen of fields and three morgen of meadows dedicated to Early Mass are assigned in the year of 1573 to the schoolmaster."

Thus, Ottersheim had a teacher who taught the children of the village in 1573 at the latest.

The school building at that time was probably the former rectory. Because the first Reformed pastor of Ottersheim, Valentin Kempfer, demonstrably lived in Knittelsheim, it seemed obvious to assign the orphaned Ottersheim rectory to the teacher. This is even more likely considering that the building, which belonged to the Eußerthal Abbey, was confiscated in 1560 by the Electoral Palatinate and administered by the Spiritual Goods Administration in Heidelberg. The assumption is corroborated by a report that Catholic priest Johann Georg Uth drew up in 1747 and effectively states:

"It is known in the local community and unanimously claimed that the actual parish place was lost in the past decrepit times. The place where the pastor now lives was originally the community school place (in other words, the schoolhouse). This place lies opposite the

church and the cemetery, and is bordered by the common road in the front, by the Eußerthal manor in the back, by the Viehtrift or the Neuweg at the top, and Theobald Weber's place at the bottom."

The teachers of that time were assistants to the pastor in the Christian instruction of the youth. As cantors, they led the community song, beat the organ,[75] and represented or assisted the pastor at baptisms and funerals. The Spiritual Goods Administration in Heidelberg was primarily responsible for their compensation through their sub-offices. The funds flowed from the rich monastic properties that were confiscated by the Elector Friedrich III in the years 1560 to 1567. In the registry book of the Hördt Monastery around 1620 we read:

School service in Ottersheim
A schoolmaster of the village is entitled to receive from the Hördt Monastery as of old:

Grain: 6 malters

From the collection in Zeiskam:

Money: 10 gulden

Note: Whatever else he is to receive depends on his competence.

Without doubt, there was not much that a teacher in Ottersheim was entitled to yearly around 1600. To feed himself and his family he, like the parish pastor, cultivated a few morgen of land, tended his garden, and raised his cattle. During the summer months, classes were held on a limited basis or they were not held.

In the 30 Years War (1618-1648), Ottersheim shared the sad fate of the District Office of Germersheim, which was hit particularly hard as the heartland of the unfortunate Winter King Friedrich V. In 1626, the Reformed Pastor Konrad Glaser had to resign shortly after he had experienced the completion of the new parish church. Pastor Glaser continued living in Ottersheim until 1628. A Reformed teacher was probably no longer tolerated, that is, provided one still existed in the chaos of war. In any case, it may be assumed as certain that at a time "where many people in Ottersheim" and other places of the District Office of Germersheim were "dying of hunger and sorrow and ruin," no scheduled instruction was given.

In 1650, two years after the war ended, Ottersheim again received a Reformed pastor who lived in Offenbach. Presumably, a Reformed teacher was again employed in the following years. No sooner had the village recovered somewhat from the consequences of the 30 Years War when soldiers of French King Louis XIV occupied the entire area south of the Queich in 1680 and in effect annexed it to France. Ottersheim became a border town

---

[75] At the time, the organ keys were up to 10 centimeters wide and up to 30 centimeters long. You could only play with fists and elbows. So they used the term "beat the organ." In the 15th century, the pipe organ was built externally more or less as we know it today.(Edith L. Lueke)

under French rule. The so-called *Queich Lines* were expanded to defend the border. These fortifications extended from Offenbach and ran directly along the north side of the village up to Germersheim.

What the Palatine Elector at one time took for himself, the Sun King Louis XIV now laid claim. He demanded that all his subjects assume the religion of the sovereign. For example, in 1684 a total of 51 families in Ottersheim became Catholic, partly voluntarily and partly through government pressure. Because the French king was not picky in the means chosen and the Catholics were favored economically, so it happened that gradually all residents of Ottersheim turned to the Catholic faith as was described in a report from the year 1699. However, it must not be denied that some of the people practiced only externally, while in their hearts they continued to belong to the Reformed faith. In 1684, the Catholics were granted the chancery of the Church and the whole house of worship in the Ryswick Peace of 1697, as it remains to this day. Presumably, already in 1684 but no later than 1686, the Reformed teacher in Ottersheim was replaced by a Catholic to whom the former school building was assigned as home and workplace. Ottersheim has had a Catholic school since that time.

When the District Office of Germersheim was returned to the Palatinate in 1697 and general religious freedom was granted in 1705, more than three-quarters of the villagers remained Catholic. The remaining portion freely professed to the Reformed faith. They bought a property in the Gröhlig using their own resources, the house at 22 Germersheimer Straße that is now inhabited by Wilhelm Hoffmann. The house was set up as a school and the barn as a makeshift church. Both the Catholics and the Reformed wanted their children to be educated in the spirit of their faith. So Ottersheim has had a Catholic and a Reformed (Protestant) school since the beginning of the 18th century.

The Catholic School of Ottersheim

The name of the first Catholic teacher in Ottersheim is not known. But we know from a visitation log of the year 1699 that the teacher was also the bell-ringer. A competency book from that time documents the individual parts of his income. According to this book, the Catholic teachers of Ottersheim were to receive in 1699:

6 malters and 6 simmers of grain:	from the producers of Germersheim
9 simmers of grain:	from the Commandery at Haimbach
6 malters and 9 simmers of grain:	from the Provost of Hördt
4 - 1/2 malters of grain:	from the pastor's share of tithes for the bell-ringer office as of old
2 gulden:	from the community from the flour scale
2 malters and 6 simmers of grain:	from the tithe supplies
16 gulden:	from the Zeiskam collection as previously received

The first Catholic teacher whose name we know was Ägidius Mau. He is named in a document of 1716. He lived and taught as did his successor, August Schultz (1727-1760), in a house on the south side of the Große Gasse that the community had bought from an Ottersheim citizen. On that spot today stands the property of Emil Brüderle at 62 Lange Straße. It was the task of the Catholic teacher to explain the catechism to the entire Catholic youth of Ottersheim, to instruct them to be virtuous citizens, and to teach them the rudiments of reading, writing, and arithmetic. Instruction began with the greeting "Praised be Jesus Christ," and was followed by a hymn. After the lessons and the homework of the previous day were checked, the new lessons in reading, writing, and arithmetic were taught. The class practiced hymns in the afternoon. Those totally unmusical had to memorize their lessons during this time. The Catechism was studied on Saturday afternoon before the start of the Salve devotions.

Regular instruction was given only during the winter months from 8-11 o'clock in the early morning and from 12-3 or from 1-4 o'clock in the afternoon. There was no school on Wednesday afternoon. During summer, the children were to come for two hours of lessons in the morning to repeat and refresh what they had covered during the winter months. But there were repeated complaints that both the students and the teachers skipped this duty to pursue their fieldwork. Thus, it is also not surprising that a visitation report from 1718 states:

"The youth of Ottersheim know nothing because they are used to learning the catechism."

An important part of the professional teacher duties was the church service. At 4 o'clock in the morning, at 3 or 4 o'clock in the afternoon and at 9 o'clock in the evening, he had to ring the bell in worship and in daily Salve devotions, beat the organ, and lead singing and prayer. During Mass, he supervised the children so that they did not "romp, wiggle, and look around." At funerals, he accompanied the priest to the cemetery, while schoolchildren or members of his family assisted him by ringing the bells. He held a lantern in front of the

Blessed Sacrament, and wore a robe and surplice when anointing the sick. Moreover, he was also responsible for the supervision of the children outside of school. He controlled not only the streets but also the spinning rooms. If a child was found in a spinning room, he was to be punished on the spot with a switch. The dance floor was monitored by the teacher so that no youth were present without authorization.

Teachers received their training in a long apprenticeship that he would complete under a master schoolteacher. Before receiving an appointment as an independent teacher, he was tested by a commission. He had to be able to read every book clearly, neatly, and true to the context of the content. He dare not make any gross spelling errors in the writing. The teacher was expected to know enough to teach the children the basic principles of arithmetic. As a person, it was expected of him that he lead a Christian and exemplary life; and as a teacher he should not quarrel, grumble, scold, or curse; and he should teach his class with love, gentleness, and patience.

But how was a teacher paid for his multi-faceted work in school and church? A list from 1747 provides insight. The annual income of a teacher in Ottersheim follows:

1. From the Provost of Hördt: 6 malters of grain.
2. From the Klingenmünster Abbey: 10 gulden
3. For bell ringer tasks from tithes: 13 malters and 4 simmers of grain
4. From 9 morgen of meadows, the teacher was entitled to the hay tithes. The meadows lay partly at the stone weir and in the Hundsloch.
5. In addition, the teacher was entitled to:
    a) From each school child quarterly: 15 kreutzers
       From each student in winter for
       heating the classroom: 2 sticks of wood
       Note well, the school fees for poor children are paid from the charity fund.
    b) For each wedding: 45 kreutzers
    c) For a christening: 15 kreutzers
    d) For the burial of an adult: 45 kreutzers
    e) For the burial of a child: 15 kreutzers
    Note well, these amounts were increased because at weddings and funerals the teacher had to beat the organ.
    Note: As the Reformed did not have their own bells, the small community bell was rung at their funerals. This was done by the Catholic teacher who had the sole privilege thereto. The Reformed had to pay him:
    For the burial of an adult: 30 kreutzers
    At the funeral of a child: 15 kreutzers
6. In addition to these incomes, a teacher had timber rights, fishing rights, and other common rights like any other citizen.

As a statement from 1744 shows, the fees amounted to approximately 10 gulden a year, and the school money to about 15 gulden a year so that the total revenue of the teacher was about 35 gulden plus 20 malters of grain and hay from a morgen of meadow. In addition, there was a free apartment and a quarter morgen of garden. If we calculate the malter of grain at 5 gulden (often it was cheaper), then the teacher had an annual income of about 150 gulden. All the while, the work in the school increased from year to year. A very detailed statistic of 1791 reported 150 schoolchildren in Ottersheim in the weekday and Sunday school, of whom somewhat more than 100 were in the Catholic school and the rest in the Reformed school. Nevertheless, the teacher at that time, Georg Adam Kirnberger, remained in the village for 19 years. It was he who remained true to the village in the stormy period of the French Revolution and in the Napoleon Era until 1810.

When the French occupied the left bank of the Rhine in 1792, they established the Department of Donnersberg to which Ottersheim also belonged. The village belonged to Canton of Germersheim in the District of Speyer at that time. The French viewed the Palatinate as part of France and introduced the same changes here as in their mother country. In fine words, they spoke of the paramount importance of the school as the top need of the people, and the first benefit that they can expect from their government. Reality was not so pretty however. According to a report of Mayor Kopf dated 4 January 1806, Catholic teacher Adam Kirnberger received from Ottersheim the following income: A free apartment, 20 malters of grain, the hay tithes from 10 morgen of meadows, and 30 gulden in cash, totaling 366 francs. Additionally, he was entitled to a half malter of grain from the community store. Each child was supposed to pay 2.15 francs in school fees but actually only 1.62 francs were paid. Even that sum was paid by only half of the children; the other half was not paid, partly due to poverty and partly due to neglecting their obligation. Moreover, each of the 80 schoolchildren were to bring 1/4 klafter of wood to the school but in fact only 9 instead of 20 klafter were brought in corresponding to a value of 97 francs. This income was also meant to cover the activity of the teacher as organist, sexton, and bell ringer, while the hay tithe was intended as compensation for the winding the tower clock. In the years 1807 to 1810, when the Ottersheim possessions of the former Spiritual Goods Administration were largely sold by the French government, the economic state of the teacher deteriorated noticeably. That is to say, many goods were sold from which the teacher had received produce through trade or barter. Therefore, the salary of the teacher was regulated according to the French model. Napoleon's Education Act from the year 1802 stipulated that the communities were required to build and to maintain the public schools. The teacher, who was chosen by the mayor and the community councils, was to receive free housing and a salary that the councils were to determine, but the parents had to finance. A statement dated 1814 reports that the contributions of the parents amounted to a total of 160.75 francs for 100 schoolchildren. The use of a garden field was estimated at 10 francs so that teacher Jakob Damen received from his work at the school a total of 170.75 francs at that time. Damen was surely happy that the remuneration for his work as bell ringer, sexton, and organist significantly increased his income, since the payments in kind that he received had only a value of 126 francs. The total income of the teacher at that time came to 296.75 francs. It was a modest sum at that time considering that a kilogram of pork cost nearly a franc and 3 kilogram of heavy grain bread cost nearly half a franc. The two statements of 1806 and 1814 clearly show how the economic situation of the teacher had deteriorated significantly as a result of the secularization of church property.

After the defeat of Napoleon, the French rule along the Rhine was ended on 1 January 1814. In the same year, Governor General Grüner restored the pre-revolutionary school order through an administrative edict. Finally, when Bavarian King Maximilian I took possession of the Palatinate in 1816, he turned his whole attention to the long neglected schools. Payment and employment of teachers remained the duty of the communities. For the internal operation of schools, he introduced a mandatory curriculum monitored by the local Spiritual and District School Inspector. School boards were formed within the local community. As in the 18th century, candidate teachers received their training privately, at first through an apprenticeship with a master teacher. The training was supplemented by two years of study at a teacher training college. Already in 1817, the first teacher training college in the Palatinate was established in Kaiserslautern. It had to accept both Protestants and Catholics. It was not until 1839 that a second college was introduced in Speyer that was intended exclusively for the Catholic teaching candidates. In the course of the 19th century, private preparation of teacher candidates was replaced by a preparatory school that lasted three-years.

In the first half of the 19th century, the Damen family provided the Catholic teacher in Ottersheim. Jakob Damen (the elder) worked from 1810 to 1815, his son Jakob taught from 1815-1831, and his brother Michael taught at the local school from 1831 to 1859. As the number of students grew steadily and already was above 100, the respective teacher himself began looking for an assistant. We are told that Jakob Damen (the elder) educated a former student to be a teacher, Johann Merdian who was born in 1798. He was then employed at the age of twenty years as an assistant teacher in Ottersheim to the highest satisfaction of all. Unfortunately, the school aides mostly remained at a place only a short time, because they could not support a family with their salary. They therefore took the opportunity to move to a place where they could find a better income as headmaster.

With the employment of a second teacher, the so-called *school aide,* the question of a second classroom in Ottersheim became a hotter issue from year to year. The old schoolhouse on the Große Gasse (property 62 of Emil Brüderle) was no place for it. So in 1827, the community bought the two-story house of impoverished former mayor Johann Kopf that had been built in 1785 and was east of the rectory. Teacher Damen (the younger) set up his living quarters on the ground floor while two classrooms and a living room for the school aide were furnished on the upper floor.

Good insight into the inner school conditions at the time can be taken from the visitation reports that were required at the end of each school year. The report of 1845 was singled out as an example. The usual final examination for the weekday and Sunday school was held on 21 April. At half past 3 o'clock in the afternoon, District School Inspector Dekan Day, Local School Inspector Father Johann Pfeiffer of Ottersheim, district police officer H. Mayr, Mayor Valentin L. Seither, the community council representatives and local school board members G. Seither, Ms. Gensheimer, A. Seither, Andr. Greiner, G. Hatzenbühler, W. Seither, and Ludwig Steegmüller appeared. The teaching staff consisted of teacher Michael Damen (1831-1859 in Ottersheim), school assistant Georg Bullinger (1840-1845 in Ottersheim), and needlework teacher Margarete Günther, who was employed at the "trade school" in 1838 as the first "vocational teacher."

The pupils and graduates from school were tested in all the subjects in which they had received instruction, including religion, biblical history, memory exercises, reading, penmanship, spelling, written essays, oral and written arithmetic, geography (especially that of the Fatherland), singing, drawing, and needle work. The report referred to Damen and Bullinger as especially capable teachers whose musical talent was outstanding. So it is not surprising that both the weekday and the Sunday school pupils received grades of very good to excellent. The two teachers had no easy job with their extremely large classes. Assistant Bullinger taught the three lower grades as the so-called *lower division* with 75 children. The upper grades of teacher Damen included 69 pupils. Each child received a bread roll in recognition of the good examination results.

In 1844, the school year had begun after Easter. During the summer months for example, from 15 April to 16 September, classes were held only in the morning. They began at 6 o'clock in the morning and lasted until 9 o'clock; afterwards, teachers and pupils worked in the fields. At harvest time, there were 14 days of vacation.

The autumn vacation lasted from 16 September to 2 November and completed the summer session. In the winter session, classes were held from 8-11 o'clock in the morning and 1- 4 o'clock in the afternoon. On Wednesday and Saturday afternoon, all the boys were free from school while the girls, partly on Wednesdays and partly on Saturdays, had needlework lessons from 12:30-3:30 o'clock in the afternoon.

Because of the practical applicability in daily life, boys were mainly taught drawing and for girls needlework. In the school year 1844-1845, one boy drew 2 barrels and a pigeon loft, another drew 2 churches and a coffee cup, a third drew a well pump, a fourth drew a castle and a column, and a fifth drew an urn and a body. The others had practiced the art of drawing in a similar fashion. In needlework craft, one girl was able to display 6 pairs of socks and an apron, a second child had made 2 pairs of socks, a pair of "wrist warmers" (pulse warmers) and an apron, a third showed 5 pairs of socks and an apron.

In spite of the strong restriction of class in the summer, there were no fewer than 773 unexcused absences recorded during the course of the session. It is therefore not surprising that the review would note that parental involvement in education left much to be desired. In contrast, health, cleanliness, and modesty of the children were highly praised. Of the Sunday schoolchildren, it was noticed that they were loitering on the dance floors during the church fair festival. All children possessed the prescribed books and writing materials. Poor children received their materials from the local poor fund. The school building, classrooms, and teaching equipment were found in good order. A school garden was also present. Teacher Damen, an avid fruit tree grower, had complained that the soil of the school was unsuitable for fruit trees however.

All children of the village had to attend school after completing the 6th year of age. Girls after their 13th the year of age and boys after their 14th year of age were released from school on weekdays. Thereafter, all up to the completed age of 18 were required to attend the Sunday and holiday school where the teaching of the week day school was continued. Classes were at 7 until 8 o'clock in the morning on all Sundays and holidays in the summer and 8 until 9 o'clock in the morning in winter. Teacher Damen taught 30 girls and assistant

Bullinger taught 24 boys in Sunday school in the school year of 1844-1845. As salary, Teacher Damen received the following:

From the community treasury in cash:	211 gulden	
20 malters of grain in kind or:	90 gulden	
Free apartment in the value of:	15 gulden	
Compensation for the church service:	19 gulden	34 kreutzers
Compensation for other services:	5 gulden	20 kreutzers
Total:	340 gulden	54 kreutzers

From the community treasury, school aide Bullinger was entitled to 200 gulden and the needlework teacher was entitled to 30 gulden.

When teacher Michael Damen retired in 1859, the community council selected his son-in-law, Anton Decker from Klingenmünster, as his successor. Decker oversaw the upper division of the 4-7 classes with an average of 70 children. He was not only an able educator but also an excellent musician, who founded the Catholic Church choir in Ottersheim and successfully led it through three decades. The beneficial work of the teachers in school and community received its deserved recognition in the awarding of the Honorary Medal of the Order of Ludwig by the Royal Bavarian government in 1886.

While Decker was active continuously for 30 years in Ottersheim, the assistants who occupied the second position changed an average of every three years. These assistants were mostly young and unmarried teachers who had just completed their training. In preparation for the profession, they had to spend five years at the Teacher Seminary in Speyer after elementary school. The first three years could be served in a preparatory school in Edenkoben, Blieskastel, Kusel, or Kirchheimbolanden. Since the year 1866, the "youth discharged with a Certificate of Qualification" from the seminary were to practice with a capable teacher in a school for a year as prospective teachers. The preparation time ended with a practical examination conducted by the responsible District School Inspector. The young teacher could be employed as a teacher's aide after passing the examination. The expectant schoolteacher would be given a position in a school after an appropriate trial period.

Since 1875, the young teachers were regularly required to attend additional training sessions that were designed and directed by the Senior Teacher of a District, later called the *District Master Teacher.* After four years of preparation time, they took an employment exam and from then on could apply for an advertised school position. The young teacher had to direct his application to the local school board or to the mayor of the town offering the position. Local councils and school boards selected the candidate most acceptable to them from any applications received, while the Chamber of the Interior of the Royal Bavarian Government declared the transfer or appointment.

Many a young assistant teacher sought and found his partner in Ottersheim. District School Inspector Pastor Hitzelberger from Lingenfeld writes about this in 1887:

"As long as there are such rich girls in Ottersheim, and hopefully it will always be so, and as long as the rich girls would gladly become Mrs. Teacher, the young inexperienced assistant teachers will be in danger of getting themselves a golden bird before they have a cottage of their own."

After marriage, the young teacher was forced to look for a better paying school position with an appropriate apartment. As assistant teacher in Ottersheim, he was entitled to 250 gulden or 428.6 marks salary plus free housing in a furnished room. However, the entitlement amounted to at least 350 gulden or 600 marks yearly as headmaster in Ottersheim. Moreover, the community had to provide him an apartment with agricultural outbuildings, a garden, and some arable land. Additionally, there was income from the church services.

Shortly before the turn of the century, a female teacher was employed in Ottersheim for the first time. She had to teach 74 boys and girls in classes 1-3. Still, Miss Luise Tabertshofer was replaced by assistant teacher Friedrich Charrois in 1899. Later, the second school position was occupied more and more often by female teachers, while school management was always in the hands of a male teacher.

Under Mayor Lorenz Föhlinger, the old schoolhouse that had served to shelter the two classes of the Catholic school for 75 years was demolished in 1902 and replaced by a stone building in the same location. In the building were three classrooms, two spacious teacher apartments, and an assistant's apartment with two rooms. The schoolhouse was occupied in 1903 by the Catholic and the Protestant school. The two barns at the rear of schoolyard continued to be available for the teachers for agricultural purposes. The house at 52 Lange Straße that is now occupied by the Dumser brothers was built from the stones of the old schoolhouse.

During the First World War in the years 1915 to 1917, when teacher Renn was drafted into the military, the upper division of the Catholic school had to be taught by Teacher Andermann and by Head Teacher Jakob Körper from Offenbach. Körper received a monthly payment of 60 marks from the income of the open position. It was not until 1917 that the position was taken by teacher Karl Leidecker from Hermersberg. The assistant teacher position also had to be carried out by outside teaching personnel, because Anton Dahl, who was the official position holder, could not take his job due to combatant service.

The defeat of Germany in 1918 and the end of the monarchy also brought a fundamental change in the status of teachers. The Free State of Bavaria signed a law in 1919 making all public school teachers government employees. Employment and compensation from then on was no longer the responsibility of the communities but that of the county governments. The church service duty was now provided at the discretion of each teacher. At the same time, the previous religion-based school inspection was transferred to civil school boards that were populated from the ranks of the teachers. The first superintendent in the district of Germersheim was Oscar Mohr who was also responsible for Ottersheim.

While the number of students initially declined as a result of the war, they increased greatly later. In 1931, 138 children had to be taught by two teachers. For this reason, Mayor Franz Steegmüller requested the construction of a third school site. The request to the community was repeated the following year because the number of pupils had risen to 156.

But not until the beginning of the 1933 school year was a third teacher ordered to Ottersheim. It was to be monastic teacher Sister Cedislava Kohl, who would teach a class in the Sisters' Home next to the church. Like all monastic schoolteachers, she had to leave the teaching profession in 1936 due to the anti-clerical policies of the Third Reich. The Catholic and Protestant denominational schools were forcibly converted into a civil public school a year later. The old state law was restored in 1949, four years after the collapse of the so-called Thousand Year Reich. The 1937-1938 school years also brought an extension of compulsory education from the current seven years to eight years. This regulation had already been implemented in the cities while in the villages the seven years of primary schooling was common until 1937.

During the Second World War, combining classes and teaching by aides was common. Particularly difficult was the situation after the collapse in 1945. At that time, two teachers had to teach up to 200 children. Not until 1949 did conditions gradually return to normal at the elementary school in Ottersheim. Head teacher Hans Gensheimer took over the school in 1948 after the transfer of Head Teacher August Foltz to Krickenbach. By March 1949, the number of students had increased to 209. That number included 31 Protestant children. This induced the District Government in June 1949 to send refugee teacher Hans Graef to Ottersheim. As a Protestant teacher, he taught in the civil school at first until he took over the re-established Protestant school with 31 pupils in November 1949. For the 178 Catholic children there were now three Catholic teachers. For the school year beginning in 1964, Ottersheim received for the first time a fourth Catholic teacher for the 150 schoolchildren. At the end of the 1964-1965 school years, Head Teacher Hans Gensheimer was transferred as Vice Principal to Landau. Only reluctantly did the population take leave of the ever-popular educator whose service to the school and also to the musical life of the village was highly recognized. "You have done more than your duty," said Mayor Wünschel at the farewell ceremony that had filled the school gymnasium to the last place. His successor was Head Teacher Berthold Feldmann from Speyerbrunn who took over as head of the Catholic School in Ottersheim.

With the shortened school year in 1966-1967, the ninth grade was introduced in Rhineland-Palatinate. If possible, students were to be brought together in classes consisting of a single grade and age. Therefore, the Ottersheim children in the ninth year of school have traveled to Bellheim since December 1966, where the boys and girls were taught with children from Knittelsheim and Bellheim but separated by gender and of their own age. The elementary school in Ottersheim therefore includes only grades 1 through 8. Since 1967, the school year has begun on August 1st in the German states, as was decided by the Minister of Culture.

After a long illness, esteemed Head Teacher Gertraud Richter died in December 1966 at the age of 48 years. She was buried in the Ottersheim cemetery.

The Catholic school head teachers
(The name of the assistants are in parentheses)

Ägidius Mau	Named in	1716
Augustin Schultz		1727-1760
Johann Baumann		1760-1777
Konrad Kern		1778-1791
Georg Adam Kirnberger		1791-1810
Jakob Damen of Knöringen		1810-1815
Jakob Damen, the son		1815-1831
Michael Damen, the brother		1831-1859
Anton Decker of Klingenmünster		1859-1889
Konrad Nieser of Waldsee		1889-1906
Robert Renn of Halberg		1906-1915
(Jakob Körper, Head teacher of Offenbach)		1915-1917
Karl Leidecker of Hermersberg		1917-1923
(Emil Cornicius of Speyer)		1923
Jakob Jäger of Arzheim		1923-1929
(Fritz Steegmüller of Ottersheim)		1929
August Foltz of Göcklingen		1929-1948
(Herbert Getto of Schaidt)		1948
Hans Gensheimer of Annweiler		1948-1966
Berthold Feldmann of Rheinzabern		1966 —

Second Catholic School

Jakob Anton Geiger	1830-1832
Franz Doniat	1832-1834
Heinrich Friedebach	1834-1839
Georg Bullinger of Herxheim	1840-1845
Karl Ludwig Mühe of Knittelsheim	1846-1847
Karl Pfeiffer	1848-1853
Friedrich Reithmayer	1853-1860
Peter Dausch of Eschbach	1860-1864
Siegmund Böhm of Hördt	1864-1865
Gustav Moßbacher	1865-1867
Gustav Schwaab	1867-1872
Ludwig Leibrecht	1872-1875
Jakob Müller	1875
Konrad Nieser of Waldsee	1875-1879
Franz Louis of Lingenfeld	1879-1884
Otto Wagner of Rülzheim	1885-1887
Friedrich Reif	1887-1891
Adam Schmidt	1892-1895
Josef Braun of Gleisweiler	1895-1898

Karl Wolf of Enkenbach	1898-1899
Luise Tabertshofer	1899
Friedrich Charrois of Thorhaus/Waldmohr	1899-1902
Josef Zorn	1902-1904
Leonhard Becker	1904-1906
Isabella Buchheit of Blickweiler	1906-1911
Amalie Öhl	1912
Paula Weis of Frankenthal	1913-1915
Georg Wesner of Speyer	1916
Ludwig Rößler of Geinsheim	1916-1918
Josef Stubenrauch	1918-1919
Katharina Amberger of Frankenthal	1919
Wilhelm Sattel of Schifferstadt	1919
August Kortz	1920-1921
Maria Wengler of Speyer	1921-1936
Wilma Wißmann of Ludwigshafen/Rhein	1937-1940
Rosa Ernst of Rodalben	1940-1950
Karl Bröhmer (born in Basel)	1950-1952
Gertraud Richter of Wirbitz/Oberschlesien	1952-1966
(Paul Laforce of Lingenfeld)	1956
(Margarete Schall of Lingenfeld)	1956-1957
Heidrun Krämer of Wollmesheim	1966—

Third Catholic School

Cedislava Kohl, School Sister (nun)	1933-1936
Annemarie Cronauer of Speyer	1936-1939
Anna Sprißler of Frankenthal (married Przybilla)	1939
Unassigned	1940-1945
Maria Neumeister of Kronach	1946-1950
Margareta Roth of Schaidt	1950-1954
Ilse Schroth, née Bohner of Speyer	1954-1962
Werner Heidenreich of Zeiskam	1962—

Fourth Catholic School

Gisela Wilhelm of Bellheim	1964—

The Protestant (Reformed) School of Ottersheim

As mentioned earlier, the present-day Protestant school in Ottersheim was initiated in the second half of the 16th century in the wake of the Reformation. It was maintained by funds that came mainly from the confiscated monastic property. The school, which was initially housed in the former rectory, very likely perished in the 30 Years War. However, it was probably already re-established in the second half of the 17th century. Under the Sun King Louis XIV of France, when 51 Ottersheim families "renounced the Calvinistic faith and returned to the Catholic Church," the school was awarded to the Catholics along with the church. Most likely, the Reformed teacher had to halt his activities in 1686 after re-catholicization took place.

Not until the Proclamation of Religious Freedom in 1705 was there again a Reformed school in Ottersheim. The Reformed villagers, who were mostly wealthy farmers, purchased a property in the Gröhlig using private funds. It was the manor property at 22 Germersheimer Straße that is occupied today by Wilhelm Hoffmann. The house was used as a school and the barn as a temporary church. That a Reformed school in Ottersheim existed in 1718 is documented in a visitation report of the time that states:

"Ottersheim has a Reformed teacher."

Also, the name of school servant Theophil Nerbel is noted in a baptismal register of that year. His successor, Christian Dunger, is mentioned in 1726. Like their Catholic counterparts, the Reformed teachers were employed by the State and salaried by the Spiritual Goods Administration.

Toward the end of the 18th century, Reformed teacher Friedrich Ruppertus lived and worked in the little schoolhouse at 22 Germersheimer Straße. He was married to Rosine Lösch. Since his income barely sufficed to live, he cultivated fields and raised livestock, as did the Catholic teacher. He designed his teaching according to the instructions of the Palatinate government; the lessons essentially matched the "Instructions for the Catholic School teachers." Besides reading, writing, and arithmetic, he had to educate the youth in the Reformed faith and to be virtuous citizens. Ruppertus had an average of 25 children to serve. Because no Reformed pastor lived in the village, the teacher took on a series of church duties. He led the songs as a cantor, and he took over the religious instruction of youth as a teacher, which the Pastor in Offenbach could not carry out. Teacher Ruppertus experienced the 1818 merger of the Reformed and the Lutherans into the United Protestant Evangelical Church of the Palatinate. This was certainly of minor importance for Ottersheim because only very few Lutherans were present and all originated from elsewhere. More important was the construction of the Protestant church at the beginning of the 19th century. Because the current makeshift church was dilapidated, voluntary donations by the Protestant inhabitants of Ottersheim comprised the largest part of the necessary funds. The new church was inaugurated on 20 August 1820 while the material from the previous building had already been auctioned in 1817. In the interim period, Catholic Pastor Märdian made the Catholic Church available to help out the Protestants.

When teacher Ruppertus retired from the teaching profession in 1831 at the age of 74 years, initially no candidate for the vacant teaching post could be found. This was probably the reason that led the community to sell the old Protestant school building in the Gröhlig and to erect a new building next to the Catholic school on the Lange Straße. It was a stone building with a classroom and a small teacher apartment. Teacher Ludwig Ecarius, who was married to a sister of the Catholic teacher Damen, moved into the house in 1832. In the thirties of the 19th century, the Protestant population reached 209 souls, nearly a quarter of the entire village population. After that, the number of Protestants steadily declined, partly due to emigration and partly due to the small number of children in Protestant families. Accordingly, the number of pupils in the Protestant school also declined.

Teacher Ludwig Ecarius, who was also a long-time town clerk, died in 1877. His daughter Amalie was needlework teacher in Ottersheim from 1865-1874. The vacant position in the Protestant school was advertised, but no candidate applied for the position. So it was, the class was initially dissolved, and the children had to be sent to the Catholic school. Religious instruction was provided by the responsible pastor from Offenbach. Even the organ service at the Protestant church was provided by the Catholic teachers. The lack of interest in the Protestant school position was due in part to the fact that the teacher received only a modest salary, and the community declined to change the teacher's aide position into a better-paid assistant teacher position. Not until 1880 was there an application for the position in the person of the teacher Karl Falk from Nördlingen. When Falk went to Oberhochstadt in 1884, new concerns arose regarding the occupation of the vacant teaching post. Temporary workers had to step in for two years until teacher Franz Stoeppler from Kirchheimbolanden was transferred to Ottersheim in 1886, after the local council and school board had voted unanimously for him. When Stoeppler went to Sondernheim in 1891, the position was given to teacher Jakob Stelzer. The Protestant school building was demolished in 1902. In place of the two schoolhouses, a new building was built with stone facing. It included two teacher apartments, an assistant's room with a side room, and three classrooms. The Protestant school was located on the ground floor opposite the lower portion of the Catholic school. Teacher Stelzer was able to occupy the new teacher's apartment in 1903.

From 1905 to 1926, Philipp Andermann of Freimersheim was the Protestant teacher in Ottersheim. When Andermann was called for military service in September 1915, his class had to be cared for by outside teachers. For this, these teachers were given a monthly allowance of 24 marks from the District fund. After the war ended, teacher Andermann resumed his service at the Protestant elementary school in Ottersheim on 1 December 1918.

During the Third Reich, the two denominational schools in Ottersheim were forcibly converted into a non-denominational school at the beginning of the 1937-1938 school years. The position of head teacher was given to August Foltz as the most senior teacher in Ottersheim, while Protestant teacher August Dewein took over one of the four classes. During the war, teacher Dewein was transferred to Kandel at his request. Because no candidate applied for the advertised position, Ottersheim remained without a Protestant teacher until 1949. Then the district government of the Palatinate assigned refugee teacher,

Hans Graef from Schirkanyen/Siebenbürgen to Ottersheim. At first, Graef worked at the non-denominational school. But when the National Socialist measures were revoked and the original denominational schools were re-opened in November 1949, he took over the single-class Protestant school with a total of 31 children. The schoolroom on the ground floor that had been used for the Protestant children before 1937 was again put into service. Unfortunately, for the Protestant population of Ottersheim, Graef applied for a school position in Landau that was given to him at the beginning of September in 1952. From 1956 to 1966, teacher Werner Frölich from Kaiserslautern was in charge of the Protestant school in Ottersheim. Because Frölich had grown up in the city, he felt so much at home in Ottersheim that his departure from the village was not easy for him. His successor was Rudolf Stubenbord from Landau who received his first teaching post in Ottersheim after graduating from the teacher seminary. He moved into the teacher's apartment with his wife.

The Protestant (Reformed) Teachers
(The name of the temporary workers are in parentheses)

Kasper Reckius		1603-1616
Hans Georg Axt		1616-1621
Simon Trenker		1621-?
Theophil Nerbel	(named to post)	1719
Christoph Dunger		1726?-1750?
Heinrich Joh. Uhinck		1750?-1780?
Friedrich Ruppertus		1780-1831
(Morgenthaler)		1831-1832
Joh. Ludwig Ecarius		1832-1877
Teaching posts vacant		1877-1880
Karl Falk of Nördlingen		1880-1884
(Friedrich Petry)		1884-1885
(J. Vogelsang)		1885
(Jakob Stelzer of Gerolsheim)		1885
(Karl Flor)		1885-1886
Franz Stoeppler of Kirchheimbolanden		1886-1890
(Joh. Michael Birnmeyer from Unterfranken)		1890-1891
Jakob Stelzer of Gerolsheim		1891-1905
(O. Munzinger)		1905
Philipp Andermann of Freimersheim		1905-1926
(Albert Wadle of Gleisweiler)		1926-1927
Ludwig Stibitz of Lauterecken		1927-1935
August Dewein of Dierbach		1935-1941

Non-denominational school	1937 to 1949
Teaching posts vacant	1941-1949
Hans Graef of Schirkanyen/Siebenbürgen	1949-1952
(Armin Schmitt of Speyer)	1952
Helmut Fischer of Insheim	1952-1956
(Otfried Müller of Freckenfeld)	1956
Werner Frölich of Kaiserslautern	1956-1966
Rudolf Stubenbord of Landau	1966 —

PUPIL NUMBERS

	Catholic elementary school						*Protestant elementary school*			
1791	~80	Students	1	Teachers	7	Grades	~30	Students	1	Teachers
1806	80	"	1	"	7	"	18	"	1	"
1814	100	"	1	"	7	"	22	"	1	"
1827	134	"	2	"	7	"	35	"	1	"
1835	152	"	2	"	7	"				
1845	144	"	2	"	7	"				
1849	152	"	2	"	7	"				
1864	128	"	2	"	7	"	33	"	1	"
1873	124	"	2	"	7	"				
1906	150	"	2	"	7	"				
1911	—	"	—	"	—	"	26	"	1	"
1913	150	"	2	"	7	"				
1915	150	"	2	"	7	"				
1924	—	"	—	"	—	"	14	"	1	"
1929	124	"	"	"	7	"	14	"	1	"
1931	138	"	2	"	7	"				
1932	156	"	2	"	7	"				
1933	152	"	3	"	7	"				
1934	146	"	3	"	7	"	23	"	1	"
1935	138	"	3	"	7	"	26	"	1	"
1936	147	"	3	"	7	"	26	"	1	"

1937 Non-denominational school with 8 grades and 4 teachers

1949 Non-denominational school with 209 children in 8 grades with 4 teachers

(~ Denotes an approximation.)

1949	178	Students	3	Teachers	8	Grades	31	Students	1	Teachers
1950	150	"	3	"	8	"	28	"	1	"
1951	143	"	3	"	8	"	33	"	1	"
1952	125	"	3	"	8	"	29	"	1	"
1953	120	"	3	"	8	"	28	"	1	"
1954	114	"	3	"	8	"	29	"	1	"
1955	98	"	3	"	8	"	22	"	1	"
1956	97	"	3	"	8	"	26	"	1	"
1957	98	"	3	"	8	"	15	"	1	"
1958	108	"	3	"	8	"	14	"	1	"
1959	116	"	3	"	8	"	13	"	1	"
1960	133	"	3	"	8	"	13	"	1	"
1961	142	"	3	"	8	"	12	"	1	"
1962	135	"	3	"	8	"	17	"	1	"
1963	138	"	3	"	8	"	21	"	1	"
1964	150	"	4	"	8	"	22	"	1	"
1965	150	"	4	"	8	"	23	"	1	"
1966	159	"	4	"	8	"	29	"	1	"
1967	169	(9) "	4	"	9	"	27	(0) "	1	"

The needlework teachers in Ottersheim

Needlework was first taught in Ottersheim in 1838. The needlework school was called Industrial School or Work School. The first needlework teachers were seamstresses. Not until in the 20th century did they receive professional and pedagogical training.

Margarete Günther of Ottersheim	1838-1861
Barbara Damen (daughter of teacher Damen)	1862-1864
(Emigrated to America.)	
Amalie Ecarius (daughter of the teacher Ecarius)	1865-1874
Katharina Glatz of Ottersheim	1874-1891
Lina Job of Ottersheim	1891-1899
Frieda Burgermeister of Ottersheim	1899-1917
Lisa Föhlinger née Hindert of Ottersheim	1917-1931
Ella Härder (Sister Sapientia) of Rülzheim	1932-1936
Science teachers	1937-1945
Maria Rinnert of Offenbach	1945-1949
Johanna Schlindwein of Bellheim	1949-1955
Gabriele Neuner née Schuster	1955-1966
Leni Steegmüller of Ottersheim	1956-1962
Cilla Kröper née Steegmüller of Ottersheim	1962—

Village Life, Past and Present

Of Mayors in Ottersheim, Schultheiß and Bürgermeister

The mayor in the medieval and early modern period was not an elected president of their community, but he was the appointed ruler responsible for the village. A mayor especially had to ensure that each villager fulfilled his obligations to the authorities. Because he had to *heißen [order]* each citizen to pay his *Schuld [debt]* on behalf of the rulers, he was called the *Schultheiß*. For example, he was responsible for ensuring that the tithe was collected and distributed properly, that the tenants of the manorial estates paid their dues, and much more.

The mayor was also the presiding judge of the village court where he led the proceedings. At least once a year, he summoned the whole community to a day of hearings that served not only court cases but also general administration. Those obliged to appear had to do so personally and could not be represented. Early exit from the meeting was prohibited. The laws or rules were not only read at this meeting, but tax obligations were brought to mind, rules for agricultural cultivation were set, and the community institutions were selected if necessary, such as the village master, the cow and pig herders, the bailiff or village servant, the land warden, and the beggar warden. The choice of a midwife was the job of the assembled women. The four Court magistrates in Ottersheim were appointed to their office by the Faut [Governor].

Old records suggest that Bellheim, Knittelsheim, and Ottersheim together shared one mayor in the 14th and 15 centuries. Not until the 16th century did a local mayor appear who was only responsible for Ottersheim. This is probably due to the fact that with the nationalization of monastery properties in the wake of the Reformation the areas of responsibility of the mayor increased significantly. The governor of Germersheim needed a man who would have exact information about local conditions. At the same time, the mayor needed to be in a dependent relationship to his superiors. It does not surprise us therefore that most of the mayoral office holders in the 16th, 17th, and 18th centuries were occupants of feudal manors and tenants of feudal properties. They were usually regarded as the richest peasants in the village. Because there was no land registry, the mayor together with the courts needed to know exactly who owned what in the community. In inheritance cases, he had to ensure that the tax liabilities were fairly distributed among the heirs.

In particular, the mayor needed to have an overview of more than a thousand morgen of manorial estate property, who held the leases of the farmed land, and how much tax was to be applied thereto. In this diverse work, the mayor was supported by the courts and by the village master. Most of these matters were handled orally. However, should a document be needed, this was provided by the State Clerk from Germersheim. Not until toward the end of the 18th century did the teacher take over the task of community clerk.

The first mayor of Ottersheim whose name we recognize was Heinrich Rormann. He is mentioned in documents from the years 1405, 1408, and 1419. Like Jörg Burggraf,

Rormann was also mayor of Bellheim. Velten Trauth, who is mentioned in documents in 1565 and 1579, seems to be one of the first mayors to reside in Ottersheim. His successor, Hans Trauth, lived in one of the two Poppelmann manorial estates on the west side of the Germersheimer Straße. He was later replaced by Simon Moock. Of Mayor Peter Trimpler, it was reported he had a lot of trouble building the new church in the years 1618-1619. Trimpler lived in the former tavern "Zur Traube," the corner house opposite the community hall. Whether or not he lived to the end of the 30 Years War cannot be determined. In any case, Hans Georg Doll was mayor of Ottersheim in 1663. Countryman Peter Grünwald stood at his side as attorney[76] or assistant.

During almost the entire 18th century, the mayor was selected from the former Eußerthal manor at 66 Lange Straße. As wealthy peasants and owners of the tavern "Zur Krone," they enjoyed a good reputation in the community. The first mayor from the Eußerthal manor was Michael Rebstock who is mentioned in documents from 1706 and 1723. He was succeeded by Wendel Müller whose private seal was carried over to the Ottersheim crest of today. His son, Georg Müller, was probably mayor of Ottersheim until 1780. Georg Kopf, father of the famous Kopp-Maire replaced him. Kopf lived east of the rectory on a large estate. His house, which he built in 1785 on the site of the old one, was later used as a schoolhouse. He was victim of an epidemic in 1795. After the death of Georg Kopf, the office of mayor in Ottersheim was vacant for two years. The work seems to have been carried out at that time by attorney Nikolaus Merdian. Because the village was occupied by the French, it seems that no farmer wanted to subject himself to carrying out the orders of the Revolutionary troops. Also, there was the anti-religious attitude of the occupying power that even forced the parish pastor to flee. Not until 1797 did unmarried Konrad Hatzenbühler take over the business of a *Bürgermeister* as a so-called *agent*. This was the first time in the history of the village that a small peasant with only two morgen of owned land stood at the head of the community. Already after three years, he was succeeded by Daniel Schott of Knittelsheim. From several documents, it can be concluded that Hatzenbühler did not truthfully report the manorial ownership situation in Ottersheim and therefore fell from favor of the French. According to his information, the fields and meadows of the Poppelmann manor and of the monastic estates had largely passed into the hands of the Ottersheim farmers as inheritance. Only a small proportion was time-leased and therefore the property of the French Republic. However, investigations by the French showed that not 600 but more than 1,200 morgen of land in Ottersheim was time-leased. As a consequence of the whole situation, even the French Minister of Finance in Paris was involved. In any event, the French consolidated Ottersheim and Knittelsheim under one *maire* (mayor) in 1800 and transferred the job to Daniel Schott from

---

[76] The mayor's assistant seems to have been referred to by a numbered of titles, among these are second mayor, attorney, assistant, and adjunct.

Knittelsheim. They installed Johann Kopf of Ottersheim as adjunct. He replaced Daniel Schott in 1805 as maire of Ottersheim and Knittelsheim.

With the incorporation of the area on the left side of the Rhine into the French Republic in 1797, not only the title of *Schultheiß* changed to *Maire* but also the legal duties of the senior position in the community. Because the French abolished the tithes, sold the manorial estates, transferred jurisdiction to its own institutions, and collected taxes through its own officials, the mayor no longer needed to perform these duties. Rather, his duty was to represent the community toward the outside, and with the help of the community council keep the income and expenditures in order, delegate community work, and further the welfare of the village. At that time, the elementary school was also placed under the control of the community for staffing as well as for content and control.

The mayor and assistant managed the village police force. They had to investigate all violations that would require up to three days in jail or sentence of three days wages. When the French controlled the Palatinate, the hunting rights that had been exclusively held by the Elector rulers were awarded to the communities. Since that time, field and forest hunting rights are publicly auctioned to the highest bidder. In addition, the office of community commissioner was created at that time. From then on, the Ottersheim citizens had to deliver their taxes to the collector in Bellheim. The *civil law notary*[77] was also an agent of the French administration. Notaries were appointed for life. They had to be over 25 years old and had to pay a security deposit in metal coins in the amount of 4,000-6,000 francs.

During the period when the French had incorporated the Palatinate into their State, Johann Kopf, the famous *Kopp-Maire,* stood at the head of the Ottersheim community from 1805 to 1815. With his assistant, Konrad Humbert, and ten local council members, he steered the fortunes of the village and its 780 inhabitants. Kopf, Humbert, and the local council were appointed by Sub-Prefect Verny of Speyer. In those days, the village was administered according to laws and regulations that applied throughout France. The fall of Napoleon was also the end of French rule on the Rhine. In 1815, Mayor Kopf, assistant Humbert, and all local council members had to make their positions available. For the next twenty years, Bernhard Flory from Großfischlingen stood at the head of the Ottersheim community.

When the Palatinate went to Bavaria on 1 May 1816, King Maximilian I decided not to apply Bavarian law broadly to the newly acquired territories. Rather, special local regulations had been in place for the Palatinate communities for decades, some of which are even in place to this day. The management practice as it evolved over time was summarized in 1869 in the municipal code for the Palatinate. According to this code,

---

[77] Civil law notaries were trained lawyers typically retained by public offices of state to provide legal advice, draft and record legal documents, and perform other forms of legal service related to noncontentious private civil law.

Ottersheim had to choose ten council members every five years. Any citizen of Ottersheim was entitled to vote. As candidates for election, a community citizen must have completed his 25th year of life. The elections were held in November or December. Elections had to be completed by 15 December at the latest so that the new council could begin work at the beginning of the New Year.

The community council members had to choose the mayor and the assistant from their ranks, who were then installed into office by the district administrative authority after confirmation by the county government. Then the mayor swore in the council members. All practiced their duties without pay. Compensation could be granted to them for their actual expenses.

During the 19th century, it was usually well-off farmers who functioned at the head of the community as mayor or adjunct [assistant]. To account for the religious composition of the population, the mayor was Catholic and his representative was most often Protestant. The average term of office of mayor was ten years. A number of community leaders held office for three or more election periods. Most of the mayors retired from service due to age. In one case or another, death prematurely ended the activity of the mayor or his assistant.

When the war ended in 1918, the King of Bavaria abdicated and Bavaria was converted into a free State; changes also occurred to the democratic state administration for the municipalities. A new electoral law was passed in March 1919. It called for twelve community council members for Ottersheim who were elected from the men and women of the village. However, the election of the first mayor was no longer the duty of the community council in contrast to conventional practice. Rather, he was to be elected directly by all eligible voters. Franz Steegmüller emerged victorious by a large majority as first mayor at that time. The choice of the assistant mayor was the duty of the community council. Taking into account the religious composition of the village, Konrad Hoffmann from the Protestant minority was chosen as assistant mayor. The elections of 1924 and 1929 yielded the same results.

A change in leadership occurred only at Christmas in 1931 when First Mayor Franz Steegmüller died quite unexpectedly at the age of 56 years. He was succeeded by Emil Zwißler who had resigned his job in 1933 against the will of the council, because after Hitler took power he did not possess the trust of the Nazi Party. By order of the District Council, former assistant mayor Konrad Hoffmann took over leadership of the village. But he was deposed already in 1934, because he had placed himself at odds with the official party position in the struggle over the cultivation of hybrid grapes. After a short term by teacher Ludwig Stibitz, landlord Edmund Bischoff was finally appointed mayor in September 1935. Bischoff oversaw the office until the total collapse of the Hitler State in 1945.

It was felt to be an act of redress in the village when Emil Zwißler again took over the leadership of the community as mayor on 1 May 1945. His deputy was farmer Josef Herrmann who had held the title of Assistant Secretary since 1946. The community council was again elected according to the democratic rule of law on 15 September 1946. Under the new municipal code, such elections were to be held every four years with 15 council members elected each time. In contrast to the twenties, the election of the Mayor was no longer the responsibility of all eligible voters but by the community council. The assistant mayor was also selected through a ballot within the community council.

After Emil Zwißler, Paul Dörzapf was chosen by the council in 1952. He held the office for twelve years until 1964 when Erwin Wünschel took over as head of the community.

The men at the head of the Ottersheim Community

Mayor (Schultheiß)		Assistant	
Heinrich Rormann	1405 Mentioned in 1408 and 1409		
Jörg Burggraf	1508 Mentioned in 1509 and 1512		
Velten Trauth	Mentioned in 1565 and 1579		
Hans Trauth	Mentioned in 1588 and 1601		
Simon Moock	Mentioned in 1604 and 1607		
Peter Trimpler	Mentioned in 1618		
Hans Georg Doll	Mentioned in 1663 and 1666	Peter Grünwald	Mentioned in 1666
Johann Reinhard	Mentioned in 1695		
Joh. Michael Rebstock	Mentioned in 1706 and 1723	Johannes Knoll	Mentioned in 1706 and 1723
Wendel Müller	1730 Mentioned in 1746 and 1753		
Georg Müller	Mentioned in 1764 and 1776		
Georg Kopf	1780-1795	Nikolaus Merdian	1780-1797

Mayor (Maire)		Adjunct	
Konrad Hatzenbühler (called anAgent)	1797-1800	Johannes Frey	1797-1800
Daniel Schott (*Knittelsheim and Ottersheim*)	1800-1804	Johann Kopf (*Knittelsheim and Ottersheim*)	1800-1804
Johann Kopf	1805-1815	Konrad Humbert	1805-1815

Mayor (*Bürgermeister*)		Adjunct	
Bernhard Flory	1815-1834	Johannes Borger	1815-1834
Valentin Seither	1835-1853	Johann Gutting	1835-1853
Georg Seither	1853-1858	Valentin Scherff	1853-1858
Georg Kröper	1858-1863	Michael Weiß	1858-1863
Valentin Seither	1863-1865	Valentin Scherff	1863-1868
Anton Job	1865-1868	Joh. Jak. Gensheimer III.	1868-1875
Ludwig Seither	1868-1880	Lösch	1875-1880
Andreas Zwißler III.	1880-1895	Valentin Ehli	1880-1885
Lorenz Föhlinger	1895-1905	Franz Weiß	1885-1905
Franz Ludwig Job	1905-1920	Georg Knoll †	1905-1912
		Valentin Seither VI.	1913-1915
		Johann Günther	1915-1920
		† = Died	

First Mayor		Deputy Mayor	
Franz Steegmüller †	1920-1931	Konrad Hoffmann	1920-1933
Emil Zwißler	1932-1933	Ludwig Stibitz	1933-1934
Konrad Hoffmann	1933-1934	Edmund Bischoff	1934-1935
Ludwig Stibitz	1934-1935	Ludwig Scheurer †	1935-1943
Edmund Bischoff	1935-1945		
		† = Died	

Mayor		Assistant Secretary	
Emil Zwißler	1945-1952	Josef Herrmann	1945-1948
Paul Dörzapf	1952-1964	Paul Dörzapf	1948-1952
Erwin Wünschel	1964 —	Hugo Steegmüller	1952-1956
		Robert Frey	1956-1964
		Alois Hörner	1964 —

The Employees of the Community of Ottersheim

The Village Master

As the mayor was the senior official of the village, he had one or two village masters as his assistants. One Ottersheim village master was mentioned by name in an agreement from the year 1599. Hans Kuntz was listed for mayor Peter Trimpler. Two village masters from the neighboring village of Offenbach are mentioned in the same document. According to the text of the *Summary of Rights in the Village of Ottersheim from the year 1740,* there seems to have been two village masters rather often. There we also discover details about the duties of the village master in community life. According to the text, he had the duty to monitor and oversee upkeep of the roads, footbridges, bridges, and culverts, among other things. He had to arrange for necessary repairs. Those who did not obey had to pay a fine of five gulden. Together with the mayor, he checked field fences, deer fences, and meadow fences for damage. The trenches were to be closed and stopped when he so ordered. If cattle from outside meadows caused any damage, then he noted the damage and estimated the cost. He also contributed to the construction of timber-framed houses. In earlier times particularly, the community gave each builder a log from which the door threshold was made. It was the duty of the village master to determine the size of the threshold and then choose a suitable tree in the forest. In addition, the village master had to calibrate the wine and dry goods measures and ensure these were fairly apportioned. He was also obliged to collect any imposed penalties from community residents and to account for the collected money. When collecting the penalties, he was assisted by the *Grimmberger [bailiff]* when necessary.

From all this, we see that the village master played an important role in community life. At the least, during the French Revolution his duties seem to have been transferred to other community institutions that led to the dissolution of this office. In any event, the 19th century documents no longer speak of a village master.

The Court People (Jurors and Magistrates)

It was the duty of the Community Assembly to choose the court people or jurors from their midst. They were usually four men who possessed the confidence of the villagers because of their knowledge and skills. They swore an oath as jurors and thereby committed themselves to reach their decisions regardless of the personal standing of the accused. Undoubtedly, these people had duties to fulfill within the realm of village justice that would be assigned to a jury today. Overseen by the mayor, specifically they had to mediate disputes and punish lawbreakers. In addition, their realm of activity was far greater than that of jurors today. They were responsible in matters of community order and community law. They exercised functions that today are carried out by the community council.

The court people monitored the district borders once a year by walking the borders and examining the border stones. They were present during surveys of the fields and meadows, and no so-called *property renovation* was carried out without them. They not only knew the size and expansion of the manorial estates, but they also knew the amount of taxes and tributes owed. They monitored and controlled the rights as written down in the village proclamation and intervened when violations occurred. Their decisions were recorded in court books at least since the 16th century. Unfortunately, no such court book from Ottersheim has been saved. However, two such court books from the neighboring community of Offenbach reside in the State Archives at Speyer.

According to a cartulary book from the Cathedral Chapter of Speyer of 1475, the villages of Ottersheim and Knittelsheim had a common court of twelve people. This common court may possibly have existed as long as the villages of Ottersheim, Knittelsheim, and Bellheim shared a common mayor. However, in the 16th century and since then there is no longer any talk of a common court, and no single resolution carries the signatures of court people from these places. Because both Ottersheim and Knittelsheim already existed as independent parishes and communities before the year 1000, it appears questionable whether they actually had a common court in the Middle Ages. However, it is conceivable that the common mayor held joint meetings for similar submitted issues. Especially likely to be discussed together would be irrigation issues. The first six Ottersheim jury members who are mentioned by name are listed in the document, *Electoral Law in Ottersheim in 1565.* One hundred years later, there were usually four court people who placed their names on the agreements and resolutions in addition to the mayor. The jurors were usually in office a very long time, some possibly until their death. Their influence on village life was quite large, because these people were prestigious and wealthy peasants. The establishment of court people also saw its end with the French Revolution at the end of the 18th century. The functions were transferred partly to the local councils and partly to border control officials. The fact that today there are still four such officials clearly shows the connection to the court people.

Ottersheim mayor and court people
(Compiled from old documents)

1565:	Velten Trauth	Mayor
	Dieter Renger	Juror
	Jakob Markh	Juror
	Mathis Ulrichs	Juror
	Wendel Grunwaldt	Juror
	Hans Trauth	Juror
	Jost Lausch	Juror

1663:	Hans Georg Doll	Mayor
	Peter Grünewald	Of the court
	Nikolaus Ludwig	Of the court
	Bastian Winkelblech	Of the court
	Hans Trauth of Offenbach	Of the court
1706:	Johann Rebstock	Mayor
	Johannes Knoll	Civil law notary
	Hans Burgermeister	Of the court
	Lorenz Ludwig	Of the court
	Johann Heinrich Hörner	Of the court
	Hans Velten Mertz	Of the court
1730:	Wendel Müller	Mayor
	Stefan Gadinger	Of the court
	Jakob Gensheimer	Of the court
	Martin Job	Of the court
1753:	Wendel Müller	Mayor
	Martin Job	Of the court
	Georg Johannes Bischoff	Of the court
	Johannes Seither	Of the court
	Claudius Kreiner	Of the court
	Jost Ludwig	Of the court
1769:	Wendel Müller	Mayor
	Martin Job	Of the court
	Velten Müller	Of the court
	Nikolaus Hatzenbühler	Of the court
	Wilhelm Job	Of the court
	Martin Job	Of the court
1774:	Georg Müller	Mayor
	Martin Job	Of the court
	Nikolaus Hatzenbühler	Of the court
	Wilhelm Job	Of the court
	Velten Seither	Of the court
	Martin Dörzapf	Of the court
1776:	Georg Müller	Mayor
	Nikolaus Hatzenbühler	Of the court
	Wilhelm Job	Of the court
	Georg Kopf	Of the court
	Johannes Seither	Of the court

The Shepherds

Like the court people, so the shepherds were originally selected by the Community Assembly. This office seems never to have been an especially popular one because it was not connected to any major sort of income. The shepherd had to be up from dawn to dusk and could hardly perform any farming on the side. Generally, there were two shepherds in Ottersheim. In the mornings, the cow herdsman went through the village streets with his horn and gathered the cows, cattle, oxen, and calves. Then he drove the herd via the *Viehtrift [Cattle run]*, the present-day Waldstraße, to the meadows north of the village. During the day, the animals remained on the common grazing land, which comprised 40 hectares that lay to the west and east of the Gänsehaardt up to the district borderline in 1788. The cattle were led to water at the Dorfbach at noon and in the evening. A watering place was located at the elevation of the Falltorweg where the brook had been widened for this purpose. A gate that closed automatically, called a portcullis, was erected to prevent the cattle from entering the Falltorweg.

The shepherd drove the cattle back to the village in the evenings where the animals were separated from the herd and returned to their stalls. The pig herder, just like the cow herder, was up early each morning. He had to drive the pigs to the forestland north of the village where the animals could wallow around and feed on the fruits of the forest. Usually the pig herder also cared for the villagers' geese. These were driven to the Gänsehaardt where an artificial pond had been built for them. In the early decades of this century, Ottersheim still had a goose and a pig herder who was employed by the community. However, the livestock owners had to pay his salary.

To protect themselves from inclement weather, the shepherds had a hut on the Gänsehaardt under which they could take shelter. The last hut of this type was built by the community in 1870. It was 3 meters long, 2 meters wide, 2.1 meters high, and cost 47 gulden and 30 kreutzers. Because the applicants for the shepherd jobs often came from outside the community, they were offered a small house for which they were charged a small fee. Thus in the copy of the *Summary of Rights in the Village of Ottersheim from the year 1674,* a little house on the Große Gasse was mentioned in which "both shepherds lived." This building was not exempt from tributes and taxes. Often the job of shepherd was inherited from father to son or son-in-law. There were families that were active for decades as cow, pig, or goose herders. The practice of pasturing the cows ended at the beginning of this century, and the goose and pig herders gave up their work in the thirties. Today, only the names Gänsehaardt and Allmend remind of times past when the village cattle were driven to common pastures north of the village from early spring to late autumn.

The Land Warden, or Field and Meadow Warden

The land warden has always been one of the most important men of the village. As the name suggests, he had to monitor the fields and meadows, and protect them. It was indeed rare in Ottersheim that a villager stole something from his neighbors, but one was not sure that foreign characters and transients would not take one thing or another from the fields. Here, it was the job of the warden to look after things. He most likely used a horse to do this as is still common in Russia. While the warden could not be everywhere at once, fear had to become the protector of the forest. For grain, hemp, and beets there was not much to watch for; however, fruit and grapes required that much more attention. In addition, Ottersheim had at that time several land areas or parts thereof where mainly garden vegetables were planted. Such plots existed in the so-called Weggärten on the Knittelsheim Straße, in the Froschau next to the Lachengärten, in the Bauernweg, in the Wasserbeiz, and in various other places. A holdover from that time is the Gänseweidegärten that extends to the Haardt meadows. In these garden plots, the land warden was always kept busy protecting the ripening fruit from theft. Because the land warden was employed by the community, he was also paid by the community for his work.

Since the beginning of the 19th century, the community council has chosen the land warden from a set of applicants for the office. A new selection was necessary only if the warden was eliminated through death or illness. In special cases, it was also possible to replace him prematurely.

Ottersheim Land Wardens

Konrad Störtzer	
Konrad Heider	-1873
Franz Walk	1873-1877
Johann Bischoff	1877-1880
Jakob Jeckel	1880-1885
Franz Adam Müller	1885-1920
Otto Kröper	1920-1944
Ludwig Gadinger	1944-1948
Otto Kröper	1948-1955
Johann Gadinger	1955-1967
Heinz Hilsendegen	1967—

The Forest Ranger

Before the French Revolution, hunting rights in the Ottersheim forest belonged exclusively to the Electoral Court Chamber in Heidelberg. A forest servant from the District Office in Germersheim had to keep watch on behalf of the sovereign. Forest and wildlife crimes were "evaluated" by Electoral officials, and the fines were collected by the State Clerk. Residents of Ottersheim were entitled to timber and grazing rights in the Ottersheim forest. They were handed down in part orally and in part written in the *Summary of Rights in the Village of Ottersheim.* According to this, no one was allowed to cut down anything "green, oaken or of beech" other than undergrowth. The "large oaks" were reserved only for those who had previously "worked" for them. Rushes and chaff could only be collected after Saint Michael's Day (29 September). Whoever needed a threshold timber to build a house was shown an appropriate tree in the forest by the village master. Every year, firewood was cut in a specific part of the forest and distributed to community residents according to predetermined timber rights.

The village master and the mayor were responsible for compliance with these rules. This all changed at the beginning of the 19th century as a result of the French Revolution when the forest was turned over to the jurisdiction of the Ottersheim community. From then on, the community could lease the forest hunting rights to private persons for an appropriate fee. The community lands that previously could only be used by community citizens possessing specific rights were transferred to the community for use as was seen fit for grazing or in some cases, leased or sold. With the new legal situation, it was also necessary to have a forest warden to oversee and protect the forest and the common lands located in front of it. Therefore, the community commissioned its own forest warden or ranger who was paid from the community treasury. The forest ranger had to make his rounds through the village forest day by day and also had to monitor it by night. At all times a danger existed that wood thieves would chop down trees and haul them away, because timber and firewood were very rare and expensive. Also deer, roe deer, and hares were not safe from being captured or shot by poachers. Therefore if he took his job seriously, the forest ranger was never without work. Moreover, it was not difficult for the community to compensate the forest ranger adequately since the forest was one of the most productive sources of revenue for the community budget up to the fifties in this century. Next to hunting, the yearly wood auction especially brought respectable sums into the community treasury. This all changed when due to technical progress, neither construction wood nor firewood was requested and the risk of timber crime barely existed. This meant that the Ottersheim community has no longer employed its own ranger since 1954. This task was taken over at that time by a district forest ranger from Zeiskam, who in addition to the Ottersheim forest, supervised those of Knittelsheim and Zeiskam. The salary was collected by the forestry associations of Zeiskam, Knittelsheim, and Ottersheim. To prevent former forest ranger Johann Gadinger of Ottersheim from becoming unemployed, he was hired and paid by the forestry association as caretaker.

Ottersheim Rangers

Jakob Hatzenbühler	-1908
Ludwig Kreiner	1908-1932
Heinrich Faath	1932-1944
Ludwig Gadinger	1944-1948
Johann Gadinger	1948-1954
Albert Humbert, District Forester from Zeiskam	1954—

The Community Servant (Policeman)

Though official offices spoke of the community servant or of policemen, the Ottersheim population has always known this community employee by the name "Bill." This name is a shortened form of *Büttel [bailiff]* that originally meant, a messenger who had to carry out the orders of the mayor and court people as minister of the village court. Such a constable was present in Ottersheim as in other villages in the Middle Ages, although this cannot be verified in documents. A village court would hardly have been able to function without someone to assist. A report from 1719 also mentions a constable from Ottersheim. Specifically, at that time a certain Georg Roth from Ottersheim was charged before the Electoral Court in Germersheim with fornication and arson. When his defender pointed to the insanity of the accused and a letter of confirmation from the University of Heidelberg, Roth was pardoned by the Elector. However, before he was set free the Elector ordered:

> "the Ottersheim constable to strike him well with a switch."

Also, in the copy of the *Summary of Rights in the Village of Ottersheim from the year 1740* there is mention of a constable under the title *Grimmberger.* It says:

> "To counter this, the village masters should have their 'Grimmberger', who forces compliance of the guilty, and who collects the fines every four weeks and delivers them to the village master."

In the official language of the 19th century, the policeman was usually called the police servant. With that, his main task was clear. To be sure, the real police power lay with the mayor and his assistants, but the constable represented the general public. This was expressed clearly by his uniform that made him stand out from the other community citizens. In addition to a colored coat and colored trousers, he wore a sword on his belt and service cap on his head. In the evening, he made his rounds through the village and announced curfew in the taverns. He also did not hesitate to lock up thieves and troublemakers in the community hall. For the young boys of the village, the "Bill" was a feared person with whom you did not want to have to deal with. Almost every day, the policeman went once or twice through the village ringing his bell and announced regulatory or other news. Only after the Second World War was he at least partially relieved of this task through the use of public notice boards.

In addition to running errands and providing news, the policeman had to ensure compliance with the various police regulations that the mayor and council had adopted to ensure cleanliness, peace, and order in the village. Inside the village for example, coaches and light vehicles had to keep a walking pace. When snow lay on the ground, the horses pulling a sleigh or carriage had to have bells on their harness. The cattle herders were forbidden to take leave of the animals on community roads and paths. All streets and alleys had to be swept twice weekly, on Wednesday and Saturday afternoon. The policeman had to monitor all this and much more, and he had to intervene when violations occurred. Today, most of these functions are handled by other offices so that the "Bill" is rightly called by the official title of "community servant."

Ottersheim police and community servants

Peter Glatz	
Andreas Kopf	-1888
Daniel Winkelblech	1888-1889
Josef Kopf	1889-1905
Anton Job	1905-1931
Otto Winkelblech	1931-1954
Robert Hindert	1954—

The Town Clerk (Secretary)

Before the French Revolution, documentation was handled by a clerk from Germersheim who was responsible not only at the District Office, but also for those communities it governed. However, at that time there was not much to document. Vital records were not kept, approvals were mostly verbally issued, and statistical surveys were very rare. Only court decisions, contracts, leases, and the like were written down. The village master kept a master list of income and expenditures. The few requests that were directed to the District Office in the course of a year were drawn up by the mayor himself, whereby he usually received help from the pastor or the teacher. That changed at the end of the 18th century when the French preferred not only paper for money but also for the communication between civil offices. The mayoral offices developed quickly into offices that could no longer do without their own clerks. At that time, the communities were required to keep extensive records of births, marriages, and deaths that were initially written in French. Through in-depth surveys, the size and yield of the manorial estates was to be documented; new taxes and levies required numerous reviews and findings. These tasks could not be handled alone by the mayor. What could be more natural than for him to turn to the teacher for help? The teacher did this quite willingly because it was an opportunity for him to earn a bit of extra income that his meager salary made urgently necessary at that time.

Thus, in Ottersheim as in other villages the first town clerks were the local teachers. It took Ottersheim only about 50 years to find a full time clerk, Adam Horn from Bellheim, who from 1845 was responsible for Bellheim, Knittelsheim, and Ottersheim. When longtime chief clerk Friedrich Engel of Bellheim retired from the service due to his age in 1920, the council chose its first clerk who was born in Ottersheim, Luitpold Stadel. Like his successor, he served the villages of Ottersheim and Knittelsheim, while Bellheim employed its own officials. Since 1946, Chief Inspector Walter Kern from Rülzheim has been employed in Ottersheim.

Significantly, in the first half of the 19th century there existed a village clerk in Ottersheim but no public office. Not until 1855 was one established through the expansion of the community hall. Before that, the district clerk worked in a room that the mayor made available in his private home. The community paid the mayor a small stipend for this space because this room needed to be heated in winter and lighted when dark. Thus, it is reported that in the year 1835, Mayor Valentin Seither received ten gulden rent for a room in his house that he made available as a community clerk office.

It was self-understood that in earlier times all documents were written by hand. To be sure, the typewriter was already invented in 1870 by Mitterhof the Austrian; however, it took many decades until the clerk's room in Ottersheim was equipped with a manual typewriter. Today, one could hardly imagine community office work taking place without such equipment and without a dedicated typist. However, the requirements that the citizens had then of their district clerk were also much lower than in our paper-driven age where each and every thing must be processed in writing.

The Town Clerks of Ottersheim

Georg Adam Kirnberger, teacher in Ottersheim	1791-1816
Jakob Damen, teacher in Ottersheim	1816-1831
Ludwig Ecarius, teacher in Ottersheim	1831-1845
Adam Horn, town clerk from Bellheim	1845-1877
Eßwein, town clerk from Bellheim	1877-1882
Friedrich Engel, chief secretary from Bellheim	1882-1920
Luitpold Stadel, secretary from Ottersheim	1920-1937
Alois Kern, inspector from Bellheim	1937-1943
Adolf Bernzott, inspector from Bellheim	1943-1945
Luitpold Stadel, inspector from Ottersheim	1945-1946
Ludwig Leicht, administrative assistant from Bellheim	1946
Walter Kern, chief inspector from Rülzheim	1946—

The Meadow Waterer (Water Manager)

Earlier, the Village Master performed the tasks of irrigating the meadows. He was responsible for maintaining the water trenches and ditches, and damming the waters of the Queich and of the Brühlgraben at certain times. The community did not hire its own water manager until the 18th century. However, this became necessary after the 30 Years War, because the strong growth of the village population required an urgent and a better utilization of the meadows and pastures. The stone weir and the Hubgraben seem to have been built at the beginning of the 18th century. This was of great importance not least for the irrigation and drainage of the back meadows, the Hinterwiesen. A plan for the Hubgraben at the time of its creation lies in the State Archives in Speyer. Unfortunately, the year is not documented so the date of origin cannot be accurately determined. The Hubgraben stretches from the stone weir to the Knittelsheim mill. From there it flowed to the confluence with the Spiegelbach; it is called the *Buschgraben* in the Bellheim district. The Hubgraben was extended not the least goal of which was to irrigate thoroughly the 128 morgen Herrenwiesen and the 33 morgen Reiterwiesen in the Bellheim district. But the Hubgraben was also of importance for the farmers of Ottersheim since with its help the marshy land to the east of the stone weir was drained and converted into fertile meadows.

As is evident from the community records in the 19th century, Ottersheim always had two water managers for its meadows. The most important of these was the one who managed the *Vorderwiesen [front meadows]* and *Hinterwiesen [back meadows]* of the district. His duties included not only closing and opening the locks but also maintaining the water and drainage ditches. These days, he is allowed to dam the Queich water and irrigate the meadows on six days of the year, specifically on the 15th and 16th of May, on the 13th and 14th of July, on the 28th of July, and the 5th of August. The Brühl meadows were previously assigned to a second water manager who had to dam the waters of the Bordgraben on certain days. In our century, this task was given over to the field warden. The water manager of the Vorderwiesen and Hinterwiesen in 1864 was August Hindert who received 50 gulden, and the water manager of the Brühl meadows was Johannes Bischoff who received 35 gulden annual salary. In 1904, Ludwig Stadel was paid 250 marks. He had to pay for an assistant from his own salary. In 1920, water manager Otto Föhlinger received 900 marks and an inflation bonus of 300 marks. Since 1952, the field warden has performed tasks of water management in Ottersheim.

Ottersheim Water Managers

August Hindert	
Johannes Bischoff	
Andreas Kopf	
Andreas Stadel	-1880
Josef Kopf	1880-1889
Georg Hindert	1889-1895
Anton Moock	1895
Daniel Heider, Linen Weaver	1895-1898
Theodor Moock	1898-1904
Ludwig Zwißler	1904
Ludwig Stadel	1904-1907
August Greichgauer	1907-1913
Fritz Gensheimer	1913-1915
Johann Föhlinger	1915-1920
Assistant meadow water manager for drafted soldier Fritz Gensheimer	
Otto Föhlinger, Day Laborer	1920-1941
Emil Job	1941-1943
Johann Gadinger	1943-1944
Alois Messemer	1944-1945
Richard Kreiner	1945-1952
Johann Gadinger	1952-1967
Heinz Hilsendegen	1967—

The Breeding Stock Caretaker

There were no Ottersheim breeding stables and therefore no stable manager before 1877. Of course, it was still necessary before then to keep and care for stock bulls. However, the peasants of the village managed this task themselves. Each fall, a public auction was held in which the stock animals were given to the cheapest bidder to manage. The leasing peasant had to accommodate the stock in his barn for at least one year and feed it with hay, oats, and other hard feed. He had to keep a suitable drop zone ready in his closed courtyard during the wintertime. The bull was put out to pasture in the warm season. The cost of keeping the stock was allocated to the livestock owners. The supervision of the bulls was done by the official veterinarian and community breeding stock commission. The Ottersheim community had three breeding animals in 1864. The care for a large animal cost the owner 113 gulden; required payment for a midsize bull was 116 gulden and 90 gulden for a bull calf.

As the number of livestock in the village grew larger, the farmers became less satisfied with the current process for care of breeding bulls. So the community council decided in 1877 to establish its own breeding stable and to transfer the care of the animals to its own caretaker. However, 10 years passed until the breeding stall was nearly complete. As a temporary solution, the community leased a barn from farmer Johannes Zwißler III in that same year. Jakob Hanck was employed as stock caretaker and acted in this role until 1907 for which he received 250 marks annually. The feed for the bulls was made available by the community. The community bought the property at 32 Germersheimer Straße from Johannes Bischoff in 1880. Construction of a barn was begun six years later at a cost of somewhat more than 3,000 marks. The breeding barn was ready for occupancy during September of 1886. Adam Winkelblech, as the bricklayer, received 30 marks in addition to his salary as recognition for good work. The cost of the barn was partially passed on to the cattle owners. At that time, 450 head of cattle were required to pay breeding money.

The situation was changed when farmer Ludwig Föhlinger was appointed as breeding stock caretaker in 1962. The new caretaker had to house the livestock in his own barns and also procure the animal feed himself. He received 1,350 deutschemarks for each animal each year as compensation for his work and expenses. The community made available one hectare of meadows for his use from the community property. The former breeding stock stables on the Germersheimer Straße were used from then on to store the fire engine and associated equipment.

The keepers of breeding stock in Ottersheim

Jakob Hanck	1877-1907
Stefan Kopf	1907-1936
Ludwig Sauther	1936-1945
Peter Kopf	1945-1949
Robert Faath	1949-1959
Manfred Kuhn	1959-1962
Ludwig Föhlinger	1962—

The Barber (Bather)

In the Middle Ages, many villages had a public bathhouse that everyone could use. The man who had the task to care for this bathhouse for the community was called the *Bader [Barber]*. He not only supervised the bathhouse, but he also cut hair, beards, and shaved male bathhouse visitors when desired. In addition, he had some skill in simpler medical tasks. He pulled teeth, bound wounds, made poultices, and attached leeches for febrile illnesses. To be sure, we do not know if Ottersheim had a public bathhouse in earlier times, but we do know there still was a barber who worked both as barber and also as a medic in the first half of our century. His name was Ludwig Hilsendegen and he lived at 1 Riedstraße. His father, Konrad Hilsendegen (1850-1916), also held this post. The villagers turned to him first for lighter illnesses before turning to a doctor for help. He extracted bad teeth using pliers.

In the village accounts of the year 1833, a certain Heinrich Günther was mentioned as a surgeon or barber in Ottersheim. He delivered twelve blood leeches to a poor person back then and attached them at the cost of the community. This was a popular way to combat fever.

238

The Community Midwife

The Old High German word *Hevianna,* that is, *Hebende [who lifts],* suggests that midwives existed already more than a thousand years ago. Originally, the midwife was chosen by the village assembly from the married women of the village. Special training was not required. However, it was expected that she be chosen on the basis of personal experience and be able to handle the new office with the help of her predecessor. The midwife was considered to be a servant of the community and was therefore paid by it. In the first half of the 19th century, she received 18 gulden a year. Since 1846, the amount increased to 25 gulden. She was paid 90 marks yearly from 1876 and 150 marks after the First World War. However, the main income of the midwife came from fees paid for the birth of a child by the relevant family.

The community council of Ottersheim hired a midwife for the last time under its own jurisdiction in 1919. Since then, a law that was enacted in 1938 regarding the education and duties of the midwife required her to be State licensed and approved by the government. The candidate had to have previously attended a training course that cost her almost 800 marks. Half of the amount was reimbursed from the village treasury. The training period at a midwife school was 18 months. The midwife profession was regarded as a free profession. The midwives are no longer servants of the community; they are dependent on the income that they earn through their work. However, the Ministry of Social Affairs guaranteed each legal midwife a monthly minimum of 300 deutschemarks.

It deserves to be noted that the Church was not disinterested in the midwife position in early times. Midwives were to provide baptism for newborns in neonatal emergencies. Therefore, each of the parishes documented in visitation reports the religion that the midwife professed. So we know that the Ottersheim midwife was Calvinist in 1718.

Ottersheim Midwives

Klara Bahlinger	-1841
Agathe Moock, widowed Job	1841-1865
Katharina Hanck née Kopf	1865-1876
Katharina Hanck née Dörzapf	1876-1919
Lisa Dörzapf née Winkelblech	1919-1955
Liesel Morio née Jeckel	1955—

The Beggar Bailiff

In the first half of the 19th century, that a beggar bailiff existed in Ottersheim can be seen in the community accounts from that time. Andreas Jost was in charge of this office in the thirties, as was Peter Lorenz in the forties. The job of the beggar bailiff was to care for the beggars. His annual compensation was eight gulden. At the beginning of the 19th century, there seems to have been a considerable number of beggars because a notice was attached to the town entrance boards in 1837 warning of the abuse of begging. The beggars' bailiff had to make especially sure that the beggars left the village on time and did not roam around at night. If traveling people or gypsies sought to stay in the district, the beggar bailiff monitored the approved times and ensured that the set departure occurred. The community declined to finance its own beggar bailiff with the decline of the beggar menace and later transferred the task to the village policeman.

The Night Watchman and Lamplighter

The night watchmen carried out their last rounds in Ottersheim on 17 January 1901. Prior to this day, the community had appointed four men to guard the village and its inhabitants every night "until further notice." The four night watchmen met each evening in the guardroom of the community hall for this purpose. The night watch lasted during the winter from 10 o'clock in the evening until 4 o'clock in the morning, and during summer only until 2 o'clock in the morning. Two guards had to make a round through the village on one-hour intervals while the other two sat in the guardroom by lantern light. A wood stove provided the necessary heat in winter. The fuel lay in the woodshed at the south entrance of the village hall.

The guards carried a signal horn in addition to their lantern when they marched through the village. With the horn, they could sound an alarm if necessary when thieves were discovered or if a destructive fire broke out. In addition to the rounds through the village, the night watchman had to sound a bell at 11 o'clock in the evening and again at 3 o'clock in the morning. The ringing at 11 o'clock in the evening notified tavern visitors to go home quickly. The ringing at 3 o'clock in the morning signaled the beginning of the workday. Each night watchman received 86 marks yearly for his work. For an extra fee, one of the night watchmen had to light and to extinguish the streetlights at a specific time. It was the task of the assistant mayor to monitor and supervise the night watchmen.

It cannot be determined exactly when the night watchman service was introduced in Ottersheim. An indication is contained in the community accounts from 1817 where the salary of the *hour-blower* is discussed. Night watchmen were called hour-blowers because they announced the time from 10 o'clock in the evening until 4 o'clock in the morning by blowing their horn. The two hour-blowers in 1836 were Georg Kröper and Johann Müller, who each received 30 gulden for their work. It is mentioned four years later that the night watch was located in the "old, dilapidated community hall."

The night watch service in Ottersheim was newly regulated by a police order in the year 1863. Henceforth, all independent male community residents who had not yet passed their 60th year were required to perform night watch service. They could be represented under certain circumstances, but "youths under 18 years of age were not allowed as substitutes." Only the mayor and the adjunct were exempted from the obligation.

At least four men were ordered to night watch service each night. The order was set by the local police authority. The guardroom, which was renovated in 1849, was located on the ground floor of the community hall. The ordinance to obligate all male community members for night watch duty seems not to have proven effective. Otherwise, this provision would not have been abolished already by 1880. At that time, the council decided that from then on four permanent night watchmen should be hired. Each of them should receive 86 marks annual compensation. However, this money had to be raised by the watch-obligated community residents in that each person paid two marks into the community treasury as *guard-money.* The following citizens were appointed as community night watchmen at that time:

Konrad Störtzer, day laborer	35 years old
Valentin Gaab, musician	43 years old
Valentin Kröper, day laborer	47 years old
Peter Greichgauer, day laborer	42 years old

The hourly time sounding that had been the rule was abolished in the year 1880. As for a reason the community account states:

"The hourly sounding disturbs the sleep of the residents and simply cannot be considered useful."

The bells of the Catholic Church were rung at 11 o'clock in the evening and at 3 o'clock in the morning from that time on as a replacement. The purpose of this ringing can be understood only if one knows that hardly anyone had a clock or an alarm clock in the home during that time, and the clock on the church tower upon which people otherwise relied was not visible at night. Night watchmen carried out their service in Ottersheim for two decades, until the watchman job was abolished forever on 18 January 1901.

However, it was not possible to give up everything that the night watchman did. A person was still needed to sound the police bell before 11 o'clock in the evening and care for the streetlights. A lamplighter was hired for this purpose. He received 100 marks annually and was responsible for cleaning, lighting, and extinguishing the streetlights. The compensation also included the daily ringing of the police bell. Delivery of the oil for the streetlights was assigned through public auction. Georg Hilsendegen was hired as lamplighter in 1901. He was replaced two years later by Peter Winkelblech; he was soon replaced by Xavier Kuntz. The last lamplighter in Ottersheim was professional weaver and goose herder Peter Bischoff who was called Bischoff *the crooked*[78] by the locals. Older villagers remember him making his rounds through the streets with ladder and oil can, caring for the lanterns. The end of his career came with the introduction of electric street lighting in 1920. Bischoff died in 1924 at the age of 75.

The Street Warden

The street warden was also originally a community servant. In the thirties and forties of the previous century, he had to monitor and maintain the highway, that is, the paved road between Offenbach and Knittelsheim that lay within the Ottersheim borders; and he had to clean the trenches. Expansion of the road was the task of the community. The highway was taken over by the District in the year 1852. Johann Eibler from Ottersheim was the community street warden until then. The District managed the maintenance of the highway after that.

Other Community Employees

At least since the beginning of the 19th century, Ottersheim had a meat inspector, a coroner, and a gravedigger. The local meat inspector had to inspect all slaughtered cattle before and after the slaughter that was intended for human consumption. He was allowed to release only healthy meat for consumption while diseased meat had to be destroyed. The community coroner had to confirm the death of a villager before he was allowed to release the body for burial. And the gravediggers dug a grave in the cemetery on behalf of the community when a body was to be laid to rest.

---

[78] Evidently there were many Bischoff's in Ottersheim and nicknames were used to distinguish among them. Peter was so named because of his infirmity brought on by age.

The Executioner of Ottersheim

Because the local language uses the word *Wasen* when referring to a *Rasen [lawn]*, one might assume that a *Wasenmeister [Lawn master]* would be responsible for the professional care and maintenance of lawns. However, the Wasenmeister was in fact anything but a harmless lawn keeper in past centuries. Rather, the name refers to the work of an executioner, which has always been a special role. The office of executioner was considered by many to be shady and dishonorable. The people looked at the office holder with superstitious shyness and wanted nothing to do with him. He was unwelcome in the taverns and had his special seat in the church that no one disputed him even if no place was free. Anyone who came in contact with the executioner was marked for life. The local vernacular he was called *Meister Hans [Master Hans], Meister Steighinauf [Master of the Climb], or Meister O [Master of Wows]*.

The executioner had to carry out the death sentences of the Blood Courts. The designation, *Wasenmeister,* reminds one that the scaffold was covered with grass. As the only full-time member of the court, he often determined the nature of the death penalty. Moreover, he was responsible for the "embarrassing questioning" of the accused. The executioner did not shy away from torture to extract a confession. Tugging, squeezing, burning, and beating were frequently used as means to force the "poor sinner" to confess. It was inevitable that the terrible pain from such torture extorted confessions from innocent people.

Understandably, no executioner was 100 percent busy in his job. Though in past centuries when the heads of the murderers, thieves, fraudsters, heretics, and sorcerers were pretty loose, the executioner was still needed only a few days during a year. Therefore, his position was usually coupled with that of a *knacker* or *skinner* and *flayer.* Management of deceased or "stale" cattle brought work on a continual basis. The animals that needed to be skinned had to be brought in from the immediate vicinity or from further away. The carcasses were partly recycled in the rendering plant and partly buried in the knackers' bone yard. The executioner of Ottersheim held that position not only in the Upper Office in the District of Germersheim, but he was also skinner and butcher in nearly thirty villages around Ottersheim. The degree to which his business flourished can be seen in that today one speaks of the "Schinnergrub" (Skinner's ditch) at the Wasserbeiz, though no cadaver has been buried there for generations.

How Ottersheim got an executioner is reported briefly in the *Summary of Rights in the Village of Ottersheim.* According to this, Governor Heinrich Riedessel of Germersheim decided to hire an executioner for the District Office of Germersheim in the 16th century. He was to live in Ottersheim because the place is conveniently located and reachable from all directions. The office of the executioner was awarded to the Franck family who most likely came from Geinsheim.[79]

---

[79] The Franck family is listed in the family book of Geinsheim (Waltraud Krieger).

In a tax book about the church, early Mass, and pastor incomes in Ottersheim from 1590, a Hans Franck is mentioned as executioner. Ninety years later, we read of Hans Peter Franck of Ottersheim in Weißenburg, who had his rights and obligations as executioner and skinner confirmed by a City Governor of Louis XIV. The employment certificate was issued on 7 December 1680. At that time, Hans Peter Franck was awarded the executioner offices for Germersheim and Billigheim for life. No one was allowed to bully him or do him harm. The executioner himself was obliged to live in peace with all men; and every year he was to deliver gloves and harness to the Royal District Office on Saint Martin's day as tribute.

Other interesting information is provided in an employment contract from 15 June 1745 that was issued by the Electoral Court Chamber in Mannheim. At that time, the executioner premises and office for the District of Germersheim was given to Johann Franck from Ottersheim, not only for himself but also for his children, grandchildren, and great grandchildren as inheritance. He oversaw the villages of Germersheim, Sondernheim, Dettenheim, Bellheim, Knittelsheim, Ottersheim, Offenbach with its three estates, Mörlheim, Bornheim, Oberhochstadt, Zeiskam, Lingenfeld, Mechtersheimer Hof, Schwegenheim, Hördt, Kuhardt, Neupotz, Leimersheim, Böbingen, Weingarten, Kleinfischlingen, Gommersheim, Freisbach, Niederhochstadt, Monastery Haimbach, Niederlustadt, and Oberlustadt.

The executioner was obliged to work with his own staff, his own vehicle, and his own tools while paying attention to cleanliness and hygiene. He was to provide carrion for wild animals and wolves. He had to keep two dogs and make them available to the hunters from the District Office, along with a driver. He was to remain silent about any interrogation of "poor sinners." He was not allowed to take any clothing, money, or other valuables from them. He was not allowed to take any gifts. Each year he was taxed 17 gulden in "Wasen" tributes. He had to pay an inheritance rights sum of 400 gulden when the employment certificate was awarded.

Of Johann Franck, who exercised his office as executioner and skinner from 1745 to 1794, we know that he owned three home sites and 12 morgen of land in Ottersheim. He lived at 30 Lange Straße. He had his skinning shop at the 31 Kleine Gasse properties. A farmhouse cost about 800-1,000 gulden, so from these figures it can be seen that the executioner/skinner had to have been a profitable enterprise. When his son was born in 1753, executioner Peter Hoff of Steinweiler was godfather. Franck had a total of 13 children; however, some died soon after birth. In view of his possessions, he was among the 25 richest peasants in the village. His income consisted mainly of fees taken from those originally sentenced for misdeeds, but later the court master paid the fees. Also, when an offender was pardoned at the last minute, he still received the executioner's wage. In later years, he was guaranteed a fixed salary regardless of whether his services had been used. Nevertheless, it was customary to pay the executioner separately for each service. Thus, an executioner earned a nice little sum of money during the year. There were also the clothes of the executed to which the executioner had always been entitled.

The skinning business was also profitable. If a horse collapsed under its rider, the riding gear and harness belonged to the skinner. He was owed a fixed amount for butchering a cow or skinning a horse. However, he had to return the skins to the peasants. The executions in which executioner Franck was involved took place mostly in Germersheim. As soon as an offender was apprehended in the country, the mayor first locked him in the local jail. Then he filed a report at the District Office in Germersheim. The detainee was not taken to the castle prison at Germersheim until official orders were received from the District Office. Then the court met, examined the case, and brought the verdict. If a death sentence was confirmed by the Electors, it was announced to the offender when the judge of the court broke the stick above him.[80] Then he handed the villain to the executioner. It was customary that the whole population escort the "poor sinner" on his way to the scaffold. The condemned was allowed to "strengthen" himself with a lush meal, the so-called *Henkersmahlzeit [Last meal]*. Before the execution, he could confess his sins and receive the Sacrament of Anointing of the Sick [Viaticum].

Usually there was a large crowd at the place of execution where children and youths were also present. A few servants were also present to assure safety. Before the executioner raised his arm to strike, he asked his victims for forgiveness for the suffering that he had to inflict for righteousness' sake. The judiciary custom demanded that the offender thank the High Court once again for the gracious sentence, thank and bless the people around him, and exit the world reconciled. For execution by the sword, it was expected of the executioner that he would sever the head from the body with a single blow swung horizontally using both hands. The body was most often buried then and there.

The executioner of Ottersheim appears to have disappeared during the French Revolution. In any case, the grandson of the above named executioner, Johann Franck, no longer practiced this job as is verified in the Employment Certificate of the year 1745. The son, Nikolaus, who had taken over the office from his father in 1809, bound up his bundle and moved with family and possessions to Russia. He founded a new life in Franzfeld along the Black Sea. But he took the two employment certificates with him and kept them. They are now in the possession of returnee Georg Wagner who is living his retirement years in Bromberg, and whose ancestors emigrated to South Russia like the Franck family.

---

[80] In the Middle Ages, the judge carried a stick in his hand as a symbol of his dignity. He was not allowed to lay it down. The accused swore an oath of truth on the Bible and the stick at the beginning of testimony. It was common practice for the judge to break the stick above the head of the convicted, then throw the parts at the feet of the condemned. (Waltraud Krieger)

Home and Citizen Rights in Ottersheim

Today, anyone can take up residence in Ottersheim or move from Ottersheim to another community. Anyone from outside the village who marries a resident has equal rights and obligations with those born in Ottersheim. He or she can participate in the community elections and they can be elected to the community council, once they live here for a half year.

Nobody would consider giving newcomers fewer rights than those of the locals. However, what now seems so obvious to us was previously unknown. We know from the *Electoral Law in Ottersheim of 1565* that not anyone could freely choose to settle in Ottersheim until the end of the 18th century. To do so prior to that time specifically required the express permission of the community and of the District Office in Germersheim. However, this permission was granted only if certain conditions were met.

So anyone who wanted to move to Ottersheim at that time had to prove "he was a free man by law; he was descended from honest parents; and was not tied to any servitude." Then he had to pay an entry fee of 60 gulden. That was quite a large sum considering that one could buy about 15 malter of grain or three fuder of wine for that amount. Only when he had paid his debt, and had vowed and sworn, was he a fully entitled community resident. Now he could use water and meadows, and he received his rights to timber in the community forest. He also had a seat and voice in the community meetings, and he could be appointed to a community office. These strict immigration rules ensured that only respectable men with no previous convictions could be citizens of Ottersheim. Should an applicant be rejected, the Office in Germersheim had to approve the decision. In addition, the District Office in Germersheim was also involved in the entry fee that was collected and documented by the district clerk.

Of course, servants, maids, and peasant workers were not prohibited from immigrating to Ottersheim. Such people were regarded as so-called *Hintersässer,* citizens with no civic rights. In particular, they were not allowed to attend the community meetings and had no grazing and timber rights. The name *Hintersässer* calls attention to the fact that they had no house but resided in the *hinter [back]* part of their landlord's property. Sometimes it also happened that a man married into Ottersheim but could not immediately pay his entry fee. In this case, he was banned from using water and meadows until he had fulfilled his obligations. Should he use community water, meadows, or other community facilities, he was punished by the community court.

When the French took possession of the Palatinate toward the end of the 18th century, these strict rules were suspended in the wake of the Revolution. The freedom to move went so far that even French soldiers could settle permanently in Ottersheim, which would have been unthinkable before. However, the French also eliminated the traditional commitment of communities to care for the incapacitated, elderly, and the sick. This was now mainly the obligation of the hospital foundations.

A modified form of the old provisions was re-initiated in 1816 when the Palatinate went to Bavaria. However, there was now a distinction between so-called *home rights* and *citizen rights.* Every member of the Bavarian State had his home right at the place where his parents last possessed their home right. A wife followed to the home of her husband, whose home she keeps if widowed. Therefore, those who moved from their home community in no way also gave up their home right. This would happen only when he became a citizen at his new community. Should this not happen, he could in case of illness, age, or disability return to his home community where he had the right to food, shelter, clothing, heating, and care. He had the right to medical care at the expense of the community if ill. The general public also had to provide support for his minor children. Servants, tradesmen, messengers, apprentices, and factory and day laborers who were employed outside their home community were supported for only three months by the community where they worked. Then the responsibility for their care fell to their original home community. If they were admitted to a hospital, then the hometown received the bill. Here the necessary funds came from the so-called *poor fund* of the municipality, which was filled when necessary by contributions.

Only under certain conditions could an outsider acquire rights of citizenship in Ottersheim. Above all, he had to be an independent adult and pay a home right fee of 100 gulden to the mayor's office; or since 1876 as Bavarian-born, pay a fee of 170 gold marks. Foreigners had to pay double the amount. The independent adult had to be granted rights of citizenship once he had lived four years in Ottersheim. During this time, he paid direct taxes to the State, fulfilled his obligations to the community fund and the fund for the poor, and neither claimed nor received pauper care in the four years. With the purchase of the home right, the newcomers also became a citizen of Ottersheim at the same time. He was allowed to vote, be elected, and partake of the community assets. The community had to provide support should he now become impoverished.

It was much more difficult for wage and salary earners to acquire the home right in Ottersheim. The wage and salary earners were mainly domestic servants, farmhands, tradesmen, and laborers. Although they were exempt from the home right fee, they must have lived and worked seven consecutive years in Ottersheim and not have been sentenced to jail by a court. Applicants for the home right had to submit an application that the community council had to decide upon. Such applications were submitted repeatedly until the year 1919.

The procedure was relatively easy if the applicant laid the fee of 170 gold marks on the table, as did Jakob Morio, Kaspar Detzel, or Johann Hoffmann. Difficulties occurred often when the applicant wanted the home right free of charge. In 1896 for example, Heinrich Huwe from Mechtersheim applied for free home rights in Ottersheim. He pointed out in his application that he had come as an employee to Ottersheim and had already lived in the village for 35 years. However, the council declined and was of the opinion that Huwe had to be regarded not as an employed servant but as an independent farmer. Huwe then appealed the local community council's decision at the Royal District Office in Germersheim. After a lengthy review of evidence and negotiation, Huwe finally prevailed in 1897. A similar case involved day laborer Michael Götz from Kuhardt. It is worth mentioning in this context that in 1897, the council in Ottersheim had decided that a newcomer without home rights could not lease any community property. In 1919, the last people to apply for and receive free home rights in Ottersheim were Ludwig Wünschel born 1879, Heinrich Faath born 1874, and Wilhelm Lutz born 1882.

The provisions relating to the home and citizen rights that had been in effect in the Palatinate since 1816 were finally repealed by the Constitution of the Free State of Bavaria on 15 September 1919. At that time, everyone received the right to reside and settle anywhere within the Bavarian State. Home fees could no longer be collected. Every citizen from then on had the right of citizenship in the community of his residence and did not need to apply for it or purchase it with money. Whoever had lived in the community for six months was eligible to vote.

This legal situation did not change after the Second World War when the Palatinate was assigned to the newly formed Rhineland-Palatinate State.

How Our Ancestors Made Cloth for Clothing and Household

Whoever needs a suit, a dress, a pair of stockings or socks, underwear, or bedding today drives into town and buys the articles in a textile store. This was not always the case. At the beginning of the 19th century, the Ottersheim residents largely made their own clothing. Only wealthy peasants could afford to purchase a wedding dress, a wedding tuxedo, a hat, or a pair of gloves in the city. Stockings, socks, shirts, sheets, blankets, tablecloths, towels, and the like were made at home from raw materials such as sheep's wool, flax, and hemp that were produced by one's own farm.

According to an old cattle statute that was renewed in 1631, a wagon owner should keep 13 sheep, a 2-wheeled cart owner should keep 7 sheep, and a hand laborer should keep 4 sheep. There were still 250 sheep in Ottersheim in 1791. The number had dropped to 35 by 1864. People processed the wool themselves and used it mainly to make stockings and socks. By contrast, clothing and underwear were made primarily from plant fibers. Not raising hemp and flax on a farm was virtually unthinkable at the beginning of the 19th century. In 1864, 20 day's work [about 6.7 hectare] of hemp and a day's work [0.33 hectare] of flax were grown in Ottersheim while 28 day's work [9.33 hectare] of tobacco was grown at that time. On an area of one day's work, about six zentners [300 kilogram] of hemp were harvested at the rate of 20 gulden per zentner. The flax harvest was slightly lower, but a zentner of flax cost 24 gulden. Flax and hemp were grown in Ottersheim 1000 years ago as indicated by the demand by the Weißenburg Monastery for the wives of the parcel dwellers to deliver linen cloth of 10 elles length and 4 elles width as tribute. Hemp and linen production seems to have been quite extensive in the 18th century. There was a reason that seven weavers and four tailors existed in Ottersheim in 1791 but only two masons and carpenters. The rural population today hardly knows what flax and hemp look like. They know even less how these plants are grown and processed.

Flax seed can be sown from April to July. Depending on when the flax was sown, one speaks of early, middle, and late flax. The flax plant has a thin stalk that grows up to a meter high and bears numerous small, narrow leaves. The spherical fruit capsules have five compartments each and contain two flat brown seeds that emerge from the sky blue flowers. Linseed oil that is obtained from the seeds is then used for the production of oil paints, varnishes, soap, and linoleum. The seeds are popular also as birdseed.

More important than the seed of the flax are the fibers from which one can produce excellent cloth. As soon as the flax stalks begin to turn yellow, the flax is plucked from the ground and laid out to dry on the field. Then the bundles are retted. The flax is pulled through an iron comb so that the fruits fall off. Now the stems are laid in water or they are spread out on the wet grass and left a few weeks in the rain and dew. This was called "roasting" and caused the damp plant parts to rot away and the fibers to separate. In Ottersheim, one seems to have preferably roasted the flax on the front lawns. For this reason, the water trench that runs through there is often called the *Flachsgraben [Flax trench]* in old documents.

The flax is dried after roasting. To be independent of the weather, artificial pits were dug, the so-called *Dulflöcher*. Fire was set in a pit and the flax was spread out over it where it quickly dried out completely. There were such pits in the 19th century at the north end of the Bauernweg and parallel to a dirt road that was therefore called *Grubenweg [Trench road]*.

After drying, the crumbly wood from the flax stalks was pounded into small pieces with the help of a breaking machine. Then the flax fibers were freed from the attached woody stalk and rind by pounding the fibers with a sword-shaped wooden tool. Finally, the whole thing was pulled through the teeth of a heckling comb. Here the long fibers separated from the short stuff, the so-called *tow*. Now the flax unraveled and the smoothed flax could be spun, which the women and girls did during the evening in the spinning room. Linen weavers made cloth from the spun flax. Then the cloth was placed on the grass, pegged at the corners, and watered diligently for bleaching. It gradually took on a white color with the help of the sun's rays. A cloth-bleaching place once stood in the Ruschgarten near the Bordgraben. Today, the "Duuchbleechpaad," [Cloth-bleaching place] in the upper village reminds of the time when the women of Ottersheim made their own *Gedüch [cloth]*.

Hemp fabric is a little coarser compared to flax. Rope, cord, and twine are made from hemp fibers. The hemp is sown in early May. The annual plant is about 1.5 meter high and has long, stalked, pinnate leaves. Male hemp was called "Fimmel" [Hops] by the locals while the female plants were called *seed hemp*. The hops were harvested after the first bloom, but the seed hemp was not harvested until mid-September. The hemp was spread on the field to dry after being plucked. Later, the female plants were packed in a cloth and threshed in the barn. The fat-rich seeds were regarded as excellent bird food. The oil was suitable for the production of soap. The hemp fibers were produced in the same way as flax. Hemp had to be roasted, dried, broken, hackled, spun, woven, and bleached. Not only clothes and underwear were made from the finished cloth but also bags and tarpaulins. There still exist malter bags on many farms that are more than a hundred years old. Some self-made linen sheets and towels are also still in use today.

At the beginning of the 19th century, cotton gradually displaced flax and hemp fibers. Spinning and weaving were no longer worthwhile, since machines could perform this work faster, better, and cheaper. Today, synthetic fibers have largely replaced cotton. While weaving is still performed now and then as a leisure activity by women and girls, spinning has entirely vanished. But where a spinning wheel still stands in a farmhouse, it is no longer a working tool but an object that decorates the living room. Soon, it will come about that only a few words and phrases remind us of flax and hemp and spinning and weaving.

The Water Supply in Ottersheim

Whoever needs water today in kitchen, barn, or garden need only to turn on the faucet and collect any amount of this important staple of life. We all have gotten so used to the water line that we do not even think it might once have been different. Yet, not until 1955 did Ottersheim come to benefit from this blessed innovation. Except for the advantaged people who previously had electricity, water had to be pumped by hand. However, in the middle of the 20th century there was hardly a property in Ottersheim that did not have at least one well. This was different in ancient times however.

At the founding of the village, residents were totally dependent on the small stream that flowed near the first houses. But over time, the Quotgraben could hardly meet the requirements that make up tasty drinking water. Therefore, the villagers probably very soon dug a common well, near where the Catholic Church is today. Most people likely drew their drinking water from there even in the 16th century. The well had to be maintained in part by the community and in part by the owners of Poppelmann manor. It is not known what the well looked like. However, we may assume that it was bordered with sandstone and protected by a small roof. The water was pulled up in a bucket with the help of a winch and a rope. A stone bench probably stood near the fountain to allow the water carrier to take a short break. Whoever found no place at the well could go to the nearby community hall to take a short rest.

Oddly, Ottersheim in medieval times had a second public well that stood on the property of the Hördt Monastery. From the *Summary of Rights in the Village of Ottersheim* from the 16th century, this well was known as the *Ried Brunnen [Reed well]*. There is an exact depiction of its location in a property plat from the year 1765. It stood to the north of the Ludwigstraße on house property number 45. The well was no longer in use at that time and was almost completely in ruins. Significant traces of this well were found by Helmut Frey during the excavation for the foundation of his new building in 1965. In about a two-meter wide circular pit, the soil was entirely blank in contrast to nearby soil. In addition, sandstones and brick fragments were found in the dirt. Even several sandstone slabs were discovered at some distance from the well. This well likely was originally used mainly for watering horses, cattle, and pigs belonging to the Hördt Monastery. The assumption is supported by the fact that the six morgen of Brühl meadows that belonged to the Provost of Hördt were located north of the well. The Ried Brunnen was also used by the inhabitants of the lower village and of the Ludwigstraße.

This is only understandable in that not only the monastery but also the community had to contribute to its maintenance, and to be exact, the community was responsible for the winch and rope, and the Hördt Monastery was responsible for the bucket. The discovery of the Ried Brunnen in the eastern half of the Ludwigstraße explains a fact that was previously shrouded in darkness. A few years ago, so it was a clay jug estimated to be over 600 years of age was found underground in a nearby field. Without a doubt, it is a water jug of the kind that was still in use at the beginning of this century in many peasant homes.

Until the end of the 17th century, the well near the church and the Ried Brunnen were probably the only wells in Ottersheim. However, given the high groundwater level it would not have been difficult to dig multiple wells. This assumption fails on the issue of casing. Because wooden casing soon rotted, it was necessary to use stone tiling that was difficult to obtain. It was not until the 18th century that the more prosperous farmers had dug wells on their properties that were also widely used by the neighbors. Many wells were also used by the residents of a whole street. So for example, the people living in the Waldstraße in the 19th and partly into the 20th century got their water from a well that stood in front of property number 7. The inhabitants of the upper village used a well near house number 86; those in Gröhlig used a well at number 22, and on the Ottostraße at number 6. In the lower village, the common well was at house number 13.

Not until the invention of concrete could relatively cheap and permanent casing be purchased. Some farmers even fabricated their own such casings. So by the middle of this century hardly a property existed where there was not at least one well. Many houses even had a second or third well so that the water supply situation was not bad on the whole. Only so, is it understandable that building a water line was not urgent.

Then as early as 1931, the District Office of Germersheim made the proposal to establish an association for water supply. However, the Ottersheim community declined. The matter was taken up again in 1950. A total of 13 communities were invited to join an association collectively. As the fourth of these 13 communities, Ottersheim declared its willingness to join the *Jockgrim Water Supply Group*. The realization of the extensive construction project understandably took a long time. The first pipes were laid in Ottersheim in late 1954. The house connections were made in the spring of 1955. Progressive farmers also had self-drinking stations built right into their barns. In June 1955, the work as a whole was finished and the first water flowed from the taps. The people said farewell to their old village wells with one eye laughing and one crying.

How Ottersheim Got Electric Light

In the early decades of the 19th century, it was still customary for the peasants in Ottersheim to direct their time according to the daily rhythm of the chickens. They went to bed with the onset of darkness, and they rose at the first cockcrow in the morning to begin the work in stall and field. One would have been very happy to stay up a few more hours at night back then, but the darkness did not allow for meaningful activities. At most, you could carry on conversations, as the saying goes "In the dark, many rumors start." Of course, in the Middle Ages one was not entirely without artificial light. Initially, chips from resinous pine were used, so-called *pine chips*. However, candles were made of beeswax in very early times, and small lanterns were fed with plant oil or animal fat. But one had to deal with the fuel sparingly, because the peasants in Ottersheim had few beehives or oil-producing plants. Food was of course more important than were oil lamps.

Not until in the course of the 19th century were wax and vegetable oil gradually replaced by cheaper petroleum oil. Soon there was no longer a farmhouse without a stall lantern present as well as an oil lamp in the kitchen or living room. While gas lighting was the first to replace the oil lamps in the cities, those in turn were replaced by electric lights. The Ottersheim residents had to wait until 1920 for the construction of an electric power network. Although the council had decided in 1909 to introduce electric lighting in the village, it took several more years before a contract came about with the Pfalzwerken [Palatinate Works] in January 1914. The first step toward the realization of this plan was the construction of housing for a transformer in the schoolyard that was begun that same year. But when the electrical cables were to be laid, the First World War broke out and everything remained the same. The people had to continue feeding their livestock by lantern light and spend their evenings by the light of kerosene lamps. Some had switched from oil to alcohol, but the alcohol lamps were not nearly as bright as the electric light later. Besides, the longer the war lasted the scarcer and expensive became the oil, alcohol, wax, and lard, so that one had to use these sparingly.

Just one year after the First World War, the Ottersheim community renewed the contract with the Palatinate Works, and construction of the lines started on Monday, 22 March 1920. The Palatinate Works in Ludwigshafen had a large working group build the electric power network, a so-called *transmission line network*. First, iron stands were set up on the barns to which the wires of the main distribution line were later attached. Finally, the connections to the individual houses were established.

In normal times, copper wire would have been used because copper conducts electric current best. It was not possible to buy this expensive metal abroad as a result of the lost war. For this reason, one was content with aluminum wires that could be produced within the country itself. Each homeowner had to install his own house connection, as far as that had not already been done before the outbreak of the First World War in 1914. The local network was fed by a transformer station that converted the high-tension power from the overland transmission lines to 220/110 volts. The high-voltage line was strung from Bellheim through Knittelsheim and Ottersheim to Offenbach. The council agreed to the installation of electric poles in the northern part of the district in May 1920.

It was a memorable day on 18 August 1920 when the local network was put into operation and 16 electric lights lit the streets of the village. Soon, the electric lights could also be turned on in the houses. The stable lanterns and oil lamps could now be put aside because these had become obsolete. Only one villager could not bring himself to connect his house to the electric line. He continued to serve himself with an oil lamp. Back then, it also happened that the electric lights of one farmer failed. As said our good David Seppl, "Oh yes, the pipe is probably clogged!"

Initially, the electric current in Ottersheim was exclusively used for illumination. Only gradually were some electric motors installed that mainly replaced the capstans used during threshing of grain. Not until later were electrical appliances incorporated into the farmhouses of Ottersheim. The local network of the Rheinelectra in Ludwigshafen was expanded in 1935 and the base connections rose from the previous 100 to 140 volts. However, the operating voltage of the system was not increased. The power consumption grew consistently after the Second World War such that a new transformer of 100 kilovolt-amperes had to be built in 1953. Two years later the local network was completely refurbished because of 310 connected households, 84 (around 26%) cooked with electric stoves. With this modification, most of the main lines were strung with copper wire having a cross section of 4x50 square millimeters and costing a total of 204,600 deutschemarks. The construction of a second substation was needed in 1956. The additional transformer was placed on the Riedweg and had an operating rating of 100 kilovolt-amperes. The operating voltage of the local network proved more and more often to be insufficient. So it was raised to 380/220 volts in September 1957. This meant that all light bulbs and many electrical appliances had to be replaced by all residents.

In March 1963, the operating rating of the transformer station in the schoolyard was increased from the previous 100 to 160 kilovolt-amperes. At the same time, the Palatinate Works rebuilt the local network, including the street lighting, at a cost of 267,750 deutschemarks. In this latest restructuring, the remaining trunk lines were strung with copper wire with a cross-section of 4x50 square millimeters. Only shorter extensions were strung in copper with 4x25 square millimeters. The number of street lamps was almost doubled and the bulbs were replaced with more economical strip lights. Most recently, the 160 kilovolt-ampere transformer in the schoolyard was replaced with another of 250 kilovolt-amperes in October 1965. Today the Ottersheim local network is designed so that it can deliver twice the performance and thus handle the growing energy needs for many years to come.

How power consumption grew since the Second World War is shown in the following overview:

1952	104,000	Kwh.		1959	245,202	Kwh.
1953	119,000	Kwh.		1960	280,585	Kwh.
1954	136,920	Kwh.		1961	320,820	Kwh.
1955	157,566	Kwh.		1962	358,980	Kwh.
1956	175,800	Kwh.		1963	441,960	Kwh.
1957	194,982	Kwh.		1964	500,760	Kwh.
1958	214,020	Kwh.		1965	570,264	Kwh.

Kwh. = kilowatt-hour

Household appliances operating in Ottersheim in 1964:

188	Refrigerators	or about	54%	of households
167	Electric stoves	or about	48%	of households
113	Washing machines	or about	33%	of households
68	Hot-water storage	or about	20%	of households

The massive increase in electricity consumption and of household appliances shows more clearly than many words how important the role of electricity is in the life of the individual, the family, and the community. It is also a sign of the extent to which the technology already influences life in the village.

Street Lighting in Ottersheim Then and Now

Since 1 September 1963, no one was needed to care for the lighting or extinguishing of street lamps any longer. When darkness fell, 49 lights in the local streets were illuminated automatically, and these lights were turned off automatically when dawn broke. In fact, turning the lights on and off was managed from a central location at the substation in Landau. The brightest lights hang above the highway from Offenbach to Knittelsheim. These are eleven mercury vapor lamps that were each mounted in the middle of the road. The lighting on the remaining streets was handled by 38 fluorescent lights.

There were still no streetlights in Ottersheim by the middle of the 19th century. Therefore, the night watchman had to carry a lantern on his tour of the village. Each citizen was required to hang a lantern on the street side of his house in the event a fire should break out, or if some other danger were on its way. A candle or oil lamp behind the window could also suffice if need be.

The community reported its spending bills for lighting, extinguishing, and cleaning the streetlights in 1873 for the first time. We may therefore assume that the streets were maintained at the expense of the community at that time at the latest. However, there were only a few oil lamps that were installed at key points in the village. Later, the numbers of lights were increased and lamps were also hung in the side streets. There were 16 street lamps in Ottersheim that were served by a lamplighter around 1900. On the main road from Offenbach to Knittelsheim hung six lamps, specifically:

1.	On the Lange Straße at house number 89	August Faath
2.	At the outbuildings of the old rectory	
3.	On the Germersheimer Straße in the corner between:	
	House number 14	Ludwig Ritter
	House number 15	Ludwig Burgermeister
4.	On the Germersheimer Straße at house number 19	Oskar Kuntz
5.	On the west side of the Protestant Church	
6.	On the Gröhlig at house number 26	Erwin Walk

Ten lamps hung in other streets, namely:

1.	On the Waldstraße at house number 10	Maria Kröper
2.	On the Lange Straße at house number 67	Eduard Steegmüller (his widow)
3.	On the Lange Straße at house number 44	Erich Kern II.
4.	On the Lange Straße at house number 21	Ludwig Gadinger I.
5.	On the Lange Straße at house number 5	Alois Messemer
6.	On Maxstraße at house number 3	Fritz Eichmann
7.	On the Ottostraße at house number 6	Julius Hoffmann (his widow)
8.	On the Ludwigstraße at house number 30	Adam Brüderle
9.	On the Ludwigstraße at house number 22	Hermann Seither
10.	On the Ludwigstraße at house number 10/11	Hugo Seither

Initially, the four night watchmen were responsible for lighting, extinguishing, and cleaning the oil lamps. The community appointed a lamplighter specifically to carry out this task after the night watchman service was canceled in 1901. Equipped with his ladder and his oil can, he was an indispensable part of the village streets before the war.

The end of the oil lamps came with the advent of electricity in 1920. Sixteen electric lamps at 60 watts each replaced the existing oil lamps. The people were so excited by the bright light that in the first few days they even read the newspaper by the light of the new lamps. Among the 16 lamps, there were two all-night lamps and 14 half-night ones. Turning them on and off was handled by a clock that was located in the stairwell of the old school building. The number of streetlights was increased to 20 with the refurbishing of the local network in 1935. There were now three all-night lights instead of two. One was still content with 60-watt bulbs at that time. The number of lights was increased again by six, taking into account especially the new building areas. Among the 26 lights were four all-night ones. With the complete reconstruction of the local network in 1963, the street lighting was renewed from the ground up. Not just the bulbs were replaced by more economical strip lights at that time, but also the number of lights nearly doubled. In view of the growing traffic, the lights burn all through the night and thus contribute their part to the safety of the villagers. The following overview shows the distribution of the 49 lighting fixtures on each of the town streets:

1. Highway Offenbach - Knittelsheim   11
2. Lange Straße (from the old schoolhouse eastward)   8
3. Waldstraße   8
4. Ludwigstraße   8
5. Riedstraße   5
6. Maxstraße   3
7. Ottostraße   3
8. Friedhofstraße   3

The Ottersheim Fire Department

The farther we go back in the history of our village, the more feared was the cry of alarm: "It's burning!" When that cry rang through the streets, the signal horn blew, the bell in the church steeple was rung, and everyone was on their feet. The adults rushed with buckets and jugs to the fire to save what could still be saved. The fire had to be prevented from spreading above all else. A fire had abundant food everywhere, because almost all the houses in Ottersheim were half-timbered buildings up to the 19th century. The thatched roofs, which were not banned until the Napoleonic period, favored the spread of flames to adjacent property in the summer.

To prevent fire catastrophes, there was already no lack of appropriate measures in the Middle Ages. There was hardly a village that did not have its fire pond. The Weet in Ottersheim provided the necessary water besides serving as a watering place for cattle and wading place for animals. In addition, the two village streams, one along the Große Gasse and the other along the Kleine Gasse, had been created not least of all to provide enough water quickly during a damaging fire. Also, the night watchman service had been put in place mainly because of fire. On their tours through the village streets, the watchmen had to look for trouble spots and alert citizens immediately in case of fire.

Nevertheless, up to the middle of the 19th century the village population was quite powerless against fire because not too much could be accomplished with water buckets, ladders, and fire hooks. From the Weet or from a village stream, the villagers formed a long chain, and buckets were passed from hand to hand. If the fire had already engulfed the whole property, then one had to be content with preventing a further spread of the fire. Most often, a damaging fire ended as described by Schiller in the Song of the Bell:

> "Burnt is the place
> Wild storm's rough bed;
> In the desolate window openings lives the horror
> And the clouds of heaven to look down into it from on high."

It is therefore not surprising that the State issued fire prevention regulations early on. This was done very thoroughly in the Napoleon Era when the first certified chimney sweeps were hired. They had to clean each chimney at least three times a year at the expense of the homeowner. In addition, all furnaces, forges, ovens, and fireplaces were examined by an expert once a year. Thereby, only fire appliances that were built from bricks were tolerated. With these regulations, the danger of damaging fire could be reduced but never completely prevented. In terms of firefighting, the year 1846 is of special significance to the Ottersheim community. It was then that the mayor bought the first "fire engine" with the consent of the community council for the not inconsiderable sum of 1,500 gulden. The price was approximately the value of 30,000 kilograms of rye. But the cost was not spared because it was hoped that this machine would save much of what would have been left to the flames. It was a pressure pump that was filled with water by the use of buckets. The fire engine was stored on the ground floor of the community hall. The open hall was bricked up in 1849 and provided with a gate to protect the pump from adverse weather conditions. A crew was needed to operate the pump of course. A few strong people were selected to operate the pump and hose, while the work-capable residents continued to be required to supply the water as far as was necessary. Direction of the work was done by older men who took their positions immediately when a fire broke out. Moreover, each villager who had a well had to make it available upon demand and to illuminate it at night. In the dark, everyone was obliged to hang a lantern on the street side of their house, or at least to provide a light behind a window. When severe cold prevailed, each owner had to keep a vessel of heated water. If the local stream was not open, then everyone had to keep a tub of water ready on his property.

It is amazing how solid that first fire pump was built because it provided not less than 107 years of service. When it was replaced in 1953 by a motorized fire engine, the neighboring community of Knittelsheim took the old pump where it was used for 5 more years. However, a single fire pump is not enough for large fires. This was shown very clearly in 1905 when not less than four barns were on fire at properties 67, 68, 71, and 74 on the Lange Straße. This fire caused then District Fire Board Manager Schott at the District Office of Germersheim to demand a second "Extinguishing-machine" for Ottersheim. But the council balked at buying another pump immediately for financial reasons. It was not until 1906 the council decided to purchase a "newer designed fire engine" with a cylinder diameter of at least 100 millimeters. Mayor Job turned to the firm of J. Vogel in Speyer who delivered such a pump for 1,630 marks that same year. Like the old, the new pump was hand-operated, and it not only pumped water upward but it simultaneously sucked in water with the aid of a hose. The pump was placed in the school barn. When the old building was demolished in 1931, this pump was also placed in the community hall.

The fire fighters had to be reorganized with the acquisition of a second fire engine. All men aged 20 to 45 years were required to perform fire service. An operations team of approximately 20 strong men was assembled for each of the two pumps. An additional water team of the same size was required to manage the water supply for the old machine. The operations team each carried belt, ax, and rope, and were equipped with two large and several small ladders. The older age groups were assigned to direct the operations. In command was a leader who was supported by several buglers. Overall, the Ottersheim fire department was between 100 and 110 men strong. The exercises took place every May early in the morning on four consecutive Sundays. The community bought helmets and belts for the fire fighters in 1909.

After the Second World War, when modernization was occurring in all areas, there was in the ranks of the fire fighters also the desire expressed to replace the two hand pumps with a motorized fire engine. Also, County Fire Inspector Hoffmann from Germersheim demanded the modernization of the fire service in Ottersheim during a visit in 1951. However, the wish was not granted until 1953 under Mayor Paul Dörzapf. It was agreed to purchase a motor-driven pump with a Volkswagen engine that was supplied by the Albert Ziegler Company of Giengen. A fourth of the cost of 4,400 deutschemarks was subsidized by the State of the Rhineland-Palatinate as a grant. The pump was transported on a trailer. Only a small but well-trained team was necessary for its operation. Therefore, the obligatory fire service in place until then was replaced by a volunteer fire department of 18 men. The volunteer fire department did their job without pay. The community gratitude is reflected in that at social events, the fire fighters receive an appropriate grant.

Since the year 1955, fire fighting again became easier when the water line was put into operation in Ottersheim. Now the hose could be connected to a hydrant so that there was always enough water available. In 1964, a new accommodation for the fire engine was located at 32 Germersheimer Straße; it had previously been the breeding stall. Since August of 1966, this shed also housed the small fire engine that the community had acquired to complete their fire extinguishing equipment. The little VW bus, including its equipment, was like the motorized pump supplied by the Ziegler Company in Giengen. The community had to supply 4,830 deutschemarks while the rest was paid by the Rhineland-Palatinate State.

Commanders of the Ottersheim Fire Department

Anton Seither	1893-1905
Franz Steegmüller	1905-1920
Ferdinand Gutting	1920-1933
Alois Kreiner	1933-1939
Fritz Gensheimer	1939-1945
Josef Lutz	1945-1951
Siegmund Glatz	1951-1959
Werner Hoffmann	1959-1962
Helmut Seither	1962 —

About the Fruit Scale and Tobacco Scale in Ottersheim

Grain, spelt (a type of wheat), barley, and oats were not weighed in ancient times but measured by volume using a measure called the *Simmer*. Similarly, wine was measured using volume measures called *Schoppen, Maß, Viertel, Ohm,* and *Fuder.* According to the *Summary of Rights in the Village of Ottersheim from the year 1565,* the village master was responsible to "calibrate and make right" the wine measures when necessary. In contrast to the volume measures, a given peasant had no way in earlier times to measure weight. For example, whoever wanted to know the weight of flour was dependent on the flour scale that presumably was located in the community hall. The current teacher probably performed the weight measurement. In a note from the year 1699, it is specifically stated that the teacher was to receive 2 gulden from the flour scale. It is remarkable that the community-owned and established fruit, seed, or onion scale of Ottersheim was preserved until the beginning of this century.

This scale was purchased and maintained by the community who was also responsible to replace it if necessary. The scale was not used by the teacher in the 19th century, but it was instead leased to the highest bidder each year at a public auction. The bidder paid 3 gulden for the lease in 1873 and 20 marks in 1884. This money gave the leaseholder the right to perform the weighing in the village for one year for appropriate fees.

For example, as payment for his work in 1884, he was able to collect six pfennigs for a zentner of onions and to demand nine pfennigs for fruit and seed goods. Noteworthy is also the fact that in the late 19th century, the scale master had to determine the weight of the leather tanning rind. This oak bark was collected in the forest and sold to a tanner in Herxheim. The scale master could reap twelve pfennigs from each zentner of bark. Whoever in the village wanted to have something weighed would invite the scale master to his home. The scale master was also often a broker. The lease-owner typically used a wheelbarrow to move the scale. Because weighing fruit, flour, seeds, vegetables, and onions was quite time consuming and financially not very rewarding, few lovers of the office of scale master could be found. The leasing of the scale was terminated in 1897. Instead, a man was selected to operate the scale; he then paid a fee to the community based on his income from the work. The service was no longer viable by the beginning of this century. The farmers bought decimal scales for themselves little by little, so that they could therefore dispense with the scale master altogether. Added to this was a weighbridge (truck scale) built south of the village hall by the Raiffeisen Cooperative in 1900 that could be used by any villager with a need. This scale was in use until 1941. Then the Raiffeisen Cooperative bought a new weighbridge that was erected on the Waldstraße in front of the current rectory. It was subsequently moved into the new warehouse on the Ludwigstraße in 1964.

In addition to the fruit scale, the Ottersheim community owned a tobacco scale. It was also used to weigh hemp in the 19th century. This scale was leased every year to the highest bidder like the fruit scale. Thus, we read that the tobacco scale brought the community a total of 99 gulden in 1873, 330 marks in 1884, and even 350 marks in 1894. The lease owner of this scale could collect a twelve-pfennig fee for each zentner of tobacco. He made a good amount in good harvest years; however, in bad years his earnings were meager. This caused the community council to end leasing of the tobacco scale in 1897, and to appoint a scale master who was paid according to the amount of tobacco that was delivered. Finally, this scale stood in an outbuilding of the "Zum Gambrinus" Inn. A fee of 10 pfennigs had to be paid to the community for every zentner of tobacco. The Tobacco Growers Association bought a new tobacco scale in 1949 at its own expense that was initially set up at the "Zum Gambrinus" Inn. Because of the increased traffic on the nearby road, this scale was moved to 1 Maxstraße in 1951 where innkeeper Otto Merdian made a shed available. A special weighing fee has not been charged since 1949. Each member of the Tobacco Growers Association paid 1% of his revenue from the tobacco harvest into the club treasury to defray the expenses.

Coins, Measures, and Weights, as Used Earlier in Ottersheim and in the Germersheim Region

1. Coins

Up until 1 January 1876 in Bavaria, and with it also in the Palatinate where the *Mark* was introduced, our forefathers used for currency the *Gulden, Kreutzer,* and *Heller.* Because the gulden was originally minted in Florence, it was also called the *Florentine-gulden* or *florin* for short. The gulden was already a known means of payment used in the 13th century. In 1618, a malter of grain cost 3 gulden in Ottersheim while a fuder of wine cost 28 gulden.

1 gulden (florin)	=	60 kreutzers	=	480 hellers
		1 kreutzer	=	8 hellers

In the 17th and 18th century, one used the *Batzen* and the *Denar* as currency. At that time, 1 batzen had a value equal to 4 kreutzers; and one denar had a value of 2 hellers. Thus, 15 batzen or 240 denars had the value of 1 gulden. In the 16th century, the *Albus* was the main coin. The albus was also called a *Weißpfennig.* At that time, 26 albus or 17-1/2 *Schilling* had the same value as 1 gulden.

2. Measures

The object to be measured determined the type of measure used. The measures included field, grain, wine, wood, oil, wax, and the like. Although a given measure was derived as a part or as a multiple of a base measure, the results were often rounded up or down so that variations had to be taken into account.

a) Field Measures

The basic measure for arable land was the *Morgen.* That was as much land as could be plowed with a team in one *Morgen [morning]*. [It was also called a *Day's work*]. In the 18th and 19th centuries, the land parcels in Ottersheim were measured by official order using a Nüremberg morgen. A Nüremberg morgen had 4 viertels [quarters] or 160 ruten. Three Nüremberg morgen were a little more than 1 hectare of land. In addition, people also calculated using a field measure of 128 ruten where a hectare comprised not quite 4 morgen.

1 Nüremberg	=	4 Viertels	=	160 Ruten	=	0.378020 Hectares
morgen						3,780.20 square meters
		1 Viertel	=	40 Ruten	=	945.05 square meters
				1 Rute	=	23.6262 square meters
1 Rute	=	10 Schuhs	=	100 Zoll	=	23.6262 square meters
		1 Schuhs	=	10 Zoll	=	2.3626 square meters
				1 Zoll	=	0.2362 square meters

b) Grain Measures

Grain, peas, and lentils were not previously weighed but like wine were measured by a volume measure called the *Simmer.* For transport, the fruits were filled into malter bags. Eight simmers of heavier produce and nine simmers of lighter produce were filled into each malter bag. This yielded an amount of weight in the sack that a man with average strength could carry away.

1	Heavy	Malter	(rye, barley)	=	8 Simmers	=		127 Liters
1	Light	Malter	(spelt, oats)	=	9 Simmers	=		142 Liters
		1 Simmer	=	4 Immel	=	32 Mäßel	=	15.8 Liters
				1 Immel	=	8 Mäßel	=	4.0 Liters
						1 Mäßel	=	0.5 Liters

c) Wine Measures

The basic measure of wine was the *Logel* or *Hotte* that contained about 35 liters. This was as much as a wine grower could carry on his back without excessive exertion. The word *Logel* comes from the Latin word *lagona* that means wine jug or bottle. All remaining wine measures are derived from the Logel.

1 Fuder	=	10 Ohm	=	30 Logel	=			1,050 Liters
		1 Ohm	=	3 Logel	=			105 Liters
				1 Logel	=			35 Liters
1 Logel	=	4 Viertel	=	16 Maß	=	64 Schoppen	=	35 Liters
		1 Viertel	=	4 Maß	=	16 Schoppen	=	8.75 Liters
				1 Maß	=	4 Schoppen	=	2.19 Liters
						1 Schoppen	=	0.55 Liters

d) Wood Measures

Earlier, the usual wood measure was the *Klafter.* It is actually not a body measure, but a measure equal to six schuhs or 1.95 meters, and denotes the width of the arms when stretched out horizontally. As a wood measure, the klafter represented about 3.8 cubic meters. It was also called *forstklafter [forest klafter].* When converting to the metric measure, 4 cubic meters, or 4 *Ster* represented 1 forest klafter. A 1-klafter pile of wood was 1 meter high, 2 meters wide and 2 meters deep.

e) Length Measures

The original length measures are *Elle* and *Schuh,* also called a *Fuß.* The mile was a Roman measure and represented a thousand steps. A number of length measurements are derived from the schuh or fuß.

1 Post mile	=	2,000 Klafter	=			4	kilometers
		1 Klafter	=	6 Schuhs	=	1.95	meters
1 Elle	=					0.56	meter
1 Schuh (Fuß)	=	12 Zoll	=			32.5	centimeters
		1 Zoll	=			2.7	centimeters

263

3. Weights

All other weights are derived from the unit weight of the *Pfund*. The word *pfund* comes from the Latin phrase *"pondus"* and means weight. The pfund previously had only 470 grams (16.57876 ounces).

1 Zentner[81]	=	108 Pfund	=	432 Viertel	=	50.440 kilograms
		1 Pfund	=	4 Viertel	=	470 grams
				1 Viertel	=	117 grams
1 Viertel	=	8 Lot	=	32 Quentlein	=	117 grams
		1 Lot	=	4 Quentlein	=	14 grams
				1 Quentlein	=	3 grams

Viticulture (Wine Growing) in Ottersheim

It is no longer possible today to determine when grape vines were first cultivated in the territory of Ottersheim. But we may assume that this occurred at the time of the erection of the church at the latest. As it was, wine was necessary when one wanted to celebrate Mass, because at that time not only the priest but also every member of the Faithful received the Communion under both forms. What could be more obvious than to cultivate wine locally rather than purchase it at expensive prices!

As in many other places, the first grape vines likely stood near to the church. The *Kirchstücke [Church fields]* are still good wine vintage sites today. Still in 1788, there was talk of a garden that stretched to the west of the church that presumably contained vines. Grape vines were also grown earlier on the hills in the Gröhlig. At any rate, there is mention in a report at the end of the 30 Years War of a vineyard on this property. The most important wine growing region in the Ottersheim district is the Kahlenberg. It lies about 20 meters higher than the village and also has soil that is amenable to growing grapes. There were vineyards there even before the 30 Years War.

The first documented evidence of viticulture in Ottersheim comes from the Commodity Listing of the Weißenburg Monastery. In *entry IX of the Liber Possessionum of Abbot Edelin,* it is mentioned that four loads of wine were to be delivered to the monastery from the vineyards in Ottersheim. Unfortunately, an exact notation that states just when this commitment was put in place is missing. But it must have been long before the year 1000 because Weißenburg had already lost its possessions in Ottersheim to Duke Otto of Worms in 991. Demonstrably, the monastery owned property in Ottersheim during 808, so probably grape vines had already been planted in Ottersheim by this time. Furthermore, in

---

[81] More recently, Germany has standardized on 1 zentner equaling 100 pfund or 50 kilograms. Thus 1 pfund is equal to 500 grams.

a report from the year 1103 there is mention of wine growing in Ottersheim when Hermann von Spiegelberg presented his fields, *vineyards,* pastures, and forests in Bellheim, Ottersheim, and other places as a gift to the Augustinian monks in Hördt.

The Eußerthal Abbey, as owners of the Ottersheim parish, had vineyards in their possession that were cultivated on the monastery property in Ottersheim. As it was, when the possessions of the abbey were confiscated in the 16th century by the Electoral Palatinate, the lease owners were required to deliver a fuder of wine yearly to the pastor of Ottersheim. This tax obligation existed until the French Revolution at the end of the 18th century.

From the *History of the Palatinate Wine Cultivation by Bassermann-Jordan,* we know that many vineyards existed in the Palatinate from the 9th to the 15th century. There were rich yields at the time, but the wine was usually of low quality. The acreage was reduced in the 16th century. Wine cultivation in the Palatinate reached its lowest point in the 17th century when the population was decimated and the land laid waste by the 30 Years War. Not until the 18th century did wine cultivation make a comeback. This also applies to Ottersheim. A survey in 1791 reports that ten Nuremberg morgen or 3.5 hectares of vineyards existed in the district of Ottersheim.

Until the French Revolution, the tithe included the obligation to deliver wine. This was done by providing a tenth of each *Hotte* of grapes during the harvest. The grape harvest was set on a specific day to control the tithe easily. In addition, the vines were guarded while maturing so that no one could bring in the harvest prematurely. During the French Revolution, the vineyards that had largely been located on church property were turned over to private owners. The following years brought obvious growth of viticulture in Ottersheim. Those who had the necessary land on the Kahlenberg would set up a vineyard in order to make wine for their own benefit. No vines were planted in early Ottersheim times for the purpose of selling it. The harvests varied considerably from year to year according to the weather conditions. Because there was not any means of chemical pest control, one could only expect a good harvest in especially hot and dry years with a good fall.

The vineyard owners of Ottersheim went together in 1834 and bought a parcel of land on the Kahlenberg for five gulden from the widow of Johann Walk. Then they had a vineyard hut built their own expense, which they intended to keep up. However, they were not angry when decades later the community took over the upkeep costs. The vineyard house still stands; and is used by the vineyard keepers and other people as a shelter in bad weather. The vineyards in the Ottersheim district in 1864 comprised 16 day's work or 5.5 hectares. In that year, all of 3,000 liters of wine were harvested. The vineyard acreage grew slowly up to World War I. That changed in the first decade after the war. At that time, vines were imported from America that were resistant to the vine louse and proved to be extremely productive. They thrived in every soil type and did not need to be treated with chemical agents. Although the hybrid grape could not produce high quality wine, the Ottersheim peasants were not concerned.

As a house drink, the hybrid wine was still better than the pomace wine[82] with which one had to make do until then. Why should one continue to buy pressed out berries from the wine growers at the Haardt, soak them in water, and sweeten them with sugar when one could brew an acceptable drink from self-grown vintage? That plan went over well as long as one was dealing with personal need. However, when the hybrid grape juice was sold, the wine growers at the Haardt feared for their *noble wine* and achieved a prohibition of the hybrid wine through the vine louse law. This led to a protracted and bitter struggle between the stakeholders. The hybrid growers in the valley banded together and created an association. When the State then forbade continued growing of the hybrid vines, and the State Court in Germersheim issued a fine for illegal importation of hybrid vines in 1930, about 3,000 wine growers of the southern Palatinate marched to the State Capitol to protest the measure, among them also many Ottersheim growers. In spite of rousing speeches by farmer Wüst of Winden, Mayor Hoffmann of Ottersheim, and association secretary Wiggers of Landau, nothing decisive could be achieved. Some growers turned to supporting Hitler because of his expected support for their American grapes. But Gau Leader Bürckel decided the matter in 1937. Without further ado, he ordered that all hybrid vines were to be ripped out. In their place, the growers were to plant noble vines. The last American vines were removed in 1941.

After the Second World War, nothing much changed in wine culture in Ottersheim at first. Vines were planted for home use and one made do with the available space as before. Only after the land consolidation did individual farmers shift more to wine while others abandoned it altogether. In 1960, there were 16 hectares of vineyards, now it has grown to about 18 hectares. A difficult situation arose in 1962 when viticulture was to be prohibited in the whole district of Ottersheim because of a wine law. In order to defend their ancestral rights, the wine growers took legal action against the land consolidation law under the leadership of the association. Success did not remain absent. The farmers of Ottersheim were allowed to cultivate grape vines by order of the Administrative Court in Neustadt an der Weinstraße in 1963. So it is now probable that a centuries-old tradition will live on in the future.

---

[82] This is wine made from a subsequent pressing of the skins, pulp, seeds and stems.

The Mechanization of Agriculture

Until the end of the 19th century, pastoral life in Ottersheim was determined by the rhythm of nature and strength of man and animal. Based on the rules and habits of tradition, the peasants cultivated the land in the spring and brought in its harvest in the fall. It was often hard and demanding work that had to be accomplished there. In particular, mowing grain and meadows, loading and unloading the hay and fruit, plowing and digging, threshing and sowing, all required what strength a man had to offer. Although such work as hoeing and heaping, setting onions and cabbage, breaking and reaping tobacco was lighter work, the peasant still had to "often eat his bread by the sweat of his brow" as is stated in the Bible. Only simple equipment such as plow and harrow, hoe and spade, sickle and scythe, rake and fork were available to ease his work.

It was not until the turn of the century that agricultural machinery was introduced to the rural landscape in Ottersheim. The first machines were small threshing machines that were initially set in motion by hand and later with the aid of a horse-driven gin. Kaspar Detzel and Franz Ludwig Job had a threshing machine before the year 1900. "Machining," as the threshing with a horse-gin was called, saved the farmers the weeklong threshing with a flail as was previously common. Nevertheless, it was quite a strenuous job for humans and animals. Therefore, it was a welcome occurrence in 1908 when Knittelsheim entrepreneurs set up a steam threshing machine in Ottersheim and threshed grain for a corresponding fee. Also, to allow poorer people access to a threshing machine, a request was made to the Raiffeisen Cooperative to purchase a steam threshing machine for collective use. But the plan could not be realized for financial reasons. Therefore, each farmer had to help himself.

Until the beginning of the First World War, there was hardly a major farm operation that did not have a grain mill behind the barn. When Ottersheim was connected to the electricity grid in 1920, many a farmer replaced the mill with an electric motor. Others also made use of a large threshing machine that was set up in Ottersheim at harvest time by an entrepreneur from Börrstadt. But because this machine was operated for only a limited period in Ottersheim, farmer Josef Job bought a large threshing machine in 1928 that was available at all times. The machine, which was set up during the harvest in a field near the Knittelsheim Straße, was originally operated by a tractor and later by an electric motor. One often had to work at night to handle the many harvest wagons. Many a farmer stored his grain in the barn first and then had it threshed in the winter by the big machine. In the fifties, three standing threshing machines were in operation in Ottersheim. A gin or mill-based machine was used for the last time during World War II by farmer Ludwig Detzel.

In 1956, Herbert Becki from Ottersheim bought a combine harvester. This opened a new chapter in the history of the grain harvest. As the name implies, this machine accomplishes not only mowing the grain but at the same time threshing, collecting the grain, and bundling the straw. The combine could harvest 60 to 80 zentners of standing crop in one hour. The new machine was so popular that Josef Job also bought a combine harvester a year later. These two monsters were often used day and night during harvest time in the Ottersheim district to prepare approximately 200 hectares of grain for milling. Their use has been made even easier by the land consolidation that had allowed for larger, contiguous field areas. Four combines were in operation in Ottersheim in 1966. They relieved the farm families of hard work that required a lot of sweat from humans and animals at the beginning of this century.

Belonging also to the most strenuous activities of the farmers in earlier times was mowing the meadows, because the first and second hay cutting was still being done by hand at the beginning of the 1920s. With scythe, whet basket, and whetstone, the men often went to the meadows to mow the grass by 3 o'clock in the morning. The women and children followed a few hours later to spread the grass and turn it. The first mower in Ottersheim was purchased by farmer Ludwig Steegmüller together with his brother Franz Steegmüller before the First World War. The machine had to be pulled by horses, oxen, or cows. This example was followed by other farmers in the twenties. There were already fifty mowers in operation in Ottersheim during 1929, including a motorized mowing machine that belonged to wainwright Julius Hoffmann. There was scarcely a farmer who did not have a mower at the beginning of the Second World War. A change occurred in the fifties when tractors replaced the draft animals. Rather than use the previous mowers, the farmers bought mowers that could be mounted to their tractors. These tractor-driven mowers had since completely replaced the earlier mowers. The scythe and sickle that were still important tools in the grain and hay harvest at the beginning of our century had now completely disappeared. Apparently, there are now farmers who never mastered the art of mowing with a scythe because they had only used mowers.

The mechanization of agriculture in recent years has been strongly influenced by tractors. Until the middle of this century, the farmer had to rely on draft animals. Horses, oxen, or cows had to not only pull plow and harrow but also the wagons and carts. While the two-wheeled carts had disappeared from the village scene already by the twenties, the four-wheeled wagons were not replaced by rubber-tired wagons until later. About fifty of these rubber-tired vehicles were already in use in Ottersheim around 1952. This was a high number compared to other rural villages of the southern Palatinate. The first tractors were three Allgaier models purchased in 1952 that were quickly followed in subsequent years by more tractors.

This prompted Master Motor Vehicle Repairman Otwin Zwißler to build a farm machine and car repair shop, including a gas station, at the south entrance of the village in 1956. The rapid development of motorization in the agricultural sector was also reflected in the fact that by 1958 there were no fewer than 51 persons, including 18 women and girls, attending a training course for truck drivers. There were only 16 tractors in operation in

1956. This number rose to a total of 64 by 1960, to 91 by 1964, and to nearly 100 tractors by 1966. The tractors are not only used for towing vehicles, but they also serve as a power source for a variety of specialized agricultural machinery. With the help of a tractor and related equipment, nowadays one can work the ground, load manure and spread it on the fields, sow seed, set young plants, spray pesticide, cultivate and ridge potatoes and turnips, harvest potatoes and beets, mow grass, turn and rake hay, second cut hay and clover, load and unload wagons, and much more.

In Ottersheim, there have also been complete potato and beet harvesters in use that were made available by outside entrepreneurs for a fee. Machines have also taken over work in the home that previously was done by hand. Thus in 1956, the first milking machines were put to use. Two Canadian-designed tobacco harvesters were bought in 1965 that eventually replaced the time consuming task of harvesting tobacco by hand. All these devices save the farmer and his wife time and energy with the various work involved in agriculture today.

Effects of Modern Traffic and News Media on Village Life in Ottersheim

The saying that "village life is quiet" is no longer correct. For several decades now, the most isolated village has been taken over by technology and transformed. A hundred years ago, there were still no bicycles in Ottersheim. Fifty years ago, there were no radios. Only the newspaper informed the villagers about events in the wide world. The people themselves rarely left their home village, and if they did, they usually visited their relatives and friends in neighboring communities or in the city. Only emigrants traveled to foreign countries. Only at the turn of the century did a new development occur.

The age of technology was heralded in Ottersheim by the bicycle. To be sure, Drais[83] had built a Draisine or running machine in 1817; and the pedal crank was invented by Fischer[84] in 1853. But a generation had passed by before Georg Gensheimer, as the first in Ottersheim to do so, bought a tricycle and demonstrated it to his admiring fellow-citizens in 1890. Four years later, Anna Böhm owned the first women's cycle. And full of pride, Ludwig Steegmüller, Josef Seither, and Konrad Hoffmann tried out their new men's bicycles in 1895. Already by the beginning of the First World War, a steel steed [bicycle]

---

[83] Karl Drais, a German inventor, is credited with inventing the "laufmaschine" [running machine], named a draisine in English. The wooden machine looked like a common day bicycle with handlebars and seat but had no pedals.

[84] Philipp Moritz Fischer, an organ builder, improved on the Drais design by adding pedals and crank.

stood in many homes in Ottersheim. These bicycles transported the lucky owners quickly and safely into the city or to villages near and far. Because of the rubber shortage during the First World War, one could not buy bicycle tires or inner tubes. This is why some people helped themselves with wooden tires mounted to the rim using steel springs. The number of bicycles in Ottersheim grew substantially after the war. Toward the end of the twenties, there were many homes with two, three, or more bicycles. They were used mainly to get quickly to work, fields, or meadows. This is still partly the case today.

With the growing number of motorized vehicles following World War II, the number of bicycles no longer increased because it was easier to get around with engine power than by strenuously pedaling the bicycle.

The propagation of automobiles in Ottersheim was much slower than that of the bicycle. After the invention of the four-stroke engine by Otto[85] in 1876, Daimler and Benz built the first gasoline car in 1885. But even in the twenties of this century, it was still rare to see a gasoline carriage drive through Ottersheim. The children stood at the roadside and marveled at the horseless vehicle with which one could travel longer distances, faster, and more conveniently than with horse and coach. Moreover, at that time a car on the highway could not be missed because it raised a massive dust cloud in dry weather that would dissipate again only after some time. The first car in Ottersheim was driven by Oskar Zwißler in 1913. Zwißler was not the owner of the car but worked as a driver for a company. The first car owner in Ottersheim was Oskar Hoffmann, whose father bought a small van for his seed store in 1927. Already a year later, there were four cars in Ottersheim. The lucky owners were Markus Benz, Oskar Hoffmann, Wilhelm Hatzenbühler, and Erwin Bischoff. While most of these were models from Opel, Markus Benz bought a used six-seat sports car from the Benz car company in 1928. The car had 28 horsepower, four gears, and steering on the right. Built in 1915, it reached a top speed of 60 kilometers per hour. A year later, he replaced this sports car with a new DKW or "Dampfkraftwagen" [Steam driven vehicle] model with three gears and four-wheel brakes. The sport model had left-hand steering and a top speed of 100 kilometer per hour. As previously mentioned, Oskar Hoffmann drove the first truck in Ottersheim during 1927. He replaced the small Bergmann model in 1929 with an Opel-Blitz that was used not only for transporting goods but also for passengers. Markus Benz bought himself a 2.5-ton Mercedes-Benz truck with 55 horsepower in 1935. The main purpose of this vehicle was to transport milk to Landau on behalf of the newly formed Milk Cooperative. With the economic boom of the fifties and sixties, the number of car owners in Ottersheim grew by leaps and bounds. At the end of 1966, there were 177 passenger cars. This meant that every second house had a car at this time.

---

[85] Nikolaus August Otto, also a German inventor, is credited with designing the first internal combustion engine which used the concept of fuel burned in a piston chamber.

The first motorcycle in Ottersheim was owned by Markus Benz in 1916. It was a 1914 DKW model motorcycle with 2.5 horsepower and one gear. In 1918, he replaced this cycle with a Wanderer model that had three horsepower and a manufacture year of 1912. Not until the thirties did motorcycle ownership by the younger people of the village visibly increase. But twenty years later, many motorcycles had been replaced by the more convenient automobile. Today, only a few use motorcycles.

The spread of radios in Ottersheim was much faster than that of motor vehicles. In 1923, the first transmitting stations were built in Germany. Installer Alois Walk of Ottersheim set up a makeshift home receiver with headphones in 1926. Eugen Hoffmann also had a small device with which you could hear a concert from Stuttgart. The first purchased radios were set up by Pastor Knöll and Ferdinand Gutting in their homes. A few years later, there were already several devices in Ottersheim with which one could quickly learn not only about the weather forecast but also about the latest world events. After taking power in 1933, Hitler was adept at making use of this news media. In most villages, public address systems were installed that carried the speeches of Hitler and Goebbels[86] into the most remote corners. As highly as the rulers of the Third Reich regarded the radio, it also had a rather unwelcome feature. With its help, you could hear not only German stations, but also foreign stations where many found out what Hitler and his propagandists would rather have concealed from the German people. So it was that in Ottersheim as in other villages, many people regularly listened to the Strasbourg station. But this was a dangerous undertaking because listening to so-called *enemy radio broadcasts* was soon prohibited and was made a criminal offense. This prohibition was strictly handled especially during the Second World War when spies were often underway to monitor receivers. However, certain people were always well informed about what was happening on the battlefields. Conversely, those who listened only to German channels heard only of German victories until Germany had "won to the death" in 1945. After the Second World War, the number of radios in Ottersheim continued to increase. One could count 190 receivers by year's end of 1966.

In the fifties, radio was joined by television. The first TV set was installed in 1954 by Ludwig Jochim at his "Zum Hirsch" Inn. His example was followed three months later by innkeeper Erwin Bischoff. Since the World Cup games were televised that year, there was also no lack of interested spectators in Ottersheim. Already in the course of a few years, the number of television sets increased significantly in Ottersheim. At the end of the year 1966, one could count 130 televisions. The devices contributed significantly to overcoming the remoteness of the village and towards publicizing the scenes and events of the wide world to the rural population.

---

[86] Joseph Goebbels rose to power in 1933. He was appointed by Hitler as his propaganda minister.

The Community Hall

First practice after the handover of the new small fire engine,
in the presence of County Administrator Weiß and
Fire District Inspector Hoffmann.

The Lower Lange Straße

The Field Chapel

Waldstraße looking toward the Catholic Church

The Extended Ludwigstraße

The Protestant Church before renovation

~Urkunde~

ZUR GRUNDSTEINLEGUNG FÜR DIE NEUE VOLKSSCHULE MIT SCHULTURNHALLE
DER GEMEINDE OTTERSHEIM bei LANDAU.

Am 13. September 1961 faßte die Gemeindevertretung den weittragenden Beschluß, zur Behebung der zunehmenden Schulraumnot sowie zur Verbesserung der Schulverhältnisse und um den Belangen der Leibeserziehung der Schuljugend Rechnung zu tragen, ein neues Schulhaus mit Schulturnhalle zu errichten.

Dem Gemeinderat gehörten zu diesem Zeitpunkt an:

PAUL DÖRZAPF, Bürgermeister
ROBERT FREY, Beigeordneter.

Die Ratsmitglieder:

BAUCHHENSS OTTO	LUTZ JOSEF
BENZ LEO	MÜLLER HUGO
FÖHLINGER KARL	SEITHER HELMUT
FÖHLINGER RICHARD	SEITHER HERMANN
HÖRNER ALOIS	STEEGMÜLLER HUGO
KRÖPER ALBERT	WÜNSCHEL ERWIN.
LERCH SEVERIN	

Das Bauvorhaben umfaßt:

Einen zweigeschoßigen Klassenbau und ein nach Süden vorgelagerter ringgeschoßiger Klassenpavillon. Beide Baukörper werden durch eine Pausenhalle verbunden, an welche sich die WC-Anlagen anschließen. Südwestlich dieser Baukörper ist die Errichtung einer Schulturnhalle vorgesehen, deren Nebenräume Verbindung mit der Pausenhalle haben. Die Kosten des Vorhabens sind auf 1.005.000,— DM veranschlagt.

Planung und Bauleitung waren an Herrn HANS H. GOLDATE, Architekt, Jockgrim, übertragen. Die stat. Berechnung wurde von PAUL REICHARDT, Hoch- und Tiefbauingenieur, vorgenommen.

Am heutigen Tag waren vergeben:

Rohbauarbeiten an Arbeitsgemeinschaft VOGEL H. und RIPP L., Erlheim / Ottersheim bei Landau. Dachdecker- und Flaschnerarbeiten an Firma LEYDECKER u. BRAND Landau / Pfalz. Elektroarbeiten an EUGEN HÖFER, Bellheim. San. Anlagen an ALOIS WALK, Ottersheim bei Landau. Heizungsanlage an Firma MÜLLER K.G., Landau i.d. Pf.

Zu dieser Zeit waren: Dr. HEINRICH LÜBKE, Bundespräsident, Dr. KONRAD ADENAUER, Bundeskanzler, Dr. PETER ALTMEIER, Ministerpräsident von Rheinland-Pfalz, Dr. EDUARD ORTH, Kultusminister von Rheinland-Pfalz, Dr. FRANZ PFEIFFER, Reg.-Präsident der Pfalz, GEORG WEISS, Landrat des Kreises Germersheim, KARL WANNER, Amtsrat, PAUL DÖRZAPF, Bürgermeister, WALTER KERN, Gemeindeinspektor, LUDWIG KELLER, Leiter der Steuer- und Gemeindekasse, JOSEF SCHERÖBL, kath. Pfarrer, WOLFGANG JUNG, evang. Pfarrer.

Lehrkräfte der

kath. Volksschule: HANS GENSHEIMER, Hauptlehrer, GERTRAUD RICHTER, Lehrerin, WERNER HEIDENREICH, Lehrer, evang. Volksschule: WERNER FRÖHLICH, Lehrer.

MÖGEN SCHULGEBÄUDE und SCHULTURNHALLE ALS STÄTTEN DER GEISTIGEN und KÖRPERLICHEN ERTÜCHTIGUNG UNSERER JUGEND AUF LANGE ZEITEN HINAUS IHREM ZWECKE DIENEN, DEN KOMMENDEN GESCHLECHTERN FREUDE und FROHSINN ZUTEIL WERDEN LASSEN und GOTTES SEGEN ALLZEIT HIER WALTEN.

Die heutige Grundsteinlegung erfolgte in schlichter Feierstunde unter Anwesenheit von Behörden- und Gemeindevertretern, der Geistlichkeit und der Gemeinschaft der Schulkinder und zahlreicher Gemeindebürger.

Worüber diese Urkunde.
Ausgefertigt am Tage der Grundsteinlegung

—6. Oktober 1963 —

(Unterschrift)
Bürgermeister

Certificate: Laying of the new elementary school corner stone

Customs and Traditions

The Spring Parade

In this age of technology, we can hardly understand that the start of the warm season was cause for celebration among our ancestors. Of course, we rejoice when snow and ice give way to spring sunshine, and we are happy when the birds return from the south and the flowers sprout from the earth. However, in our domestic and professional life, changes with the beginning of spring are usually very few. We artificially generate the heat that the sun failed to provide us in the winter, and very likely nobody has seriously frozen during the cold winter. Our ancestors in earlier centuries certainly did not have it so easy. Wintertime for them meant a hard time when people were constantly struggling with the cold. One need only remember that the medieval castles had round holes instead of windows, and that only the women's chambers in the castle were heated. But in the peasant homes, fuel was always rare and expensive until well into the 19th century. So it was all too understandable that everyone yearned for the spring when one no longer needed to shiver. Therefore, one had good reason to celebrate joyfully the "summer day," a day when spring began.

Today, the summer fest is usually held on Laetare Sunday, the fourth Sunday of Lent. Surely, this day was also chosen because the Catholic Church calls for joy on this day in spite of the Lenten season. Moreover, experience has shown that this Sunday is also suitable for the summer festival because it usually falls in the middle of the awakening spring. As long as one can remember, on this Sunday the children of Ottersheim decorate a stick with colored ribbons and a pretzel, and roam the streets singing. Though a real parade is held today, this custom is only a few decades old. It dates back to the former head of the Ottersheim Gymnastics Club, Peter Hindert, who had witnessed this practice in Speyer at a young age, and who called something similar into being in Ottersheim with the support of the Gymnastics Club. In 1929 for the first time, he succeeded to collect about 200 children on Laetare Sunday and to march with them through the village streets. Peter Hindert also paid a former baker to provide each child with a pretzel. It was therefore no surprise when a sizable crowd of children assembled for the Summer Day Parade in the following year.

The band participated in the children's parade for the first time in 1933. At that time, 240 pretzels were distributed, whereby the public did their part in contributing to the cost. The Summer Day Parade was canceled during the construction of the West Wall and during World War II. Not until three years after the war did the practice begin again. "Spring" rolled through the village streets on a float that was pulled by a team of horses. It was followed by a float depicting "Winter" pulled by cows. Singing children with colorfully decorated summer day sticks accompanied the unlike pair. When the parade was over, a battle was held in the schoolyard between winter and summer that ended when winter went up in flames. Unfortunately, for the children there were no pretzels at that time because of the bad times. This was not possible until 1950 when the situation had improved somewhat.

Since that time, the pretzels have been sponsored alternately by the Raiffeisen Cooperative, the Tobacco Growers Association, and the Milk Suppliers' Cooperative. Participation of children at the Summer Day parade was especially strong in 1962. Although the baskets had been abundantly filled, so many boys and girls marched through the village singing with the band that there were insufficient pretzels. Since then, the Summer Day parade has become an integral part of rural life in Ottersheim. It would be a shame if this beautiful custom would one-day fall victim to the practical thinking of our times.

Mischief in the Night before 1 May

In the evening of 30 April, the night before 1 May, the boys of the village carry out all kinds of harmless and less harmless pranks according to an ancient custom. They create mischief within the homes and on the streets while the children and the older people are asleep. For example, they remove window shutters, pull tiles from roofs, remove roofs from garden sheds, take wagons apart and put them back together on top of a barn, carry away yard gates, and smear walls with paint or chalk. In addition, they bring in birch trees from the woods and setup the so-called *bouquet* in front of the house of their beloved.

No one understands exactly why this all happens on the night before 1 May. Few people know that this strange custom dates back to our pagan ancestors and their belief in witches. In fact, centuries ago it was still firmly believed that evil spirits lived in the forest and were not well disposed to the people. The witches were to blame when the cows gave no milk, if children suddenly became ill, when an 'abnormal child' was born, when a plague swept away man or animal, or if the water was undrinkable. According to the belief of our ancestors, the witches were especially active in the night before 1 May, when they gathered together on the Brocken, the highest mountain in the Harz. They crawled up the chimney and flew with moans and croaks through the air on their broomsticks. They could romp once again to their heart's content before sunrise, but they had to retreat into the darkness by day. What remained of the witches' night out were missing doors and shutters, broken bricks, and roofless huts, tools lying in disarray, and disassembled wheelbarrows and wagons.

Today, the boys of the village perform these witching tasks, when they carry out their pranks in the night before 1 May. The depth of this superstition that was once rooted in our people is seen in that through the centuries the Church has not been able to eradicate it completely. To be sure, as in other cases a holy festival was set on that day. The canonization of the Virgin Mary is celebrated on 1 May, as is Saint Walpurga from England (710-779) who served as a missionary in Bavaria. But the people did not forget their witches, and they let them continue to ride to the Brocken on Walpurga's Night. In fact, in later centuries the belief in witchcraft grew even stronger. Many were convinced in all seriousness that women and girls could turn into witches and then inflict all sorts of evil in their environment. Therefore, those witches were pursued and burned at the stake, after a confession had been previously extorted under torture. Many an innocent woman or innocent girl had departed from this life in this way. The abuse of witchcraft was especially commonplace in and after the 30 Years War. Only gradually did the State and Church authorities manage to bring this superstition under control and prohibit the burning of witches. A remnant of the ancient belief in witchcraft is still present in the custom to perform mischief in the village during the night before 1 May, as is still the case in Ottersheim.

Baptismal and Marriage Customs

Up until the thirties of this century, the *Taufe [baptism]* of a child was an event over which little fuss was made. It usually took place on a weekday morning after the Mass. Accompanied by the midwife, the godmother carried the new child into the church where the pastor performed the baptism according to the church rites. Not until under Pastor Knöll did the baptismal rite become more solemn. It took place when possible on a Sunday afternoon so that children and adults could participate. Nowadays, it is usually late enough to allow the child's mother to be there. At the entrance to the church nave, the child to be baptized is received by the pastor with a speech directed to the family, and after several prayers, the godparents and infant are accompanied to the sanctuary of the church where the actual baptism takes place. After the baptism, young and old line the main aisle of the house of worship to form a corridor through which the newly baptized is carried outside by the godmother. Outside and on behalf of the parents, the midwife distributes a large bag of candy to those children who have gathered for the christening.

In the selection of godparents, close relatives such as an uncle and aunt are usually preferred. With the baptism, the *Petter [Godfather]* and *Götel [godmother]* take over the obligation for the religious upbringing of the child should the parents die prematurely, or due to chronic illness not be able to care for the child. Moreover, it is customary that the godparents provide gifts at Christmas and Easter as long as the child is in elementary school. On the first Christmas holiday, the godchild collects his "Christ Child" from the godparents and on Easter Sunday his "Easter bunny."

The choice of name was quite easy in earlier times. As a rule, a boy received the first name of his godfather and a girl the name of her godmother. The result was that only rarely were new names given, and it was typical to distinguish locals having the same name by using Roman numerals. The selection is handled more freely today, but the given name of the godfather or godmother is often added as a middle name to honor the godparents. Already in very early times, the day of baptism and the name of the child were recorded in the baptismal record book of the pastoral office. As far as this was done before the French Revolution, these books are invaluable sources for family history research.

Much richer than in baptism are the customs and practices at a *Hochzeit [wedding]*. As the name implies, it is a *Hoch [high] zeit [time]* that initiates a new phase in one's life. Early on, that parents played a key role in the choice of a spouse is well known. More important than the affection of bride and bridegroom for each other was often the intention to keep land parcels intact, and to assist the young couple in getting a good start financially, because "whoever marries nothing and inherits nothing, remains a poor devil until he dies." So it happened that now and then, marriages among relatives took place though the Church did not relish providing dispensations for these. That one cannot speak of inbreeding on a large scale in Ottersheim is easily demonstrated by the surnames. Spouses from elsewhere are an everyday occurrence today. The engagement is usually celebrated only in small circles, as far as the bride and groom do not skip it entirely. An announcement is posted at the mayor's office four weeks before the wedding. Soon after, the names of the couple appear in the "Notices" at the Community Hall. Friends and acquaintances take the opportunity to decorate the notice with bouquets of flowers, the number of which speaks to the popularity of the bride and groom. Previously, the couple was also "announced" during church services by the pastor. Today, we are content with an entry in the church bulletin. The wedding itself usually took place during a time when the farmer is least busy. Popular weeks include prior to carnival [which ends on Ash Wednesday], the time between Easter and Pentecost, and the autumn months. Weddings are celebrated only in exceptional cases during Advent and Lent.

Guests are invited personally by the bride or the groom. An unjustified refusal would be seen as insulting the bride and groom. The guests gather in front of the "wedding house" on the day of the wedding and form pairs prior to the procession to the church. No one dare exclude himself from this because "whoever does not help grace the wedding procession, need not smear his face [partake of the food]." As soon as the bells sound, the procession begins with the children in front, the bride in white dress and veil, and then the groom, earlier in wedding tuxedo and today in a black suit.

Many villagers line the road while good friends follow the course of the wedding procession with gun salutes. The bride walks to the right of the bridegroom when entering the church; however, during the ceremony itself she kneels on the left. After the usual wedding ritual, the participants stand in the middle aisle of the nave, after which they go home. However, they may not leave the church until they have presented the Mass servers with a gift of money. So that no one omits this obligation, the attendees must pass a rope that two Mass servers have strung across the aisle. Outside the church, friends and relatives congratulate the young couple. Then the wedding procession starts moving again. The festival is usually celebrated in the home of the bride where food and beverages are plentiful. Before dinner, the wedding party marches through the village streets and sings folk songs that have been handed down. The wedding celebration itself usually lasts until late into the night.

As a rule, the cost of the meal is shared by the parents of the bride and of the groom. The guests show their gratitude in that they present the young couple with more or less valuable items for their new household. If the bridegroom is part of a musical or choral society, his friends are not deterred from serenading the couple. That they then get to taste the wedding wine is a matter of course. Sometimes young people also play jokes or pranks with the young couple. So it happened that in 1952 during the wedding celebration, friends of the groom, a blacksmith, carried his anvil and complete set of smith tools into the bedroom and set them up there. In another case, the beds and cabinets were completely taken apart and laid out in the bedroom. Once it also happened that during the ceremony, a tree trunk was laid in front of the yard gate. The couple had to saw through the tree trunk to get into the house.

In addition, the friends and neighbors of the house are not forgotten, even if they could not be invited to the ceremony itself. Children are sent to them with pieces of cake and sweets so that in this way they may also share in the festivities.

Wedding Presents

Franz Steegmüller, Mannheim

A peasant wedding as of old, that is the second greatest holiday,
A feast of very special rank. We sit then often for hours and hours,
From early morning 'till late at night, here the aunt, there the uncle.
People gossip about this and that, the mouth nearly 'runneth over'.
There is never a pause, never a missing piece, and everyone knows a juicy bit.
Everyone has something in store, everyone knows another 'winner'.
From the good old days, one learns all there is to know.
Therefore, the young and the old chat so eagerly,
About the weather, about the time, about money and about the people.
There is laughter, chatter, and song, for the old, for the young.
Are you well seen and esteemed as uncle or aunt by the relatives,
Then you will certainly be an especially honored guest at such a festival.

All that is right and just and fair, but it calls for more;
Every time the thorny question, every time the same story.
If you think seriously, practically, give something for the household,
Maybe something quite ordinary something personal,
Or something very special, something individual.
For her, for him alone, something for both?
Yes, the gifts and presents bring one to despair,
Gives you headaches from thinking and thinking about the wedding presents.
To help with the dizziness, until at night around eleven,
I cogitated and dissembled, collected and noted,
Until morning around three, I had a complete litany.
Hearken forth and pay good attention, now I'm putting wrappers on it:

Noodle rack, cake pans - coal shovel, egg cups,
Baking pan, hoe, pick - saucers, hair curlers,
Louse comb, gray baskets and brooms - things to drink and to eat,
Pitch fork, scythe, trowel, garden fork - clog socks, ear muffs,
Butter churn, wash machine - clothes hanger blue, green,
Coal bucket, woolen slippers – Charcoal briquettes - pot holders,
Kitchen scale, Christmas crib - record player, wheel barrow,
Canning jars, seed keeper - ladder wagon with ladder hooks,
Shirt with starched front and cuffs - Cases for cigarettes

Coffee bowl, nicely named - for the Papa, for the Mama,
Camel hair shoes from the department store - chairs with back that reclines,
Pudding powder, red jello - a squeaky new dining service,
A chamois beard and folklore blouse - canned applesauce,
Oil paintings, watercolors - for hanging and for setting,
Marble bust and sculpture - Italian plaster figure,
Clothes brush, sewing material and thread - stockings for the calves,
Sofa pillow and reading lamp - High-heel shoes and heel-less shoes,
Hanging rods for curtains - gift basket with oil sardines,
Collar buttons and socks for dancing - cognac and champagne,
Fine soap three pieces in a box - a hit record, a television,
A grandfather clock that chimes - a gem on a wedding day.
Pralines, filled, extra fine - shoe horn, clothesline,
An ultra-super radio - impressive to see and to hear,
A four-door closet cupboard - three meters high and just as long
A colander and a curtain pulley reel - a sieve for seed and one for flour,
Mittens, rolled ham - a hen with 19 young chicks,
A complete medicine cabinet - a bathroom bowl or a sink,
Night lamp, a little sow - an onion rake,
A barrel, vat or jug - a brand new front end plow,
A flower bouquet or a plant - an extra fine wheel barrow frame,
A nicely polished coffee mill - embroidered pillows for the chairs,
Flower vases of all kinds - spatula for the wedding cake,
Rotating or other cake plate - shaving cream for the model husband,
A few rolls of new towels - homemade bed sheets,
Rugs for around the bed - table cloth for company,
Pull-through elastic, oxford shoe strings - a special egg pan,
Picture frames, large, small – hot water bottle and a candy jar,
If we want something to laugh about - or to pull a prank,
Night pot, cigar stumps - just big enough for under the bed,
And things packaged in box after box, - needs to be at every wedding,
In addition, pail, pitcher, appliances - for washing and for bathing the feet.

When thinking a bit further - one will come up with other wedding gifts:
What about blankets, diapers, with things for little ones?
With rompers, cute sweaters - shirts and jackets?
With bonnet, bottle or cap - with socks, bootees or slippers?
With rattles, doll buggies - and other children's things?

Who still is thinking - and has not yet found a wedding gift,
For the happiness of bride or groom - I'm so very sorry for him.

Pork Bouillon and Harvest Roast

As long as one can remember, bouillon or soup from freshly slaughtered pork has provided for a festive event for the peasants in Ottersheim, where not only the family partakes but also relatives and friends. Because there was no butcher in the village before 1902, the people had every reason to long for the day when they could again feast on meat and sausage at will. Therefore, young and old happily looked forward to this celebration of fresh pork bouillon. Today, you can of course buy fresh meat at the store throughout the year. Because it costs money however, the portions are always somewhat smaller than when one could rely on his own product.

A home slaughter usually took place during the cold season. The farmer and so-called *Advent butcher* agree on a day for the slaughter. He does not forget to invite family and friends to the feast on time. The trough and incline are picked up and erected in the yard the evening before. The Advent butcher arrives at the farmer's house early the next morning and the work begins immediately. The fat pig is captured in the barn and bound with a rope. All available forces are needed to help scrape off the bristles once the animal is killed and the blood is drained. Then the butcher suspends the pig and cuts it up. A portion of the meat is cooked in a kettle. The family members and their guests gather in the kitchen to feast on the boiled meat once the meat is cooked. They all stand around the table. Each person serves himself by cutting off as much as he wants of the farmer's bread and kettle meat, then salts and eats the meat with the bread. For thirsty souls, the farmer brings a jug of wine from the cellar. Those in the know and a sure eye find the tastiest cuts of meat, while the novice usually goes for the big chunks.

It is expected of the guests that they not only do well with the fresh meat, but that they also then help with cutting the bacon and rind. The more hands to help the sooner the butcher can begin making sausage. In the past, only real intestines were used for this, but today artificial skins and cans are also used. The sausages and stomach rinds are also cooked in a kettle like the boiled meat. As a conclusion to the slaughter festival, a meal is usually shared in the afternoon where the bouillon soup, fresh sausage, sauerkraut, and potatoes are served. In addition to their own family members, relatives and friends take part in this meal that is the climax of the slaughter festival.

It is still customary in Ottersheim to give the parish priest and the teacher some of the soup. This custom dates back to the blood tithes of old that obliged the people to surrender a portion of meat from slaughter to the rulers. Although the population now knows nothing of this old custom, they still follow the example of their ancestors. The Nurses' Station is also often provided with a small gift. In addition, relatives and friends also get a pot of soup and from case to case a sausage to taste.

When the slaughter fest has ended, the sausages and headcheese are brought into the smokehouse and smoked. However, the hams and side pieces [bacon] are salted on the following day. For this, a *Stande,* pronounced *Stanne* in Ottersheim, is used that is usually set up in the basement. The Stande was a barrel-formed wooden drum. It stood on three extended staves and it was closed at the top using a wooden lid. The ham and bacon pieces are left in brine inside the drum for six weeks. Then the pieces are brought to be stored in the smoke chamber where these are smoked with the help of sawdust.

In recent years, it has become customary for many farmers to slaughter in the warm season. But this is only possible if you own a freezer where the fresh meat can be protected from deterioration. While previously the farmer lived almost only from smoked meat during the summer, now fresh meat is also available to eat during the hot season.

De Ernbrore [The Harvest Roast]

Separate from the slaughter festival, the harvest roast is held by the community only once a year in Ottersheim. It is the traditional community Thanksgiving. Special public celebrations were previously uncommon. Instead, they originally contented themselves with a festive meal in the home after completion of the harvest. In 1927, when the church dedication festival was moved from Saint Martin's Day to the next-to-last Sunday in August, a harvest roasting was celebrated in November with public dance music. It was not until the thirties that the State ascribed greater importance to the feast of Thanksgiving. It was celebrated as a festival in town and country in early October. It was in most cases connected to a public gathering of the farmers.

To prevent a secularization of Thanksgiving, Pastor Knöll took up the idea and sought to integrate it into the church service. At his suggestion, the villagers brought a selection of all field and garden crops to the church and placed them on a table in the church sanctuary. In conjunction with the service, the gifts were blessed and God was thanked in prayer for the harvest. This custom has remained to this day. The harvest festival is usually celebrated on the first Sunday in October.

The Lorenz Hole

When the feast of Saint Lorenz [Lawrence] is celebrated on 10 August, the youth of Ottersheim are already looking forward to the following Sunday when the Lorenz bread is distributed in Herxheim. After the morning worship service, young and old set off on foot, by bicycle, or by car on country roads to the Lorenz Hole near Herxheim. According to ancient tradition, the Ottersheim residents will be presented with a large amount of consecrated bread. And the reason is as follows:

In 1660, when the terrible consequences of the 30 Years War had not yet been overcome in our country, the plague raged in Herxheim. The Black Death swept away many of the inhabitants of this village. The *Leergasse [Empty lane]* of today was completely depopulated by the plague back then. Herxheim was quarantined because of the danger of contagion; no one was allowed in, no one out. Desperate cries for help from the hungry people did not go unheard in neighboring communities. Although they themselves possessed only the bare minimum, the people of Ottersheim, Knittelsheim, and Offenbach shared their scanty bread supplies with the needy from Herxheim. Thereafter, those of Ottersheim were distinguished by their exceptional generosity. They brought the food in baskets to the quarantine border of Herxheim and set them on the so-called *Diebsweg [Thieves' road]*. Only from afar could one speak with the residents of Herxheim. The Herxheimers took the food as soon as the benefactors were gone. The place was called the *dark hole* at that time because it still lay in the dark forest.

In their unspeakable need, the inhabitants of Herxheim conducted beggar processions in the village and gave the following promise:

> *"If hunger and plague should come to an end, we will consecrate the first bread of our harvest each year forever, and bring a two-horse wagon full to the dark hole where it should be distributed among the benefactors."*

This promise of gratitude has been held ever since by Herxheim. On the Sunday after the feast of Saint Lorenz, the bread is collected in the village and consecrated at the main church. Then it is driven to the *Lorenz Hole* or *dark hole* and distributed. People from neighboring communities of Ottersheim, Knittelsheim, and Offenbach take the bread home where it is distributed among the family members. Everyone gets a slice, because everyone should have a share in the blessing of God resting within the consecrated bread.

Herxheim only once did not keep its promise in 300 years. But in that year, the entire crop was destroyed by a storm. Herxheim has been true in fulfilling the vow of their ancestors since then.

The Palm Spray

The Catholics hold a solemn procession on the Sunday before the Easter celebration [Palm Sunday] to commemorate the triumphant entry of Jesus into Jerusalem before his Passion and Death. It represents a tribute to Christ the King and is a sign of devotion to the Incarnate Son of God. Just as the children of the Hebrews hailed the Messiah with palm reeds in their hands, so now the boys and girls march with their own palms.

As long as one can remember, the following plants have been used in Ottersheim to represent the palm reeds.

Local Name	Genus species	Common name
Boxwood	Buxus sempervirens	Boxwood
Ivy	Hedera helix	Ivy
Periwinkle	Vinca minor	Periwinkle
`Blessing´ Juniper	Juniperus Sabina	Savin Juniper
Oak	Quercus pedunculata	Stem or summer oak
Hazelnut shoot	Corylus avellana	Hazelnut bush
Elderberry shoot	Sabucus nigra	Elderberry
Currant shoot	Ribes vulgare	Currant bush
Pussy willow	Salix caprea	Pussy willow

While an herb spray consists mainly of herbs, the palm spray is made of the plants that either live through the winter or that bud or bloom in the spring. We primarily use boxwood, ivy, periwinkle, and branches of juniper as a substitute for real palm trees, which do not thrive in our climate. These evergreen plants are supplemented by branches of the oak tree, which as we all know does not shed its withered leaves during winter. To these are added roots of the shrubs that bud out very early in the spring. The male flowers or catkins of the hazelnut and pussy willow, and the young leaves of the elderberry and currant bush are used to represent the new life. A cross was placed in the middle of the palm spray that the children made themselves from elderberry bush twigs.

In the week before Palm Sunday, the boys and girls are eager to gather the various plants for the palm spray. No one takes the easy way out to get the best possible result. Boxwood can be found in every yard, but one has to look around for the juniper because it is not very common. What is sought is the so-called *Savin Juniper* or *Savin shrub,* known locally as the *Stink Juniper* because of its distinctive smell. It differs from the cypress above all in its needles, which are very small and grow individually on the branches. The name commemorates the blessing that is bestowed when the branches are brought into the house after the consecration and hung from the ceiling.

Once the bells start to ring for worship on Palm Sunday, the children flock with their sprays to God's house where the bundles are blessed. Then led by the youth, the whole congregation proceeds while singing, through the old cemetery, to the Sisters' Home across the street, then back to the church.

After the service, the boys and girls proudly take their palm spray home. There the blessed twigs are usually tucked under the roof tiles. At the Consecration of Fire during the Easter Vigil, it is common that some "palms" from the previous year are burned. The ashes are blessed and kept until Ash Wednesday. At the beginning of Lent, the priest marks a cross on the forehead of the faithful with these ashes to remind them of the impermanence of the world.

The Gärrerbuben of Ottersheim

On Maundy [Holy] Thursday, after the Gloria of the Solemn Mass when the bells "fly to Rome,"[87] the time has come for the *Gärrerbuben [Rattle boys]*. For weeks, the boys from the last class of the elementary school have prepared for this day. They have come together alternately in the homes of members of their class and rehearsed the old songs and chants that they will recite to the villagers on the last three days before Easter. They are the same songs and chants that have been sung for generations before them. No song can be changed or be replaced by another.

The rattle boys step into action at noon on Holy Thursday for the first time. In groups of three to five boys, they parade through the streets of the village and urge the people to pray the "Angel of the Lord." At the instruction of the leader, the rattles are set in motion. Then they chant together as follows:

> *Hear Ye People, it is prayer time!*
> *Ave Maria, is how the Lord greets the Virgin Mary.*

After completion of the chant, the group moves on for a reasonable distance to swing the rattles again. Then a song follows in Latin:

> *Ave, ave, ave, ave, ave Maria gratia plena*
> *Dominus tecum, Dominus tecum.*

Similarly, the Angelus bells during the Mass are replaced in the evening by the rattles and song.

On Good Friday, the rattle boys are on their feet very early in the morning. When people are still in bed, the group is already marching through the village singing the traditional songs. Some of these hymns are long gone from hymnals of today. The collection of these songs can be neither increased nor shortened. These include:

1. *Arise, in the name of our Lord Jesus Christ!*
   The bright day is come,
   The light of day that watches over us.
   God gives us all a good day,
   A good day, a happy time,
   Blessed be God forever!

---

[87] This is a reference to the Angelus bells that go silent during the Holy Masses from Holy Thursday until the Easter Vigil.

2. Melchisedech appeared, according to the priest's duties,
   To give thanks by offering bread and wine.
   In this way, from pure bread and wine
   Christ the Eternal Priest offered the supreme sacrifice.

3. Lord, You who at the foot of the cross
   Innocent as a lamb
   Have offered Yourself as dear ransom
   For the sin of the entire world
   Willingly, for our salvation.
   The redeemed flock brings their love to the altar of atonement.
   Look upon, O Saviour, graciously
   The poor, who glowing in thanks
   Now dedicate to You the weak victim's offering.

4. Come, dear Christian throng, with humble hearts.
   See here the Saviour's death pains.
   At each station you see what God's Son
   Suffered out of love for you!
   Reflect on this, hasten not away!

5. O sacred cross of love
   Bowed at your feet
   Let us greet you with kissing.

6. How shall my feeling of pain pour out in sorrow?
   The tears that flow so hot from my eyes,
   Drown the words and sound of my song.
   O God, take my tears as a song to Your praise!

7. On the Mount of Olives in the stillness of the night
   Surrendered Himself to the will of His Father
   To drink the cup of suffering,
   To pay our debts;
   Saturated with bloody sweat,
   So He began,
   O my Jesus, what pain are You suffering!

8. Christ's mother stood in pain
   At the cross and cries from the heart,
   As her beloved Son was hanging.
   Full of sorrow to the soul,
   Cutting under deathly fear,
   Now the sword of sorrow went.

Before each Mass and prior to each devotion, the rattle boys march through the village three times calling:

> This is the first time (call) to church!
> This is the second call to church!
> This is the third and last call to church!

In the morning on Holy Saturday, the boys again use the rattles and chant in the streets. In the afternoon, the long awaited moment has come when the rattle boys gather together to collect a large laundry basket with which to store their reward in the form of eggs and money. As they go from house to house, they sing:

> We have gone with rattles to the grave
> Give us therefore an Easter gift
> Not too big and not too small
> That it fits into the basket;
> Not too small and not too big
> That they force a hole in the basket.

When the rattle boys receive a gift in a house, they sing upon departing:

> The people have given us gifts.
> May they see much joy this year,
> They and their children, they and their household.

Should the very rare case occur that the rattle boys are rejected at a house, they are not exactly squeamish with evil wishes. Then they sing upon departing:

> The people have given us nothing.
> May the brew run down their ...
> They and their children, they and their household.

Once the collection is completed, the eggs and the money are distributed evenly among the rattle boys. It is not uncommon that a given boy may receive fifty or more eggs. An illustration of the popularity that Garrer is enjoyed among the youth is the following true story:

> In 1923, when the graduating class was preparing for the Garrer, a father told his son, "If you do not participate in the Garrer, I will give you a gold watch for Easter." Without hesitation the boy replied, "I would like to have a gold watch, but I'd rather take part in Garrer."

Less pleasing is another incident that occurred during World War II. At that time on Holy Saturday of 1942, an overzealous, Nazi-minded policeman from Bellheim was watching the rattle boys as they marched through the village streets with their laundry basket receiving the usual gifts. When the collection was completed, the policeman ordered the boys to come with him into the community hall. He questioned them and wrote down their names. Then he took all the eggs and all the money in the amount of 100 marks. At the same time, he announced to them that they would be punished for illegal gathering. Apparently, the policeman found little understanding for his actions among his superiors. That same evening, the policeman from Ottersheim received an order from the police station at Bellheim to return the confiscated money to the rattle boys plus 8.5 pfennigs for each confiscated egg. Delight prevailed in Ottersheim for young and old, and the old custom was preserved.

The Herb Bundle

When the feast of the Assumption is at hand in mid-August, the village youth go in search of herbs for the herb bundle. According to tradition, only certain plants can be gathered and tied in a bunch. The *Mullein* is the center and the focal point of the herb bundle. These along with the other herbs were medicinal plants that were used to restore the health of humans and livestock. Our ancestors were of the opinion a specific herb existed for treating any illness. They brewed tea from the *Mullein* to treat coughs and abdominal pain. The seeds of *Sorrel* were cooked in red wine and used as a remedy for diarrhea. Those who had intestinal worms could drink a tea made from *common Tansy*. *Lovage* was thought to support the stomach and force sweating, while *Toadflax* was used to treat tuberculosis. *Agrimony* was used as a bath to treat intestinal problems. *Peppermint* tea is still popular, especially to treat bloating or gas in small children. *Millet* was placed on a person suffering from tooth or abdominal pain, while the *wild Carrot* was used for gallstones. *Centaury* was so sought after as a remedy for dyspepsia and indigestion that it is almost extinct in some areas. For anemia, jaundice, and gout, *Wormwood* was thought to help. *Yarrow* was used primarily for colic and diarrhea in domestic animals, while *Saint John's Wort* was used to keep livestock healthy.

One did not always content oneself with relying only on the natural healing properties of herbs. Even with Christianity, it had not been possible until this century to eradicate superstition in the villages. However, certain plants played an important role in "Customs." So you could banish witches from yard and stables if you picked *Saint John's Wort* at the midnight hour. It was believed that injured horses could be cured with *Hazelnut twigs*. How to do this is indicative of the superstitions of past centuries. The instructions were:

> *"If a horse is injured, one cuts off three Hazelnut twigs. While reciting the three names of the Divine Trinity, dip the cut end into the bleeding wound and hang them on the stove pipe or chimney. Once the Hazelnut twigs have dried the wound will be healed."*

Just as strikingly strange to us is the recipe to treat cows that give no milk.

> *"One need only to chop up Vermouth, Dill, Garlic, and Masterwort (Imperatoria), then let the cow lick it. Immediately all will be well again."*

Understandably, the church was in constant battle with the popular superstitions of the population. Because nothing could be achieved with banning anything however, the heathen customs were instead reinterpreted with a Christian meaning. The consecration of the herbs was meant to point the people to the fact that ultimately only God can help those in need due to illness, if one turns to Him with sincerity.

The consecrated herb bundle brought God's blessing into house and barn. Therefore, the herbs are kept for the whole year under the roof where they are supposed to protect the house from lightning. Sometimes the flowers are rubbed into the drinking trough of calving cows so that the cattle remain protected from disease.

The consecration of herb bundles was already common everywhere in our homeland in the Middle Ages. Fortunately, the custom in Ottersheim has continued to this day. At the Feast of Assumption, boys and girls compete to see who can bring the largest Mullein into the church. No less important is to possess all the usual herbs, especially the rare Centaury. According to tradition, the following herbs should be included in the herb bundle:

	Local Name	Genus · species	Common name
1.	Virgin Mary Kunkel	Verbascum thapsiforme	Mullein
2.	Old horse	Rumex acetosa	Sorrel
3.	Young horse	Rumex acetosella	Sheeps Sorrel
4.	Blue Blood Drops	Scabiosa Succisa	Devil's Bit Scabious
5.	Red Blood Drops	Sanguisorba officinalis	Burnet
6.	Fox tail	Lythrum Salicaria	Purple loosestrife
7.	Hazel nut twigs	Corylus Avellana	Hazelnut
8.	Wild oats	Avena sativa	Oats, oat straw
9.	Tansy	Tanacetum vulgare	Tansy
10.	Amber/Chase-devil	Hypericum perforatum	Saint John's Wort
11.	Lovage	Levisticum officinale	Lovage
12.	Maria bed straw	Linaria vulgaris	Toadflax
13.	Eurasian walnut	Juglans regia	Walnut
14.	Agrimony?	Agrimonia Eupatoria	Agrimony
15.	European birthwort	Aristolochia clematis	Birthwort
16.	Peppermint	Mentha aquatica	Peppermint
17.	Garden Rue	Ruta graveolens	Common rue (herb of grace)
18.	Pearlwort	Achillea ptarmica	Achillea (sneeze weed)
19.	Red Sheaf	Origanum vulgare	Oregano
20.	White Sheaf	Achillea millefolium	Yarrow
21.	Red deer	Panicum miliacum	Millet
22.	Wormtongue	Epilobium angustifolium	Great willowherb (fireweed)
23.	Common centaury?	Centaurium erythraea	Centaury
24.	Bird nests	Daucus carota	Wild carrot
25.	Vermouth	Artemisia culgaris	Mugwort/wormwood

The Church Dedication Festival in Ottersheim

The church dedication festival is of religious origin as the name suggests. As a religious festival, it is still celebrated every year on a Sunday in the Liturgy. Because the Ottersheim church is dedicated to Saint Martin, the church dedication festival was celebrated in past times on the Sunday after Saint Martin's Day. The death of Saint Martin on 11 November was a mandatory holiday in ancient times that was celebrated with High Mass and Vespers. It was preceded by a special day of Reconciliation. The secular festival of dedication took place on the following Sunday. This was a feast that young and old especially looked forward to because the Saint Martin festival signaled the end of the year for the farmers. The harvest had been brought in, the grapes were pressed, and the meat larder filled. The lease was paid and the income for the year could be enjoyed in barn, cellar, granary, and storage shed.

The Church Dedication feast was preceded by a great cleaning day. The yard was strewn with fresh sand, the rooms were thoroughly washed, and fresh curtains hung up. Feast cake and new wine dare not be missing. For the main meal at noon, there was soup made with flour ground from unripe spelt, grain with meat dumplings, pork chop or roast, potatoes and cabbage. The relatives met over coffee and cake in the afternoon. Young and old enjoyed themselves to waltz, polka, or Rheinländer in the taverns. At the community hall stood the riding school in the middle of the street while booths awaited the sweet tooth at the street sides. The festive activities lasted for two days until the feast was officially ended on Tuesday afternoon.

The Church Dedication feast was the largest village festival. It was still celebrated even when Ottersheim was a Reformed community and there was no intent to dedicate the church, which was newly built in 1619. How the church dedication festival became secular in the minds of the people becomes clear from the fact that in the 19th century, not the religious church authority but rather the secular community council set the date of the celebration. It was decided in 1881 to celebrate the feast on the Sunday after Saint Gall's Day (16 October) instead of Saint Martin's Day. Through this change, the peace between pastor and congregation was to be restored. It had been lost due to the secular nature of previous celebrations at an otherwise religious festival. With the change of the pastor in 1897, the church dedication festival was once again celebrated on Saint Martin's Day, so it remained until 1927.

After the First World War, a Veteran's Day celebration was set on the second Sunday in November in all of Germany. Out of respect for the dignity of this day, public dances were prohibited everywhere on this Sunday. Since the Saint Martin's feast fell mostly on the same Sunday, the festival could not be celebrated in the usual context. Therefore, the council decided to move the festival to the second to last Sunday in August. After the Second World War, the feast was again moved in 1947 to the old date in November. This choice could be maintained for only a few years; however, because of the nationally set Memorial Day that often coincided with Saint Martin's feast day. So in 1952, the third Sunday in October was set as the date for the celebration of the Church Dedication feast. This date has remained in effect to this day.

The Celebration of Saint Martin

Every year on 11 November, the Catholic parish in Ottersheim celebrates the feast of its patron, Saint Martin. The celebration of the saint was previously held on the Sunday following the 11th. In the fifties however, Pastor Kern was able to win over the population to celebrate the date of the Franconian Bishop's death as a local holiday. Menial work is voluntarily waived on this day and the people gather in the morning and afternoon for a communal church service. On the evening before or on the evening of the feast day itself, the popular Saint Martin parade takes place. The village youth meet with lanterns, lights, and lighted pumpkins in the old schoolyard at dusk. When Saint Martin arrives on horseback, he is greeted by the children with song and poetry. After the thank-you speech of the rider, the parade begins to move to the strains of the young peoples' band. Even men and women from Ottersheim and from neighboring villages mingle with the carriers of burning Saint Martin lamps.

On the eastern part of Lange Straße where the Bauernweg enters, a beggar awaits the parade. As soon as this beggar sees Saint Martin, he asks him for help. Without hesitation the rider parts his own coat and gives the poor man one-half for which the beggar sincerely thanks him. The children follow the acts of the saint attentively. But watching alone is surely not enough. Since the war ended, it is common that the participants in the Saint Martin parade bring an offering themselves for the poor and needy. Initially, food was donated that was then given to hospitals and orphanages. Today money is given, especially for the needy of the Soviet zone.

After the beggar scene, the children parade back through the Ludwigstraße and the Deich to the old schoolyard where a fire has been kindled. The youth surround the burning pyre as the flames rise to the sky. The impressive ceremony is completed with songs and chants. Then three men choose the six best Martin's lamps and present awards. Whoever wants an award has to make the lamp himself and to carry it in the parade. However, for all children who participate in the parade there is a tasty pretzel at the end. The parish covers the costs.

The celebration of Saint Martin in Ottersheim is a relatively young tradition. It goes back to Reverend Knöll who started the tradition in the thirties. Because the rulers of the Third Reich wanted no public events with a church character, the children gathered with their lanterns in the old cemetery and from there moved solemnly into the church where they remembered the Saint with prayer and song. As the boys and girls prepare to leave the church at the end of the celebration, they were given butter cookies shaped in the form of Saint Martin's geese as they exited through the bell tower door. After the Second World War, the school also participated in service of the good cause. Since that time, there has been a parade around the village, where fortunately numerous members of the Protestant population of Ottersheim also take part. Riders and beggars were present at the ceremony for the first time in 1948. The Saint Martin pageant was also introduced at that time and had since repeatedly attracted spectators from near and far.

Associations and Cooperatives

The Saint Cecilia Society of Ottersheim

As is apparent from the description of the parish, in 1856 there was a loose association of singers comprised of about 24 men and 16 girls, out of which the *Cäcilienverein [Saint Cecilia Society]* of Ottersheim emerged in 1860. The club owes its origin to teacher Anton Decker from Klingenmünster. In 1859, he took over the school position in Ottersheim of his father-in-law, Michael Damen, that he then held for a full thirty years. Decker was then 43 years old and had earned his education at the Catholic Teachers' Seminary in Speyer. He began the work already in 1859. The *Katholische Sangverein [Catholic Singing Society]* as it was called then was launched on 1 January 1860. The founding members were:

1.	Martin Böhm	(1814-1904)
2.	Theobald Brucker	(1801-1867)
3.	Johannes Gutting	(1808-1876)
4.	Konrad Hatzenbühler	(1821-1890)
5.	Augustin Hanck	(1800-1875)
6.	Johannes Job	(1810-1879)
7.	Franz Leonhard Job	(1802-1868)
8.	Stefan Kopf	(1813-1879)
9.	Andreas Kreiner	(1800-1880)
10.	Nikolaus Kreiner	(1831-1887)
11.	Peter Kreiner	(1810-1888)
12.	Theobald Kreiner	(1828-1897)
13.	Valentin Kröper	(1813-1889)
14.	Rudolf Merdian	(1825-1892)
15.	Franz Adam Seither	(1838-1903)
16.	Theobald Seither	(1821 —?)
17.	Jakob Anton Waçon	(1798-1869)
18.	Andreas Zwißler	(1811-1900)
19.	Georg Zwißler	(1806-1884)
20.	Johannes Zwißler (called 'Large')	(1831-1917)
21.	Peter Zwißler (Manager of Tavern 'Hirsch")	(1839-1907)
22.	Wendelin Zwißler III. (called 'Sing Wendel')	(1832-1887)

Among the leading men of the newly formed church choir:

1.	Pastor Matthäus Dotterweich	as president
2.	Teacher Anton Decker	as conductor
3.	Secondary teacher Peter Dausch	as deputy conductor
4.	Konrad Hatzenbühler	as committee member
5.	Johannes Zwißler	as committee member
6.	Johannes Job	accountant

In its statutes, the Saint Cecilia Society set itself the task of embellishing the worship service and other religious celebrations with its songs. Practice sessions were held in one of two classrooms that were located on the upper floor of the schoolhouse.

The inclusion of a new member into the Catholic Singing Society was subject to certain conditions that were handled very strictly during the initial years. The candidate had to not only have certain singing ability but also have the appropriate character and behavior for a church choir member. For a long time the choir could consist of no more than two dozen singers because space on the balcony of the church was rather crowded. At that time, there were still a considerable number of men and young men who waited eagerly to be admitted to the Saint Cecilia Society. Thus, we are told that seven candidates were available for three deceased members in 1869, four of which could not be considered. Thirty kreutzers were to be paid into the club treasury upon admission. Six kreutzers in dues were to be paid quarterly.

A female singer was mentioned in the Minutes Book of the association for the first time in 1880. Thus, a mixed choir developed from the original men's choir, which is undoubtedly a result of the introduction of the Universal German Society of Saint Cecilia in the Diocese of Speyer in 1877. The first few passive members were recorded at that time.

In addition to multiple-voice song, the single-voiced hymns were especially cultivated in the first decades of its existence. This was mainly caused by the fact that the newly formed Diocese of Speyer, created on the left bank of the Rhine through an act of the Vienna Congress, was comprised of five older bishoprics. It was no wonder that Diocesan Administrator Johannes Geissel, later Cardinal of Cologne, wrote in 1833 that "The church music in the Diocese of Speyer was in a Babylonic state." These following hymnals were simultaneously in use at that time: the Mainz, the old Palatinate, the old Weißenburg, the new Bruchsal, the Strasbourg, the Metz, the Trier, and the old Worms. After extensive preliminary work, the "Catholic Hymns for the Diocese of Speyer" appeared at last in 1842 under Bishop Nikolaus von Weis. This hymnal was obviously not familiar to all churchgoers in the village when the Saint Cecilia Society was founded in Ottersheim, although 18 years had elapsed since the publication of the book. This gap was quite quickly closed with the help of the church choir.

Of course, multi-voiced singing was practiced from the outset. That this included only a few choruses or Mass hymns is easy to derive from a song list. School administrator Gustav Schwaab received three gulden wages for copying three music booklets in 1870. In 1883, it is mentioned that two, four-part Mass hymns were included by the bookbinder. A four-part Mass by Schweizer was purchased in 1866 and practiced. Special love and care was given to learning the German Passion for Holy Week. The required music book was paid for by each of the singers from their own pockets. In addition to church music, secular song was not left out. Usually the singing practice sessions, which were held by petroleum light in the school hall, ended with a multi-voice folk song.

Of particular importance for the positive growth and prosperity of the Saint Cecilia Society in Ottersheim was that the music-loving founder of the choir, teacher Anton Decker, was also able to serve the singing flock for over 30 years.

When he retired to his birthplace of Klingenmünster at 73 years of age in 1889, the church choir had grown to a tradition-minded community. The legacy was assumed in 1889 by teacher Konrad Nieser from Waldsee, while the spiritual leadership lay in the hands of Reverend Ettmüller who had been transferred to Ottersheim in the same year. From 1906 to 1915, teacher Robert Renn was conductor of the Saint Cecilia Society. On the whole, the church choir in Ottersheim experienced an encouraging upswing by the beginning of our century in spite of several crises. At the outbreak of World War I in 1914 for example, there were 41 active singers in addition to 51 passive members. During 1912, it was reported in the protocol that 68 practice sessions were held and the choir sang with multiple voices in the church 17 times. In addition to the annual outing, popular family entertainment was enjoyed on Prince Regent's Day, on Corpus Christi, and on the second Christmas holiday.

After the First World War, the Saint Cecilia Society developed another enjoyable activity. When the liturgical movement took root in Ottersheim under Pastor Knöll, who came to the community in 1929, the church choir willingly stepped up in service of the new form of singing and prayer. After the difficult years of World War II, when most men were drafted into military service, the Cecilia Society quickly took up its activities again in even stronger form. In 1948, it found a choir director in supervising teacher Hans Gensheimer, whose impressive musical skills helped continue not only the tradition of previous decades but also expanded in terms of the liturgical reform.

The Saint Cecilia Society in Ottersheim celebrated its centennial in 1960. The multi-voiced *Missa Gregoriana* by the contemporary composer Hermann Schroeder was sung in alternation with the congregation at the festive divine service on 20 November. At the celebration of church music in the afternoon and at the evening gala concert, the choir gave samples of its capabilities, providing eloquent testimony to the high level of education it possessed. In its anniversary year, the Cecilia Society counted 53 active members, consisting of 19 male singers and 34 female singers as well as 215 passive members. The head was Pastor Scherübl, board chairman was Erwin Wünschel, and choir director was teacher Gensheimer.

The choir directors of the Saint Cecilia Society

Teacher	Anton Decker	from	1860 - 1889
Teacher	Konrad Nieser	from	1889 - 1906
Teacher	Robert Renn	from	1906 - 1915
Teacher	Karl Leidecker	from	1917 - 1923
Teacher	Jakob Jäger	from	1923 - 1929
Teacher	Fritz Steegmüller		1929
Head teacher	August Foltz	from	1929 - 1948
Head teacher	Hans Gensheimer	from	1948 —

The United Singers of Ottersheim

The United Singers of Ottersheim originated in 1933 through the merger of the two male choirs, the *Gesangverein Ottersheim [Singing Club of Ottersheim]* and the *Sangesfreunde Fröhlich Pfalz [Merry Palatinate Friends of Song]*. While the men's Singing Club of Ottersheim was founded in 1864, the Merry Palatinate Friends of Song, which emerged from a vocal department of the Catholic Workers' Association, did not assume the form of an organized club until 1924. The merger of the two choirs was encouraged and promoted by the government, and it happened in such a way that the two clubs brought into the new club not only their members but also their flags and their fortunes. Thus, a very capable male voice choir was formed that included as its members the most enthusiastic and most willing singers among the men and young men of the village.

The beginnings of multi-part, male singing in Ottersheim dates back to the sixties of the 19th century. In 1860, then Headmaster Anton Decker of the Catholic school founded a church choir that consisted solely of men. After the conversion of the Saint Cecilia's Society into a mixed choir, apparently a number of men and young men had the desire to continue to maintain a multi-voiced male choir. So in 1864, they founded their own club that they called the *Männergesangverein [Men's Singing Society]*. Former school administrator Friedrich Reithmayer, who was active in Ottersheim from 1853 to 1860 and whose wife came from Ottersheim, made himself available as conductor. The newly formed club received a good response within the population. Because the Cecilia Society could only accommodate a limited number of men, the remaining song-loving villagers gathered in the singing club, Catholics and Protestants alike. In 1866, a club flag was purchased and dedicated. The positive trend continued until the Franco-German war of 1870-1871. But from this point on, things went backwards to the point that singing activity stopped completely because a capable conductor was lacking.

That changed in 1886 when former Offenbach teacher Franz Stoeppler transferred to the Protestant school in Ottersheim and took over the post of conductor. The Men's Singing Club overhauled its statutes at that time and assumed the name *Singing Club of Ottersheim*. A year later, school administrator Friedrich Reif replaced teacher Stoeppler as conductor. He then led the choir until his transfer in 1891. The male chorus consisted of 36 active and 10 passive members out of 1,008 villagers in 1890. From 1899 to 1902, School Administrator Friedrich Charrois earned special merit with the Singing Club of Ottersheim. Very musically talented, he spared neither time nor effort to train the choir and lead it to a golden age. Unfortunately, after his departure no one could be found who had the talent to continue the work he had begun. Thus, in the next two decades the club led a fairly modest existence.

The club's activity stopped almost completely during the First World War. In 1918, the flag that had faithfully accompanied the club since 1866 was actually lost on its way through the joys and sorrows of time. With the retreat of the western front in November 1918, Hungarian, Slovak, and Bosnian troops came through Ottersheim. These soldiers stole like magpies. So under cover of darkness, they dragged away the club flag with which they probably could not do anything.

The choir was once again brought to life after the First World War. During 1920, Teacher Karl Leidecker made himself available as conductor so that again regular singing practice could take place. The first Forest Festival since the war was held in 1921, and the club took part for the first time in a singing evaluation in Rheinzabern in the same year. Meanwhile, a new flag had been ordered whose dedication was celebrated in May of 1922. That the choir still found time to prepare for the Federal Speyer Valley Fest on 14 May 1922 in Landau, and in addition the associated singing evaluation, proves once again what a singing community is capable of when it is animated by the right spirit. When teacher August Jäger assumed the conductor's baton in January 1924, the confused political situation forced them to limit club life, although good will was not lacking. It became necessary in 1924 to cancel the 60th anniversary celebration.

Of 16 clubs registered to attend the festival, the occupation authorities approved only eight. The representative of the national chairman was banned from giving a speech at the presentation of a certificate of honor. Therefore, the club management decided to postpone the anniversary observance by one year. It was held in June 1925 and was associated with a singing contest in the form of a morning concert. Teacher Albert Wadle was head of the men's choir from 1926 to 1927. He was replaced by teacher Ludwig Stibitz under whose leadership the 65th anniversary festival was held in June 1929.

Ludwig Gaab was chosen as head of the men's choir in 1931. He accumulated more than three decades of outstanding service to the men's choir. Thanks to his well-balanced personality, the merger of the two male choirs in Ottersheim during 1933 to form the *United Singers* was carried out without bitterness or resentment. Because Ludwig Gaab always saw the main tasks of the men's choir as love of song and sociability, he was able to keep the club together in turbulent times. Even during the Second World War (1939-1945), the club activities did not have to come to a complete standstill, although many active members had been drafted into the military. Under the acting leadership of head teacher August Foltz, former singers made themselves available so that the club could meet its major obligations. Unfortunately, during the occupation of the village by Americans and Frenchmen in 1945, almost the entire set of scores was destroyed. However, the presence of mind of some men resulted in bringing the club piano and the two flags to safety so that a new start was possible later. However, several years passed until that happened. After the collapse, all clubs were disbanded and banned by the occupying powers.

Individual organizations, beginning with cultural ones, were not allowed to resume their activities until 1948. So it happened that on 15 January 1949, the second founding of the United Singers of Ottersheim took place. A month later, head teacher Hans

Gensheimer, who meanwhile had been transferred to Ottersheim, was hired as musical director of the choir. With this talented and energetic conductor, the club experienced a new golden age that achieved a memorable climax at the foundation centennial celebration in 1964. Under the baton of head teacher Gensheimer, the United Singers held its annual concerts and recitals on a regular basis. It involved well-known soloists, instrumentalists, and the school choir. The club hosted its own choral celebrations and also took part in such events outside of Ottersheim. At the 90-year anniversary, the famous *Enkenbach Boys' Choir* was guest with its conductor, Albert Hoffmann, who was president of the Palatinate Choral Society. Finally, the United Singers repeatedly took part in concerts with neighboring clubs and with their Swiss singing friends from Hägendorf near Olten. Not least, the association took part in all choral singing competitions and concerts in the Palatinate and participated actively in the Federal Song Festival at Pirmasens in 1958.

The 100-year foundation celebration of the United Singers in Ottersheim was an important milestone in the history of the club. The festivities began on 7 June 1964 with a commemoration at the new cemetery for the deceased and fallen members of the choral society. In the festival marquee on the playing field, a ceremony took place on Saturday June 13th at which the band, the Saint Cecilia Society, and the male choirs of Bellheim, Herxheim, and Hayna participated alongside the men's choir. The musical highlight of the centennial celebration was the choral presentation on Sunday morning that included the *Weinkehlchen,* a children's choir from Neustadt. At the afternoon parade, numerous neighboring clubs marched by music through the flag-bedecked streets of town and expressed their solidarity with the United Singers of Ottersheim. A friendship concert at the festival location in the woods concluded the successful anniversary celebration. Contributing to the success of the festival were not only the 52 active singers under their conductor Hans Gensheimer and its board director Ludwig Gaab but also other cultural associations of the village and the entire population of the Ottersheim community. They all spared no effort to ensure the success of the centennial celebration. This must be especially highly regarded in an age when many are only interested in their personal welfare.

Board members and conductors of the Choral Society of Ottersheim
(The data are incomplete because some documents were lost.)

Board members		*Conductors:*	
		Teacher Frederich Reitmayer	1864
		Teacher Franz Stoeppler	1886
Johann Seither	1889-1890	Teacher Friedrich Reif	1887-1891
Jakob Lösch	1890-1904	Teacher Friedrich Charrois	1899-1902
Franz Steegmüller	1904-1910		
Edmund Bischoff	1910-1911		
Franz Adam Job	1911-1912		
Ludwig Job	1912-1920		

From August 1914 until January 1920 the association's activities rested.

Ed. Winkelblech	1920-1921	Teacher Karl Leidecker	1920-1923
Ludwig Gensheimer	1921-1922		
Herm. Bischoff	1922-1928	Teacher Jakob Jäger	1924-1926
		Teacher Albert Wadle	1926-1927
Wilh. Hatzenbühler I.	1928-1929	Teacher Ludwig Stibitz	1927-1935
Karl Detzel	1929-1930		
Wilh. Hatzenbühler I.	1930-1931		
Ludwig Gaab	1931-1965	Teacher Armin Frey	1935-1936
		Teacher Fritz Steegmüller	1937-1939
		Head Teacher August Foltz	1939-1945

During the Second World War, the association's activities were limited mainly to burials. From 1945-1948, the association's activities were forbidden. On 15 January 1949 the club was brought back to life.

Ludw. Steegmüller	1965 —	Head Teacher Hans Gensheimer	1949 —

The Band of Ottersheim

The Ottersheim band was founded on 20 February 1932 at the "Zum Hirsch" Inn. At that time, 16 young men banded together to form a music club, the purpose and goal of which was to perform simple brass music to embellish church and secular celebrations. At that time, inspiration for the founding of the band was young teacher Fritz Steegmüller, who came from his work location in Niederstaufenbach and served the practice sessions as conductor in his hometown of Ottersheim. The first members committed themselves not only to learn to read music and to play an instrument but also to carry the not insignificant financial costs for the purchase of instruments. Only through such great personal sacrifice was the start possible. Founding members of the band were:

1.	Fritz Steegmüller	Conductor
2.	Markus Benz	Trombone
3.	Ferdinand Benz	Baritone
4.	Leo Benz	Clarinet
5.	Jakob Gadinger	Tuba
6.	Ludwig Gaab	Trumpet
7.	Emil Ößwein	Trumpet
8.	Clemens Kröper	Trumpet
9.	Franz Anton Kröper	Alto Horn
10.	Ludwig Kramer	Trumpet

11.	Otto Kreiner	Baritone
12.	Alois Messemer	Clarinet
13.	Hugo Steegmüller	Alto Horn
14.	Ludwig Steegmüller	Trumpet
15.	Karl Wünschel	Clarinet
16.	Ludwig Wünschel	Bass Trumpet

At the inaugural meeting, Hugo Steegmüller was elected president of the board and Markus Benz was elected vice-president. Before long, additional members joined the society. Franz Kröper took over the drums and Heinrich Bischoff a brass instrument. Childless farmer Valentin Seither supported the band with a large amount of money. When Ludwig Kramer and Leo Benz left the club after two years, Wilhelm Gadinger and Richard Föhlinger took over their instruments.

Already three weeks before the official founding meeting on 31 January 1932, the club presented music performances to the public for the first time. Although the presentation of the marches, dances, and songs was somewhat loud and not always completely in tune; nevertheless, the event had the undivided support of the villagers. The effort was worth it and all were determined to continue the work that had begun. It was not long until the band had won a permanent place in village life. At festivities and other events of the choirs and the Gymnastics Club, at the Summer Day parade, and at dances, one could no longer imagine the band not being there. It accompanied the first communicants to the church on White Sunday; it accompanied the chants of the faithful on Corpus Christi; and it marched with the procession to the cemetery on All Saints Day. It is no wonder that the participation of the band at church festivals was especially viewed by the local Party officials in the Third Reich with suspicion. The music club was to be brought into line like all clubs. The officials threatened to dissolve the band in case of refusal. The local party leadership was finally satisfied when teacher Foltz took over the presidency because there were no followers of Hitler among the club members.

Ludwig Steegmüller began to recruit new members in 1936 who would take over from their elders after a training period. Twelve young men were willing to learn to play. They made good progress and soon gradually replaced the older players. Then World War II broke out in 1939. Large portions of the players were called immediately for military service and the remaining players were called later. So the musical activities almost came to a complete standstill. That changed in the middle of the war however when Ludwig Steegmüller was dismissed from military duty after a serious injury and returned to the homeland. He began with the installation of a new band already in August 1942 that was composed of young men not yet old enough for conscription. The military and economic collapse of the German Empire in 1945 was not conducive to the music scene. However, it did not completely stop the activities of the band led by Ludwig Steegmüller. Nine brass players never returned to their homeland from the war, these were:

Erwin Detzel	Clemens Kröper
Theo Föhlinger	Franz Anton Kröper
Emil Ößwein	Ludwig Stadel
Ludwig Kramer	Ernst Winkelblech
	Ludwig Wünschel

A noticeable upturn was experienced by the band in 1951 when head teacher Hans Gensheimer decided to take the post of conductor and offered his musical knowledge and proven skills in service of the good cause. Gensheimer found in board leader Oskar Kröper an energetic supporter. A survey in 1953 showed that the club had a total of 40 members. The music club of Ottersheim joined the Palatinate Music Association in 1956. It successfully took part in a band competition in Neustadt a year later. The club celebrated its 25th anniversary on the 18th and 19th of May 1957, which had opened on Saturday with a gala concert at the "Zum Gambrinus" Inn. The band performed with 19 active players who were professionally conducted by head teacher Hans Gensheimer. A celebration was held on Sunday at the festival grounds in the woods with the active participation of the villagers; numerous outside guests were also present. The music club celebrated its 30th anniversary in 1962 with an impressive event. At the subsequent general assembly, then board president Fritz Steegmüller noted with pride that the band had taken part in public secular celebrations twelve times in the past year. Added to that was the involvement of the band at church events. The band continued its cultural activities in the following years by serving the community successfully in the same way. It must be emphasized that the youth were always ready and willing to continue the tradition so that the band has so far been spared recruitment problems. This is not least also thanks to conductor Gensheimer who ensures junior players from among the schoolchildren.

The conductors of the band

Fritz Steegmüller, teacher	1931-1939
Ludwig Steegmüller	1942-1951
Hans Gensheimer, head teacher	1951 —

The board members of the band

Hugo Steegmüller	1931-1934
August Foltz, head teacher	1934-1945
Oskar Kröper	1945-1961
Fritz Steegmüller	1961-1962
Hans Dörzapf	1962 —

The Gymnastics Club of Ottersheim

Forty years after the death of the father of gymnastics, Friedrich Ludwig Jahn (1778-1852), about thirty young men founded the Gymnastics Club of Ottersheim on 5 June 1892. The general statutes were set at the first annual meeting and were based on existing associations. The club continued with the direction set by Jahn, that is, to educate its members in mind and body as fresh, pious, happy, and free people. They sought to provide a healthy body for a healthy mind. This objective was to be achieved through regular gymnastic exercises, by instruction, by travel to gymnastic functions, and by socializing. By joining the association, each member assumed the obligation to take appropriate part in the activities.

At the first meeting, a board was elected with the following men and young men as members:

1.	Josef Seither	Board president
2.	Ludwig Kreiner	Board vice president
3.	Josef Müller	First coach
4.	Eugen Zwißler	Second coach
5.	Johann Zwißler	Record keeper
6.	Adam Gensheimer	Property manager
7.	Philipp Benz	Treasurer
8.	Ludwig Jochim	Committee member
9.	Friedrich Reinhardt	Committee member

Each active member was to pay an initial fee of one mark. The monthly fee was set at 20 pfennigs. Ages 13 to 16 years were considered pupils and were not contributory. At 24 years, it was possible to belong to the Gymnastics Club as a passive member. Also, only males could be members of the Gymnastics Club.

It was planned to hold a gymnastics festival every year on the last Sunday of the month of May that was to end with a dance in the evening. It was the duty of the coach and his deputy to carry out the gymnastics instruction and gymnastics tours. Because no room was initially available for apparatus, exercises were limited to calisthenics, running, jumping, and throwing. The gymnastics lessons took place on a makeshift exercise field. From 1907, we are told that a Miss Kreiner made her farmyard on the Ludwigstraße available to this end for a monthly fee of one mark.

Additionally, strict discipline was enforced. Non-members were not allowed onto the exercise place except to watch a gymnastics display after paying an entrance fee. Anyone of the active gymnasts who left without permission before the exercises were completed had to pay a penalty of 10 pfennigs into the club treasury. A similar fate befell anyone who stayed away from exercises for no good reason.

Every year at the prescribed time, the general assembly of the Gymnastics Club took place at which a new coach was elected. It is striking that in the first decade, the boards, coaches, record keepers, and the like changed often in contrast to later practice. In 1904, a club flag was purchased for 350 marks and officially dedicated. Because the Gymnastics Club had neither a gym nor sufficient practice facilities, the club operation subsided over time. The situation seems to have gotten somewhat better in 1907 when teacher Robert Renn took over as head of the association. At that time, the club rented the ballroom at the "Zum Gambrinus" Inn and held two weekly gymnastic sessions there. At that time, 16 young men and 8 pupils participated in apparatus exercises. Coach Josef Nann held a total of 84 gymnastic sports lessons in 1907. For the month of July, a large gymnastics display was planned in the forest that was attended by 14 clubs with more than 350 gymnasts. Accompanied by the dance band - *Gaab,* prizes were distributed in the evenings at the "Zum Gambrinus" Inn. At the District Gymnastics Festival in Neustadt in 1907, Ottersheim was represented by 19 gymnasts who took fifth place among 36 clubs.

President Renn brought a request to the community in 1908 to provide one of the two school barns for practice. But the council rejected the application because the barn was part of the official residence of the teacher. A workable solution was not found until a year later that had the agreement of all parties. For an annual fee of 30 marks that was payable to the principal of the Catholic School, the Gymnastics Club was awarded the right to use the west barn as a makeshift gymnasium. At the expense of the Gymnastics Club, a brick wall was to be erected between the two floors, and the roof of the barn was to be boxed out. Then the horizontal bar and parallel bars were set up in the gym. In addition, a few small apparatus were housed, such as ball weights and shot put. A pommel horse was purchased in 1913 after the money had come together in a rather original way. Namely, that year the Gymnastics Club set up a shooting range at the church dedication festival that brought in 86 marks net profit. The remaining 34 marks for the horse were paid by the club treasury. The club bought a gun that same year to accommodate shooting sports.

When the First World War broke out in 1914, the Ottersheim Gymnastics Club had 114 members of which 103 were called to the military, one part immediately and one part a little later. Seventeen members died for the fatherland, three remained missing, and eight were taken prisoner. An Honor Roll from the year 1927 keeps alive the memory of the dead and missing members of the gymnastics family. A regular gymnastics operation was unthinkable during the war. Only the so-called *youth army* looked after the physical training of school graduates. This youth corps in Ottersheim consisted of about 60 teenagers who were supervised by coaches Konrad Störtzer, Jean Benz, and Josef Nann.

The gymnastics operation was not started again in Ottersheim until 1920 with Jean Benz as board president and Paul Dörzapf as head coach. These two men, gymnastics lovers, stood at the top of the club and quickly unleashed new life in the ranks of the gymnasts. The gym was repaired and fitted with electric light. Gradually added were mats, stone, springboards, drums, fist balls, javelin, horizontal bar, shot put, a new parallel bar, and twelve pairs of juggling clubs. The jumping sand pits were restored on the old festival grounds in the "alders." Gymnastic practices were held every Tuesday and Friday evening that were also well visited.

When various members of the Gymnastics Club wanted to start a soccer department, a makeshift playing field was created on the Gänsehaardt. At the outfitting of the field in particular, 22 soccer players participated under their leader, Wilhelm Hellmann. However, the soccer department of the Gymnastics Club was not particularly viable over time, so it stopped operation after a few years.

The Gymnastics Club was the strongest club in Ottersheim by 1922. Every year it conducted a festival in the woods at which many outside clubs were involved in addition to the local population. Ottersheim sent a nine-person team to the Palatinate Gymnastics Festival in Ludwigshafen in 1925. They succeeded in winning the second prize in horizontal bars, in running, and in free exercise. The club competition in August 1925 had the largest participation since the founding of the club with 38 active members. In this year, 110 practice sessions were held with an average of 15 participants per session. Was it any wonder that the call for a new gymnasium became louder? In spite of many attempts, unfortunately it took four more decades until the wish was finally fulfilled. In 1927, the Gymnastics Club bought a building lot in the Faselbrühl, but it was sold again in 1929. In 1930, an attempt was made to build a hall on the Landauer Straße at the Mühlweg, but this plan failed also due to the lack of funds. That was all the more regrettable when the school barns had to be demolished in 1931 because these were dilapidated. So no exercise facility was available for gymnastics from then on.

Meanwhile, a new sports branch emerged among the youth of the gymnasts club that became more popular from year to year - handball. The game was started in the Gymnastics Club in November 1927 and it grew within a very short time to amazing heights. The team made its first public appearance in 1928 at the Ottersheim Handball Promotion event. Where there were 17 handball games in 1928, this number rose to triple that in 1929. There were three handball teams in Ottersheim at times. By comparison, gymnastics declined sharply since 1931 due in great part to the lack of a facility.

However, the handball court on the Gänsehaardt was also lacking. So it is not surprising when the Gymnastics Club approached the community in 1929 with a request to be allowed to extend the playing field. This wish was fulfilled. Between Mayor Franz Steegmüller and Board President Jean Benz, an agreement was made in 1931 to provide sufficient room on the Gänsehaardt for the Gymnastics Club, free of charge. The location was bounded on the north by the compost pile, on the east by the Neuweg, and the west by the Gänseweiher [Goose pond]. It extended to the south about 80 meters. Once the legal status was clarified, the expansion of the sports facility could be started. This occurred mainly in the years between 1932 and 1933 with the help of volunteer service work. The labor office contributed a total of 4,000 marks to help cover costs.

Drainage ditches were dug and the grounds leveled out. In addition, a dressing cabin was built and a footpath was created. With these, the external conditions for a successful handball operation were present. When Hitler took over power in 1933, the Gymnastics Club in Ottersheim was not useful. Although physical training of youth was an important item of National Socialist policies, in Ottersheim it was evident that sports activities diminished. In 1933, 26 members left the Gymnastics Club and in the following year 28 members so that the club counted 54 members by 1 January 1935. Even the long-standing and successful Jean Benz resigned from the board. Although the Nazi leadership very carefully went to work with enforcement of political conformity, only a few actively wanted to support the Nazi State through their participation, as it was prescribed in the statutes that went into effect in 1937. The minutes from 1938 indicate that all club activity had stopped. Gymnastics having already come to an end, so also the handball activity had to be stopped due to the construction of the West Wall. Although games were recorded again on a small scale in 1939, now the Second World War put an immediate end to every sporting activity. Even the club flag was lost in 1945. As it was, about 50 Moroccans were quartered with former Board President Jean Benz. When the soldiers left the village on 1 April 1945, the club flag was missing along with the accessories.

Not until 3 March 1946 was the activity of the former Gymnastics Club taken up again as the newly founded *Sportverein [Sports club]*. Elected to the first board were President Karl Wünschel, Vice President Peter Hindert, Secretary Jean Benz, and Manager Erwin Winkelblech. In addition to social events, the club wanted mainly to play handball. At the beginning of 1947, the club already had 107 members, which grew rapidly to 141. At the general assembly, Jean Benz stated the association had in the past mainly focused on entertainment, theater, and dances but must now focus more on sport and the physical education of youth. For this purpose, the playing field again needed to be rebuilt above all. To that end, the Becht Company from Hördt was hired in March of the following year and they began work on the Gänsehaardt. The work was successfully completed in a relatively short time. The formal inauguration of the field was held on 18 May 1948 with the participation of the band. In the same year, the sports club again took up the tradition of the Gymnastics Club and held a Summer Day parade that enjoyed extraordinary popularity and participation. It was similar in 1949 when in addition to the band, riders and wagons were decorated, and a group of cyclists also took part.

Changing rooms were built on the new playing field in 1950 for which the Handball Association granted 800 marks. Given that a suitable facility for gymnastics was missing, the handball game remained the most important branch of the sports club since 1950, as described in a decision by the general assembly. When the Gymnastics Club flourished once again soon after World War II, this was due to the merit of Peter Hindert who, as board member from 1947 to 1951, spared neither time nor effort to help move things forward. When he moved to Germersheim in 1951, a beech tree was planted in his honor near the sports field, which is called the *Hindert Beech.*

The 60th foundation anniversary of the Gymnastics Club and the 25th anniversary of the handball division were celebrated in 1952. The festivities were held on 29 June and were well organized by then board president Oskar Hoffmann. In the morning, triathlon events and individual competitions were conducted. In the afternoon, a gymnastics exhibition was held with the participation of visiting clubs. The top award from the Ottersheim community was taken home by the Herxheim Gymnastics Club as the winner in the 8 by 100 meter relay. A fireworks display shown for the first time in Ottersheim concluded the festival. Present at the club anniversary in Ottersheim was Ruprecht Job, the son of honorary member Peter Job from the United States. He promised to donate a new flag to the Gymnastics Club and to return to Germany to attend the dedication. Job kept his promise and the new flag was dedicated in his presence during July of 1954. To commemorate the occasion, the noble founder was presented the letter of honor and a painting of the village of Ottersheim in gratitude.

The club began gymnastics activities again in 1954. But sessions had to be held elsewhere because no suitable space was available in Ottersheim. At that time, a section for female gymnasts was created. At the same time, the statutes were amended to the effect that in the future, women and girls would have equal rights within the Gymnastics Club as with men. But the more gymnastics flourished, the greater was the lack of a gymnasium perceived by the club members. Mayor Paul Dörzapf considered a plan to construct a hall in the schoolyard. As in previous years, this plan failed due to the lack of funds.

Thus, handball continued to be the main focus of the Gymnastics Club. At times, Ottersheim was able to handle five handball teams that achieved considerable success in handball tournaments. The highlight of this development was the year 1958 when the first team emerged from the competition as district champion. In 1963, the B-youth were able to win the Palatinate championship. Since 1955, the Gymnastics Club organized the annual National Youth Games in Ottersheim that were always associated with a small festival in the forest. In the summer of 1960, the National Youth Games again took place on the sports field with the participation of boys and girls. To the chagrin of the board president, few club members were present at the parade. Although the festival on the sports field went quite harmoniously, Hoffmann handed in his resignation as head of the Gymnastics Club. His mission was taken over by vice president Josef Weimann until the next general assembly.

Former score keeper Richard Föhlinger was selected as board president of the Gymnastics Club in 1961. Not only did Föhlinger actively want to continue the work already begun but also to realize a new plan - the Sports Club of Ottersheim should get a marching band. On 25 June, the resolution was passed at a meeting of the board and was also soon realized.

The registrations for the marching band exceeded all expectations so that soon practice sessions could be started under the direction of celebration bandleader Werner Nägele from Germersheim. Not only the club members but also the players had considerable financial sacrifice when purchasing of instruments. A year later, the marching band performed together for the first time in the home community at the 30-year foundation anniversary of the Ottersheim band. Due to its good discipline and brisk playing, it gained the recognition and the applause of the population. On the 11th and 12th of May 1963, it celebrated its Foundation Festival at which the marching band of the Abenberg Sports Club near Nuremberg participated. Since that time, the marching band participated in a number of festivals in Ottersheim and in other places in the Palatinate.

The year 1961 will remain memorable in the history of the Gymnastics Club. On 13 September of that year specifically, the community council made the decision to build a new schoolhouse with a gymnasium. With this, the decades old wish of the Ottersheim gymnasts would finally come true. On 23 October 1965, the new building was given over to its purpose. Now after so many failed approaches, a space was available not only to use the equipment and perform floor exercises but also to play indoor handball. Fortunately, the community agreed to provide the spacious gymnasium as a place to practice at no charge to the gymnasts and athletes. As was previously the case, now it was no longer necessary for physical education teacher Brodrück to travel with his handball players to Haßloch for practice. Meanwhile, gymnastics practice was taken up in the hall. While the girls and women were cared for by Mrs. Gertrud Benner, coach Hellmann from Bellheim conducted regular gymnastics sessions for men and young men. So it was expected that gymnastics with apparatus would again rise to the levels that it enjoyed in the twenties in Ottersheim.

True to its statutes, the Gymnastics Club of Ottersheim supported not only the physical training of youth through sports and gymnastics but also socializing. At many forest festivals, usually a large part of the village population gathered with the gymnasts to spend a few happy hours with music, song, and conversation. Theater performances often took place at Christmas time or New Year's that were attended by young and old.

Only reluctantly did club members and their families miss the chance to attend a ball. This local custom is also in place thanks to the gymnasts. If today at the start of spring a Summer Day parade is held regularly, this tradition is the work of the former board president Peter Hindert who encouraged it and also personally organized it. Thus, without the Ottersheim Gymnastics Club, the cultural life of the village is hardly imaginable. However, the anniversary year 1967, when the club celebrated its 75th, the handball department its 40th anniversary, and the marching band celebrated its 5th year, not only was the end of a glorious past celebrated, but also the beginning of a hopeful future in the spirit of those men who brought the Gymnastics Club of Ottersheim to life in 1892.

The leading men of the Gymnastics Club

First Board of Directors:		Coach:	
Josef Seither	1892-1893	Josef Müller	1892-1893
Lorenz Föhlinger	1893-1895	Eugen Zwißler	1893-1894
Ludwig Weiß	1895-1902	Jakob Jochim	1894-1895
		Eugen Zwißler	1895-1896
		Anton Walk	1896-1902
Edmund Bischoff	1902-1904	Johann Kopf	1902-1905
Anton Walk	1904-1907	Ludwig Hindert	1905-1907
Robert Renn, teacher	1907-1910	Josef Nann	1907-1908
		Ferdinand Gutting	1908-1909
Anton Walk	1910-1911	Heinrich Brüderle	1909-1911
Johann Müller	1911-1913	Josef Nann	1911-1913
Konrad Störtzer	1913-1914	Otto Kreiner	1913-1914
	First World War from 1914-1918		
Johann Benz	1920-1934	Paul Dörzapf	1920-1924
		Richard Jeckel	1924-1925
		August Walk	1925-1927
		Richard Hindert	1927-1929
		Hugo Steegmüller	1929-1932
Robert Winkelblech	1934-1939	Ruprecht Hindert	1932-1935
Karl Wünschel	1939-1940	Clemens Kröper	1935-1936
	Second World War from 1939-1945		
Karl Wünschel	1946-1947		
Peter Hindert	1947-1951		
Oskar Hoffmann	1951-1960		
(Josef Weimann, vice president)	1960-1961		
Richard Föhlinger	1961 —		

Gymnastics Club member count:

1892:	~30	1915:	87
1901:	36	1920:	128
1902:	84	1925:	161
1903:	105	1930:	101
1904:	138	1935:	54
1905:	108	1945:	51
1906:	100	1950:	164
1907:	102	1955:	228
1908:	105	1960:	203
1909:	99	1965:	230
1910:	76	1966:	238

(~ Denotes an approximation.)

The Kolping Family of Ottersheim

The precursor of the Kolping Family of Ottersheim was the Catholic Workers' Association founded in Ottersheim during 1911. This association had set itself the goal to bring together Catholic workers and artisans and to educate them in the spirit of Catholic social teaching. An additional goal was to prevent the complete movement of working people to the Marxist camp. Head of the Catholic Workers' Association was the respective parish priest, while a layman led the association. Following a succession of presidencies was Wilhelm Lutz, Leo Herrmann, Josef Ripp, and Wilhelm Jennewein. The club, which counted about 30 members, was able to celebrate its flag dedication in 1928. But it had to halt its activities five years later due to Hitler's takeover, as did so many other Catholic organizations. The treasury was seized in 1933, but the small amount of money was returned a few months later. However, the association's work came to a complete halt. Also, it was no longer taken up again after the capitulation in 1945.

Not until 1952 did then Pastor Bernhard Kern of Ottersheim create the plan again to bring together the working men and young men in the village. A Catholic social club would be started this time in the spirit of the Father of Apprentices, Adolf Kolping. The family-like community set itself the goal of educating their young unmarried members to be capable master tradesmen, competent fathers, and efficient citizens, while the older married members should be supported as Christians in work, family, nation, and state. A *Kolping Family* is comprised of three groups based on the age and marital status of members: *Jungkolping, Kolping,* and *Altkolping.* The *Jung [Young] Kolping* group included adolescents from 12 to 17 years and was the preliminary stage of the Kolping family. The *Kolping* group included any unmarried Catholic Kolping man who was at least 17 years old, had no independent business, and had not exceeded the 30th year of life. Whoever was married, owned an economically independent business, or had passed the 30th year belonged to the *Alt [Old] Kolping* group. New members to the Kolping family could join on either the first of May, the feast day of Saint Joseph, or the Kolping Memorial Day, which is the first Sunday in December. Active love was the law of life in the Kolping family. It could be practiced in many ways. If they were in their travels as journeymen, members were provided with accommodation and meals free of charge where possible. As a rule, a group meeting took place once a week. The head of the Kolping group was called, *Senior,* the head of the Altkopling group was called, *Altsenior,* while the Jungkolping group was led by a young Kolping leader. The respective local parish Priest stood at the head of the Kolping family as the *Präses.*

The Ottersheim Kolping Family was founded on 1 June 1952 in the presence of the Diocesan Präses, Pastor Schlachter from Großbockenheim. A total of 29 members joined the association. Sixteen unmarried young men formed the Catholic Kolping group; and thirteen married men formed the Altkolping group. Pastor Kern became präses while the lay leader of the two groups was Karl Dumser. In that same year, Walter Kreiner took over as Senior of the Kolping group.

Pastor Kern made the outbuilding of the rectory available for the meetings. From the beginning, the Kolping sons dedicated their work especially to vocational training. In addition, they held social hours and presented amateur theater. Several times a year they undertook bicycle trips into the Palatinate Forest. Since 1956, no year passed in which at least one play was performed in public. In this, Leo Lutz had done great service as leader and organizer of the amateur theater group. The response of the population was usually so large that the performances had to be repeated.

The number of members had grown to 43 by 1962. On 1 April 1967, there were a total of 59 Kolping sons, including 18 supporting members and 9 members in the group of young Kolping. Thanks to their great enthusiasm, the Kolping Family of Ottersheim had won a significant position in the cultural life of the village. May their sons henceforth guard the heritage of the journeyman's father, Adolf Kolping!

Präses of the Kolping Family

Pastor Bernhard Kern	1952-1959
Pastor Josef Scherübl	1959 —

Altsenior		Senior	
Karl Dumser	1952-1957	Walter Kreiner	1952-1954
Ernst Müller	1957-1961	Franz Lutz	1954-1955
Leo Lutz	1961—	Franz Seither	1955-1960
		Klaus Kreiner	1960-1965
		Reinhold Becki	1965 —

Raiffeisen Cooperative of Ottersheim

On 13 March 1898, the 80th birthday of Friedrich Wilhelm Raiffeisen (1818-1888), 81 farmers from Ottersheim founded the *Savings and Loan Association*, registered as a cooperative with unlimited liability. According to Raiffeisen, rural cooperatives should ensure economic self-reliance and independence of farmers in the capitalist era. Savings of the farmers should primarily be used for the benefit of the economy in the village. In addition, they wanted to protect the club members from exploitation through joint purchasing of seeds, fertilizers, animal feed, and consumer goods. The purchase of agricultural machines for common use was also considered. Each member had to pay ten gold marks to the cooperative.

At the inaugural meeting, Valentin Leingang and teacher Jakob Stelzer were elected as club president and club administrator, respectively. Appointed as board members were:

Josef Seither   Georg Seither

Johannes Seither Josef Hanck

On the oversight board was Kaspar Detzel, Georg Dörzapf, Franz Anton Dörzapf, Johann Dörzapf, Valentin Gadinger, Valentin Seither, Valentin Steegmüller, Johann Steegmüller, and Martin Wingerter. The confidence in the new association can be observed in the fact that the membership had reached 134 by December of 1898.

The beginning was difficult since the cooperative had neither an office nor a warehouse. The accountant had to work from his apartment, and the storekeeper had to provide storage in his barn. The association purchased a building site at 26 Lange Straße from mason George Kreiner in 1905 and built a warehouse there that was in use until 1961.

Fertilizer, seed, and feed were purchased wholesale. These had to be picked up by specially appointed carters at railroad stations in Bellheim, Offenbach, and Landau or be picked up directly at the Dreihof[88]. Shipping charges were reimbursed depending on the distance at 7 to 20 pfennigs per zentner. When a wagon with coal or briquettes arrived, the members picked up their own fuel loads from Offenbach or Bellheim. To facilitate weighing the goods, the Raiffeisen Cooperative built a weighbridge south of the village in early 1900. The scale master was initially association accountant Jakob Stelzer, and then Franz Müller performed the task from 1906 to 1929.

The accountant and head of the cooperative changed during 1902. At the will of the general assembly, Josef Seither assumed leadership of the association. With great diligence and selflessness, he managed his office through 36 turbulent years. Johann Dörzapf was cooperative accountant for 26 years. When the warehouse was built near his apartment in 1905, he also took over the duties of storekeeper. As accountant, Dörzapf worked without the technical aids available today. He had to calculate interest on savings deposits and loans by hand. It was fortunate that the interest rates remained the same through the course of many years. In general, interest paid was 3.75% for savings and 4.5% for loans. It was perceived as a simplification measure when the Raiffeisen Bank got a phone connection in 1912. The confidence of the population in the cooperative was again expressed in that it had over 200 members by 1912. As an aside, Pastor Schwarz from Ottersheim made the proposal in 1905 to encourage the thrift of the children by issuing savings stamps.

Early on, the purchase of agricultural machinery was seen as an important task of the association. Already by 1898, it was decided to buy a seed cleaning and sorting machine. Agriculture Teacher Hoffmann from Bellheim held a lecture at the general assembly in 1902 about the Trieur seed-cleaning machine. The purchase of a fertilizer spreader and a steam threshing machine was discussed in 1908; however, these had to be postponed for

---

[88] The Dreihof was a farmstead between Offenbach and Hochstadt, which was also the nearest station to Ottersheim.

financial reasons. Two cultivators were purchased in 1911 and a ridging plow in 1912. After the First World War, a seeding-drill was purchased in 1925, and it was followed by an onion-sorting machine and a modern seed-filtering machine ten years later. Finally, a carrot-washing machine was put into operation.

The general economic development in the first half of this century was reflected in the economic ups and downs of the Raiffeisen Cooperative. Before the First World War, it went slowly but steadily upward. The annual profits of the association were usually a few hundred marks of which a part was always used for charitable purposes. The 1914-1918 war brought a stagnation of business at first. But then the funds flowed abundantly from year to year, until they eventually reached astronomical heights in 1923. At that time, the total revenue of the association came to 2,303,366,890.82 marks and the expenditures were 2,251,977,592.59 marks. Unfortunately, not even a pencil could be purchased in 1923 from a net profit in the amount of close to 17 million marks.

With the introduction of the rentenmark on 1 January 1924, the savings were worthless and the reserves of the association were destroyed. With an empty treasury and an empty warehouse, one had to "start from scratch" as they say. While people could throw around billions and trillions in 1923, money was scarcer than ever a year later. The association paid 9% interest for deposits, and they demanded 12% for loans. At the same time in the private sector, rates of 18 to 20% were not uncommon. Only slowly did things get better again. In 1926, the interest rates on savings deposits could be reduced to 6% and to 8% for loans. But already in 1929 there was a new economic crisis at the Ottersheim Raiffeisen Cooperative that reached its peak in 1933. The club had 130,000 reichsmarks in outstanding loans to members. However, some borrowers could not meet their obligations on time because of the faltering economy. Fearing a collapse, some farmers gave notice to end their membership in the cooperative and others wanted to follow their example. It required great efforts from the board members to stop a number of members from taking ill-considered steps.

The crisis came to an end faster than expected. The efforts of the Third Reich to support the population as much as possible by using its own products gave a significant boost to local agriculture. A new directive guaranteed that farmers could sell their goods at a fixed price. All products were delivered to the local collection center that was affiliated with the Raiffeisen Cooperative. Head of this collection center was cooperative accountant Jean Benz. In 1935, a new warehouse had to be built on the Altsheimer Weg, because the old warehouse could no longer accommodate the machinery and fertilizers. The favorable trend also continued after the outbreak of the Second World War in 1939. In 1941, the cooperative purchased a new weighbridge that was set up in front of the current Catholic rectory on the Waldstraße. Due to the shortage of manpower, a water pump was purchased in 1942 and made available to the people throughout the village. By the year 1943, the supply of fertilizer and seed potatoes for farmers was good. But then the difficulties became noticeably larger until the total collapse of the war fronts in 1945. Economic life also came to a standstill. In 1945, the activities of the Raiffeisen Cooperative stopped entirely. It paid no interest, although the savings were quite large.

At the general assembly in 1946, current board president Ludwig Gensheimer was replaced by Paul Dörzapf. The statutes had to be modified in accordance with the new circumstances. Accountant Jean Benz was able to report little good news about the economic activities of the cooperative in the previous two years. Profit had decreased significantly and sales were without significance. Only the inventory had seen growth.

Black and barter sales had affected the sales at the vegetable collection point, even though the majority of producers had complied with their obligation to deliver.

In spite of the poor harvest in 1947, things got slowly better in subsequent years. The 50th anniversary of the cooperative was remembered with gratitude during the general assembly on 13 June 1948. Accountant Jean Benz provided a look back at the checkered history of the association, while Spiritual Council Steegmüller added his own experience and insights as a known and proven Raiffeisen member. The economic life of the Raiffeisen Cooperative again took a normal course with the currency reform of 1948. Membership grew and sales increased from year to year. Under the energetic leadership of board president Paul Dörzapf, a freezing plant was built and furnished in 1958 on Germersheimer Straße for a total of 51,000 deutschemarks. A site for a new warehouse was purchased on the Ludwigstraße in 1959. The construction started in 1960 and the new warehouse was put into operation in 1961. The association moved into the new office building on 1 January 1964, and the weighbridge was moved from the Waldstraße to the Ludwigstraße in April. Adhering to Father Raiffeisen's principle of "All for one and one for all!," the Raiffeisen Cooperative of Ottersheim was the largest association in the village in 1965 with over 300 members.

Board members of the Raiffeisen Cooperative

Valentin Leingang	1898-1902
Josef Seither	1902-1938
Ludwig Gensheimer	1938-1945
Paul Dörzapf	1945 —

Accountants

Jakob Stelzer, teacher	1898-1902
Johann Dörzapf	1902-1929
Hermann Zwißler	1929-1933
Jean Benz	1933-1960
Norbert Benz	1960 —

Storekeeper (Warehouse manager)

Ludwig Seither I.	1898-1901
Franz Walk I.	1901-1905
Johann Dörzapf, accountant	1905-1923
Ludwig Zwißler	1923-1936

Ludwig Gadinger	1936-1941
Hermann Gaab	1941-1944
(Representative for Gadinger)	
Ludwig Gadinger	1944 —

Storerooms

41 Lange Straße	(Ludwig Seither I.)	1898-1901
10 Germersheimer Straße	(Franz Walk I.)	1901-1905
26 Lange Straße		1905-1961

The warehouse was built in 1905. In 1963, Mrs. Erna Hoffmann from Lindenholzhausen near Limburg bought it for the sum of 8,500 deutschemarks.

| 34 Germersheimer Straße | 1935-1961 |

The storage shed was used as additional space for machinery and fertilizer.

| 33 Ludwigstraße | 1961 — |

The warehouse was put into service in 1961. The office building was occupied on 1 January 1964.

Member Count			*Savings*	
	81	founding members		
1898	134			
1900	165			
1905	182	1905	180,705	marks
1910	193	1910	197,005	marks
1915	201	1915	371,365	marks
1920	248	1920	1,384,070	marks
1925	238	1925	36,155	reichsmarks
1930	255	1930	177,000	reichsmarks
1935	238	1935	134,000	reichsmarks
1940	245	1940	315,000	reichsmarks
1945	259	1945	1,269,000	reichsmarks
1950	287	1950	85,000	deutschemarks
1955	279	1955	382,000	deutschemarks
1960	290	1960	943,000	deutschemarks
1965	323	1965	2,454,000	deutschemarks

The Tobacco Growers Association of Ottersheim

American tobacco came to Germany via France in the 16th century. Hatzenbühl was the first German town where the chicanery weed was grown in the fields. This was said to be as early as 1573. During the 30 Years War, the soldiers contributed greatly to the spread of smoking and sniffing tobacco in Germany. So the demand for tobacco grew steadily. Already in the 17th century there were several villages in the southern Palatinate and Alsace where tobacco was grown in larger amounts. Presumably, Ottersheim did not belong to this group however. Not until the 18th century did tobacco seem to have found its way here. So in the report from the Ottersheim parish from the year 1747, it is mentioned that each grower had to deliver the tenth *Bert*[71] *[bundle]* from the tobacco harvest. However, no mention is made of tobacco in a special register of all agricultural products in 1791. Hereby must be taken into account that a kind of tobacco monopoly existed in the Electoral Palatinate until the French Revolution, and that tobacco cultivation was overseen by the State. It was not until the Napoleonic period that farmers were able to do as they saw fit.

So it is no surprise that tobacco was grown on a large scale in Ottersheim during the twenties of the 19th century as in other villages of the southern Palatinate. This is likely to be found in the fact that at the time not only the cultivation of dyer's madder became increasingly unprofitable but also flax and hemp. Tobacco was a replacement for the small growers in Ottersheim. In 1864, 28 day's work or about 9 hectares of tobacco were grown in the Ottersheim district. About 12 zentners [600 kilograms] was harvested on one day's work [one morgen] at a price of 12 gulden per zentner. Tobacco cultivation in the southern Palatinate reached its height in 1873 with 5,000 hectares. However, the prices did not keep pace with the harvest. In fact, toward the end of the century prices sank steadily, because more, cheaper, good quality tobacco was imported from foreign countries. Often a mere 15 marks was paid for an entire zentner. Thus, the tobacco farmers found themselves in a bad situation even though the German Empire provided some protection for the domestic tobacco growers through a tobacco excise tax.

For this development, the farmers blamed above all others the traders who bought up the tobacco at the time of harvest. Now the local, district, and regional brokers of that time were certainly not innocent of certain intrigues. They often set firm high prices in favor of the tobacco processing companies without taking the quality of the tobacco into consideration. In addition, the dealer had no objections to lowering the price later if it had declined between the time of purchase and the time of weighing the raw tobacco. This sometimes led to circumstances that were hard to beat in ugliness and repulsiveness. To control this scourge, many tobacco farmers joined together in 1897 with the so-called *Palatinate Tobacco Cooperative* that had its seat in Schifferstadt. Some Ottersheim farmers joined this association. But ten years later the cooperative had to explain its insolvency. Thus, some 162 shares amounting to 8,910 marks were lost to members in Ottersheim.

An outstanding patron of tobacco cultivation in the Palatinate at the turn of the century arose in agriculture teacher Philipp Hoffmann from Bellheim who was the son of a small tobacco farmer himself. Hoffmann recognized that improvement in the tobacco economy must focus not on the sales organization but on tobacco cultivation itself. In his opinion, only good quality domestic tobacco could compete with foreign competitors. So he began with attempts to improve the cultivation of local tobacco in 1897. He reported his findings not only in class but also in lectures in the various tobacco growing communities. At his suggestion about 15 farmers from Ottersheim joined together with the *Tobacco Growers Association* in 1906 under the leadership of former agricultural student Kaspar Detzel. The members pledged to grow their tobacco following the instructions of agricultural teacher Hoffmann. Above all, strict adherence to the prescribed use of fertilizer was followed in order to raise the quality of the tobacco. Understandably, they questioned whether the effort would pay off since the improvement of quality could only be achieved at the expense of weight. All this was very uncertain at the beginning because the tobacco industry had the last word in the matter. They were forced to take up discussions with the tobacco buyers.

This difficult situation could not be solved by a single association. Therefore, on the advice of the agricultural teacher Hoffmann the current association decided in 1909 to join together with other local clubs to form the regional *Association of Palatinate Tobacco Growers.* At the inaugural meeting in Bellheim, the representatives of nine local tobacco growers groups were present, among these were Büchelberg, Dudenhofen, Hatzenbühl, Hayna, Herxheimweyher, Minfeld, Ottersheim, Rheinzabern, and Wörth. Another club joined during the same year so that in 1909 the association consisted of ten clubs with about 150 members. The acreage of the organized tobacco growers at that time was 50.5 hectares and the harvest was at 2,020 zentners [101,000 kilograms] of tobacco.

In addition to improving the quality of the tobacco, the attention of the association focused above all on sales. Presentations were made to tobacco companies and much effort was invested to raise their interest in the concerns of the association. In fact, some companies in Speyer, Mannheim, and Strasbourg were willing to pay a surcharge of one mark per zentner for association tobacco of good quality. Five years later, the good experience with this system had led the tobacco companies ready to pay excess prices of 2 to 2.5 marks. That meant at a base price of 30 marks per zentner, a 6% to 8% surcharge was paid. When the tobacco cultivation in Germany was compulsive-managed in 1916, club tobacco first received a markup of 8%, 12% a year later, and 18% in 1918. However, deductions in the same amount were also threatened for poor product.

From the year 1920, sales meetings for the first time were held in Speyer that were attended by the club board members and representatives of the companies. A premium of up to 20% over the basic price is said to have been paid for good product. That was a powerful incentive to grow for quality and at the same time a deterrence for the delivery of inferior product. This provision was retained in all subsequent years. The so-called *registrations*[89] that are still commonly used developed out of the sales meetings in 1922. These meetings were first held in the "Sternemoos" Inn, then in the "Wittelsbacher Hof," and finally in the community hall in Speyer.

In spite of some setbacks, more and more tobacco farmers found their way to the Ottersheim Tobacco Growers Association. This development was favored by the bad experiences that had been had from time to time in the free market. There the traders paid 35 marks a zentner of tobacco in 1925 but only 20 marks a year later. Since prices depend not only on quality but also on the quantity of the harvest, it was decided in 1929 to impose quotas on tobacco growing. From the year 1930, a farmer was allowed to grow only as much tobacco as he had planted on average in the previous three years. From this, an acreage was calculated for each community that could not be exceeded. If a tobacco farmer gave up his allocation, another farmer could be awarded his allotment. There were 131 Ottersheim tobacco growers at the time who were members of the Tobacco Growers Association.

In 1934, the "Council of Palatinate Tobacco Growers Associations," which in turn belonged to the "State Association of Bavarian Tobacco Councils," built a tobacco shed in Ottersheim that could be used for a fee. Moreover, during the Third Reich it was compulsory for all tobacco growers to join the Tobacco Council. As part of the market order of 1937, tobacco prices were set by the State. For this purpose, the average price of the last three to four years was calculated, that then was declared to be the future fixed price, which in Ottersheim was about 60 marks. As before, premiums or penalties of up to 20% were allowed. From then on, only distribution meetings were held to which the tobacco growers were not consulted.

Nothing changed initially relative to this scheme even after the Second World War. From 1945 to 1948, all tobacco in the French zone was seized and had to be delivered for a fixed price. The quota also remained in place. However, the growing restrictions gradually declined in importance. In the fifties and sixties, many small farmers gave up on agriculture while others turned more to growing vegetables. In 1955, a total of 48 hectares were cultivated by 236 tobacco growers, ten years later it was only 23.5 hectares; meanwhile, the permitted acreage for Ottersheim stood at around 50 hectares. The decline in tobacco cultivation is made clear in the following overview:

Year	Permitted acreage		Allocated acreage	
1951	49.5	hectares	49.5	hectares
1952	49.3	hectares	47.5	hectares
1953	45.0	hectares	44.0	hectares
1954	53.0	hectares	52.2	hectares
1955	54.0	hectares	48.0	hectares
1956	54.0	hectares	49.0	hectares

---

[89] Initially the tobacco meetings resulted in verbal quality, price, and sales agreements. The term *registrations* refers to the records created when these agreements were documented using written protocols.

318

Year	Amount 1		Amount 2	
1957	54.0	hectares	41.0	hectares
1958	54.0	hectares	41.0	hectares
1959	54.0	hectares	41.0	hectares
1960	48.0	hectares	35.0	hectares
1961	unlimited	hectares	19.0	hectares
1962	unlimited	hectares	16.0	hectares
1963	unlimited	hectares	18.0	hectares
1964	unlimited	hectares	20.0	hectares
1965	unlimited	hectares	23.5	hectares

What is striking is the decline of the tobacco acreage in the years 1961 and 1962. This is mainly a consequence of blue mold that occurred as a complete surprise in 1960 and decimated the tobacco heavily. This fungal disease would probably have put an end to tobacco cultivation had a remedy not been quickly found that effectively protected against the pest when used at the appropriate time. This saved tobacco cultivation from total collapse.

In the 19th century and the first half of the 20th century, only *Geudertheimer* cigar tobacco was planted in Ottersheim. But as the demand for cigar tobacco declined and the prices sank, *Burley* cutting tobacco was tried. So it was that in 1955 with 48 available hectares of land, 19 were planted with Burley for the first time. Ten years later, the cutting tobaccos had supplanted the cigar tobaccos almost entirely in that only 6.4 hectares of Geudertheimer and 17.1 hectares of Burley were planted in 1965. Naturally, this development is due to the fact that a hectare of Burley brought about 14,300 deutschemarks gross receipts while the same acreage of Geudertheimer brought only 9,800 deutschemarks.

In Ottersheim, the tobacco was grown mainly by small and medium farmers. The cultivation on a large scale failed mainly due to the large amount of work connected with this special culture. For one hectare of tobacco, approximately 3,500 hours of work are needed before the goods can be offered for sale. Only with the use of modern sowing machines in 1966 had the demand for labor been somewhat reduced. But even then, most of the work was done by hand. The work began in the spring when the seeds are sown. To prepare the young plants as early as possible, they are started in covered beds, then set out in the fields at the end of April or early May. The seedlings gradually grow into large stalks with proper fertilization. The howing and plowing is done today using a cultivator. By contrast, the leaves are still broken by hand. The most time consuming work previously was bringing in the harvest.

While children and old people strung one leaf after another during the day, the remaining family members were busy doing this during the evening and often well into the night. Often the strings were then hung in a shed or barn loft where they dried during late summer and autumn. Only at the present time has the effort been made to ease the collection and hanging of the tobacco through technical means. Beginning in early

November, the dried tobacco leaves are taken down. But only at weighing time does the work come to an end for the tobacco farmer.

The leaders of the Ottersheim Tobacco Growers Association:

Kaspar Detzel	1906-1919
Franz Steegmüller	1919-1931
Bernhard Kröper	1931-1933
Ludwig Gensheimer	1933-1945
Franz Kröper	1945-1951
Hugo Steegmüller	1951 —

Status of Tobacco Growers Association in 1955

Board of Directors:	Hugo Steegmüller
Secretary:	Otto Morio
Honor board of directors:	Franz Kröper
Number of tobacco growers:	236
Size of Area:	48 hectare
Quantity of tobacco produced:	1,860 zentners
Average price per zentner:	123 deutschemarks
Total income of all members:	229,000 deutschemarks

Status of the Tobacco Growers Association in 1965

Board of Directors:	Hugo Steegmüller
Secretary:	Otto Morio
Number of tobacco growers:	57
Size of Area:	23.5 hectare
Quantity of tobacco produced:	365 zentners (Geudertheimer)
Average price per zentner:	160 deutschemark
Quantity of tobacco produced:	910 zentners (Burley)
Average price per nwh.:	270 deutschemarks
Total income of all members:	300,000 deutschemarks

The Milk Suppliers' Cooperative of Ottersheim

On 16 February 1934, 54 local farmers established the *Milk Suppliers' Cooperative* in Ottersheim. As the statute of the association stated, the members wanted to process the milk produced on their farms at common expense and at common risk. All the milk that was not used for one's own household was to be delivered to the cooperative who sold it to the dairy processor in Landau. The leadership committee was to consist of three members and was to be elected by the general assembly. The first committee consisted of Alois

Kreiner, August Hilsendegen, and Wilhelm Hatzenbühler. Alois Kreiner was chair. On the supervisory board were Konrad Hoffmann, Karl Kröper, and Ludwig Gensheimer.

At the first meeting of the leadership committee and the supervisory board, it was decided to establish a milk collection center at 35 Germersheimer Straße, the location of existing milk dealer Richard Winkelblech, and to appoint Winkelblech himself as collector. Cooperative members could deliver milk there in the morning and evening between 7-8 o'clock. The milk was then hauled to the dairy processor in Landau. The necessary milk cans were to be collectively purchased. Already at the first meeting, a plan was made to construct a cooperative collection area in the middle of the village. For this purpose, a small garden was purchased at 79 Lange Straße that same year from farmer Ludwig Föhlinger for 200 marks; there a collection space was built. A small tobacco shed that was previously located on the property was demolished at the expense of the Milk Suppliers' Cooperative. Convinced of the importance of the cooperative, another 82 farmers joined within a year after the founding of the association so that the number of members more than doubled. Former accountant Ludwig Gensheimer also became chair of the cooperative in 1936, the position he held until the end of the Second World War in 1945. The quantity of milk delivered increased considerably during this time. There was 234,548 liters delivered in 1935, and 416,831 liters were dropped off at the collection point by the year 1940. After the collapse of the front in March 1945, the Ottersheim Milk Suppliers' Cooperative stopped its activity for the time being. The delivery of milk at the collection point had to resume in April 1945 by order of the occupying power. For this, each family had to take its turn every three days.

With the end of the war, the senior posts in the Milk Suppliers' Cooperative were newly appointed. The chairmanship was taken over by then Deputy Mayor Josef Herrmann, Hugo Zwißler became collector, and the accountant was Ludwig Steegmüller. Transportation of milk to the dairy processor in Landau was now carried out by the Landau dairy itself. When starving townspeople came by the hundreds to the village begging for food in the early postwar years, milk deliveries increased very little at the collection point. Only after the currency reform in 1948 did they gradually return to their old level. The previous collection area was demolished and newly built in 1957 by Master Mason Ripp from Ottersheim using plans by Architect Wilhelm Thibaut from Bellheim. A small piece of land was purchased from farmer Ludwig Föhlinger and added to expand the premises. The collection point was given a contemporary interior when the new building was erected. The dairy and eggs agency of the Rhineland-Palatinate in Kaiserslautern provided a milk cooling system. Also included was a new milk scale with the necessary accessories. For skim milk, a container for returns was purchased as well as a hand cart for the handling of milk cans. The milk collection center was converted to tank pick-up in 1964 that the dairy processor in Landau itself managed since 1965.

Today, rural life can no longer be imagined without the Milk Suppliers' Cooperative. Hardly anyone still remembers the time when the milkman drove through the village streets, purchased the milk at his own expense from the farmers, and then sold it in the city.

However, only some of farmers sold their milk to the milk dealer. Many processed their own milk by making butter because this seemed to be the most profitable. For this purpose, the milk was let stand in earthen bowls until the cream had collected on the surface. Then they scooped off the cream and poured it into a pot. Butter was churned once or twice a week. This was done by pouring the cream into a butter churn where butter was made with the help of a plunger. Churning took up to half an hour. The dealers bought what was not used and sold it in the city. Only as an exception did Ottersheim farming women bring their own country butter to market. The buttermilk served humans and animals as a refreshing drink. In the period after World War II, many country folk bought a cream separator that accelerated and facilitated removal of the cream from the milk. Today, churns and centrifuges have disappeared from the farm houses. Churning butter is left to the dairy processor. The townspeople get their butter and cheese from there, which not the least means measurably less work for the hard working farmer's wife.

Cooperative Members:		Quantity of the delivered milk:		Amount paid to the members was:		Price per liter or per kilogram:	
1934:	54						
1935:	136	234,548	liters	36,680	reichsmarks	~16	pfennigs
1940:	198	416,831	liters	72,242	reichsmarks	17	pfennigs
1945:	202	164,572	liters	29,346	reichsmarks	18	pfennigs
1950:	194	325,627	liters	87,718	deutschemarks	27	pfennigs
1955:	197	493,351	kilograms	149,424	deutschemarks	29	pfennigs
1960:	197	722,329	kilograms	252,746	deutschemarks	35	pfennigs
1964:	175	791,364	kilograms	328,586	deutschemarks	41	pfennigs
1965:	175	701,662	kilograms	281,198	deutschemarks	40	pfennigs

(~ Denotes an approximation.)

Chairmen of the Milk Suppliers' Cooperative:		Accountants of the Milk Suppliers' Cooperative:	
Alois Kreiner	1934-1936	Ludwig Gensheimer	1934-1945
Ludwig Gensheimer	1936-1945	Ludwig Steegmüller	1946 —
Josef Herrmann	1946-1947	*Drivers:*	
Ludwig Burgermeister	1947 —	Richard Hoffmann	1934-1940
Collectors:		Mees from Zeiskam	1940-1945
Richard Winkelblech	1934-1945	Landau Dairy	1945-1959
Hugo Zwißler	1945-1962	Markus Benz	1959-1965
Willi Röhrig	1962 —	Landau Dairy	1965 —

The Palatinate Farmers and Vintners of Ottersheim

Mention was first made of an agricultural society in 1864. However, it was a regional group to which only one farmer from Ottersheim belonged. It was landowner and innkeeper Johannes Zwißler of 79 Lange Straße. Five additional farmers from Ottersheim joined the association that same year. The aim of the association was to promote better agriculture and animal husbandry through better tillage and fertilization. An agricultural calendar was produced every year that recommended to the members measures for increasing the production of their products. So began a slow but perceptible modernization of farming. This development continued for over a hundred years and reached its peak in the second half of the 20th century. The farmers probably would not have found the connection to the scientific and technological world if left on their own. Here the State and the economy provided vigorous development assistance. Occupational and agricultural colleges emerged as did numerous experimental farms where new methods were tested. The agricultural cooperatives and associations contributed their part to the modernization of the enterprises.

As in other places after the First World War, farmers in Ottersheim joined together to form a *Christian Farmers Association.* Political reasons played a large role in this. In the newly created democratic political system, the farmers also wanted to be heard and to further their own interests. The Christian Farmers Association was in concert with the Bavarian Peoples' Party, which was then the ruling party in the Free State of Bavaria and therefore also in the Palatinate. Some of the farmers sympathized with the opposition and joined the so-called *Free Farmers.*

All agricultural organizations were dissolved after Hitler took power in 1933 and a compulsory organization of farmers called the *Reichsnährstand [Reich Nutritional Regulation]* was brought to life. A local farm leader was appointed in each village who had considerable power, especially during the war. He had to make especially sure that only the products desired by the government were cultivated and that these were delivered on time for fixed prices. Also, after the collapse in 1945 the main provisions of the Reich were still in force. In particular, in the French zone of occupation the farmers had to deliver their products at fixed prices as in the Third Reich.

After the famine years of 1946 and 1947, when the occupying power loosened the reigns somewhat and the administration was largely in German hands, many farmers joined the *Palatinate Farmers and Vintners Association* to better represent their interests.

A local chapter of this association was also founded in Ottersheim on 11 February 1948. On that day, 65 Ottersheim farmers joined the association at the "Zum Hirsch" Inn. Elected were Alois Kröper as Board President and Hugo Steegmüller as Vice President. At the first general assembly in December 1948, six more farmers joined the club so that the local group then had 71 members. The club dues were set by the amount of land in cultivation.

The Palatinate Farmers and Vintners Association primarily represented the interests of its members. For this purpose, an office was set up in Landau where every farmer could get advice and information.

A qualified person was available for legal questions. Upon request, the manager held explanatory presentations on agricultural issues in the various local groups. Particularly appreciated by every farmer was the ability to seek advice on tax and insurance issues in the office of Landau. The Palatinate Farmers and Vintners Association also produced a weekly newspaper, *The Palatine Farmer*. Printed in Waldfischbach, the paper informed the members on all issues of politics, economics, and law that affected them.

The activity of the local group primarily consisted of discussing current farming issues at public meetings. So in the past few years, discussions at the meetings centered on appropriate fertilizers, pesticides, sugar beet cultivation, taxation, old-age insurance for farmers, and the like. In this way, the local chapter of the Palatinate Farmers and Vintners Association played its part in keeping the Ottersheim farmers up to date.

President		*Vice President*	
Alois Kröper	1948-1962	Hugo Steegmüller	1948 —
Helmut Seither	1962 —		

The Raiffeisen Machinery Ring of Ottersheim

Farmers in the second half of the 20th century could no longer get along without a large machinery. The shortage of labor alone forced every farmer to purchase machinery. In addition, only a mechanized operation could remain competitive in the long run. But agricultural machinery costs money, often more money than a smaller or medium-sized farm could afford. For this reason, such small operations either refrained from purchasing a set of expensive machines entirely or took upon themselves the excessive purchases and maintenance costs. Usually the machines for small and medium farmers were also under utilized, because the acreage used for certain products was relatively small. A quite different situation existed for a larger enterprise, where for example an area of about ten hectares of potatoes is under cultivation. The use of a harvester was profitable here, because the machine paid for its purchase price within a few years.

To make the advantages of a large company also available to smaller farms, *machinery rings* or associations had been launched in recent years, particularly in Bavaria and Lower Saxony. These are associations of small and medium farmers with the goal to make better use of their agricultural machinery. Joining the machinery ring is voluntary. All machines remain the property of the individual members of the ring. Not every member purchases as much machinery as he can, but only a few purchase machines that are then made available to the other members of the ring. The renumeration for the use of the machine was transferred by the Raiffeisen Bank according to a predetermined price list. Depending on the case, either the work was performed entirely by a member or only the machine itself was rented out. For seldom used machines, it is sufficient when only one member of the ring buy one. However, multiples of frequently used machines were usually available.

The Ottersheim Machinery Ring was founded in 1965 by seven young farmers. The leadership of the ring was taken over by young farmer and Master Agriculturalist Fritz Steegmüller.[90] Already two years after its founding, 16 members belonged to the ring. This significant increase shows that the association had paid off. Though badly managed farms cannot be saved by the ring, rings do help the smaller and middle-size operations to farm more efficiently. The members of the Ottersheim Machinery Ring have the following agricultural machines: a harvester for sugar beets, a fertilizer spreader, a hay press with loader wagons, a forage harvester, a manure loader and manure spreader, a disc harrow, a sprayer, and a combination harrow and drag, among other things.

---

[90] This was not the author of this book but his nephew, the son of the author's brother, Hugo Steegmüller.

Ottersheim in 1740

Ottersheim -1740
Showing the ramparts and moat of the Queich Lines
(Provided by Bernhard Steegmüller)

The External Appearance of the Village

The Village Streets

Ottersheim currently has nine village streets carrying the following names:

1. Germersheimer Straße
2. Lange Straße
3. Ottostraße
4. Ludwigstraße
5. Maxstraße

6. Waldstraße
7. Riedstraße
8. Friedhofstraße
9. Schulstraße

For most of these streets, the local people use their own names that in some cases have been customary for hundreds of years and hopefully will not die out in the future. The streets are listed not by their size and importance but by their age.

1. The Germersheimer Straße [Germersheimer Street]

This street extends from the south-eastern exit of the village to the Catholic Church and is 330 meters long. Before the 30-Years War, only the piece from the Ludwigstraße of today up to the church was built and it was called the *Deich [Dike]* while the southern part was called "Im Gröhlig." The Deich is without doubt the oldest village street in Ottersheim. Already over more than a thousand years ago, the water of the Quot- or Bordgraben was dammed by means of an artificial dirt hill so that a *Weet* or pond was created. The Weet served simultaneously as livestock watering hole, livestock bath, and fire pond. Between the Weet and the church lay the Poppelmann feudal manor that belonged to the Palatine Electors. On the east side stood the ancient manor of the Benedictine Abbey of Klingenmünster. The Deich, a through way from the Rhine to the Haardt, was paved with stones at a very early date. However, this was not regular paving but larger stones of gneiss or melaphyre that gave stability to the soil.

The Gröhlig was undeveloped for a long time. The houses on the west side were built mainly in the 18th century. The field on the east side of the road was owned from 1808 by the Protestant religious community of Ottersheim who built their church there on the corner of the Ludwigstraße. Not until our century was the remaining free site traded for another site so that this part of the Germersheimer Straße could be built. The walk path from the Catholic church to the west exit of the village also belonged to the through way or *Hauptstraße [Main street]* as it was sometimes called in the past. Here there were of course no houses until the 18th century. In 1788, the *Tuchbleichpfad [cloth bleaching path]* was still the western border of residential building while the properties on the north side all emerged in the 19th and 20th centuries. This part of the former Landauer Straße was also fortified early on with hard stones.

Paving of the Germersheimer Straße began in 1841. Pavement Masters Franz Gerst from Maikammer and Johann Dunschen from Rülzheim had taken the contract for 3,083 gulden. First they had to break up and smash the stones of the old pavement that was 90 meters long and 7 meters wide. The new pavement was to be 120 meters long and 8.7 meters wide, and the stones were brought in from the quarries at Albersweiler. In the

328

course of the work, the bridge at the Weet was repaired for 207 gulden by carpenter Reinhold Weber from Landau. In 1842, the lining of the village stream was begun from the Protestant church to the south entrance of the village at a cost of over 1,000 gulden. Probably the last piece of Germersheimer Straße in the Gröhlig was paved at that time also.

Because of the busy through traffic, it was not surprising that by the year 1863 the bridge at the Weet was in need of repair. From oral tradition, we know that carriages had to drive through open water there at that time, so 334 gulden was spent to renew the bridge. Unfortunately, the pavement got bumpier from year to year. After the First World War, the condition of the Germersheimer Straße and the exit to Offenbach had so badly deteriorated that a renewal could no longer be delayed. So in 1921, the road from the west exit of the village up to the Catholic Church was repaired and the Germersheimer Straße was repaved four years later. After the Second World War, maintenance through the village was acquired by the State who then became responsible for the condition of the highway. So in 1959, the Germersheimer Straße was paved with an asphalt surface at the expense of the State.

2. The Lange Straße [Long Street]

This street follows a slight curvature from the north-eastern end to the western end of the village and is the longest street of the village at 750 meters. The Große Gasse [Big alley] as it generally used to be called originally reached only from the Catholic Church up to the present Riedstraße. It was then about 500 meters long. Already in the Middle Ages it had this length. The Lange Straße did not grow slowly from west to east as one would assume. Rather, the development took place from the two ends toward the center. As it was, the two courtyards of the Hördt cloisters, which were separated from each other by the Riedgässel, stood already in very early times on the eastern side. In 1600, there was still an empty lot between these courtyards and the Eußerthal courtyard in the western part of the Lange Straße where the reeds grew up to the street. So the Lange Straße was a really large alley already in the Middle Ages. That it was once called the Hintergasse [Back alley] suggests that the Deich was the most important street in the village because the designation Hintergasse only makes sense when the Deich would be seen as the Vordergasse [Front alley], that is, the core and center of the village. By the way, until the 19th century, this alley was never called a street because at no time did it serve through traffic. Its importance is underscored by the fact that the Große Gasse was the only street that in the 16th century had an artificial water canal. The Dorfbach, or village stream, was a trench built by people to direct water from the Queich to supply water to the village.

In 1832, the Dorfbach was lined with dressed sandstone, at first to a length of 200 meters. The lining was extended to the east later. The sandstone blocks had to be brought from the quarries of Gleisweiler. At the same time, a paved drain channel was built on the north side of the street while the street surface was fortified with gravel and sand. The paving stones came from quarries in Albersweiler where they were picked up by horse-drawn wagons.

From 1837 to 1839, the Große Gasse was paved in four phases. The contractor was Master Paver Matthäus Müller from Landau. The transportation of stone from

Albersweiler to Ottersheim was taken over by farmers Friedrich Gensheimer and Valentin Ehli, while Johannes Hilsendegen and Philipp Konrad Hatzenbühler brought in the sand for the 20 centimeter thick cover. This sand came from the five-morgen community sand pit near the present-day Rechhagwiesen. Because the old pavement drainage channel on the north side of the Große Gasse lay too deep, it was broken up. The Riedgässel was later paved using these stones.

In the years 1860, 1862, 1865, and 1873 the enclosure around the Dorfbach in the Große Gasse was thoroughly repaired because the blocks had partially collapsed or had moved. The street's drainage channel pipes were repaired and covered with iron plates in 1868. After the First World War, the Dorfbach enclosure was again repaired and updated. The street itself was to be paved again in 1939. However, it did not happen because the Second World War broke out in the meantime. The Lange Straße received a new asphalt pavement cover in 1958. The old pavement was grouted, and the road was laid out with tarred chipping on its entire width.

3. The Ottostraße [Otto street]

You have to be lucky to find an Ottersheim resident who knows where to find the Ottostraße. But everyone knows it as the *Riedgasse [Reed alley]* or *Pariser Gässel [Paris alley]*. As small as this street may be at 150 meters it is still pretty old. In the Middle Ages, it separated the two Hördt cloister yards that lay at the east end of the village. The upper Hördt yard stood to the east and the lower Hördt yard to the west of the Riedgässel. The houses that were built there were in part outbuildings of the monastery courtyards.

The name of Ottostraße dates from the 19th century. With this name the community wanted to express its solidarity with the Bavarian royal family whose founder was Palatine Count Otto von Wittelsbach (1180-1183). The term *Riedgässel,* or small reed alley, comes from the sedge grass that covered the swampy land up to the Quot- or Bordgraben. The name, *Pariser Gässel,* did not appear until the past century. It is a reminder of the Gensheimer brothers, who worked as shoemakers in Paris at one time and then later returned to the house of their parents on the Riedgasse. They lived next to the *Pariser Pädel [Paris path]* that is also named after them.

By the year 1840, the Ottostraße connection to the Große Gasse was paved. The stones from the old gutter of the Lange Straße were used for this. A blacktop surface was laid in 1956.

4. The Ludwigstraße [Ludwig street]

This street was named Ludwigstraße in the 19th century in honor of the Bavarian royal family. Locally it was either called the *Andere Gasse* or *Annergaß,* meaning *Other alley,* or the *Kleine Gasse [Little alley]*. This street is not mentioned in the *Summary of Rights in the Village of Ottersheim from the year 1599*. It was probably created after the 30-Years War. In 1745, eight properties stood on the south side of the Ludwigstraße and nine on the north side, and there were already thirteen and fourteen houses respectively in 1788. Until the 20th century, the development boundary lay at the point where the connecting path from the Riedgässel joins with the Ludwigstraße. Paving of the Kleine Gasse was started in 1840, a short time before the Dorfbach enclosure had been completed. The commission was carried out for 1,686 gulden by pavers Franz Gerst from Maikammer and Johann Dunschen from Rülzheim. Because the Ludwigstraße experienced no through traffic, the pavement remained without major damage for quite a long time. The Dorfbach was leveled in 1949 because most of the time it no longer carried any water. In 1954, the extended Ludwigstraße was surveyed up to the Riedstraße and released for construction. A year later, this part of the Kleine Gasse was fortified and covered with blacktop.

5. The Maxstraße [Max street]

Rarely does an Ottersheim resident use the word *Maxstraße*. The name was selected in the 19th century in honor of the Bavarian King Max. For the villagers, the Maxstraße is the *Bauernweg [Peasant road]*, as it has been called since as early as the 16th century. As late as 1788, only one house stood on the street behind the present property of Wilhelm Lutz at 21 Lange Straße. All the other houses on the Bauernweg were built in the 19th and 20th centuries. The name Bauernweg cannot be interpreted with certainty. The name has nothing to do with the French fortification system that crossed over the Maxstraße. Probably this road was preferred by the peasants for their carts and carriages because the Neuweg that also stretched northward to the forest was only intended for cattle being driven to pasture. The Bauernweg received a paved gutter and the surface was fortified in 1843. Not until 1956 was it turned into a street and provided with an asphalt surface.

6. The Waldstraße [Forest street]

Until 1952, the Waldstraße was officially named *Teichstraße [Pond street]*. This name refers to a second Weet that could still be seen at the end of the road at the level of the drop gate in the middle of the 19th century. The pond was an artificial extension of the Dorfbach and served as a watering place and wading opportunity for cattle, pigs, and geese when they returned from the north pasture. In the local language, the Waldstraße is called the *Neuweg [New road]*, as was common already in the 16th century. Originally the road was called *Viehtrift [Cattle run]* because it was used to drive the cattle out to pasture. When the Viehtrift was expanded and renamed to Neuweg cannot be accurately determined. At any rate, this road was already called Neuweg in the 16th century.

At the beginning of the 19th century there were no houses on the present Neuweg. The fields on the west side belonged to the Poppelmann estate while the property to the east was owned by the Eußerthal Monastery. Moreover, because the larger Poppelmann estate was crisscrossed with fortifications, it could not be readily used as a building site. First, the so-called *Queich Lines* that lay parallel to the Dorfbach had to be leveled. The Neuweg was made passable in 1858. Four years later, work was begun to enclose the Dorfbach along the Waldstraße. The work was completed in 1864 and cost the community 1,438 gulden. It was decided to fortify the Neuweg in 1870 and the first phase of work was completed that same year. The necessary limestone was brought from Arzheim. The second section was finished in 1873. Total cost of the fortifications was around 1,000 gulden.

Until the middle of this century, the houses on the Waldstraße reached only up to the Falltorweg. Then in 1955, the northerly part of the street was approved for construction and developed into a street. In 1958 the Neuweg received an asphalt road surface.

7. The Riedstraße [Reed street]

In contrast to the *Riedgässel [Small reed road - the Ottostraße]*, the Riedstraße was listed in the record book of 1788 as the *Große Riedgasse [Big Reed road]*. Construction had not begun on it until this century. Previously, the Riedgasse formed the eastern boundary of the Hördt upper manor yard and the abbey farm lands which ran up to the highway. Similar to the Deich, this road was created to dam the water of the Quot- or Bordgraben and make it available for irrigating the Brühl meadows. The cattle of both Hördt cloisters grazed year in and year out on the fenced Brühl meadows that stood on the east end of the Lange Straße. The expansion of this road in the Middle Ages was probably also intended to provide access from the county road to the Hördt upper manor yards, which was also a collection point for the taxes of the tenants of the monastic fields and meadows. To this day the oral tradition recalls a tithe barn that stood on the monastery property at 12 Lange Straße. Once the Riedstraße was declared a construction area in 1961, it received an asphalt surface. Meanwhile, the bridge over the Quot- or Bordgraben was renewed.

8. The Friedhofstraße [Cemetery street]

Heinrich Faath was the first to build a house on the old *Feldweg [Field road]* after the First World War. Later the road was widened somewhat. The council decided to name this road *Friedhofstraße* in 1952 after more houses had been built there. The Friedhofstraße was widened to its present dimension as part of the land consolidation in 1964. It was expanded and paved in 1965.

9. The Schulstraße [School street]

The community council decided to rename the Falltorweg [Drop gate road] to Schulstraße in 1962 after a new kindergarten and a new school building were constructed on this street. So far the street has been neither fortified nor expanded. The name Falltorweg reminds of a gate that closed by itself of its own weight after having been opened [a portcullis]. The gate stood at the west exit of the road where today one of the two stone pillars from the gate can still be seen. The second pillar was unearthed decades ago and placed behind the new cemetery as a footbridge across the Waalengraben [Flowing trench]. Oral tradition has it that on the site where the tobacco shed now stands there was a large fenced area where the cattle rested from grazing. In the middle of the last century, the cow herder who kept the community cows and breeding stock is said to have herded his animals for watering at the Weet via the portcullis, and then drove them to rest on the free area near the present-day tobacco shed in the afternoon. The Falltorweg is not mentioned in the record book of 1788. Rather, it is known there as the Mittelschorweg [Middle passage road].

Street name signs and house numbers were not mounted until the beginning of this century. At that time, the house numbers for the whole village were reviewed. The difficulty in numbering new buildings led the community to carry out a reorganization in 1952. From then on each street is numbered separately.

The Houses and Their Inhabitants (Overview)

(As of March 1967)

Germersheimer Straße

West side		East side	
1	Community Hall	2	Milk collection point
3	Catholic Church	4	Emil Hilsendegen (his widow)
7	Walter Fischer		Walter Dörzapf
	Eugen Mohr	5	Robert Frey
8	Franz Ludwig Walk		Marie Frey
	Julius Gütermann	6	Karl Hermann
10	Alois Walk		Anna Hermann
12	Bernhard Kröper (his widow)		Hedwig Hermann
	Hermann Hilsendegen		(Post office)
	August Gaab	6A	Hiltrud Kreiner (widow)
14	Ludwig Ritter		Herbert Disqué
	Karl Ritter (his widow)		Anna Job (widow)
15	Hugo Burgermeister	9	(Karl Ettmüller (owner))
	Ludwig Burgermeister		County and Municipal Savings
18	Robert Kröper		Bank of Germersheim,
			Ottersheim Branch
19	Oskar Kuntz	11	Werner Hoffmann I.
	Otto Kreiner I. (his widow)		Josef Hoffmann
19A	Freezer facility of the	13	Ludwig Jochim
	Raiffeisen Cooperative		Georg Jochim (his widow)
20	Paul Dörzapf		Elisabeth Jochim
	Markus Dörzapf	16	(Ferdinand Glatz)
21	Albert Kröper	17	Ferdinand Glatz
	Fridolin Kröper	23	(Building site Oscar Zwißler)
22	Wilhelm Hoffmann II.	28	Oskar Zwißler
24	Hugo Gutting (his widow)		Heinz Zwißler
	Franz Gutting	31	Leo Herrmann
25	Fritz Gensheimer		Werner Kaiser
	Fritz Dörzapf		
26	August Walk (his widow)		*South Side*
	Erwin Walk	34	Heinz Hilsendegen
27	Eduard Kröper	35	Edwin Benz
	Willibald Kuhn (his widow)	36	Ludwig Gaab
29	Eduard Jeckel I.		Klaus Gaab
30	Severin Lerch	37	Oswald Gensheimer
32	Communal property		Ludwig Gensheimer (his widow)
	Agnes Münster (widow)	39	Otwin Zwißler

33 (August Gaab (owner))
   Hugo Gaab
   North side
38 Armin Hoffmann
   Berta Marz (widow)

Lange Straße

North side		*South side*	
1A	Herbert Merdian	2	Gustav Nikolaus
1	Aug. Winkelblech (his widow)		Konrad Störtzer (his widow)
3	Artur Winkelblech (his widow)	4	Wilhelm Hoffmann I.
	Katharina Winkelblech	8	Otto Winkelblech
5	Alois Messemer	6	Otto Morio
7	Richard Gaab (his widow)		Jakob Morio
7A	Alois Ries, Offenbach	9	Johann Kuntz
10	Ludwig Winkelblech (his widow)	11	Richard Kreiner
	Hilmar Winkelblech		Maria Kreiner
13	August Kuhn (his widow)	12	Alois Reichling
	Auguste Günther (widow)	15	Albert Becker
14	August Zwißler		Anna Sauther
17	Otto Bauchhenß	16	Wilhelm Breßler
	Werner Bauchhenß	19	Franz Schwaab
18	Otto Merdian	20	(Franz Schwaab)
	VIVO Grocery	22	Franz Benz
	Store of Erwin Walk		Fritz Benz
21	Ludwig Gadinger I.	24	Alois Wingerter
	Erwin Kramer	26	Warehouse of
21	(rear building)		Peter Hoffmann
	Wilhelm Lutz (his widow)	27	Emil Hünerfauth
	Walter Kuhn (his widow)		Günter Hünerfauth
23	Eduard Dörzapf		Johann Brüderle (his widow)
	Anna Dörzapf	29	Tilbert Kröper
25	Eugen Job I. (his widow)		Josef Müller (his widow)
	Edwin Job	31	Helmut Winkelblech
28	Theodor Weisbrod	32	Franz Josef Kröper (his widow)
	Josefine Weisbrod	34A	Franz Moock I. (his widow)
	Barbara Kröper		Karl Schwarz
30	Julius Job	34	Otto Job I.
33	Otto Glatz (his widow)		Artur Josef Märdian
35	Alfons Zwißler	36	Josef Berwanger
	Norbert Zwißler		Anton Zwißler
37	Oskar Hoffmann	38	Eugen Jochim
	Günter Benner	39	Eugen Jochim
40	Richard Hoffmann	41	Stefan Hörner

Adolf Burg

40 (rear of building)

Josef Dörzapf

42 Alwin Seither

Frieda Kröper

44 Erich Kern

46 Julius Seither

Erich Seither

Hildegard Seither

48 Franz Föhlinger

49 Willi Röhrig

51 Josef Weimann

Anton Weimann

Peter Schwendemann

Juliane Dolezal

(Second residence)

54 Alfred Scherff

56 Otto Job II.

58 Titus Schuhmann (his widow)

59 Walter Kopf

61 Alois Hilsendegen

Otmar Detzel

63 Willi Hindert

65 Eugen Gensheimer

Otto Gensheimer

Berta Gensheimer

67 (Ed. Gensheimer (his widow))

68 Ed. Steegmüller (his widow)

71 Joh. Josef Job

Eugen Job II.

74 Rudolf Metzger (his widow)

Gustav Lösch

76 Georg Kruppenbacher

78 Old Schoolhouse

Berthold Feldmann

Rudolf Stubenbord

Emil Korn

Charlotte Sablotny

80 Former Catholic

Rectory (demolished)

81 Erwin Bischoff

82 Alois Winkelblech

84 Markus Ößwein

43 Albert Hilsendegen (his widow)

Franziska Huwe

45 Erwin Wünschel

Ludwig Detzel

47 Magd. Weinmann (widow)

Elfriede Götz née Ansorg

Alfred Heß (second residence)

50 Edwin Hilsendegen

52 Richard Dumser

Alois Dumser

53 Dumser Brothers

55 Alois Kopf (his widow)

Martin Jennewein

57 Eduard Lavo (his widow)

Vinzenz Gläßgen

60 Unoccupied (Sold to the

neighbors)

62 Emil Brüderle

Otmar Breßler

64 Eugen Seither (his widow)

Emil Rund (his widow)

66 Emil Gutting

Rolf Gutting

Ferdinand Gutting (his widow)

69 Friedrich Blattmann

Amalie Weiß

70 Ludwig Kreiner (his widow)

Dietmar Kluge

72 (Franziska Huwe (owner))

Franz Uterhardt

73 Willibald Faath (his widow)

75 Severin Zwißler (his widow)

77 Alois Hörner

Gertrud Zwißler

79 Lud. Lorenz Föhlinger

Ludwig Föhlinger (his widow)

83 Saint Elisabethen Club

Catholic Sisters' Home

85 Franz Müller (his widow)

Elis. Winkelblech (widow)

87 Otto Ettmüller (his widow)

Walter Bullinger

89 August Faath

	Anna Ößwein (widow)	91	Wilhelm Dotterweich
86	Markus Ößwein (his widow)		Josef Dotterweich
88	Karl Walk	93	Robert Hilsendegen
90	Emil Hatzenbühler		Rosa Reichling (widow)
	Ewald Kern	95	Hubert Kröper
92	Georg Kröper (his widow)		Philipp Müller
	Franz Xaver Kröper	98	Karl Hoffmann
94	Herbert Becki		Werner Hoffmann II.
	Johann Knoll (his widow)	100	Johann Benz
96	Emil Zwißler		Edmund Groll
	Maria Zeyer		Klaus Scheib
97	Peter Müller	101	Leo Benz
99	Markus Benz I.		Hilda Benz
99A	Ferdinand Benz	102	Franz Freudenstein (his widow)
	Norbert Benz		Erwin Kröper
103	Alois Kröper		Oskar Faath
	Walter Kröper (his widow)	104	Wilhelm Burkard
105	Fritz Föhlinger	106	Hugo Steegmüller
	Maria Lang (widow)		Fritz Steegmüller
107	Wilhelm Jennewein		Lina Job
		108	Oscar Kröper
			Karl Kröper

Ottostraße

West side

3	Hubert Gadinger
	Alois Gadinger (his widow)
5	(Hubert Gadinger)
6	Julius Hoffman (his widow)
8	Ferdinand Job
	August Job
10	Oswald Moock
	Jakob Moock

East side

1	Emma Sauther heirs
2	Paul Romanowski
4	Albert Winkelblech (his widow) heirs
7	Edwin Disqué
	Karl Disqué (his widow)
9	Hermann Zwißler
	Anna Zwißler
11	Bernhard Stadel
	Maria Stadel
12	Leo Lutz

Ludwigstraße

North side

2	Arnold Zwißler
4	Ferdinand Föhlinger
6	Jakob Eichenlaub (his widow)
	Karl Moock
8	Ruprecht Hindert
10	Hugo Seither

South side

1	Protestant Church
3	Ludwig Hermann
	Kurt Zwißler
5	Alois Benz
	Klara Job
	Hildegard Benz

11	(Hugo Seither)		7	Hubert Kramer
13	Hermann Kröper			Arnold Kramer
15	Hugo Müller (front house)			Gustav Kramer
	Emma Müller		9	(Elisabeth Job (owner))
	Klaus Müller			Kurt Kröper
15	Ruprecht Job (rear house)		12	Alois Merdian
				Katharina Merdian
18	Eugen Dörzapf			Emil Diebold
20	Ludwig Disqué		14	Helmut Seither
22	Hermann Seither		16	Hermann Nist
	Franz Seither		17	Franz Ludwig Dörzapf
23	Emil Kern		19	Bernhard Detzel
	Walter Kern			Karl Detzel (his widow)
24	Ferdinand Kröper		21	August Schaller
	Ewald Kröper			Ludwig Braun
27	Building site Wilhelm		25	Franz Hatzenbühler
	Hatzenbühler I.		26	Edgar Dörzapf
29	Helmut Brüderle			Albert Dörzapf
30	Adam Brüderle		28	Josef Michalczyk
32	Werner Wenzel			Roland Winkelblech
33	Raiffeisen Bank warehouse		31	Peter Bischoff (his widow)
35	Alfons Seither, building site			August Schreiber
36	Alfons Seither, building site		34	Heinrich Bischoff
41	Jakob Gadinger		38	Otmar Kröper
43	Markus Moock		40	Alois Wünschel
45	Helmut Frey		42	Gunter Schuhmann
	Elsa Frey		44	Willibald Richter
47	Robert Faath			Rudolf Zeisberger (his widow)
	Johann Dörzapf		46	Karl Föhlinger
49	Maria Kröper née Job		48	Franz Knebl
	building site			Sebastian Knebl
51	Josef Lutz			Jakob Knebl (his widow)
			50	Otto Hilsendegen (his widow)
			52	Robert Ripp
			53	Erich Hellmann

Maxstraße

West side

4	Clemens Kröper (his widow)
5	Otto Dörzapf children (owners)
	Hans Kröper
7	Hch. Bischoff. (owner)

East side

1	(Weighing Hall)
2	Richard Kuntz
	Fritz Eichmann
6	Viktor Becki (his widow)
	Reinhold Becki

	Walter Weimert		Klaus Kreiner
9	Heinrich Greichgauer	8	Friedrich Job
12	Hermann Kreiner	10	Alois Morio
	Robert Kreiner	11	Alois Kreiner (his widow)
		13	Otto Kreiner II.
	North side		Hugo Kreiner
15	Heinrich Kröper	14	Josef Mayr
	Otto Kröper (his widow)	16	Otto Kreiner III.
			Werner Heidenreich
		17	Werner Heidenreich
			building site

Waldstraße

West side		*East side*	
1	Robert Winkelblech	5A	Catholic parsonage
2	Alois Glatz		Josef Scherübl, pastor
	Josef Glatz		Martha Scherübl
	Luzia Glatz	7	Frieda Moock
	Franziska Winkelblech		Emil Moock
3	Eugen Uhrig	9	Ludwig Störtzer (his widow)
	Paul Föhlinger (his widow)		Ludwig Störtzer
4	Lorenz Hilsendegen (his widow)		Emilie Störtzer
5	Ernst Müller	11	Hugo Dörzapf (his widow)
	Barbara Müller		August Dörzapf (his widow)
	Berta Müller	13	Heinrich Stadel
6	Robert Hindert		Anna Stadel
	Auguste Morio (widow)	15	Josef Kopf (his widow)
8	Edwin Greichgauer		Johann Meyer
	Emil Greichgauer (his widow)	17	Heinrich Kaiser
10	Maria Kröper	19	Wilhelm Jeckel
	Waldemar Brauner	21	Wilhelm Hatzenbühler
	Maria Morisak (widow)		Rudi Hatzenbühler
12	Jakob Glatz	23	Emilie Föhlinger
14	Peter Föhlinger (his widow)		Georg Föhlinger (his widow)
	Kurt Holdermann (his widow)	25	Otto Stadel
16	Siegmund Glatz	27	Ludwig Wünschel
	Alfred Neugebauer		Walter Wünschel
18	Eduard Jeckel II.	29	Alois Föhlinger
	Hugo Jeckel (his widow)	31	Ludwig Steegmüller
20	Karl Gaab (his widow)	33	Hans Kiefer
22	Heinrich Jeckel		Jakob Kaiser (his widow)
	Erwin Jeckel	37	Emil Kröper
24	Wilhelm Stadel		Richard Kröper
26	Hermann Hatzenbühler	37A	Building site

	Kurt Breßler	38	Fridolin Föhlinger
28	Otto Sauther	39	Jakob Weiß
	Erich Sauther	40	Richard Hindert
30	Friedrich Scheurer (his widow)	40A	Building site
	Reinhold Scheurer	41	Hugo Müller
32	Otto Detzel (his widow)	42	Klara Wünschel
	Albert Krauß		Bertold Wünschel
34	Eduard Hilsendegen	43	Oswald Föhlinger
	Franz Hilsendegen		Kath. Hellmann (widow)
35	August Josef Faath	43A	Building site
	Johann Gadinger	44	Emil Job (his widow)
35A	Robert Stadel		Alfred Hilsendegen
36	Richard Föhlinger	45	Robert Jeckel
45A	Fritz Dörzapf		

Riedstraße

West side

1D	Alois Seither
2	Hugo Zwißler
	Eugen Müller
2A	Heinrich Kurt Bolleyer
3	Richard Jeckel
4	Leo Kreiner
	Hermann Bischoff (his widow)
5	Ludwig Winkelblech II.
	Horst Winkelblech
7	Franz Zwißler
	Willi Zwißler
10	(Zwißler Garden)

East side

1	Maria Hilsendegen
	Amalie Messemer (widow)
1A	Rudi Moock
1B	Hugo Kröper
3 ½	Eugen Disqué
4A	Karl Ludwig Lutz
6	Eugen Hoffmann
8	Johann Sentz
9	(Dolezal building site)
11	August Jäger (his widow)
	Fritz Jäger
	Elisabeth Steegmüller
	Auguste Heist (widow)
12	Erich Winkelblech
13	Markus Benz II.
14	Ludwig Gadinger II.
	Franz Gadinger
15	Hubert Gadinger, (Factory)

Friedhofstraße

(All the houses on the east side)

1	Heinrich Faath II. (his widow)
	Leo Pfaff
2	Ludwig Ripp
2A	Erich Peter Messemer

3	Reinhold Job
4	Building site
5	Building site
6	Josef Schmitz
7	Engelbert Puhl

House Inscriptions

House inscriptions are usually found in old houses, barns or sheds. They usually give an indication of the builder and the year.

On the Germersheimer Straße

1	Community Hall:	The gate arch bears the date `1555´
7	Walter Fischer:	The main beam of the house has an unreadable inscription: `1788 wohnte dort Anton Bischoff´ [In 1788 Anton Bischoff lived there]
15	Ludwig Burgermeister:	Earlier, the house had a plaque with the inscription: `Wirtschaft "Zur Pfalz," erbaut von Johannes Bischoff, 1875 geschlossen´ ["Zur Pfalz" Inn built by Johannes Bischoff, 1875 closed] Inscription in the barn gate: `H. B. H. K. F.N. 1808´ [In 1788 Konrad Hatzenbühler the unmarried, lived there.] Door beam in the pig stall: `1831 JMS KK´
19	Oscar Kuntz:	Inscription on the barn beam: `DIESEN BAU HAT ERBAUT 1832 JOH. KRÖPER + MARIA KATHARINA GEB. HATZENBÜHLER´ [This building was built in 1832 by Joh. Kröper + Maria Katharina née Hatzenbühler]

On the Lange Straße

16	Wilhelm Breßler:	Gate beam: `1803´
20	Franz Schwaab:	House beam: `Dieses Haus wurde erbaut von Franz Wingerter und dessen Ehefrau Ursula Kopfin im Jahre 1816´ [This house was built by Franz Wingerter and his wife Ursula Kopf in 1816.]
25	Eugen Job I. (his widow):	Barn beam: `DIESE SCHEIER HAT ERBAUT MARIA HUCKIN IM JAHRE CHRISTI 1741´ [This barn was built by Maria Huck in the Year of Christ 1741]
28	Theodor Weisbrod:	Stone plaque on the house: `Mit Gottes Hilf und Segen hat dieses Haus erbaut ... Anna Maria Knoll im Jahre 1889´ [With God's help and blessing this house was built by ... Anna Maria Knoll in year 1889]
30	Julius Job:	Barn beam: `17 Johannes Franck und Catarina Franck 78´

		The executioner Johannes Franck lived there in 1788.
33	Otto Glatz (his widow):	On the gate pillar that has since disappeared, the year `1562´ was imprinted.
40	Josef Dörzapf:	`1835´ `1829´
44	Erich Kern:	On the soffit of the small courtyard gate that has since been demolished, was an eight-pointed star with the year `1570´
48	Franz Föhlinger;	Barn beam: `Klaudius Dürzapf und Katharina Dürzapfin beide Eheleute 1780´ [Klaudius Dürzapf and Katharina Dürzapf both spouses 1780]
50	Edwin Hilsendegen:	Barn beam: `1836 DIESEN BAU HAT GEBAUT JOHANNES STADEL UND SEINE EHEFRAU BARBARA MUTHIN´ [This building was built in 1836 by Johannes Stadel and his wife Barbara Muth] Small outbuilding: `ICH HAB DIES WEITERGEBAUT 1804´ [I extended this in 1804] Barn beams: `17 STEFAN WILHELM UND SEINE HAUSFRAU DOROTHEA 50´ [17 Stefan Wilhelm and his housewife Dorothea 50]
56	Otto Job II.:	Beam barn with indistinct inscription: `ICH B UND SEIN FRAU LEBAU E 1802´ (I B and his wife Lebau E 1802)
59	Walter Kopf:	On a piece of the beam stands: `Jakob Moser und Catarina Moser 1728´ [Jakob Moser and Catarina Moser 1728]
60	Eugen Leingang: (Former Owner)	`DIESES HAUS HAT GEBAUT VALENTIN KROEPER UND SEINE EHELICHE HAUSFRAU CATARINA HATZENBÜHLER A(nno) 1815´ [This house has built Valentin Kroeper and his wedded housewife Catarina Hatzenbühler Year 1815]
64	Emil Rund (his widow)	Barn beam: `Diese Scheuer haben gebaut Seither und Maria seine Hausfrau im Jahre 1766´ [This barn was built by Seither and Maria his wife in 1766]
65	Eugen Gensheimer:	Well stone bearing the date `1735´
66	Emil Gutting	Piece of an old barn beam: `Meister Christof Rebstock Erb. 1686´ [Master Christof Rebstock builder 1686]

69	Friedrich Blattmann:	Dates located on the shed: `1822´ `1896´
		Date on the barn: `1851´
		Name: `Ehli´
79	Ludw. Lor. Föhlinger:	At the cellar door: `1609´ with two letters: `M´ (?) and `S´
		Dates on barn and shed: `1632´ `1663´ `1727´
85	Franz Müller (his widow)	Barn beam:

`Diese Scheuer baute Hanes KREPER und seine Frau Katharina Hoffmann 1788´

[This barn built in 1788 Hanes KREPER and his wife Katharina Hoffmann]

On the Ludwigstraße

| 2 | Arnold Zwißler: | At the old house, now demolished stood: |

`Dieses Haus hat erbaut Joh. Philipp Peter Seither und seine eheliche Hausfrau A. Kath. eine geborene Himmerlin im J. 1700´

[This house was built by Johann Philipp Peter Seither and his wedded housewife A. Kath. née Himmerl in year 1700]

9	Elisabeth Job (owner):	House Beam: `J.H. Job 1819´
		"Kurt Kröper Eva K. Störtz"
21	August Schaller:	`ANNO 1761 JAKOB DOLL UND SEINE HAUSFRAU ABELONIA DOLLIN´

[In the year 1761 Jakob Doll and his house wife Abelonia Doll]

On the Waldstraße

| 7 | Frieda Moock: | Illegible writing: `1715´ |

The house was purchased in Bellheim, torn down there, and rebuilt in Ottersheim

The Poppelmann Estate of Ottersheim

Presumably founded by Kaiser Konrad II, the builder of the Cathedral in Speyer, a Kaiser Fortress existed already in the 11th century in Germersheim. Under Rudolf von Habsburg (1273-1291), a bailiff was first mentioned who was employed as manager of the fortress. He had the task of securing the peace, supervising the fortifications, and commanding the garrison at the fortress. Under the bailiff were the *fortress men* who were appointed by the king. They served as weapons carriers and received for this a fief. From around 1400, two directories of Germersheim fortress men have been handed down to us. Therein are listed names that are also of importance to Ottersheim. First, an Ottmann Sturm is mentioned whose family probably owned the lands "Im Sturm." However, more important for Ottersheim was the Poppelmann family of knights who owned a large feudal manor. As property of the Electoral Palatinate, for several centuries the Poppelmann estate was in the hands of the Poppelmann family who lived in Weingarten around the year 1400. It is therefore not surprising that the name Poppelmann to designate this property is still alive in the minds of the villagers and will most likely remain so for several more centuries. By the way, the Poppelmann family also possessed a large amount of land in Knittelsheim.

Two feudal manors that stood at the "common alley" called the Deich also belonged to the Poppelmann estate in Ottersheim around the year 1600 and were separated from the church yard by a *Weinberg [hill growing grapes for wine]*. Back then, there was still empty land up to the Quotgraben that was part of the adjacent Brühl meadows belonging to the Poppelmann estate. In 1599, Ottersheim Mayor Hans Trauth occupied one house of the estate while the second house was owned by farmer Martin Ludwig. The two had bought the houses from the Electoral Court Chamber as hereditary property. The properties had several good stables but only one barn. Thus, it was difficult to set clear boundaries between these properties (7 and 10) on the west side of the Deich for subsequent inheritances that is noticeable even today.

In early times, the Poppelmann estate comprised 37.2 hectares of land within the district of Ottersheim. The fields consisted of a total of 20 parcels of which 6 were in the Oberfeld, 5 in the Niederfeld, 7 in the Obersand, and 1 plot each in the Mittelsand and Niedersand. Larger contiguous cultivated land parcels belonging to the Poppelmann estate included 11 morgen in the Elfmorgen, 6 morgen in the Knopfgewanne, 8 morgen in the Hintergrund, 4 morgen on the Kahlenberg, and 3 morgen in the Schlägel. Add to these the so-called *Großstück [Big piece]* to the west of the Neuweg that was 36 morgen and thereby the largest contiguous land area belonging to one owner. Before 1800, the Großstück stretched from the Landauer Straße to the Rechhag and from the Neuweg to the Mühlweg. Some of the land was used by the French to build the fortress lines. Along the Landauer Straße, in the upper village and west of the Neuweg, 1 morgen and 22 ruten of land were "buried" during the building of the Queich Lines.

Also mentioned in a document from the Poppelmann estate was a piece called the *Schäfereigut [Shepherd's property]*. It is possible that this term refers to the Großstück, which before the 30 Years War, perhaps served as a sheep pasture and was therefore also fenced in. It seems the Rechhag screened the terrain to the north. The sheep farm seems to have vanished during the 30 Years War. In any case, nowhere in later documents is there mention of a sheep farm. The administration of the Poppelmann estate was apparently in the hands of the mayor. Every year, 110 malters of oats had to be supplied by the community to the Electoral Chamber of Accounts. It was the duty of the mayor to collect the natural goods from the tenants and to transport them to the designated collection point.

As did the monastic possessions, the Poppelmann estate was sold at auction during the Napoleonic period. The Großstück seems for the most part not to have found a well-funded buyer in Ottersheim so it was auctioned to outside buyers. Later, at least part of the "Landauer fields" were sold to Ottersheim farmers.

The name Poppelmann also stood on two ancient boundary markers that were found on the Landauer Straße. On one stone was the inscription ‘GP 1731’ and on the other ‘GP 1768’. The abbreviation GP stands for Gut [Estate] Poppelmann. After the land consolidation of 1964, part of the former Großstück was named "Im Poppelmann." This place name should keep the Poppelmann name alive among the village population and later generations during the coming centuries and serve as a reminder of the existence of the Poppelmann estate in Ottersheim.

The Feudal Manor of the Klingenmünster Abbey in Ottersheim

Although we have no reliable historical evidence, we may assume that the former Benedictine Abbey of Klingenmünster and the Abbey of Weißenburg originated in the time of the Merovingians. Perhaps either King Dagobert I (623-639) or his successor Dagobert II (639-678) was founder of the Klingenmünster Monastery. The rich gifts that the abbey possessed in the near and extended surroundings would have come from the royal founder and other high nobles. The documents speak of 11,000 hube[10] or hufe [parcels] of land distributed over more than thirty villages of the southern Palatinate.

In spite of the great wealth of the monastery, it fell into financial distress during the difficult times of war in the Middle Ages so that it often had to pawn its lands. At the instigation of members of the Order and of the Palatine Elector, the Benedictine Monastery of Klingenmünster was turned into a secular monastery in 1491. Due to this change, the spiritual occupants were no longer obligated to maintain communal living space, food, and property. In 1567, Elector Friedrich III of Heidelberg closed the monastery completely. The goods were confiscated and from then on managed by officials of the Spiritual Goods Administration.

As in Offenbach, Mörlheim, Wollmesheim, Göcklingen, Insheim, and other southern Palatinate villages, the Klingenmünster Abbey also owned an estate in Ottersheim. At the time of secularization, the property of the estate consisted of 41.5 hectares of land and three manorial properties. The households included the respective houses, barns, stables, and outbuildings that were on the "common road through the middle of the village." These were probably the properties 5, 6, and 8 on the Germersheimer Straße opposite the former Poppelmann estate. As stated in the abbey documents, the manorial property of the Klingenmünster Abbey in Ottersheim also served as a collection point. That is to say, that the lease had to be delivered in the form of farm goods. It is no coincidence that the barn at house number 6 was still called the *Zehntscheune [Tithe barn]* during our times. It became a victim of flames in the middle of the Second World War on 22 April 1943.

The 154 morgen of farmland and 12 morgen of meadows in Ottersheim that belonged to the Monastery of Klingenmünster were distributed throughout the district. The arable land consisted of 63 quite different parcels: 21 parcels were in the Oberfeld, 17 in the Niederfeld, 15 in the Obersand, 3 in the Mittelsand, and 7 in the Niedersand. They included about 14 morgen of vineyards.

In 1571, soon after the closure of the Klingenmünster Abbey by Elector Friedrich III, the Ottersheim manor was given to three families of the village as hereditary property for appropriate fees. These were the peasants Gangolf Dörzapf, Velten Doll, and Adam Moock. Since the estate consisted of three houses with their respective outbuildings, each of these farmers received a complete household and farm.

From this time on, these three families also cultivated the fields of the monastery. However, the land was periodically leased out by the Electoral Court Chamber in Heidelberg after the 30 Years War.

A series of documents mentions such leases. So for example, from 1700 to 1706 Sebastian Hatzenbühler, Paul Burgermeister, Sebastian Job, David Kuhn, and a few other farmers held the fields, pastures, and vineyards of the Klingenmünster manor in their possession. The lease costs by year were as follows:

1700:	18 malters of grain	and	8 malters spelt
1701:	20 malters of grain	and	10 malters spelt
1702:	22 malters of grain	and	12 malters spelt
1703:	22 malters of grain	and	10 malters spelt
1704:	20 malters of grain	and	12 malters spelt
1705:	20 malters of grain	and	12 malters spelt
1706:	26 malters of grain	and	12 malters spelt

The grain had to be delivered as so-called *commercial goods* to the storage places in Landau. If the Electoral Court Chamber stipulated a different collecting site, this site could not be more than four hours from Ottersheim.

In 1757, the Klingenmünster estate was leased for 12 years and in the ensuing years for periods of 9 years each. The tenants in the second half of the 18th century were not only willing to deliver 40 malters of grain and 70 malters spelt per year but also to make 12 trips for the Spiritual Goods Administration.

Like the other government property in Ottersheim, the Klingenmünster estate was confiscated and sold by the French during the French Revolution. The houses were kept by the former owners while the fields and meadows were largely bought by the respective tenants. As far as they could not raise the purchase price, the lands went to cash-rich local farmers or to outside buyers.

The Eußerthal Estate in Ottersheim

When Saint Bernhard von Clairvaux was in Speyer during the Christmas season of 1146 and called the Christians to a crusade, presumably the decision was also made to found a Cistercian Monastery in the Diocese of Speyer. To that end, Knight Stefan von Mörlheim and the Dukes Hartmann and Otto gifted the Gray Monks of Weilerbetnach near Metz the Sülz or Eußer valley near Albersweiler. The construction work began in 1148. Other nobles gave the abbey a handsome forest district a few years later. A special friend of the Eußerthal Monastery was Emperor Friedrich Barbarossa (1152-1190). He took the abbey under the special protection of the kingdom and employed the Eußerthal monks as fortress chaplains of the Trifels. The Cistercians were at the same time the guardians of the crown jewels that were kept in the Trifels fortress.

As a result of numerous donations, the Eußerthal Abbey was considered one of the richest monasteries of the Middle Ages. For example, Eußerthal monks had large land holdings in Mörlheim, Offenbach, Ottersheim, Bellheim, and Mechtersheim. In spite of this wealth, the industrious Cistercians personally led an austere life. They used most of their revenue for cultural and charitable purposes. Besides art and science, charity work for the poor, sick, and travelers passing through, consumed the economic power of the monastery, often to complete exhaustion.

During the Reformation, Elector Friedrich III of Heidelberg dissolved the Eußerthal Monastery in 1561 and transferred the administration of the monastery properties to an Electoral caretaker. In 1705, the income of the former Eußerthal Monastery was incorporated into the Catholic Spiritual Goods Administration of the Palatinate.

The manoral estate of the Monastery of Eußerthal in Ottersheim was located on the Hintergasse and included two manors and associated outbuildings. In all probability, these were the current properties 64 and 66 on the Lange Straße, which are still listed in the stock book of 1788 as a single property. One such property was transferred in 1595 as a hereditary estate to Ottersheim citizens Simon Nauerth and Petronella, the widow of Christof Deidesheimer, for 250 gulden and an annual property tax of 20 schillings plus two geese and two capons (fattened roosters). The second property was acquired by peasants Heinrich Dachenhäuser and Sebastian Degen for 250 gulden and other annual charges.

Included with the two manors were about 100 morgen of fields and meadows that were also given to citizens of Ottersheim as a long lease for which they had to pay 700 gulden in cash. The tenants also had to deliver a fuder of wine to the pastor of Ottersheim as a yearly tax, among other things. The tenants at that time were Mayor Hans Trauth and the peasants Velten Trauth, Jost Grünewald, and Melchior Velten Kuhn. The fields of the Eußerthal estate comprised 47 parcels that were up to 3 morgen in size. The parcels included 14 each in the Oberfeld and Niederfeld, 11 in the Obersand, 5 in the Mittelsand, and 3 in the Niedersand. The Eußerthal monks owned almost 10 morgen of meadows in the Ottersheim district. In 1723, Mayor Michael Rebstock and Rudolf Kröper were owners of the Eußerthal manor properties on the Große Gasse. At that time, the estate consisted of 91 morgen of fields and approximately 9 morgen of meadows. Regarding the delivery of goods required by the lease, the produce had to be delivered to the Eußerthal manor in Mörlheim, the Wendelinushof of today.

During the French Revolution, the Eußerthal estate was sold by the French State to private individuals. The two manors went without any formality to the owners of the houses while the fields and meadows were mostly purchased by the current tenants. Thus, the annual delivery of a fuder of wine to the pastor of Ottersheim came to an end.

The Hördt Cloisters in Ottersheim

Around 1100, Knight Hermann von Spiegelberg, whose castle stood east of Kramer's Mill in Bellheim, erected on his land in Hördt a parish church for the accommodation of the clergy, along with the necessary administrative buildings. The ministry was to be provided by the Augustinian Canonical Order. These were priests who led their lives as a community in the spirit of Saint Augustine with poverty, chastity, and obedience. Hördt was the first monastery of the Augustinian Canonical Order in the Diocese of Speyer. A school was connected with the monastery that was attended mainly by future knights.

On 9 February 1103, Hermann von Spiegelberg gave the Hördt Monastery to the Cathedral Church of Speyer. Bishop Johannes ordered that the convent should not be headed by a dean but by a pastor. For the maintenance of the clergy, the Noble von Spiegelberg gave the Augustinians his farm fields, vineyards, pastures, and forests in Hördt, Kuhardt, Bellheim, Ottersheim, and other nearby places. Further donations from lords of the nobility and from spiritual men followed over time. Thus in 1231, the Monastery of Hördt received from the Cleric Hugo from the Allerheiligenstift [All Saints Monastery] in Speyer, his manorial properties in Essingen and Ottersheim. In 1318, the Augustinian clerics leased all the properties of Katharina Rohrhaus, widow of Ulrich von Rohrhaus of Speyer, and delivered from these 200 malters of grain and 50 malters of spelt annually. These properties were in Knittelsheim and Ottersheim. In 1327, the heirs of the Rohrhaus properties relinquished their possessions in Ottersheim and Knittelsheim before the Council at Weißenburg in favor of the Monastery of Hördt. A year later, Provost Jakob von Hördt exchanged a monastery-owned property in Mühlhausen near Landau for a corresponding property in Ottersheim. This would complete the acquisition of land in the Ottersheim district by the Hördt Monastery. In the following period, the Provost of Hördt acquired a field only in isolated cases when one had been offered for sale by Ottersheim peasants. A document from 1543 describes a land exchange. At that time, the Ottersheim community gave the Provost of Hördt nine morgen of meadows, the "Auf den Stöcken" at the edge of the forest and received in return nine morgen of the "Biengarten" meadows as community meadows.

When Provost Wendelin von Remchingen died, Elector Friedrich III of Heidelberg occupied the Monastery of Hördt in 1566 and confiscated all its possessions. The Augustinians, who were devoted to the Catholic faith, were forcibly expelled from the convent. The possessions of the priory were secularized and from then on managed by a caretaker who was subordinate to the Spiritual Goods Administration in Heidelberg. It was not until the Napoleonic period that the properties were dispersed by the French State and auctioned to the highest bidder.

A series of documents from the 16th, 17th, and 18th centuries provide insight about the location, size, and amenities of the Hördt monastery in Ottersheim. According to these, the Provost of Hördt had two independent properties in Ottersheim that were next to each other but were separated from each other by the Riedgässel [Ottostraße] of today. The Hördt upper manor stood on the "Hintergasse" at the end of the current Lange Straße between the Ottostraße and the Riedstraße. Buildings present were a house, a courtyard, stables, several barns, and several outbuildings.

The upper manor was bordered in the front by the "common alley" and in the back by the Quotgraben. The present timber-framed house at 15 and 16 Lange Straße is probably the former living quarters of the Hördt upper manor, although the present building was probably not built until the 18th century. Apart from a large garden, three morgen of Brühl meadows that lay to the south of the manor courtyard belonged to the upper manor. Around the year 1600, it was reported that the Brühl was "discontinued and a meadow was made" of it.

The Hördt lower manor stood to the west of the Riedgässel. It is probably property 27 on the Lange Straße where Emil Hünerfauth now lives. This house still stands as the only building on the Lange Straße that is not set an equal distance from the street with the other houses but is set about 20 meters back. Like the upper manor, the lower manor consisted of a house, a courtyard, several stalls, and barns. The lower manor was bordered by the "Im Ried" to the west. It is thus clear that the two Hördt manors were not directly connected with the rest of the village but lay a bit away from the village center and the church. The lower manor also included three morgen of Brühl and was separated from meadows of the upper manor by a living fence. From a land plat sketch of 1765, we know that on the north side of the extended Ludwigstraße there was a well located at the border of the two manors that was in a bad state already at that time. Remains of walls were found in 1965 when digging the foundation for the new Frey building. The fact that there was a well at the east end of the Ludwigstraße also makes it understandable that not too long ago a water jug was found there at a building site. Experts have examined the pieces and put the age of the jug at about 600 years. This proves that a well stood on the Hördt manor property already in the 14th century.

In contrast to the common convention, the names *upper manor* and *lower manor* do not originate from their locations; otherwise, then the upper manor would face toward the Haardt and the lower manor would face toward the Rhine. In fact the name, *upper manor,* makes it clear that this manor played a privileged role in the administration of the monastery properties. Here is where the administrators of the Provost of Hördt sat and where they received the tithe goods from the tenants. It was not by chance that the upper manor stood next to the so-called *Zehntscheuer [Tithe barn]* on property 12. An old document speaks of a collecting location "wherein the tithes were initially brought."

The wood that was needed for the construction of houses, stables, barns, and sheds on the monastery courtyards came largely from the Hördt forests. This can be determined from a lawsuit in 1538 by Provost Sigismund von Wittstadt against the Hördt community over the Auwald forest. In the contract that was signed at that time is stated that: "Other than construction timber for the monastery buildings in Ottersheim and Knittelsheim, no wood could be freely removed from the district." It is therefore possible that one or another oak beam in current buildings came from the Hördt forests because for even new renovations the acceptable wood is reused.

Very extensive land holdings in Ottersheim belonged to each of the two monastery properties. According to a document from 1569, the upper manor owned 387 morgen of fields and meadows while the lower manor was slightly larger with 401 morgen of land. A record book from 1788 contains precise information about the distribution of the lands within the Ottersheim district. According to it, the cultivated land of the two manors consisted of 197 parcels of quite different dimensions: 70 parcels were in the Oberfeld, 76 in the Niederfeld, 29 in the Obersand, 9 in the Mittelsand, and 13 in the Niedersand. The Provost of Hördt owned, among other things:

	First area		Second area		Third area	
Am Altsheimer Weg:	12	morgen	6	morgen	3	morgen
Am Altsheimer Weg zum Scheid:	4.5	morgen	6	morgen		
In der Hochangewanne:	7	morgen	4	morgen	4	morgen
In den Kurzen Zwanzigmorgen:	12	morgen				
In den Zwanzigmorgen:	20	morgen				
In der Langgewanne:	15	morgen	8	morgen	3	morgen
Im Schlittweg:	9	morgen	8	morgen	1	morgen
In der Muld:	14	morgen				

Meadows belonging to the Provost of Hördt were 10 morgen in the Mühlwiesen and 9 morgen in the Stockwiesen, among others.

Had a land consolidation been carried out back then, the Hördt Monastery would have comprised a third of the cultivated fields and meadows or a quarter of the entire district with 189.6 hectares. And yet, the Augustinian Canonists hardly purchased any properties in addition to what was given to them by the nobility of the time. Such purchases are mentioned a few times in documents. For example, the widow Breid of Ottersheim sold a field to the monastery in 1508 for 30 gulden. Similar sales are reported in 1509 by Hans Michels and his wife, in 1596 by Martin Doll, in 1598 by Stefan Trauth, and in 1601 by Velten Doll.

Although the monastery with its rich farm lands was owned by the Augustinian Canonists in Hördt, they were probably never cultivated by members of the monastery. Rather, the farmyards and associated lands were leased out to local farmers who had to deliver grain, spelt, and other farm products to the Provost of Hördt. The Hördt Monastery assigned the oversight of the goods to an administrator. After secularization in 1566, the property was managed by an administrator. As tenants of the farms at that time, Georg Trauth and Jakob Antoni are mentioned. To avoid the costly obligations for maintaining the buildings, the two farmsteads were given as hereditary properties to a number of Ottersheim community residents in 1602 for a price of 4,674 gulden. In those days, 4,674 gulden was a considerable sum that one individual would not have been able to raise.

Therefore, an entire extended family took part in the purchase and also inhabited the farmsteads together. Some buildings were shared while others were divided by family. This went well as long as close family relationships existed. Difficulties arose at marriages or inheritances. Then they were forced to stake out boundaries or to erect new buildings. In such cases, it was possible that the exit from one house led over the yard of another as is still the case today for house numbers 2 and 4 on the Ottostraße.

The fields and meadows of the Hördt farms were leased for several years at a time to Ottersheim farmers. A list of tenants from the year 1602 has been preserved.

Peter Apfel	Jost Grünewald	Jost Schaller (his widow)
Adam Burggraf	Jost Hatzenbühler	Bernhard Steimer
(the farmer)	Hans Kuntz	Hans Steinlein
Heinrich Dachhäuser	Jost Lausch	Theobald Stibich
Bastian Degen	Georg Ludwig	Velten Trauth
Georg Doll (the old)	Jakob Ludwig	Lorenz Trauth
Georg Doll (the boy)	Jakob Metz	Hans Trauth
Martin Doll	Simon Moock	Stefan Trauth
Theobald Doll	Jakob Moock	Bernhard Trauth (his widow)
Velten Doll	Georg Nauhard	Wendel Trauth
Wendel Doll	Simon Nauhard	Georg Trauth
Mathäs Doll	Stefan Österreich	Simon Trauth
Georg Dörzapf	Jakob Renger	Peter Trimpler

On Saint Martin's Day, these farmers together had to deliver 190 malters of grain and 190 malters of spelt to the administrator of the Hördt Monastery, whereby the grain was usually driven to the convent barns in Hördt. The burden was acceptable considering that for every morgen of land about 1/2 malter of grain and 1/2 malter spelt were due for the lease. After the 30 Years War, the levy was reduced by almost half. Delivered in the years 1667-1669 were 100 malters of grain and spelt, 105 malters in 1670-1672, and in the following years 110 malters of grain and 110 malters of spelt. For the 12-year lease in the year 1742, the administrator demanded 123 malters of grain and 280 malters of spelt, and from 1780 until 1789 it was 155 malters of grain and 370 malters of spelt.

To simplify the leasing process, at least in the 18th century, all the fields and meadows of the monastery manor were divided into parcels called *Pflüge*. On average, one pflug amounted to about 15 morgen of farmland and 1.5 to 2 morgen of meadows. The Hördt estate included 46 pflüge. At public auctions, each pflug was given in lease to the highest bidder for 6, 9, or 12 years. But it was common that a given family leased the same parcel and therefore felt as though they owned or had inheritance rights to the piece even though it was in fact only time-leased.

In 1765, the Spiritual Goods Administration considered a strange plan. They wanted to build dwellings, barns, and stables for six tenant farmers on the monastery grounds on the far side of the Quotgraben in the eastern part of the Kleine Gasse. This would have meant building on the field from what is today the Raiffeisen warehouse up to the Riedstraße. Along the north side of the Kleine Gasse, six houses were planned, each with two rooms, a kitchen and a bedroom. Six barns were planned 60 meters to the north while the two sides were to be enclosed by horse, cattle, and pig stables. For each of the six barns was expected 16 to 18 horses and cattle, and 12 to 16 pigs. But soil tests revealed that the ground was rather poor for building. So the plan was to construct the farms to the south of this area between the Kleine Gasse and the district road. However, before the plan was implemented the French Revolution broke out. With this, the fate of the Hördt monastery was sealed forever.

The two properties were given to their former tenants as inheritance property. The tenants of the individual parcels were also allowed to keep their land for a moderate sum. But when the French found out through a detailed investigation that the Hördt properties were not hereditary but time-based leases, they demanded a back payment of 43,000 francs. Most likely, only some of the tenants were able to pay their portion in cash over the course of a few years. Thus, many fields and meadows changed owners through auction. A portion of the land went to outside bidders, but most fields and meadows were acquired by wealthy farmers from Ottersheim. In particular, former mayor of Ottersheim Johannes Kopf (Kopf-Maire) bought so much land that he could walk anywhere from the village exit up to the Kahlenberg and half way to Herxheim and still be on his own property.

The Ottersheim Spelt Property of the Cathedral Chapter of Speyer

Until the French Revolution, the Cathedral Chapter of Speyer had about 2 hectares of land in Ottersheim consisting of two fields and two pastures. One field of about 2 morgen lay in the Froschau and a second on the Haardt below the village. A meadow of about 2 morgen was located in the Hörsten and a smaller meadow in Schuster's Eck near the Rödel. It can no longer be determined who gave these fields and meadows to the Cathedral Chapter of Speyer. We know that the little property was in the possession of the Cathedral Chapter long before the year 1500. In 1502, it was given to citizens of Ottersheim as hereditary property. The lease consisted of four malters of spelt and was to be paid annually on the Blessed Mother's birthday, but it could also be settled with two malters of "white grain." A main collector had to bring the grain to the granaries at the Cathedral Chapter of

Speyer. Because the payment was always made with spelt through the centuries, the leased land was called the *Spelzengütlein [Little spelt parcel]*. The hereditary lease contract was renewed in 1591.

The tenant family had vanished after the 30 Years War. Therefore, the property was returned to the Cathedral Chapter that from then on only leased the fields and meadows as a time-based lease. So Cathedral Administrator Neudecker gave the spelt property in Ottersheim to Master Butcher Theobald Weber on a six year lease in 1742. After this lease elapsed, the property was given for nine years to Theobald Weber, Rudolf Knoll, Nikolaus Hatzenbühler, and Ludwig Busch. From 1773 on, only three malters of spelt had to be delivered as rent instead of four. The last tenants were Rudolf Hatzenbühler and Anton Knoll. Then in 1800, the French declared the fields and meadows to be national property of the French Republic and sold them to private individuals. The proceeds flowed into the French treasury.

The Community Hall in Ottersheim

The oldest building in Ottersheim is the community hall. If one is to believe the date on the archway at the entrance to the fire house, then the building was built in 1555. It is 63 years older than the Catholic Church that was built at the outbreak of the 30 Years War in 1618. The stately building was formerly called the *Rathaus [Town hall]* with pride. In a copy of the *Summary of Rights in the Village of Ottersheim from the year 1676* the following is said of this building:

> *"The community hall, which has stood for more than a hundred years for common use, at all times mortgage free, stands between the churchyard and the common road or street."*

It is no coincidence that the community hall emerged in the 16th century. This was a time of transition from medieval to modern times that has left its mark in our villages. The rural people felt more and more as citizens who wanted to have their community hall and mayor as did the city dwellers. So it is not surprising that at that time, new community halls were also built in other places and have been partially preserved to this day. The community halls were usually built in the center of the village near the church.

The Ottersheim community hall was formerly at the center of town. Before 1555, there was probably a large linden tree under whose leafy canopy the community citizens came together for meetings and court sessions. While the linden tree was not sacred to our ancestors it was revered. It was carefully nursed and when aged it was supported by rods or by stone substructures. Tables and benches that stood under the linden tree were made of stone slabs and built to outlast a lifetime. As we know from ancient records, a village well stood near where the community hall stands today. Here, the residents of the Deich and the

Hintergasse (Lange Straße) got their drinking water. The people of the lower village used their own well that was located in the eastern part of the Ludwigstraße at house number 45, that of Helmut Frey.

The construction of a community hall in 1555 was an important event for the small town of Ottersheim that counted about 300 souls. The new construction was probably actively supported by the Electoral District Office in Germersheim. The village residents had to cut and bring the sandstones free of charge. The stone walls are nearly two feet thick. That solid work was done here is shown by the 400 year history of the community hall. The outer walls had to be newly plastered from time to time during the many years, but they never had to be totally renewed. They will survive centuries to come provided they are not destroyed by force.

The community hall was intended in some ways to replace the former village linden tree. The meetings which previously were held under the linden tree now took place on the ground floor. These sessions had to be public. The ground floor of the community hall consisted of an open arbor to enable the whole community to participate. Such arcades can still be seen at the community halls in Leinsweiler and Ilbesheim. The Ottersheim community hall originally had an open hall on the ground floor, presumably in which stood stone benches. One could enter the arcade through archways. In the 19th century, at the wall to the east there were still three semi-circular openings instead of the current door and the two rectangular windows. In the center of the ground floor there was a round pillar with a simple capital upon which oak beams rested. This created a hall-like room that was open on three sides. Part of the previous column is still visible within the stone separating wall that was constructed on the ground floor in 1849.

From the arcade, a wooden staircase leads to the upper floor that originally consisted of one room where community affairs were discussed and decided. For example, the timber auctions and leasing of manorial estates took place here; and documents that provided insight into affairs of the community and its residents were kept there in a trunk. A community hall of this type is still preserved in its original form as a single space in Ilbesheim. It is currently used as a school hall. There probably was a detention room on the ground floor of the Ottersheim community hall from the beginning. For when an offender was arrested in Ottersheim, the mayor had to put him behind bars and report to the District Office. Not until requested was the offender taken to the castle prison in Germersheim. The community hall was also storage place for the tools used by the village court: the oath tablet, judge's staff, policeman's lance, and a stick for carrying out lower court punishments. Also, very probably the village scales and corresponding weights stood on the ground floor of the community hall.

The community hall and community square were also the center of village social life. While drawing the daily water supply, the latest events were discussed and experiences exchanged. On warm summer evenings, the elderly could get together for a chat on the

354

stone benches while the youth delighted in a folk dance. At the church dedication festival, dealers set up their booths in the community hall arcade while the fair visitors and local villagers enjoyed themselves on the square in front of the community hall. There was hardly any danger that the people would be disturbed in their celebration by vehicles passing through. In abnormal times, there may have been soldiers standing guard on the ground floor, but the community hall was at no time considered to be a fortress. Markets were also never held there because Ottersheim had at no time any rights to hold a market, with the exception of a horse market.

In the middle of the 19th century, the community hall was completely renovated and redesigned on the inside. The work began in 1849. First, a separating wall was constructed on the ground floor from north to south. While the western section was built as a shed for the fire engine, the eastern part was to be more usefully organized for the night watchmen. At this end, three separate rooms were created there, a guards' room, a detention room, and a wood pile room. The guards' room was equipped with a door while the window of the detention room was secured with bars. To protect the fire machine that had been purchased in 1846, the stone archway on the north side received a wooden gate. A part of the wall had to be knocked out to allow the gate to open and close. This leads to the assumption that the archway originally had no gate.

The upper floor that was formerly a single room was remodeled and refurnished in 1855. Three walls were added so that an office, a community hall room, and a lavatory were created. Then the stairs to the upper floor were renovated and a small window was added to the lavatory. The community hall was equipped with wicker chairs and a cupboard a year later. The outside plaster was renewed in 1861. More than 1,000 gulden were spent for the reconstruction and expansion of the village hall at that time. Since that time, the Ottersheim community hall has not undergone any more fundamental changes. In 1906, 18 new chairs were set up because the old ones had become useless. A central heating system was installed in 1947, and the building received the present exterior plaster in 1953.

It would be too bad should one day the community hall disappear entirely or give way to a new building. This oldest structure in the village should not be demolished because of its historical value, even if the local government should move to another building. One might even consider returning the arcade on the ground floor to their original form and remaking the upper story into a community archive. In any case, a community that has no older buildings than the church and the community hall should not shy away from the maintenance costs but should muster all that is needed to keep the 400 plus year old community hall for a long time.

The Old Cemetery

Before 1824, all the deceased of the Ottersheim community were buried on the raised ground around the present-day Catholic Church. This conformed to an old Christian custom to bury the dead as close as possible to the house of God, in testimony to the unity with the struggling, suffering, and triumphant Church. With the cemetery near the church, the faithful could easily visit the graves of their relatives after services and pray for their souls. In addition, it was customary at a funeral that the body was brought into the church and laid out before the altar. After the services for the deceased, the body was carried to the cemetery and buried. Setting up a *Tumba*[41] at the first Mass for the Dead reminds us of this custom that was common until recently.

Although the village of Ottersheim had little more than 300 residents in the Middle Ages, in the course of around 1,000 years a considerable number of dead have been buried in the churchyard. Since the beginning of the 18th century about 10 people died each year, and in the 19th century about 15 to 20 villagers. This number multiplied during epidemic years. For example, in 1794 alone 76 died and in 1822 a total of 54 people died. They all would have found their last resting place in the old cemetery. Under these circumstances, it was not possible to keep a grave for decades and beyond. Instead of grave stones, simple wooden crosses were used that could be easily removed. Moreover, the graves were hardly deeper than 60 centimeters [about 2 feet]. So it is not surprising that when digging new graves, bones of the dead often came to light. Unless an ossuary was present, as for example in Deidesheim, the bones were collected at a special place. Only so can be explained that numerous bones were found when digging the foundation of the nearby Sisters' Home.

It is said that the cemetery has been filled several times. The soil was taken from the Brühl meadows at the eastern end of the Kleine Gasse. In fact, the old cemetery was enlarged only once after the construction of the present church in 1618 and that was during the expansion of the church in 1789. At that time, the cemetery previously ended at about the side entry ways of the church, so it was extended to the west and surrounded with a new wall. A lot of soil had to be brought in to align the newly acquired piece of land to the existing cemetery. Other cemetery fillings of which the locals speak refer to the new cemetery where in fact many a load of soil was added in the years 1859 and 1867. The artificial hill near the church was at its present height at least since 1618; otherwise, the base of the nave would stick much deeper into the ground. Also, the height of the cemetery cross, which was set up in 1747 under Pastor Uth, fits well with the surrounding terrain. Its base does not indicate that soil was heaped up around it several times.

Because of its value as historical art, the impressive cemetery cross was illustrated and described in the book "Kunstdenkmäler der Pfalz" [Art Treasures of the Palatinate]. On its base is the following sentence:

ICh hab gefUnDen beII ChrIstI WUnDeN eWIg rUhlge StUnDen.
[Ich habe gefunden bei Christi Wunden ewig ruhige Stunden.]
[I have found in Christ's wounds eternally quiet hours.]

Of the capital letters in the inscription there are 3 - D's, 2 - C's, 4 - U's (as V's), 2 - W's (as double V's), and 7 - I's. If one considers these as Latin (Roman) numerals then one can calculate: 3 x 500, plus 2 x 100, plus 4 x 5, plus 2 x 5 x 2, plus 7 x 1 resulting in 1747.[91] At the foot of the cross, we see Adam and Eve pleading to the crucified Savior for salvation from purgatory. In 1853, the cross was repaired by a mason and a blacksmith. The famous parish benefactor, widow Knöll née Burck, had it renewed from the ground up in 1898. Another renovation was carried out under pastor Knöll in 1931.

The cemetery was used as a burial place for the last time in the years 1822 and 1823. We are told that at that time the cemetery was completely covered with graves. During that period, an epidemic had claimed no fewer than 54 victims. So it is understandable that the call for a new and larger burial ground became more and more urgent. Actually, the community would have been required to place the cemetery outside the village during the Napoleonic period. An Imperial Decree of 1804 regarding funerals had prescribed specifically that no more burials should take place in churches, chapels, or within boundaries of populated areas for reasons of hygiene. Rather, new burial grounds should be created 35 to 40 meters outside the city wall in all places. Many towns and villages in those days complied with this order and moved the cemeteries. In Ottersheim, more time was taken until a state of emergency forced them to act. The new cemetery at the western exit of the village was dedicated by Pastor Märdian in 1824.

The former cemetery was left in its old state for the time being. It was not until 1854 that it was leveled and laid out in the manner of an English garden. It was provided with paths and planted with shrubs. Seven horse chestnut trees were planted to eventually provide shade for visitors. The three existing grave stones of Peter Burgermeister, Barbara Gutting, and Eva Maria Winkelblech were left standing. At that time, the cemetery was considered an ornament of the church and the entire village. A lattice fence was even added to protect the gardens. Two slatted gates allowed entry to the cemetery. However, less joy was experienced with the cemetery wall. As early as 1835, the 14 meter-long piece south of the church threatened to collapse. It had to be removed and replaced. An almost equally long piece along the Germersheimer Straße had become dilapidated by 1859. Mason Adam

---

[91] It is no coincidence this calculates to the year the crucifix was erected in the cemetery.

Winkelblech of Ottersheim was commissioned to demolish it and rebuild it from the ground up. It is possible that the wall was set back somewhat at this time. In any case, the wall was not built in alignment with the old wall. There is no mention of transport costs for removal of leftover soil in the invoices however. This could lead to the assumption that at this site the wall already had one knee.

Although the community set aside an annual amount for the care of the cemetery grounds, it could not be avoided that the grounds slowly became overgrown. This development was fostered especially during the turbulent years of the First World War and the years thereafter. This led then Deputy Mayor Konrad Hoffmann, with the help of unemployed, to thoroughly renew the cemetery in 1925 by creating new pathways, and planting young trees and ornamental shrubs. The maintenance of the cemetery was also of special concern for Pastor Knöll (1929-1939). He had the grounds dug up and decorated with flowers and shrubs in 1931.

During the horrors of World War II, Katharina Kopf of Ottersheim decided to give her hometown a statue of Saint Konrad of Parzham as a gift. Brother Konrad (1818-1894) came from a family with many children and was a simple gateman in the Capuchin Convent at Altötting for over 40 years. Miss Kopf wanted to entrust the village to the intercession of this saint during and after the difficult years of the war. The statue was made by a blind artist in Blieskastel and was brought to Ottersheim during the war. To protect it from destruction by bombs it was initially buried in the old cemetery. Not until after the war did it find its final place in the northern part of the church yard. After the Second World War, the statue of Saint Konrad von Parzham was set up in the northern part of the cemetery.

In her youth, Miss Kopf was active as a supporter of the future Bishop Busch in Speyer. However, severe muscle disease forced her to abandon her position and return home. Since no doctor could help her, she sought and found healing on a pilgrimage to Lourdes. After her recovery, Miss Kopf was a nurse in the mental hospital of Klingenmünster for 33 years. In 1908, she had a Lourdes grotto erected in the church tower in gratitude. She had bought the statue at Lourdes. It now adorns her own grave in the new cemetery.

In 1945, the old cemetery was again put to its original use after more than 120 years. At that time, former pastor Jakob Knöll of Ottersheim was laid to rest behind the cemetery cross. How it came about is so memorable that it deserves to be handed down to coming generations. From 1929 to 1939, Pastor Knöll was in charge of the Catholic parish in Ottersheim. At the age of 29, which he counted at his installation, he was the first young pastor in Ottersheim for many decades. He soon won the esteem of the whole community through his zeal, his simplicity, his modesty, and his selfless love. His transfer in 1939 to Landau as parish priest shortly before the outbreak of the Second World War was seen very reluctantly. In his rectory at Saint Maria's Church, he was the victim of an enemy air attack on 16 March 1945. Pastor Knöll had sought protection in the basement of the rectory with his family. A bomb destroyed the house and buried the people beneath it. The responsible

358

offices in Landau gratefully accepted an offer of help to exhume the deceased and to bring him to Ottersheim. It was not possible to do the digging during the day due to artillery and air attacks.

Therefore, on the evening of 19 March 1945 and the Feast of Saint Joseph, about 50 Ottersheim men, women, and girls came together to exhume their former pastor. They saw a sad scene of destruction upon arriving in Landau. The rectory was reduced to a pile of rubble with the exception of the entry way. The search for Pastor Knöll and his dead relatives began by the thunder of artillery and the light of the moon. While the men risked their lives digging a path downward with picks and shovels, the women and girls prayed constantly for the success of the work. After the brother of the pastor and two other deceased persons were removed, and after a long and difficult search, they finally found Pastor Knöll whose feet were covered by a large stone. It was midnight before the corpse could be removed and laid on a makeshift stretcher. Some messengers rushed to Ottersheim to get a wagon that arrived at about 3 o'clock in the morning in Landau. The dead were immediately brought to Ottersheim where they were placed in the rectory. The burial had to be postponed to the evening of 20 March 1945 because of the air raids and bombings.

At 9 o'clock in the evening, the whole community gathered in the church where Pastor Knöll lay before the altar. Two candles burned on the coffin. Because the electric power had failed, these two candles were the only lighting in the church. After prayers and hymns, the coffin was accompanied by the deeply mourning believers and carried from the church to the cemetery. At night, he was lowered into the grave with no bells, eulogy, cross, or relatives. Only the silver moon hung over the cemetery and shared the great grief of the bystanders as they bid farewell forever to the highly respected and beloved priest.

The New Cemetery

At the west end of the village and to the south of Landauer Straße lies the new cemetery of Ottersheim. The land was purchased in 1824 by the community for about 200 gulden because the old cemetery at the Catholic Church was no longer sufficient. The cemetery was extended twice over time. In 1866, the community purchased the adjacent field to the west from Theobald Knoll for 926 gulden, and in 1870 an additional property of Jakob Günther also to the west. The original cemetery was dedicated by Pastor Märdian (1817-1839) and the two extensions by Pastor Dotterweich (1863-1875). The new cemetery was also used from the beginning by Catholics and Protestants alike as was the old cemetery.

On the north side, the cemetery is bordered by a handsome stone wall and an iron lattice gate while it is bordered on the sides and back by a living fence. The two-meter wide iron gate was made in 1849 and cost 54 gulden. Already in 1828 a large cemetery cross was erected bearing the following inscription:

"Weder Holz noch Stein beten wir an, nur Jesum, der gestorben daran."
[Neither wood nor stone do we worship, only Jesus who died on it.]

This cross was renovated in 1932 under Pastor Knöll (1929-1939). The attentive observer will not fail to notice that the rear part of the cemetery is higher than the surrounding fields. Already in 1859, 190 cubic meters of earth were brought in to fill the back of the original church yard and this was followed by a total of 344 cubic meters of additional landfill soil in 1867.

Thirty years after its the dedication, all the graves at the new cemetery were still marked with a simple wooden cross. In 1853, Elisabeth Cambeis had the first grave stone installed for deceased pastor Rudolf Märdian. This example was followed little by little by more affluent residents of the village. Today, the cemetery is tastefully decorated with numerous grave stones that were mostly erected in the past few decades. Among the few grave monuments from the 19th century is a grave stone with the name of Ludwig Steegmüller of Weingarten (1797-1860) that still stands in the back row. This is the ancestor of all Steegmüllers in Ottersheim and Göcklingen. The graves of the Catholic priests who died in Ottersheim are still fairly well preserved. Until now, seven local priests have found their resting place at the new cemetery. They are:

Pastor	Rudolph Märdian	died 1839
Pastor	Johannes Pfeiffer	died 1859
Pastor	Joh. Georg Ullrich	died 1863
Pastor	Matthäus Dotterweich	died 1875
Pastor	Sebastian Ettmüller	died 1896
Pastor	Joh. Rudolf Schwarz	died 1909
Pastor	Heinrich Theobald Eckel	died 1916

The priests Ettmüller, Schwarz, and Eckel, who most recently passed away, were buried immediately at the cemetery cross while the graves of the earlier priests lie to the east of the cross. Before the cemetery was expanded, they of course lay in the middle of the cemetery with their dead parishioners. Deacon Steegmüller, who most recently had been Spiritual Council in Edenkoben, was laid to rest in 1951 and the only clergyman buried to the west of the cross. As a son and honorary citizen of Ottersheim where he spent his youth and his retirement years, he desired to be buried in his home community. Very few of the many teachers who were active in Ottersheim have been buried at the new cemetery. The grave of Protestant teacher Ludwig Ecarius (died 1877) no longer exists. By contrast, the grave of head teacher Jakob Jäger of Arzheim (died 1929) is still in good condition. In 1966, teacher Gertraud Richter was buried in the new cemetery. After the Second World War, relatives of fallen soldiers created a simple hero's grave and adorned it with a steel helmet in memory of their beloved dead who rest in foreign soil. A young oak tree was planted at the head of the memorial. The Iron Cross that hangs from the oak tree is to remind people of the sacrifices that the dead made for their homeland. On All Saints Day, when the whole community marches with brass-band music to the flower-decorated cemetery, the prayers include those who rest in foreign soil far from home. The ceremony for the dead ends each year when *Lied vom guten Kameraden [Song of the Good Comrade]* is played for them.

The Post Station in Ottersheim

An auxiliary post office was established in Ottersheim on 14 March 1899. It was located in the annex of the "Zur Traube" Restaurant that belonged to Lorenz Föhlinger who was mayor at the time. The auxiliary post office was converted into a post office substation on 15 November 1900 and was initially supervised by the mayor's daughter, Auguste Föhlinger Heist. While earlier a postman walked from Bellheim to Ottersheim and brought the mail to the homes of the recipients, now the postmaster in Ottersheim assumed this task. Beginning in 1900, a small postal car traveled regularly on weekdays between Bellheim and Ottersheim bringing the letters, parcels, and newspapers while taking the outgoing mail. Because this postal car took only mail and not persons, the community had already expressed the wish for a postal bus in 1902. This wish was not fulfilled so that people had to get to Offenbach, Landau, Bellheim, or Germersheim by walking until 1921. Only those who had their own horse and carriage could spare themselves the walk.

In 1901, the Ottersheim post office received a telephone line so that anyone could talk with friends and relatives in other places when necessary. The private connections of country produce retailer Philipp Benz, innkeeper Theobald Bischoff, and seed dealer Konrad Hoffmann followed hesitently. In 1908, the City Council decided that a telephone in the community hall was unnecessary because three private connections were present in the village in addition to the public telephone station. Fifty years later, there were telephones not only in all public offices and businesses but also in many private residences. There was a total of 27 telephones in 1965. The phone booth at the community hall was set up in 1967.

In contrast to post offices, the postal substation in Ottersheim never had its own building. Each postmaster instead had to set up a room in his home as a mail room. Here, the people could bring cards, letters, and packages to be mailed, buy postage stamps, and transfer money. In addition, a mail box at the community hall provided people the opportunity to mail their letters and cards at any time of the day. This was especially important when the post station was located on the Ludwigstraße in the upper village or in the Gröhlig.

The first postal bus line of the Palatinate was begun in 1909 between Landau and Eschbach, while Ottersheim had to wait until 1921 to get such transportation. While talks were held in 1912 between the community and the postal administration in Landau on this topic, they remained without result from 1914 to 1918 because of the war. Finally the time had come, the first postal bus traveled from Landau via Ottersheim to Neupotz on 1 March 1921. After World War II, traffic increased more and more so that the line had to run several times a day. So it was, the coach was highly used by students from the villages of Hördt, Bellheim, Knittelsheim, and Offenbach to get to the secondary schools in Landau. The post bus is still a popular and affordable transportation means for bringing commuters daily to their workplace.

Where before the year 1900 there was no postal substation, without a doubt the residents of Ottersheim still mailed and received their letters, although the amount of mail was significantly smaller than today. Whoever in the Middle Ages desired to forward an oral or written message had to hire a messenger, unless friends or relatives took the message as a favor during a trip. In 1508, Emperor Maximilian with the help of the Thurn and Taxis families set up a regular messenger service for the first time between his widely separated dominions. The public postal system later developed from this. From the District Office of Germersheim, we are told that in the early 17th century post riders brought the correspondence between the larger towns, while post drivers took over transportation of packages towards the end of the century. By the middle of the 18th century, there were already 'extra' postmen who traveled between Landau and Germersheim and accepted letters and packages as needed and forwarded them.

The central post office was administered by an official messenger in the 18th century. Thus we read that in 1792 the application of the Reformed congregation for approval of the church building in Ottersheim was brought by the Klingenmünster messenger to Germersheim and was delivered there to the post office. When the French occupied the left bank of the Rhine, news delivery was organized according to the French model. In Germersheim, a canton messenger was hired who had to organize delivery between the central district city and the various rural communities. This district messenger brought the official mail to the mayor offices twice a week and took the outgoing mail. When the Palatinate went to Bavaria in 1816, the messenger service based on districts or cantons had

362

basically remained the same. The messengers were now called *Landboten [District messengers]* and were distinguished by a brass plate on the left side of the shirt. The district messengers reported to the rural police stations that hired and paid them. They had to deliver official mail to the recipients free of charge. Therefore, the municipalities were obliged to raise a portion of the messengers' salaries. The messengers were also permitted to take private mail as long as it did not interfere with their official service. They could charge a fee for private letters for which an amount was not specified. Generally, 2 kreutzers were paid for the forwarding of a letter. On 1 November 1849, the first postage stamps were introduced in Bavaria and thus also in the Palatinate.

Beginning on 24 October 1816, a parcel wagon came through Ottersheim every fourth day. It traveled from Speyer via Germersheim to Landau and from there via Neustadt and Bad Dürkheim to Kaiserslautern. The round trip took 40 hours, whereby the horses and the coachmen were replaced in the larger cities. Nine horses and three carriages were stationed at the Germersheim post stall. Landau also had a post stall at that time. In addition, a messenger had to ride from Germersheim to Landau three times a week to get the mail. Only letters and packages were transported between Landau and Germersheim until the year 1855. Then a horse-drawn bus was introduced that also took passengers for remuneration. This post bus traveled twice daily between Landau and Germersheim. In doing so it also traveled through Ottersheim. Old and young garnered pleasure in the handsome postilion who drove his yellow coach carefully over the rough pavement. He announced his coming with a signal call from his post horn.

When the *Landau-Germersheim Railway Line* started operation in 1872, travel by post bus on this route was halted. The *Germersheim-Lauterburg Line* was opened four years later. Since that time, a postman from Bellheim had to bring the mail on foot to Ottersheim to distribute it to the recipients. He had to voluntarily report to the mayor's office and perform the mail service free of charge, as did the former *Landbote* or district messenger. For this, the community contributed their share to the postman's salary. Private mail could be deposited in a mailbox that was attached to the community hall. All municipalities were required to install such mail boxes since 1858. Whoever needed stamps had to buy them from the postman. Of the last postman from Bellheim named Settelmeyer, it is said that he did not take a lot of care in distributing the mail in Ottersheim. It was therefore generally welcomed when the post station was established in the village at the turn of the century. Now the mail was delivered regularly and conscientiously, and one did not need to wait for the postman to buy a stamp. It was now also possible to mail packages in Ottersheim that previously was allowed only in Bellheim or Landau.

The postmasters in Ottersheim

Auguste Heist née Föhlinger   1899-1902
> The post station was located in the annex of the "Zur Traube" Inn,
> at 79 Lange Straße. Valentin Föhlinger helped to deliver the mail.

Valentin Leingang   1902-1909
> The post station was located at 6 Ludwigstraße from 1902 to 1906
> and at 79 Lange Straße from 1906-1909.

Franz Ludwig Job, Mayor   1909-1913
> The post station was located at 5 Ludwigstraße.

Wilhelm Seither   1913-1917
> The post station was located in the "Zum Pflug" Inn at 58 Lange
> Straße

Eduard Heider and Emma Heider née Kaiser, married Freudenstein   1917-1945
> The post station was located at 89 Lange Straße. When Emma
> Heider moved to 102 Lange Straße after her marriage, the post
> station was also moved there.

Eduard Jeckel   1945-1955
> The post station was located at 29 Germersheimer Straße. Jeckel
> was previously a broker for farm products.

Karl Herrmann and Anna Herrmann   1955 —
> The post station is located at 6 Germersheimer Straße. Postmaster
> in civil service rank is Karl Herrmann while his sister as an
> employee saw that the mail was delivered. The Post Office pays rent
> for the postal space.

Note: The last Landau Postillion, Heinrich Gensheimer, was born in Ottersheim.
Before the First World War, his yellow post coach was part of the 'street landscape' in
Landau. In his lifetime, Gensheimer drove many very important persons, including the
last King of Bavaria, Ludwig III. He died in August 1940 at the age of 71 years.

Guest Houses (Inns) in Ottersheim

That there were already guest houses in Ottersheim centuries ago is attested in the *Electoral Summary of Rights in Ottersheim from 1565.* Therein is stated specifically that the Electoral Palatinate in Ottersheim is entitled to *das Ungelt [the Tax],* as with other villages within the Germersheim District. This tax was mainly a beverage tax that was levied mostly on wine and beer. No innkeeper was allowed to bring in a barrel of wine or beer without the knowledge of the Germersheim Office. Rather, he was required to let the tax collector know, show him the barrel, and swear under oath what the beverage cost him and what other expenses it engendered. According to the tax rules of Elector Friedrich II from 1549, the tax on a liter of beer or wine was set at 1 pfennig. A fuder could be compensated with two gulden and eight albus, or two pfund. Every 14 days, the tax collector settled accounts with the innkeeper in the presence of the mayor. He put the money into a locked box that was opened on a quarterly basis at the District Office and emptied.

A census from the year 1792 counted three *Schildwirte [signed innkeepers]* in Ottersheim. These were taverns or inns that were approved by the District Office and were denoted by a *Schild [sign].* Unlike a vintner or wine cellar owner, who was only allowed to sell his own products, the sign innkeepers got their beverages from the wine merchants and breweries. The three inns in Ottersheim were:

> The "Zur Krone" Inn at 66 Lange Straße
> The "Zur Traube" Inn at 79 Lange Straße
> The "Zum Pflug" Inn at 59 Lange Straße

The "Zur Krone" [To the Crown] Inn is derived from the former Eußerthal Monastery that passed into state ownership in 1561. This monastery property most likely offered both board and lodging to travelers from its founding, and the Eußerthal Monastery was especially obliged to provide hospitality to transients as owners of the Ottersheim parish. This tradition continued even when the two properties changed as hereditary property to private owners in 1595. Foreigners and locals gathered in the large rustic dining room for a glass of wine or beer. The profit margin for the innkeepers was small so that only the affluent could afford to own and operate an inn. The "Zur Krone" seems to have been a central location for the social life in the 18th century because three generations of owners were also the mayor of Ottersheim. These mayors were Michael Rebstock, Wendel Müller, and Georg Müller. One of them expanded the ground floor of the inn by adding a window to the west so that additional space was gained. Since there was no office for the mayor in the community hall at that time, the mayor's official duties were carried out in these rooms. It is therefore not surprising the record book from 1788 was kept in this house to the present-day. The "Zur Krone" closed its doors to guests and passing tourists after the death of its owner in 1870.

Another of the old inns in Ottersheim is the "Zur Traube" [To the Grape] that was adjacent to the Klingenmünster feudal manor. If we are to believe the date that is over the entry to the cellar, then the decorative half-timbered structure was built in 1609. Its builder was very likely then Mayor Peter Trimpler who led the construction of the new church in 1618. In its day, this inn was definitely the biggest and most beautiful building of the village. Here, not only the men and young men of the community gathered for discussions and entertainment, but the inn was also a refreshing rest stop for passers-through because this house stood immediately on the through street between Landau and Germersheim. Throughout the 19th century, "Zur Traube" was the most important meeting place for locals and outsiders. Preachers and teachers, mayors and council members, farmers and craftsmen, all came on Sundays and on long winter evenings to play cards and seek entertainment with wine and beer. The well-run kitchen was known far and wide so that outsiders also enjoyed stopping here. In spite of the brisk business, profits were not high. So it is understandable that Ludwig Föhlinger, as heir of the house, let the business die in 1917 after the death of his parents.

The third inn that was run by an inn keeper in the 18th century was the "Zum Pflug" [To the Plow] at 59 Lange Straße. Records from the year 1785 show that auctions were held there. This guest house was closed in 1878. The premises were later used for the post station.

The "Zur Pfalz" [To the Palatinate] Inn seems to have been erected on the site of the former Poppelmann manor at 15 Germersheimer Straße around the year 1800. Its owner at the time was Konrad Hatzenbühler who was agent (mayor) of Ottersheim from 1797 to 1800. Since this property belonged to the Palatinate for centuries, the name "Zur Pfalz" is not a surprise to history experts. The restaurant remained in operation until 1875. Then the "Zum Hirsch" [To the Deer] Inn took over the tradition of the "Zur Pfalz." This inn was opened in 1875 by Peter Zwißler at 13 Germersheimer Straße. The "Zum Hirsch" was the only inn at the time that possessed a large room that could be used as a theater and dance hall. Georg Jochim took over the inn from his father in 1902 and set up a butcher shop next to the inn. He had the ballroom expanded eastward in 1930 and added a 9-pin bowling alley. The last time the restaurant was redesigned was in 1960 when the hall and dining room were connected by a sliding door and the butcher shop was made a little larger.

The newest restaurant in Ottersheim is the "Zum Gambrinus" [To the God of Beer]. It was built in 1895 by Theobald Bischoff at 81 Lange Straße on the grounds of the former fortifications. Previously, Bischoff had operated the "Zum Engel" [To the Angel] Inn on the Riedgässel that was popularly known as the "Alm" [Pasture]. The "Zum Gambrinus" was located on the ground floor near the south gated entrance while upstairs there was a dance hall. Edmund Bischoff, the son of the builder, opened a butcher shop next to his inn in

1914. The dance hall was extended by half in 1925. The inn was remodeled most recently in 1954, during which the gated entrance on the south side was removed. This space was added to the main dining room as an annex.

While the "Zum Hirsch" and "Zum Gambrinus" are currently the only guesthouses in the village, in addition to the cafe-restaurant *Becki* that opened in 1966, the "Zum Schwanen" [To the Swan] Inn closed in 1964. The building was built in 1887 by Christine Job at 18 Lange Straße and was used as an inn immediately upon its completion. Son-in-law Franz Böhm took over the "Zum Schwanen" in 1899. Then ownership went to Jean Bentz and his wife Therese née Hitschler in 1928, who in turn passed it on to Otto Merdian in 1935. It is probable that the building that previously stood on this spot already was an inn with a small guest room. A hall was not available. Old people can still remember how the landlord at that time had an original method to overcome this. During the church dedication festival, he simply blocked off the village street in front of his house, laid boards over the pavement, and stretched a tarp over the dance floor. He left a pathway open on the opposite side of the street for pedestrians only. This "bear stall" as it was jokingly called was popular with locals and outsiders alike and was a central location for church dedication festival activities. There was no need to worry about traffic at that time because during the church dedication festival there were no vehicles to be seen on the streets.

While there were usually three taverns in Ottersheim during the 18th and 19th centuries, in the 20th century there were about a dozen. It is amazing when you consider that the people were quite poor at that time and had better uses for their money than for wine, beer, and liquor. Partly to blame for this trend seems to be the legislation that was much more generous in the approval of taverns than the Palatine Electors of yore. Apparently there was a perception that each village street should have its inn. As previously mentioned, the "Zum Engel" Inn, which the people called the "Alm," was in operation at Riedgässel number 6 until 1896. The building stood on the site of the former lower courtyard of the Hördt monastery. The "Englischer Garten" [English Garden] Corporation in Landau bought the Riedgässel Inn during 1889 from former owner Georg Konrad Reichling. The new landlord hired Theobald Bischoff to run it. In 1892, Joseph Merdian wanted to manage the inn. The council approved the proposal because it was thought that the "Zum Engel" Inn exhibited the "nicest furnishings." However, following the opening of the "Zum Gambrinus," the inn on the Riedgässel closed its doors forever.

There was another inn at the site of the former Hördt lower courtyard in the 19th century at 27 Lange Straße. It seems not to have been of great importance. Most recently it was operated by the "Kanierbawett."[92] The upper village also had its own inn at 93 Lange Straße. Even the Waldstraße did not want to miss out. Its residents met in the evenings at house number 17 where a certain Kerp served wine, beer, and liquor. Of this host was told that he once went to the Haardt to buy wine. As the full barrel was already on the cart, he

---

[92] The most senior resident of Ottersheim indicates *Kanierbawett* is a local reference to Barbara Seither.

pulled out his wallet and behold it was empty. The winemaker was of the opinion Kerp had forgotten to put in the necessary money. Although the buyer wanted to unload the barrel, the seller asked him to take the wine and pay for it later. Only with mock disgust did Kerp accept this proposal. However, the wine grower is still waiting for the agreed price!

In the 19th century, the Gröhlig also had its own inn at 25 Germersheimer Straße. To be sure, the "Zur Sonne" [To the Sun] shed no warming rays on the local residents but it did supply the thirsty with wine, beer, and liquor. Presumably the "Zur Sonne" Inn was closed in 1883. Finally, there was also once a "Zum Löwen" [To the Lion] in Ottersheim. This inn was at 15 Ludwigstraße. From the former landlady, Gretel Augustin, the following 'ditty' is still sung today:

> "And the Kaspern [daughter of Kaspar Detzel] says Fäje [threads], and Gretel Augustin has only Mäje [girls]."

Most of these inns were already closed by 1892. A report from that time states that in Ottersheim there were still four inns. These four were listed, "Zur Traube," "Zum Schwanen," "Zum Engel," and "Zum Hirsch." Of these four inns, only the "Zum Hirsch" has survived to the year 1967. The second village inn that still exists today is the "Zum Gambrinus" that was built in 1895. Herbert Becki opened a cafe-restaurant in 1966 at 94 Lange Straße. So that Ottersheim currently has three public inns or restaurants.

Blacksmiths in Ottersheim

Schmied [Blacksmith] and *Müller [Miller]* were the first craftsmen in our villages. Therefore, the names Schmied (Schmitt, Schmidt, Schmitz) and Müller are among the most common family names in Germany. Ottersheim also had a village blacksmith very early. He had to shod horses, attach wheels to carts, forge plowshares, make nails and chains, sharpen scythes, and much more. In early times, no farmer could do without a blacksmith. It is therefore understandable that every community ensured they had a blacksmith and provided him with a community-owned workshop for a small fee. A document dated 1674 states that in Ottersheim such a blacksmith shop stood "at the large stream" near the Weet. It had always been free from taxation. Owner of the workshop at the time was blacksmith Hans Jakob Rebstock who paid 1 gulden annually to the community for the little house.

The site of this ancient village smithy was property 21 on the Germersheimer Straße where Albert Kröper now lives. Before the present building was erected in 1956, the forge area was still clearly visible. The forge was at the front of the house and was originally entered from the village street through a large gate. So the blacksmith was easy to find from outside by wagoners. The house itself was behind the workshop and was set apart from it in width and height. The village blacksmith shop was in the possession of the Dörzapf family over several generations. Shortly before his death in 1873, Andreas Dörzapf gave up his business and sold the blacksmith business to Konrad Kröper who continued it until 1890. After Konrad Kröper, Johann Kröper took over all the equipment and used it to set up a new facility at 18 Germersheimer Straße. This shop still exists today and is run by the grandson of Johann Kröper. Konrad Kröper converted the old blacksmith shop into a room that was intended to serve as his retirement home. But before the table that was intended for the room could be constructed, Konrad Kröper died in April 1891. Of his two sons, neither was allowed to perform any blacksmith work according to a written agreement between Konrad Kröper and Johann Kröper. And so it happened that the ancient village blacksmith workshop at the Weet was probably closed for good in 1890.

Until the beginning of the 18th century, there was only this one blacksmith workshop in Ottersheim. But when the number of village residents more than doubled during the course of the 18th century, so also did the number of artisans grow. There were verifiably three blacksmiths in Ottersheim in 1791. One of them was Philipp Scherff who had moved here in 1775 from Bodenheim in present-day Rheinhessen. This Scherff lived at 42 Lange Straße where he probably also had his workshop. His descendant practiced the craft at 3 Ludwigstraße next to the Protestant Church until 1904.

A blacksmith was located at 18 Lange Straße during the second half of the 19th century where later the "Zum Schwanen" Inn stood. It was opened by Johann Job and was operated until his death in 1884. To this day, a grinding wheel by the village stream in front of the Schwaab home reminds of this blacksmith workshop. Peter, the son of Andreas Dörzapf, learned the blacksmith trade from the village blacksmith at the Weet, "Jobeschmied" [the blacksmith named Job]. Peter Dörzapf then opened a blacksmith shop at 40 Lange Straße behind the Hoffmann seed business. His son, Josef Dörzapf, later took over this business and continued to run it into the sixties of our century. Another blacksmith shop once stood at 27 Lange Straße. It belonged to Fritz Gensheimer, also called *Fritzelschmied.* That shop was closed in the twenties of this century. It had opened in 1880.

The newest blacksmith shop in Ottersheim was opened in 1919 at 3 Ottostraße. Its owner, Alois Gadinger, learned the blacksmith trade before the First World War from Franz Kröper at 18 Germersheimer Straße. As an apprentice, he had to work from 6 o'clock in the morning to 9 o'clock in the evening and received 50 pfennigs weekly during his first year. Because Gadinger was not busy enough in Ottersheim, he worked from 1923 on, four days a week, in the training workshop of the state education center in Queichheim, until he had to give up his duties there in 1946. His son, Hubert, took over the Ottersheim workshop in 1953 and ran it until 1960. Then he converted the workshop into an automated turnery. So this blacksmith shop is the latest to fall victim to technological progress. As in previous centuries, Ottersheim had only a single fully operational blacksmith shop in 1967. The limited demand in farming could scarcely support a second blacksmith shop in the long run.

The discussion of the horse shoe smiths would not be complete without mentioning the tinsmiths who appear in Ottersheim for the first time at the turn of the century as independent craftsmen. The first tin smith of the village was Jakob Zwißler who opened his business at 52 & 53 Lange Straße in 1892. His work consisted less in patching damaged household appliances than in making new buckets, watering cans, pots, roof gutters, etc. The workshop was associated with a general store where you could buy almost everything that can be used in a farmhouse. Electrician Karl Dumser from Herxheim married into the business in 1919. Although for many years no one has been engaged in the tinsmith business, people still bought their goods "at the tinsmith's."

In 1898, Jakob Walk opened a tinsmith shop at 10 Germersheimer Straße where his father previously made wooden clogs. His son, Alois, was an electrician and took over the business after his father's death. This workshop included a general store where you could buy everything from the flower vase to a motorcycle.

The Master Vehicle Mechanic Otwin Zwißler could be called the modern "smith" as he has operated a farm machinery and auto repair shop, including a gas station, at 39 Germersheimer Straße since 1956. As the blacksmith was once responsible for horse and wagon, the vehicle mechanic is responsible for tractors and vehicles of all kinds, and he also supplies the "food" for the gas and diesel engines of these modern horses. Thus, workshops reflect the technical development and changes in the farming business.

Bakers in Ottersheim

According to statistics from 1791, there was at the time no *Bäcker [Baker]* in Ottersheim. A baker was not absolutely necessary because in earlier times each family baked its own bread. A brick oven still stood in many houses in the thirties of our century. By contrast, now one can only occasionally find such an oven in the kitchen, basement, or in an annex. Friday was the day for baking for many farm wives at one time. The baking form was set up in the kitchen and filled with sifted flour on the evening before. Then the so-called *pre-dough* was stirred then mixed with sour dough and a bit of yeast. The actual baking began at dawn. Water was added to the flour in the baking form and the mixture was thoroughly kneaded by hand. Once the dough had "risen" enough, the bread loaves were formed on the baking tray then set into straw baskets where the sour dough could continue working.

Meanwhile, the oven had been fueled for over an hour using vines, board, and fire wood. If the floor and walls of the oven were hot enough, the embers were removed and the oven temperature was tested using three "ears" of grain. If the ears were lightly browned then the loaves could be inserted using a wooden paddle after having previously been brushed with water. The freshly baked bread was so tasty that you could eat it with pleasure without spread. The loaves were round, had a diameter of about 40 centimeters, and weighed 8 to 10 pfund [4-5 kilograms]. The bread was usually kept in the cellar. In order to protect it from mice, some people hung their bread on a "bread hanger."

After the bread baking was completed, the hot oven was then used to bake cake. In addition to braided wreaths and "covenant cake," tasty cream cakes were particularly popular. In order to have plenty of sourdough for the next baking day, a stone bowl was filled with dough and sprinkled with salt. This "sourdough starter" was kept in the cellar during the week.

The Ottersheim peasant wives have made their bread in this or in a similar manner for centuries. Servants or laborers who also lived in the village but had neither flour nor oven ate at the table with the farmer. Sometimes baked goods were obtained from Bellheim where there were bakers at the beginning of the 19th century. Thus we are told that in the forties, baker Michael Doll from Bellheim delivered the rolls each year that were distributed to the elementary school children on final examination day.

The first baker in Ottersheim came from Bellheim in 1850, having established himself at 25 Germersheimer Straße. His name was Friedrich Born. This baker died after a few years and left a widow who would have had to close the business without assistance. But journeyman baker Jakob Frey from Dalland in Baden filled the missing position. He soon married the widow Born and ran the bakery under his name.

From this marriage was born a son in 1858, Franz, who learned the bakers' trade as a young man. Franz Frey took over the family business at 25 Germersheimer Straße. However, when the space became too small for his large family, he bought the house at 5 Germersheimer Straße and set up his bakery there. He worked there until the beginning of the First World War. In 1916, the "Freybäcker" [Baker Frey] closed his business forever. Frey baked not only rolls and bread but also *Lebkuchen [gingerbread]* that he sold on his own behalf as far as Alsace. The gingerbread was made late in the year and was brought to the customers using a light wagon, the "char à bancs." After Christmas, Frey collected the money himself.

Valentin Burgermeister from Ottersheim opened a bakery in the village around the same time as Jakob Frey. The business seems not to have brought in much because Burgermeister emigrated to America in 1867. Presumably the operation was continued by Andreas Bischoff. But this baker also gave up his trade in Ottersheim after a few years and moved to Germersheim. Not until 1891 did a second baker settle down next to Franz Frey in Ottersheim. He was Johann Hoffmann from Offenbach. Hoffmann opened his shop in the upper village at 82 Lange Straße. He operated it about 25 years. Like Frey, Hoffmann closed his bakery at the beginning of World War I, thus Ottersheim had no bakery from then on. That lasted about ten years. As was the case for the school graduations, so the community had to purchase the necessary pretzels elsewhere for the dedication of the bells in 1924. A corresponding newspaper article resulted in several bakers reporting an interest in Ottersheim. The first to move to Ottersheim was Peter Hindert from Speyer who opened a bakery at 59 Lange Straße in 1926. Georg Kopf took over the business six years later. He passed it on to his son, Walter Kopf, in 1939 who still operates the bakery today. When Kopf was drafted during the war, Karl Ettmüller ran the business for a few years. A second bakery was opened in 1920 by Josef Hoffmann at 11 Germersheimer Straße. His son Werner Hoffmann, runs the business today. Finally, Otto Leingang opened a bakery at 60 Lange Straße in 1936 but it was also closed at the beginning of the war and did not subsequently reopen because the owner was killed. Thus, Ottersheim has had only two bakeries since the war as was the case for decades before the First World War.

Of Shoemakers and Tailors in Ottersheim

Shoemakers and tailors were indispensable craftsmen in every village as long as there were no shoe shops and clothing stores. Their job above all was to make new shoes and new clothes. In addition, they also performed repairs. Ottersheim had four shoemakers and four tailors for its 650 residents in 1791.

Even though the people at that time had only the bare essentials of shoes and clothes, the craftsmen were never without work because making new garments took a long time. The need for leather shoes in Ottersheim was relatively small in the past. During the cold season specifically, old and young ran around all day in wooden clogs. These wooden clogs were made from birch wood by the clog maker, while the peasant women knitted the woolen socks that were worn with the wooden clogs. Still in the twenties of this century, all children went to school in wooden clogs. In the hallway of the school building there was a special cupboard where the wooden clogs were placed. Leather shoes were worn only on Sunday and on special occasions.

To the same degree that shoe factories were created in the 19th century, the work of the shoemakers in the villages declined. Instead of having shoes made to measure, the residents covered their needs cheaper in the shoe stores. So for the local shoemakers, the only remaining task was to sole and repair used shoes. In Ottersheim up to the fifties of our century, this was done by two shoemakers of about the same age, August Müller at 5 Waldstraße and Franz Müller at 85 Lange Straße. There was only one shoemaker in Ottersheim since 1959. He was Ernst Müller who lived at 5 Waldstraße like his father. Müller served not only the residents of Ottersheim but also those of Knittelsheim where there had been no shoemaker for some time. As an aside, the first carriers of the names Föhlinger, Greichgauer, Ößwein, and Jennewein came to Ottersheim as shoemakers.

Not quite so sweeping was the development of the tailor trade in Ottersheim. There were four tailors in the village around 1791 and today there are still three, of whom only one is directly from Ottersheim. Heinrich Bischoff of 34 Ludwigstraße learned his craft from the famous "Schützen-Schneider,"[93] Johann Müller, who carried out his profession at 15 Ludwigstraße until 1958. The other two tailors settled in Ottersheim after the Second World War. Werner Wenzel, who was expelled from Stettin, operated his business at 32 Ludwigstraße. And Peter Schwendemann, the refugee from Yugoslavia, had his workshop at 51 Lange Straße.

---

[93] This was the local nickname for the *Schneider* (tailor), Johann Müller, who was the son of the *Feldschützen* (Field warden).

Of Masons, Carpenters, Joiners and Other Craftsmen in Ottersheim

Whoever wants to build a new home today needs not only an architect but also at least a dozen other construction workers like masons, carpenters, roofers, joiners, glaziers, plasterers, tilers, fitters, plumbers, electricians, heating mechanics, painters, and wall paper hangers. That was not so in earlier centuries. Whoever wanted to build a house in the village in those days relied entirely upon himself, his relatives, and his neighbors. All helped when a house was being built. For the foundation and the base, one drove to the quarries at the Haardt or got sandstone from crumbling ruins. The wood for the timber-framed building came from the forest. The threshold at the front door was always donated to each builder by the community. Carving the timber was originally left to the builder himself to accomplish. Later when the houses were built a little more elaborately, a local resident who was the most skilled and could handle an ax and a saw took over this job. From this the occupation of carpenter eventually developed. Masons who lived entirely from their craft did not exist in the village. However, they did find enough work in the city to earn their living. For farmhouses, the owner usually built the foundation and the base himself. Also, filling the spaces between the beams of the timbered house did not require a trained craftsman. This was done by the owner himself using cob [earth and straw]. Not until the 18th and especially the 19th century were trained craftsmen used more often for constructing houses in the village, not the least because farmhouses were being built more and more from stone rather than from wood.

There were two Ottersheim masons in 1791. The first was Nikolaus Walk who came from a local family. The second was Pankraz Hindert who emigrated from Switzerland in 1782. Jakob Jeckel from Waldhambach became the third mason in 1810. During the 19th and at the beginning of the 20th century, the Winkelblech family carried out the most masonry work in Ottersheim. Additionally, Jakob Eibler, Georg Dörzapf, Anton Glatz, and several others worked in this profession. The first fully trained mason in Ottersheim with a Master's Certificate was Joseph Ripp, who came from Scheibenhardt in 1918 and married in Ottersheim. His son Ludwig, who has a construction business located at 2 Friedhofstraße, currently employs six journeymen. A second masonry operation in Ottersheim is run by Hugo Kröper; and Master Mason Kurt Kröper has worked since April 1967 at a major construction business in Lingenfeld.

Carpenters were once more important to the village than masons because most farmhouses were built as timber-framed buildings. So by 1791 there were already three carpenters in Ottersheim. One of them was Paul Zwißler who came from Erbes-Büdesheim near Alzey in 1740. This was the first Zwißler in Ottersheim. In the 19th and in the first half of the 20th century the Zimmermann, Glatz, and Stadel families did most of the carpentry work in the village. Today, Hubert Merdian, the son of carpenter Otto Merdian, owns the only carpentry business in Ottersheim. He built his own home at 1A Lange Straße in the Black Forest style, which demonstrates what a competent carpenter can accomplish in his profession.

Surprisingly, earlier in Ottersheim there were few joiners, even though there were no furniture stores at that time where one could buy tables, chairs, cabinets, benches, chests, and beds. All these items had to be individually made by joiners. One joiner worked in Ottersheim in 1791; however, a hundred years later there were already three. They were all building and furniture makers. Before the First World War, six joiners were active in Ottersheim, three of whom moved here from elsewhere. Johann Kuhn came from Rheinzabern, Wilhelm Lutz from Knittelsheim, and Heinrich Faath from Offenbach. By contrast, Peter Kröper, August Dörzapf, and August Hindert were local craftsmen. Two of them completed their apprenticeship under joiner Peter Hanck. There are still three Ottersheim joiner businesses today. Ruprecht Hindert, the son of August Hindert, practices his craft at 8 Ludwigstraße. August Faath, the son of Heinrich Faath, works at 89 Lange Straße, and Ludwig Lutz, son of Wilhelm Lutz, operates his carpentry shop at 4A Riedstraße.

Little weight seems to have been placed on decorative walls, doors, and shutters in earlier times. This can be seen in the fact that it was not until 1867 that the first painter settled in Ottersheim. This was Ludwig Kuntz from Herxheim. Before this time, painting and varnishing work was borrowed from outside craftsmen, they were for example, Franz Müller and Andreas Arbogast from Germersheim, and Jean Busch from Offenbach. Already around 1900 there were three Ottersheim painters namely, Ludwig Kuntz, Karl Jeckel, and Wilhelm Stadel. Even today, Ottersheim still has three painters, two of whom had moved here. Gustav Nikolaus of Herxheimweyher married around 1927 in Ottersheim, and Vinzenz Gläßgen from Wernersberg came in 1960. The most recent painter was Hilmar Winkelblech of Ottersheim who opened his paint shop at 10 Lange Straße.

The first wheelwright in Ottersheim was Georg Heinrich Reichling who came from Bellheim in 1808. His son, Johannes, also practiced this craft later. There were two wheelwrights in Ottersheim in the first decades of the 20th century, Otto Dörzapf and Valentin Hoffmann. Due to the conversion of agriculture to tractors and rubber-tired wagons, a wheelwright could no longer exist from this profession. So wheelwright Hermann Seither worked only occasionally in his workshop because he lacked the necessary work orders.

There are no longer any coopers in Ottersheim, although in the year 1791 there were two of them. The last cooper in Ottersheim to exercise his craft was Anton Walk at 8

Germersheimer Straße. When he died in 1923, his son Franz worked another two years in this profession. Then he gave up the cooperage and took a job in an outside business.

Still working in his craft in Ottersheim today as the only saddler is Alois Winkelblech at 82 Lange Straße. Hermann Bischoff, the second saddler in the village, died in 1963 without a successor for his craft.

Up until the thirties of our century, the barbers Ludwig Hilsendegen, Alois Glatz, and Ludwig Wünschel went every Wednesday and Saturday from house to house and shaved their customers or cut their hair. Following an administrative regulation, the barbers had to set up a service room and practice their craft from there. To meet the requirement from then on, Hilsendegen used the neighboring house at 79 Lange Straße, and Glatz worked temporarily from his home. Not until after the Second World War did two trained barbers open their businesses in Ottersheim. The barbershop of Eugen Disqué was first located on the Leingang estate at 60 Lange Straße. Disqué moved into his new house at 3½ Riedstraße in 1963 where customers were served in a well-furnished salon. Markus Ößwein, who previously worked in Mannheim, opened his business in 1964 at 84 Lange Straße. He built a new building with a modern barbershop two years later. Thus, Ottersheim today has two barbershops that meet all requirements of the male and female population of the village.

Of Shopkeepers and Merchants in Ottersheim

There was only one merchant in Ottersheim in 1791. His name was Markus Lorentz and he lived at 64 Lange Straße. Whether he was a broker or a shopkeeper, no one can say with certainty today. We first hear of general merchandise stores in Ottersheim around the middle of the 19th century. Konrad Hatzenbühler, Johann Georg Kopf, and Jakob Anton Waçon each owned a small general store about that time. The general store of Konrad Hatzenbühler was located at 12 Germersheimer Straße. It was later used by David Hatzenbühler, then taken over by Elisabeth Hatzenbühler, and finally by Frieda Kröper. Today, August Gaab owns the store that is one of the oldest shops in Ottersheim.

The general store of the Dumser siblings at 53 Lange Straße seems to be relatively old because it was already there in 1892 when Jakob Zwißler opened his tinsmith shop. The general store of Frieda Hindert née Weiß at 8 Ludwigstraße was founded in 1911 by the father of the current owner. In the same year, the general store of Lisa Hindert at 7 Waldstraße was opened. It is now run by Frieda Moock. The newest food business in Ottersheim was set up at 18 Lange Straße in 1964, which was the former "Zum Schwanen" Inn. VIVO opened a store there that is operated by the Erwin Walk family.

Here it must be mentioned that in the past hundred years, several little shops were opened and after a shorter or longer life were closed. There were for example the little shops of Lina Job at 6 Germersheimer Straße, in the house of Anna Böhm at 32 Lange Straße, of Therese Zwißler and Franziska Huwe at 72 Lange Straße as well as Emma Sauther at 1 Ottostraße.

Konrad Hoffmann started a seed store at 40 Lange Straße for wholesale and retail customers in 1902. Today, his son Oscar runs his father's business at property number 37. There was also a country products wholesale business in Ottersheim at 83 Lange Straße from 1893 to 1939. It belonged to Philipp Benz (1865-1932) whose father, Markus Benz, came here from Zeiskam as a broker in 1863. For four decades in the person of Peter Seither (1862-1930), Ottersheim also had a bookbinder from whom the schoolchildren could buy their notebooks. Seither built himself a house at 97 Lange Straße in 1910 where in addition to the bindery he raised bees. The property is now in the possession of his nephew Peter Müller.

The Field Chapel of Ottersheim

About 500 meters south of the village on Kapellenweg [Chapel road], at the heart of the village plat there is a small chapel with a hipped roof and an open porch. Inside there is a Pieta. The chapel owes its existence to farmer Johann Rudolf Kröper who married Maria Katharina Dörzapf in 1790; he was 22 years old and she was of the same age. A total of thirteen children were born from the marriage, three died soon after birth and two others as small children. In the epidemic year of 1822, no fewer than six sons and daughters lay prostrate with the illness. Within fourteen days, death snatched away three children ages 17, 23, and 25 years. There was little hope of recovery for the other children. In his need, Kröper vowed to build a chapel on his land in the "Lach" should at least some of his children remain alive. In fact, the disease claimed no more victims.

Kröper fulfilled his promise in 1827. In memory of his dead children, a picture of the sorrowful Virgin Mary weeping for her dead son was placed inside the chapel and flanked by two candles. The chapel was unlocked and opened to the public every Sunday afternoon.

After the death of the founder, the chapel went into the possession of his son Franz Adam. With the inheritance, Franz took on the commitment to keep the chapel in good structural condition, to open it for visitors every Sunday, and to provide the necessary wax. For this, his siblings gave him a half morgen of arable land from the parental legacy. Around the middle of the century, Franz Adam Kröper decided to emigrate to America with his family. Before he left, he thoroughly renovated the chapel and placed a plaque. The inscriptions read,

> *"This chapel was built by Johann Rudolph Kröper in 1827. In 1853 the chapel was renovated by his son Franz Adam Kröper before his departure."*

On 13 January 1854, Kröper departed with his wife and five children seeking his fortune in the New World and bidding farewell to his homeland forever. Previously, he had sold the property and the chapel to farmer Johannes Gib from Ottersheim. Gib obliged himself to provide for the maintenance of the chapel. In 1860 and at the request of the community, the chapel was consecrated to the Blessed Mother of Sorrows [Blessed Virgin Mary]. The chapel centennial was commemorated in a simple celebration in May 1927. Nearly all the community residents participated in the procession.

The "Saint Mary's Chapel" was completely renovated in 1966. Interior plaster, floors, pillars, ceiling, and roof were renovated and the Pieta redone by a trained person. The chapel was until recently in possession of farmer Franz Kröper, a descendant of the builder. After his death, the property with the chapel was handed over to Erwin Kröper.

The Field Crucifix on Rülzheimer Weg

The great benefactor of the parish of Ottersheim, the childless widow Barbara Knöll née Burck (1848–1916, a widow since 1889) was also the provider of the field cross on Rülzheimer Weg. She purchased the property at the intersection of the Rülzheimer and Herxheimer field roads for this purpose and bequeathed it in her will to the Catholic Church. She commissioned the Hohneck Company of Landau to make the stone cross for which they charged 500 gold marks. The cross was solemnly consecrated by Pastor Ettmüller on the Feast of Saint Joseph, 23 April 1893. The whole community proceeded to the cross while singing hymns; and while there the pastor performed the consecration. The participants gathered in the church for homily and worship upon returning to the village.

The parish memorial book reports that the solemn celebration sank deep into the minds of the participants. The cross was newly painted at the suggestion of Pastor Knöll in 1932. The resulting costs were covered by the faithful through voluntary donations. During the land consolidation, the parish lands were laid mostly in the vicinity of the field cross at Rülzheimer Weg.

The Field Crucifix on the Waldstraße

Whoever goes to the woods via the Neuweg will see a simple field cross on the left hand side near the Gänsehaardt, on a small artificial hill. The cross was not always at this place. It was originally built by the Wingerter family on their own property at the end of the populated part of the Waldstraße. Due to the land consolidation in 1964, the land fell to a different owner so the location of the monument was therefore changed.

The cross owes its existence to a young soldier from Ottersheim who was killed near Moscow as a participant of the Russian campaign. His name is recorded on the back of the cross.

HUGO WINGERTER,
BORN ON 14 APRIL 1921,
DIED ON 27 DECEMBER 1941 NEAR MOSCOW.

The horrors of the Second World War had impressed the young man so much that he asked his parents in a letter to erect a field cross in the homeland should he find his final resting place in Russia.

The desire of their only son was a sacred obligation for the parents. The cross was consecrated by Pastor Funk on 7 May 1944; it had cost 3,200 reichsmarks. The inscription reflects the attitude of the believers at that time of killing and destruction. It reads,

"The cross will remain, even if the world goes to pieces."

The Sport and Festival Grounds of Ottersheim

It took many years before Ottersheim got its present beautiful sport and festival grounds. At the beginning of our century, the village geese still grazed free where today hand ball games are played and song festivals are celebrated. This also is why the area is called *Gänsehaardt [Goose forest]*. At one time, this land belonged to the large meadow that lay north of the village stretching from Offenbach up to the Knittelsheim border, and as *Allmend* property, it belonged to the community at large. In the first half of the 19th century, the Gänsehaardt served also as the community sand pit. A remnant of that era was the *Gänseweiher [Goose pond]* that lay in the midst of the Gänsehaardt.

The plan to transform the unused site into a sports field was created after World War I. At that time, the game of soccer was becoming more and more popular in Germany. In Ottersheim also, a number of young men who were members of the Gymnastics Club joined together to form a soccer team in 1921. Coach of the 22 players was Wilhelm Hellmann. The game of soccer was to be carried as a branch of the Gymnastics Club. For this reason, the Gymnastics Club intended to provide for a playing field. The club submitted a petition to the community council that was approved. The Gymnastics Club was given permission to use a part of the Gänsehaardt as a playing field. However, they were responsible for the leveling and preparation of the field. Thanks to the voluntary participation of the club members, especially the soccer team, the site was prepared well enough that games could be played there in good weather. But the soccer team did not reach a high level of success. So it is not surprising that the soccer department soon became less active and finally ceased altogether. One reason for this was certainly the fact that the leaders of the German Gymnastics Association were more interested in the game of handball rather than soccer.

In 1927, Ottersheim launched a handball team and in November began practice games. The leveled field on the Gänsehaardt served as the playing field. As the handball game continued to flourish, the Gymnastics Club improved the playing field accordingly. In 1928, they built a hut for dressing and undressing and outfitted the two goals with wire mesh. The field was extended to the north the following year with the permission of the community. Nevertheless, it was still far removed from fulfilling all the requirements of the handball players. The high water table and poor subsoil led to water drainage problems again and again when it rained, such that the water did not drain away and the soil became soaked. Nothing definitive was done until 1932. At that time there were unemployed in Ottersheim, those who had to live from unemployment insurance or those for whom insurance had expired and thus relied on government support. To prevent the working capabilities of these people from being wasted, crisis jobs were created everywhere. In addition, the volunteer work service, Freiwillige Arbeitsdienst (FAD), was launched. Following an agreement between the Gymnastics Club of Ottersheim and the employment office, twelve men from the FAD began work on expanding the sports field on 17 June 1932. After the area had been slightly enlarged, drainage ditches were installed and the field was filled. Up to 35 people were employed at times. After the leveling, new broad jump paths were created, locker rooms expanded, and the playing field partly surrounded by a railing. The employment office contributed 3,500 reichsmarks to the project. The volunteer work service again performed activities on the sports field in April 1933. With a grant of 500 reichsmarks from the employment office, the fields were improved, the railing completed, the roof of the locker room tarred, and the footpath refilled.

During the construction of the Western Wall in 1938, the playing field could no longer be used by the handball team. The dressing rooms had been seized by the flak troops and antitank barriers were erected on the roadway along the length of the field. Although handball games were resumed in 1939, they ended a year later because most players had been drafted into the military. When the war ended, the changing rooms at the sports field were so damaged that the cabins had to be completely demolished. Nevertheless, the handball games were resumed in 1946 after the grounds had been provisionally repaired by the players. At the instigation of Gymnastics Club president Peter Hindert, the Becht Company from Hördt was commissioned in March 1948 to renovate the grounds thoroughly for use by the club. Already in May the sports field could be given over to its intended use. Finally, the handball federation provided a larger grant to build new changing rooms in 1950.

Because the sports field and the adjacent area were also to serve as a festival ground, a plan to build a natural stage there was created in 1953. For this purpose, the representatives of the community and of the local clubs met at the sports field to determine the location. The stage was to be 36-40 square meters in size and be suitable for both gymnastic and vocal performances. In view of the 90th foundation celebration of the "United Singers," the members declared their willingness to contribute to the construction of the stage with hand and team labor while the community pledged their financial support. Also, access to the festival site was to be built. The desired objective was achieved by the joined forces. In 1956, the community expanded the extended Waldstraße up to the Gänsehaardt and provided it with blacktop paving. It covered the cost of the electric line to the sports field a year later. Today, because of the quiet forest location and its convenient access at the entrances, Ottersheim is in possession of a well-developed sports and event venue for which it can be justly proud.

That was not always so. When the male voice choir wanted to hold a forest festival in 1886, it had to make do with the "Kuhnen" north of the fishpond. Later, they set up a festival location in the "Stöcken." This place is still recognizable by the ditches that were dug at the time for water drainage. In 1910, when the grounds were retired in favor of new festival grounds at the "Erlen," this was planted with spruce trees that still mark the former location. The festival site at the "Erlen" southwest of the present-day sports field served the performances of both the singers' festivals and gymnastic events. It had facilities for long and high jump. Horizontal and parallel bars were set up for the respective events. Amidst the festival grounds was a natural stage, last expanded and raised in 1921 using soil and grass from the fishpond. Ball games were not conducted on this relatively small space. It is therefore understandable that the Gymnastics Club sought a new practice facility after the First World War, and that the choirs soon followed that example.

The Ottersheim Fishpond

In the first half of the 19th century, Ottersheim had large sand pits that were leveled in 1846 and 1847. These were located to the west and east of the Waldstraße just before the present-day Gänsehaardt and in the cow pasture at the sports field. As a replacement, the Allmend in the upper Haardt was released. The fishpond originated from this sand pit later. We do not know who created the first pond. It is known that collector Philipp Pfeiffer from Bellheim leased it for nine years in 1892. The fish lease cost 60 marks annually. The pond received its water from the Dorfbach that flowed by there. On the south side, an avenue of chestnut trees had been planted. As early as 1897, Pfeiffer wanted to dissolve his contract because to his chagrin the pond was completely muddy and full of silt. With the consent of the community council, the fishpond was then used to obtain scattering. It was to be leased for twelve years in 1901. No reports are available telling whether or not an interested person was found. At any rate, no one paid any attention to the pond until 1921.

At that time, a small group was formed that had set a goal to bring the pond back in order. For that purpose Luitpold Stadel, Jean Benz, Markus Benz, Edmund Bischoff, Oskar Zwißler, Eugen Job, and Josef Job leased the property in February 1921 for a period of 15 years. The annual rent was 720 marks. By joining forces, mud and sand were removed, drainage ditches dug, bridges built, and two boats were bought in Maximiliansau for 1,900 marks. Water was let into the pond on Friday, 8 April 1921. On the following Sunday, a large number of villagers went to the fishpond to enjoy a boat ride that brought the lease owners 250 marks. Also, in the following period the pond remained a popular destination for Sunday afternoon walks.

The tenants also expected corresponding income from raising fish in the pond. To this end, they set out a good number of breeding fish and young fish. But they had been deceived. The fish did not thrive in the polluted Queich water as had been expected.

Moreover, since the water flow to and from the pond was poor, the fishpond was so silted by 1926 that the setup gradually became dilapidated. After the Second World War, the area was used as a garbage dump. The avenue of chestnut trees on the south side was cut down and only the chestnut tree that stood in the middle of the pond remained standing. Currently, the old fishpond is rather far from being an ornament to the village. Because parts of a West Wall concrete bunker were also sunk there, it would be difficult to make use of the site for meadow or field land. But one could reforest the space, therein turning it back to its original use before the beginning of the 19th century: Haardt, i.e. forest.

The Names of the Ottersheim Field Plots and Their Meanings

The cultivated land belonging to the Ottersheim district was originally a large forest where an industrious population had already lived and worked for their daily bread for centuries. The first inhabitants of the village presumably settled on the Deich near the Quotgraben and began clearing the forest. The felled trees were partly used as fuel and partly used to build wood houses, barns, and stables. The entire population had to participate in cutting down the trees and turning the forest floor into arable land, whereby an average of 6 hectares of forest was claimed. Thus, field upon field was created until finally the largest part of the district had been turned into fields and meadows. The deforestation apparently began in the village center and continued in the southern district in the Oberfeld and Niederfeld. Only in recent centuries was the land to the north of the village put under the plow. For example, the present Haardt fields as well as the Wasserbeiz fields were communal pastureland in 1788. The growth of the plots corresponded generally to the growth of the population. It took place without basic planning and was therefore subject to many contingencies. It may be assumed to be fairly certain that the shape and size of the plots have remained in their original state up to our century. Only by subdivision into separate fields due to sales and distribution have these estates experienced certain changes. It was not until the land consolidation of 1964 that roads and boundaries were eliminated that were for the most part well over 1,000 years old. Like the plots, so also their names have remained relatively unchanged until the present century. Written documents from earlier centuries use primarily the same name expressions that are still common today. Only in the spelling do they tend to differ from the current form. Many plot names are still readily understandable today. Others are more difficult to interpret because the connections are often not known. The following section attempts to explain and interpret in detail the Ottersheim land plot names as they were before the land consolidation.

A: Farmland

1. Fields named for their size.

In den Elfmorgen [In the Eleven morgen] [G-1].[94]

In den Achtmorgen [In the Eight morgen] [H-1].

In den kurzen Zwanzigmorgen [In the short Twenty morgen] [H-2].

In den langen Zwanzigmorgen [In the long Twenty morgen] [H-1].

Auf dem Großstück [On the Big piece] [E-3]: It covered 36 morgen (9 hectares) of contiguous land and belonged to the Poppelmann family as a fief [feudal property].

2. Fields named from the nature of the soil.

In der Goldgrube [In the Gold mine]: This plot was also called the *Löchel [Little hole]* and was marked by a small but noticeable depression in the ground. The name *Goldgrube* suggests that perhaps gold coins were found there. It is possible that this gold came from inhabitants of the lost village of Altsheim that probably lay close by.

Auf der Hochangewanne [On the High attached fields] [G-1]: The plots at Altsheimer Weg are probably the oldest plots in the *Oberfeld [Upper fields]*. Plots attached to them lay slightly higher and therefore these were called *Hochangewanne.*

In der Knopfgewanne [In the Button fields] [I-2]: The fields of this small plot lay horizontally to the surrounding fields of the adjoining plots. Together, they form a button, or a knot.

Über dem Höhlchen [Over the Little Hollow] [I-3]: This plot is located at the *Höhlchen,* that is, at a small ravine or hollow that leads into the Hintergrund [Back lands].

In der Mulde [In the Mold] [J-1]: This conspicuous depression in the ground runs from west to east and has similarity to a [half-cylinder] baking mold.

Auf dem Berg [On the Mountain] [I-3]: This field is slightly higher than the rest of the area. Where everything is almost flat, even a small hill looks like a mountain to the attentive observer.

Auf dem Brett [On the Board] [I-4]: In contrast to the nearby Berg, the surface of this field resembles a board.

In der Froschau [In the Frog valley] [E-1]: In 1788, this field is still called, *In der Froschau und den Lachengärten [In the Frog valley and the Puddle gardens]*. The land was marshy and in wet weather formed a large puddle of water where there were many frogs. Later, the field was drained by a ditch.

In der Wasserbeiz [In the Water hunt] [D-4]: In 1788, this field did not exist as an arable plot. At that time it was still forestland, most of which was covered with pools of water. Wild ducks, coots, and geese could only be hunted with the help of trained falcons. Such a hunt was called a *Beiz*. After the forest was cleared, the name *Wasserbeiz* was given to the newly acquired fields.

---

[94] This is a coordinate for the location the named parcel if it is shown on page 396. The parcel can be located within the area above the alphabetic and to the right of the numeric coordinate.

Im Ried [In the Reeds] [F-4]: On the sour marshy ground on either side of the Quotgraben, to the west of the present-day Riedstraße, sedge grass was the main plant growth. The hard, cutting-sharp leaves provide poor quality food. In 1600, the *Im Ried* probably stretched from the west of the lower Hördt court up to the Große Gasse.

3. Fields named for their shape.

In den Spitzäckern [In the Pointed fields] [G-2]: This plot at the Altsheimer Weg, which belonged to the Cathedral Chapter of Speyer, seems to have been cleared very late. When the lands were divided, the irregular shape of the plot resulted in some pointy shaped fields.

Im Gärn [In the Blade] [G-3]: Earlier the term *Gärn* referred to a lance or a triangle. Until the land consolidation, this land plot was shaped like a medieval blade of a halberd.

Im Offenbacher Zipfel [In the Offenbach Corner] [H-1]: The plot protruded like a lobe into the Ottersheim district.

In den Scheeräckern [In the Broken fields]: In Middle High German, *Scheer* means as much as hole, nick, crack, or break. At the *Scheeräckern,* the clearing was done with a deep pick. Later this cut was extended accordingly.

Im Zwerchsack [In the Crooked sack] [I-1]: This small plot lay like a sack among the other fields. Its fields are twisted and crooked. A permanent access road was not present.

In der Langgewanne [In the Long plot] [I-2] Earlier, the fields of this plot were more than one hundred meters long and usually very narrow.

Im Reiterspieß [In the Rider's Halberd or Reuter's Halberd] [G-5]: This field was in the form of a medieval halberd, a rider's spear.

Bei der Mittelschor [At the Middle break]: Schor, Scheer or *Scharte* in the Middle Ages meant as much as break, crack or dent. Before the land consolidation, the course of the lands to the north of the Falltorweg looked like such a slice or dent.

Im Bogen [In the Curve] [G-5]: This field must have been shaped like an curve. If you think of the term curve in the sense suggested by a crossbow, it is at least strange that the *Reiterspieß [Rider's Halberd]* lay in the immediate vicinity while the adjoining Knittelsheim plots are called *Kaiseräcker [Emperor fields]* and *Reiterspiel [Rider's game].* Prof. Christmann suggested that *Reiterspiel* means *Reuters Bühl,* that is, hill of a man named Reuter. Anyone who knows the area knows that all the fields in the area there are as flat as a board. It is therefore still not completely unthinkable that perhaps this was a medieval tournament site. Because Ottersheim lay roughly in the middle of the upper Palatinate and every village was home to a knighted family, this possibility cannot be ruled out completely. It is also noteworthy that the roads to Rülzheim, Herxheim, Insheim, Offenbach, and Knittelsheim converge near the *Reiterspiel.*

4. Fields named after their former owners.

Poppelmanns Großstück [Poppelmann's Large plot]: The Poppelmann knights were first mentioned in documents of 1282. In 1347, a Rudolf Poppelmann appears as Burgmann [castle warden] at Germersheim, who was a subject of the castellan there. He received a fief from royal lands for his services. From 1400 to 1410, a Hans Poppelmann was castle warden in Germersheim. The Poppelmann family owned nearly 150 morgen (37.2

hectares) of fields and meadows in Ottersheim. The largest contiguous area was the 9-hectare *Großstück* that stretched from the Neuweg to the Landauer Straße. Around 1600, this area was used as a sheep pasture. In 1788, there was still no house on this land.

Im Sturm [In the Sturm] [F-5]: Like the Poppelmann family, so the Sturm family belonged to the castle men of Germersheim. The plot "Auf dem Sturm" seems to have been a part of the fief that the Sturm family received as a reward for their services at the castle in Germersheim. In 1788, of the 21 morgen Sturm plot, 14.5 morgen belonged to the Monastery of Hördt.

Lorenz Ludwigs Wingert [Lorenz Ludwig's Vineyard] [I-3]: As early as 1705, Lohrs Vineyard is named in documents. It is likely that an ancestor of the Ludwig family created these vineyards. In the 16th century, Ludwig was already a common surname in Ottersheim.

Im Baumann [In the Baumann]: Around the year 1600, several bearers of the Baumann surname appear in Ottersheim as landowners. We may assume that a Baumann family was especially wealthy there.

Im Engelsgarten [In the Engel's gardens] [F-1]: In 1788, the Engel's gardens plot was still owned by the Ottersheim community. The small plot was presumably worked by a family named Engel.

5. Fields named after their original use.

In den Linsenäckern [In the Lentil fields] [H-2]: The primary crop in these land was lentils. With the end of formal planting rules, the connection between the name of a plot and its use was lost in the consciousness of the people. Thus, the *Linsenäcker* became the *Lissenäcker.* In a document dated 1706, the name "In denen Linßenäckern" is still correct.

Auf dem Kahlenberg [On the Bald mountain] [J-1]: This name appears in a document already in 1590. Presumably this small hill that forms the highest point in the district was originally bare. It was later planted with vineyards.

Im Schlägel [In the Small clearing] [D-4/H-4]: A small *Schlag* is a copse or clearing. Perhaps the Schlägel was still forest when the nearby areas were already cleared. In any event, the Schlägel east of the Gänsehaardt was still covered with forest in 1788.

In den Weggärten [In the Road gardens] [F-4]: The plot lies at the southern exit of the village on the road to Knittelsheim. Probably there were several gardens there belonging to less wealthy farmers.

In den Ruschgärten [In the Elm gardens] [F-3]: In a document from the year 1590, this field was called "Im Rustgarten." *Rusch* is also called *Rust* or *Rüster.* These were formerly common names for elm. Most likely there were elms near the Quotgraben from which the gardens there got their names. Today, this field is also called "Duuchbleech," meaning *clothbleach,* because in early times the self-woven cloth was bleached there. Even in our century housewives washed clothes at this place.

In den Gänseweidegärten [In the Goose pasture gardens] [E-3]: The goose pasture that belonged to the public lay to the north of these gardens. The goose herdsman drove all the geese of the village to pasture there during the warmer seasons. The parcels are still small and are mostly used as gardens.

In den Lachengärten [In the Puddle gardens]: Froschau and *Lachengärten* were still one plot in 1788. Before a drainage ditch was built, this field was swampy and was covered with puddles of water when it rained. Less well off farmers had created gardens near these puddles.

In den Stockstücken [E-1] (See *In den Stockäckern* below).

In den Stockäckern [In the Bush fields] [E-1]: In 1788, the *Stockäcker* with 9.7 hectares of land was still community property, meaning these belonged to the public. From this it can be concluded that they were cleared very late. Previously they were covered with *Stöcken,* that is, bushes, hedges and small trees. Presumably the forest and pasture land was previously already called "In den Stöcken" as a part of the Hinterwald [Back forest] is still called.

In den Haardtstücken [In the Forest fields] [D-2]: The *Haardtstücke* belonged to the public for use as grazing. Only after 1788 were they cleared and brought under cultivation. Before, they were covered with *Hart,* that is, forest. The lower Haardt was also formerly forest and pasture land and was there for all to use as community property.

6. Fields named after random features.

Bei den Quittenbäumen [At the Quince trees] [G-3]: The cultivation of quince trees in the Ottersheim district was nothing ordinary. When a farmer planted them on a large scale for the first time, he could not foresee that he would give the name to a field.

Im Bild [At the Shrine] [I-2]: This plot lay on the district boundary to Offenbach. The Insheimer Weg was built up to that point. Probably there stood on this prominent place a base for a crucifix or a saint's image that invited the visitor to a prayer.

Auf dem Schwalbenberg [On the Swallow's mountain] [J-3]: The Hintergrund [Back lands] were probably the last to be made arable. It is assumed that Bank Swallows once nested on the Schwalbenberg.

Im Langenstein [In the Long stone] [H-4]: It is likely that the district border toward Knittelsheim was marked by a high stone. It is also conceivable that in Celtic times a so-called *Megalithic stone* or *Menhir* stood there that probably served some religious purpose. Similar megalithic stones have been preserved in the northern and western Palatinate up to our times.

In den Kappenäckern [In the Capon fields] [H-4]: These lands were near the Schlägel [Small clearing]. The tenants had to pay the rent in the form of fattened roosters [capons]. The capons were popularly known as *Kappen.*

Bei Hörners Griebelnußbaum [At Hörner's walnut tree] [G-4]: The walnut tree from which the name of this plot was derived belonged to the Hörner family. A *Griebelnuß* was a small (stunted) nut.

Bei der Rehdarr [At the Madder Kilns] [G-4]: It is hardly conceivable that deer may have been dried at this place. The correct spelling is not *Rehdarr but Rötdarr. Röt* was the name our ancestors used for the madder plant from which a red dye was made. Already in the 16th century, much madder was cultivated in Ottersheim, Bellheim, and

Knittelsheim. The color was extracted from the root system that was pulled out of the loosened soil, shaken off, and then spread on the field for preliminary drying. Then the underground stems were heated on trays in large kilns until they were very dry. Such a kiln stood at the south entrance of the village. This was probably a handsome building with three floors.

For a long time madder cultivation was a very profitable business that earned the farmer a multiple of what he could otherwise get from the fields. The dried roots were processed in madder mills to make a red dye. For example, such a madder mill was located around the year 1800 in the Saint Guido Monastery in Speyer. The cultivation of madder in the Palatinate gradually declined with the advent of artificial dye.

Im Gröhlig [In the Ravine] [F-3]: This plot is very likely one of the oldest of the village and lies between the Quotgraben and Altsheimer Weg on the west side of the village. The name can no longer be interpreted with certainty due to its age. The plot was called "In Kröling" in 1590. Professor Christmann assumes that the term *Gröhlig* comes from *Krinneling.* But in earlier centuries, *Krinne* referred to a gutter, a ditch, or a ravine. It is possible that the bed of the Dorfgraben at Altsheimer Weg gave the plot its name. Also, a document from 1863 states there were formerly vineyards in the Gröhlig.

Im Rechhag [In the Deer hedge] [D-2]: This plot was mentioned in a document already in 1590. Earlier, there were forests to the north and west of the Rechhag fields. It was therefore quite possible that deer roamed at night and early morning on the fields looking for food. The farmers certainly did not like to see this, especially because they themselves had no hunting rights. Therefore, they planted a thick hedge fence around their fields to protect them from wildlife damage. The plot name *Rechhag* was derived. It should also be noted that in Middle High German, the word *Reh [deer]* was pronounced *Reech.*

Am Birnbaum [At the Pear tree] [E-1]: The name of the plot came from a striking pear tree. In the Record Book of 1788, a plot "Am Birnbaum" is not mentioned.

7. Fields that were named after nearby roads

Am Altsheimer Weg [At the Altsheimer road] [F-2]: Between Ottersheim and Offenbach, there was at one time a small village called Altsheim that had disappeared before the 30 Years War. Whether the disappearance was caused by a war, a plague, or economic reasons can no longer be determined. Only the Altsheimer Weg reminds of the former settlement.

Über dem Insheimer Weg [Along the Insheimer road] [G-2].

Über dem Herxheimer Weg [Along the Herxheimer road].

Im Schlittweg [The Hauling road] [G-3]: A connection or a road through a field was formerly called a *Schlidweg.* It was not a public road. Only those with land at the road had the right to *schleifen [pull or haul]* their agricultural implements to their land.

Über dem Niederherxheimer Weg [Above the lower Herxheimer road] [G-4].

Am Knittelsheim-Herxheimer Weg [At the Knittelsheim-Herxheimer road].

An der Landauer Straße [At the Landauer road]: Landau is much younger than Ottersheim. In 1290, King Rudolf von Habsburg gave the city its freedom. Like the city of Landau, it seems that the Landauer Straße originated rather late. It is in any case unusual that the fields on both sides of the road run uniformly from south to north.

Über der Landauer Straße am Scheid [Above the Landauer road at the district boundary]: The district boundary is called *Scheid* or *Scheed.*

Außer der Straße [On the far side of the road].

Außer dem Mühlweg [On the far side of the Mill road] [F-2]: The *Mühlweg [Mill road]* that began at the western end of the village ran in a northwesterly direction toward the *Neumühle [New mill]* or *Fuchsmühle [Fox mill].*

Über dem Mühlweg [Above the Mill road].

Am Gartenweg [At the Garden road] [E-4]: The garden road seems to have already existed when the Neuweg was still unpaved and was used to drive cattle to pasture. It connected the village with the Gänseweidegärten [Goose pasture gardens].

Am Falltorweg [At the Drop gate road]: In 1788, the present-day Falltorweg [renamed Schulstraße in 1962] was still called *Mittelschorweg [Middle break road].* The name reminds of a portcullis gate that by virtue of its own weight closed automatically when it was opened by human hands. Such gates are still common today in Alpine country to access fenced pastures. The portcullis would prevent the cattle from running into the village when they were driven at noon to the resting place near the present-day tobacco shed.

Über dem Bauernweg [Above the Peasant road] [E-4]: Already by 1590, the name Bauernweg occurs in documents. But it was a dirt road at that time. It was undeveloped as late as 1788. Only one house stood at that time at the point where the weigh station stands today.

Außer dem Grübenweg [On the far side of the Trenches road] [E-4]: In 1788, the Grüben or Grubenweg is not yet mentioned. In the 19th century, there were *Grüben [trenches]* or deep holes there in which flax and hemp were processed.

Unter dem Bauernweg am Knittelsheimer Weg [Below the Peasant road at the Knittelsheimer road].

Am Knittelsheimer Weg [At the Knittelsheimer road] [E-5].

Über dem Knittelsheimer Weg [Above the Knittelsheimer road].

Unter dem Bauernweg [Below the Peasant road].

8. Fields that were named for their location.

Im Hintergrund [In the Back lands] [J-3]: The plots that lie at the district border to the south are called the *Hintergrund [Back lands].* They spread out far from the village behind the *Mittelgrund [Middle lands].*

Auf dem Oberfeld im Hintergrund [On the Upper field in the Back lands].

Auf dem Niederfeld im Hintergrund [On the Lower field in the Back lands] [J-3]: The names of *Oberfeld [Upper field]* and *Niederfeld [Lower field]* relate to the position of the fields toward the Haardt or the Rhine. The streams come from above [the west] and flow below [to the east].

B) Meadows

1. Meadows named for their size.

In den Sechsmorgen [In the Six morgen] [B-5]: These lie beyond the Hubgraben. This trench, which takes up two-fifths of the Queich waters, was probably created artificially in the 18th century. A plan to this effect is located in the State Archives at Speyer but it contains no date. The Hubgraben joins downstream with the Spiegelbach.

2. Meadows named after the nature of the soil.

Im oberen Brühl [In the upper Swampy meadows] [F-1]: The record book from 1788, calls these meadows "Oberer Brühl [Upper Swampy meadows] and Viehweide [Cattle pasture]." The meadows stretch from the Offenbach boundary up to the Weet. They include 9.75 hectares of land. In 1788, 18 contiguous morgen (4.5 hectares) were owned by the community as pastureland, 3 morgen (0.75 hectares) belonged to the Eußerthal Monastery, 6 morgen (1.5 hectares) to the Hördt Monastery, and 3 morgen (0.75 hectares) to the Poppelmann estate. The Brühl meadows were mostly wet meadows that served as an outlet for the cattle of the manor. They were watered from the Quot- or Bordgraben. Peasants were obliged from ancient times to care for these meadows by raking, fencing, mowing, harvesting, and grazing.

Im mittleren Brühl [In the middle Swampy meadows]: These meadows were at the Quot- or Bordgraben between the Deich (Germersheimer Straße) and the Riedgasse. They were 1.75 hectares in size. Six morgen (1.5 hectares) of these belonged to the Hördt Monastery. Today, the middle Brühl has largely been converted to gardens.

Im niederen Brühl [In the lower Swampy meadows] [F-5]: These meadows were also called the *Faselbrühl [Breeding meadows]*. In 1788, of the 3.28 hectares of meadows in the lower Brühl, 3 morgen (0.75 hectares) belonged to the Hördt Monastery. Another 3 morgen (0.75 hectares) were owned by the community as the *Farrenbrühl [Bullock meadows]*.

In den Waalen [In the Waves]: These meadows begin in the Offenbach district and run along the Quot- or Bordgraben into the Ottersheim district. In contrast to the Viehweide and the Brühl, the Waalen were formerly not cared for well. Water seeped up high in the marshy ground. This surge of water would have led to the name *Waalen (Wallen)* or wave.

In den Wasserbeizwiesen [The Water hunt meadows]: In 1788, these meadows were part of the so-called *Niederweide* or lower pasture. As community property, everyone was allowed to graze their cattle there. The land was once probably very wet and marshy. Therefore, the hunt for ducks or coots had to be carried out with trained hawks. Such a hunt was called a *Beiz.*

Im Hundsloch [In the Miserable puddle] [C-4]: The *Hundswiesen* or miserable meadows, as these were called in a document from 1602, were part of the Niedervorderwiesen [Lower front meadows]. *Loch* is the local dialect word for puddle. The meadows seem to have been of particularly bad quality. (Compare to, Hundwetter [miserable or beastly weather], Hundstage [dog days], etc.)

Auf den Seemorgen [On the Lake morgen] [C-5]: There were probably smaller standing waters or lakes in this area. Derived from these lakes were the names of the *Seemorgen, Seewiesen* (at the Hubgraben) and the adjacent forest.

Auf den Seewiesen [On the Lake meadows]: (Compare to Seemorgen!) Until the artificial Hubgraben was built, the water could not flow off at this point. This is why lake-like water collections formed here during wet weather.

Im Dämmel [In the Dark forest] [B-1]: In 1788, these meadows were called 'In den Dümmelswiesen." The words *Timmel* or *Demel* denoted a deep, dark forest. That name was transferred to the meadows that were created after clearing there. This alludes also to the expression *Dämmelswiesen [Dark forest meadows]* that were once common. In 1932, an additional part of the Dämmel was cleared. It was the last clearing in the Ottersheim community to this day.

Im Schwenkpfuhl [In the Changing pool] [A-2]: The term *Pfuhl* formerly referred to a depression in the land where water or sewage accumulated. Because the Schwenkpfuhl lay near the Queich, the water level in the depression changed very frequently. The water level in the depression was high when the Queich water level was high; the amount of water in the depression fell when the Queich water level fell. The frequent ups and downs of the water levels probably led to the name *Schwenkpfuhl. Schwenken* comes from *schwingen* and means as much as "to cause to swing" or change. In 1788, the Schwenkpfuhl belonged to the Rohrbusch [Reed thicket]. It was owned by the community at that time and was therefore exempt from tributes and taxes.

3. Meadows named for their shape.

In den Stock- und Scheerwiesen [In the Bush- and Break Meadows] [C-3]: *Scheer, Schor,* or *Schäre* means something like nick, crack, or break. The shape of the Scheerwiesen shows that deforestation in fact started with a triangular cut. Before it was cleared, these were called the Stockwiesen because the area was covered with *Stock* or *Steck,* that is, smaller trees, shrubs, and hedges. Today, the adjacent forest is still called "In den Stöcken."

In Schuster's Eck [In the Shoemaker's Corner] [B-1]: The meadows lie between the Rohrbusch and the Hinterwiesen, and have more or less the shape of a triangle. The owner was a certain Weiß from Ottersheim who by trade was a shoemaker.

4. Meadows named after their former owners.

In den Abtswiesen [In the Abbot's meadows]: In the land register of 1788, the Abtswiesen is not specifically mentioned, but these meadows were a part of the Obervorderwiesen [Upper front meadows]. In the Middle Ages, the abbots of Klingenmünster and Hördt owned almost 10 morgen (2.33 hectares) of contiguous meadows here.

In Schuster's Eck [B-1] (See in 3 above).

5. Meadows named after their original ground cover.

In den Stock- and Scheerwiesen [C-3] (See in 3 above).

Auf den Hörsten [In the Scrub forest] [C-1]: In Middle High German, *Hurst* or *Horst* means as much as scrub forest. Presumably, this forest was divided up for clearing so that several smaller areas of scrub were created from the larger one. This presumption is the more likely in that the meadows together comprise about three times the acreage of a normal meadow plot (9.52 hectares).

Auf den Börstwiesen [On the Bristled meadows] [B-1]: In 1788, these meadows were called "Auf den Berschwiesen." It seems that initially only bristly, short, stiff grass grew on these meadows.

Im Rohrbusch [In the Reed thicket] [B-1]: Only reeds grew in the wet subsoil.

In den Haardtwiesen [In the Forest meadows] [D-3]: In 1788, this area belonged to the communal cattle pasture. It was overgrown with Haardt, that is, shrub forest.

6. Meadows named after random features.

In den Rechhagwiesen (Rechhackwiesen) [In the Hedge meadows]: These meadows are located north of the larger Poppelmann manor plot near the forest. To protect the grass from grazing deer, the peasants planted a *Hag* or *Heck [hedge]* fence. Both the meadows and the fields were named after this hedge fence.

In den Niederalmen-Wiesen [In the Lower public meadows] [C-5]: *Oberallmend [Upper public]* and *Niederallmend [Lower public]* were names for the large pasture that spread west and east of the Gänsehaardt [Goose forest]. The pasture belonged to the *Allmend [Public]*. The Niederalmen-Wiesen was part of the former Niederweide [Lower meadow].

Auf den Mühlwiesen [On the Mill meadows] [C-4]: The *Summary of Rights in the Village of Ottersheim from the year 1599* mentions a ford or passageway on the provost's Mühlwiese, or mill meadows. In 1602, these meadows were called "Uf der Mühlwiese." With 10 morgen of meadows, almost half of the land still belonged to the Hördt Monastery in 1788. A mill probably stood near the Mühlwiesen in the early Middle Ages.

Auf dem Rödel [On the Small Clearing] [B-3]: The meadows "auf dem Rödel" are mentioned in a document from 1590. A *Rod* used to designate an area that has been cleared. A small *Rod* was called a *Rödel*. This name is justified because the Rödel with 1.8 hectares of land represented the smallest meadow size in Ottersheim.

Auf den Neuwiesen [On the New meadows] [B-4]: These are mentioned in a document from 1590. It can no longer be determined when these were actually 'new' meadows. Like the Rödel, these meadows seem to have originated after the actual Queich meadows.

Auf den Freiwiesen oder Amtmannswiesen [On the Free meadows or Magistrate's meadows] [A-5]: These lie beyond the Hubgraben to the east of the Queich in the direction of the Zeiskam mill. Originally, these 30 morgen (7.5 hectares) of meadows belonged to the Knights of Saint John Monastery of Haimbach, which was located two kilometers north of Zeiskam, and indeed, right at the intersection of the Hochstraße and Freimersheim Straße.

Today there are some mature trees in prominent wilderness there while the fishpond is used as a garbage dump. The meadows of the Commanders of the Haimbach Order were exempted from the tithe burden. Therefore, the meadows were called *Freiwiesen*, or free meadows.

The designation *Amtmannswiesen* has its own significance. In 1512, the Commander of the Order in Haimbach, Johann von Hattstein, was elevated to Grand Master and Grand Prior of Germany. The Order of the Knights of Saint John in Haimbach was consequently dissolved and converted into a Commandery managed by a magistrate. However, the Grand Prior, as Lord and owner of the Haimbach house, lived in Heitersheim in the Breisgau.

In the eyes of the population, the warden of Haimbach was owner of the Freiwiesen, which he could lease as he saw fit. The *Amtmannswiesen* were auctioned during the Napoleonic period. Buyers were the Reformed adjunct Konrad Humbert of Ottersheim, the citizen Bernhard Bernion of Germersheim, and a certain Josef Spitz from Speyer. The purchase price was 10,200 francs. It was mainly Ottersheim farmers who later either owned or leased these meadows. For this reason, the Amtmannswiesen have been counted as Ottersheim district property since 1809, although they originally belonged to Haimbach.

7. Meadows named after rivers running past.

Über der Queich [Above the Queich] [A-3]: In 1788, these meadows were called *Über der Queichbach*.

Unter der Queich [Below the Queich].

Ober der Queich [On the far side of the Queich]: In 1788, these meadows were called *Jenseits der Queichbach [On the other side of the Queich]*.

8. Meadows named for their location.

In den Gärtelswiesen [In the Garden meadows]: Small gardens were located near these meadows.

Auf den Niedervorderwiesen [On the Lower front meadows] [C-4]: This name is already mentioned in a document from 1705. *Vorderwiesen [Front meadows]* is a collective term for all the meadows that are located in front of the *Hinterwald [Backwoods]*. The term *Niedervorderwiesen* refers to the part of the meadows that spreads out to the east toward the Rhine.

In den Obervorderwiesen [In the Upper front meadows] [C-3]: This term refers to the part of the *Vorderwiesen* that lies in the direction of the Haardt.

Auf den Hinterwiesen [On the Back meadows]: This term refers to the collection of meadows that lies beyond the *Hinterwald [Back woods]* along the Queich.

C) Forest

Ottersheim has a *Vorderwald [Front woods]* and a *Hinterwald [Back woods]*. The back lower woods, which are still mentioned in 1788, had been cleared. Those woods lay near the Wasserbeiz on the Knittelsheim district border. Today we distinguish the following wooded areas:

1.) In the Front woods:

In den Birken [In the Birches] [D-2]: This area is largely forested by birch trees.

In den Oberalmen [In the Upper public meadows] [C-1]: This area is a part of the *Oberweide* or upper meadows that belonged to the community at large.

Im Viehtrieb [In the Cattle run]: This area was also a part of the former *Oberweide,* or upper meadows where the cattle were driven to graze.

In den Erlen [In the Alders] [D-3]: The existence of this rich alder forest plot indicates wet, poor soil.

2.) In the back woods:

In den Stöcken [In the Bushes] [B-2]: Because the forest had to provide building and firewood for the whole population, it seems that large trees were rare. *Stöcken* or *Stecken* refers to smaller trees and bushes that were the main growth in this area.

Im Dämmel [In the Dark Forest] [B-1]: The Dämmel already appears in a document dated 1602. *Timmel* or *Demel* means a deep, dark forest.

Im Rödel [In the Small Clearing] [B-3]: This area got its name from the adjacent small clearing where trees were cut down to create meadows.

Im Neuwiesenschlag [In the New meadow clearing] [B-4]: This forest is also named after the adjacent meadow, the Neuwiesen.

Obere Waldstücke [Upper forested areas] [C-4]: This forest is located in the western part of the district and faces the Haardt.

Untere Waldstücke [Lower forested areas] [C-5]: This forest is located in the eastern part of the district and faces the Rhine.

Im Mühlwiesenschlag [In the mill meadow clearing] [C-4]: The forest is named after the adjacent Mühlwiesen, or mill meadows.

Im See [In the lake] [B-5]: Like the adjacent *Seewiesen,* or Lake Meadows, this land plot was once covered with standing water.

Area names after the land consolidation of 1964

A) Pastures

(The numbers indicate the section in which the land plot names were listed and explained in the previous pages.)

Am Altsheimer Weg	7	In der oberen Haardt	5
Ober dem Bauernweg	7	In der niederen Haardt	5
Im Baumann	4	In den neuen Haardtstücken	5
Auf dem Berg	2	Im Hintergrund	8
Im Bild	6	In der hohen Angewanne	2
Am Birnbaum	6	Ober dem Höhlchen	2
Im Bogen	3	Auf dem Kahlenberg	5
Auf dem Brett	2	Im Kaisersmorgen	New
Im Engelsgarten	4	In den Kappenäckern	6
An der Friedhofstraße	New	Am Knittelsheimer Weg	7
In der Froschau	2	In der Knopfgewanne	2
In den Gänsweidegärten	5	An der Landauer Straße	7
Im Gärn	3	In der Langgewanne	3

Am Gartenweg	7	In den Linsenäckern	5
Am Griebelnußbaum	6	Im Mittelgrund	New
Im Gröhlig	6	In der Mulde	2
Auf dem Großstück	1	Am Mühlweg	7
Außer dem Grübenweg	7	Im Niederfeld im Hintergrund	8
Im Oberfeld im Hintergrund	8	Im Schlägel	5
Im Poppelmann	4	Am Schlittweg	7
Bei den Quittenbäumen	6	Auf dem Schwalbenberg	6
Im Rehhag	6	In den Stockstücken	5
Im Reiterspieß	3	Im Sturm	4
An der Riedstraße	New	Im Tal	New
Bei der Rötdarr	6	An der Waldstraße	New
Im Ruschgarten	5	In den Weggärten	5
In den Scheeräckern	3	Im Zwerchsack	3

B) Meadows

In den Abtswiesen	4	In den Mühlwiesen	6
In den Allmendwiesen	6	Auf den Neuwiesen	6
In den Amtmannswiesen	6	Über der Queich	7
In den Börstwiesen	5	Im Rödel	6
Im Dämmel	2	Im Rohrbusch	5
Auf dem Faselbrühl	2	Im Schwenkpfuhl	2
In den Freiwiesen	6	In den Sechsmorgen	1
In den Gärtelswiesen	8	In den Seemorgen	2
In den Haardtwiesen	5	In den Seewiesen	2
Auf den Hinterwiesen	8	In den Stock- and Scheerwiesen	3
Auf den Hörsten	5	In den Waalen	2
Im Hundsloch	2	In den Wasserbeizwiesen	2

The land consolidation that ended in 1964 has changed the image of the Ottersheim district, sometimes dramatically. While the old land plots that developed over the centuries clearly bore the characteristics of their origination, the land consolidation for the first time had created a distribution defined on a drawing board with usefulness first and foremost in mind. The increased use of farm machinery required not only the consolidation of smaller parcels to larger cultivated areas but also required good access to each plot. While in the past it was not possible to reach every single plot even from a dirt road, after the consolidation as a rule, most plots could be reached by two access roads, one of which was paved. Attention was also paid to ensure that the length and width of a field were in reasonable proportion to facilitate the use of machines.

Regrettable is the fact that because of the land consolidation, hundreds of trees were felled. Fruit trees are certainly an obstacle to machine cultivation of the soil. But it should not be overlooked that treeless landscapes are more threatened by desertification than areas with trees. Disappearing with the trees and hedges are nesting opportunities for our songbirds, the eager helper of the farmer in controlling destructive insects. So where possible, trees and hedges should again be planted.

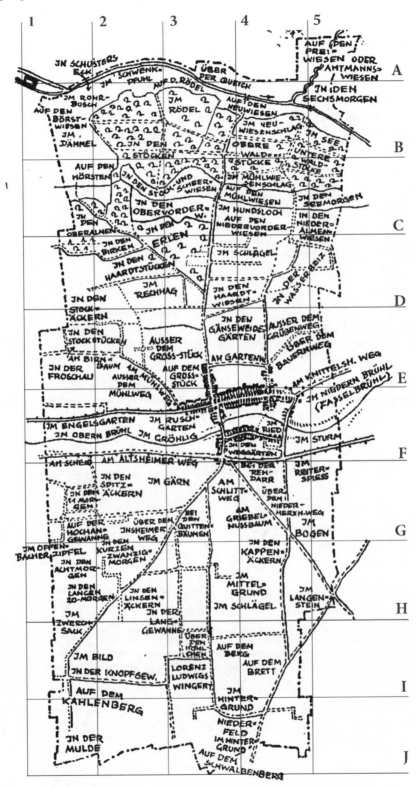

Ottersheim parcels before the land consolidation in 1964

With the land consolidation there was also the danger that the traditional place names would disappear in favor of mere numbers. Fortunately, this fear was not confirmed. All involved parties agreed at a meeting that the old names should be retained as much as possible. Some of the old plot names had to be given up because the number of plots was reduced. In this process, the more or less colorless names were given up while the old characteristic plot names remained. As the table on pages 394 and 395 shows, six new plot names were added. Their interpretation poses hardly any difficulty. From the names of nearby roads were derived the following plot names: "An der Friedhofstraße," "An der Riedstraße," and "An der Waldstraße."

The term "Im Mittelgrund" [H-4] [In the Middle ground] was already commonly in use. However, it was not the name of a land plot but was the collective term used for the fields on the near side of the Hintergrund. For the plot name "Im Tal" [In the Valley], the nature of the land was decisive. The plot name "Im Kaisersmorgen" was adopted from the Knittelsheim district. Professor Christmann assumes *Kaisermorgen* at one time belonged to a family named *Kaiser*. But he has to admit that the name *Kaiser* cannot be found in Knittelsheim in the past 400 years. Moreover, the local vernacular speaks not of a Kaisermorgen but instead of a *Käsermorgen*. Peculiar in any case is the fact that the plots Kaisermorgen, Reiterspiel, Bogen, and Reiterspieß all lie close together, although they belong partly to the Knittelsheim district and partly to the Ottersheim district. After all, could these have been royal estate lands that were once used for conducting tournaments? We do not know. At any rate, it provides food for thought that the adjacent land plot "Im Sturm" to the north of the highway belonged to the Palatine Electors in earlier times who provided it as fief land to their castle wardens.

The Land Consolidation in Ottersheim

A land consolidation is certainly not an invention of our century or only the result of mechanized agriculture. Already in 1886, Bavaria issued a law concerning land consolidation in the Palatinate through which "better use of land through consolidation of plots or through the regulation of roads" was to be achieved. The land consolidation could be carried out any place where the majority of property owners wished this measure. The management was entrusted to a commission appointed by the King at the Chamber of the Interior.

Until the mid-20th century however, hardly anyone in Ottersheim was seriously interested in land consolidation. While true that the fields and meadows of the individual farmers were almost always scattered throughout the district and the roadways were not always laid in the most appropriate fashion, as long as the farmers used their horses and cows for their fieldwork and most of the work had to be done by hand, they did not expect any appreciable help from a land reorganization. They therefore waived any redistricting, although it would have been possible decades before. That changed only when tractors and agricultural machinery replaced draft animals and displaced many of the traditional tools. For example, with a combine you could often accomplish very little on the small, irregular parcels; and tractors can only work efficiently when the fields are sufficiently large and both sides are accessible. The benefits of land consolidation could be observed daily by the Ottersheim farmers at the neighboring town of Offenbach that redrew their entire district area in the fifties. A drawback against a land consolidation was first and foremost the high cost that would be incurred in spite of significant federal and state grants to individual landowners.

The first push for Ottersheim land consolidation was under Mayor Paul Dörzapf during his meeting on 22 May 1957. Of the 15 council members, ten spoke in favor of a land consolidation that was followed up with a corresponding application directed to the Department of Culture in Neustadt an der Weinstraße. Almost exactly a year later, an educational meeting of all landowners was convened on 14 May 1958 at the "Zum Gambrinus" Inn where a representative of the Cultural Office spoke about the organizational side of land consolidation, the rights and obligations of the parties, the costs, and the expected funding from federal and state government.

The well attended meeting served only as education while decisions would be made a week later at another meeting. In the meantime, lively discussions for and against land consolidation took place among the landowners. On 21 May 1958, the meeting hall at the "Zum Hirsch" Inn had hardly sufficient space to hold all the voting claimants and interested parties. In addition to youth, men and women of all ages had come to vote on a measure that was of crucial importance to the future of the farmers. Regardless of the size of the property, each owner was granted one vote. The count resulted in 153 voting no, 89 yes, and eight invalid. That led the progressive-minded Young Farmers Organization in the following weeks to collect petition signatures from the medium and large farmers in Ottersheim. It was found that of the area farmers who owned 624 hectares of cultivated land, a total of 356 hectares of land or 57% favored land consolidation.

However, this signature collection would not have been necessary. Even before the list was filed at the Cultural Office of Neustadt an der Weinstraße, the Ministry for Agriculture, Viticulture and Forestry, and the Department of Land Management office in Mainz had officially ordered land consolidation for Ottersheim on 10 July 1958.

So the State decided a matter that was otherwise apt to drive a wedge between the people and to cause strife within the village. After the die was cast, the Cultural Office of Neustadt an der Weinstraße began the necessary preparatory work. The Knittelsheim district was also to be reorganized together with Ottersheim. On 7 October 1959, a meeting of the participant communities was held at the "Zum Hirsch" Inn where six Ottersheim and five Knittelsheim board members were selected. From Ottersheim the following board members were elected: Robert Frey, Hugo Steegmüller, Paul Dörzapf, Oswald Gensheimer, Helmut Seither, and Alois Föhlinger. Paul Dörzapf was appointed Chairman of the General Committee of both communities, his deputy was Johann Eichmann of Knittelsheim. Selected as road architects were Hugo Steegmüller for Ottersheim and Fritz Steimer for Knittelsheim.

In April 1960, the entire Board of the General Committee assembled for its first meeting at the invitation of the Cultural Office of Neustadt an der Weinstraße where the order of the activities was discussed. First, the meadow lands were to be reorganized and then an unpaved road was to be built in a southerly direction from each of the villages of Ottersheim and Knittelsheim. The remaining roadways were to be built after that. A rather difficult task was the equitable distribution of the fields and meadows among the individual landowners. Specifically, everyone involved should have land of approximate value equal to their current property in terms of value, yield, and distance from the village after consolidation. On the other hand, the assignments only made sense if the land of individual farmers could be consolidated into the largest possible area. It was therefore necessary to conduct a thorough ground analysis in the district. This was conducted by officially appointed estimators with the appropriate support staff. The Commission began work in 1961. The land was given grades depending on the location, yield value, and soil composition with the best land receiving Grade I and the worst Grade VII. For example, if land of better quality had to be exchanged for land of lesser quality, the difference was made up by increasing the amount of land. Moreover, every farmer's opinion on the proposed redistribution of the land was heard. In this way, it was possible to satisfy most of the affected persons, especially because with larger properties each farmer received land in both good and lesser locations.

In the summer of 1964, the time came when the land could finally be surveyed and marked. Then the parcels were assigned to their new owners who were allowed to cultivate it immediately, although the entries in the land register were not made until later. In the difficult tasks associated with the land consolidation, Head Survey Consultant Grießemer of the Cultural Affairs Office in Neustadt an der Weinstraße deserves special recognition. Through his expertise and negotiating skills, he was able to balance opposing views and to bring the project to a positive conclusion.

The cost of land consolidation for Ottersheim and Knittelsheim amounted to about 2.4 million deutschemarks of which about half was attributable to infrastructure construction. In Ottersheim alone about 13 kilometers of concrete roads were constructed. The water resource development projects cost about 0.6 million deutschemarks. The landowners in Ottersheim and Knittelsheim had to come up with about 1.3 million deutschemarks. A hectare of the best land was worth about 1,800 deutschemarks while the worst brought only about 550 deutschemarks. Over a million deutschemarks were provided by the Federal and

State governments. About 750,000 deutschemarks in expenses that arose from the consolidation was to be made payable by the Ottersheim landowners over several years.

The land consolidation had changed roads and land plots that for the most part were more than a thousand years old. That the district was not divided into more rational parcels at an earlier time is due mainly to the rules and laws of ownership in previous times. In the Middle Ages, large parts of the upper and lower fields belonged to the monasteries of Hördt, Klingenmünster, Eußerthal, and to the Palatine Electors. But the citizens of Ottersheim had no rights over these properties. Also, the road network was adequate for the existing property rules. That changed in the course of the 19th century when the manorial estates were turned over to private owners and then were gradually fragmented more and more through inheritance. Thus in many cases, narrow belts of land evolved such as the Langgewanne where some fields were 500 meters long but only four to five meters wide. Such misshapen plots have been removed by the land consolidation. As a rule, the lengths and widths of the fields are such that agricultural machinery can be used without difficulty

Unfortunately, with the land consolidation many fruit trees are gone that once adorned the top end of the land parcels and gave the district a varied appearance. Although important reasons against planting fruit trees along the roads exist, at the same time ways and means should be found to prevent a total lack of trees and shrubs along the fields. This is required not only to protect birds but also serves to preserve the climatic conditions in the Rhine valley. The treeless but especially fertile Ukraine and its dreaded drought years should be a warning.

Rosenhof and Gärtnerhof, the Relocation Farms of Ottersheim

Not only were the farm lands largely merged as a result of the land consolidation, but also provided were opportunities to build farm houses and buildings on the newly formed properties within the district. Two Ottersheim farming families took advantage of the opportunity and settled near the concrete road south of the field cross. Eduard Kreiner established his farmstead in the "Baumann," while Artur Trauth built his farm on the opposite side to the west of the concrete road. The two farmers had already informed the land consolidation office at the Ministry of Culture in Neustadt of their wishes so the relocation farms could be part of the planning activity. Eduard Kreiner (1967 deceased) and his wife Paula née Benz began the extensive construction project in November 1964 after the consolidated land was turned over to them for their use. Mason Ripp built the house and farm buildings according to standardized plans in just under ten months so that it could be occupied in October 1965. The house comprises 115.5 square meters of floor area with approximately an equal-sized cellar and storage rooms. The outbuilding is 30 meters long and 20 meters wide. The southern half contains appropriate stables for cattle and pigs while the north side contains a large dairy barn and a feed room. In a later phase of construction, a retirement home of about 40 square meters was planned to be built. A well of 29 meters depth provided the farm with the necessary water for drinking and farm use. It delivered 14 liters of water per second. Electric current was provided by the Bellheim-Herxheim line while the Federal Post Office provided a telephone connection. Belonging to the farm were about ten hectares of valuable farmland. In addition to grain and vegetables, the Kreiner family mainly raised sugar beets.

Without substantial grants and a subsidized State loan, it would have been hardly possible for a young farm family to set up such a large property with a value of around 160,000 deutschemarks in such a short time. The power supply and the installation of the well was completely covered by the state. The low-interest loans were to be repaid in the course of 35 years.

Artur Trauth built his farm on the west side of the concrete road under similar conditions. As a gardener's son from Herxheim, he married Gisela Glatz, an Ottersheim farmer's daughter. Trauth wanted to devote himself mainly to growing vegetables with his newly built greenhouse and also to raise a few pigs. He had an architect create his design blueprint, unlike his neighbor Kreiner.

The decision about the names of the two relocated farms was made in 1966. At the request of the Kreiner family and with the permission of the District government, their property was henceforth known as *Rosenhof,* and the Trauth family house was to be called *Gärtnerhof.* In spite of names, the owners and their relatives do not even consider making themselves so independent as to restrict their relations with the villagers to a minimum. Quite the contrary! The two relocated families come into the village very often and take an active part in community life. Also, they are quite often visited by their relatives and acquaintances in Ottersheim so any feeling of abandonment cannot possibly arise. Moreover, when working in their kitchens or fields, they always have the familiar silhouette of their beloved home village before them, and with binoculars they can even see the time of day on the church tower. And the children regularly attend school in Ottersheim, getting to know their age-mates there. Under these circumstances, the risk of alienation is very low.

Ottersheim Family Names Index of 1965

The following index shows the first recorded bearer of the surname in Ottersheim. The living persons today are descended from him in direct line. Protestant families are marked with a superscript [P] to the right of the family name.

Bauchhenß [P]	Theobald from Bellheim. Marriage about 1797 with A. Barbara Gensheimer.
Becker	Rudolf, forest technician from Schaidt. Marriage in 1952 with Elfriede Kuhn.
Becker [P]	Albert, carpenter from Oberlustadt. Marriage in 1958 with Hildegard Sauther.
Becki	1. Viktor from Bellheim. Marriage in 1930 with Elisabeth Kröper. 2. Herbert, driver from Bellheim. Marriage in 1948 with Ottilie Job.
Benner [P]	Günter from Pirmasens. Marriage in 1954 with Gertrud Hoffmann.
Benz	Markus from Zeiskam. Marriage in 1863 with Katharina Zwißler.
Bischoff	1. Anton from Ottersheim. Marriage in 1757 with Magdalena Job. 2. Georg Jakob, weaver from Offenbach. Marriage in 1815 with Katharina Winkelblech.
Blachut [P]	Josef, hometown expellee from Weimar. Moved here in 1953.
Blattmann [P]	Friedrich Theobald from Offenbach. Marriage in 1911 with Emma Weiß.
Braun	Ludwig from Offenbach. Marriage in 1916 with Amalie Seither.
Brauner	Waldemar from Göcklingen. Marriage in 1959 with Anna Maria Kröper.
Breßler [P]	Wilhelm from Oberhochstadt. Marriage in 1925 with Katharina Scheurer.
Brüderle [P]	Johann (Lutheran) from Bockschaft near Sinsheim. Marriage in 1813 with Eva Margareta Job.
Bullinger	Walter, farmer from Herxheim. Marriage in 1963 with Mathilde Ettmüller.
Burgermeister	Peter from Ottersheim. Marriage in 1760 with Ursula Hahn from Steinfeld.
Burkard	Wilhelm from Wernersberg. Marriage in 1943 with Hildegard Jochim.
Detzel	Kaspar from Herxheim. Marriage in 1884 with Anna Job.
Diebold	Emil, a farmer from Harthausen. Marriage in 1959 with Gertrud Merdian.
Disqué [P]	Ludwig from Knittelsheim. Marriage in 1895 with Anna Maria Barucker.
Dörzapf	1. Wendelin from Ottersheim. Marriage in 1757 with Elisabeth Störtzer.

	2. Konrad from Ottersheim. Marriage in 1771 with Margareta Maier from Herxheim.
Dotterweich	Josef, miller from Geiselwind near Bamberg. Marriage in 1875 with Eva Rösch.
Dumser	Karl, an electrician from Herxheim. Marriage in 1919 with Anna Zwißler.
Eichenlaub	Valentin from Herxheimweyher. Marriage in 1874 with Anna Maria Kröper.
Eichmann	Friedrich from Knittelsheim. Marriage in 1954 with Emily Schwaab.
Ettmüller	Sebastian from Sarregemünd. Marriage in 1908 with Anna Hilsendegen.
Faath	Heinrich, carpenter from Offenbach. Marriage in 1900 with Lina Kopf.
Fischer	Walter, laborer from Hördt. Marriage in 1958 with Luise Kuntz.
Föhlinger	Stephen, shoemaker from Herxheimweyher. Marriage in 1748 with Christine Dörzapf.
Freudenstein	Franz, railroad worker from Westheim. Marriage in 1920 with Emma Heider.
Frey [P]	Jakob, baker from Dalland in Baden. Marriage in 1858 with Barbara Stephan.
Frölich [P]	Werner of Kaiserslautern. A Protestant teacher in Ottersheim since 1956.
Gaab	Georg Peter, musician from Siebeldingen. Marriage in 1805 with Maria Katharina Witz.
Gadinger	Rudolf from Ottersheim. Marriage in 1752 with Maria Barbara Dörzapf.
Gensheimer	Christoph, weaver from Offenbach. Marriage in 1823 with Ottilie Dörzapf.
Gensheimer [P]	Jakob from Ottersheim. Marriage in 1707.
Gläßgen	Vinzenz, painter from Wernersberg. Marriage in 1960 with Maria Renate Lavo.
Glatz	Georg from Ottersheim. Marriage in 1765 with Margareta Ullrich from Kleinfischlingen.
Greichgauer	David, shoemaker from Wollmesheim. Marriage in 1829 with Anna Maria Hoffmann.
Günther [P]	Abraham from Ottersheim. Marriage in 1747 with Maria Barbara Diehl from Bellheim.
Günther	Wilhelm, assistant mechanic from Herxheim. Marriage in 1944 with Auguste Kuhn.
Gütermann	Julius from Mörlheim. Marriage in 1952 with Paula Walk.
Gutting	Andreas from Ottersheim. Marriage in 1783 with Maria Elisabeth Gadinger.

Hatzenbühler	1. Nikolaus from Ottersheim. Marriage in 1743 with Eva Maria Benz.
	2. Valentin from Ottersheim. Marriage in 1747 with Katharina Dörzapf.
Hatzenbühler [P]	Johann from Ottersheim. Marriage in 1743 with Katharina Bähr from Haßloch.
Heist	Auguste née Föhlinger. Moved here in 1960 from Bensheim.
Hellmann	1. Erich, bricklayer from Herxheimweyher. Marriage in 1950 with Aloisa Gadinger.
	2. Oskar from Herxheimweyher. Marriage in 1952 with Ruth Nikolaus.
Herrmann	Jean from Hördt. Marriage in 1897 with Rosa Job.
Hilsendegen	Valentin from Ottersheim. Marriage in 1757 with Agathe Kröper.
Hindert	Pankraz, bricklayer from Switzerland. Marriage in 1782 with Anna Maria Dörzapf.
Hoffmann	Johann, baker from Offenbach. Marriage in 1891 with Magdalena Jünger of Ruchheim.
Hoffmann [P]	Philipp Dieter from Bellheim. Marriage in 1833 with Katharina Job.
Hörner	Stephan from Bellheim. Marriage in 1923 with Maria Seither.
Holdermann	Kurt Alfons from Speyer. Marriage in 1962 with Angela Glatz.
Hünerfauth [P]	Emil, a carpenter from Zeiskam. Marriage in 1937 with Paula Brüderle.
Huwe	Heinrich from Mechtersheim. Marriage in 1883 with Katharina Zwißler.
Jäger	Jakob, Head Teacher from Arzheim. Transferred in 1923 to Ottersheim, died in 1929.
Jeckel	Jakob, bricklayer from Waldhambach. Marriage in 1810 with Katharina Merdian.
Jennewein	Wilhelm, shoemaker from Offenbach but born in Pirmasens. Marriage in 1919 with Maria Faath.
Job	1. Nikolaus from Ottersheim. Marriage 1732 with Barbara Müller.
	2. Salomon from Ottersheim. Marriage in 1724 with Anna Maria Kreiner.
Jochim	1. Johann from Knittelsheim. Marriage in 1871 with Anna Maria Gutting.
	2. Peter from Knittelsheim. (Innkeeper at the `Hirsch´). Marriage in 1872 with Katharina Müller.
Kaiser	Jakob from Offenbach. Marriage in 1915 with Karolina Gotz.
Kern [P]	Michael from Bellheim. Marriage in 1897 with Katharina Barucker.
Knebl	Jakob, expellee from Yugoslavia. Moved here in 1952.
Knoll	Johann from Ottersheim. Marriage in 1755 with Margareta Huck.

Kopf	1. Konrad from Ottersheim. Marriage in 1762 with Elisabeth Walk. 2. Georg from Ottersheim. Marriage in 1763 with Ursula Hahn. Konrad and Georg Kopf were brothers.
Korn	Emil from Pirmasens. Moved here in 1946.
Kramer	1. Gustav, miller from Bellheim. Marriage in 1910 with Maria Seither. 2. Erwin, builder from Bellheim. Marriage in 1961 with Helene Gadinger.
Krauß	Albert, blacksmith from Enkenbach. Marriage in 1938 with Rosa Stadel.
Kreiner	Stephan, tailor from Ottersheim. Marriage in 1756 with Elisabeth Glatz.
Kröper	1. Michael from Ottersheim. Marriage in 1749 with Agathe Benz. 2. Nikolaus from Ottersheim. Marriage in 1756 with Anna Maria Gadinger. Michael and Nikolaus Kröper were brothers. 3. Jakob from Knittelsheim. Marriage in 1750 with Elisabeth Seither.
Kruppenbacher	Georg from Knittelsheim. Marriage in 1924 with Anna Kreiner.
Kuhn	Johann, carpenter from Rheinzabern. Marriage in 1878 with Eva Katharina Wendel of Hainfeld.
Kuntz	Ludwig, painter from Herxheim. Marriage in 1867 with Margareta Dörzapf.
Lang	Cyrill from Eppenbrunn. Marriage in 1938 with Maria Müller.
Lerch	Severin from Offenbach. Marriage in 1940 with Elisabeth Kopf.
Lösch [P]	Heinrich from Offenbach. Marriage in 1854 with Barbara Weiß.
Lutz	Martin from Knittelsheim. Marriage in 1873 with Elisabeth Gadinger.
Märdian	Artur Josef from Oberhochstadt. Marriage in 1959 with Cäcilia Job.
Merdian	Jakob from Knittelsheim. Marriage in 1738 with Anna Maria Müller.
Mayr	Josef, a carpenter from Waal in Bavaria. Marriage in 1939 with Berta Zwißler.
Messemer	Johann, dairyman from Offenbach. Marriage in 1903 with Barbara Steimer from Knittelsheim.
Metzger [P]	Rudolf from Ilbesheim. Marriage in 1948 with Lydia Lösch.
Meyer	Johannes from Herxheim. Marriage in 1963 with Annemarie Münster.
Michalczyk	Josef from Eisenau in Upper Silesia, expellee. Marriage in 1951 with Gertrud Winkelblech née Glatz.
Mohr [P]	Eugen from Mechtersheim. Moved here as a joiner in 1962.

Moock	1. Georg from Ottersheim. Marriage in 1735 with Barbara Hatzenbühler.
	2. Franz from Offenbach. Married in 1904 with Barbara Wünschel.
	3. Karl from Bellheim. Married in 1948 with Erna Eichenlaub.
Morio	Jakob from Ranschbach. Marriage in 1907 with Elisabeth Reichling.
Morisak	Franz, locksmith from Bolonka/Yugoslavia, expellee. Moved here in 1959.
Müller	1. Johann from Offenbach. Marriage in 1775 with Katharina Huck.
	2. Michael, butcher from Bellheim. Marriage in 1884 with Magdalena Hoffmann.
	3. Eugen, locksmith from Offenbach. Marriage in 1952 with Melitta Zwißler.
	4. Rudolf from Rheinzabern. Marriage in 1963 with Gertrud Steegmüller.
Münster	Franz from Würzburg. Marriage in 1952 with Agnes Kopf.
Nikolaus	Gustav, whitewasher from Herxheimweyher. Marriage in 1927 with Maria Störtzer.
Ößwein	Franz Peter, shoemaker from Kuhardt. Marriage in 1865 with Christina Seither.
Pfaff	Leo, laborer from Alsenborn. Marriage in 1959 with Elisabeth Faath.
Puhl	Engelbert from Fremersdorf/Saar. Marriage in 1949 with Maria Glatz.
Reichling	Georg Heinrich, wheelwright from Bellheim. Marriage in 1808 with Magdalena Moock.
Richter	Willibald, bookkeeper from Seesitz/Außig, expellee.
	Mrs. Gertraud Richter has been a teacher in Ottersheim since 1952.
Ripp	Josef, mason from Scheibenhardt. Marriage in 1918 with Frieda Hilsendegen.
Ritter	Karl, heating technician from Hagenbach. Marriage in 1927 with Elisabeth Kröper.
Röhrig	August, locomotive engineer from Steinfeld. Marriage in 1910 with Maria Woock.
Romanowski [P]	Paul, blacksmith from Klinken/East Prussia. Moved here has an expellee in 1950.
Rund	Emil from Bellheim. Marriage in 1953 with Ida Seither.
Sablotny [P]	Charlotte from Freistadt, Kreis Rosenberg. Moved here as expellee in 1948.
Sauther [P]	Nikolaus from Oberhochstadt. Marriage in 1784 with Anna Barbara Hatzenbühler.
Schaller [P]	August from Bayreuth. Marriage in 1947 with Lydia Braun.
Scherff [P]	Philipp (Lutheran), blacksmith from Bodenheim near Mainz. Marriage in 1775 with Katharina Dörr.

Scherübl	Josef from Zweibrücken. Catholic priest in Ottersheim since 1959.
Scheurer ^P	Jakob from Haßloch. Marriage in 1818 with Barbara Ludwig.
Schmitz	Josef from Lövenich near Cologne. Marriage in 1946 with Anneliese Winkelblech.
Schreiber	August, gardener from Nußdorf. Marriage in 1938 with Susanna Glatz.
Schwaab	Johann from Alsterweiler. Marriage in 1902 with Anna Wingerter.
Schwarz	Karl, painter from Offenbach. Marriage in 1956 with Hildegard Job.
Schwendemann	Josef from Karawukowo in Backa. Moved here as expellee in 1951.
Schuhmann	Titus from Insheim. Marriage in 1938 with Ottilie Kopf.
Seither	1. Johann from Ottersheim. Marriage in 1752 with Apollonia Job. 2. Johannes from Ottersheim. Marriage in 1763 with Barbara Hörner.
Sentz	Johann from Lovas/Yugoslavia. Moved here as expellee in 1958.
Stadel	Georg Jakob. Marriage in 1776 with Christine Hatzenbühler.
Steegmüller	Johann Ludwig from Weingarten. Marriage in 1823 with Margareta Knoll of Herxheim. His grandfather Hartard Steegmüller was baker and innkeeper in St. Leon near Heidelberg.
Störtzer	Konrad, tailor from Ottersheim. Marriage in 1749 with Elisabeth Kröper.
Trauth	Artur from Herxheim. Marriage in 1951 with Gisela Glatz.
Uhrig	Eugen, woodworker from Offenbach. Marriage in 1961 with Eugenie Elisabeth Föhlinger.
Utherhardt ^P	Franz from Berghausen, Kreis Angermünde. Came as an expellee.
Walk	Nikolaus, mason from Ottersheim. Marriage in 1749 with Katharina Mesmer from Herxheimweyher.
Weimann	Josef from Karawukowo/Yugoslavia. Moved here as an expellee in 1950.
Weisbrod	Theodore from Hainfeld. Marriage in 1921 with Maria Kröper.
Weiß ^P	Philipp Jakob, cooper from Schwegenheim. Marriage in 1771 with Anna Maria Gensheimer.
Wenzel	Werner Theo, tailor from Stettin. Marriage in 1944 with Paula Bißon.
Wingerter	Franz from Knittelsheim. Marriage in 1806 with Ursula Kopf.
Winkelblech	Daniel from Ottersheim. Marriage in 1815 with Eva Geidlinger and in 1824 with Katharina Dörzapf.
Wünschel	Johann, boardmaker from Leimersheim. Marriage in 1863 with Barbara Glatz.
Zeisberger	Rudolf, railway official from Oderberg/Silesia. Came as an expellee in 1952.
Zeyer	Maria from Frankenthal, Moved here in 1944.
Zwißler	Paul, carpenter from Erbes-Büdesheim near Alzey. Marriage in 1740 with Regina Hatzenbühler.

Origin and Meaning of Surnames

Until the late Middle Ages, people in Germany had only a given name. Many of these names were taken from the Bible while others came from ancient Germanic heritage. Individual family names did not appear until 1100 A.D. These spread more rapidly in the cities than in the small, manageable villages. The surname was used to distinguish its bearer from other people of the same given name. It was added to the given name and considered less important than the given name. This is confirmed by a list of Ottersheim names from 1590. That list is laid out alphabetically. In contrast to current practice, not the surnames but the given names are sorted. The surnames are explanations for the given names in a sense. Based on their origin, the following major surname groups can be distinguished:

1. Titles of trades and government offices

Many Ottersheim surnames are derived from a trade or office. *Bäcker [Bakers], Müller [Millers], Schuhmacher [Shoemakers],* and *Schmiede [Smiths]* exist everywhere. It is therefore not surprising that these became the most common surnames. That *Kröper, Seither,* and *Dörzapf* are also names derived from professions is no longer recognized at first glance.

2. Names depicting place of origin

Those who moved from one village to another place and married there were often named after their place of origin. A Konrad Geinßheim (Geinsheim) is listed in a document from 1508. He is probably the ancestor of all the *Gensheimer* families who live in Ottersheim and the surrounding area. At the same time the name *Hatzenbühler* (Hatzenbühel) appears, meaning immigrants from Hatzenbühl. Moreover, in 1323 there was a Speyer citizen who called himself *Ottersheimer.* It is likely that he moved from Ottersheim to Speyer; there he was named after his place of origin. Meanwhile, the family has vanished.

3. Patronymic - named after the father

To describe a son more accurately, a father's given name was often added to his son's name. So for example, the son *Jakob* of the father *Gunther* was called *Jakob Günther.* Similar name formations are still possible today though they are not officially registered, for example, Philip Marx (Benz), Jean Marx (Benz), Philipp Jean Franz (Job).

4. Attribute names

Some surnames go back to a distinctive feature of the original carrier. *Lang [Long] and Kurz [Short], Weiß [White] and Schwarz [Black], Groß [Large],* and *Klein [Small]* are quite frequent surnames of this type. Our ancestors certainly were not squeamish. The bald-headed they called *Glatz* and the quarrelsome *Greiner.*

5. House names

The surnames *Bär [Bear]*, *Ochs [Ox]*, and *Schaf [Sheep]* do not imply that their previous carriers have behaved like bears, oxen, or sheep. Rather, here we are dealing with old house names. Before there were house numbers, the houses were marked with an eagle, a sheep, an ox, a horse, a deer, and the like, especially in the city. Thereafter, the inhabitants of a given house was called *Adler [Eagle]*, *Schaf [Sheep]*, *Ochs [Ox]*, *Roß [Horse]*, or *Hirsch [Deer]* depending on the house mark. The use of such house names has been preserved in the tavern signs.

6. Role names

Many a surname reminds of the role that its first carrier took on at the annual recurring plays during Lent, Easter, and Christmas and probably continued playing for decades. Thus the names *Kaiser [Emperor]*, *König [King]*, *Bischof [Bishop]*, *Graf [Count]*, and so on arose.

7. Nicknames

Also, nicknames occasionally became family surnames. For example, whoever constantly used the phrase "Daß Gott erbarm" [Lord have mercy], did not need to wonder why he was generally called *Gotterbarm*.

In addition to German names, foreign names also exist in Ottersheim. In the reign of Louis XIV (1643-1715), many French Protestants (Huguenots) fled to the Palatinate and settled there. These refugees have kept their French surnames. The end of the Second World War brought a large influx from the East. The names of these expellees mostly have a Slavonic sound so that they appear to us now as strange names, although they often are of German origin.

1. Family names that come from trades or official offices

Becker:	A baker.
Benner:	The word *Benne* previously described braid made of willows. The maker of baskets, panniers, and back packs were called *Benner*.
Bleimaier:	A *Meier* in the Middle Ages was a supervisor and head of a feudal estate, a *Meierhof*. Later, a bearer of the name *Meier* was a lead caster.
Burgermeister:	The head of the citizens. He was also known as *Schultheiß [mayor]* or *Schulze* because he was responsible for the collection of debts (tithes, etc.).
Dörzapf:	A man named *Dörr* who served beer or wine from the *Zapf* or *Zapp [tap]*, that is, an innkeeper. He owned a tavern keeper pin and thus was conferred the official right to pour out drinks. *Dörr* comes from the old German name *Dioro*, which means dear or precious.

Hoffmann:	A *Hoffmann* was either a servant at the court of a nobleman or a peasant who was rewarded with a manorial property.
Holdermann:	A man standing in a fiduciary relationship. The Middle High German word *Holde* means a person who performs services, such as a porter.
Hünerfauth:	The *Hühnerfaut* or chicken bailiff had to collect the tithe chickens (capons or caps) on Ash Wednesday, in May, and in November.
Korn:	A *Körner* was a grain dealer. Maybe also a nickname for farmers.
Kröper:	A craftsman who makes cooking pots of clay or metal.
Kramer:	An owner of a general store.
Leingang:	Perhaps a man who was employed in shipping on the Rhine and who had to monitor the towpath.
Lösch:	An arbitrator who mediated disputes and made peace.
Mayr:	Bavarian form of *Meier*. The administrator of an estate was called a *Meier* in the Middle Ages. The word comes from the Latin word *Major* meaning, the Greater. The French word *Maire* (as in Burgermeister) is also derived from the Latin word *Major*.
Messemer:	A sacristan or sexton. The Swiss expression for the sacristan is *Sigrist*.
Metzger:	A butcher.
Meyer:	(See Mayr above.)
Müller:	An owner of a mill.
Richter:	In Eastern Germany, the *Richter* is a village church elder or magistrate. As such, he is an organizer, director, or judge.
Ritter:	A *Ritter* was a knight or horseman of the King. *Ritter* may also indicate a person who in folk theater plays the role of the knight.
Sauther:	*Sutter, Sauther,* or *Seither* is the the old name for seamsters and menders. Most often this meant a cobbler.
Scherübl:	A Bavarian farmer who grew mostly *Scherr* beets (fine cooking beets).
Scheurer:	Supervisor of a *Scheuer* (manorial barn) or administrator of the whole estate.
Schmitz:	The Rhenish form of *Smith* or *Schmitt.*
Schreiber:	Official recorder for a city, administration, or guild. A notary, accountant, or broker.
Schwendemann:	A servant who cleans the meadows of bushes through burning.
Schuhmann:	A shoemaker.
Seither:	(See Sauther above.)
Stadel:	A supervisor over a *Städel [barn]* or a stately storehouse.

Steegmüller:	Owner of a *Stegemühle,* that is, a mill with equipment for commercial work for which strong flowing water is required. Stegmühl is still the name of 15 places in Bavaria. A charter of 1357 speaks of the "Stegmul in den Oren" (Öhringen).
Störtzer:	In Switzerland, the tinsmith or plumber is called *Störtzer.* The name is also used to denote a land traveller, such as a vagabond.
Weisbrod:	A baker who produced mainly white bread.
Winkelblech:	A tinsmith who lived "Im Winkel," that is, off the main path.

2. Family names derived from place or country of origin

Berwanger:	*Berwangen* is a place name in Baden.
Blattmann:	A *Blattmann* or *Blatter* is a resident of a house that is situated on a stone ledge that is devoid of plant growth.
Breßler:	In South Tyrol, *Preßler* is a native of Brixen. Otherwise, it denotes someone from *Breslau.*
Dotterweich:	*Dotterweich* is a place name in Wuerttemberg, which today has been changed to Dorneich.
Eichenlaub:	An ancestor lived in *Eichenlau* or *Eichenloh,* that is, in the oak woods.
Eichmann:	The settlement was marked by *Eichen [oaks].*
Ettmüller:	*Ettmühle* or *Öttlmühle* is a place name in Bavaria.
Föhlinger:	*Felling* is a place name in Bavaria. The name *Föllinger* is common in Tyrol. *Föhlinger* migrated from there to the Palatinate.
Freudenstein:	*Freudenstein* is a place name near Maulbronn.
Gadinger:	*Kading* is a place name in Bavaria.
Gensheimer:	*Geinsheim* is a village in the Palatinate.
Greichgauer:	The fertile hill country between the Black Forest and Odenwald is called the *Kraichgau.*
Hatzenbühler:	*Hatzenbühl* is a village in the southern Palatinate.
Hellmann:	The term *Hell* was used to denote a hidden place, a wild gorge or a remote location.
Hilsendegen:	*Hülse* means holly or buckthorn. *Degen* once denoted a young warrior, follower, or servant. The *Hilsendegen* was thus a follower or servant who lived along a road covered with holly.
Hindert:	Residents of *Hinterhaus [back building],* or a *Hintersasse [resident without citizenship].*
Hörner:	*Hörn* is a common place name, especially in the Alps.
Kruppenbacher:	*Grubenbach* is a place name in Upper Hesse.
Münster:	A very common place name.
Puhl:	*Buol* or *Bühl* is a place name.

Rund:	In Westphalia, *Rund* or *Runte* denotes a cut in the landscape, in the heath or in the forest. Those living there were called *Rund* or *Runte.*
Sablotny:	A Polish name. It describes a person who lived in an unkempt place.
Schwaab:	The ancestors came from Swabia.
Utherhardt:	In Low German, *Ut der Haardt* means originating in the Haardt [forest].
Wingerter:	An ancestor is from *Wingerte,* as in *Weingarten [Wine garden].*
Wünschel:	Diminutive form of *Wünsch, Winsch,* or *Wunsch.* Denotes people of Wendish origin. Related are the names *Wendt, Windt* and *Windisch.* The name *Wünschel* is especially common in Eastern Germany.
Zeisberger:	*Zaißberg* is a place name near Rosenheim.
Zwißler:	*Zwiesel* is a land and place name located in Bavaria. It means a fork, such as a fork in a road.

3. Family names derived from the first name of the father

Bauchhenß:	*Henß* is the North German form of *Johannes.* The first to carry this name seems to have had a *Bauch [an extensive belly].*
Benz:	Short form of the old German name *Berchtold* or *Berthold,* meaning, the illustrious ruler.
Braun:	Old German first name *Bruno* meaning, shining, sparkling, or brilliant.
Brauner:	Descendants of *Braun* or *Bruno.* (See Braun above.)
Burkard:	Old German first name *Burkhard* meaning, the courageous protector of the castle.
Detzel:	Term of endearment for *Dietrich* meaning, the people's prince.
Diebold:	Old German given name *Theobald* meaning, a man who excels through courage in the army and among the people.
Faath:	Short form of *Servat. Servatius* is the Latin term meaning, the rescued.
Gaab:	The old German name *Gabo* is similar in Greek to *Theodor* meaning, the gift of God.
Gaube:	The Swabian form of the first name *Gabo.* (See Gaab above.)
Gläßgen:	Diminutive of the Greek name *Nikolaus* meaning, the people's victor. Other forms are *Klaus, Klaas, Kläsgen.*
Günther:	The old German name *Gunther* or *Günther* meaning, hero in battle.
Gütermann:	Local form of the old German given name *Guotmann* or *Gutmann.* In the Middle Ages, an armed vassal or a fief owner was called a *Gütermann.*

Gutting:	Sons or descendants of *Godo* meaning, the good or the friend of God.
Heist:	Short form to *Matheis, Matthäus, Matthias.* The Aramaic word *Matthäus [Matthew]* meaning, gift of God.
Herrmann:	*Hermann* or *Herimann* is a warrior, a man in the army.
Jeckel:	Pet form of *Jakob* meaning, the heel-holder.
Jennewein:	Distorted form of *Saint Ingenuinus* meaning, the free-born. The saint is especially revered in Brixen. Jennewein is a Tyrolean name.
Job:	German form of Old Testament name of *Hiob* meaning, the attacker.
Jochim:	Germanized form of the Hebrew name *Joachim* meaning, God will raise him up.
Kern:	Old German name *Chemo.* It is sometimes also a collective name for an industrious, down-to-earth person.
Kopf:	*Kopf* or *Kopp* is the short form for *Jakob,* that is, the heel-holder.
Kuhn:	Short form of *Konrad, Kuno, Kunz, Kurt* meaning, a consultant to the tribe.
Kuntz:	Like *Kuhn* it is a short form of *Konrad,* a consultant to the tribe.
Lutz:	Short form of *Ludwig* or *Chlodwig* meaning, the glorious warrior.
Märdian:	Alemannic form of *Martin* meaning, son of the war god - Mars.
Merdian:	(See Märdian above.)
Michalczyk:	Slavic form of *Michael* meaning, who is like God.
Morisak:	Perhaps a Slavic form of *Moritz, Mauritius.*
Morio:	Morio is a Latin word meaning a fool, jester, jesters, or joker. It can describe a person's character, or his job as court jester, or his role in church drama.
Nikolaus:	The Greek name *Nikolaus* meaning, people's victory.
Ößwein:	*Answin, Oswin, Öswein* meaning, protected by *Äsen,* friend of the gods.
Reichling:	*Reichlin, Reuchlin, Richelin.* Diminutive of *Richard* meaning, the rich, strong, brave prince.
Ripp:	Old German name *Ripo, Riprecht, Ruprecht, Rupert* meaning, the splendid or glorious.
Röhrig:	Old German given name *Roridi, Rurik* meaning, the glorious prince or the splendid. The name Röhrig is very common in the middle Rhine area. It can therefore also mean, he who lives in the Röhrich [Reeds].
Romanowski:	Slavic form of *Roman* meaning, the Roman.
Scherff:	Old German given name having the meaning, reckless, sharp, rough.
Sentz:	Short for *Vinzcenz* meaning, the winner.

413

Trauth:	Old German given name *Drudo, Trut, Trutwin, Trautwein* meaning, love or confidante.
Uhrig:	Old German given name *Ulrich, Udalrich, Odalrich* meaning, the ruler of the hereditary goods. The widespread use of the name is due to Bishop Ulrich of Augsburg, the winner over the Hungarians. Bishop Ulrich was canonized in 993.
Walk:	Old German given name *Walko, Wolfgang* meaning, the man who walks with the auspicious wolf.
Weimann:	Silesian form *Wigman, Wichmann, Weikmann* meaning, the fighter, warrior, hero, valiant fighter.
Wenzel:	Short form of *Wenzeslaus* meaning, the famous hero. Wenceslaus is the patron saint of Bohemia.
Zeyer:	Swabian form of the Greek name *Cyriakus* meaning, belonging to the Lord.

4. Family names derived from a distinctive feature

Becki:	The name *Becki* comes from the French name *Beccue.* The name was Germanized into *Becki* because the Palatine pronunciation of Beccue sounds like Becki. It could mean, a man with a long nose or hooked nose.
Blachut:	Slavic form of *Blauhut.* Blue was the color of fools.
Disqué:	The French name *Disqué* literally means, the scholar, he who knows. Originally the name was pronounced *Dikee [Dikay].*
Dumser:	A person who lives remote from man.
Frey:	A free-born, belonging to the free, in contrast to the many half-free and not free, or bonded.
Frölich:	A man with a cheerful, happy personality.
Glatz:	The first bearer of this name was generally noticed by his bald head.
Huwe:	The Alemannic word *Huwe* means, the night owl. Perhaps the first bearer of this name was a night owl, that is, he never went to bed on time. Under certain circumstances, *Huwe [Owl]* could have been a house sign from which its residents were named.
Knebl:	A rough, clumsy fellow.
Knoll:	A somewhat awkward man.
Krauß:	A man who attracted attention by his kinky, curly hair.
Kreiner:	A man who twists his mouth and snarls, a complainer or whiner.
Lang:	A strikingly tall person.
Lerch:	Instead of *Lerche* the people used to say *Lerch [Lark].* Metaphorically, this refers to a person who expresses his good mood in song.
Moock:	A small, quiet person who is a bit rough.

414

Schaller:	A crier or herald. The name is also used in the role of boaster or gossip.
Schwarz:	A man who attracted attention by his especially black hair.
Weiß:	A man who developed gray hair early or a had remarkably white skin.

5. Family names derived from house names

Bißon:	Literally, the French word *Bisson* means, wild ox or buffalo. This was probably a house name that became a family name.
Kaiser:	Even today, Inns "Zum Kaiser" [To the Emperor] are common. But it can also be a role name.

6. Family names derived from role names

Bischoff:	Surely, the first bearer of this name was not a real bishop. Instead, he played the role of bishop at the popular religious plays, as they are still preserved in the Oberammergau Passion Play. It is also conceivable that name is derived from an inn called "Zum Bischof" [To the Bishop]. Such inns were common in the Middle Ages.
Pfaff:	Until the Reformation, *Pfaff* was the commonly used word for a priest or pastor. It was in no way derogatory as it is today. (See Pfaffengasse in Speyer.)

7. Family names derived from nicknames

Brüderle:	Diminutive of *Bruder [Brother]*. This name has emerged from confidential, affectionate salutation

Appendix

Altsheim, the Lost Village between Ottersheim and Offenbach

Whoever wants to take the shortest walking route from Ottersheim to Offenbach should use the Altsheimer Weg that runs just south of the Brühlgraben from east to west. It would have been obvious to call this dirt road the Offenbacher Weg as has been done with the Insheimer, Herxheimer, Rülzheimer, or Knittelsheimer Weg, because it connects the two villages of Offenbach and Ottersheim directly with each other. But since time immemorial the Offenbach and Ottersheim residents both have called it the Altsheimer Weg. This suggests that once there was a settlement between the two places that was called Altsheim. Significantly, there is a second Altsheimer Weg in the Herxheim district. It leads from the north side of the Herxheim village, over the Altsheimer mountain, to the Offenbach district boundary. Its imaginary extension to the north crosses the former road [the one from Ottersheim] at about the district boundary between Offenbach and Ottersheim. This suggests that the defunct place of Altsheim lay near this intersection. This assumption is also confirmed by a note in the "Pastoral Description of Offenbach" from 1866. There, Protestant Pastor Scherer writes the following:

> "From the boundary description of the land plots in the old court book, the location of the village of Altsheim, which has completely disappeared, can be determined. According to the record, Altsheim was about halfway between Offenbach and Ottersheim, beyond the Altsheimer creek, which is probably identical with the present-day so-called Brühlgraben."

Although there is no longer any trace of Altsheim to be seen, the historians are still able to report some things about this lost settlement. Thus, under Item 407 in his calendar entries, Glasschröder mentioned a document from the year 1529 in which it is noted that early Mass readers from Offenbach should read the Mass once every 14 days in Altsheim. In Heintz, we learn that the monasteries of Eußerthal and Hördt owned larger estates in Altsheim. He also points out that the famous war officer, Colonel Bastian Vogelsberger, was born in the little village of Altsheim near Herxheim. And Frey reports that the victorious Elector Friedrich I pitched his war camp in Altsheim after his departure from Heidelberg in 1455. However, Frey believes here that a different Altsheim is meant, which he believed to lie in the vicinity of Herxheim. There are no obvious reasons for this assumption however. The location of this second Altsheim would have been the Altsheimer mountain, one kilometer north of Herxheim. In this case, we would be dealing with the first settlement in the southern Palatinate that would not have been built at a creek. That man and animal would have gotten their water only from an artificial well would be very improbable. Also missing on the Altsheimer mountain are the grazing pastures on which the medieval peasant always placed great weight. In addition, it is very unlikely that two neighboring settlements would have the same name. Also, the distinction between *Altheim* and *Altzheim* does not help because the population of Ottersheim, Offenbach, and Herxheim have to this day only used the name Altsheim. So it should hardly be doubted that in this area there was just one village of Altsheim, and that this settlement was located near the Brühlgraben that lay between Ottersheim and Offenbach. If the place was still frequently called *Altsheim bei Herxheim,* this was certainly due to the fact that Ottersheim and Offenbach were still small, insignificant places in the 16th century while Herxheim was the seat of a Church District (Deanery) and was known well beyond the narrow district borders.

When searching for the probable location of the lost village of Altsheim, a view of the district borders before the land consolidation can help a little. While nearly all the fields along the Altsheimer Weg are laid out from south to north, the so-called Spitzäcker [Pointed fields] diverge strikingly from that rule, although the nature of the soil provides no reason for this. In this plot near the district border, the fields lay not only in various directions, but there are also six fields that run together into one single point. Even more remarkable is that no regular dirt road led to these fields from either side, and the owners had to be content with a narrow pathway through the neighboring properties. The random layout is only understandable when one assumes that there were once houses on this land whose inhabitants cultivated the surrounding area. This assumption is supported by the fact that sandstones of the type previously used for the construction of foundations or wells were found at the Spitzäcker during the excavation of beet fields.

Also noteworthy is the name and location of the land plot *Goldgrube [Gold mine]* at the district border toward Offenbach. The nature of the soil of this small area does not differ from that of the surrounding fields. There was therefore no reason to call the area Goldgrube because of any particular soil fertility. But if one interprets the name literally, one must assume that at one time gold coins or gold ornaments were found there. This is quite possible considering that houses once stood on the property. In addition to the Spitzäcker and the Goldgrube, the so-called *Viehweide [Cattle pasture]* also points toward a settlement. The *Vehwäd,* as they are locally known, comprise the Brühl meadows near the district border north of the Spitzäcker. The location already indicates that the area was not used for regular grazing of Ottersheim cattle, because that area lay north of the village on both sides of the present-day Gänsehaardt. While the Ottersheim Allmend [public] pasture was 41 hectares in size, the Viehweide pasture at the district boundary consisted of only 5 hectares of Brühl meadows. The location and size of this pasture suggests that the land once belonged to the village of Altsheim, and only after the demise of the community did it fall to Ottersheim.

We have only very meager historical evidence about the foundation and the fate of the village of Altsheim. Like other local villages on the Brühlgraben, this little one was probably a Frankish settlement from the time of the Merovingians. Christmann suggests that the name itself alludes to *Home of Alto* or *Oldo*. It seems that larger parts of the surrounding lands transferred into the ownership of monasteries. For example, Heintz reports that in 1200, the Monastery of Hördt owned assets there that had been transferred over by a Knight Konrad von Ried (Rippurg). In addition, the Monastery of Sinsheim had an estate in the little village of Altsheim that it sold in 1248 to Domscholaster Adelvolk in Speyer. This noble bequeathed the estate to his nephew, Diocesan Administrator Albert von Lachen, who then donated the property in 1290 to the Hördt Monastery. In fact, a record book of 1788 shows rather extensive estates owned by the Monastery of Hördt at the district border near the lost village of Altsheim. The Provost of Hördt owned 7 hectares to the east of the Spitzäcker fields in the plot called "Am Altsheimer Weg," 4 hectares to the west of the Spitzäcker fields toward the district boundary, and approximately 9 hectares of land to the south of the Spitzäcker, not to mention the extensive lands of the Hördt Monastery toward the more southerly lying Wingertsberg. But it is striking that the Monastery of Hördt, like the Monastery of Klingenmünster, only owned a half hectare of land in the Spitzäcker.

Heintz also reports that the Cistercian Abbey of Eußerthal also had extensive property at Altsheim. The monastery bought the land in 1256 from Konrad von Steinach for the considerable sum of 700 pfund-heller [700 gulden]. Indeed, the Eußerthal Abbey still owned many fields in the lands to the west, east, and south of the Spitzäcker in 1788. Under these circumstances, it is not surprising that little land remained for the people of Altsheim. This is probably the reason why the place remained very small compared to Offenbach and Ottersheim. Add to this is that the spiritual properties of the large monastic estates were managed from the neighboring villages. So Altsheim remained a tenant village without its own church, without its own mayor, and without its own court. It probably had a chapel where early Mass readers of Offenbach and Ottersheim alternately read a Mass on Sundays. Surely the settlement had a well from which the inhabitants were able to draw their drinking water. It is therefore not impossible that buried remains of a well could be found in the ground at the Spitzäcker.

That the village of Altsheim still existed in the 16th century has been verified. The allocation of an early Mass reader in 1529 confirmed that the place was not yet dying. The demise of the settlement can probably be attributed to the 30 Years War. Many a man or young man would have followed the example of the famous soldier from this community, Colonel Bastian Vogelsberger, and fought as a mercenary; and perhaps losing his life. Meanwhile, the women and children would have left the scarcely protected place and fled to safety elsewhere; unless they were killed during the looting. In any case, no one returned to the small town after the war. The abandoned property probably returned to the Palatinate when the peace was announced in 1648. Indeed, the Spitzäcker was under the management of the winery of Germersheim in the 18th century. During a review in 1768, new boundary stones were erected with the following characters: *CPEB,* meaning *Cur Pfalz Erb Bestand [Electoral Palatinate Hereditary Property].* From that time on, the mayor and court of Ottersheim managed the Viehweide near Altsheim. In the seventies of the 18th century, Ottersheim farmers tried to convert a portion of pasture into arable land but the mayor and court wanted to prevent this. A dispute arose that was finally decided by the Electoral Court Chamber in Mannheim to the benefit of the farmers.

But what happened to the houses, barns, and stables in Altsheim? Most likely, some of them went up in flames, while the rest was carried away by the inhabitants of surrounding villages as building material. Probably not one stone remained upon another since the procurement of sandstone has always been very difficult and expensive for the inhabitants of the valley. It is therefore not surprising that today nothing is visible any longer from the village of Altsheim. The name *Goldgrube* suggests that later generations have searched the site of the defunct town deliberately for valuables and apparently also had some success. This is really surprising when you know that Altsheim was mainly inhabited by tenants and small farmers. However, the fact that a wealthy and prominent mercenary leader came from Altsheim sheds new light on the relationship. Specifically, Altsheim was the birthplace of the famous military commander, Bastian Vogelsberger, who gained considerable wealth in his lifetime. Although it is not historically attested, we may assume that he in his fortune did not forget his poor relatives in his native town. Many a piece of gold may have found its way to Altsheim that its owners then buried in the ground as was commonly done during times of war. Because whole families died out in the 30-year struggle in the early 17th Century however, surely some coins remained in the ground until they were rediscovered by chance.

Bastian Vogelsberger, the Great Son of the Defunct Village of Altsheim

Far more historical evidence has been handed down about the great son of Altsheim, Colonel Bastian Vogelsberger, than about the defunct village near Ottersheim. This important mercenary leader of the 16th century was born in Altsheim in 1505 and grew up in relative poverty. His father was probably a peasant who lived by leasing farmland like most of his fellow citizens. We do not know how `small´ Bastian found his way into the `big´ world. At any rate, we know that as a young man he could not only read and write but also spoke relatively good French and Italian, even though Altsheim, Ottersheim, and Offenbach all lacked a school. Around 1529, he taught young people French and Italian in Straßburg, which was still a German city then.

In the long run however, the teaching profession did not satisfy the talented and driven Vogelsberger. Therefore, he entered into the service of Count Wilhelm von Fürstenberg, the Lord of Hausen in the Kinzig Valley, as a mercenary. Because of his ability, in particular his language skills, the Count favored him over the other writers and entrusted him with important management tasks. In 1536, Vogelsberger separated from his former superiors and accepted the leadership of a 6,000-strong German infantry in the service of King Franz I of France. This was absolutely nothing extraordinary at that time because such soldiers did not fight for their country and fellow citizens but for the Lord who paid them. The captain swore with his regiment to "serve the king faithfully, excepting nobody except the Holy Roman Empire." This he did, and tacked so many victories to his flags that he was finally promoted to *Kriegsoberst [War Colonel].* In this way, he made true his pronouncement that "God and luck can raise people from poor heritage to positions of high command." In addition to his fame, Bastian Vogelsberger also acquired a considerable fortune. In 1539, he was able to advance the Bishop and Elector to Mainz 28,000 gulden, an extraordinary sum in those days.

In 1540, the war colonel and his family built a handsome house of hewn stones, all in Rhenish Renaissance style and taste, in the German town of Weißenburg on the left bank of the Lauter at Anselmannstaden. At the front of the house under the oriel [bay window], he placed images of two men in full armor, one of himself to the left and to the right one of his faithful battle companion, Captain Thomas Wolf from Heilbronn. Between these hung his coat of arms, a bird resting on a mountain. The house and image are well preserved and can be seen in Weißenburg.

In 1542, Vogelsberger bought citizenship for himself in Weißenburg. Palatine Elector Friedrich II held Colonel Vogelsberger in such esteem that in 1544, Friedrich appointed him as lifelong war council and govenor of the Saint Remigius castle. In 1546, the Colonel purchased the beautiful Wasserburg castle at Friedelsheim near Wachenheim with the knowledge and consent of the Elector and the Prince Bishop of Speyer. Like other castle owners and noblemen, Vogelsberger owned vineyards and had timber rights in the Wachenheim forest. Yes, he even had serfs in the villages of Gönnheim and Weidenthal. The Palatine Elector soon presented him the Friedelsheim castle as a hereditary fief because of his loyal service.

The great son of Altsheim also had great enemies. Most of all, he fought his former boss, Count Wilhelm von Fürstenberg. This Count even wrote a pamphlet against him and spread it everywhere. Vogelsberger continued along his way in spite of this. After the death of French King Franz I, his successor, Heinrich II, called him to the coronation at Reims in 1547. Vogelsberger was to protect him with a few thousand mercenaries because the new ruler feared unrest. Vogelsberger recruited ten companies of soldiers, mostly from Saxony, and marched with them to France. This aroused the indignation of the Emperor Charles V, who felt threatened by these recruitments and the dubious attitude of the new French king, and who therefore even called off the planned siege of Magdeburg. But already in the autumn of 1547, Vogelsberger removed his troops from Reims and returned to his family in Weißenburg.

On 31 October 1547, Emperor Charles V sent a letter with instructions to arrest Vogelsberger within 14 days so that he could explain his position and answer questions; since not unjustly, the Emperor saw in the new French king a dangerous rival in the upcoming battles over the Burgundian inheritance. Imperial Steward Lazarus Schwendi received the order to capture Vogelsberger and jail him. He did not dare face the colonel openly but treacherously lured him into a trap. Vogelsberger was taken prisoner on 21 January 1548 at Gutleutehof near Weißenburg. Then he was brought into the city where he was imprisoned for a week. Without seeing his wife and children again, he was taken to Augsburg by 200 mounted Spanish marksmen where he was immediately thrown into the city jail. Meanwhile, his cause had been handed over to an Imperial court. Torture was used to extract a confession. But his strong body and the conviction of his innocence withstood all the tortures. He repeatedly insisted that his recruitments for the French king were never directed against the Emperor. Nevertheless, the court handed down a death sentence on the famous Colonel Bastian Vogelsberger.

The execution took place in Augsburg on 7 February 1548. Unbowed, the brave warrior stepped onto the scaffold that was surrounded by a large crowd of people of all classes. All the bystanders were struck by this lofty military figure, his even-built body, his noble clear face, and his flowing black-brown beard. In his black velvet clothing and his Welsh hat embroidered with silk, he delivered a heartfelt speech to the bystanders from the scaffold, the text of which has been preserved. Most of all, he regretted that they had denied him a confessor and was allowed no food for the journey to the afterlife. Aware of his innocence, he hoped to find a merciful judge there. He asked the bystanders to pray the Our Father and the Creed, which was also granted. Standing erect, he then received the fatal blow from the executioner. The same fate was suffered by his two faithful followers, Thomas Wolf from Heilbronn and Jakob Mantel from Landau. The Emporer wanted the sentence to have a deterring effect. So the executioner proclaimed in the face of the dead to all the people:

> *"Who serves the King of France will suffer the same fate as Vogelsberger, Wolf, and Mantel."*

Nevertheless, after the bloody drama the sympathy of the people belonged not with the Emperor but to Colonel Vogelsberger and his faithful followers, because everyone sensed that innocent people were sacrificed here to dynastic interests. Vogelsberger's mercenaries also did not forget their brave colonel after his death. After his body had long since rotted away, they sang:

> *"A sad song about the Colonel called Vogelsberger,*
> *Who though innocent, was executed by the sword. "*

A fellow Palatine citizen wrote this song, and it was also first sung in the Palatinate.

The wife and children of Colonel Vogelsberger awaited an unenviable fate after the death of their breadwinner. Elector Friedrich II declared the Friedelsheim castle as confiscated in 1550 and sold it to Count Ludwig von Leinigen-Dachsburg. A year later, the city of Weißenburg acquired the residence of the Vogelsberger family. It is said that the widow and her children left Weißenburg in 1554 and moved to Bergzabern where their descendants led a life in poverty until 1816. King of France Heinrich II sought revenge for his brave Colonel Vogelsberger however. He therefore allied himself with the rebellious German nobility under the leadership of Moritz von Saxony and supported them in their struggle against Emperor Charles V. Heinrich II also carried out severe reprisals on the city of Weißenburg, because according to his conviction it was complicit in the capture and execution of Vogelsberger. When Weißenburg was occupied by his soldiers in 1552, its residents had to pay a penalty of 8,000 gulden. Then the king ordered the city to be burnt and then pillaged by his troops. No doubt the inhabitants of Altsheim did not forget their son, in spite of his disreputable end. But when the village died out during the 30 Years War, so also did the name of this famous man who played a role not only in the history of Germany but also in European history.

Sources and References

Manuscript sources

Ottersheim Family books
>Created by the Spiritual Counselor Otto Steegmüller, Ottersheim

Minutes of community council meetings in Ottersheim
>Started in 1875

Community of Ottersheim - List of bills
>Started in 1816

House booklet of Dieter Job of Ottersheim
>Written down in 1821

Parish Memorial Book of the Catholic Parish of Ottersheim
>Started in 1856 using old documents

Description of the Protestant Parish of Offenbach
>Started in 1866

Books containing minutes of the local associations and cooperatives in Ottersheim

School diaries of Catholic and Protestant schools in Ottersheim

Diaries of Jean Benz of Ottersheim
>Started in 1914

Archives

State Archive Speyer

>*Archives Department Electoral Palatinate*

>121 Description of the District Office of Germersheim
>129A Tax Books of the District Office of Germersheim
>1524 Ottersheim:
>>Statistical Tables, 1791
>>Plats - General-upkeep and vacant land in the so-called Hinterlands, 1778, 1779
>>The Cattle pasture, 1775
>>Privileges and Rights of the Village of Ottersheim, 1565, 1599
>>The Poppelmann Feudal Property, 1565
>>Debentures and Private Loans
>>Comparison between Ottersheim and Offenbach regarding a water sluice, 1517
>>District plat review from 1738
>>Review and hereditary properties, the Spitzäcker, 1769
>>Separation of the parishes Ottersheim and Knittelsheim, 1785

>*Archives Department Spiritual Goods Administration*

>186
>>a) Reversal of hereditary status of the Eußerthal Feudal property in Ottersheim 1596
>>b) The court review of the estate and its manor yards in 1723.
>>c) Inventory of goods, 1723-1768
>>d) Records and plan for two meadows adjoining to the estates of the House of Haimbach and the Monastery of Hördt in 1789

Literature

Bader,   Dorfgenossenschaft und Dorfgemeinde
  Karl Siegfried: [Village Cooperative and Village Community]
            Böhlau-Verlag, Köln, 1962

Becker,   Die Pfalz und die Pfälzer
  August: [The Palatinate and the Palatinates]
            Leipzig 1858

Biundo,   Bellheim im Wandel der Zeiten
  Georg: [Bellheim Through the Ages]
            Selbstverlag, Bellheim, 1930

Biundo,   Pfälzisches Pfarrer- und Schulmeisterbuch
  Georg: [Book of Palatinate Pastors and School Teachers]
            Kaiserslautern 1930

Brechenmacher, Etymologisches Wörterbuch der Deutschen Familiennamen
  Josef: [Etymological Dictionary of German Family Names]
            Limburg Bd. I, 1957-1960; Bd. II, 1960-1963

Christmann, Die Siedlungsnamen der Pfalz, Teil I,
  Ernst: [Palatinate Settlement Names, Part I]
            Speyer 1953

Frey,   Versuch einer geographisch-historisch-statistischen Beschreibung des
  Michael: königl.-bayerischen Rheinkreises, Teil I
            [Attempt at a Geographical-Historical-Statistical Description of the Royal
            Bavarian Rhinelands, Part I]
            Speyer 1837

Geib,   Handbuch für die Gemeindebehörden der Pfalz
  Adalbert: [Manual for the Municipal Authorities of the Palatinate]
            Kaiserslautern 1885

Glasschröder, Urkunden der pfälzischen Kirchengeschichte des Mittelalters
  Franz Xaver: [Palatinate Church History Records of the Middle Ages]
            München-Freising, Bd. I, 1903
            München-Freising, Bd. II, 1930

Gottschald, Deutsche Namenskunde
  Max: [Onomastics-Science of German Names]
            Berlin 1954

Gümbel,   Die Geschichte der protestantischen Kirche der Pfalz
  Theodor: [History of the Protestant Church in the Palatinate]
            Kaiserslautern 1885

Haeberle,   Die Wüstungen der Rheinpfalz
  Daniel: [The Lost Villages of the Rhine Palatinate]
            Kayser, Kaiserslautern, 1921

Harrer,   Wahrhafte und gründliche Beschreibung des Bauernkrieges
  Peter: [Truthful and Thorough Description of the Peasants' War]
            Kaiserslautern 1936

Heuser, Emil:	Der Bauernkrieg 1525 in der Pfalz [The Peasants' Revolt in 1525 in the Palatinate] Neustadt 1925
Heintze / Cascorbi:	Die Deutschen Familiennamen [German Family Names] Halle / Saale in 1933
Keller, Albrecht:	Der Scharfrichter in der deutschen Kulturgeschichte [The Executioner in German Cultural History] Verlag Schroeder, Bonn und Leipzig, 1921
Keller, Conrad	Die deutschen Kolonien in Südrußland [The German Colonies in South Russia] Odessa in 1905
Leidner, Eduard Eugen:	Entwicklung der katholischen Religionsverhältnisse in der Kurpfalz von den Reunionen bis zur Kirchenteilung (1680-1707) [Development of the Catholic Religion Relations in the Palatinate from the Reunions to the Church Division (1680-1707)]
Linnartz, Caspar:	Unsere Familiennamen, Bd. I; Zehntausend Berufsnamen im ABC erklärt [Our Family Name, Volume I; Ten Thousand Job Names Explained Alphabetically] Verlag Dümmler, Bonn, 1957
Pfeiffer, Albert:	Stoffsammlung zur pfälzischen Volksschulgeschichte [Palatine Elementary School History Materials Collection] Speyer 1911
Probst, Josef:	Geschichte der Stadt und Festung Germersheim [History of the Town and Fortress of Germersheim] Speyer 1898
Remling, Franz Xaver:	Urkundliche Geschichte der ehemaligen Abteien und Klöster [Documentary History of the Former Abbeys and Monasteries] München 1913
Solleder, Friedrich:	Obrist Bastian Vogelsberger, ein Opfer der Politik Kaiser Karl V. [Colonel Bastian Vogelsberg, a Victim of the Imperial Policies of Charles V.] Verlag Schmidt, München
Sprater, Friedrich:	Die Pfalz in der Vor- und Frühzeit [The Palatinate in Prehistoric and Early Times] Speyer 1948
Stamer, Ludwig:	Kirchengeschichte der Pfalz Teil I-IV [Church History of the Palatinate, Parts I-IV] Speyer, 1935, 1949, 1955 und 1964
Steinmetz, Heinrich:	Das linksseitige Rheingebiet unter der Herrschaft der Franzosen 1792-1813 [The Left Side of the Rhine Area Under French Rule 1792-1813] Alsenz 1913

Widder, Goswin:	Versuch einer vollständigen geographischen-historischen Beschreibung der kurpfälzischen Pfalz am Rhein
	[Attempt at a Full Geographical-Historical Description of the Electoral Palatinate on the Rhine.]
	Frankfurt und Leipzig, 1788
Wilde, Julius	Die Pflanzennamen im Sprachschatz der Pfälzer
	[Plant Names in the Vocabulary of the Palatinate]
	Neustadt, 1923

Fritz Steegmüller (1910-2002)

Fritz Steegmüller was one of ten children born in Ottersheim to Franz Steegmüller and Lisa née Föhlinger. Besides son and sibling, his life experience would bestow upon him the additional titles of teacher, veteran, husband, father, prisoner of war, author, historian, and "Honorary Citizen of Ottersheim," to name just a few. Fritz acquired an appreciation for Ottersheim while growing up there as a child and making regular trips back to the community to visit family and relatives as an adult.

His early education began in 1916 in the Ottersheim elementary and middle schools. Ottersheim had no secondary

Fritz Steegmüller (about 1960)

schools, so Fritz left Ottersheim in April of 1923 to attend the Catholic Teacher's Seminary in Speyer to begin his training as a teacher. During the course of the next six years, he developed a love for studying and learning. He excelled academically and achieved above average performance in all subjects. He loved music, and in addition to singing in choir groups, he loved to play the piano and organ.

Fritz received his "Certificate of Qualification" in April of 1929 and thus began a series of training assignments over the next five years in many local schools as a teaching candidate, the first of which was his old primary school in Ottersheim. After becoming an accredited Assistant Teacher, he was accepted to teach at the Catholic Elementary School at Hatzenbühl in April of 1934 where within a short time he took over the role of headmaster.

While at Hatzenbühl, Fritz fell in disfavor with the National-Socialist Party for speaking out against Party interference in Catholic school affairs. To escape the scrutiny of oppressive local party officials, Fritz left teaching in October of 1935 for a year of military service. Returning from that service, Fritz taught at the Teacher Seminary in Speyer for a time and eventually got back to the Hatzenbühl Catholic Elementary School in April of 1938.

Fritz was drafted into the German army in August of 1939. Prior to being deployed to the front, he took leave to marry Elisabeth Holz whom he had met in Speyer. He survived several conflicts during the war, but was captured by the Russian Army in April of 1945 and held for 4 years and eight months.

Fritz returned to Speyer in December of 1949 where he reunited with his wife and 5-year-old son, Bernhard, whom he had not seen until this time. After a short respite, he returned to teaching and held several positions as head teacher throughout the district. He maintained his home in Speyer with his wife and family to which was added another son and daughter, Hermann and Monika. In 1956, Fritz became Chief Administrator of the County and City Schools of Speyer. Ten years later, he was appointed Government Inspector and held that position until his retirement in 1974.

In retirement Fritz wrote additional books on such topics as the history of the Teacher Seminary in Speyer, the memories of his captivity during the Second World War, a history of the Cathedral Choir in Speyer, and histories of the Steegmüller and Föhlinger families.

This book is but one testament to his legacy.

A

Batzen	A batzen was a small silver (later alloy) coin. One batzen was equal to 4 kreutzers or 16 pfennigs or 32 hellers; 15 batzen was equal to 1 gulden.
Elle	An elle was a unit of dry measure equaling the distance from the elbow to the tip of the middle finger.
Franc	The franc was the unit of currency used by the French beginning in 1795.
Fuder	A fuder was either a cartload or an oak barrel having a volume of approximately 1000 liters.
Gulden:	The gulden was the currency used in the Palatinate during the Late Middle Ages. One gulden was equal to 60 kreutzers or 15 batzen or 240 pfennigs, 480 hellers, or 1 pfund-heller.
Hectare	The hectare, abbreviated (Ha.), is a unit of land area equaling 10,000 square meters.
Heller	A heller was a small copper-based coin. Its value to other coinage was 480 hellers to 1 gulden; 32 hellers to 1 batzen; 8 hellers to 1 kreutzer, 2 hellers to 1 pfennig.
Hufe or Hube	A hufe was an old German measure of land area. It was considered that amount of land necessary to support and maintain a farmer and his family. It could vary in size from 7.5 to 30 hectares depending on the region and soil quality. Hube is a regional variation of hufe and has the same meaning.
Jauchert	A jauchert was a parcel of land equivalent to a morgen.
Klafter	A klafter was a unit of measurement equal in length of the outstretched arms, fingertip to fingertip, or about 2 meters (6 feet).
Kreutzer	A kreutzer was a small silver coin. One kreutzer was equal to 4 pfennigs or 8 hellers; 4 kreutzers were equal to 1 batzen; 60 kreutzers were equal to 1 gulden.
Malter	A malter was a measure of volume. A light malter was equivalent to 142 liters while a heavy malter was equivalent to 127 liters.
Morgen	A morgen was a common unit of land measure having an inconsistent area depending on the region. A morgen could range from 1/4-to-1 hectares.
Pfennig	A pfennig was a small silver coin. One pfennig was equal to 2 hellers; 4 pfennigs was equal to 1 kreutzer; 16 pfennigs was equal to 1 batzen; 240 pfennigs was equal to 1 gulden.
Pflug / Pflüge	Pflug was a composite land measure which averaged about 15 morgen of farmland and 1.5 to 2 morgen of meadows. Pflüge is the plural of pflug.
Schilling	A schilling was a silver coin having a value of 17-1/2 pfennigs.
Schuh	A schuh was the distance from the back of the heel to the tip of the toe of an average sized shoe, boot, or foot.
Zentner	A zentner was the unit for mass for weighing crops. Also called hundred-weight, it was equal to 100 pfunds (pounds) or 50 kilograms. One pfund is 1/2 a kilogram.

Present Day Ottersheim Region

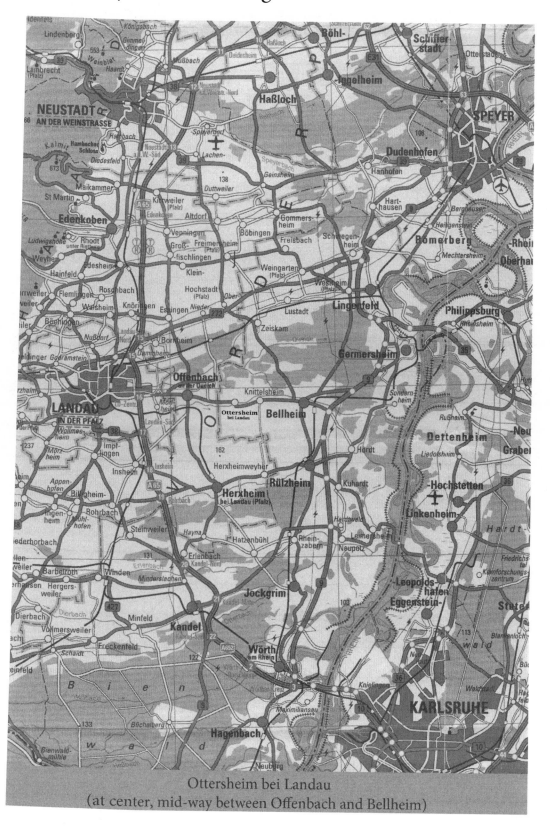

Ottersheim bei Landau
(at center, mid-way between Offenbach and Bellheim)

D